Research Directions in Parallel Functional Programming

Springer
*London
Berlin
Heidelberg
New York
Barcelona
Hong Kong
Milan
Paris
Santa Clara
Singapore
Tokyo*

Kevin Hammond and Greg Michaelson (Eds)

Research Directions in Parallel Functional Programming

 Springer

Kevin Hammond, BSc, PhD
Division of Computer Science, University of St Andrews, North Haugh, St Andrews, Fife, KY16 9SS, UK

Greg Michaelson, BA, MSc, PhD
Department of Computing and Electrical Engineering, Heriot-Watt University, Riccarton, Edinburgh, EH14 4AS, UK

ISBN 1-85233-092-9 Springer-Verlag London Berlin Heidelberg

British Library Cataloguing in Publication Data
Research directions in parallel functional programming
  1.Functional programming (Computer science) 2.Parallel
  programming (Computer science)
  I.Hammond, Kevin II.Michaelson, Greg
  005.1'14
  ISBN 1852330929

Library of Congress Cataloging-in-Publication Data
Research directions in parallel functional programming / Kevin Hammond
  and Greg Michaelson (eds.).
      p.   cm.
  ISBN 1-85233-092-9 (alk. paper)
  1. Parallel programming (Computer science)--Research.
  2. Functional programming (Computer sceince)--Research.
  I. Hammond, Kevin. II. Michaelson, Greg 1953- .
  QA76.642.R48 1999   99-29081
  005.2'75--dc21

Apart from any fair dealing for the purposes of research or private study, or criticism or review, as permitted under the Copyright, Designs and Patents Act 1988, this publication may only be reproduced, stored or transmitted, in any form or by any means, with the prior permission in writing of the publishers, or in the case of reprographic reproduction in accordance with the terms of licences issued by the Copyright Licensing Agency. Enquiries concerning reproduction outside those terms should be sent to the publishers.

© Springer-Verlag London Limited 1999
Printed in Great Britain

The use of registered names, trademarks etc. in this publication does not imply, even in the absence of a specific statement, that such names are exempt from the relevant laws and regulations and therefore free for general use.

The publisher makes no representation, express or implied, with regard to the accuracy of the information contained in this book and cannot accept any legal responsibility or liability for any errors or omissions that may be made.

Typesetting: Camera ready by contributors
Printed and bound at the Athenæum Press Ltd., Gateshead, Tyne & Wear
34/3830-543210 Printed on acid-free paper SPIN 10696976

To Vicki and Nancy

Contents

Foreword XIII

Overview XVII

Part I. Fundamentals

1. **Introduction** 3
   1.1 Introduction 3
   1.2 Language Issues 8
   1.3 Architectural Issues 14
   1.4 Implementation Issues 20
   1.5 Proof Issues 24
   1.6 Summary 29

2. **Foundations** 31
   2.1 Introduction 31
   2.2 A Basic Introduction to Haskell 31
   2.3 λ-Calculus 39
   2.4 Strict Evaluation and the SECD Machine 47
   2.5 Lazy Evaluation and Graph Reduction 50
   2.6 Dataflow 58

3. **Programming Language Constructs** 63
   3.1 Introduction 63
   3.2 Overview 63
   3.3 Implicit Parallelism 66
   3.4 Controlled Parallelism 76
   3.5 Explicit Parallelism 81
   3.6 Conclusion 91

4. **Proof** 93
   4.1 Introduction 93
   4.2 The Basis of Functional Programming: Equations 95
   4.3 Pattern Matching, Cases and Local Definitions 96

	4.4	Structural Induction and Recursion	99
	4.5	Case Study: A Compiler Correctness Proof	100
	4.6	General Recursion	105
	4.7	Partial Languages	107
	4.8	Semantic Approaches	108
	4.9	Strong Functional Programming	115
	4.10	Conclusion	118
5.	**Realisations for Strict Languages**		**121**
	5.1	Introduction	121
	5.2	Concurrent Program Execution	123
	5.3	System Architectures	131
	5.4	Systems Supporting Strict Languages	136
6.	**Realisations for Non-Strict Languages**		**149**
	6.1	Introduction	149
	6.2	Worked Example: the G-Machine	150
	6.3	Analecta of Abstract Machines	162
	6.4	Realisations of the Technology	175
	6.5	Conclusion	186

Part II. Current Research Areas

7.	**Data Parallelism**		**191**
	7.1	Introduction	191
	7.2	Data Parallel Combinators	192
	7.3	Active Data Structures	201
8.	**Cost Modelling**		**207**
	8.1	Why Model Costs?	207
	8.2	Why is Cost Modelling Hard?	208
	8.3	Easy Cost Modelling	211
	8.4	An Example	214
	8.5	Hard Cost Modelling	214
	8.6	Summary	218
9.	**Shaping Distributions**		**219**
	9.1	Introduction	219
	9.2	Shape Theory	222
	9.3	The FISH Language	223
	9.4	Aspects of the Design of GOLDFISH	227
	9.5	Distributions	228
	9.6	Cost Modelling	231
	9.7	Conclusion	232

10. Performance Monitoring ... 233
10.1 Introduction ... 233
10.2 Analysing an Example Using Current Tools ... 233
10.3 Data Modelling Parallelism ... 239
10.4 Conclusions and Future Work ... 246

11. Memory Performance of Dataflow Programs ... 247
11.1 Introduction ... 247
11.2 The Dataflow Model of Computation ... 247
11.3 Programming Languages ... 249
11.4 Programming Issues ... 251
11.5 The Benchmarks ... 251
11.6 Conclusions and Future Work ... 264

12. Portability of Performance in the BSP Model ... 267
12.1 Introduction ... 267
12.2 The BSP Programming Model ... 267
12.3 Simplicity by Restriction ... 269
12.4 BSP Programming ... 270
12.5 The BSP Cost Calculus ... 271
12.6 BSP Design: Parallel Scan ... 275
12.7 BSP Design: Sample Sorting ... 277
12.8 BSP and Functional Programming ... 283
12.9 Conclusion ... 285

13. Algorithmic Skeletons ... 289
13.1 Introduction ... 289
13.2 Patterns of Parallel Computation ... 289
13.3 Challenges in Skeletal Programming ... 290
13.4 From Theory into Practice ... 292
13.5 The Way Ahead ... 303

14. Coordination Languages ... 305
14.1 Introduction ... 305
14.2 Caliban: A Common Framework ... 305
14.3 Simple Example: Ray Tracing ... 308
14.4 Implementing Caliban ... 311
14.5 Performance and Performance Tuning ... 314
14.6 Discussion ... 320
14.7 Future Directions ... 320

15. Parallel and Distributed Programming in Concurrent Clean ... 323
15.1 Introduction ... 323
15.2 Parallel Programming in Clean ... 323

15.3 Distributed Programming in Clean 331
15.4 Conclusion 338

16. Functional Process Modelling 339
16.1 Introduction 339
16.2 Modelling Functions as Processes 341
16.3 Decomposition Strategies for Pipelined Parallelism 344
16.4 Parallel Decomposition of Map 345
16.5 Parallel Decomposition of Directed Reductions 352
16.6 Related work 359
16.7 Conclusion 359

17. Validating Programs in Concurrent ML 361
17.1 Introduction 361
17.2 Program Analysis 361
17.3 Concurrent ML 363
17.4 Behaviours 366
17.5 A Case Study 372
17.6 Conclusion 377

18. Explicit Parallelism 379
18.1 Motivations 379
18.2 Design Choices 380
18.3 A Caml Interface to MPI 385
18.4 An Example 391
18.5 Lessons and Perspectives 393
18.6 Related Work 395
18.7 Conclusion 396

Part III. Conclusion

19. Large Scale Functional Applications 399
19.1 Introduction 399
19.2 Purely Implicit Parallel Applications 400
19.3 Semi-Explicit Parallelism 405
19.4 Coordination Languages 413
19.5 Explicit Parallelism 416
19.6 Derivational Approaches 419
19.7 Conclusion 423

20. Summary 427

Glossary 465

Index 481

Foreword

Programming is hard. Building a large program is like constructing a steam locomotive through a hole the size of a postage stamp. An artefact that is the fruit of hundreds of person-years is only ever seen by anyone through a 100-line window. In some ways it is astonishing that such large systems work at all.

But *parallel* programming is much, much harder. There are so many more things to go wrong. Debugging is a nightmare. A bug that shows up on one run may never happen when you are looking for it — but unfailingly returns as soon as your attention moves elsewhere. A large fraction of the program's code can be made up of marshalling and coordination algorithms. The core application can easily be obscured by a maze of plumbing.

Functional programming is a radical, elegant, high-level attack on the programming problem. Radical, because it dramatically eschews side-effects; elegant, because of its close connection with mathematics; high-level, because you can say a lot in one line. But functional programming is definitely not (yet) mainstream. That's the trouble with radical approaches: it's hard for them to break through and become mainstream. But that doesn't make functional programming any less fun, and it has turned out to be a wonderful laboratory for rich type systems, automatic garbage collection, object models, and other stuff that *has* made the jump into the mainstream.

Parallel functional programming is the same, only more so. The rewards are even greater. Parallel functional programs eliminate many of the most unpleasant burdens of parallel programming. In particular, programs are determinate: if they give the correct answers on a serial machine they will do so on a parallel machine too[1]. That is a truly wonderful property, because it means that debugging a parallel program is no harder than debugging a sequential one. (*Performance* debugging — that is, figuring out why your allegedly-parallel program runs more or less sequentially — remains challenging, but at least it is a separable issue.) Furthermore, the side-effect-free functional style encourages (but definitely does not ensure) relatively independent computations, with fewer artificial dependencies.

---

[1] There are a few non-functional languages that share this property, such as Cilk and High Performance Fortran.

Parallelism without tears, perhaps? Definitely not. It is easier to describe the nice properties of parallel functional programs than it is to implement them. Two things have become clear over the last 15 years or so. First, it is a very substantial task to engineer a parallel functional language implementation. The very high-level nature of a parallel functional program leaves a large gap for the implementation to bridge.

Second, the always dubious "feed in an arbitrary program and watch it run faster" story is comprehensively dead. For a start, arbitrary programs are rarely parallel. Quite a bit of work needs to go into designing and expressing a parallel algorithm for the application. Then there is often too much parallelism, or the granularity is too small, or the data communication costs dominate, or one sequential thread dominates...the list goes on. All the interesting work these days is about how to gain control over these resource allocation issues, without throwing the baby out with the bath-water and reverting to manual allocation of everything.

There are also interesting wide-open semantic questions: some parallel algorithms (e.g. branch and bound) are *internally* non-deterministic while having deterministic results; other parallel algorithms (notably graph algorithms) seem to be most naturally expressed in an imperative fashion. In both cases the overall determinacy (i.e. purely-functional behaviour) of the result is a deep property of the algorithm. It is not clear how to express and reason about such algorithms in a purely-functional setting.

The chapters in the bulk of this book are all about exercising carefully-chosen control over parallel functional programs. What is interesting is how many different approaches there are to doing so. Part II covers SPMD programming, shapely programming, BSP, skeletons, dataflow, `par` and `seq` combinators, explicitly concurrent processes; it also has chapters on performance modeling and measurement. And that does not exhaust the field: SISAL and NESL are two other prominent successes.

Interestingly, not one of the chapters is about completely-automatic parallelisation, a long-time goal of the parallel functional programming community. Why not? Negatively, because it has turned out to be technically extremely difficult for a compiler to infer appropriate parallelism from a vanilla functional program. (By "appropriate" I "enough, but not too much", and "of large enough granularity", and "not involving too much communication", and so on.) More positively, once the programmer has dreamt up a parallel algorithm, they want to be able to express that parallelism in an explicit way in the program. Writing a vanilla functional program, and hoping that a cunning compiler will be able to figure out your intentions, is not good enough, even if (implausibly) the compiler is indeed cunning to get it "right" most of the time. Nevertheless, some automatic inference may help a compiler to "fill in the gaps" in a program whose main parallel structure is explicitly exposed by one or more of the techniques discussed by contributors to this book.

Another interesting absence from the book is any discussion of special-purpose hardware to support parallel functional languages, something which in which I had a personal stake ten years ago, in the form of the GRIP machine. It is usually a mistake to pronounce something a dead end, but special-purpose hardware for parallel functional programming is certainly now very unfashionable, and for good reasons. The world has changed decisively: it is simply impossible to complete with the billion-dollar investments that now go into mainstream microprocessor designs, and multiprocessors have become commodity items. This is not something to mourn — it is delightful to have a lot of the work done for us!

Where does that leave us? Is parallel functional programming any good? If I am honest, I have to say that the jury is still out. The applications described in Part III are encouraging, certainly way beyond what was being done ten years ago, but the march of the killer micros means that desktop uniprocessors are still getting faster so quickly that the 10-processors-in-every-PC situation is still a way off; and while parallel processing is the preserve of the big, high-value programs, the low-pain/moderate-gain tradeoff of parallel functional programming has yet to find an economic niche.

Is it worth bothering, then? Emphatically, yes! Functional programming, including parallel functional programming, is a place where theory and practice meet particularly fruitfully. That alone makes it fascinating territory. The early euphoria of parallel functional programming has worn off, but the fun has not. This book presents an up-to-date picture of the state-of-the-art in a field that is still advancing on many fronts. Enjoy.

Simon Peyton Jones, August 1999

Overview

Motivation

This book provides a state-of-the-art survey of research trends in parallel functional programming. It is aimed at practitioners and researchers, providing a thorough source reference of recent activity and new directions.

A fundamental aim of the book is to provide not only an overview of current research, but also to survey the range of choices which led to the development of those areas, in the hope that these may profitably be explored by future researchers.

Parallel functional programming has been a significant stream of Computing research for the best part of 25 years. It is an area of international activity with many well established groups, in particular across Europe and North America, forming a lively community which shares results through numerous specialist conferences and workshops. However, the significance of parallel functional programming extends well beyond this community. Parallel functional programming spans Computing Science in general and has had notable impacts in computer architecture, language design, compilation techniques and operating systems, for concurrency and parallelism. For example, Darlington's ALICE informed the UK Flagship which informed the EU European Declarative System which informed ICL's commercial Goldrush.

It is therefore timely to try and provide an integrated account of this engaging field by:

- Surveying foundational concepts and techniques;
- Evaluating successes and failures to date;
- Presenting contemporary research;
- Speculating about future trends.

However, it would be highly misleading to present this book as a seamless, uniform, all-embracing canon. Precisely because parallel functional programming is such a large and diverse area, there is no definitive state-of-the-art but rather numerous overlapping, complementary and, above all, synergistic strands. Instead, the editors have sought contributions from a wide variety of established international researchers on their current activities and situated these within a common context.

Structure of the Book

This book has three levels, split for convenience, though not orthogonally, into three parts. Part I covers parallel functional programming fundamentals. The first chapter represents the top level, providing some essential background for non-specialists (Chapter 2).

The remaining chapters of Part I form the second level, providing more focused and detailed surveys of the common key aspects of parallel functional programming: parallel programming constructs (Chapter 3); proof techniques (Chapter 4); and realisations for strict and non-strict languages, respectively (Chapters 5 and 6).

Part II forms the third level and covers a number of current research areas in more depth, providing insight into research results and directions. The authors refer back to Part I for background, which enables them to concentrate on presenting their current research. Part III provides a summary and assessment of the preceding chapters, describing the applications of functional programming. It is followed by an integrated bibliography, which is common to all chapters, and a glossary of major terms and concepts.

We will now survey each part in turn.

Part I. Fundamentals

Foundations. In this chapter, underpinning material is presented by the Editors and Chris Clack.

We have decided to adopt the contemporary lazy functional language Haskell as a common notation throughout the book. Here, we provide a practical account of the main Haskell constructs used in subsequent chapters.

All functional languages acknowledge Church's λ-calculus as a common formal basis. In this section, short appreciations of the λ-notation, normal order and applicative order β-reduction, and normal forms are given, along with summaries of the Church-Rosser properties which characterise the λ-calculus.

Functional languages may be broadly characterised as strict, if β-reduction is carried out in applicative order, or as non-strict (lazy) if normal order is used. Here we present Landin's SECD machine, the first abstract machine for strict evaluation, and, with Chris Clack, a simple graph reduction system for lazy evaluation. We also provide a short account of dataflow implementation.

Programming Language Constructs. A wide variety of approaches have been taken to exploit parallelism in functional programs, from attempting to identify implicit parallelism in pure programs, through extending extant functional languages with various forms of notations and constructs for making different aspects of parallelism explicit, to designing new functional languages intended primarily for parallel programming. In this chapter, Rita Loogen surveys parallel functional programming from a language construct perspective, giving short accounts of the major parallel functional languages through examples that illustrate their distinctive constructs.

Proof. A much vaunted strength of functional languages lies in the comparative ease with which formal techniques may be used to prove properties of and manipulate programs. While techniques specifically oriented to parallel programs are still in their infancy, those for sequential functional programs are widely used and adapted within parallel functional programming, in particular for program refinement and transformation. Here, Simon Thompson discusses the main inductive techniques for reasoning about functional programs through worked examples, and surveys other contemporary approaches.

Strict and Non-Strict Realisations. The strict/non-strict distinction between functional languages is based on fundamental semantic properties, as noted above. In order to tease out the practical implications of these properties, we have chosen to focus on a continuum of realisations, characterised by abstract machines at varying degrees of conceptual distance from a language and the physical computer on which it is ultimately animated. This contrasts with the traditional implementation/architecture distinction, based on a simple division between software and hardware.

Werner Kluge discusses strict realisations. Starting with a simple conceptual model of strict concurrent evaluation, he develops abstract primitive operations for concurrent task management and considers conservative and speculative evaluation on shared- and distributed-memory machines. He then uses these to discuss extant realisations of strict functional languages.

While strict languages map relatively naturally onto von Neumann machines, there has been considerably more research into non-strict realisations of functional languages, which Chris Clack surveys. After detailed discussion of the G-Machine as an archetypical graph reduction system, he provides overviews of the major non-strict abstract machines and concrete realisations.

Part II. Current Research Areas

Data Parallelism. John O'Donnell considers parallel functional programming through data parallel combinators on aggregate data structures. His approach is oriented to SIMD and SPMD programming and is based on equational reasoning.

Cost Modelling. Accurate performance prediction is crucial for developing efficient parallel programs. David Skillicorn's work on compositional cost modelling draws on the formal underpinnings of functional languages in elaborating an algebraic cost calculus. Here he surveys approaches to parallel cost modelling and discusses the challenges it presents.

Shaping Distributions. Barry Jay's FISH language is based on shapely types to enable precise cost modelling and efficient compilation of array programs. In this chapter, he discusses the theoretical background to and key features of FISH, and the design of GOLDFISH, a new shapely language with combinators for data parallel programming.

Performance Modelling. In contrast to static cost modelling, performance modelling enables the dynamic analysis of program behaviours. In this chapter, Nathan Charles and Colin Runciman discuss the design and use of the parallel profiling tools for lazy functional languages, through layered conceptual data models for concurrent graph reduction.

Memory Performance of Dataflow Programs. Poor memory use is a common criticism of functional language implementations. Here, Wim Böhm. and Jeff Hammes analyse the space behaviour of scientific algorithms written in the dataflow language Id on the Monsoon Dataflow Machine, and discuss the use of destructive updates to reduce memory inefficiencies.

Portability of Performance in the BSP Model. The Bulk Synchronous Parallel (BSP) model is used for general SPMD programming and has much in common with the dataflow and skeleton approaches to parallel functional programming. Here, Jon Hill discusses the use of the BSP cost calculus in enabling portability of performance of scalable parallel applications.

Algorithmic Skeletons. Murray Cole's characterisation of algorithmic skeletons and their close relationship to higher-order functions has been the basis of considerable international research into parallel functional programming. In this chapter, he considers current challenges in skeletal programming, and surveys both language and implementation implications of skeletons.

Coordination Languages. Paul Kelly's Caliban was one of the first languages to use functional constructs to coordinate the parallel behaviours of interconnected sequential components. Here, he and Frank Taylor provide a critical appreciation of Caliban's design and implementation.

Parallel and Distributed Programming in Concurrent Clean. The Clean Project exemplifies the integrated design and implementation of a functional language intended for parallel as well as sequential programming. In this chapter, Rinus Plasmeijer and his collaborators present Clean's parallel and distributed programming constructs.

Functional Process Modelling. It is important to have a framework in which to reason about the operational behaviour of a parallel program. In this chapter, Ali Abdallah relates common higher-order functions to an underlying process semantics in CSP. The chapter considers not only the commonly specified data parallel constructs, but also ones based on control parallelism including parallel filters, folds and pipelines.

Validating Programs in Concurrent ML. Parallelism adds a new layer of difficulty to reasoning about programs. In this chapter, Flemming Nielson considers how the type and effect systems for Concurrent ML may be extended to enable the automatic deduction of the behavioural properties of communication within parallel programs.

Explicit Parallelism. A pragmatic approach to parallel functional programming is to provide wrappers for appropriate primitives in an underlying communications library. Here, Jocelyn Sérot discusses the design and implementation of an interface to MPI for Objective Caml.

Part III. Conclusion

Large Scale Functional Applications. In this substantial concluding chapter, Phil Trinder, Hans-Wolfgang Loidl and Kevin Hammond provide a major survey of significant applications of functional programming technology. They show how the approaches and techniques discussed in the rest of the book have been put to good use in solving significant practical problems, and demonstrate the wide range of applications to which they have been applied.

Summary.

Finally, the editors attempt to draw some conclusions from the book, and speculate briefly about future problems and potentials for parallel functional programming.

Readership

This book is intended for three types of readers, all of whom will have a background in Computer Science to at least undergraduate degree level. First of all, the book will provide a useful starting point for new researchers in this area, especially postgraduate students. In particular, Part I gives a survey of the whole field with pointers to essential further reading on particular topics, the glossary introduces important terms, and the bibliography provides a useful initial research base. Secondly, this book will be of interest to a broader Computer Science audience, in industry as well as in academia, who wish to find out more about particular areas of parallel functional programming research from the Part II chapters and who may find Part I and the glossary helpful in providing more context to a focused project. Thirdly, established researchers in parallel functional programming will find definitive descriptions of other groups' projects of benefit in situating and developing their own research.

List of Contributors

Dr Ali Abdallah is a Lecturer in the Department of Computer Science at The University of Reading. He was previously a Research Officer at the Computing Laboratory Oxford University, where he received his DPhil in Computation. His main research interests include functional parallel programming. He serves on the Euro-Par Conference Advisory Board.
URL: http://www.cs.reading.ac.uk/cs/people/aea/

Dr Wim Böhm worked from 1984 at Manchester University on the SISAL to Dataflow Compiler, instruction set, and throttling. In 1990, he moved to Colorado State University and worked on multithreading. He is now designing SA-C: a single-assignment language for Image Processing targeting (FPGA based) reconfigurable systems.
URL: http://www.cs.colostate.edu/~bohm/

Nathan Charles received his BSc in Mathematics and Computer Science from the University of Kent at Canterbury. He is now a DPhil candidate in Computer Science at the University of York. One of his main research interests is the design of tools for the practical analysis of parallel functional programs. **URL:** http://www.cs.york.ac.uk/~nathan/

Chris Clack is a Senior Lecturer in the Department of Computer Science at University College London. He is co-author of several books and numerous research articles in the areas of programming languages and systems, with particular emphasis on parallel functional programming. In the 1980s, he worked on the use of strictness analysis to detect implicit parallelism in functional programs, on the design and implementation of the GRIP system, and on the Four Stroke Reduction Engine. In the early 1990s, he worked on the design and implementation of the DIGRESS system (an object-oriented test-bed for distributed-memory graph reduction) and profiling techniques for lazy functional languages (Lexical Profiling). Chris is currently concentrating on memory management issues for run-time systems, especially with regard to guarantees on worst-case behaviour. He is a founder member of the IFIP WG2.8 working group on functional languages and has served on the executive board of the London and South-East Centre for High Performance Computing. **URL:** http://www.cs.ucl.ac.uk/staff/C.Clack/

Dr Murray Cole is a Senior Lecturer in the Division of Informatics at the University of Edinburgh. His research interests concern the design and implementation of programming language constructs which facilitate the structured expression and analysis of parallel programs, notably through the use of *algorithmic skeletons*. **URL:** http://www.dcs.ed.ac.uk/home/mic/

Dr Kevin Hammond is a Lecturer in the Division of Computer Science at the University of St Andrews. He has worked on parallel functional programming since the mid-1980s, contributing to research projects that include the

ZAPP and DACTL parallel systems at the University of East Anglia (whence he obtained his PhD in Computer Science in 1989), and the novel GRIP architecture and Glasgow Parallel Haskell (GpH) language at the University of Glasgow (where he worked on the GUM and GranSim parallel implementations). He has also been heavily involved in the design and implementation of the non-strict functional language Haskell.
URL: http://www.dcs.st-and.ac.uk/~kh/kh.html

Jeff Hammes worked from 1989 at Los Alamos National Laboratory studying the performance of functional languages for parallel numerical codes, including Id on the Monsoon dataflow machine. In 1993, he moved to Colorado State University and continued work on functional language performance. Jeff is now designing the optimising compiler for SA-C.
URL: http://www.cs.colostate.edu/~hammes/

Dr Jon Hill is a director and founder of Sychron Ltd, an Oxford based company that develops system software for scalable parallel servers. He received his PhD in Computer Science in 1994 from Queen Mary and Westfield College, London. He was previously a research officer at Oxford University Computing Laboratory, responsible for the design, implementation and optimisation of systems software and software tools for BSP computing.
URL: http://www.sychron.com/people/hill/

Dr Barry Jay has a BSc (Mathematics) from the University of Sydney, a doctorate in category theory from McGill University, learnt about computing at the Laboratory for the Foundations of Computer Science in Edinburgh, and is now at the University of Technology, Sydney, as an Associate Professor, and Reader in Computer Science. His primary research interest is in converting semantic ideas, such as shape, into programming tools.
URL: http://www-staff.socs.uts.edu.au/~cbj

Dr Paul Kelly has a BSc (UCL, 1983) in Computer Science, and a PhD (Westfield College, 1987) in parallel functional programming. He has worked in the avionics industry, in distributed systems on Project Universe, and, in 1986, came to Imperial College, where he is now a Senior Lecturer, to work on wafer-scale integration and parallel functional programming. He has published in programming languages, program transformation, operating systems, computer architecture, compilers, debugging and tools for parallel computing. His consultancy work has covered computer architecture and Internet quality of service management. He serves on the Euro-Par Conference Advisory Board. **URL:** http://www.doc.ic.ac.uk/~phjk

Prof. Werner Kluge is Professor of Computer Science at the University of Kiel in Germany. He became interested in functional programming as early as 1975 when he teamed up with Klaus Berkling to build the GMD reduction machine which was the first of its kind worldwide. Since then he has continued to work on the implementation of functional (reduction) languages and systems, among them parallel and distributed architectures. His current interests also include system modelling and architecture in a broader sense.

Dr Hans-Wolfgang Loidl received his PhD from the University of Glasgow in 1998 for his work on Glasgow Parallel Haskell (GpH), notably on the GranSim parallel simulator and on a new approach to granularity analysis. He is currently a Visiting Research Fellow at Heriot-Watt University.

Prof. Dr Rita Loogen works as a university professor at the Philipps-University, Marburg. She received her diploma in Informatik in 1985 and passed her doctoral examination in 1989 at the University of Technology in Aachen. In 1993 she received the venia legendi (Habilitation) from the University of Technology in Aachen and moved to the Department of Mathematics and Computer Science at Marburg University. Her current research interests are in the fields of declarative programming languages and parallel systems. She is especially interested in the design, analysis and implementation of parallel declarative languages.
URL: http://www.mathematik.uni-marburg.de/~loogen

Dr Greg Michaelson is a Senior Lecturer in Computer Science at Heriot-Watt University. His research interests span functional languages and programming, in particular the development of parallel implementations from functional prototypes, and compilation and implementation techniques for automatic parallelisation. **URL:** http://www.cee.hw.ac.uk/~greg

Dr Flemming Nielson is an Associate Professor at the University of Aarhus. He received his PhD from Edinburgh University (in 1984) and his DSc from the University of Aarhus (in 1990). He is the co-author of several books and numerous journal and conference articles within the area of programming languages. His main research interests are semantics, program analysis, type systems, and applications to the validation of systems with concurrency. **URL:** http://www.daimi.au.dk/~fn

Dr John O'Donnell has a BS from the California Institute of Technology and MS and PhD from the University of Iowa. He is currently a Lecturer in Computing Science at the University of Glasgow. His research concerns the design process for parallel programs and digital hardware, including data parallelism and synchronous digital design. Much of his research is based on the applications of formal equational reasoning in pure functional languages.
URL: http://www.dcs.gla.ac.uk/~jtod/

Simon Peyton Jones is a researcher at Microsoft Research Ltd, Cambridge, England. His main research interest is in the design, implementation, and application of functional programming languages, especially Haskell. He plays a leading role in the international functional programming community, and leads the group that develops and maintains the widely-used Glasgow Haskell Compiler. **URL:** `http://research.microsoft.com/~simonpj`

Marco Pil is a member of the Clean research project in the Computing Science Department at the University of Nijmegen.

Prof Rinus Plasmeijer is Head of the Computing Science Department at the University of Nijmegen and Head of the Software Technology Research Group. He has directed the Clean research project since its inception in 1984. **URL:** `http://www.cs.kun.nl/~rinus`

Dr Colin Runciman is a Reader in Computer Science at the University of York, where he leads the Programming Languages and Systems group. Most of his current research is connected with functional programming.

Pascal Serrarens is a member of the Clean research project in the Computing Science Department at the University of Nijmegen.

Dr Jocelyn Sérot was born in France in 1966. He graduated from IRESTE, Nantes in 1989 and received the PhD degree from the University of Paris-Sud in 1993. He was appointed Assistant Professor at Blaise Pascal University, Clermont-Ferrand, France in 1994 and joined the computer vision group of the LASMEA (Laboratoire des Sciences et Materiaux pour l'Electronique, et d'Automatique) CNRS laboratory. His major research interests are in functional programming, parallel architectures and computer vision.

Dr David Skillicorn is a Professor in the Department of Computing and Information Science at Queen's University in Kingston, Canada. His research interests are in general purpose parallel computing and its application to areas such as structured text/hypermedia, and data mining. This involves the interaction of a wide range of issues in areas such as: formal methods, transformation systems, compilation, run-time systems, and architecture design. He is also involved in the ongoing development of the BSP programming model. **URL:** `http:www.cs.queensu.ca/home/skill`

Frank Taylor finished his PhD in Computer Science at Imperial College in 1996, working in the area of coordination languages, compilers and partial evaluation applied to parallel functional programming. He is now with TECC Ltd, a North London middleware and Internet consultancy, specialising in actor-based middleware and Internet information systems.

Dr Simon Thompson is a Reader in Logic and Computation at the University of Kent, UK. His research has explored links between logic and programming, and particularly functional programming, with recent interests including type theories and integrating computer algebra and reasoning. He is the author of three books, most recently "Haskell: The Craft of Functional Programming", second edition (1999).
URL: `http://www.cs.ukc.ac.uk/people/staff/sjt`

Dr Phil Trinder is a Lecturer in the Department of Computing and Electrical Engineering at Heriot-Watt University, Edinburgh. His primary areas of research are parallel functional languages and their application to databases. Current work includes the design, implementation, and reasoning about Glasgow Parallel Haskell (GpH). **URL:** http://www.cee.hw.ac.uk/~trinder/

Dr Marko van Eekelen is in the Computing Science Department at the University of Nijmegen. He has been a leading member of the Clean research project since its inception in 1984. **URL:** http://www.cs.kun.nl/~marko

Acknowledgements

The editors would like to thank all the contributing authors for their active participation and cooperation in this project. We would also like to thank the anonymous referees for their helpful comments and suggestions, and the long suffering editorial and technical staff at Springer, especially Rosie Kemp, Beverley Ford and Karen Barker, for their understanding and forbearance. Finally, but by no means least, we are grateful for the generous assistance offered by Tony Davie, Alex Hulpke, Vicki Ingpen, Sahalu Junaidu and Álvaro Rebón and others in proof-reading and correcting drafts of this book, in suggesting useful improvements, in constructing the index and in providing essential machine resources and support.

Greg Michaelson would like to thank the School of Computing Sciences at the University of Technology, Sydney, and the Department of Computer Science and Electrical Engineering at the University of Queensland for their hospitality during the final frantic integration of this book.

The editors and authors have waived all royalties from the sale of this book which will form a fund for a prize at the annual International Workshop on the Implementation of Functional Languages (IFL).

World Wide Web Page

Errata and other material relating to this book will be maintained on-line at http://www-fp.dcs.st-and.ac.uk/pfpbook.

Part I

Fundamentals

1. Introduction

Kevin Hammond[1] and Greg Michaelson[2]

1.1 Introduction

1.1.1 Why Parallel Functional Programming Matters

In his seminal paper [292], Hughes argues that functional programming is important because it promotes modular programming. Hughes identifies a number of significant advantages to using functional languages, which include:

- Ease of program construction;
- Ease of function/module reuse;
- Simplicity;
- Generality through higher-order functions ("functional glue").

Experience suggests that a number of other points can be added:

- Ease of reasoning/proof;
- Ease of program transformation;
- Scope for optimisation.

While these motivations are also important in a parallel setting, there are several additional reasons why functional programming matters to a parallel programmer [246]:

- Ease of partitioning a parallel program;
- Simple communication model;
- Absence of deadlock;
- Straightforward semantic debugging;
- Easy exploitation of pipelining and other parallel control constructs.

We will see later in Sections 1.2 and 1.4 of this chapter and in the separate chapters on programming language constructs and realisations (Chapters 3–6) that some language and implementation design choices affect these points, and may even render them invalid. For now, we will concentrate on a minimalist set of choices that represent something of an ideal parallel programming environment (*non-strict, purely functional, implicitly parallel*). The motivation for these choices and a discussion of the alternatives is given in later sections.

In compensation for the advantages of functional programming for parallel programming that are listed above, there are a number of problems which,

---

[1] School of Computer Science, University of St Andrews, UK.
[2] Department of Computing and Electronic Engineering, Heriot-Watt University, UK.

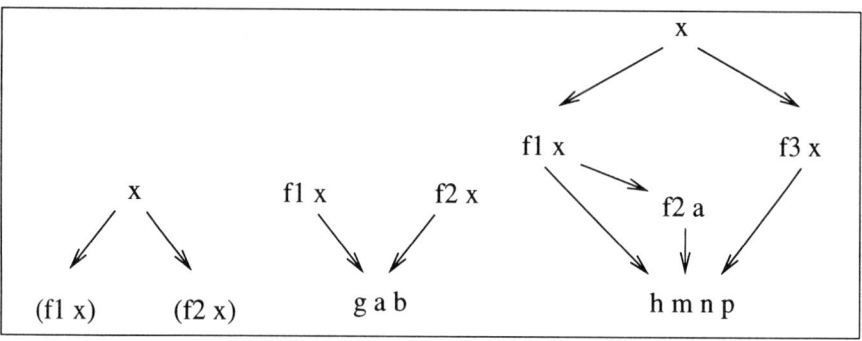

Figure 1.1. Simple data dependencies in the definition of `parallel` (left), argument dependencies in the definition of `parg` (centre), and complex dependencies in the definition of `pdep` (right)

while not entirely new to functional programming, are of greater relative importance in this context. These essentially correspond to the behavioural rather than semantic aspects of parallel programming, and include:

- Performance monitoring;
- Cost modelling;
- Locality.

These problems are addressed specifically in Chapters 8 and 10 as well as generally throughout the book.

Ease of Partitioning a Parallel Program. In principle, any two subexpressions of a *purely functional* program can be executed in parallel. This is because there are no implicit control dependencies between those subexpressions, such as are introduced by assignment. All sequential dependencies are captured either by data dependencies between subexpressions or by explicit control dependencies.

For example, given the definitions below (the notation used here is explained further in Chapter 2),

```
parallel x = (f1 x, f2 x)
f1 y = y + 1
f2 z = z * 3
```

the two subexpressions f1 x and f2 x can be executed in parallel, since neither expression depends on the other. Both subexpressions depend, however, on the value of x, and consequently there exists a data dependency between the two subexpressions and this value as shown in Figure 1.1. This dependency means that the value of x must be produced before either of the two subexpressions can be evaluated. This forces sequential evaluation.

A classic situation occurs when a function depends on its arguments. Consider the definition of `parg` below:

1.1 Introduction

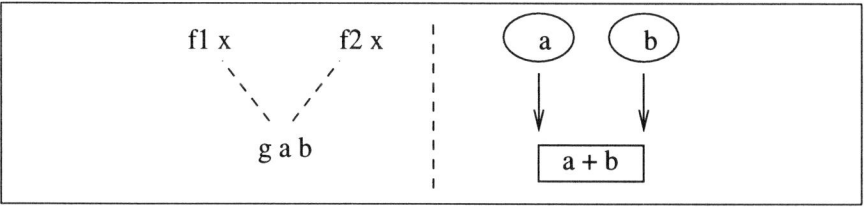

Figure 1.2. Data dependencies and communication

```
parg x = g (f1 x) (f2 x)
g a b   = a + b
```

Assuming that + needs both its arguments, as usual, then the corresponding dependencies for g are as shown in Figure 1.1 Clearly both of g's arguments can be evaluated in parallel, but both arguments must have been evaluated before the value of g can be produced. This simple observation is, in fact, the basis for most parallelism in a *strict* functional language, as discussed in Section 1.2.2.

Of course, in more complicated examples, there may be complete or partial data dependencies between subexpressions that inhibit parallel evaluation. For example, consider the definition of pdep below:

```
pdep x = let a = f1 x in
         h a (f2 a) (f3 x)
h m n p = m + n + p
```

As can be seen from Figure 1.1, such dependencies quickly become too complicated for the programmer to manage easily. Unfortunately, the parallel time and space behaviour can depend crucially on dependencies of this kind.

Simple Communication Model. Data dependencies can be seen as introducing sequential demands on the production of values. Alternatively, they may be seen as potential communication channels. In this latter view, a communication channel is created when a needed expression demands the value of another expression that is already being evaluated by another parallel task. When the latter task completes, the demanding task is notified of the appropriate value and the communication channel can be discarded. Figure 1.2 shows this correspondence: executing tasks are represented by circles, suspended tasks are represented by boxed expressions and communication channels by arrows.

Straightforward Semantic Debugging. Purely functional programs have the same semantic value when evaluated in parallel as when evaluated sequentially. This value is independent of the evaluation order that is chosen. Conversely, if a program terminates with error (yields an undefined value, often shown as ⊥) when run sequentially, then it will also yield an undefined value (though not necessarily the same one!) when run in parallel.

This property of *determinacy* means that it is possible to have a great deal of faith in the answer that a parallel functional program produces. Unlike in more conventional parallel languages, it is not necessary to consider order of communication or race conditions when testing or debugging a program. The result of the program will always be the same regardless of system issues such as variations in communication latencies, or the intricacies of scheduling parallel tasks.

An important consequence of program determinacy is that it is possible to test and debug a functional program on a sequential machine and then compile and run it on a different parallel machine. The only thing that will change is the execution time. It is, of course, also possible to exhaust resources on one machine configuration that would not be exhausted on another. For example, as illustrated in Chapter 11, a parallel program may require more (or sometimes less) dynamic heap than its sequential counterpart. The solution may lie in the development of better performance monitoring tools and programmer awareness.

Absence of Deadlock. In contrast to an imperative parallel program, it is impossible to introduce deadlock by simply parallelising a purely functional program. Any program that delivers a value when run sequentially will deliver the same value when run in parallel. To those who have spent fruitless hours discovering why a simple program deadlocks, or pored over complex bisimulations, this is no doubt a significant advantage! Despite this, however, an *erroneous* program (i.e. one whose result is *undefined*) may fail to terminate, when executed either sequentially or in parallel.

Easy Exploitation of Pipelining and Other Parallel Constructs. There is a direct analogy between function composition and a parallel pipeline. This is an immediate corollary of the simple communication model noted above. If a function f depends on a value e then a communication channel can be created linking f with e (Figure 1.3, left). Where the function needs successive values of a data structure and this is computed by the argument, a parallel pipeline can be created. Figure 1.3 shows how a producer (from 2 10) and a consumer (squares) can be composed to give a simple pipeline and that this principle can be extended to give a pipeline of arbitrary length. The definitions of squares and from are as below. Both from and squares use the list construction operator (:) that prefixes a value (the head) to a list (the tail) to give a new list with one extra element. squares also uses (:) as a pattern to extract the head and tail of a list.

```
squares (x:xs) =   x*x : squares xs
from m n =         if m == n then [] else m : from (m+1)
simplepipe =       squares (from 2 10)
twostagepipe =     squares simplepipe
threestagepipe =   squares twostagepipe
```

1.1 Introduction 7

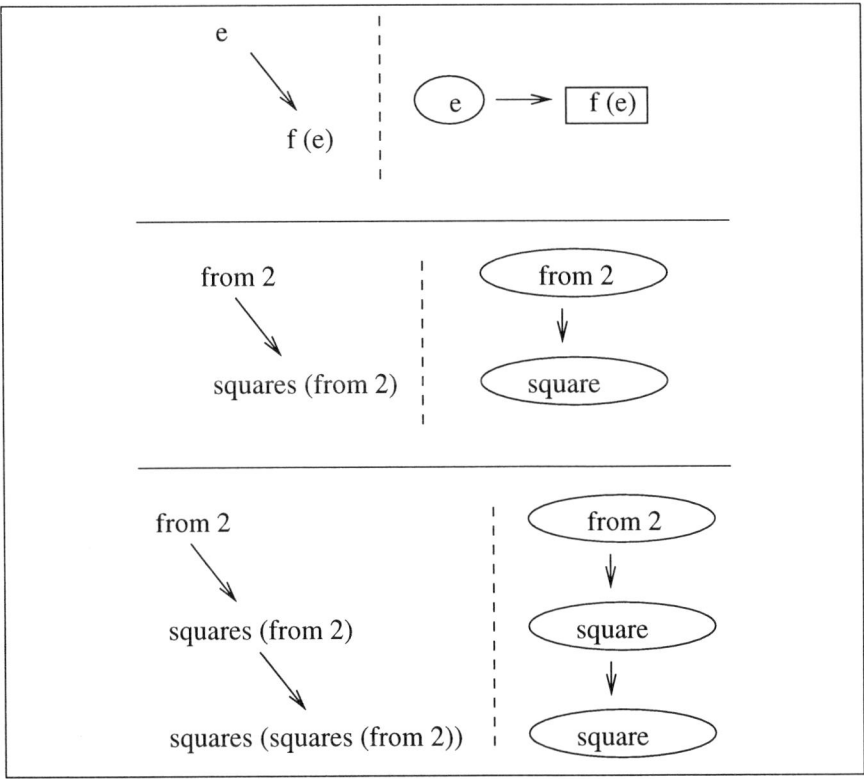

Figure 1.3. Parallel pipelining (top), with one-stage pipeline (centre), and two-stage pipeline (bottom)

Recognising a pattern such as pipelining in a program amounts to detecting the parallel control structure or *skeleton* of the program. Chapter 13 studies much more complicated patterns of parallel computation, and shows how these patterns can be mapped to particular parallel architectures.

1.1.2 Parallelism or Concurrency?

The terms *concurrency* and *parallelism* have sometimes been used interchangeably in the past. Both types of system involve executing processes or tasks at the same time. Modern usage [44], [497] is, however, to use the term "concurrency" for systems which involve a number of independent, but collaborating, processes, such as graphical user interfaces or operating systems. The term "parallelism" is used for systems involving the cooperation of a number of inter-dependent tasks on a single activity.

The purpose of concurrency is to support abstraction and to improve security by separating activities which are logically independent processes, but which may take place simultaneously. The purpose of parallelism, in contrast, is to improve performance, usually in terms of speed, throughput or response time by creating subtasks to deal with units of work.

Explicitly parallel languages such as Eden, Concurrent ML (Chapter 17) or Scampi (Chapter 18) can often be used to program concurrent activities, and must face similar issues of deadlock, starvation etc. Implicitly parallel languages such as SISAL or SAC can avoid such problems, but are not suitable for dealing with the abstractions required by concurrent systems.

1.2 Language Issues

Much darkness has been cast on the crucial choices facing functional language designers, fuelled by acrimonious debate between devotees of one particular set of language features countering arguments propounded by those of another set. This section attempts to dispassionately dissect these fundamental decisions, and to reveal them as genuine language design choices rather than purely dogmatic positions. In the process, it should become apparent that these choices are not entirely orthogonal, and that based on our current understanding, some sets of design choices are not as desirable as others. The choices are revisited in Chapter 3, which considers the general issue of language constructs to support parallelism.

1.2.1 Functional versus Non-Functional

At a public exhibition, we were asked by an eminent psychologist why we had chosen to focus our research on *functional* languages. Carefully we explained the advantages of clean semantics, the ability to reason about those languages, and the higher-level programming that was possible by an experienced practitioner. The psychologist was unconvinced. But why, he asked, in a manner that clinched the argument and left us momentarily unable to respond, had we chosen to research such a narrow area rather than the much more interesting and encompassing field of *dysfunctional* languages?

In spite of the fact that it is easy for us to distinguish functional from non-functional languages, it is surprisingly hard to define the characteristics of a functional language in an absolutely precise way. We will follow the general trend in defining a functional language to be one where the principal building block is the function definition, and where the primary mechanism for constructing more complex programs is the higher-order function and function composition ("functional glue").

1.2.2 Strict versus Non-Strict

The level of *strictness* supported by a language can crucially affect parallelism.

1.2 Language Issues

In a strict language all arguments to a function are needed, and may therefore be evaluated in parallel both with each other and with the evaluation of the function body. Data dependencies will, however, restrict the available parallelism to some extent.

In a non-strict language on the other hand, not all function arguments are necessarily needed, and consequently analysis may be required to determine which expressions can be executed in parallel. Such analyses must be conservative since it may be unsafe to evaluate an expression which is not needed (the program might fail unexpectedly in this case), and therefore will not usually detect all possible parallelism.

This language decision feeds through to the implementation. For a strict language, the main problem is restricting the amount of available parallelism so that sensibly sized computations are run in parallel. For a non-strict language on the other hand, the problem usually lies in detecting enough potentially parallel computations. Once this fundamental problem is solved, however, there are strong similarities in the implementation approaches that can be taken in each case.

Given that non-strict languages restrict the parallelism which is abundant in a strict language, the observant reader may now be wondering why we chose to restrict our attention to non-strict languages rather than strict ones. The reason is mainly pedagogical: it is much simpler to motivate the discussion of data dependencies and the corresponding model of communication in a non-strict context – in strict languages we are much less inclined to think in terms of data dependencies. We note, however, that strict languages have a more predictable execution order, and are therefore more amenable to explicitly controlled parallelism.

There are also algorithmic implications to the choice of strictness properties. For instance, functions written in a strict language must take account of the context in which they are used and provide explicit limits to computation rather than relying on lack of demand to limit the amount of computation that must be performed. This can lead to code duplication as shown below. In a parallel context, it may be necessary to provide even more versions of a function to allow for all possible combinations of parallel and sequential use.

1.2.3 Impure versus Pure

Purity is clearly a loaded term. What right-thinking person would buy *impure fruit juice* or promote *impure thoughts* in the young? In the functional language community it has also assumed something of the status of a moral term, implying criticism rather than description to some researchers. In addition it is almost as ill-defined as the word functional itself. However, the term *purity* has a well-known intuitive definition and we have therefore chosen to use it in this book in the usual sense of excluding implicit side-effects such as assignment, I/O or exceptions.

In a parallel setting, side-effects are, of course, anathema to automatic or semi-automatic parallelisation since they inhibit easy program decomposition into parallel tasks and introduce new dependencies between tasks which can be difficult or impossible to disentangle without using explicit parallel control.

Because a purely functional program has no side-effects, it is relatively easy to partition programs so that sub-programs can be executed in parallel, as we have shown in Section 1.1. Any computation which is needed to produce the result of the program may be run as a separate task. The control dependencies which are implicit in the language serve to enforce any sequential behaviour, and also to limit the creation of excess parallelism to some extent.

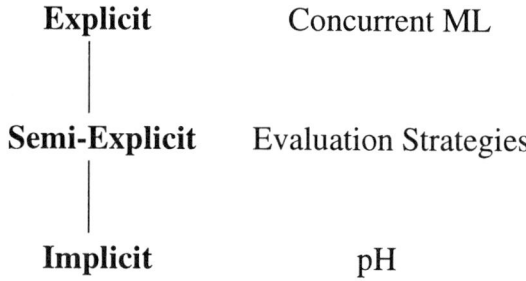

Figure 1.4. Hierarchy of explicit and implicit approaches to parallelism

1.2.4 Level of Control

The two extremes of parallel control are typified by fully explicit approaches, where all behavioural details are specified, including parallel partitioning, task and data distribution, load management and communication, and fully implicit approaches where the compiler makes all such decisions. In between lies a wide range of choices, as shown by Figure 1.4.

Purely Implicit Approaches. The most implicit approaches, requiring least programmer input are exemplified by pH [426] or evaluation transformers [98], [100]. pH is an implicitly parallel language based on Haskell, which provides dataflow-style loop-constructs and I-structures (see Section 2.6). The arguments to a function are evaluated in parallel, and each iteration of the parallel loop-construct is similarly executed as a separate task.

Evaluation transformers exploit the properties of non-strict languages, but rely on the system being able to generate good strictness information. Each function is provided with a set of evaluation transformers, one for each formal argument. Each transformer is a forcing operation that will evaluate

1.2 Language Issues

an actual argument to the extent required by the function, perhaps evaluating it to weak head normal form, or forcing evaluation of the spine of a list. In any context where the function is used, these transformers can be applied in parallel to the corresponding actual arguments.

Restricted Implicit Approaches. Restricted implicit approaches match certain language characteristics with desirable program properties. For example, in the skeleton approach alluded to earlier (see Chapter 13 for a full exposition), certain patterns of computation are recognised and matched with suitable templates of parallel behaviour. A simple example might be matching a function composition in the source with a parallel pipeline implementation, as in Section 1.1. More typically, the patterns that are detected are predefined higher-order functions, which the programmer has parameterised on some algorithmic component. For example, consider:

```
let doubles = map double (from 3 20) in
consume doubles
```

The `map` function applies its first argument, a function, to each element of its second argument, a list, in turn, giving a new list as its result. The list `doubles` is thus created by applying `double` to each element in the list `from 3 20`.

The `map` function could be matched to a number of different parallel implementations, perhaps creating a process farm, or a bounded buffer pipelined in parallel with the `consume` function.

Other examples of restricted implicit approaches include the data parallel language NESL [61], SAC [236] and SISAL [391]. All three languages are strict, purely functional languages, all three obtain parallelism from bulk types such as lists or arrays. NESL provides nestable data parallel operations over lists; SISAL uses control parallel loop-constructs over arrays; SAC uses control parallel With-loops.

Controlled Parallelism. Annotation-based approaches may fall either side of the implicit/explicit divide. If an annotation is a directive to the compiler, then this is clearly an example of explicit parallelism. If the annotation is a suggestion, however, that may perhaps be checked by the compiler or even ignored entirely, then the construct lies more in the realm of implicit parallelism. This is not merely a technical distinction: in implicitly parallel systems, overall control lies in the hands of the compiler and run-time system (which is automatic parallelisation), whereas in an explicitly parallel system overall control rests squarely in the hands of the programmer (which is manual parallelisation).

Other controlled approaches include evaluation strategies [571] and first-class schedules [404]. In these systems, functions are used to control parallel behaviour. These functions are higher-order functions that manipulate sequential or parallel program components to yield a more complex parallel program behaviour, but whose definition is entirely within the normal semantics of the sequential programming language.

Explicit Approaches. In explicit approaches, not only is every detail of the parallel execution under the programmer's control, but it *must* be specified in the parallel program. In principle, this allows a skilled programmer to produce a highly optimised parallel program for some architecture. This is usually achieved by providing new parallel control constructs to deal with parallel partitioning, communication, and task placement etc. Chapter 18 describes one such approach that combines the functional language Caml with the MPI message passing library, while Chapter 17 describes the different approach taken by Concurrent ML, in which new language constructs are introduced to deal with process creation and communication.

Coordination Languages. Coordination languages fall somewhat outside the classification introduced above, though controlled languages may be seen as a kind of coordination language. Rather than introducing language constructs to control parallelism, this is effected through a special purpose control language. Caliban is the most widely known functional coordination language [331]. In the case of Caliban, the coordination language is very closely related to the functional language that it controls, and is used to determine a static mapping of parallel tasks to processors. Other approaches such as Linda [214] introduce a completely new coordination language layer that controls the dynamic execution of sequential program fragments written in a conventional programming language (often C or Prolog). These approaches are discussed in Chapter 14.

1.2.5 Type System

While the choice of type system can have a major impact on language design and usability, it seems to have little impact on parallelism in general. There are, however, a few systems which have taken advantage of the flexibility offered by modern type systems to distinguish parallel and sequential computations using separate types, or to provide types to capture behavioural information. Examples of such systems include Loogen's Eden language [85] or Mirani and Hudak's first-class schedules [404]. Types may also be used to derive behavioural information about a program. For example, we have devised a cost (granularity) analysis for parallel programs that exploits the notion of sized types to obtain information about the cost of executing subexpressions [366]. This information can be specialised for particular contexts using a mechanism similar to that used for normal parametric polymorphism.

There also seem to be strong software engineering reasons for preferring strongly typed languages to ones which are weakly typed. Firstly, although programs may take longer to write in a strongly typed language, they are more likely to be correct. Secondly, implementations of strongly typed languages can often take advantage of type information to produce more specific

1.2 Language Issues

compiled code for certain cases. Finally, polymorphism (whether parametric or ad-hoc) allows generic code to be written, which reduces program complexity, enhances ease-of-construction, and promotes modularity. This book therefore concentrates on statically typed functional languages such as Standard ML and Haskell, but we note that most of the material covered here applies equally to dynamically typed languages such as Lisp.

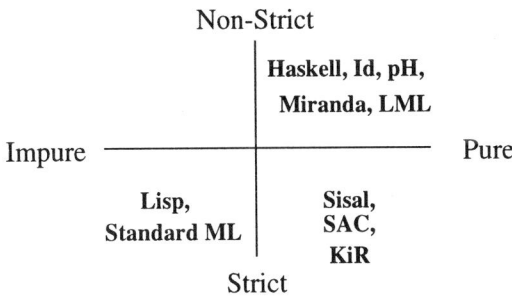

Figure 1.5. Purity and strictness

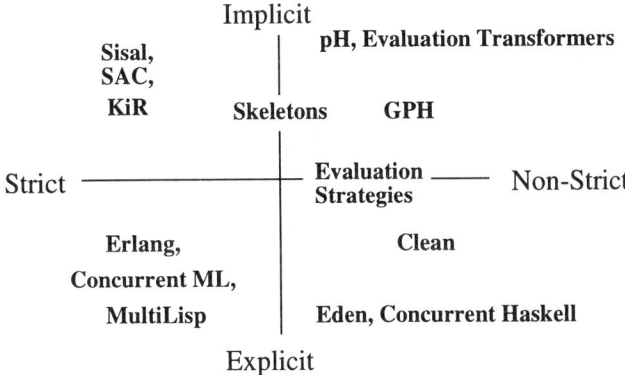

Figure 1.6. Explicitness versus strictness for parallel functional languages

1.2.6 Combinations of Language Choices

As hinted earlier not all combinations of language choice are equally good. Figures 1.5 and 1.6 chart the major parallel functional language designs. The majority fit into the strict, impure or non-strict, pure areas. The majority of the strict, impure languages use an explicit programming model, while the majority of the pure languages use implicit models.

The reason why is quite interesting. All languages need to perform I/O. In a purely functional setting, this was traditionally done by mapping lazy streams onto normal O/S files. In a non-strict language, lazy streams can be easily modelled by normal lists. In a strict setting on the other hand, streams require a special implementation. This is the approach that is taken by SISAL and SAC. Other strict languages, such as Standard ML, Lisp or Erlang have accepted the use of side-effect in order to obtain a more conventional I/O model, as well as the availability of explicit assignments for sequential programming. A consequence is to render non-explicit parallel programming much harder. The recent use of *monads* [588] to support explicit side-effects in non-strict languages like Haskell breaks apart the issues of side-effect, serialisation and composition, so allowing the prospect of implicitly parallel programming in the presence of a rich I/O system.

The remaining issue that was raised earlier (typing) seems to be entirely orthogonal to the other issues that have been covered in this section. We know of very few attempts to exploit parallelism that are confined only to either strongly-typed or weakly-typed languages (an exception is the shapely types approach that is introduced in Chapter 9). Typing issues are therefore considered where appropriate in the later chapters.

1.3 Architectural Issues

From the earliest days of computing, the use of parallel hardware has been seen as a cost-effective way to enhance CPU performance. Apart from isolated small-scale examples such as the Illiac IV [38], however, parallel computing was not really viable until the early 1980s. From that time on, a number of designs have become available, spurred largely by the widespread availability of cheap, powerful microprocessors and user demand for more raw CPU power than can be obtained easily from a single CPU. This section outlines the basic issues in parallel computer architecture. The interested reader is referred to Culler and Singh's book for more detailed coverage [151].

1.3.1 Data and Control Parallelism in Computer Architectures

It is common to distinguish control and data parallelism at the language level, and there is a corresponding distinction in hardware. In the SIMD (Single Instruction Multiple Data) model all parallel processors execute the same instruction at each clock cycle; there is a single shared instruction stream and a single program counter. Parallelism is obtained from executing the instruction on many data items simultaneously.

1.3 Architectural Issues

In contrast, the MIMD model (Multiple Instruction Multiple Data) allows each processor to execute instructions independently, with each processor having its own program counter and other local state. In the most general case, each MIMD processor could be executing a different program, though it is more common for the processors to be running independent copies of a single program – this is SPMD (Single Program Multiple Data).

The original SIMD (Single Instruction Multiple Data) concept of all processors on a parallel machine executing identical instructions seems to have evolved over time. It is now probably best to see SIMD as an architectural model rather than a physical realisation. It is entirely conceivable that a SIMD program could execute on a machine that was originally designed to run MIMD programs, though such an architecture is unlikely to run the SIMD program optimally. It is also likely that modern SIMD processors are fully-featured microprocessors rather than simpler devices as was often envisaged in the past. In effect, SIMD has evolved somewhat towards SPMD.

The SIMD model is thus one of data parallelism rather than the more common control parallelism, applying a single, usually large and complex, operation to all elements of a data structure in parallel. Operations may be conditional, and can often be combined so that results of one phase are used in a later phase. For suitable applications, where operations on data items can essentially be carried out without encountering dependencies on other items SIMD architectures can achieve impressive performances.

Table 1.1. Relative latency and bandwidth for typical communication systems

Type	Latency	Bandwidth Per Processor
Uniprocessor	1	100%
Shared-Memory	5–20	50%–100%
Distributed-Memory	500–5,000	20%–50%
Distributed Network	50,000–1,000,000	3%–30%

1.3.2 Communication System

The structure of the communication system is a fundamental characteristic of a parallel architecture, with profound implications for a language implementation or even language design that is intended to execute on that architecture.

The two primary attributes of any communication system are its latency and its bandwidth. The latency is simply the time taken for a communication to arrive at its destination. The bandwidth is the limit on the volume of data that can be transferred through the system simultaneously (usually in Mb/s or Gb/s). For comparison purposes, Table 1.1 lists these characteristics for a number of modern communication systems in relative terms. The different types of system will be covered in subsequent sections.

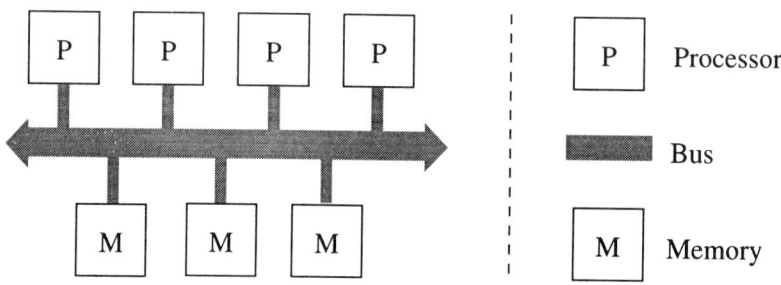

Figure 1.7. Shared-memory architecture

Tightly-Coupled, Shared-Memory Systems. Tightly-coupled systems are ones where the network supports reliable transmission over short distances, and where the parallel machine is best viewed as a single system rather than as a collection of connected components. The simplest such designs are shared-memory systems as shown in Figure 1.7.

Shared-memory systems have the twin virtues of low latency and ease of programming. It is therefore not surprising that they have proved to be relatively popular as commercial designs, often being used as central file-servers or shared compute-servers. They have also proved relatively successful platforms for straightforward parallel implementations of functional languages, often allowing near-linear relative speedup for small numbers of processors.

Shared-memory machines are usually built around a fast internal bus. This is both a strength and a weakness. The primary limitation of a shared-memory machine is that it will only allow a small number of processors to be used. Typical designs will support approximately 16 processors before the bus bandwidth becomes inadequate. When this happens, the communication system thrashes in a manner similar to overloaded virtual memory.

In fact, the model shown in Figure 1.7 is extremely simplistic. Modern shared-memory machines commonly provide some memory that is local to each processor, either in the form of dedicated memory banks, or simply in the form of processor cache memory. This enhances locality of memory access, improves access times and reduces memory traffic across the bus at the cost of requiring that all local copies of shared memory locations must be kept up to date with the master versions (cache coherency). Perhaps surprisingly, maintaining good locality can be very important to shared-memory performance. This is because accesses to shared memory are usually significantly slower than accesses to unshared memory, especially if the latter is cached,

1.3 Architectural Issues

and because the available bus bandwidth must be shared between all the parallel processors.

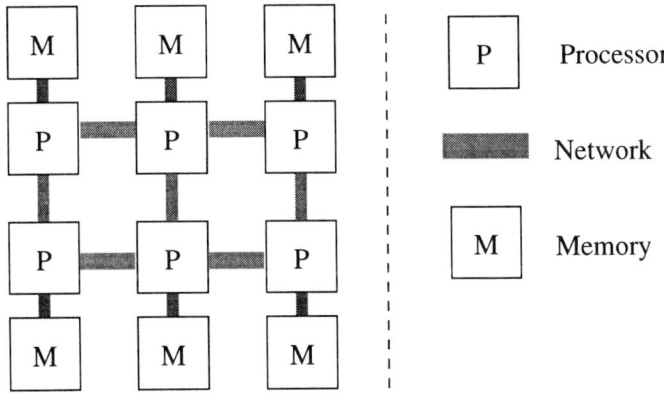

Figure 1.8. Distributed-memory architecture

Tightly-Coupled, Distributed-Memory Systems. Distributed-memory machines have a higher latency, but higher bandwidth network than shared-memory machines (Figure 1.8). The advantage of such designs is that they are more scalable, allowing more processors to be connected through the network. The cost of such a machine is, however, much greater than a shared-memory machine for two reasons. Firstly, the network is much more complicated than that for a shared-memory machine: in order to yield good performance, it is fairly common to provide four or more dedicated point-to-point connections from each processor. While each connection can be simpler than a bus, the sheer number of connections makes the total network cost much greater than a single bus. Secondly, each processor needs its own memory bank. This must typically be large enough to hold a complete copy of the program plus working data.

Loosely-Coupled, Distributed Systems. A recent development is to treat networks of workstations as parallel machines, as shown in Figure 1.9. This is possible because workstations have become increasingly cheap and powerful, and commodity networking solutions are now widespread. The advantages of this approach are that the system is cheap to construct – comprising a few standard workstations and a LAN, such as Ethernet or ATM, to connect them – and that it is easily reconfigured to match varying system resources. It is even possible to configure *heterogeneous* systems – ones which use processors of different types, and in extreme cases, these processors may themselves be tightly-coupled parallel machines.

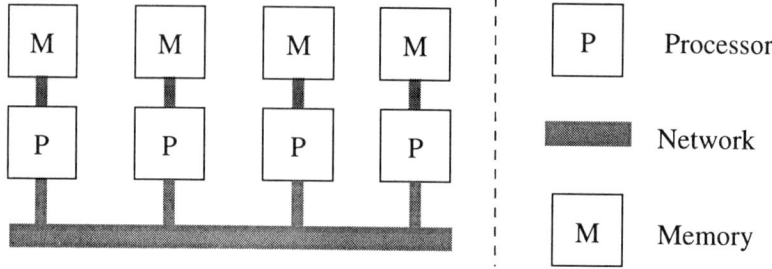

Figure 1.9. Distributed network used as a parallel machine

Given a coarse-grained parallel program decomposition, a loosely-coupled system can work well as a parallel machine, and there have been many cases of people using such systems to solve large, regular problems in parallel. Indeed, there are several instances where the Internet has been used to harness surplus machine resources in what is effectively a very large-scale parallel computation.

The disadvantages of using a loosely-coupled configuration are that it has both very high latency and very low bandwidth. Unless the implementation is designed to handle unreliable transmission, or the network is unusually reliable, the underlying transport protocol must also deal with communication failures. The overheads for such support can be considerable, in extreme cases perhaps doubling latency or halving bandwidth.

Network Topology. The *topology* or shape of the computer network is crucially important to network performance, and matching the pattern of computation to the network is a major implementation issue. While early work on parallel machines considered many interesting topologies such as rings, toroids, butterfly networks and cubes of varying dimensions, shared-memory systems now predominantly use buses, and distributed-memory systems normally use meshes or hypercubes. Figure 1.10 shows some sample network topologies. Each box represents a processing node: a processor-memory combination.

In general, it is possible to combine network topologies to produce a layered or clustered topology. In these systems the bottom layer is usually a small shared-memory cluster, which is then connected to other clusters using another topology, often a mesh or hypercube. This approach exploits cheap low-latency communication within a cluster, whilst providing a scalable approach to building larger systems.

There have been many attempts in hardware to minimise the impact of network topology on an implementation. These attempts are often spurred by a desire to obtain cheap speedups for imperative legacy code written in languages such as Fortran or C, which usually assume constant and cheap

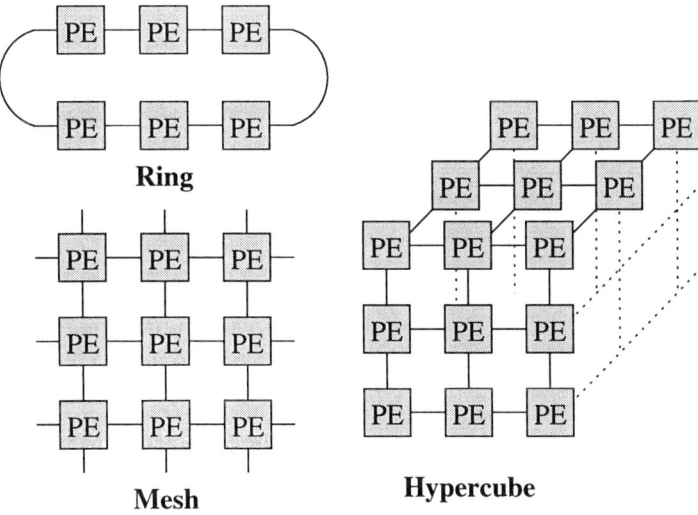

Figure 1.10. Some standard network topologies

memory access times. The best-known technique is cache coherency for a shared-memory machine, which ensures that all local caches are consistent with the globally shared memory.

In order to overcome the scalability problem with shared-memory systems, some vendors have extended this idea to distributed-memory machines to produce virtual shared memory or distributed shared memory systems [151]. These systems provide a uniform memory addressing framework with non-local memory accesses automatically transferred to the appropriate node. In practice, such systems have not yet proved successful, since they hide locality information, and this information is crucial to obtaining good performance.

1.3.3 Novel Architectures

The 1980s saw the construction of a number of novel parallel architectures which were specifically designed to execute functional programming languages efficiently. Examples include ALICE [146], GRIP [251], the Manchester dataflow machine [238] and MIT's Monsoon dataflow machine [270]. Although these designs were interesting from an architectural perspective and progressed our knowledge of parallel computing, they were generally overtaken very quickly by rapid developments in stock hardware and by similar advances in compiler technology for conventional architectures. The modern trend is to exploit high-quality compiler technology for off-the-shelf hardware. This is both faster and more cost-effective than designing and constructing a novel architecture and also allows general improvements in hardware design to be tracked more easily.

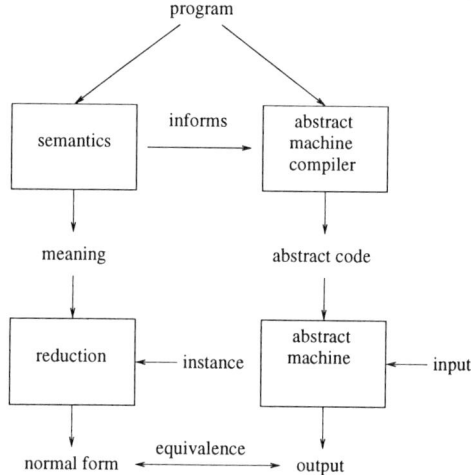

Figure 1.11. Overview of the implementation process

1.4 Implementation Issues

1.4.1 From Semantics to Architecture

From a programmer's point of view, a programming language implementation may be thought of as an animation of a language's semantics. A program is a general mapping from inputs to outputs which is brought alive when an implementation dynamically applies it to a specific input instance. An analogy with animated film is useful in that a language implementation is responsible for generating the "in-betweening" sequence of behaviours that links the input "frame" to the output "frame". Programmers are not normally concerned with the actual details of that "in-betweening" provided they are reassured that the process is a true reflection of the language's semantics. It may be useful for "in-betweening" to be visible during program development, to enable tracing and debugging, but it should be presented in terms of the language semantics independently of specific implementation details.

The implementor has the unenviable task of realising the semantics in a concrete form on a specific architecture. The implementation must optimise performance on the underlying architecture whilst staying true to the semantics. A useful way to characterise an implementation is as an abstract machine straddling both the semantics and the architecture, even if an abstract machine is not an explicit part of a particular implementation. The implementation may then be viewed as the coupling of one component that maps a program onto abstract machine instructions to another that maps abstract machine instructions onto a concrete architecture. The choice of abstract machine and its relative distances from the semantics and the architecture then becomes the locus for key implementation decisions.

1.4.2 Between Church-Rosser and von Neumann

The well-rehearsed benefits of (pure) functional languages derive from the Church-Rosser property of reduction order independence through unchanging associations between names and values. This leads to pleasingly simple semantics through what are, at heart, rewrite systems that successively reduce nested function applications to some normal form. However, direct implementations based on rewriting are hopelessly inefficient in both time and space consumption.

History suggests that von Neumann architectures are, this side of quantum computing [173], the most efficacious physical realisations of Turing computable functions, but von Neumann architectures are quintessentially lacking in Church-Rosserness. Thus, a central problem for functional language implementation lies in the efficient realisation of time order independence in a program through time ordering on a von Neumann architecture.

Unlike quantum computers, von Neumann implementations cannot draw on the simultaneous reduction of all applications: rewrites must be performed in some order. Since Church [125], a primary distinction is made between normal order (leftmost outermost application first) and applicative order (leftmost application first) reduction: this distinction and its implications for language design are discussed above. To gloss: normal order avoids unnecessary evaluation of unselected subexpressions but may result in repetitive evaluation of a single actual parameter at different sites of formal parameter use; applicative order avoids multiple evaluation of a single actual parameter but may result in unnecessary evaluation of unselected subexpressions, with particular implications for termination.

For practical implementations, a corresponding distinction is usually made between the lazy graph reduction machine for normal order evaluation (Section 2.5), with its relatively close correspondence to rewrite semantics, and the SECD machine for applicative order (Section 2.4), with its relatively close correspondence to von Neumann architectures. An immediate implication is an emphasis in graph reduction on mapping graphs onto von Neumann architectures and in the SECD machine on mapping program constructs onto SECD instructions.

In both models, efficiency depends on the realisation of name/value associations, in particular the instantiation of multiple sites of formal parameter use with an actual parameter value. The Church-Rosser property implies that the evaluation of the same expression in different places results in the same final value. Thus, the multiple evaluation of multiple instances of the same actual parameter value may be avoided through some sharing mechanism: in graph reduction with all instances of a formal parameter sharing the same actual parameter subgraph; in the SECD machine through efficient access to environments mapping formal to actual parameters.

Note that in practice these two models are not mutually exclusive. Thus, much research in graph reduction involves removing unnecessary laziness through the introduction of constructs for strict evaluation. Similarly, all supposedly applicative languages actually have normal order conditional expression evaluation and there are standard SECD machine extensions to encompass normal order and laziness. Nonetheless, these models do represent two different traditions in functional language implementation, as will become clear in the rest of this book.

1.4.3 From Abstract to Concrete Machine

Ultimately, an abstract machine must be realised in some sense on a concrete architecture. The number of levels of abstraction between them has manifold implications for the timeless tussle between compilation effort, run-time efficiency and portability.

At its simplest, an abstract machine might directly mirror the language semantics and be implemented through an interpreter for abstract syntax trees, for example as in many early Lisp implementations. This minimises compilation and maximises portability but at considerable cost to efficiency.

The next stage is to identify a lower-level abstract machine and then to compile from the language into abstract machine code for subsequent interpretation. This approach is most common for non-strict languages, for example through variations on the TIM [189] and the G-Machine [314], while noting Cardelli's influential FAM implementation [117] of strict ML. Here compilation effort and efficiency both increase with little impact on portability.

Finally, abstract machine code may be rendered into concrete machine code. This again increases compilation effort and maximises efficiency but at some cost to portability: the abstract to concrete code translator must be reconstructed for each new CPU.

A growing trend is to combine a high level language like C++ or Java with a communications model like MPI [544] or PVM [212] to form a basis for object code, relying on the widespread availability of relatively consistent compilers and communications libraries to avoid explicit code generation and to enable portability. Interest is also growing in language-independent, functionally oriented object languages.

1.4 Implementation Issues

1.4.4 All for One or One for All

The addition of parallelism to a functional language compounds the above sources of difficulty. As with all forms of parallelism, the main problem lies in optimising the balance of communication and processing, which in turn depends on how parallelism is located. Here, functional parallelism may be realised within programs, through some correspondence between functions and processes and between composition and inter-process communication, or through the abstract machine itself: typical design choices for parallel strict and lazy evaluation based on SECD machines or graph reduction.

This distinction is orthogonal to that between control flow and data flow implementations. In a control flow model, parallelism is located in activity specific processes passing data between themselves. In a data flow model, parallelism is located in multiple instances of general purpose abstract machine processes, being activated by data nodes seeking specific processing. While control flow is commonly identified with strict parallelism, and data flow with lazy graph reduction, in practice all distributed memory parallel architectures boil down to processors communicating explicitly with each other.

While lazy graph reduction through data flow is a simpler, more natural model for functional parallelism, it tends to be less efficient than explicit control flow, as it is at a higher level of abstraction than von Neumann machines. Considerable effort goes into reducing the inherent inefficiencies in data flow lazy functional parallelism through compile-time techniques such as strictness and liveness analysis, and into finding optimal run-time task sparking policies. However, control flow implementations either involve the programmer in deep understanding about topology and performance, or the compiler writer in identifying appropriate general purpose communication and process placement mechanisms which are still optimal for particular applications.

For further discussion of strict and non-strict realisations of functional languages, see Chapters 5 and 6 respectively. For discussion of the dataflow tradition, see Section 2.6 and Chapter 11.

1.4.5 How Fast is Fast

The normal objective of parallel programming is to make individual programs run faster. Thus, for the broad project of parallel functional programming to be deemed successful, its protagonists must demonstrate that this latent promise is actually realised. Two complementary approaches can be taken: compile-time performance prediction (covered in Chapters 8 and 9) and run-time performance monitoring (covered in Chapter 10).

Ideally, all useful parallelism should be identifiable statically at compile time but in practice, this is undecidable for Turing computable languages. A variety of static cost models have been developed but their efficacy usually depends on restricting the forms of parallelism that are supported, for example through requiring regularity in the shape of data. Static analysis may be augmented with sequential instrumentation on typical and pathological data. The accuracy of prediction depends crucially on an appropriate choice of data and exhaustive testing is infeasible. However, broad identification and pessimistic interpretation of communication costs usually suffice to clarify whether or not parallelism is useful, since communication on real architectures is usually substantially more costly than processing. Instrumentation itself may be on a specific concrete implementation or on an abstract interpreter, for example based on the language semantics; the latter enabling implementation independence and instrumentor portability.

For both static analysis and dynamic instrumentation, a relationship must be found between the derived information and the corresponding behaviour on the intended architecture. Typically, this takes the form of a general performance model which is parameterised on machine characteristics and instantiated either by appeal to the manufacturer's specifications or through the use of benchmarking test suites on the target machine.

Given that analysis and instrumentation, when available, cannot provide total accuracy, they may be complemented by post-hoc profiling. Indeed, instrumentation on the target architecture is precisely profiling. Here again, the choice of test data is fundamental. Profiling is crucial for understanding the general characteristics of a parallel implementation but may be less desirable than analysis and instrumentation for program development: profiling is application-specific and may lead to an undue focus on a program's final implementation rather than the original design.

1.5 Proof Issues

1.5.1 Introduction

The motivation for developing formal models of programming languages is to provide mechanisms to demonstrate that:

- Programs meet their specifications;
- Programs are equivalent;
- *Transformation sequences* from programs to programs preserve meaning;
- *Refinement sequences* from specifications to programs also preserve meaning.

A latent assumption in this bland statement of intent is that there exists a clear distinction between meta-apparatuses for reasoning about programs and the programs themselves. Here, functional programming has a curiously privileged status, drawing strongly on mathematical logic and computability theory that has been developed from the mid-1930s onwards, including λ-calculus [125], recursive function theory [338], and combinatory logic [153], and, more recently, on theoretical developments within Computer Science

1.5 Proof Issues

itself, for example: symbolic reasoning; denotational semantics [549]; or constructive type theory [379]. These influences may be identified in concepts, notations, programming techniques and implementations. Indeed, functional programming is often presented as straddling the theory and practice of Computing: it might be better characterised as torn between them.

Pragmatists [513] see functional languages as vehicles for executable specification. A formal specification relates inputs to outputs. Given an input instance, a specification may then be reduced to a normal form equivalent to the output. And what is reducing an instantiated specification to a normal form if not executing a program? In contrast, purists [262] argue that mathematics and hence specification encompass non-computable as well as computable functions. Thus, it is possible to specify "computations" which can never be implemented. At best any programming language can only embody an impoverished subset of all possible specifications. Constructivism [433] provides a middle path which is, in principle, acceptable to both camps. Finitistic techniques are used to derive a program from a specification in a formalism which is simultaneously a specification notation, a (functional) programming language and a programming logic. However, this approach depends on restrictions to the expressive power of the formalism which satisfy neither pragmatists nor purists. Epistemological break? Parlour game? Certainly a source of mud slinging. Let us note simply that the formal status of functional programming is by no means straightforward.

Nonetheless, functional languages benefit strongly from their roots, bringing relative ease of formal manipulation compared with imperative languages. Von Neumann time ordering necessitates special extensions to predicate calculus to enable program proof and transformation reflecting an explicit evaluation sequence: Floyd's loop invariants; Hoare's inductive assertions and axiom of assignment; Dijkstra's weakest preconditions and predicate transformers.

In contrast, formal techniques for functional languages draw directly on the antecedent theories. For example, from Church's λ-calculus, abstraction and reduction lead to Burstall and Darlington's fold/unfold approach [103], and reduction is the basis for "partial application". For example, from Peano arithmetic and Kleene's recursive function theory, a variety of induction schemes inform recursion and structural induction. Indeed, the comparative simplicity and purity of functional languages enable a pleasing opportunism in the choice of formal techniques. A more detailed and more formal coverage of proof techniques is found in Chapter 4.

1.5.2 Proof and Functional Parallelism

The degree to which properties of parallel functional programs may be formally verified depends fundamentally on how parallelism is expressed, if at all, within a functional framework. In purely implicit approaches, parallelism is totally transparent to the programmer. There are no specifically parallel properties which may be investigated at the program level and attention is focused on the underlying implementation. However, run-time profiling may identify significant loci of parallelism for modification through program transformation.

For explicit functional parallelism with communication constructs or libraries, the main concerns are with synchronisation properties, as in explicit imperative parallelism. A variety of approaches are available, for example through a proof system oriented to parallelism and concurrency like CSP [284] or CCS [400], or via a formal specification notation for communication protocols like Estelle [297] or the CCS-related LOTOS [298]. Closer to home, the π-calculus [402] has a strongly functional flavour and may be used as a parallel object language for the λ-calculus.

For controlled functional parallelism, synchronisation properties can again be determined at the implementation level. However, performance modelling and prediction may clarify whether or not the parallelism that has been nominated is efficiently exploitable and, as with purely implicit parallelism, consequently enable guided program transformation.

1.5.3 Functional Program Transformation

Perhaps the main formal strength of functional languages lies in the rich theoretical basis for semantics preserving program transformation, which comes into its own in higher-order parallel functional programming. For example, Backus' FP [28] and the Bird-Meertens Formalism (BMF) [53] provide unified approaches to the transformation of composed higher-order functions. There are well known associations between higher-order functions and parallel schema, characterised by Cole as skeletons [139]. The transformation of composed higher-order functions leads to equivalent reconfiguration of the corresponding skeletons. Coupled with cost modelling techniques like Skillicorn's (Chapter 8), this enables rigorous strategies for manipulating programs to optimise sites of parallelism.

For example, consider the map function that was mentioned in Section 1.2.4. This higher-order function applies its argument function f to every element of an initial list [e1,e2, ... eN] to return a final list [f e1,f e2, ... f eN]. Consider also the definition of the *function composition* operator (.):

   (f . g) x = f (g x)

where the result of one function g is the argument for another f.

Note that map distributes over composition:

   (map f) . (map g) ⇔ map (f . g)

so applying g to every element of a list and then applying f to every element of the resulting list is the same as applying g followed by f to each element of the original list.

1.5 Proof Issues

For parallel programming, map is equivalent to a parallel process farm:

```
map f [e1 ... eI ... eN] ==>
```

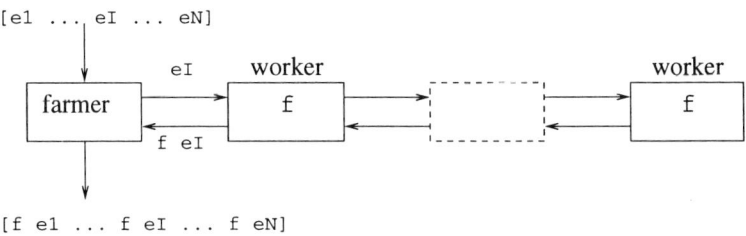

and composition is equivalent to a process pipeline:

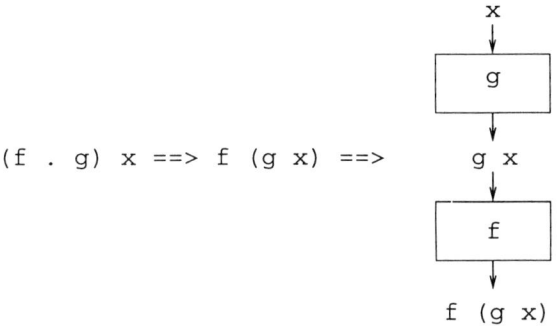

Thus map/compose distributivity is equivalent to changing a pipeline of farms for (map f) . (map g) to a farm of pipelines for map (f . g):

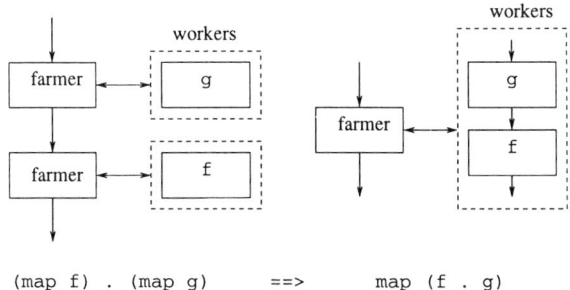

Starting with (map f) . (map g), if either map f or map g has a very large communication-to-processing ratio then f and g might be combined within a single map. Conversely, starting with map (f . g), if f . g has a very small communication-to-processing ratio, then the maps for f and g might be separated. Similarly, bracketing nested compositions is equivalent to grouping the corresponding processes. Thus, the trivial transformations:

f . g . h ⇔ (f . g) . h ⇔ f . (g . h) ⇔ (f . g . h)

are equivalent to rearranging the equivalent process pipelines:

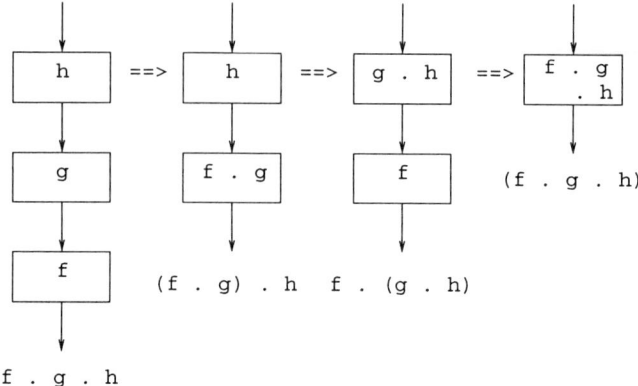

1.5.4 Explosion in a Cathedral

The number of possible transformations grows rapidly with the number of higher-order constructs and it is necessary to prove the correctness of each proposed transformation to ensure that it is truly semantics-preserving. This may be alleviated to some extent by the use of families of higher-order functions with associated families of transformations. For example, transformations for *shapely* list operations will have equivalents for the corresponding *shapely* operations on other types (see Chapter 9).

Nonetheless, a considerable burden of proof is implied by transformational parallelism optimisation, which may be eased by automatic and computer-assisted theorem proving. Identification of likely transformations might also be aided by computer assistance.

Furthermore, the number of possible transformation applications grows rapidly with the size of program. For example, there are 2^{N-1} ways of grouping N composed functions onto up to N processors. In particular, there are 2^{N-1} ways of grouping N composed maps: if the *Ith* grouping involves $M(I)$ maps then there are a further $2^{M(I)-1}$ ways of grouping the argument functions after applying the map/compose transformation.

To render this potentially vast search space tractable, substantial automation of program transformation is required, utilising heuristics to select transformations, based on the change each transformation makes to the processing/communication balance of the construct it is applied to. This, in turn, necessitates the modelling of the effects of each transformation, a process which might itself be automated by combining cost models for the components on both sides of a transformation.

1.6 Summary

This chapter has given an overview of the choices that must be made by parallel functional language designers, implementors and users. It has identified the important characteristics of parallel functional programming, motivating the use of functional languages for parallel programming, considered the primary choices that face the designers of parallel functional languages, outlined the main implementation approaches that have been used to date, surveyed the architectural issues that affect these implementations, and indicated the proof techniques that are appropriate to parallel functional programmers. As befits an introductory chapter, the material presented here is necessarily terse and somewhat elliptic. The remaining chapters in Part I of this book provide more detailed expositions of this material, focusing on each of the four main areas identified here of language, strict and non-strict implementations and architectures, and proof, preceded by common foundational material on Haskell, λ-calculus, the SECD machine and graph reduction.

2. Foundations

Greg Michaelson[1], Kevin Hammond[2] and Chris Clack[3]

2.1 Introduction

This chapter is intended to provide a background in functional programming. In a book of this nature (and size), it is not appropriate to provide a tutorial introduction to all aspects of functional programming. We have therefore been selective in covering the most essential ground, and refer the reader who wishes to discover more to the many excellent texts on functional programming and *lambda*-calculus that have already been produced, e.g. [51], [564], [459].

Section 2.2 introduces a basic version of the Haskell language that will be used for many of the examples in later chapters of this book. Section 2.3 is a simple introduction to the λ-calculus, introducing the theory that underlies functional programming and discussing issues related to parallel execution of functional programs. Sections 2.4 and 2.5 cover fundamental implementation concepts for strict and non-strict languages respectively. Finally Section 2.6 covers basic issues relating to dataflow programming.

2.2 A Basic Introduction to Haskell

Haskell is a non-strict, purely functional language designed by an international committee of functional programmers [457]. This section introduces a minimal version of the Haskell language capable of explaining the basic notation used in the examples throughout this book. The full Haskell language is much larger and more complex, including technically advanced features such as type classes for systematic overloading [590], and monads for clean input/output and state manipulation [588]. Two good introductory text books covering the full Haskell language are those by Thompson [564] and Bird [51].

2.2.1 Basic Types

The full Haskell language possesses a rich array of numeric and non-numeric types. However, only a few basic types are needed to understand the majority of the programs presented in this book. The most basic, unstructured types are `Int`, `Float`, `Char` and `Bool`, representing fixed precision integers, floating point numbers, ASCII characters and Boolean truth values respectively.

---

[1] Department of Computing and Electronic Engineering, Heriot-Watt University, UK.
[2] School of Computer Science, University of St Andrews, UK.
[3] Department of Computer Science, University College, London, UK.

Fixed-Precision Integers: Int. The type Int comprises integers in the range minBound...maxBound. Integer constants are written in the conventional way ...-1, 0, 1, ...

The standard arithmetic operations on integers are all provided and have their usual meanings: (+), (-), (*), abs, div, mod. The normal set of comparison operators is also provided to test for equality (==), inequality (/=), or the obvious orderings (<), (<=), (>), (>=).

Constants and operators can be used to produce value definitions. For example:

```
height, width, area :: Int
height = 120
width  = 50
area   = height * width
```

defines height, width and area to be values of type Int. height and width are simple constants, area is defined to be the product of these two values.

Floating-Point Numbers: Float. The type Float comprises single precision floating point numbers. Constant Floats may be written in a variety of standard ways, e.g. -1.234, 0.1e-3. Integral Floats can also be written using integer constants (e.g. 1000). The arithmetic and comparison operations provided for Float are similar to those provided for Int, except that integer division (div) is replaced by floating division (/) and there is no modulus operator (mod).

Floating point operators and values are used in definitions in a similar way to their integer counterparts. For example:

```
pi, radius, area :: Float
pi     =   3.14159
radius = 20
area   =   pi * radius * radius
```

Double precision values and arithmetic can also be used in exactly the same way. In this case the type is Double.

Characters: Char. Character constants of type Char are written using single quotes, thus 'x'. There are a few special escape characters for newline ('\n'), tab ('\t'), single quote ('\''), backslash ('\\') etc.

The same comparison operators are provided for Chars as for Ints and Floats. Standard functions are also provided to convert characters to Ints (ord) or vice-versa (chr).

```
first, next :: Char
first = 'a'
next  = chr (ord first + 1)
```

2.2 A Basic Introduction to Haskell

Strings: String. Strings (of type `String` – see also Section 2.2.3) are written as sequences of characters, with the same escapes as for character constants. Strings also have all the standard comparison operators, plus operations to give the length of a string (`length`), concatenate two strings (`++`), or to return a prefix or suffix of a string (`take` and `drop`, respectively).

```
filename, basename, objname :: String
filename = "test.hs"
basename = take (length filename - 3) filename
objname  = basename ++ ".obj"
```

Note that the arguments to `take` and `length` are given by juxtaposition rather than by bracketing into comma-separated lists, as is common in imperative or object-oriented languages, so `take` has two concrete arguments (`length filename -3`) and `filename`, and `length` has the single argument `filename`.

Booleans: Bool. Boolean values of type `Bool` may be either `True` or `False`. These are returned by comparison operators such as (`<`), logical operators such as (`&&`) or (`||`), which represent logical *and* and *or*, respectively, and may also be used directly. For example:

```
high, otherwise :: Boolean
high = height > 20
otherwise = True
```

2.2.2 Tuples

Values can be built into record-like structures using *tuples* of a certain length.

```
haskell, turing :: (String,Int,Int)
haskell = ("Haskell B. Curry",1900,1982)
turing  = ("Alan Turing",1912,1954)
```

declares two three-tuples, each of which contains a `String` and two `Int`s. Haskell also provides a more complicated record notation with named fields, but this will not be used in this book.

2.2.3 Lists

The basic data structure in Haskell, as in most functional languages, is the list. Lists are normally written as comma-separated lists of values, all of which must be of the same type. For example:

```
primes :: [Int]
primes = [1,2,3,5,7,11]
```

declares the function `primes` to be a list of `Int`s.

Lists are in fact built from two components: `[]` represents a null list; and the infix function (`:`) prefixes a new component to an existing list (this constructor is also sometimes known as *cons*, from its origin in Lisp). We can therefore write `primes` instead as a series of integers joined onto `[]` by the (`:`) operator.

```
primes = 1 : (2 : (3 : (5 : (7 : (11 : [])))))
```

or, since (`:`) is right-associative, as:

```
primes = 1 : 2 : 3 : 5 : 7 : 11 : []
```

There is no limit on the extent to which lists may be nested, and lists may also freely contain tuples or vice versa. For instance:

```
birthdays :: [(String,Int,Int)]
birthdays = [("Kevin",17,6),("Greg",24,9)]

dead, live :: Char
dead = ' '; live = '*'
life :: [[Char]]
life = [[dead, live, dead],
        [live, dead, live],
        [dead, live, dead],
        [dead, dead, live]]
```

Strings as Lists. Strings are actually defined as lists of characters – the type `String` is defined to be equivalent to the list type `[Char]` in the Haskell prelude. All the standard list operators can therefore also be used for strings. For example:

```
length "Haskell"              == 7
drop 11 "Manchester Baby"     == "Baby"
```

2.2.4 Functions

Recursion. Since purely functional languages cannot directly express iteration (the value of a variable cannot change within a function definition), the usual way to construct programs that require loops is to use recursion. For instance:

```
sum :: [Int] -> Int
sum [] = 0
sum (x:xs) = x + sum xs
```

defines a function to sum the elements of an integer list. The type of the function (`[Int] -> Int`) indicates that it takes a list of integers `[Int]` as its argument and returns an integer as its result. Each of the two lines in

the function definition gives one of the two possible cases for the value of
the argument. In the first case, the list is empty and the result will be 0. In
the second case, the list is a cons cell whose head is a and whose tail is as).
These two values are used in the body of the definition.

The sum function can be used in an expression (*applied* to a concrete argument) in exactly the same way as the standard take, length etc. functions.
So:

```
      sum [1,2,3]
   ⇒  sum (1 : (2 : (3 : []))) -- uses second rule of sum
   ⇒  1 + sum (2 : (3 : []))   --         -- " --
   ⇒  1 + 2 + sum (3 : [])     --         -- " --
   ⇒  1 + 2 + 3 + sum []       -- uses first rule of sum
   ⇒  1 + 2 + 3 + 0
   ⇒  6
```

Pattern Matching. The definition of sum has used patterns for its list argument. In general, any constructor, including primitives such as integers and
floats or tuples, can be used as a pattern for any argument to a function definition. If a function is defined as a series of overlapping patterns, then the
patterns are matched in turn from top-to-bottom, left-to-right. A variable
matches any constructor. So, for example, to join two lists of floats into a
new list, the following function of two arguments could be used:

```
append :: [Float] -> [Float] -> [Float]
append []     fs2 = fs2
append fs1    []  = fs1
append (f:fs) fs2 = f : append fs fs2
```

Conditionals and Guards. Conditional functions can be introduced in two
ways:

- Using conditional expressions if...then...else...;
- Using guarded definitions.

Examples of the two styles are:

```
max1, max2 :: Float -> Float -> Bool
max1 x y = if x >= y then x else y
max2 x y | x >= y     = x
         | otherwise = y
```

Like patterns, guards are also tested in order from top to bottom. The
result of a function is the expression attached to the first guard that succeeds
(evaluates to True). The special guard otherwise always succeeds. Guards
can be combined with patterns if required.

```
positives :: [Int] -> [Int]
positives [] = []
positives (x:xs) | x >= 0    = x : xs
                 | otherwise = xs
```

Local Definitions. Local definitions are introduced using `where` or `let`.

```
gcd :: Int -> Int -> Int
gcd x y = gcd' (abs x) (abs y)
          where gcd' x 0 = x
                gcd' x y = gcd' y (x 'mod' y)
```

Currying and Partial Application. Currying describes the mechanism by which functions of multiple arguments are represented by functions of a single argument. This improves generality by allowing functions to be always treated as functions of a single argument that perhaps return a function as their result, rather than needing to deal with differing numbers of arguments. *All* functions take exactly one argument.

A consequence of allowing Currying is that it is now possible to *partially apply* a function (supply it with some, but not all, arguments, in the expectation that it will acquire the remainder at some later point during execution).

2.2.5 Polymorphism

Polymorphism is derived from Greek, meaning "having many forms". In Haskell, polymorphic types are used for functions that may take or return values of arbitrary types. The simplest polymorphic function is the identity function

```
id :: a -> a
id x = x
```

which just returns its argument. The type variable `a` stands for any type; in the case of `id` both the argument and the result must be of the same type. Other useful polymorphic functions act as selectors over data structures:

```
fst :: (a,b) -> a; snd :: (a,b) -> b
fst (x,y) = x
snd (x,y) = y

head :: [a] -> a; tail :: [a] -> [a]
head (x:xs) = x
tail (x:xs) = xs
```

So, for example:

```
(head [1,2,3],head "abcd") == (1,'a')
```

2.2.6 Higher-Order Functions

Polymorphism is especially useful with *higher-order* functions (ones that take functions as their arguments or return functions as their result), such as the standard `map` function, whose definition is:

2.2 A Basic Introduction to Haskell

```
map :: (a->b) -> [a] -> [b]
map f [] = []
map f (a:as) = f a : map f as
```

The `map` function takes two arguments, a function `f` and a list `as` and applies the function to each element of `as` in turn. The function `f` can be *any* function. Its argument type is `a`, and its result type is `b`, where these can be the same or different concrete types. The argument list `as` must be a list of values that can be given as arguments to `f`, and hence has type `[a]`. Similarly the overall result of the map is a list of results generated by `f`, and hence has type `[b]`. For example:

```
even :: Int -> Bool
even n = n 'mod' 2 == 0

evens :: [Int] -> [Bool]
evens ns = map even ns
```

so `evens [1..10] == [2,4,6,8]`, where `[m..n]` is the list of values between `m` and `n` inclusive.

Three other standard higher-order forms are filters, folds and scans. The `filter` function filters out those elements of a list that do not conform to the predicate which is its first argument.

```
filter :: (a -> Bool) -> [a] -> [a]
filter p [] = []
filter p (x:xs) | p x =       x : filter p xs
                | otherwise =     filter p xs
```

This can be used to construct other functions, such as one to return the positive integers in a list:

```
positives :: [Int] -> [Int]; positive :: Int -> Bool
positives = filter positive
positive n = n >= 0
```

Note the use of partial application in the definition of `positives`.

Folding functions are used to apply a function to all elements of a list working from a base case. The usual version is `foldr` which applies a binary function `f` to the first element of the list `x` and the recursively defined result of folding the rest of the list `foldr f z xs`, and so on until the base case is reached at the end of the list.

```
foldr :: (a -> b -> b) -> b -> [a] -> b
foldr f z [] = z
foldr f z (x:xs) = f x (foldr f z xs)
```

so `foldr 0 (+) [1,2,3] == (1 + (2 + (3 + 0)))` (where `(+)` and `(*)` is the standard addition operator used as a function).

The similar foldl function starts with the base case, applying the function f to the result that has been accumulated to date z and the first element of the list x. This is then passed as the first argument to the recursive call to foldl. When the end of the list is reached, the result is the value that has been accumulated in z.

```
foldl :: (a -> b -> a) -> a -> [b] -> a
foldl f z [] = z
foldl f z (x:xs) = foldl f (f z x) xs
```

so foldl 0 (+) [1,2,3] == ((0 + 1) + 2) + 3. This is an example of the use of an *accumulating parameter*.

The use of *fold* functions makes it possible to define many new functions over list elements in a very simple way. For example:

```
sum, product :: [Int] -> Int
sum = foldr (+) 0
product = foldr (*) 1
```

Scanning functions generalise the folding functions introduced above, by returning not only the final result of the fold, but also all intermediate results. Like the folding functions, scanning functions over lists come in left and right associative versions.

```
scanr :: (a -> b -> b) -> b -> [a] -> [b]
scanr f q0 [] = [q0]
foldr f q0 (x:xs) = f x (head qs) : qs
    where qs = scanr f q0 xs
```

So scanr (+) 0 [1,2,3] == 1+(2+(3+0)) : 2+(3+0) : 3+0 : 0.

The first element of the result of a scanr is the same as the result of the equivalent foldr, while the last element of the result of a scanl is the same as the result of the equivalent foldl.

```
foldr f z l == head (scanr f z l)
foldl f z l == last (scanl f z l)
```

These functions are often used in data parallel functional computations (see Chapter 7.

2.2.7 User-Defined Data Types

So far we have only used list and tuple types. However, new data types can be easily introduced using data definitions. For example:

```
data Colours = Cyan | Yellow | Magenta | Black
```

introduces a new data type Colours whose legal values are the *constructors* Cyan, Yellow, Magenta and Black. Unlike function names, constructor names always begin with an upper case letter.

Data types may be polymorphic:

```
data Array index value = Array [(index,value)]
```
defines an array type to be a list of pairs associating an index with a value. Data type declarations may also be recursive, so
```
data Tree a = Leaf a | Node (Tree a) (Tree a)
```
defines a type of tree whose leaves are of some polymorphic type and whose nodes contain two polymorphic subtrees.

Functions defined on data types usually use pattern matching to select components of the types.
```
minval :: Tree Int -> Int
minval (Leaf v) = v
minval (Node lt rt) | ml <= mr  = ml
                    | otherwise = mr
       where ml = minval lt
             mr = minval rt
```

2.3 λ-Calculus

2.3.1 Introduction

Alonzo Church [125] developed the λ-calculus in the 1930s as a formalisation of the concept of effective computability. Subsequently, it has had a profound influence throughout Computer Science, in particular as a basis for functional languages. This section presents a brief overview of basic properties of the λ-calculus. For fuller formal accounts see the standard work by Barendregt [35] or Hankin's succinct text [253]; for more practically oriented accounts see Peyton-Jones [459] on functional language implementation or Reade [488] on functional programming.

2.3.2 Overview

The λ-calculus is essentially a notation for identifying and specialising abstraction points in expressions. The pure type-free λ-calculus has just three constructs:

$exp \to ident$: variable
  $(\lambda ident \, . \, expression)$: function
  $(\, exp_1 \, exp_2 \,)$: application

To simplify presentation we will omit the enclosing (...)s from a top-level function or application, and where the body of a function is an application. We then assume that application is left associative.

A *variable* is an abstraction point in an expression. For simplicity, we will allow any alpha-numeric sequence starting with an alphabetic character, e.g.:

x y omega R66 legs11

A *function* identifies its bound variable *ident* as a locus of abstraction in its body *exp*. To simplify presentation, we will omit intermediate .λs in nested sequences of functions. For example:

λx.x : Identity
λx y.y : First
λs.s s : Self
λf a.f a : Apply

In Identity, the bound variable is x and the body is just that bound variable x. In First, the bound variable is x and the body is another function λy.x. Note that the body has no occurrences of its own bound variable. In Self, the bound variable is s and the body s s is an application of s to itself. In Apply, the bound variable is f and the body is a function λa.f a which applies the outer bound variable f to the inner bound variable a.

An *application* applies its *function expression*, exp_1, to its *argument expression*, exp_2, through a process called *β-reduction*. The function expression is evaluated to return a function. Some form of the argument expression then replaces all appropriate occurrences of the function's bound variable in its body. We will write → for one β-reduction step.

For example, consider the application:

(λf a.f a) (λs.s s) (λx.x) →
(λa.(λs.s s) a) (λx.x) →
(λs.s s) (λx.x) →
(λx.x) (λx.x) →
λx.x

Analysing this application, the function expression is:

(λf a.f a) (λs.s s)

This is reduced through the replacement of f in f a with λs.s s giving:

λa.(λs.s s) a

The original expression is now:

(λa.(λs.s s) a) (λx.x)

with λa.(λs.s s) a as the function expression so a in (λs.s s) a is replaced withλx.x giving:

(λs.s s) (λx.x)

This is reduced through the replacement of s in s s with λx.x giving:

(λx.x) (λx.x)

Finally, x in x is replaced with λx.x giving:

λx.x

2.3.3 β-Reduction and α-Conversion

In the above informal account of β-reduction there was a vague reference to replacing *appropriate* occurrences of the bound variable in the body with the argument, which we will now clarify. A variable is *bound* in an expression if it is in the body of a function which introduces it as the bound variable. Otherwise it is *free* in the expression. For example, f is bound in:

λf a.f a

as it is introduced by the outermost function but free in:

λa.f a

Note that a variable may have both bound and free occurrences in the same expression. For example, in the application:

(λf a.f a) (λf.f a)

the occurrence of a in the function expression is bound but the occurrence in the argument expression is free.

If all bound variables are unique identifiers then the appropriate occurrences for replacement are the only occurrences. However, bound variables need not be unique. A variable is in *scope* in the body function that introduces it as a bound variable, until an inner function reintroduces it: only those occurrences of a bound variable which are in scope should be replaced during β-reduction. For example, in:

(λa.a (λa.a) a) (λx.x)

a is introduced twice as a bound variable in the function expression. If we label the variables to show which bound variable they correspond to:

(λa_1.a_1 (λa_2.a_2) a_1) (λx.x) → (λx.x) (λa_2.a_2) (λx.x)

then only occurrences of a_1 should be replaced by λx.x.

We can now be somewhat more precise:

> To β-reduce *(λident.exp_1) exp_2*, replace all free occurrences of the bound variable *ident* in the body *exp_1* with some form of the argument expression *exp_2*.

The free occurrences of *ident* in the body correspond to the outer bound variable. Any bound occurrences must have been introduced by a function within the body.

There still remains a potential problem if the same identifier is used to represent different variables in different scopes in the same expression; a free occurrence may become bound as a result of β-reduction. For example, consider:

(λf a.f a) (λf.f a)

once more. Following the replacement of f in f a with λf.f a:

λa.(λf.f a) a

the free a in λf.f a has been moved into the scope of the function expression's inner bound variable a and may be replaced inappropriately by a subsequent β-reduction.

This may be circumvented through α-*conversion*, the consistent introduction of new identifiers to ensure that all variables are unique:

> To rename *ident* as *ident'* in λ*ident.exp* through α-conversion, where *ident'* is not the same as the bound variable *ident* and does not occur in the body *exp*, replace all free occurrences of *ident* in *exp* with *ident'*, and replace the *ident* after the λ with *ident'*

Note that in an application where a variable which is free in the argument expression is bound in the function expression, α-conversion should be applied to the function rather than the argument.

For example, α-conversion of a to b in the function expression in:

(λf a.f a) (λf.f a)

followed by β-reduction gives:

(λf a.f a) (λf.f a) $\to^\alpha$
(λf b.f b) (λf.f a) $\to$
λb.(λf.f a) b

thus avoiding free variable capture.

An alternative to α-conversion is the use of de Bruijn indices to label λ-bound variables in expressions with the depth below their defining λ-abstraction [169]. This gives a unique (relative) number for each variable that can be exploited to give rapid stack-based substitution for bound variables.

2.3.4 Church-Rosser Theorems

A reducible expression of the form *(λident.exp$_1$) exp$_2$* is termed a *redex* and an expression that contains no redexes is said to be in *normal form*. Reducing a λ-expression to normal form through repeated β-reduction is directly analogous to running a program with data until it terminates. Just as it is undecidable whether or not a program terminates on arbitrary data as a consequence of the Halting Problem, it is undecidable whether or not an arbitrary λ-expression has a normal form.

In a λ-expression with many redexes, there are many different sequences in which β-reduction may be applied to try and find a normal order. The *first Church-Rosser theorem* established that β-reduction has the *diamond property*, or *confluence*:

If λ-expression M β-reduces to both M' and M'', then M' and M'' must both β-reduce through a series of steps to a common λ-expression M'''s. In

2.3 λ-Calculus

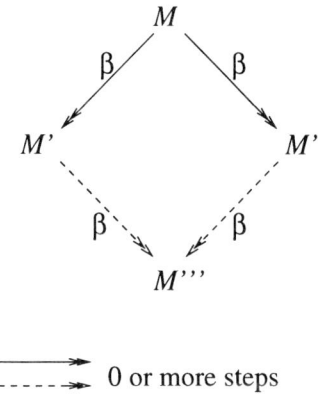

Figure 2.1. Diamond property

other words, if a λ-expression has a normal form then it is unique and some sequence of β-reduction will indeed find it.

The *Church-Rosser property* of *evaluation order independence* is one of the distinguishing characteristics of pure functional languages, with crucial implications for this book. Thus, Wegner [596] notes that the Church-Rosser theorem:

> "...essentially states that lambda expressions can be evaluated by *asynchronous multiprocessing* applied in arbitrary order to local subexpressions."(p. 185)

2.3.5 Normalising Reduction Orders

Establishing that β-reduction is Church-Rosser is less satisfactory than at first might appear. It tells us that if there is a β-normal form for an expression, then some sequence of β-reductions will find it. The trouble is that there are an awful lot of different β-reduction sequences to consider in an arbitrary expression and not all may terminate. Hence, there is considerable interest in the properties of different well-defined reduction *strategies*, in particular in identifying *normalising* reduction strategies which will reach the normal form for an expression in a finite number of steps, if there is one to reach.

Reduction strategies may be characterised in terms of the order in which the redexes in an expression are reduced, typically in terms of the relative position of redexes in an expression, for example one redex being to the *left* or *right* of another. Curry and Fey's *standardisation theorem* [153] proved that *standard* β-reduction, which reduces the *leftmost* redex at each stage, will find a normal form if there is one. *Normal β-reduction* is standard β-reduction resulting in a normal form.

2.3.6 Normal Order Reduction

Normal β-reduction is the basis of *normal order* reduction where the leftmost outermost redex is reduced at each stage. Consider an application:

   $exp\ exp_1$

Initially, all leftmost redexes must be in *exp* so it is reduced to normal form. Suppose this results in a function:

   $(\lambda ident.exp_2)\ exp_1$

whose body exp_2 contains no redexes. The leftmost rule leads to the unreduced exp_1 replacing free occurrences of the bound variable *ident* in the body exp_2.

Simple normal order reduction may be very inefficient. Every free occurrence of a function's bound variable in its body is replaced by the unreduced argument expression: for multiple occurrences there will be multiple copies of the argument expression, each of which may eventually be a leftmost outermost redex for evaluation. For example, consider:

   $(\lambda x.x\ x)\ ((\lambda y.y)\ (\lambda z.z))\ \xrightarrow{n}$
   $((\lambda y.y)\ (\lambda z.z))\ ((\lambda y.y)\ (\lambda z.z))\ \xrightarrow{n}$
   $(\lambda z.z)\ ((\lambda y.y)\ (\lambda z.z))\ \xrightarrow{n}$
   $(\lambda y.y)\ (\lambda z.z)\ \xrightarrow{n}$
   $\lambda z.z$

Here $(\lambda y.y)\ (\lambda z.z)$ is evaluated twice.

2.3.7 Applicative Order Reduction

A more efficient alternative to normal order evaluation is applicative order where the leftmost innermost redex is reduced at each stage. Thus, in:

   $exp\ exp_1$

all redexes in *exp* are reduced, as for normal order. Again suppose that *exp* has been reduced to a function:

   $(\lambda ident.exp_2)\ exp_1$

whose body exp_2 contains no redexes. Further leftmost innermost redexes must be sought in the argument exp_1 which is next reduced to normal form, say to exp_3:

   $(\lambda ident.exp_2)\ exp_3$

Finally, exp_3, the reduced form of exp_1 replaces all occurrences of the bound variable *ident* in the body exp_2. Thus, any redexes in argument positions will only be reduced once. For example, consider:

2.3 λ-Calculus   45

(λx.x x) ((λy.y) (λz.z)) $\xrightarrow{a}$
(λx.x x) (λz.z) $\xrightarrow{a}$
(λz.z) (λz.z) $\xrightarrow{a}$
λz.z

Here, (λy.y) (λz.z) is only evaluated once.

However, applicative order is not normalising: there are expressions with normal forms for which applicative order will not terminate because they contain non-terminating redexes which are not actually needed as part of the final normal form. For example, consider:

(λx y.x) (λx.x) ((λs.s s) λs.s s))

Note that the internal redex:

(λs.s s) (λs.s s) → (λs.s s) (λs.s s)

reduces to itself and hence has no normal form.

In applicative order:

(λx y.x) (λx.x) ((λs.s s) (λs.s sx)) $\xrightarrow{a}$
(λy x.x) ((λs.s s) (λs.s s)) $\xrightarrow{a}$
(λy x.x) ((λs.s s) (λs.s s)) $\xrightarrow{a}$
...

the argument redex is evaluated endlessly so reduction never terminates.

In contrast, using normal order reduction, while there may be multiple copies of argument expressions, some never become a leftmost outermost redex for reduction, typically because they have been discarded through binding with a non-occurring bound variable. Repeating the previous example in normal order:

(λx y.x) (λx.x) ((λs.s s) (λs.s s)) $\xrightarrow{n}$
(λy x.x) ((λs.s s) (λs.s s)) $\xrightarrow{n}$
λx.x

the non-terminating redex is discarded as there are no free occurrences of y in the body of the λ-expression.

2.3.8 Normal Forms

As discussed above, an expression has been reduced to normal form when it no longer contains any more redexes. For practical purposes, however, it may not be necessary to fully reduce an expression. For example, in real functional languages, multi-component structures are often represented as *constructors* applied to expressions for each component. It is unnecessary to evaluate any component expression until is is selected for use [267], [204]; the basis of *lazy evaluation*.

Lazy functional language implementations usually reduce expressions to *weak head normal form* (WHNF) [592]. Here the final expression may be a function:

$\lambda ident.exp$

whose body *exp* is an arbitrary expression, or an application:

$ident\ exp_1\ exp_2\ ...\ exp_N$

with a variable function expression *ident* and arbitrary argument expressions.

Note that an expression in WHNF is not a redex but may contain redexes: in essence, function bodies are not reduced.

WHNF is a weaker variant of the earlier notion of *head normal form* (HNF) [591]:

$\lambda ident_1\ ...\ ident_N.ident_I\ exp_1\ ...\ exp_M$

where the final expression is a function whose body is not a redex but which may contain redexes.

Note that an expression in HNF is also in WHNF but an expression in WHNF is not necessarily in HNF.

Note for an expression there may be several equivalent expressions in HNF or WHNF. However every expression has a unique *principal* HNF. Suppose an expression is of the form:

$\lambda ident_1\ ...\ ident_N.(\lambda ident.exp_0)\ exp_1\ ...\ exp_M$

$(\lambda ident.exp_0)\ exp_1$ is called the *head redex*. The unique principal HNF for an expression is found by successively reducing head redexes.

2.3.9 Parallel Reduction, Neededness and Strictness Analysis

As noted above, the Church-Rosser property implies that λ-expressions may be evaluated by β–reduction in arbitrary order, including through the simultaneous evaluation of arbitrary subexpressions. However, as noted above, not all reduction sequences may terminate.

Given an application $exp_1\ exp_2$, the simplest form of parallelism is to evaluate exp_1 and exp_2 at the same time in normal order. This will find a normal form for both subexpressions if they exist. Furthermore, it may not matter if there is no normal form for exp_2 provided it is not *needed*, that is, selected for reduction, during the application of the function from exp_1 to it. However, if exp_1's normal form is not needed then there is no point in reducing it in the first place.

Alas, it is undecidable in general whether or not a redex is needed in an expression as this depends on determining whether or not an arbitrary expression has a normal form, which is equivalent to solving the Halting Problem. There are heuristics for finding some, if not all, needed redexes in an expression.

A closely related concept to neededness is that of *strictness*. Suppose $\bot$ is the undefined value, corresponding to non-terminating reduction sequences such as:

(λs.s s) (λs.s s)

A function of one argument *f* is said to be *strict* in that argument if:

$$f \perp = \perp$$

That is, if the argument does not have a normal form then neither does the function application. Thus, the argument must be reduced for successful reduction of the application, so the function expression that leads to *f* and the argument expression may as well be reduced at the same time. Where there are many strict arguments to one function, the evaluation of all such arguments may proceed concurrently without altering the lazy semantics.

As with neededness, it is in general undecidable whether or not a function is strict in an arbitrary argument. However, *strictness analysis* will identify some, if not all, strict arguments, for example through techniques based on *abstract interpretation* [415], [101], [134], [6].

2.4 Strict Evaluation and the SECD Machine

2.4.1 Overview

Peter Landin's SECD machine [353] was the first abstract machine for the λ-calculus and was originally designed for applicative order evaluation. The following account draws heavily on that given in Field and Harrison's book [194].

The SECD machine is named for its Stack, Environment, Control and Dump structures. The stack holds intermediate values, typically closures or return values. The environment holds identifier/value associations, created by binding function bound variables to arguments. The control holds expressions under evaluation. The dump holds enclosing contexts for nested function applications, consisting of old stacks, environments and dumps.

These are all stacks, which we will model as LIFO lists. We will model an SECD machine state as a four-tuple, (S,E,C,D), and describe its behaviour as a set of transition rules operating on λ-calculus abstract syntax trees.

For an identifier on top of the control, push its value from the environment onto the stack:

(S,E,*ident*:C,D) → (find(*ident*,E):S,E,C,D)

For a function on top of the control, push a *closure*, to associate its bound variable, body and environment, onto the stack:

(S,E,λ *ident.exp*:C,D) → (clo(*ident,exp*,E):S,E,C,D)

Note that a closure is effectively a λ-function in a binding context:

clo(*ident,exp*,(*id1,value1*):(*id2,value2*)...) ⇒
let *id1*=*value1*
and *id2*=*value2*

...

in λ *ident.exp*

For an application on top of the control, push an apply operator, the argument expression and the function expression onto the control:

(S,E,*(exp1 exp2)*:C,D) → (S,E,*exp2:exp1*:@:C,D)

The argument expression will be evaluated before the function expression. Eventually, the function value will be above the argument value on the stack with the corresponding apply operator on top of the control.

For an apply operator on top of the control, with a closure above an argument value on the stack:

- Push the stack below the closure and argument, the environment, and the control below the apply operator onto the dump
- Create a new control from the function body from the closure
- Create a new environment from an association between the closure bound variable and the argument from the stack, and the closure environment
- Create an empty stack

(clo(*ident,exp*,E'):*value*:S,E,@:C,D) →
([ ],(*ident,value*):E',[*exp*],(S,E,C):D)

For an empty control, with a context on the dump and a value on top of the stack, restore the stack, environment and control from the dump, with the value from the former stack on top of the restored stack:

(*value*:S,E,[ ],(S',E',C'):D) → (*value*:S',E',C',D)

For an empty control and dump, the computation has finished and the result is on top of the stack:

(*value*:S,E,[ ],[ ]) → *value*

2.4.2 Example

For example, consider evaluating (λ s.s (λ y.y s)) (λ x.x). We start with an empty stack, environment and dump, with the expression on top of the control:

([],[],[(λ s.s (λ y.y s)) (λ x.x)],[])

The argument expression, function expression and apply operator replace the expression on the control:

([],[],[λ x.x,λ s.s (λ y.y s),@],[])

A closure for the argument expression, a function, is pushed onto the stack:

([clo(x,x,[])],[],[λ s.s (λ y.y s),@],[])

2.4 Strict Evaluation and the SECD Machine

A closure for the function expression, a function, is pushed onto the stack:

   ([clo(s,s (λ y.y s),[]), clo(x,x,[])],[],[@],[])

The function closure is applied to the argument value. The old stack, environment, and control are pushed onto the dump. A new empty stack is created. A new environment is formed from the association of the closure bound variable, argument value and closure environment. The closure body is pushed onto an empty control:

   ([],[(s,clo(x,x,[]))], [s (λ y.y s)],[([],[],[])])

The argument expression, function expression and apply operator replace the expression on the control:

   ([],[(s,clo(x,x,[]))], [λ y.y s,s,@],[([],[],[])])

A closure for the argument expression, a function, is pushed onto the stack:

   ([clo(y,y s,[(s,clo(x,x,[]))])],
   [(s,clo(x,x,[]))],[s,@],[([],[],[])])

The value of the function expression, an identifier, is found from the environment and pushed onto the stack:

   ([clo(x,x,[]),clo(y,y s,[(s,clo(x,x,[]))])],
   [(s,clo(x,x,[]))],[@],[([],[],[])])

The function closure is applied to the argument closure. The old stack, environment and control are pushed onto the dump. A new empty stack is formed. A new environment is formed from the association of the closure bound variable and the argument value in the closure environment. The closure body is pushed onto an empty stack:

   ([],[(x,clo(y,y s,[(s,clo(x,x,[]))]))],
   [x],[([],[(s,clo(x,x,[]))],[]),([],[],[])])

The value of the function closure body, an identifier, is pushed onto the stack:

   ([clo(y,y s,[(s,clo(x,x,[]))])],
   [(x,clo(y,y s,[(s,clo(x,x,[]))]))],
   [],[([],[(s,clo(x,x,[]))],[]),([],[],[])])

The control is empty so the inner application s (λ y.y s), where s is λ x.x has been fully evaluated with the result on the stack. The old stack, environment and control are restored from the dump:

   ([clo(y,y s,[(s,clo(x,x,[]))])],
   [(s,clo(x,x,[]))],[],[([],[],[])])

The control is empty so the outer application (λ s.s (λ y.y s)) (λ x.x) has been fully evaluated with the result on the stack. The old stack, environment and control are restored from the dump:

([clo(y,y s,[(s,clo(x,x,[]))])],[],[],[])

The control and dump are empty so the final result is popped from the stack:

clo(y,y s,[(s,clo(x,x,[]))]) → let s=λ x.x in λ y.y s

which, substituting from the context for the free variable s is:

λ y.y (λ x.x)

2.4.3 Extensions and Variations

Field and Harrison [194] discuss extensions to the basic SECD machine for built-in operations for arithmetic and logic, corresponding to λ-calculus δ-rules, and for other evaluation regimes. A conditional expression may be represented by a new operator to indicate the delayed evaluation of option branches. For non-strict evaluation, *suspensions* are introduced to associate unevaluated expressions with enclosing environments. When a suspension is found in the function expression position in an application, its expression must be evaluated in the corresponding environment. For call-by-name, raw suspensions are manipulated so identical copies may proliferate and be evaluated repeatedly. For call-by-need, suspensions are accessed indirectly via shared pointers. When a suspension is evaluated, it is effectively overwritten by its resultant value, thus avoiding repeated evaluation.

Reade [488] discusses the relationship of the SECD machine to other functional language implementations. In particular, he cites Cardelli's FAM for Standard ML [116] as a highly optimised SECD machine, and notes that Curien's Categorical Abstract Machine [152] is very similar to a SECD machine.

2.5 Lazy Evaluation and Graph Reduction

Laziness is an implementation technique that encompasses both normal order evaluation (in that it pursues a leftmost outermost reduction strategy to achieve (weak) head normal forms) and sharing (in that β-reduction is achieved using *call-by-need* rather than *call-by-name*); the latter is necessary so that, for example, in the expression $\lambda x. (x+x)$ the argument x is only evaluated once. In practice, the normal order evaluation of function arguments also extends to data constructors so that, for example, (1/0) : [] does not evaluate (1/0) unless, and until, the head of the list is demanded.

Whilst it is possible to introduce *lazy evaluation* into the SECD machine [95], [264], [266], [167], it is far more common to use an elegant method formulated by Wadsworth known as *graph reduction* [591]. Specifically, Wadsworth's technique increases the efficiency (in terms of the number of reduction steps) of normal order reduction by introducing sharing via graph pointers.

2.5 Lazy Evaluation and Graph Reduction

With graph reduction, a program is held in the heap as its syntax tree — individual syntactic elements are represented as heap cells containing pointers to other heap cells. Each node of the syntax tree is either:

- A binary application node denoted by @, with two branches pointing to the operator and operand respectively;
- A λ-abstraction denoted by the symbol λ, followed by the name of the bound variable and a pointer to the body of the abstraction; or
- A terminal node which is either a constant, such as 3, or an operator, such as + (this is an extension of the pure λ-calculus).

The type of a node determines which operations may be performed on it and the permitted data components for that node:

- A binary application node supports two selectors $s1$ and $s2$ (for the operator and operand branches respectively) and has no components;
- A λ-node supports one selector $s3$ (for the function body) and has one component — the name of the bound variable;
- A terminal node supports no selectors but has one component — the name of the terminal.

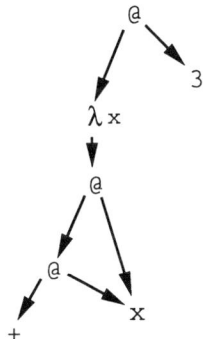

Figure 2.2. Example graph demonstrating sharing

Wadsworth defines the graph as $(X, s1, s2, s3, Z)$, where X is the (finite) set of nodes, $s[123]$ are the selector functions defined above, and Z is the root node of the graph. A straightforward implementation of such a graph would ensure that terminals only exist as separate nodes and that each selection function $s1, s2$ and $s3$, therefore, always returns a node; this is known as a "boxed" implementation [459] (because terminal values are held inside whole nodes). However, most modern implementations achieve high performance by using a more efficient "unboxed" representation where terminal values may be held in the operand branch of an application node or the function branch of a λ-node.

Lazy evaluation is achieved through a combination of: (a) a left-to-right depth-first traversal and on-the-fly transformation via β-reduction of this graph, which corresponds to normal order evaluation, and (b) the implementation of sharing through the use of pointers (for example, consider the expression $(\lambda x.\ (x+x)3)$ as illustrated in Figure 2.2).

2.5.1 Operation of Graph Reduction

In order to understand how the above reductions may be implemented, we introduce the notion of an abstract machine which has access to (i) a stack of pointers to the nodes that it has previously visited, and (ii) the graph.

Indirection Nodes. In addition to the graph described above, we also incorporate Wadsworth's notion of an "indirection node" (a node containing a single pointer to another node), which becomes necessary for the implementation of those functions where no new graph is built (e.g. projection functions). An indirection node is denoted by *IND* and supports a single selector $s4$ which dereferences the indirection. This avoids the loss of sharing whenever a projection function is used (the root node of the redex would be overwritten with a copy of the argument rather than a pointer) — furthermore, if the argument were an unboxed value, it would need to become boxed.

Graph Reduction Without Constants. The simplest graph reducer operates on the λ-calculus without constants. Each λ-abstraction is a function of a single argument and the reducer needs merely to find the leftmost outermost application of an abstraction to an argument, β-reduce the application, and continue to find the next redex. This mechanism is illustrated by the following state-transition rules: the machine state is given by the two-tuple $< S, G >$ comprising the stack (of pointers to graph nodes) and the graph (a set of graph nodes); the stack may either be empty (denoted by ()) or may contain an item at the top of the stack followed by the rest of the stack (denoted $p.S$, the dot operator being right-associative so that $p.q.S$ denotes the top two items on the stack); pointers to graph nodes may be shown as an identifier (p) or as an identifier together with a description of the referenced node (denoted by $p \rightarrow nodetype$), or as the result of a selection operation on another pointer (denoted by $s1(p)$); the graph may be augmented with new graph using set union (denoted by $\cup$) and may be modified by overwriting the cell referenced by a pointer with new contents (denoted $G[newcontents/pointer]$).

$$< (p \rightarrow @).S, G > \quad \longrightarrow \quad < (s1(p).p.S), G >$$

$$< (p \rightarrow IND).S, G > \quad \longrightarrow \quad < (s4(p).S), G >$$

2.5 Lazy Evaluation and Graph Reduction

$$< (p \to \lambda x).q.S), G > \quad \longrightarrow \quad < (r.S), G[IND(r)/q]$$
$$\cup \{newgraph\} >$$

where

$$\{newgraph\} \equiv copy(s3(p))[INDs2(q)/x]$$
$$r \to newgraph$$

The above transition rules execute a left-to-right depth-first traversal of the graph until the leftmost outermost λ-node is reached; then the application of that λ-abstraction to its argument is β-reduced. The path from the root node of any redex (including the root of the whole program) to the leftmost outermost operator is known as the *spine* of that application; the process of traversing down the spine is known as *unwinding*.

In this simplistic example, the β-reduction is entirely unoptimised and, for example, new indirection cells will be created for projection functions. The action of the above reducer may be illustrated by considering the expression $(\lambda x.((\lambda x.x)x))(\lambda x.x)$. This will be represented by the graph in Figure 2.3 and will be evaluated by a reducer whose initial state comprises (i) a stack containing a single pointer to the top node of the graph, and (ii) a graph containing eight nodes (viz: G = $\{(N1 : @N2N3), (N2 : \lambda xN4), (N3 : \lambda xN5), (N4 : @N6N7), (N5 : x), (N6 : \lambda xN8), (N7 : x), (N8 : x)\})$.

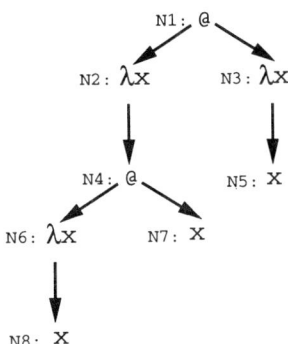

Figure 2.3. Example graph

Nodes $N5$, $N8$ and $N9$ are never observed by the reducer except within the routine which effects the β-reduction. The sequence of states for the reducer is:

```
    < (q->N1).(),   G >
=>  < (p->N2).(q->N1).(),   G >
=>  < (r->N9).(),
```

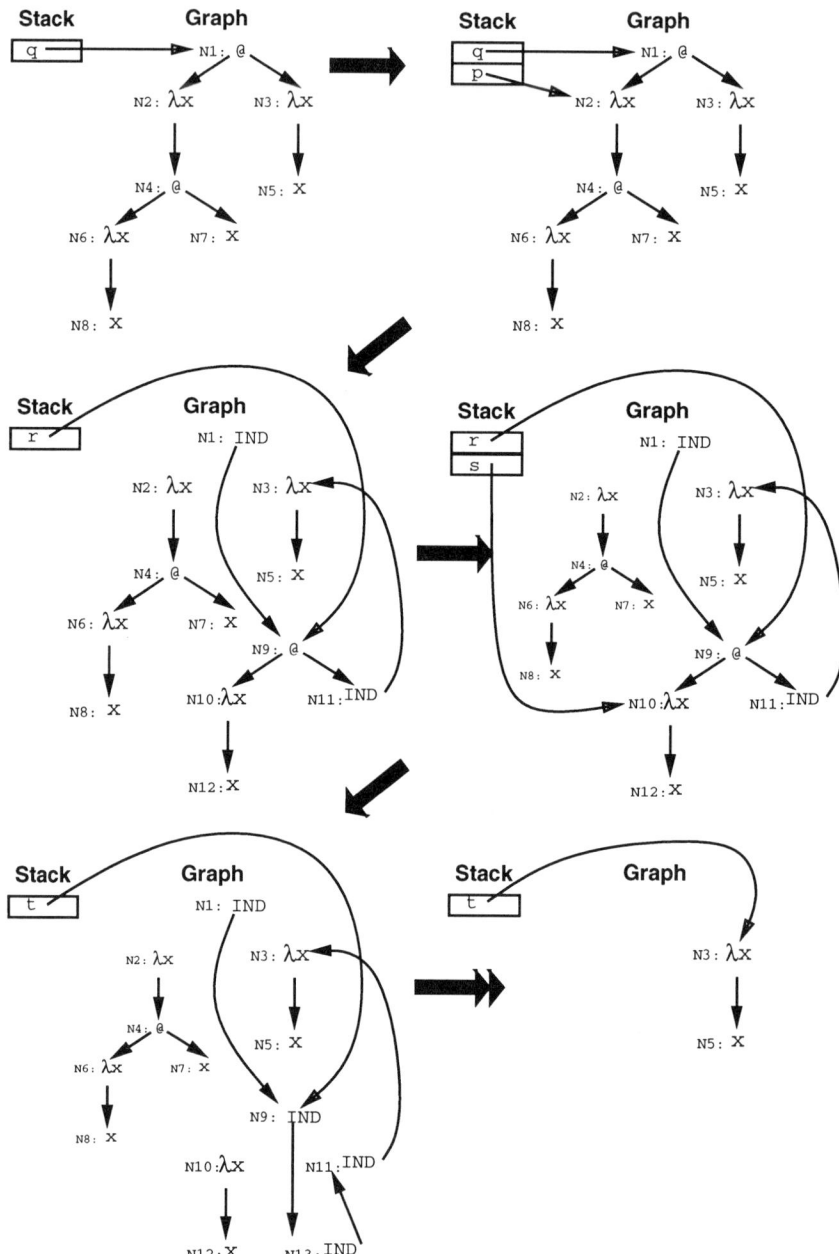

Figure 2.4. Example evaluation

2.5 Lazy Evaluation and Graph Reduction

```
            G[IND(r->N9)/q] U {newgraph} >
         where
         {newgraph} = copy(N4)[IND N3/x]
                    = {N9, N10, N11, N12}
   =>   < (s->N10).(r->N9).(),
           G[IND(N9)/q] U {N9, N10, N11, N12} >
   =>   < (t->N13).(),
           (G[IND(N9)/q] U {N9, N10, N11, N12})[IND N11/r]
           U {newgraph}>
         where
         {newgraph} = copy(N4)[IND N3/x]
                    = {N13}
   =>   < (t->N11).(),
           (G[IND(N9)/q] U {N9, N10, N11, N12})[IND N11/r] >
   =>   < (t->N3).(),
           (G[IND(N9)/q] U {N9, N10, N11, N12})[IND N11/r] >
```

At this stage, the contents of the stack do not match any left-hand side of any rule (because there are too few items on the stack), so the reducer stops. The result is $\lambda x.\ x$, as expected. Note also that the reduction rules given above are overly simplistic, in that the *copy* function creates a new indirection cell for the projection function. The evolution of the stack and graph are shown in Figure 2.4 (the final graph shows only the live nodes).

Through sharing, a single λ-node could be used in many different contexts with different values for the bound variable. Thus, it is necessary to make a copy of the body of the λ-node; β-reduction is then applied to this copy, replacing all free occurrences of the formal variable name with the actual value of the variable (this will be a pointer to a graph node, unless unboxed representations are allowed). The β-reduction must, of course, manage any name clashes by applying α-conversion as required. The application node of the root of the redex is then overwritten with an indirection to the new graph and depth-first traversal continues into the new graph (since the result of the reduction may be another application node). The overwriting of the redex node ensures that the evaluation of this redex is shared by any other expressions which point to this cell.

Graph Reduction with Constants. Graph reduction becomes slightly more complex when the λ-calculus is extended with constants (such as integers with primitive arithmetic operators which require δ-rules). In particular:

- Many primitive operators require their arguments to be evaluated before they can return a result; this must either be achieved before the appropriate δ-rule is applied (requiring a modification to the normal order evaluation strategy), or must be included as part of the δ-rule for the primitive (requiring the δ-rule and the evaluator to be mutually recursive, which is not entirely satisfactory);

- Many primitive operators take more than one argument, so that the root of the redex must be searched for on the stack (the act of upwards traversal to find the root of the redex is often called *rewinding*);
- While an argument to a primitive operator is being evaluated, the environment for the application of the primitive must be saved; this is done by pushing the current stack onto a "dump" (a stack of stacks). After the argument has been evaluated, the previous stack is popped from the dump.

The impact of the dump mechanism on a real abstract machine (the G-Machine) is shown in Chapter 6.

2.5.2 Combinator Graph Reduction

Combinatory logic [153] provides another elegant basis for the implementation of functional languages. In fact, most modern implementations of lazy sequential and non-strict parallel functional languages are based on combinatory logic rather than the λ-calculus:

- There is a clear correspondence between combinators and λ-abstractions, between combinator expressions and λ-expressions, and between the normal order reduction of combinator expressions and the normal order reduction of λ-expressions [574];
- The optimisation of using cyclic pointers in place of the fixpoint operator Y was first proposed and later proven [190] in the context of combinatory logic;
- Combinator reduction can also be implemented via graph reduction (in this context also known as "graph rewriting", a variant of term rewriting systems [583]);
- Since combinator expressions have no free variables and no internal λ-expressions, they therefore do not suffer from name-clash problems.

SK-combinators. Early implementations of functional languages exploiting combinatory logic used a fixed set of pre-defined combinators (such as S and K). We use the term "SK-combinator reduction" to refer to any combinator reduction method that uses a fixed set of pre-defined combinators.

The first practical implementation of SK-combinator graph reduction was described by Turner [574]. The MaRS system [118] is an example of a parallel implementation that uses SK-combinators. However, the simplicity of the technique means that code size is large, granularity is small, many intermediate results are constructed in the heap and rapidly discarded, and there is no opportunity to exploit local or global static analysis of the program. As a result, SK-combinator implementations are slow; in practice, modern implementations use *supercombinator* reduction instead.

2.5 Lazy Evaluation and Graph Reduction

Lambda Lifting and Supercombinator Graph Reduction. Lambda lifting [315], [290] is a transformation of the program text which turns each function of the original program into a combinator: first it abstracts all free variables as extra formal parameters (the free variables are passed as explicit extra arguments whenever the function is called), and then it lifts all λ-expressions to the top level. The resulting program comprises these (possibly mutually recursive) *supercombinators* together with an expression to be evaluated. As a result of the transformation, λ-abstractions may not occur in expressions.

Two key advantages of lambda lifting are:

1. It increases the granularity of combinator graph reduction, thereby providing increased performance;
2. It simplifies the passing of values from the environment into a function.

Supercombinator Instantiation. A key result of lambda lifting is that the environment which provides the binding for variable names is completely flattened, so that the entire environment for a function is embodied in its arguments. Furthermore, since there are no free variables and there are no λ-abstractions embedded in the function bodies, name clashes do not occur. This greatly simplifies the strategy for identifier lookup; to apply a supercombinator to its arguments, it is sufficient simply to create a copy of the body of the supercombinator with pointers to the appropriate arguments substituted for occurrences of the formal parameters (the original application node — the root node of the redex — is overwritten with an indirection to the new copy).

This technique is significantly faster than β-reduction (which must resolve name clashes). However, there are some disadvantages:

1. There may be needless passing of values (or pointers to values) that are not used for a long time (for example, they may only be used at the end of a recursion), which may lead to needless inter-processor communication in a parallel context;
2. There is a slight increase in complexity since many arguments must be substituted at once;
3. The numbers of arguments to functions may increase dramatically, so some static analyses (such as abstract interpretation) will perform poorly unless carried out before lambda lifting the program. However, this would require additional complexity to carry through the analysis information during lambda lifting.

Interpretive and Compiled Graph Reduction. Supercombinator instantiation may be achieved either in an interpretive fashion by copying the graph node-by-node (template instantiation), or the procedure may be effected by compiled code. The latter is clearly more efficient. Similarly, the traversal of the graph can to some extent be compiled such that a stack rather than the heap is used wherever possible (for example, where the result of a reduction is another redex whose cells could be built on the stack rather than in the heap).

This is sometimes referred to as "compiled graph reduction". The first examples of this approach can be found in Cousineau et al's Categorical Abstract Machine (CAM) [142] and Johnsson and Augustsson's G-Machine [316], [24] (see Sect. 6.2). The resultant abstract machines are also sometimes known as "stack-based" graph reduction systems.

2.5.3 Non-Strict Parallel Graph Reduction

At first sight, lazy evaluation would seem to preclude parallel evaluation (since normal order traversal is inherently sequential). However, it is often possible to choose a non-sequential evaluation order which is guaranteed to provide exactly the same result as lazy evaluation, i.e. that it finds weak head normal forms, that it always finds a normal form if normal order evaluation would do so, and it does no more work than lazy evaluation (for example, it evaluates arguments to functions, at most, once). One mechanism for determining a non-sequential evaluation order which preserves the lazy semantics is *strictness analysis* (Section 2.3.9).

Systems that use non-sequential evaluation to provide what is essentially a lazy semantics, are called *non-strict*. Non-strict parallel implementations have much stronger termination guarantees than strict parallel implementations (which routinely evaluate subexpressions whose values are not required by the program), whilst also supporting the lazy programming style (e.g. with infinite objects).

These ideas will be revisited in Chapter 6 which covers parallel realisations of non-strict functional languages in more depth, including discussion of abstract machines for parallel graph reduction.

2.6 Dataflow

The evaluation models we have seen so far are control-driven: expressions are evaluated when the evaluator determines that they are needed as a result of following the flow of control through the program. *Dataflow* models differ in being *data-driven*. In such models *any* function application (including applications of built-in functions) may be evaluated as soon as all its arguments are available. The remainder of this section provides a brief introduction to dataflow implementation techniques. The forthcoming text by Arvind and Nikhil [424] gives much more detailed coverage of dataflow, including many examples of programming using implicit parallelism in the pH dataflow variant of Haskell [426].

2.6.1 Dataflow Graphs

In conventional compiler technology, dataflow graphs are used to track the lifetimes and usage patterns of individual data entities. Graph nodes represent operations, with arcs representing data dependencies. Dataflow execution models use such dataflow graphs to actually drive program computation. Dataflow *tokens* are introduced for each instance of an operation. When all arguments to the token become available (values are present on all of the arcs), the token becomes active and may be evaluated. The value of the token is then passed to those tokens that depend on it, which may themselves be activated. The process continues until there are no more active tokens in the system.

Early *static dataflow* was restricted to fixed dataflow graphs [170]. Modern approaches use *dynamic dataflow* graphs, in which the shape of the graph varies at execution time, in order to support recursion and other control structures.

2.6.2 Synchronised Memory: I-structures and M-structures

Two mechanisms for handling synchronised memory have found widespread use in dataflow systems: I-structures are used for single-assignment variables and M-structures are used for multiple-assignment variables.

I-structures. In order to implement non-strictness in a dataflow system, it is necessary to introduce some notion of delay. I-structures (Incomplete structures) [20] are single-assignment variables, which may take two states. In the initial unassigned state, all attempts to read the value of an I-structure will block. As soon as a value has been assigned to the I-structure, however, all outstanding reads can proceed, and any future attempt to read the I-structure will receive the assigned value. Thus there will be exactly one assignment to each I-structure. The effect is similar to the *graph reduction* implementation of lazy evaluation (Chapter 6), except that reading an unevaluated I-structure will cause the current thread to block, whereas reading a similarly unassigned lazy variable will cause it to be evaluated immediately through the propagation of demand.

M-Structures. M-structures [40] differ from I-structures in that they can potentially be assigned several different values during the course of a single program execution. Thus they implement conventional imperative variables – the value that is returned when an M-structure is read is the value that has most recently been assigned to the M-structure. like I-structures, but unlike conventional variables, M-structures have an initially unassigned state. Any attempt to read an M-structure before it has been assigned an initial value will therefore block rather than returning an error.

2.6.3 Dataflow Machines

Several early realisations of dataflow techniques were tightly bound to hardware designs. The first successful dataflow machine was built at Manchester [238]. This demonstrated good relative speedup for several small applications, and provided much basic data on task scheduling. The substantially similar MIT tagged token dataflow architecture (TTDA) [17] was never realised in hardware, but a much revised design was eventually built at MIT in the shape of the Monsoon machine [446]. The most recent MIT designs (P-RISC [18] and *T [427]) are based on conventional RISC processors augmented with special mechanisms to manage parallel threads.

A number of dataflow-inspired machines were also produced in Japan. One such machine was the SIGMA-1 [602], which was specifically designed for scientific computations. Other similar machines produced in Japan include the PIM-D and ELS machines, which were specifically designed to execute logic programming languages based on Horn clauses.

2.6.4 Compilation for Dataflow

As described above, most of the early dataflow implementations targeted special-purpose dataflow hardware. Compilation for such systems essentially comprised constructing the initial dataflow graph and seeding the initial tokens. Special purpose hardware was provided to manage the token pool, matching tokens with arguments, and identifying and scheduling active tokens, as in the Manchester dataflow machine. More recent approaches, such as the MIT Monsoon machine [446] used conventional non-associative memory for the token pool, however. In Monsoon, the arguments to each token were held in a token-specific *activation frame* with presence bits used to indicate the arguments that had been provided. Tokens could be activated once all arguments were available.

Since token-based approaches lead to very fine granularity, compilation techniques have since concentrated on aggregating tokens into larger tasks (*macro-dataflow*) or identifying tasks as single loop iterations. The modern trend is to compile dataflow languages for more or less stock parallel architectures, perhaps subdividing tasks into several independent lightweight threads. In some cases, dataflow-based approaches have crossed over to conventional compiler technology. Culler et al.'s TAM (Threaded Abstract Machine) [150] provides cheap support for multithreading, using a hierarchy of control structures: *inlets* provide entry points which are used for synchronisation; threads perform single indivisible computations; and tasks aggregate threads.

Granularity Control. Dataflow programs typically produce much fine-grained parallelism, which must be managed carefully to avoid memory exhaustion and excessive scheduling overheads [149]. One solution is to increase granularity by combining operations into larger "basic blocks" that can be

2.6 Dataflow

treated as individual dataflow nodes [511] (so-called *macro-dataflow*). The resulting parallelism is still relatively fine-grained, however. An alternative approach used by the Manchester dataflow team [503] is to throttle the system by using workload measures to control which tokens are activated. In an unloaded system, tokens are scheduled in a breadth-first fashion, corresponding to parallel evaluation. In an overloaded system, tokens are matched in a depth-first manner, which corresponds to sequential evaluation.

These approaches are predominantly dynamic. More recent work has focused on static analysis techniques to automatically partition dataflow programs into sequential threads based on granularity information [569].

Another dynamic approach that has been used successfully by several systems, including both SISAL [391] and Id [425], is loop-bounding [149] (often referred to as k-bounded loops). Loop-constructs can give rise to one parallel thread per iteration. In the case where the loop has a large number of iterations, thread creation can be throttled by limiting the number of simultaneously executing threads to some pre-defined constant k. As threads terminate, so more threads are created for the remaining loop iterations. This limits the number of parallel threads that are executed simultaneously. SACs With-loop construct is similar [517]. k-bounded loops have been found to be very effective when they are applicable [148] but can be difficult to use in practice [529].

Latency Hiding Through Multithreading. An example is Arvind and Nikhil's lambda-S calculus, which has dispensed entirely with dataflow graphs as an internal intermediate form, and which provides a number of communication and control structures.

Having combined instructions into coarser-grained tasks, and having opted to use more or less conventional hardware, the issue of delays due to communication latency becomes much more important. One solution is to divide tasks into even smaller parallel units (threads) that share the same task state, but which can be executed entirely independently [150]. When a thread becomes blocked as a result of performing a communication, another thread can then be executed. This effectively hides the communication latency by performing useful work at the same time as the communication is taking place. The blocked thread may then be resumed as soon as the result of the communication becomes available. TAM [150] supports a finer level of latency hiding, using *inlets*. In this model, threads do not block as soon as they communicate, but may continue execution (perhaps performing additional communications). When a value that has been requested is needed, the thread must then suspend. When a communication is set up, the communication system is given an inlet continuation to execute when the communication completes. Each such inlet decrements a count of the communications that are outstanding for the thread, and either terminates if it is non-zero or continues with the main continuation for the thread. Threads are thus scheduled without needing a heavyweight scheduling mechanism.

3. Programming Language Constructs

Rita Loogen[1]

3.1 Introduction

Functional languages offer abstraction, expressiveness, referential transparency, and a clear semantic model. They allow algorithms to be expressed at a high level of abstraction and thus support the task of program development substantially. Research in parallel functional programming also tries to provide these advantages in the context of parallel program development. Following the idea of declarative programming, the main task of a parallel programmer should be to specify *what* has to be evaluated in parallel and not *how* the parallel evaluation has to be organised. Consequently programmers should not deal with *low level* details of process management such as process creation and placement, communication and synchronisation.

Research in the area of parallel functional programming ranges from exploiting implicit parallelism to adding explicit parallel constructs. This chapter describes and compares several mechanisms and language constructs that have been proposed and presents some representative languages in detail.

3.2 Overview

Chapter 1 discussed several design choices that can be taken for functional languages. Impure languages, i.e. those with side-effecting constructs, are opposed to pure languages, and non-strict languages, i.e. those in which function arguments are not necessarily evaluated, to strict ones. In the context of parallelism one may additionally distinguish several levels and types of parallel control. Fully explicit approaches specify all behavioural details, while fully implicit approaches rely on the compiler and run-time system in this respect. Data parallel approaches exploit inherent parallelism in special (data parallel) operations, while control parallel approaches allow arbitrary parallel control flows to be expressed. The design space is large and thus it is not straightforward to give an appropriate classification of parallel functional languages. Figure 3.1 classifies the approaches discussed in this chapter with respect to both the level of control and the type of parallelism.

In *implicit* approaches the system tries to exploit parallelism that is inherent in the reduction semantics or, in the case of data parallelism, in the semantics of special operations. The parallelism is semantically transparent, and is usually introduced through relatively low-level language constructs.

---

[1] Philipps-Universität Marburg, Germany.

	control parallelism	data parallelism
implicit	automatic parallelisation annotation based languages	data parallel languages
↕ controlled ↕	para-functional programming evaluation strategies skeleton languages	high-level data parallelism
explicit	process control languages message passing languages concurrent languages	

Figure 3.1. Classification of parallel approaches by level of control and type of parallelism

The transparency property also holds for *controlled* approaches, but in this case the programmer is aware of parallelism and higher-level parallel constructs are provided.

Finally, in languages with *explicit* parallelism there is an explicit notion of a process and there are also language constructs for the definition of process systems. Of course there are no strict borders between these classes and further features could be considered to classify the various approaches, e.g. the kind of process systems and the level of abstraction and purity.

Shapiro [527] distinguishes between transformational and reactive concurrent process systems. A *transformational* system or program receives some input at the beginning of its operation and yields an output at its end. Even if some basic interactive input/output is performed, the central task of such a system is to compute a final result. In contrast, the purpose of a *reactive* system is not necessarily to obtain a final result, but to maintain some interaction with its environment. Many reactive systems ideally never terminate and in this sense never yield a final result. Operating systems, for example, fall into this category. Based on this distinction, parallel systems can be defined as a special case of concurrent systems: concurrent systems with transformational behaviour are called *parallel*.

The main goal of parallel systems is to speed up computations, while in concurrent systems, the focus is on structuring software. Most functional programs define transformational systems. Parallel functional languages which are based on semantics-preserving parallel constructs only consider the parallelisation of such systems. Concurrent functional languages incorporate nonfunctional constructs to cope with general concurrent systems, such as a nondeterministic choice construct. There have been attempts to define operating systems purely functionally [576] using streams, but so far it has proved necessary to use some kind of nondeterministic merge operator in order to model time-dependent interactive behaviour.

3.2 Overview

Another important feature of parallel or concurrent functional languages is whether they allow dynamically evolving process systems to be defined or whether they consider only systems whose structure is statically determined.

In the rest of this chapter, we follow the above classification of parallel functional languages and explain the specifics of each approach. To compare the language features, we use two simple running examples. The first is a simple integer function that defines the binomial coefficient and represents a typical divide-and-conquer algorithm.

Example 3.2.1. The following recursive Haskell program computes a binomial coefficient $\binom{n}{k}$ for natural numbers n and k, which denotes the number of ways of choosing k objects from a collection of n objects.

```
binom                     :: Int -> Int -> Int
binom n k | k == 0 && n >= 0 = 1
          | n <  k && n >= 0 = 0
          | n >= k && k >= 0 = binom (n-1) k + binom (n-1) (k-1)
          | otherwise        = error "negative parameters"
```

As a second example we consider the multiplication of sparse matrices with dense vectors.

Example 3.2.2. Sparse matrices can be represented by lists of rows, where each row is specified by a list of (column number, value) pairs of the non-zero values in the row.

```
type SparseMatrix a = [[(Int,a)]]
type Vector a       = [a]
```

An example matrix and its list representation are

$$\begin{pmatrix} 1 & -0.5 & 0 & 0 \\ -0.5 & 1 & -0.5 & 0 \\ 0 & -0.5 & 0 & 0 \\ 0 & 0 & -0.5 & 1 \end{pmatrix}$$

```
[ [(0,1),(1,-0.5)],
  [(0,-0.5),(1,1),(2,-0.5)],
  [(1,-0.5)],
  [(2,-0.5),(3,1)] ]
```

The multiplication of sparse matrices with dense vectors can easily be expressed using the map function over lists (see Chapter 2).

A function which multiplies the non-zero matrix elements with the corresponding vector elements is mapped over each row. The resulting list is summed using the sum function:

```
sum :: Num a => [a] -> a
sum =   foldr (+) 0
```

The composition of the sum function and the map application is then mapped over the list of row representations:

```
matvec       :: Num a => SparseMatrix a -> Vector a -> Vector a
matvec m v = map (sum.map (\ (i,x) -> x * v!!i)) m
```

3.3 Implicit Parallelism

The *Church-Rosser property* guarantees that every expression in a purely functional program has, at most, one normal form and that it is possible to evaluate independent subexpressions in arbitrary order and thus in parallel (see Chapter 2). This source of parallelism is called *implicit*, because it is inherent in the reduction semantics. It forms the basis for the automatic parallelisation of functional programs and for annotation-based parallel functional languages.

In contrast to this approach data parallel languages are based on special parallel functions that apply some basic operation to all elements of some data structure. The parallelism is inherent in these functions and restricted to their applications. There are many applications, for instance several numerical algorithms, where this kind of implicit parallelism is sufficient (see Chapter 19).

In this subsection we discuss these forms of implicit parallelism.

3.3.1 Automatic Parallelisation

In general a functional program contains much potential parallelism, the exploitation of which is, however, not always worthwhile. It strongly depends on the complexity of expressions and the characteristics of the underlying parallel system whether the overhead of parallel evaluations will be compensated by the gain in execution time and space. Each parallelising compiler must, therefore, incorporate some *granularity* or *cost analysis* to decide for which expressions a parallel evaluation might be advantageous (see also Chapter 8).

Example 3.3.1. In the binomial coefficient program the recursive calls of `binom` are independent subexpressions which can be evaluated in parallel. This is a source of divide-and-conquer parallelism. Moreover the comparisons in the case analysis of `binom` could, in principle, be evaluated in parallel. This would, however, lead to very fine-grain parallelism that would carry excessive overhead on most parallel systems.

Strictness Analysis. *Lazy* functional languages embody an additional obstacle that renders parallelisation more difficult. The lazy evaluation strategy only allows the evaluation of subexpressions whose value is necessary to determine the overall result. The evaluation process is demand-driven and thus inherently sequential. Demand for the evaluation of subexpressions is propagated step-by-step outside-in. Thus laziness hinders easy correct parallelisation. In order to avoid wasting resources due to the evaluation of unneeded subexpressions (*speculative parallelism*) some additional analysis is necessary to detect the maximal parallelism in programs. Strictness analysis (see Chapter 2) provides a way out of this dilemma. The parallel evaluation of a strict function argument can safely be initiated, because the strictness property guarantees that if this evaluation is undefined or fails to terminate then the whole function application is undefined. A parallelising compiler for lazy functional languages usually incorporates some kind of strictness analysis.

Example 3.3.2. In the binom example the strictness of the predefined function (+) guarantees that both recursive calls must be evaluated in order to compute the overall result. Furthermore it can be inferred that the binom function is strict in both arguments. Thus, the parameters of the function could also be evaluated in parallel, but their low complexity implies that this strictness should only be used to replace lazy evaluation by eager evaluation, i.e. call-by-need by call-by-value parameter passing.

The basic definition of function strictness must be refined for an appropriate *handling of data structures*. For data structures, several levels of definedness can be distinguished. The basic strictness definition distinguishes only between the bottom value $\bot$ and non-bottom values, i.e. between the totally undefined structure and structures for which the weak head normal form (WHNF) exists, and thus for which at least the top level constructor is defined. Many intermediate levels of definedness could be distinguished, e.g. structures for which the normal form (NF) exists, i.e. which are totally defined (finite with defined entries), or structures for which the spine normal form (SNF) exists, i.e. which are finite, but may contain undefined entries.

Example 3.3.3. Detailed strictness analysis of the sparse matrix vector multiplication example which takes into account the context of function calls leads to the following results.

The function map is strict in its list argument, i.e. whenever this argument is undefined, the result of the map application will also be undefined. Analysing the definedness of a map application depending on the various possible levels to which the list argument may be defined gives more detailed information: the evaluation of a map application to weak head normal form also requires the evaluation of the list argument to weak head normal form. The same is true for the spine normal form. The evaluation of a map application to full normal form, however, only requires that the list argument is evaluated to normal form when a *hyper-strict* function is mapped over the list (a function is *hyper-strict* when it requires all of its argument, as opposed to simply the weak head normal form of that argument — in this case, this is significant if the list argument contains sub-lists or other elements of constructed types, but not if it is a list of ground types such as integers). Otherwise, it is only possible to deduce that the list argument must be evaluated to spine normal form.

The idea of relating the evaluation degree required by a function application to the evaluation degrees that are necessary for the arguments of this application was introduced by Burn's *evaluation transformer* approach [98]. An evaluation transformer maps the evaluation degrees required for function applications to those evaluation degrees which are consequently necessary for the arguments of the application. For the map function, the evaluation transformer defines the following mapping:

evaluation degree (map fct list)	evaluation degree	
	fct	list
WHNF	—	WHNF
SNF	—	SNF
NF	WHNF	NF if fct is hyper-strict SNF otherwise

The strictness behaviour of the function sum is much easier. This function always evaluates its list argument to normal form.

The fact that the multiplication function (*) is strict in both its arguments[2] and that the index operator (!!) is strict in its second argument implies that the function (\ (i,x) -> x*v!!i) is strict in both its arguments (the vector v is a global variable in this expression). Mapping a hyper-strict function over a list means that this list will be evaluated to normal form. The composition of the sum function and the map application is thus a function that also evaluates its argument (a row representation of the sparse matrix) to normal form. As this composed function is mapped over the matrix, the matrix argument of matvec can be evaluated to normal form before the function call whenever the result of this call of matvec must be evaluated to normal form. This is not true for the vector argument. The application of matvec may be well-defined even if the vector argument is $\bot$.

If only the weak head normal form or spine normal form of (matvec m v) is needed, the strictness properties of map imply that the matrix expression m will also be evaluated to weak head normal form or spine normal form.

The inherent parallelism in the matrix vector multiplication lies within the higher-order functions map and foldr. The strictness results show that parallelisation is only sensible when these are used to produce a full normal form.

The development of strictness analysis methods has been a very active field of research that has produced many interesting theoretical results. We will not go into further details here but refer the reader to the text by Nielson, Nielson and Hankin [419] if additional background is required.

3.3.2 Indicating Parallelism

Implicit parallelism can be made explicit in various ways: parallel let-expressions, annotations or predefined parallel combinators. These methods,

---
[2] Note that the potential non-strictness of the multiplication function which results from the fact that one could define $0 * \bot = 0$ and $\bot * 0 = 0$ is usually not considered.

3.3 Implicit Parallelism

which we call *annotation-based* have in common that the parallelism constructs are semantically transparent, i.e. they advise the compiler to generate parallel code, but do not change the semantics of programs. In general the "parallel" code does not actually enforce parallel evaluation. Most parallel functional systems decide at run-time depending on the current workload, whether a "parallel" expression is going to be evaluated in parallel or not.

Parallelism can be detected and indicated by a parallelising compiler, but nowadays it is common for programmers to indicate parallelism manually.

Parallel let. In functional programs the let-construct is used to introduce local definitions within expressions. In various projects [224], [369], [119] a parallel let-expression of the form

```
letpar var_1 = expr_1
       ...
       var_p = expr_p
in expr
```

has been introduced to express parallelism explicitly. The letpar expression means that the expressions expr_1, ..., expr_p may be evaluated in parallel. Thus, p parallel processes may be spawned at run-time, while the process evaluating the letpar expression continues with the evaluation of expr. In any case the evaluation of the subexpressions will be initiated, either sequentially or in parallel. Thus, in a lazy system they should be strict subexpressions.

Example 3.3.4. A parallel version of the binom program is as follows:

```
binom                          :: Int -> Int -> Int
binom n k | k == 0 && n >= 0 = 1
          | n <  k && n >= 0 = 0
          | n >= k && k >= 0 = letpar v = binom (n-1) (k-1)
                               in binom (n-1) k + v
          | otherwise        = error "negative parameters"
```

The second recursive call has been abstracted out of the addition expression in order to make clear that it should be considered for parallel evaluation.

The advantage of letpar expressions is that a special compilation scheme can be used which is independent from the evaluation order of the sequential compiler. However, the parallelisation requires a program transformation which may cause a small overhead due to the additional indirection when a "parallel" subexpression is evaluated sequentially. The letpar construct can be further decorated with information on how to allocate the processes to processors or with information about the degree of safe evaluation.

Example 3.3.5. In the sparse matrix vector multiplication example it would be wise to place letpar expressions in the code of the higher order functions map or foldr and to introduce parallelized versions of these functions, e.g. a parallel map:

```
parmap f []     = []
parmap f (x:xs) = letpar y = (f x)   -- only if NF evaluation
                  in  y : (parmap f xs)
```

During the evaluation of this function a parallel process may be created for each list element transformation.

The restricting comment indicates that the `letpar` should only allow a parallel evaluation if the whole expression is evaluated to normal form. This information could be propagated during runtime or special function definitions could be prepared for different evaluation contexts. One could also inline the code of the higher order functions `map` and `foldr` and thus produce specialised first-order code before the parallelisation.

Annotations. The easiest way to indicate parallelism within a functional program is by placing appropriate annotations to show the compiler which subexpressions should be evaluated in parallel. Annotations only affect the run-time behaviour of programs: the program semantics remains unchanged. Furthermore the program can still be compiled sequentially by simply ignoring the parallelism annotations.

Since functional programs do not specify evaluation order, the annotations must therefore be chosen in such a way that the parallel execution occurs for any evaluation order implemented in the compiler. Consequently, annotations are usually provided not only to indicate potential parallelism, but also to influence the order of sequential evaluations.

A typical example is the three primitive process annotations provided in Concurrent Clean (see also Chapter 15). The {|P|} and {|P AT location|} annotations lead to the creation of a parallel process which evaluates the annotated expression to root normal form (which corresponds to weak head normal form). This process is preferably allocated on another processor. The location directive `AT location` explicitly determines the processor on which the new process has to be created. The expression `location` has the type `PROCID`, with predefined functions such as `CurrentP` or `NeighbourP` yielding objects of this type. The process locations influence only the process allocation on a machine, but never the result of a program. The {|I|} annotation initiates the creation of an interleaved process, i.e. a process which will be executed on the same processor as the generator process.

Example 3.3.6. The following Concurrent Clean program defines a parallel version of the `binom` function:

```
Binom :: !Int !Int -> Int
Binom n k | k == 0 && n >= 0  = 1
          | n <  k && n >= 0  = 0
          | n >= k && k >= 0  = (binom (n-1) k) + {|P|} parproc
          | otherwise         = abort "negative parameters"
          where
             parproc = binom (n-1) (k-1)
```

3.3 Implicit Parallelism

The second recursive call of Binom can be evaluated in parallel on another processor. The strictness annotations (shown by "!") in the type declaration force the evaluation of the argument expressions (n-1) and (k-1) before the parallel process is created. The Clean system handles annotations in such a way that parallelism is maximised, i.e. although the annotation is put on the second argument of (+) the parallel process will be started first and then the computation will continue with the evaluation of the first argument.

The sparse matrix vector multiplication can simply be parallelised by using a parallel map function, which generates a parallel process for each element of the result list. This function corresponds to the parmap function described before, except that it does not depend on the evaluation context:

```
ParMap :: (a -> b) [a] -> [b]
ParMap f []     = []
ParMap f [x:xs] = [ {|P|} f x : {|I|} ParMap f xs ]
```

The {|I|} annotation is placed on the tail of the result list in order to force the evaluation of the whole list by creating an interleaved process. Without this annotation, the evaluation of a ParMap application will stop as soon as the top level constructor node of the result list is computed.

Parallel Combinators. Another simple way to indicate parallelism is to introduce special identity functions which influence the evaluation of their arguments. In Glasgow parallel Haskell (GpH) [571] the following combinators are used to cope with parallelism:

```
par, seq :: a -> b -> b
```

The par function indicates potential parallelism. An expression par e1 e2 means that a so-called *spark* is created for e1 which shows that e1 may be evaluated in parallel. The value of the whole expression is the same as e2. Usually, e1 will be referenced by e2. The seq combinator (a standard function in Haskell 98) corresponds to sequential composition. An expression seq e1 e2 means that first e1 is evaluated to WHNF and then e2 is returned. Semantically both functions correspond to projections on their second arguments, but operationally the compiler is instructed to initiate either parallel or local expression evaluation.

Example 3.3.7. A GpH version of the binom function can thus be specified as follows:

```
binom                       :: Int -> Int -> Int
binom n k | k == 0 && n >= 0 = 1
          | n <  k && n >= 0 = 0
          | n >= k && k >= 0 = let b2 = binom (n-1) (k-1)
                               in b2 `par` ((binom (n-1) k) + b2)
          | otherwise        = error "negative parameters"
```

This code will create a parallel task for the evaluation of the second recursive call and then go on evaluating the expression ((binom (n-1) k) + b2). The parallel task may, but need not, be evaluated on another processor depending on the workload within the whole system.

If the arguments of the addition function are evaluated from left to right, the other recursive call will be evaluated next. Otherwise the parent task will simply wait for the result of the sparked expression and no parallelism will be exploited.

Since evaluation order is not specified in Haskell and either operand of the addition could consequently be evaluated before the other, it is better to use the seq function in order to be explicit about evaluation order in this case.

Example 3.3.8. The following GpH version of the binom function explicitly specifies that the second recursive call can be evaluated in parallel and that the evaluation continues with the evaluation of the first recursive call, before the sum of the recursive results is returned:

```
binom :: Int -> Int -> Int
binom n k | k == 0 && n >= 0  = 1
          | n <  k && n >= 0  = 0
          | n >= k && k >= 0  = let b1 = binom (n-1) k
                                    b2 = binom (n-1) (k-1)
                                in b2 'par' b1 'seq' (b1 + b2)
          | otherwise         = error "negative parameters"
```

The effect is similar to the one of the letpar construct.

3.3.3 Data Parallelism

The ability to operate in parallel over sets of data is called *data parallelism* (Chapter 7 gives a fuller description of this style of programming). Usually the same operation is performed on many different data sets. This form of parallelism naturally scales with the problem size. In contrast the parallel evaluation of independent subexpressions (as considered in the preceding subsections) is commonly referred to as *function* or *control parallelism*. Data parallelism often occurs in scientific computing and thus most data parallel functional languages have been developed with such applications in mind. Typical structures that have to be represented efficiently are matrices and vectors. Thus data parallel languages support array structures and provide implicitly parallel operations on arrays like transformation or reduction operations. In the context of implicit parallelism, the data parallel functional languages SISAL [532] and Id [425] are the most closely related. Both not only support data parallelism, but also the inherent expression parallelism in the functional kernel language. While SISAL relies on an applicative-order evaluation strategy, Id is based on a concurrent execution model with non-strict data structures.

3.3 Implicit Parallelism

SISAL (Streams and Iterations in a Single Assignment Language) has been designed as a single assignment language for expressing solutions to large-scale scientific problems [532]. It provides loop-constructs and arrays with data parallel operations adopted from FORTRAN 90. SISAL 90 [193] supports types, higher-order functions and a foreign language interface. Determinism in the language kernel is retained but nondeterminism can be imported by foreign language calls.

A central goal of the language designers was that the compilers for the language must be able to produce highly efficient code. SISAL is not explicitly targeted to multiprocessors. The low-level parallelism provided in uniprocessors through multiple functional units or vector instructions will also be beneficial in SISAL implementations.

The extraction of parallelism is the responsibility of the compiler and may depend on the target architecture. The programmer may influence the compilation through the constructs chosen for the specification of the algorithm, but there is no way to control the parallelism that is extracted by the compiler. The following sources of parallelism are distinguished:

- *Data parallelism:* "forall" expressions, and iterative-style loops can generate parallelism on fine-grained parallel machines;
- *Stream or pipeline parallelism:* producers and consumers of streams can execute concurrently, controlled by synchronisation added by the compiler;
- *Function parallelism:* independent subexpressions can be evaluated in parallel, especially function applications that might represent large quantities of work. Low-level parallelism, such as that found within a single expression, can also be exploited by dataflow computers and by *super-scalar* conventional machines that overlap the execution of multiple functional units.

Differences in machine architecture may make some forms of parallelism more attractive than others.

Example 3.3.9. The following sample code for the sparse matrix vector multiplication in SISAL looks much like imperative code. The sparse array A is in the form of an array of rows. Each row contains only the non-zero values and is stored in an array of variable length with entries of type real. index is an array of integer arrays with the same shape as A containing the column indices for the non-zero values in A. Let (a_{ij}) be the original sparse matrix. Then:

$$\text{index}[i,j] = k \text{ if and only if } A[i,j] = a_{ik}.$$

A vector b consisting of the array-vector product is returned.

```
type vector = array[real];
type sparsearray = array[array[real]];
type sparseindex = array[array[integer]];

function spvmul(A: sparsearray; index: sparseindex; x: vector;
```

```
                    returns vector)
% loop over rows
  for i in 1, array_size(A)

    % loop over non-zero elements of each row
    b := for j in 1, array_size(A[i])
           c := A[i,j] * x[index[i,j]];
         returns
           value of sum c
         end for;
  returns
    array of b
  end for
end function
```

Note that the for-loops are forall expressions, i.e. that the loop bodies can be instantiated independently. The inner loop returns the value of a sum reduction on the array c. It depends on the compiler how the inherent loop-parallelism in this program is exploited.

The functional dataflow language Id (Irvine Dataflow) [425] and its Haskell successor pH (parallel Haskell) [426] are based on a concurrent evaluation strategy: any redex not in the body of a λ-abstraction or conditional will be reduced. Although not only those redexes whose results are known to be needed are reduced, this strategy implements a non-strict semantics provided that no redex has its evaluation delayed indefinitely.

Id is a layered language. It has a functional core with arrays created by array comprehensions which are similar to Haskell's list comprehensions. The functional kernel is extended by so-called I-structures (see Section 2.6.2), which provide write-once storage locations. I-structures do not compromise the Church-Rosser property of the language. The second extension is by so-called M-structures (see also Section 2.6.2) which provide updatable storage locations the use of which destroys the Church-Rosser property. Accesses to I- or M-fields are combined with synchronisation in order to simplify their use in a parallel environment.

Id exploits inherent expression, loop and function parallelism in a similar way to SISAL. Due to the concurrent evaluation strategy and the non-strict semantics of data structures, it is possible to allow dependencies between the elements of array comprehensions in Id. The SISAL language is more restrictive in this respect, since it allows only non-circular structures.

In the strict functional language SAC (Single Assignment C) [516] array operations can be defined using a dimension-invariant form of array comprehensions called With-loops. These allow the element-wise definition of operations on entire arrays as well as on subarrays selected through index ranges or strides. A high-level optimization called With-loop-folding [517], which eliminates the creation of superfluous intermediate array structures in combined array operations, leads to substantial improvements in run-time. The inherent data parallelism within the array operations has been exploited in a compilation scheme which transforms With-loops into multithreaded target code [236].

3.3.4 Discussion

The exploitation of implicit parallelism is a neat and simple idea. It is closest to the ideal approach where the programmer need not think about parallelism at all. However, its implementation requires powerful and complex run-time systems which support the dynamic creation of parallel processes for the evaluation of subexpressions, the automatic transfer of data to and from remote processors and the automatic synchronisation of parallel processes. These systems often provide a global address space which is automatically distributed during execution when subexpressions are evaluated on another processor. Communication takes place automatically when a computation demands the value of such subexpressions.

Thus, in an implicit (control or data) parallel system many tasks related to parallel execution are managed by the run-time system, leaving the programmer to specify only what has to be evaluated and to what extent, or to use the appropriate data parallel operations and constructs, respectively. Nevertheless it turns out that the correct and effective indication of parallelism by programmers is not as easy as it seems at first glance, but may require some knowledge about the internals of the parallel run-time system. In particular, the programmer may need to be explicit about evaluation order in order to achieve the desired parallelism or he/she may need to restructure the program in order to avoid sequential bottlenecks (see e.g. Chapter 11).

The primitive low-level constructs that are used to reveal implicit parallelism have in common that they preserve the semantics of the original program, but they may change the structure of the program. Parallel *let*-expressions or parallel combinators have the disadvantage that a program transformation is necessary to specify the dynamic behaviour. In principle, annotations could simply be placed in the sequential program without any reorganisation, but in many cases it is also necessary to restructure the original program in order to make the exploitation of parallelism possible. Low-level parallelism indications, such as par and seq combinators, scattered through the program code tend to obscure the structure of the parallel program. The same is true for data parallel languages (see Chapter 7). In the following section we discuss higher-level approaches which try to overcome these difficulties.

Up to now we have taken the view that a "sequential" functional program is parallelised by the programmer or a compiler. Apart from the fact that this is only reasonable when the program has been written in such a way that it contains implicit parallelism, this view is rather restricted and we now wish to turn to the question of how to specify "parallel" algorithms in a functional language. This is related to the desire for higher-level parallel constructs.

3.4 Controlled Parallelism

In this section we consider approaches to parallel functional programming where parallelism is under the control of the programmer. Higher-level constructs are used to express parallel algorithms. One might classify these approaches as *semi-explicit,* because parallelism is explicit in the form of special constructs or operations, yet at the same time details are hidden within the implementation of these operations and constructs. There is no explicit notion of a parallel process. Parallelism is not a matter of the denotational semantics which remains unchanged, but a matter of the implementation which takes advantage of the parallelism.

3.4.1 Para-functional Programming

In [288] Hudak argues that a parallel functional language needs explicit mechanisms to express:

- The scheduling of a computation, i.e. a specific partial ordering on program execution;
- The mapping of the program onto a machine, i.e. on which processor a particular part of a program is to be executed;
- The distribution of data.

He introduces *para-functional programming*, an extension of the functional paradigm, which is based on scheduling and mapping annotations.

A *scheduled expression* controls the evaluation order of an expression. It has the general form `exp sched sexp` where `sched` is a keyword and `exp` is the expression whose evaluation order is determined by the schedule expression `sexp`. A schedule defines a partial order on *events*. Parallelism is introduced by the event `Dlab` which represents the demand for the evaluation of the expression referenced by `lab`. Further events are the start and the end of the evaluation of an expression. Schedules can be composed by concatenation "." (sequential composition) and concurrency "|" (parallel composition).

A *mapped expression* `exp on pid` means that `exp` is to be evaluated on the processor `pid`. The expression `pid` must evaluate to a processor identifier which may be modelled by integers assuming a predefined mapping from those integers to the physical processors. The programmer can manipulate processor identifiers using conventional arithmetic operations, for instance, by defining

```
left  pid = 2 * pid
right pid = 2 * pid + 1
```

in order to model the neighbour connections in an infinite binary tree.

Example 3.4.1. A parallel version of the `binom` function can be expressed as follows using these para-functional extensions:

3.4 Controlled Parallelism

```
binom                        :: Int -> Int -> Int
binom n k | k == 0 && n >= 0  = 1
          | n <  k && n >= 0  = 0
          | n >= k && k >= 0  = b1 + b2       sched   Db1 | Db2
          | otherwise         = error "negative parameters"
     where b1 = binom (n-1) k       on left  self
           b2 = binom (n-1) (k-1)   on right self
```

The schedule Db1 | Db2 has the effect that the recursive calls of `binom` will be evaluated in parallel. The mapping annotations lead to their evaluation on the left and right children on a virtual tree topology.

Para-functional programming allows the programmer to specify a parallel algorithm in a very high level language. There is a clear separation between the purely functional specification of what has to be computed and the annotations introduced to control the dynamic behaviour and the mapping onto a parallel system. The extremely fine control over parallel behaviour may however lead to cumbersome programs and sometimes it is necessary to restructure a program for better parallel performance.

3.4.2 Evaluation Strategies

A clear separation of the algorithm specified by a functional program and the specification of its dynamic behaviour is also the goal of Glasgow parallel Haskell (GpH), which uses *evaluation strategies* defined on top of the combinators `par` and `seq` for that purpose [571]. Evaluation strategies allow the programmer to influence the dynamic behaviour, e.g. by overruling lazy evaluation and forcing normal form evaluation in favour of parallelism. Strategies can be used to specify parallelism/sequencing as well as the degree of evaluation. In contrast to the schedule expressions of para-functional programming, they abstract from the start and the end of expression evaluation, and control the evaluation degree instead.

Formally, a strategy is a function taking as an argument the value to be computed. It is executed purely for effect, i.e. its result is irrelevant and therefore simply ():

```
type Strategy a = a -> ()
```

A strategy is applied by the `using` function which applies its second argument, a strategy, to its first argument, the result expression, and then returns this:

```
using     :: a -> Strategy a -> a
using x s = (s x) 'seq' x
```

Example 3.4.2. Using these predefined constructs the parallel `binom` function can be expressed as:

```
binom :: Int -> Int -> Int
binom n k | k == 0 && n >= 0  = 1
          | n <  k && n >= 0  = 0
          | n >= k && k >= 0  = let b1 = binom (n-1) k
                                    b2 = binom (n-1) (k-1)
                                in (b1 + b2) 'using' strat
          | otherwise         = error "negative parameters"
                                where
                                strat _ = b2 'par' b1 'seq' ()
```

In this definition there is a clear separation between the algorithm and the strategy which describes how to evaluate the recursive function calls. The program has, however, to be restructured slightly to name the subexpressions which are referenced by the strategy.

Individual evaluation strategies can be used to specify the amount of evaluation that should be done on an expression explicitly. The most basic strategies define no evaluation, evaluation to weak head normal form (WHNF) (the default in Haskell) or to normal form (NF) for structures:

```
-- no evaluation
r0      :: Strategy a
r0 _  = ()

-- evaluation to WHNF
rwhnf   :: Strategy a
rwhnf x = x 'seq' ()

-- class of data for which normal form strategy is defined
class NFData a where
  rnf :: Strategy a
  rnf =  rwhnf          -- default

-- evaluation of lists to NF
instance NFData a => NFData [a] where
  rnf []     = ()
  rnf (x:xs) = rnf x 'seq' rnf xs
```

As strategies are simply functions, they can also be passed as parameters in the definition of higher-order strategies.

Example 3.4.3. The parallel evaluation of each element of a list using a strategy passed as a parameter can be defined by the parList strategy:

```
parList                :: Strategy a -> Strategy [a]
parList strat []       = ()
parList strat (x:xs)   = strat x 'par' (parList strat xs)
```

This function can be used to define a parallel map function:

```
parMap              :: Strategy a -> (a->b) -> [a] -> [b]
parMap strat f xs = map f xs 'using' parList strat
```

3.4.3 High-level Data Parallelism

High-level control over data parallelism is provided by languages such as GOLD-FISH (see Chapter 9), which uses information on the shape of data structures for optimisation purposes, and NESL [60], a data parallel language based on ML, which provides special support for nested data structures. NESL uses one-dimensional arrays called *sequences* as primitive parallel data types. Parallelism is achieved exclusively through operations on these sequences:

1. A parallel map construct called *apply-to-each* that applies a function to each element of a sequence in parallel;
2. A set of parallel functions that operate on sequences, e.g. summing the elements of a sequence or permuting the order of the elements.

A high-level set-like notation similar to list comprehensions in Haskell is used for the parallel map construct. The key feature which distinguishes NESL from other data parallel languages is its ability to express *nested data parallelism*. Any user-defined function can be applied over the elements of a sequence, even if the function is itself parallel and the elements of the sequence are themselves sequences.

Example 3.4.4. We consider the problem of multiplying a sparse matrix by a dense vector. In NESL sequences play the role of lists so the sparse matrix is represented as a sequence of rows which are themselves sequences. The parallel multiplication of the non-zero elements of a row with the corresponding position in a vector x is defined by:

```
{v*x[i] : (i,v) in [(0,-0.5),(1,1),(2,-0.5)] }
```

The code for multiplying a sparse matrix A by a dense vector x uses nested parallelism:

```
{ sum( {v*x[i] : (i,v) in row})  :   row in A }
```

The predefined function sum sums all elements of a sequence in parallel.

By using the parallel map construct and parallel reduction operations the programmer explicitly specifies the parallelism within his/her program. Nevertheless, this parallelism is hidden within the implementation of the data parallel constructs and it may be difficult for the programmer to assess the parallel evaluation of the nested parallel constructs. Therefore, NESL supplies a mechanism for deriving the theoretical running time directly from the code for an algorithm. The performance model is based on the notion of work and depth of computations instead of run-time. See Chapter 8 for other approaches to cost modelling.

NESL does not preserve referential transparency. It provides a parallel write function on sequences to modify several values in a sequence in parallel. The function takes the sequence and a list of (index,value)-pairs as arguments. If an index is repeated, one value is even written non-deterministically.

3.4.4 Skeletons

Skeletons are higher-order functional forms with built-in parallel behaviour (see Chapter 13). They define common parallel computation schemes at an abstract level. Many parallel algorithms can simply be expressed as instantiations of these schemes without any explicit reference to parallelism. The best-known skeleton is perhaps the divide-and-conquer scheme:

```
d&c :: (p->Bool) -> (p->s) -> (p->[p]) -> ([s]->s) -> p -> s
d&c trivial solve divide conquer problem
    = if trivial problem then solve problem
      else conquer (map (d&c trivial solve divide conquer)
                        (divide problem))
```

Example 3.4.5. The binom example is a special instance of this general scheme, where:

```
trivial     :: (Int,Int) -> Bool
trivial (n,k) = (n >= 0 && (k == 0 || n < k)) || n < 0 || k < 0

solve                   :: (Int,Int) -> Int
solve (n,k) | k == 0 && n >= 0 = 1
            | n < k && n >= 0  = 0
            | n < 0 || k < 0   = error "negative parameters"

divide      :: (Int,Int) -> [(Int,Int)]
divide (n,k) = [(n-1,k),(n-1,k-1)]

conquer :: [Int] -> Int
conquer =  foldr (+) 0
```

This example shows that the programmer has to express the parallel algorithm he/she has in mind as an instance of the skeletons provided in the skeletal language he/she intends to use. In the simple binom example the overhead does not seem to be worthwhile, but for more complex algorithms it may be beneficial to make use of predefined parallel schemes instead of expressing parallelism directly using lower-level methods. This can already be seen from our second running example where the straightforward parallelisation simply replaces the map function with a parallel variant, which is, in fact, a skeleton.

A big advantage of skeletal programming is that the compiler can provide special support for the predefined skeletons. Each skeleton defines a regular computational structure which is statically determined and can be predistributed. This kind of parallelism is reasonably simple to implement, but it can only be applied to programs with the requisite structure. If the program's structure is not appropriate, it must be transformed to the required structure. This complicates the programming process.

Chapter 13 gives more detail on SCL, Darlington et al.'s Structured Coordination Language [162] and P3L, the Pisa Parallel Programming Language [27]. SCL provides *elementary skeletons* which abstract data parallel operations over distributed arrays and *computational skeletons* which express parallel control flow. Data partitioning, placement and movement, as well as control flow, are handled explicitly on a high level of abstraction.

As common in data parallel languages, parallelism is restricted to predefined operations and skeletons. Most languages work with a layered program structure, i.e. skeletons introduce parallelism on the top level, but they cannot be called from the sequential code on the lower level.

3.4.5 Discussion

The higher level of abstraction in the parallel approaches presented in this section gives the programmer high-level control over the parallelism and the dynamic behaviour of programs. The evaluation strategy approach is very flexible. It allows the programmer to define arbitrary evaluation strategies. The control over the parallelism and the functional specification of what has to be computed are cleanly separated. This is similar to the para-functional approach. Skeletons and data parallel operations can be defined using special higher-order functions, but will not necessarily be implemented efficiently.

While evaluation strategies and para-functional programming support general dynamic process networks, data parallel and skeletal languages work with special predetermined process structures. Data parallel languages usually exploit rather fine-grain parallelism.

Skeletal programming is reasonably simple to implement. However, it can only be applied to programs with the requisite structure. Other programs must be transformed to such a form. This complicates the programming process.

Another problem with the approaches discussed so far is that the class of algorithms that can be expressed is restricted to so-called *transformational systems*, i.e. deterministic algorithms that transform some input to some output without any interaction with the environment. The large class of interactive and distributed systems cannot be specified without some explicit notion of concurrency. Typical examples include master/worker algorithms in which a master process controls a bench of tasks which have to be distributed to various worker processes which deliver their results back to the master process. In order to specify such algorithms functional languages must be extended by constructs for handling processes and their communication or interaction explicitly.

3.5 Explicit Parallelism

The restrictions of implicit and controlled parallelism motivate the use of explicit constructs for the appropriate modelling of arbitrary process structures and general concurrent, i.e. interactive, systems. Languages and systems which exploit implicit and controlled parallelism mainly aim at speeding up the execution of transformational systems. In contrast, functional languages with explicit parallelism aim at improving the expressiveness of the functional kernel language. Examples include the so-called concurrent functional languages that aim to integrate functional and concurrent programming. Concurrent programming focuses on the structuring of software into components that run concurrently and perform separate subtasks. It does not necessarily regard programming of parallel algorithms and improving the efficiency of programs. Nevertheless distributed implementations of such languages are feasible.

3.5.1 Streams and Process Networks

Higher-order functions and laziness are powerful abstraction mechanisms of functional languages which can also be exploited with respect to parallelism. Lazy lists can be used to model communication streams and higher-order functions to define general process structures or *skeletons* (Section 3.4.4).

The idea of defining dynamically evolving process networks using a functional framework and streams as communication channels derives from the seminal work of Kahn and MacQueen [324]:

> "The language presented here provides concise and flexible means for creating complex networks of processes which may evolve during execution. The key concepts are *processes* and structures called *channels* which interconnect processes and buffer their communications."

This idea has been used in functional operating systems [576] and for modelling interactive input/output in functional languages.

With respect to parallelism, process networks have been mainly considered for distributed-memory parallel computing. In the following we present two approaches. The first, Caliban [331], uses a declarative annotation scheme to provide explicit control over process placement and communications. It is, however, restricted to static functional process networks which can be configured at compile-time. The second, Eden [85], extends the functional language Haskell by a coordination language for the definition of parallel, interacting processes. Both approaches have in common that interaction between processes is explicitly modelled using streams, i.e. lazy lists. Their main concern is parallel functional programming, although Eden also provides language constructs for concurrent programming. We call these languages *process control languages*.

Caliban. Caliban is an annotation language for the definition of process networks which has been built on top of Haskell. The process networks consist of processes which evaluate named expressions connected by communication links which are modelled by head-strict lazy lists. These links ensure that only normal form values are sent between processes. The network structure

3.5 Explicit Parallelism

is described declaratively using annotations. Coordination is expressed using `moreover` clauses, whose purpose is similar to that of the `using` function for an evaluation strategy. Bundle annotations are used to indicate which expressions should be evaluated on the same processor and which should not. `Arc` annotations define which interconnections have to be installed. Using data dependency analysis the need for communication between process nodes can be determined automatically. The `Arc` annotations are only used for explicit documentation and consistency checking. Each process is evaluated eagerly by its processor. Functions, so called "network forming operators", can be used to construct annotations. We consider here only a very simple example. A more detailed description of Caliban is contained in Chapter 14.

Example 3.5.1. In order to evaluate the function `binom` with a process system consisting of two processes which evaluate the top level recursive call, we can write the following Caliban program:

```
parbinom     :: Int -> Int -> Int
parbinom n k =  if n >= k && k >= 0
                then parsum else binom n k
                moreover Bundle [parsum,b1] And Bundle [b2]
                                            And (Arc parsum b2)
                where    parsum = b1 + b2
                         b1     = binom (n-1) k
                         b2     = binom (n-1) (k-1)
```

The Bundle annotations specify that the expressions `parsum` and `b1` are evaluated on the same processor and that the expression `b2` should be evaluated on a different processor. The `Arc` annotation indicates that `b2` is consumed by `parsum`.

At compile time the Caliban compiler evaluates the annotations and extracts the process network which, consequently, cannot change during execution. Thus, the compiler has complete information about processes, process allocation and communication requirements and can try to optimise the mapping of the process network to the machine platform.

Eden. Eden [86], [85] takes a similar approach to Caliban. Process networks are defined declaratively and lazy lists are used to model communication channels. However Eden supports dynamically evolving process systems and does not consider the bundling of process expressions.

Eden is a two-layered language which adds a *coordination layer* with explicit processes to the *computation language* Haskell [457]. The Eden coordination language contains *process abstractions*, which define a scheme for a process in a functional style, and *process instantiations*, which are expressions that generate processes and yield the respective outputs as their result.

A process that maps inputs $in_1, \ldots, in_m$ to outputs $out_1, \ldots, out_n$ can be specified by the process abstraction:

process $(in_1, \ldots, in_m)$ -> $(out_1, \ldots, out_n)$
where $equation_1 \ldots equation_r$

The optional where part of this expression is used to define auxiliary functions and common subexpressions which occur within the output expression.

Process abstractions have the type Process a b, where Process is a newly introduced type constructor and the type variables a and b represent the input and output interface of the process, respectively. A process can have as input (respectively, output) tuples of channels and data structures of channels [84]. In the latter case, annotations < and > are used to indicate channels in types.

Example 3.5.2. A simple process computing the scalar product of a vector and the row of a sparse matrix is defined by:

```
rowVecProd   :: (Num a, Transmissible a) =>
                [a] -> Process [(Int,a)] a
rowVecProd v =  process row -> sum (map (\ (i,x) -> x * v!!i) row)
```

The context Transmissible a ensures that functions for the transmission of values of type a are available. The argument vector v will be passed as a parameter at process creation time, while the row of the sparse matrix will be passed as a stream via a communication channel after process creation. The process outputs a single value.

A *process instantiation* forms the counterpart of a process abstraction. It creates a process and the corresponding communication channels. In the expression below, a process abstraction p is applied to a tuple of input expressions, yielding a tuple of outputs. (#) : Process a b -> a -> b is the operator for process instantiation.

$(out_1, \ldots, out_n)$ = p # $(input\_exp_1, \ldots, input\_exp_m)$

The child process uses n independent threads in order to produce these outputs. Likewise, the parent process creates m additional threads that evaluate $input\_exp_1, \ldots, input\_exp_m$.

Communication channels are unidirectional and connect one writer to exactly one reader. Only fully evaluated data objects are communicated and lists are transmitted as streams. Threads that try to access data that is not yet available will be suspended.

Example 3.5.3. A parallel version of the function map can easily be defined as follows. The function parmap instantiates a process abstraction p given as a parameter with each element of a list.

```
parmap :: Process a b -> [a] -> [b]
parmap  p []     = []
parmap  p (x:xs) = p # x : parmap p xs
```

A parallel Eden version of the sparse matrix vector product can then be simply defined using the parmap function and the process abstraction defined above:

3.5 Explicit Parallelism

```
matvec     :: Num a => SparseMatrix a -> Vector a -> Vector a
matvec m v = parmap (rowVecProd v) m
```

This represents the inner loop of the `matvec` function of Section 3.2.

The evaluation of an Eden process is driven by the evaluation of its output expressions, for which there is always demand. This rule overrides normal lazy evaluation in favour of parallelism. Furthermore, each process immediately evaluates all *top level* process instantiations. This may lead to speculative parallelism and again overrules lazy evaluation to some extent, but speeds up the generation of new processes and the distribution of the computation. If the demand-driven evaluation of certain inner process instantiations obstructs the unfolding of the parallel process system, the programmer has the possibility to lift them to the top level where they are immediately evaluated.

Nevertheless the process network will still be influenced by the demand for data: a process with all its outputs closed will terminate immediately. On termination its input channels will be eliminated and the corresponding outputs in the sender processes will be closed as well [83].

Additionally, Eden incorporates special concepts for defining reactive systems and for handling time-dependency. The *dynamic creation of reply channels* simplifies the interactive communication in reactive systems. A predefined non-deterministic process `merge` is used to model many-to-one communication in process systems, e.g. in master/worker systems where a master process collects results from several worker processes and the order of the incoming results is not relevant. Non-determinism is only introduced at the process level and it is encapsulated inside processes, i.e. non-deterministic processes cannot be used within the body of functions but only within the body of processes (see [85] for details).

Apart from its ability to define concurrent systems, there are three major properties which distinguish Eden from other parallel functional languages. In Eden:

1. It is possible to create stable process systems with efficient direct communication between the component processes instead of an indirect exchange of values via a logically shared, but physically distributed, memory;
2. Communication is strict, which means that input values are evaluated to normal form by the sender (streams are possible) and sent without further inquiries to the receiver (push messaging instead of pull messaging);
3. Memory is really distributed, which means that there is not a single distributed heap with a global address space forming a virtual shared heap but n independent heaps (where n is the number of processors).

3.5.2 Explicit Message Passing

In process control languages like Caliban and Eden, processes and their communication topology are clearly specified, but communication commands remain implicit. The next lower level of abstraction is to work with explicit message passing in a functional framework. This leads to languages where communication must be explicitly specified by the programmer. Such languages are especially appropriate for distributed programming.

In this subsection we refer to two approaches which introduce mechanisms for the communication between functional programs without the support of general evolving process systems.

The Scampi approach described in Chapter 18 (Simple Caml interface to MPI) is based on a library that provides MPI features to the Objective Caml language. It shows how to produce a portable parallel programming environment building on an existing functional language and a standard message passing library. The Scampi model is based on a simple static SPMD model, i.e. each processor runs the same program and communication is done using MPI routines. There is no dynamic process creation. This method leads of course to a programming style dominated by imperative parallel programming, although Sérot points out several benefits resulting from the use of a functional host language.

The advantages of functional programming can even be better exploited with higher-level communication primitives, such as those introduced in Clean for distributed programming (see Section 15.3) [526]. Clean provides message passing primitives for distributed applications, i.e. independent, but communicating programs running on different processors. Any data structure and any function can be exchanged in a type-safe manner. This is achieved using *dynamic typing*.

Communication channels are split into so-called send and receive channels, which are provided using abstract data structures:

```
:: SChannel a
:: RChannel a
```

and which can be used for sending and receiving messages, respectively. A communication channel may connect several send channels to several receive channels. A message sent on a send channel will be broadcast to all programs which have a corresponding receive channel. Nondeterminism occurs, if several senders use the same channel. The channels for inter-program communication are maintained in a table for each local network. To install a channel the following functions are provided:

```
:: ChName    :== String
:: Maybe a =  Just a | Nothing

createRChannel :: ChName *World -> (Maybe (RChannel a), *World)
findSChannel   :: ChName *World -> (SChannel a,         *World)
```

The function `createRChannel` creates a new entry in the table. If the name already exists, the function call returns `Nothing`, otherwise it returns an receive channel. The function `findSChannel` waits until the channel name is available in the table and then returns a send channel. The argument

3.5 Explicit Parallelism

of type *World ensures a controlled serial execution of these side-effecting operations. A program will have the type *World -> *World.

For message passing functions send and receive are available:

```
send    :: (SChannel a) a *World -> *World
receive :: (RChannel a)   *World -> (a, RChannel a, *World)
```

The function send is non-blocking. It sends the message argument to the receive channels corresponding to the send channel. The function receive is blocking. If messages are available, it retrieves the first message value and returns a new receive channel which can be used to receive the rest of the messages. Otherwise, it waits until a message value arrives.

The message passing facilities of Concurrent Clean allow the programmer to write distributed applications with a number of programs located on different processors which can exchange messages of arbitrary type using channels with several senders and several receivers. Communication actions must be explicitly specified, but the transfer of typed data is managed by the system. Even infinite structures can be sent, because message passing is based on a technique called lazy normal form copying. Further details can be found in [526] (see also Chapter 15).

3.5.3 Concurrent Functional Programming

In order to improve the expressiveness of functional languages with respect to interactive applications such as programs with graphical user interfaces, some functional languages have been extended by explicit concurrency constructs taken from process calculi such asCCS [400], TCSP [91] or the π-calculus [402] (e.g. constructs (e.g. [565], [492], [466], [15]). The main purpose of these languages is not to speed up computation through parallelism. Nevertheless there is a close relationship with parallel functional programming, because there is no reason why the concurrent processes within such approaches could not be evaluated in parallel.

Typical concurrent functional languages are Facile [565] and Concurrent ML [492], [445] (Chapter 17) which both extend ML and both employ synchronous communication, while Concurrent Haskell [466], a concurrent extension of Haskell, is based on an asynchronous model. Erlang [15] is a concurrent programming language designed for prototyping and implementing reliable real-time systems. It has been influenced by ML and the concurrent logic language Strand [202]. In contrast to the previously mentioned languages Erlang does not incorporate a higher-order, typed functional language, but is based on a first-order untyped functional kernel. It provides a special syntax for referring to time (time-outs), and explicit error detection capabilities. While there are experimental parallel versions of Erlang [263], these have not yet found widespread use.

Further approaches like K2 [22], PICT [470], or ProFun [211] use calculi like CCS or Petri nets as top level framework for a concurrent language and functional features just for describing computations within concurrent components. In PICT [470], a concurrent language based on the π-calculus, functional features like λ-abstraction and application are, for instance, encoded using processes and communication. A similar approach is considered in Chapter 16.

In the following we concentrate on concurrent functional languages which extend functional languages by primitives for:

- The creation of new threads (or processes) in the sense of evaluations which can be performed concurrently;
- The creation of communication media (channels);
- Communication operations like send and receive.

Generally speaking, the function and concurrency levels are clearly distinguished in these languages. Predefined operations are used to embed functional expressions into concurrent computations or vice versa.

Facile [565], for instance, is a symmetric integration of the functional language Standard ML and a model of concurrency based on the process calculus CCS [400] with its higher order and mobile extensions such as the π-calculus [402]. Facile's concurrency level comprises processes, channels and guards. The latter are used for selective communication. The behaviour of processes is defined by so-called *behaviour expressions*, which are different from expressions and do not denote values.

The simplest behaviour expression is `terminate`. It denotes a process which does nothing and terminates immediately. A process that evaluates an expression `exp` is defined by the behaviour expression `activate exp`. The expression `exp` must be of type `scr` and thus evaluate to a process script. The `activate` construct allows expressions (of type `scr`) to be embedded in behaviour expressions, while a construct `script` converts behaviour expressions into values of type `scr`. The concurrent execution of two processes with behaviours `b1` and `b2` is described by the behaviour expression `b1 || b2`.

Processes will be created from scripts using the primitive function:

```
val spawn : scr -> unit
```

Communication between processes is channel based. A channel enables a handshake communication which transmits a value from one sender to one receiver. A new channel is created using the primitive function:

```
val channel : unit -> 'a channel
```

Channels are typed, i.e. all values communicated over a channel must be of the same type. They can be used bidirectionally and even for multi-party communication. Two primitive functions:

```
val send    : 'a channel * 'a -> unit
val receive : 'a channel      -> 'a
```

3.5 Explicit Parallelism

are provided for sending and receiving values over channels. Processes that attempt a communication on a channel will be blocked until a communication partner becomes ready.

Example 3.5.4. A simplified explicitly parallel version of the `binom` example can be defined in FACILE as follows:

```
proc binomp (c_in1, c_in2, c_out) =
  let fun binom n k =
          if (k=0) and (n>=0) then 1 else
          if (n<k) and (n>=0) then 0 else
          if (n>=k) and (k>=0)
          then
             let val inp1 : int channel = channel();
                 val inp2 : int channel = channel();
                 val out  : int channel = channel()
             in spawn (send(out,binom(receive(inp1),
                                       receive(inp2)));
                        terminate);
                send(inp1,n-1);
                send(inp2,k-1);
                (binom (n-1) k + receive(out))
  in send(c_out,binom(receive(c_in1),receive(c_in2)))
  end;
activate binomp(c_in1,c_in2,c_out)
```

The notation `proc f pats = b` is equivalent to:

```
fun f pats = script(b)
```

Each communication must be defined explicitly using the `send` and `receive` primitives. Sequential composition is used extensively to specify the order in which the expressions have to be evaluated. Chapter 5 covers Facile in more detail, while Chapter 17 is dedicated to the similar language Concurrent ML.

Concurrent Haskell [466] uses I/O monads to describe concurrent behaviour. Communication is modelled by an abstraction of shared memory cells which serve as one-value channels. The following primitives are added to Haskell:

- `forkIO :: IO () -> IO ()` starts a new process which performs the I/O action given as an argument concurrently with the continued execution of the parent.
- The new primitive type `MVar a` is used to introduce mutable locations which may be empty or contain a value of type `a`. The following primitive operations are provided on `MVars`:
  - `newMVar :: IO (MVar a)` creates a new `MVar`.

- `takeMVar :: MVar a -> IO a` blocks until the location is non-empty, then reads the location and returns the value, leaving the location empty.
- `putMVar :: MVar a -> a -> IO ()` writes a value into the specified location which must be empty.

More abstract concurrency constructs can be defined on top of these primitives, for example channels with unbounded buffering (see [466]).

A substantial question in concurrent functional programming is how choice is supported or how selective communication can be organised. In many applications it is necessary to express that a concurrent activity, i.e. a thread or process, determines what to do next based on which of a number of communications are ready to proceed. The process must be ready to communicate with one of several possible processes or on one of several possible channels.

The Facile choice operator `alternative` bases its selection on readiness for synchronisation upon channel communication. As there are two basic forms of synchronisation, sending and receiving, there are two forms for constructing so-called *guards*:

```
val sendguard : 'a channel * 'a * (unit -> 'b) -> 'b guard
val recvguard : 'a channel     * ('a   -> 'b) -> 'b guard
```

The guard values produced by these functions indicate the need for synchronisation and the computation to be performed upon synchronisation. The function:

```
val alternative : 'a guard list -> 'a
```

takes a list of guard values and selects one non-deterministically. The call-by-value discipline of parameter passing is applied, i.e. the list elements are evaluated to guard values before `alternative` is called. A guard can only be selected when it can synchronise. The process calling `alternative` will be blocked, if no guard can synchronise immediately. Facile provides time-out mechanisms on communications which can be used to unblock processes.

Process creations or communications performed during the guard evaluations do not trigger the selection of the corresponding alternative and they will not be undone after another alternative has been chosen. This may lead to undesirable side effects and complicates the use of the choice construct.

The treatment of choice in CML is similar to the Facile approach. A new abstract type of values, called *events*, is used to represent potential communications (see also Chapter 17). Events only perform their communication when a thread uses them for synchronisation. Special combinators allow to construct more complex events from simpler ones.

In contrast to Facile and CML, Concurrent Haskell does not provide a primitive choice operator. Application-specific choice constructs must be defined by the programmer using the nondeterminism already provided by `MVars`. This avoids the costly implementation of a general choice construct and the problems arising with partially completed actions of compound guards expressions.

3.5.4 Discussion

The languages considered in this subsection work with an explicit view of communicating processes. The programmer gets the chance to control the process system completely. But he/she now has to define processes and their interaction explicitly. In contrast to the implicit and semi-explicit approaches discussed in the previous subsections, the notion of a parallel process is explicit in all these languages.

The various approaches differ in the level of abstraction and the techniques which are used for the specification of process systems. Naturally, the level of abstraction is lower than that of the implicit and semi-explicit approaches. This is due to the fact that the programmer must be precise about the process system he/she has in mind. At least, the process granularity and the interconnection scheme must be determined. In languages like Caliban and Eden functional constructs are used for that purpose. Thus, the topology of the process network and the necessary exchange of data are still specified in a declarative way. Concrete communication instructions (send/receive) will be automatically derived and inserted by the compiler.

In concurrent functional languages the programmer specifies his/her process system on an even lower level of abstraction. Constructs from imperative process calculi are adopted for the definition of processes and communication media. Low level communication commands must be used to specify the interaction of processes explicitly. This reduces the programming comfort and is more error-prone. The main concern of these languages is however not the high-level programming of parallel systems, but an efficient handling of reactive systems.

3.6 Conclusion

This chapter has considered the range of programming constructs that are provided by parallel functional languages. At the simplest level, programs may be implicitly parallel or simply require the programmer to exploit some predefined construct or skeleton (Chapter 13). Such approaches are attractive, but may necessitate some code manipulation in order to expose parallelism to the compiler. In our present state of understanding, such approaches also seem unlikely to yield optimal parallelism in the general case, though as described in Chapter 19, they can be highly effective in specialised application domains such as numerical computation. Such approaches are exemplified by the dataflow languages Id and SISAL and the functional languages KiR (Chapter 5) and SAC.

The desire for more flexible expression of parallel algorithms has led to approaches that we term "semi-explicit" or "controlled", in which the programmer can indicate some parallelism, but does not have complete control over the parallel evaluation, communication patterns etc. Such approaches are exemplified by para-functional or annotation-based approaches, such as Concurrent Clean (Chapter 15) or GpH. They have been applied to a wide range of applications, with a reasonable degree of success (Chapter 19). Para-functional programming and evaluation strategies separate the specification of the problem to be solved from the control of parallelism. Caliban (Chapter 14) takes a similar approach, but goes even further by explicitly specifying static process networks.

More extreme requirements for control lead to explicit approaches, where the programmer both has control and is required to exercise control over the parallel evaluation. Such approaches are especially suitable for reactive and distributed systems, where both processes and communication are semantically important. Examples of functional languages that incorporate explicitly parallel constructs are Concurrent ML (Chapter 17) and our own Eden language. An alternative approach is to add support for parallelism through explicit calls to parallel library or higher-level communication primitives. This is described for the Scampi system in Chapter 18 and for Concurrent Clean in Chapter 15.

4. Proof

Simon J. Thompson[1]

4.1 Introduction

In this chapter we examine ways in which functional programs can be proved correct. For a number of reasons this is easier for functional, than for imperative, programs. In the simplest cases functional programs are equations, so the language documents itself, as it were. Beyond this we often have a higher-level expression of properties, by means of equations between functions rather than values. We can also express properties which cannot simply be discussed for imperative programs, using notations for lists and other algebraic data types, for instance.

Apart from the general observation that proofs carry over directly to implicitly parallel functional systems, what is the particular relevance of proof to parallel functional programming? Two particular points are emphasised in this chapter:

- Lazy evaluation gives infinite and partial data structures, which can be viewed as describing the data flowing around deterministic networks of processes (see Section 3.5); Section 4.8.3 gives a proof that a process network produces the list of factorials; the bisimulation method used here forms a link with verification techniques for process algebras, which give a declarative treatment of parallelism and non-determinism, which are surveyed in Section 4.8.4;
- There is an important thread in the development of functional programming, going back at least to Backus' FP [28], which argues that it is best to eschew explicit recursion and to program using a fixed set of higher-order, polymorphic combinators, which are related to programming skeletons (see Section 3.5). The properties of these combinators can be seen as logical laws in an algebra of programming [53]. These laws can also be seen to have intensional content, with a transformation from left- to right-hand side representing a change in the cost of an operation, or in the parallelism implicit there (see Chapter 8 for more details of cost modelling). This topic is examined further in Section 4.9.3.

The equational model, explored in Section 4.2, gives the spirit of functional program verification, but it needs to be modified and strengthened in various ways in order to apply to a full functional language. The pattern of the chapter will be to give a succession of refinements of the logic as further features are added to the language. These we look at now.

---

[1] Computing Laboratory, University of Kent at Canterbury, UK.

The defining forms of languages are more complex than simple equations. Section 4.3 looks at conditional definitions (using "guards"), pattern matching and local definitions (in let and where clauses) each of which adds complications, not least when the features interact.

Reasoning cannot be completely equational. We need to be able to reason by cases, and, in general, to be able to prove properties of functions defined by recursion. Structural induction is the mechanism: it is discussed in Section 4.4, and illustrated by a correctness proof for a miniature compiler in Section 4.5.

With general recursion, examined in Section 4.6 and which is a feature of all languages in the current mainstream, comes the possibility of non-termination of evaluation. In a non-strict language general recursion has the more profound effect of introducing infinite and partial lists and other data structures.

In both strict and non-strict languages this possibility means, in turn, that in interpreting the meaning of programs we are forced to introduce extra values at each type. This plainly affects the way in which the logic is expressed, and its relation to familiar properties of, say, the integers. The background to this is explored in Section 4.7.

Section 4.8 gives an overview of the two principal approaches to giving meanings to programs – denotational semantics and operational semantics – and their implications for program verification. A proof of correctness for a function defined by general recursion exemplifies the denotational approach, whilst operational semantics underpins a proof that a lazy process network generates the list of factorials. This last proof forms a link with the process algebra approach to parallelism, which is also discussed in this section.

Because of the complications which non-termination brings, there has been recent interest in terminating languages and these are introduced in Section 4.9. Of particular relevance here is the transformational approach of Backus, Bird and others.

A fully-fledged language will allow users to interact with the environment in various ways, but, at its simplest, by reading input and writing output. This is supported in a variety of ways, including the side-effecting functions of Standard ML (SML) and the monads of Haskell 98. SML also allows mutable references and exceptions. In this chapter we cover only the pure parts of languages, but refer readers to [226] for a perspicacious discussion of program verification for various forms of input/output, including monadic I/O. Recent work on modelling SML-style references can be found in [475].

This chapter does not try to address all the work on verification of parallel imperative programs: Sections 8.9 and 8.10 of the exhaustive survey [144] more than do justice to this topic, and put it in the context of imperative program verification in general. On the other hand, links with process algebra are examined in Section 4.8.4.

4.2 The Basis of Functional Programming: Equations

In this section we examine the basis of functional programming and show how the definitions of a simple functional program can be interpreted as logical equations. An examination of how this approach can be modified and extended to work in general forms the main part of the chapter.

A functional program consists of a collection of definitions of functions and other values. An example program using the notation of the Haskell language [457] is:

```
test :: Integer
test = 42

id :: a -> a
id x = x

plusOne :: Integer -> Integer
plusOne n = (n+1)

minusOne :: Integer -> Integer
minusOne n = (n-1)
```

Execution of a program consists of evaluating an expression which uses the functions and other objects defined in the program (together with the built-in operations of the language). Evaluation works by the replacement of subexpressions by their values, and is complete when a value is produced. For instance, evaluation of:

```
plusOne (minusOne test)
```

will proceed thus:

```
plusOne (minusOne test)
  => (minusOne test) + 1
  => (test - 1) + 1
  => (42 - 1) + 1
  => 41 + 1
  => 42
```

where it can be seen that at each stage of the evaluation one of the defining equations is used to rewrite a subexpression which matches the left-hand side of a definition, like:

```
minusOne test
```

to the corresponding right-hand side:

```
test - 1
```

The model of evaluation for a real language such as Haskell or ML is somewhat more complex; this will be reflected by the discussion in subsequent sections.

In each step of an evaluation such as this equals are replaced by equals, and this points to the basis of a logical approach to reading functional programs. The use of the equals sign in function definitions is indeed suggestive, and we can read the definitions as *logical statements* of the properties of the defined functions, thus:

$$\text{id x} \equiv \text{x} \tag{id.1}$$

for all x of type t, and so on. Note that we have used the symbol "$\equiv$" here for logical equality to distinguish it from both the "definitional" equality used to define objects in the language, =, and the "calculational" Boolean equality operation of the language, ==.

Logical equations like these can be manipulated using the rules of logic in the standard way, so that we can deduce, for instance, that:

```
id (id y)
  ≡ {by substituting id y for x in (id.1)}
id y
  ≡ {by substituting y for x in (id.1)}
y
```

In linear proofs we shall use the format above, in which the justification for each equality step of the proof is included in braces $\{\cdots\}$.

So, we see a model for verification of functional programs which uses the defining equations as logical equations, and the logical laws for equality: reflexivity, symmetry, transitivity and substitution:

$$\frac{\text{P(a)} \quad \text{a} \equiv \text{b}}{\text{P(b)}} (Subst)$$

to make deductions. Note that in giving the substitution rule we have used the convention that P(a) means an expression P in which a occurs; the appearance of P(b) below the line means that the occurrences of a in P have been replaced by b. An alternative notation which we use later in the chapter is P[b/a] which is used to denote "b substituted for a in P".

The logical versions of the definitions given here contain free variables, namely the variables of the definitions. In the remainder of the chapter we will also use a closed form given by taking the universal quantification over these variables. (id.1) will then take the form $(\forall \text{x::a})(\text{id x} \equiv \text{x})$ for example.

4.3 Pattern Matching, Cases and Local Definitions

The purely equational definition style of Section 4.2 can be made to accommodate case switches, local definitions and pattern matching by means of the

4.3 Pattern Matching, Cases and Local Definitions

appropriate higher-order combinators. Indeed, this is one way of interpreting the work of Bird and others, discussed further in Section 4.9.3. However, for reasons of readability and conciseness, most languages offer syntactic support for these facilities, and with this additional syntax comes the task of giving it a logical explanation.

This section gives an overview of how pattern matching, cases and local definitions are rendered logically; a more detailed examination can be found in [563], which addresses the same question for Miranda. Note that here we are still considering a small (terminating) language, rather than a full language.

4.3.1 Pattern Matching

Pattern matching serves to distinguish cases, as in:

```
isEmptyList :: [a] -> [a]
isEmptyList [] = True
isEmptyList _  = False
```

(where "_" is a wildcard pattern, matching anything), and also to allow access to the components of a compound object:

```
tail :: [a] -> [a]
tail []     = []
tail (x:xs) = xs
```

In the example of `tail`, where the patterns do not overlap (are exclusive) and cover all eventualities (are exhaustive), the definitions can be read as logical equations.

In the general case, we need to take account of the *sequential* interpretation which is usually applied to them. Looking at `isEmptyList`, the second equation in which the "_" will match any value will only be applied should the first clause not apply. We therefore need to give a description of the complement of a pattern, here [], over which the remaining equations hold. The complement of [] will be the non-empty list, (x:xs), and so we can rewrite the definition of the function to give its logical form thus:

```
isEmptyList []     ≡ True
isEmptyList (x:xs) ≡ False
```

As another example, consider the pattern (x:y:ys). This will match lists with two or more elements, and its complement is given by the two patterns [] and [_]. The full details of the way in which pattern matching definitions can be translated are to be found in [563].

4.3.2 Cases

Definitions can have alternatives depending on the (Boolean) values of guards, in a Haskell style:

```
f args
  | g1          = e1
  | g2          = e2
    ...
  | otherwise = e
```

If the (actual values of the) parameters args satisfy g_1 then the result of f args is e_1; should g_1 be False then if g_2 is True, e_2 is the result, and so on. In logical form we then have:

$$(g_1 \equiv \text{True} \Rightarrow \text{f args} \equiv e_1) \land$$
$$((g_1 \equiv \text{False} \land g_2 \equiv \text{True}) \Rightarrow \text{f args} \equiv e_2) \land \ldots$$

which renders the definition as the conjunction of a set of conditional equations.

4.3.3 Local Definitions

A local definition, introduced either by a let or a where introduces a name whose scope is restricted. An example is given by the schematic:

```
f :: a1 -> a2
f x = e
        where
          g :: a3 -> a4
          g y = e'
```

The function g is in scope in the expression e as well as the where clause. It is also important to realise that its definition will, in general, depend upon the parameter x. It is translated thus:

$$(\forall \text{x}::a_1)(\exists \text{g}::a_3 \text{ -> } a_4)((\forall \text{y}::a_3)(\text{g y} \equiv e') \land \text{f x} \equiv e)$$

in which the locally defined value(s) are existentially quantified, and the universal quantification over the argument values for f and g are shown explicitly.

4.3.4 Further Issues

The features discussed in this section can, when they appear in real programming languages such as Haskell, have complex interactions. For instance, it is not necessary to have an otherwise case in a guarded equation, so that it is possible for none of the guards to hold for a particular set of arguments. In this situation, the next guarded equation (and therefore pattern match) has to be examined, and this is particularly difficult to explain when the guards also refer to local definitions – an example is presented in [563].

The translation given here goes beyond the equational, giving axioms which involve arbitrarily deep alternations of quantifiers. In practice, these quantifiers will be stripped off, allowing conditional equational reasoning to take place; the effect of the quantifications is to ensure that the scoping rules of the language are obeyed, while the conditions reflect the guards in the definitions of the language. Pattern matching is supported by the substitution mechanism of the logic.

4.4 Structural Induction and Recursion

In this section we consider how to strengthen our language to accommodate recursively defined functions and types while retaining the property that all computations will terminate.

At the heart of modern functional programming languages are built-in types of lists and a facility to define "algebraic" data types built by the application of constructors. If we wish to build a simple-minded representation of integer arithmetic expressions — as part of a calculator or a compiler, say — we might write, using Haskell notation:

```
data IntExp = Literal Int |
              Binary Op IntExp IntExp

data Op = Add | Sub | Mul
```

which describes a type whose members take two forms, built by the two constructors of the type, Literal and Binary:

- The first is Literal n, where n is an Int (integer);
- The second form is Binary op ex1 ex2 where ex1 and ex2 are themselves IntExps and op is one of Add, Sub or Mul (representing three binary arithmetic operators);

An example of the type, representing the arithmetic expression (4+3)-5, is:

```
Binary Sub (Binary Add (Literal 4) (Literal 3)) (Literal 5)
```

To define a function over Op it is sufficient to give its value at the three possible inputs, so that:

```
opValue :: Op -> (Int -> Int -> Int)

opValue Add = (+)
opValue Sub = (-)
opValue Mul = (*)
```

serves to interpret the arithmetic operators. In a similar way, if we wish to prove that some logical property holds for all operators it is sufficient to prove that the property holds for the three values of the type.

Now, the type IntExp is rather more complicated, since it is recursively defined, and has an infinite number of members. However, we know that the only ways that elements are constructed are by means of a finite number of applications of the constructors of the type. This means that an arbitrary element of the type will take one of the forms:

```
Literal n
Binary op ex1 ex2
```

where `ex1` and `ex2` are themselves elements of `IntExp`.

Because every element is built up in this way, we can deduce how to define functions over `IntExp` and how to prove that properties hold for all elements of `IntExp`. To define a function we use *structural recursion*, as exemplified by a function to evaluate an arithmetic expression:

```
eval :: IntExp -> Int

eval (Literal int) = int                              (eval.1)
eval (Binary op ex1 ex2)
  = opValue op (eval ex1) (eval ex2)                  (eval.2)
```

Here we see the pattern of definition in which we:

- Give the result at `Literal int` outright; and
- Give the result at `Binary op ex1 ex2` using the results already defined for `ex1` and `ex2` (as well as other components of the data value, here `op`).

It can be seen that a finite number of recursive calls will result in calls to the `Literal` case, so that functions defined in this way will be total.

In an analogous way, we can use structural induction to prove a property for all `IntExps`. This principle is stated now.

Structural Induction. To prove P(e) for all e in `IntExp` we need to show that:

- **Base case.** The property P(Literal int) holds for all int;
- **Induction case.** The property P(Binary op ex1 ex2) holds *on the assumption that* P(ex1) and P(ex2) hold.

Given any `IntExp` t we can see that a finite number of applications of the induction case will lead us back to the base case, and thus establish that P(t) holds.

In the next section we give examples of various functions defined by structural recursion together with verification using structural induction over the `IntExp` type.

4.5 Case Study: A Compiler Correctness Proof

In this section we give a proof of correctness of a tiny compiler for arithmetic expressions using structural induction over the type of expressions, given by

4.5 Case Study: A Compiler Correctness Proof

```
data IntExp = Literal Int |
              Binary Op IntExp IntExp

data Op = Add | Sub | Mul

opValue :: Op -> (Int -> Int -> Int)

eval :: IntExp -> Int

eval (Literal int) = int                               (eval.1)
eval (Binary op ex1 ex2)
  = opValue op (eval ex1) (eval ex2)                   (eval.2)
```

```
data Code = PushLit Int |
            DoBinary Op

type Program = [Code]

compile :: IntExp -> Program

compile (Literal int)
  = [PushLit int]                                      (compile.1)
compile (Binary op ex1 ex2)
  = compile ex1 ++ compile ex2 ++ [DoBinary op]        (compile.2)

type Stack = [Int]

run :: Program -> Stack -> Stack

run [] stack
  = stack                                              (run.1)
run (PushLit int : program) stack
  = run program (int : stack)                          (run.2)
run (DoBinary op : program) (v2:v1:stack)
  = run program (opValue op v1 v2 : stack)             (run.3)

run _ _ = []                                           (run.4)
```

Figure 4.1. A simple interpreter and compiler for expressions

Base case ───

```
run (compile (Literal int) ++ program) stack
    ≡ { by (compile.1) }
run ([PushLit int] ++ program) stack
    ≡ { by definition of ++ }
run (PushLit int : program) stack
    ≡ { by (run.2) }
run program (int : stack)

run program (eval (Literal int) : stack)
    ≡ { by (eval.1) }
run program (int : stack)
```

Induction case ───────────────────────────────────────

```
run (compile (Binary op ex1 ex2) ++ program) stack
    ≡ { by (compile.2) and associativity of ++ }
run (compile ex1 ++ compile ex2 ++ [DoBinary op] ++ program) stack
    ≡ { by the induction hypothesis for ex1 and associativity of ++ }
run (compile ex2 ++ [DoBinary op] ++ program) (eval ex1 : stack)
    ≡ { by the induction hypothesis for ex2 and associativity of ++ }
run ([DoBinary op] ++ program) (eval ex2 : eval ex1 : stack)
    ≡ { by (run.3) and definition of ++ }
run program (opValue op (eval ex1) (eval ex2) : stack)

run program (eval (Binary op ex1 ex2) : stack)
    ≡ { by (eval.2) }
run program (opValue op (eval ex1) (eval ex2) : stack)
```

Correctness theorem ──────────────────────────────────

```
run (compile e) []
    ≡ { substitute [] for both program and stack in (goal) }
run [] [eval e]
    ≡ { by (run.1) }
[eval e]
```

──

Figure 4.2. Proof of compiler correctness

4.5 Case Study: A Compiler Correctness Proof

the algebraic data type IntExp. In developing the proof we explore some of the pragmatics of finding proofs.

It is instructive to compare this program and proof developed in a functional context with a similar problem programmed in a modern imperative language such as C++, Java or Modula 3. The advantage of the approach here is that modern functional languages contain explicit representations of recursive data types, and so a proof of a program property can refer explicitly to the forms of data values. In contrast, a stack in an imperative language will either be represented by a dynamic data structure, built using pointers, or by an array, with the attendant problems of working with a concrete representation of a stack rather than an appropriately abstract view. In either case it is not so easy to see how a proof could be written, indeed the most appropriate model might be to develop the imperative program by refinement from the verified functional program presented here.

4.5.1 The Compiler and Stack Machine

The program is given in Figure 4.1, in two halves. In the first half, we reiterate the definitions of the IntExp type and its evaluation function eval, which is defined by structural recursion over IntExp.

In the second half of the figure we give a model of a stack machine which is used to evaluate the expressions. The machine operates over a stack of integers, hence the definition:

```
type Stack = [Int]
```

The instructions for the machine are given by the type Code, which has two operations, namely to push an element (PushLit) onto the stack and to perform an evaluation of an operation (DoBinary) using the top elements of the stack as arguments.

An expression is converted into a Program, that is, a list of Code, by compile. The compile function compiles a literal in the obvious way, and for an operator expression, the compiled code consists of the compiled code for the two expressions, concatenated by the list operator ++, with the appropriate binary operator invocation appended.

The operation of the machine itself is described by:

```
run :: Program -> Stack -> Stack
```

and from that definition it can be seen that if the stack fails to have at least two elements on operator evaluation, execution will be halted and the stack cleared.

4.5.2 Formulating the Goal

The intended effect of the compiler is to produce code (for e) which when run puts the value of e on the stack. In formal terms:

            run (compile e) [] ≡ [eval e]   (compGoal.1)

Now, we could look for a proof of this by structural induction over e, but
this would fail. We can explain this failure from two different points of view.

Looking first at the problem itself, we can see that in fact the compiler
and machine have a rather more general property: no matter what the initial
configuration of the stack, the result of the run should be to place the value
of the expression on the top of the stack:

            run (compile e) stack ≡ (eval e : stack)

This is still not general enough, since it talks about complete computations
– what if the code is followed by more program? The effect should be to
evaluate e and place its result on the stack prior to executing the remaining
program. We thus reach the final formulation of the goal:

            run (compile e ++ program) stack
                ≡ run program (eval e : stack)   (compGoal.2)

An alternative view of the difficulty comes from looking at the failed proof
attempt: the induction hypothesis turns out to be insufficiently powerful to
give what is required. This happens in the case of a binary operation, when
we try to prove (compGoal.1) where e is, for example, Binary Add ex1 ex2.
In this case we need to prove that:

            run (compile ex1++compile ex2++[DoBinary Add]) ≡ [eval e]

so that we will need a hypothesis about compile ex1 *in context*:

            run (compile ex1 ++ ...)

rather than in isolation.

This leads us to formulate the generalisation (compGoal.2) — this is
examined in the next section and again it is shown there how a failed proof
attempt leads to a suitable formalisation of the induction hypothesis.

A guide to the form of hypothesis is often given by the form taken by the
definitions of the functions under scrutiny; we will discuss this point after
giving the full proof in the next section.

4.5.3 The Proof

Our goal is to prove (compGoal.2) for all values of e, program and stack.
As a first attempt we might try to prove (compGoal.2) by induction over
e, for arbitrary program and stack, but again this will fail. This happens
because the induction hypothesis will be used at different values of stack
and program, so that the goal for the inductive proof is to show by structural
induction on e that:

            (∀program,stack)(run (compile e ++ program) stack
                ≡ run program (eval e : stack))   (goal)

holds for all e.

The proof is given in Figure 4.2 and follows the principle of structural induction for IntExp presented in Section 4.4 above. In the first part we prove the base case:

$$\begin{aligned}&\texttt{run (compile (Literal int) ++ program) stack}\\&\equiv \texttt{run program (eval (Literal int) : stack)} \quad \text{(base)}\end{aligned}$$

for arbitrary program, stack, thus giving the base case of (goal). The proof proceeds by separately rewriting the left- and right-hand sides of (base) to the same value.

In the second part we show:

$$\begin{aligned}&\texttt{run (compile (Binary op ex1 ex2) ++ program) stack}\\&\equiv \texttt{run program (eval (Binary op ex1 ex2) : stack)} \quad \text{(ind)}\end{aligned}$$

for arbitrary program, stack using the induction hypotheses for: ex1:

$$\begin{aligned}&(\forall \texttt{program,stack})\texttt{(run (compile ex1 ++ program) stack}\\&\equiv \texttt{run program (eval ex1 : stack))} \quad \text{(hyp)}\end{aligned}$$

and ex2. It is instructive to observe that in the proof the induction hypothesis for ex1, (hyp), is used with the expression:

```
compile ex2 ++ [DoBinary op] ++ program
```

substituted for program, and that for ex2 it is used in a similar way. Again the proof proceeds by separately rewriting the left- and right-hand sides of (ind).

The third part of Figure 4.2 shows how our original goal, (compGoal.1), is a consequence of the more general result (compGoal.2).

How might we be led to the goal (goal) by the form of the program itself? If we examine the definition of run we can see that in the recursive calls (run.2) and (run.3) the stack parameter is modified. This indicates that the stack cannot be expected to be a parameter of the proof, so that the general formulation of the induction hypothesis will have to include all possible values of the stack parameter.

4.6 General Recursion

In the preceding sections we saw how structural recursion and induction can be used to define and verify programs over algebraic data types. Functions defined in this way are manifestly total, but there remains the question of whether these limited forms of recursion and induction are adequate in practice. An example going beyond structural recursion over IntExp is a function to rearrange arithmetic expressions so that the additions which they contain are associated to the left, transforming:

(4+2)+(3+(7+9))   to   (((4+2)+3)+7)+9

The function is defined thus:

```
lAssoc :: IntExp -> IntExp

lAssoc (Literal n) = Literal n
lAssoc (Binary Sub ex1 ex2)
    = Binary Sub (lAssoc ex1) (lAssoc ex2)
lAssoc (Binary Add ex1 (Binary Add ex3 ex4))
    = lAssoc (Binary Add (Binary Add ex1 ex3) ex4)   (lAssoc.1)
lAssoc (Binary Add ex1 ex2)
    = Binary Add (lAssoc ex1) (lAssoc ex2)
```

(where the Mul case has been omitted). Each clause is structurally recursive, except for (lAssoc.1), in which the top-level expression ex1+(ex3+ex4) is transformed to (ex1+ex3)+ex4. Once this transformation has been effected, it is necessary to reexamine the whole rearranged expression, and not just the components of the original. The reader might like to experiment with the example expression in order to convince themself of the necessity of making a definition of this form, rather than a structural recursion.

Now, what is the lesson of examples like this for the design of functional programming languages and for the verification of systems written in them? There are broadly two schools of thought.

The predominant view is to accept that a language should allow arbitrary recursion in the definitions of functions (and perhaps other objects). Mainstream languages such as Haskell, Miranda and Standard ML are all of this kind. With arbitrary recursion come a number of consequences:

- The semantics of the language becomes more complex, since it must now contain an account of the possible non-termination of programs;
- Moreover, the evaluation mechanism becomes significant. If all programs terminate, then the order in which programs are evaluated is not an issue; if non-termination is possible then strict and lazy evaluation strategies differ, and thus give strict and non-strict languages different semantics;
- As far as the topic of this chapter is concerned, the complexity of the semantics is reflected in the logic needed to reason about the language, for both strict and non-strict languages.

For these reasons there has been recent interest in terminating languages — Turner's notion of "strong" functional languages [577] — because such languages have both a simpler proof theory and full freedom of choice for evaluation strategy, which is, of course, of relevance to the field of parallel functional programming.

In the remainder of this chapter we will explore the effect of these two alternatives for functional program verification, first looking at the mainstream, partial languages.

4.7 Partial Languages

This section gives an informal overview of the effect of admitting general recursion into a programming language, and emphasises the consequent split between strict and non-strict languages. This serves as an introduction to the overview of the semantic basis of languages with partiality in the section to come.

4.7.1 Strict Languages

In a strict language such as (the pure subset of) Standard ML arbitrary forms of recursive definitions are allowed for functions. A definition of the form:

```
undefFun :: a -> a
undefFun x = undefFun x                           (undefFun.1)
```

(using Haskell-style syntax) has the effect of forcing an undefined element at every type. What effect does this have on evaluation and on the logic? Take the example function:

```
const :: a -> b -> a
const x y = x
```

and consider its logical translation. Our earlier work suggests that we translate it by:

```
const x y ≡ x                                     (const.1)
```

but we need to be careful what is substituted for the variables x and y. If we take x to be 3 and y to be undefFun 4 then it appears that:

```
const 3 (undefFun 4) ≡ 3
```

This is contrary to the rule for evaluation which states that arguments need to be evaluated prior to being passed to functions, which means that (undefFun.1) should be undefined when applied to undefFun 4. The translation (const.1) can therefore only apply to *values* (of type Int) rather than arbitrary *expressions* of that type as was the case earlier. This can be made clear by reexpressing (const.1) thus:

$$(\forall_v x, y)(\text{const } x\ y \equiv x)$$

where the subscript in the quantifier "$\forall_v$" serves as a reminder that the quantifier ranges over all (defined) values rather than all expressions, including those which denote an undefined computation.

4.7.2 Non-Strict languages

In a non-strict language like Haskell, the definition of undefFun (undefFun.1) also gives rise to an undefined element at each type. This does not, however, affect the translation of const given in (const.1) above, since in a non-strict language expressions are passed *unevaluated* to functions. In other words, the evaluation mechanism can truly be seen to be one of substitution of expressions for expressions. (For efficiency, this "call-by-name" strategy will be implemented by a "call-by-need" discipline under which the results of computations are shared.)

Nevertheless, the presence of an undefined expression in each type has its effect. We accept as a law the assertion that for all integers x:

```
x+1 > x
```

but this will not be the case if x is an undefined computation. We will therefore have to make the distinction between defined values and all expressions as in Section 4.7.1.

The result of combining lazy evaluation and general recursion are more profound than for a strict language, since data structures can become partial or infinite. The effect of:

```
nums = from 1
from n = n : from (n+1)
```

is to define the infinite list of positive integers, [1,2,3,...]. If nums is passed to a function, then it is substituted unevaluated, and parts of it are evaluated when, and if, they are required:

```
sft :: [Int] -> Int
sft (x:y:_) = x+y                                        (sft.1)

sft nums
  => sft (from 1)
  => sft (1 : from 2)
  => sft (1 : 2 : from 3)
```

At this point the pattern match in (sft.1) can be performed, giving the result 3. Our interpretation, therefore, needs to include such infinite lists, as well as "partial" lists such as (2:undefFun 2). Note that under a strict interpretation all infinite and partial lists are identified with the undefined list, since they all lead to non-terminating computations.

In order to give a proper account of the behaviour of languages with non-termination we now look at the ways in which a formal or mathematical semantics can be given to a programming language.

4.8 Semantic Approaches

This section surveys the two semantic approaches to functional programming languages with the aim of motivating the logical rules to which the semantics lead.

4.8 Semantic Approaches

4.8.1 Denotational Semantics

Under a denotational semantics, as introduced in the textbook [599], the objects of a programming language — both terminating and non-terminating — are modelled by the elements of a *domain*. A domain is a partially ordered structure, where the partial order reflects the degree of definedness of the elements, with the totally undefined object, $\bot$, below everything: $\bot \sqsubseteq x$. Recursion, as in the definition:

    f = C[f]

can then be explained by first looking at the sequence of approximations, f_n, with:

    f₀ ≡ ⊥

and:

    f_{n+1} = C[f_n]

A domain also carries a notion of limit for sequences (or indeed more general "directed sets"), so that the meaning of f, $[\![f]\!]$, is taken to be the limit of this sequence of approximations:

    f ≡ ⊔_n f_n

Another way of seeing this is that $[\![f]\!]$ is the *least fixed point* of the operation:

    λf.C[f]

with a domain having sufficient structure to provide fixed points of (monotone) operators over them.

All the data types of a functional language can be modelled in such a way, and reasoning over domains is characterised by fixed-point induction, which captures the fact that a recursively defined function is the limit of a sequence. Before stating the principle, an auxiliary definition is needed.

A predicate P is called *inclusive* if it is closed under taking limits, broadly speaking. Winskel, [599], provides a more detailed characterisation of this, together with sufficient conditions for a formula to be an inclusive predicate.
Fixed-point Induction. If P is an inclusive predicate and if f is defined as above, then if:

- $P(\bot)$ holds; and (FPI.1)
- $P(f_n)$ implies $P(f_{n+1})$; (FPI.2)

then P holds of the limit of the sequence, that is P(f).

As an example we look again at the lAssoc function, defined in Section 4.6 above. We would like to show that rearranging an expression will not change its value, that is:

    (∀e)(eval (lAssoc e) ≡ eval e)   P₀(lAssoc) (where eval is defined in Section 4.4). Equations are inclusive, but, unfortunately, we cannot prove the inductive goals in this case. Take the case of (FPI.1); this states that the property should hold when the function lAssoc is replaced by the totally undefined function, $\bot$, so that we should prove:

$(\forall e)(\text{eval } (\bot \text{ e}) \equiv \text{eval e})$

which, since the $\bot$ function is undefined on every argument, is equivalent to:

$(\forall e)(\text{eval } \bot \equiv \text{eval e})$

which is plainly not the case.

We can modify the property to say that *if the result is defined* then the equality holds, namely:

$(\forall e)((\text{lAssoc e} \equiv \bot) \lor \text{eval (lAssoc e)} \equiv \text{eval e})$ P(lAssoc)

It is interesting to see that this is a *partial correctness* property, predicated on the termination of the lAssoc function, for which we have to prove a separate termination result. We discuss termination presently.

To establish this result we have to prove (FPI.1) and (FPI.2) for this property. A proof of (FPI.1) is straightforward, since P($\bot$) states:

$(\forall e)((\bot \text{ e} \equiv \bot) \lor \text{eval } (\bot \text{ e}) \equiv \text{eval e})$

and $\bot \text{ e} \equiv \bot$ holds, as discussed earlier. A proof of (FPI.2) requires that we show that P(lAssoc$_n$) implies P(lAssoc$_{n+1}$) where (omitting the Mul case):

```
lAssoc_{n+1} (Literal n) = Literal n                              (1A.1)
lAssoc_{n+1} (Binary Sub ex1 ex2)
    = Binary Sub (lAssoc_n ex1) (lAssoc_n ex2)                    (1A.2)
lAssoc_{n+1} (Binary Add ex1 (Binary Add ex3 ex4))
    = lAssoc_n (Binary Add (Binary Add ex1 ex3) ex4)              (1A.3)
lAssoc_{n+1} (Binary Add ex1 ex2)
    = Binary Add (lAssoc_n ex1) (lAssoc_n ex2)                    (1A.4)
```

Now, our goal is to prove that:

$(\forall e)((\text{lAssoc}_{n+1} \text{ e} \equiv \bot) \lor \text{eval (lAssoc}_{n+1} \text{ e}) \equiv \text{eval e})$

on the assumption that:

$(\forall e)((\text{lAssoc}_n \text{ e} \equiv \bot) \lor \text{eval (lAssoc}_n \text{ e}) \equiv \text{eval e})$

We look at the cases of the definition in turn. For a literal we have by (1A.1):

lAssoc$_{n+1}$ (Literal n) $\equiv$ Literal n

from which we conclude immediately that:

eval (lAssoc$_{n+1}$ (Literal n)) $\equiv$ eval (Literal n)

Now, looking at subtraction, and assuming that the function terminates, we have:

4.8 Semantic Approaches

```
eval (1Assoc_{n+1} (Binary Sub ex1 ex2))
   ≡ { by (1A.2) }
eval (Binary Sub (1Assoc_n ex1) (1Assoc_n ex2))
   ≡ { by definition of  eval }
eval (1Assoc_n ex1) - eval (1Assoc_n ex2)
   ≡ { by termination and the induction hypothesis}
eval ex1 - eval ex2
   ≡ { by definition of  eval }
eval (Binary Sub ex1 ex2)
```

The tricky case is (1A.3), which is the non-structurally recursive clause. Now, again assuming termination, we have:

```
eval (1Assoc_{n+1} (Binary Add ex1 (Binary Add ex3 ex4)))
   ≡ { by (1A.3) }
eval (1Assoc_n (Binary Add (Binary Add ex1 ex3) ex4))
   ≡ { by termination and the induction hypothesis}
eval ((Binary Add (Binary Add ex1 ex3) ex4))
   ≡ { by the associativity of  + }
eval (Binary Add ex1 (Binary Add ex3 ex4))
```

The final case – which corresponds to (1A.4) – follows exactly the proof for the (1A.2) case, with Add replacing Sub. This establishes the induction step, and so the result itself.

How do we prove that 1Assoc terminates on all arguments? We need to have some "measure of progress" in the recursive calls. In all calls but (1Assoc.1) the recursive calls are on structurally smaller expressions, but in (1Assoc.1) the call is to an expression containing the same number of operators. What is changed in the recursive call is the arrangement of the expression, and it is easy to see that on the right hand side of the Add in the recursive call there are fewer applications of Add than in the same position on the left hand side:

This reduction means that there can only be a finite number of repeated calls to (1Assoc.1) before one of the structural cases is used. Informally, what we have done is to give an ordering over the expressions which is *well-founded*, that is, has no infinite descending chains (like the chain $-1 > -2 > \ldots > -n > \ldots$ over the integers). A recursion will terminate precisely when it can be shown to follow a well-founded ordering.

Further details about denotational semantics can be found in [599], [451]. We also refer back to denotational semantics at the end of Sect. 4.8.3

4.8.2 Operational Semantics

The structured ("SOS") style of operational semantics pioneered by Plotkin describes a programming language by means of deduction rules which explain how expressions are evaluated. This style has been used to describe real languages, notably Standard ML [403], and it arguably gives a more readable and concise description of a language than a denotational semantics. The account given in this section relies on Gordon's thesis, [226], which serves as an introduction to the way that these ideas are applied to the description of functional programming languages.

SOS descriptions give reduction rules (describing "one step" of the computation), as in:

$$((\lambda x.M)N) \longrightarrow M[N/x]$$

or can provide a description of the evaluation of an expression to a value (the "big step" rules), thus:

$$\frac{L \Longrightarrow (\lambda x.M) \quad M[N/x] \Longrightarrow V}{(L\ N) \Longrightarrow V}$$

These rules are related, with $\Longrightarrow$ representing arbitrarily many steps under the relation $\longrightarrow$. From these rules an equality relation can be generated: two expressions are equal, $L \simeq M$, if whatever context $C[\_]$ they are placed in, $C[L] \Longrightarrow V$ if, and only, if $C[M] \Longrightarrow V$. Now, the issue becomes one of finding ways of deducing, for given expressions L and M, that $L \simeq M$ holds. Abramsky [5] had the insight that this relation resembled the bisimulations of process calculi. This characterises the equivalence as a *greatest* fixed point.

Rather than look at the general theory of bisimulations, we will here look at how it applies to infinite lists. We take an infinite example because in the finite case the flavour of proof is similar to the denotational style, so that the proof of correctness for 1Assoc would follow similar lines to that in Section 4.8.1; it is in the infinite case that a distinctive style emerges.

The equality relation over infinite lists, "$\simeq$", is the greatest fixed point of the definition

$$\text{xs} \simeq \text{ys} \iff_{df} \text{ there exist z, w, zs, ws so that xs} \longrightarrow (\text{z:zs}),$$
$$\text{ys} \longrightarrow (\text{w:ws}), \text{z} \equiv \text{w and zs} \simeq \text{ws}.$$

where the symbol $\iff_{df}$ is used to mean "is defined to be".

Now, the greatest fixed point of a relation can be characterised as the union of all the post-fixed points of the relation, which in this case are called *bisimulations*. The relation $\mathcal{S}$ is a bisimulation if

$$\text{xs } \mathcal{S} \text{ ys} \implies \text{ there exist z, w, zs, ws so that xs} \longrightarrow (\text{z:zs}),$$
$$\text{ys} \longrightarrow (\text{w:ws}), \text{z} \equiv \text{w and zs} \equiv_\mathcal{S} \text{ws}.$$

where $\equiv_\mathcal{S}$ is the smallest congruence generated by the relation $\mathcal{S}$. It is now the case that

4.8 Semantic Approaches   113

Coinduction for Infinite Lists.
  xs ≃ ys   ⟺   there exists a bisimulation $\mathcal{S}$ such that xs $\mathcal{S}$ ys.
In the next section we give an example of a proof using this coinduction principle for infinite lists.

4.8.3 An Example of Coinduction

In this section we give proof of the equality of two lists of the factorials of the natural numbers. The first is a mapping of the factorial function along the list of natural numbers:

```
facMap :: [Integer]
facMap = map fac [0..]

fac :: Integer -> Integer
fac 0 = 1                                                         (fac.1)
fac (n+1) = (n+1) * fac n                                         (fac.2)
```

The second, facs 0, gives a recursive definition of the list in question. The definition uses the function zipWith which runs in lock step along two lists, applying a function to the elements chosen.:

```
zipWith f (x:xs) (y:ys) = f x y : zipWith f xs ys
zipWith f _      _      = []
```

so that, for example:

```
zipWith (*) [1,1,2] [1,2,3] = [1,2,6]
```

In fact, a more general function is defined, which gives a recursive definition of the list of factorials from n!:

```
facs :: Integer -> [Integer]
facs n = fac n : zipWith (*) [(n+1)..] (facs n)                   (facs.1)
```

To prove the equality of the two lists facMap and facs 0 we first prove an auxiliary result, namely that:

```
zipWith (*) [(n+1)..] (facs n) ≃ facs (n+1)                       (zipFac)
```

for all natural numbers n. In order to do this we take the relation:

$\mathcal{S} \equiv \{(\text{zipWith } (*) \; [(n+1)..] \; (\text{facs n}), \; \text{facs } (n+1)) \mid n \in \text{Nat}\}$

and show that it is a bisimulation. Expanding first the left-hand side of a typical element we have:

```
zipWith (*) [(n+1)..] (facs n)
 => zipWith (*) (n+1:[(n+2)..]) (fac n : (tail (facs n)))
 => (n+1)*(fac n) : zipWith (*) [n+2..]
                                 (zipWith (*) [(n+1)..] (facs n))
 => fac (n+1) : zipWith (*) [n+2..]
                                 (zipWith (*) [(n+1)..] (facs n))
```

On the right-hand side we have:
```
facs (n+1)
  => fac (n+1) : zipWith (*) [n+2..] (facs (n+1))
```
Now observe the two expressions. They have equal heads, and their tails are related by $\equiv_S$ since they are applications of the function:
```
zipWith (*) [(n+2)..]
```
to lists which are related by S, namely:
```
zipWith (*) [(n+1)..] (facs n) ≃ facs (n+1)
```
This establishes the result (zipFac), and the consequence that:
```
facs n ≃ fac n : facs (n+1)
```
Now we prove that:
```
facs n ≃ map fac [n..]
```
by showing that the relation:
$$\mathcal{R} \equiv \{ \text{(facs n, map fac [n..])} \mid n \in \text{Nat} \}$$
is a bisimulation. Taking a typical pair, we have:

```
facs n                          map fac [n..]
  ≃ fac n : facs (n+1)            => fac n : map f [(n+1)..]
```

which establishes that $\mathcal{R}$ is a bisimulation and in particular shows that:
```
facs 0 ≃ map fac [0..]
```
as we sought.

It is interesting to observe that recent work has shown that coinduction principles can be derived directly in domain theory; see [474] for more details.

4.8.4 Process Algebra

Of the many approaches to describing concurrency and non-determinism, most extend the imperative model of computation. Distinctive, therefore, are the process algebras (or process calculi) CSP [284] and CCS [400], which take a declarative model of concurrent processes. Although they differ in substantial details, their similarities outweigh their differences, and therefore the discussion here will concentrate on CCS. The use of CSP is described in detail in Chapter 16.

Processes (or, rather more accurately, states of processes) are represented in CCS by expressions, with definitions of the form:
```
A = (a.A + b.(B|C))
```

The process A is defined so that, performing the action a, A can evolve to A, or (+), performing the action b, it can evolve to the parallel composition B|C. One can see the sequencing operation, ".", as generalising the lazy ":" which appears in definitions of infinite lists like:

    natsFrom n = n : natsFrom (n+1)

The usual form of reasoning about CCS is equational, with equality characterised by a bisimulation relation, generalising the description in Section 4.8.2, and so one can view the lazy-stream characterisation of processes as embedding this part of functional programming in a general view of deterministic concurrency.

The set of processes in a CCS expression is fixed; in the π-calculus – which axiomatises name passing in a CCS style – processes can be created, destroyed and reconfigured, again in a declarative manner. A general introduction to the π-calculus and other action calculi is given in [401].

4.9 Strong Functional Programming

We have seen that the potential for non-termination makes program verification more complicated. Because of this there is interest in programming languages which are "strong" in the sense of providing only the means to define terminating functions.

These languages are also attractive to the implementor, since if all programs terminate, however they are evaluated, there is a substantially wider choice of safe evaluation strategies which can be chosen without there being a risk of introducing non-termination; this applies in particular to adopting parallel implementation strategies.

In this section, we give a brief overview of various research directions. A general point to examine is the degree to which each approach limits a programmer's expressivity.

4.9.1 Elementary Strong Functional Programming

Turner [577] proposes a language with limited recursion and co-recursion as a terminating functional language which could be used by beginner programmers (in contrast to alternatives discussed later in this section). The language proposed will have compile-time checks for the termination of recursive definitions, along the lines of [382], [561]. The language also contains co-recursion, the dual of recursion, over co-data, such as infinite lists (the greatest fixed point of a particular type equality). An example of co-data is given by the definition of the infinite list of factorials:

    facs = 1 : zipWith (*) [1..] facs

This definition is recognisable as a "productive" definition, since the recursive call to `facs` on the right-hand side is protected within the constructor ":", and so there is a guarantee that the top-level structure of the co-datum is defined. Proof of the properties of these corecursive objects is by coinduction, as discussed above.

Note the duality between these productive definitions over co-data with primitive recursive definitions over data, as exemplified by the definition of the function which gives the length of a (finite) list:

```
length (x:xs) = 1 + length xs
```

Here the recursive call to `length` is on a component of the argument, `(x:xs)`, which is contained in the application of the constructor ":"; thus primitive recursive definitions require at least one level of structure in their arguments whilst productive definitions give rise to at least one level of structure in their results.

The disadvantage of this approach is that it must rely on the compile-time algorithms which check for termination. It is not clear, for instance, whether the earlier definition of the `lAssoc` function is permitted in this system, and so the expressivity of the programmer is, indeed, limited by this approach. On the other hand, it would be possible to implement such a system as a "strong" subset of an existing language such as Haskell, and to gain the advantage of remaining in the terminating part of the language whenever possible.

4.9.2 Constructive Type Theories

Turner's language eschews the more complex dependent types of the constructive type theories of Martin-Löf and others [433], [562]. These languages are simultaneously terminating functional languages and constructive predicate logics, under the Curry/Howard Isomorphism which makes the following identifications:

Programming		Logic
Type		Formula
Program		Proof
Product/record type	&	Conjunction
Sum/union type	\/	Disjunction
Function type	->	Implication
Dependent function type	$\forall$	Universal quantifier
Dependent product type	$\exists$	Existential quantifier
...		...

in which it is possible in an integrated manner to develop programs and their proofs of correctness.

From the programming point of view, there is the addition of dependent types, which can be given by functions which return different types for different argument values: an example is the type of vectors, `Vec`, where `Vec(n)` is

4.9 Strong Functional Programming

the type of vectors of length n. Predicates are constructed in a similar way, since a predicate yields different logical propositions – that is, types – for different values.

Predicates (that is, dependent types) can be constructed inductively as a generalisation of algebraic types. We might define the less than predicate "<" over Nat – the type of natural numbers – by saying that there are two constructors for the type:

```
ZeroLess :: (∀n::Nat)(0 < S n)
SuccLess :: (∀n::Nat)(∀n::Nat)((m < n) -> (S m < S n))
```

This approach leads to a powerful style of proof in which inductions are performed over the form of proof objects, that is, the elements of types like (m < n), rather than (say) over the natural numbers. This style makes proofs both shorter and more readable, since the cases in the proof directly reflect the inductive definition of the predicate, rather than being over the inductive definition of the data type, which in this case is the natural numbers.

A more expressive type system allows programmers to give more accurate types to common functions, such as a function which indexes the elements of a list:

```
index :: (∀xs::[a])(∀n::Nat)((n < length xs) -> a)
```

An application of index has *three* arguments: a list, xs and a natural number n — as for the standard index function — and a third argument which is of type (n < length xs), that is, a *proof* that n is a legitimate index for the list in question. This extra argument becomes a *proof obligation* which must be discharged when the function is applied to elements xs and n.

The expressivity of a constructive type theory is determined by its proof-theoretic strength, so that a simple type theoretic language (without universes) would allow the definition of all functions which can be proved to be total in Peano Arithmetic, for instance. This includes most functions, except an interpreter for the language itself.

For further discussions of constructive type theories see [433], [562].

4.9.3 Algebra of Programming

The histories of functional programming and program transformation have been intertwined from their inception. Serious program manipulations are not feasible in modern imperative languages which allow aliasing, pointer and reference modifications, type casting and so forth.

More suited are current functional languages which support the definition of general operations – such as map, filter and fold over lists – as polymorphic higher-order functions. Indeed, these higher-order operators can be sufficient to define all functions of interest. This was the insight of Backus in defining FP [28], and has been developed by a number of researchers, most notably by Bird and Meertens, [49], who are responsible for the Bird-Meertens formalism

(BMF). Their approach is to build a calculus or algebra of programs built from a fixed set of combining forms, with laws relating these combinators expressed at the function level, such as:

map (f . g) ≡ map f . map g (mapComp)

These laws are expressed in a logic which extends the definitional equality of the programming language, and, essentially, equational reasoning in that logic allows transformations to be written down in a formal way. On the other hand, laws such as (mapComp) will themselves be proved by structural induction; for a proof of this result and many other examples of properties of list-based functions see [564].

What is the intensional reading of a law like (mapComp)? It shows that two traversals of a list structure, map f . map g is equivalent to a single traversal, map (f . g); this clearly has efficiency implications. In a similar way, the fold of an associative operator into a non-empty list enjoys the property:

foldr1 f (xs ++ ys) ≡ (foldr1 f xs) 'f' (foldr f ys) (foldAssoc)

in the case that xs and ys are themselves non-empty. The intension of (foldAssoc) is dramatic, with the left-hand side representing a single left-to-right traversal of a list and the right-hand showing that this can be computed by means of two parallel computations over the two halves of the list.

Many of the combining forms of BMF correspond to skeletons (Chapter 13), and so the laws governing these forms will transfer to skeletons.

The most recent development of this work is Bird and de Moor's [53] in which they use the constructs of category theory to express their functional programming language. Their categorical approach means that they are able to provide general rules for equational program manipulation at a very high level. For instance, they are able to formulate in a data type independent way a "fusion" law by which a function is absorbed into a *primitive recursively* defined function. A review of [53] which explains this work in more detail can be found in [477].

4.10 Conclusion

This chapter has given an introduction to the methods used in verifying functional programs, including references to further work in axiomatising more complex aspects of the functional paradigm. These methods can, in most cases, be transferred to parallel functional programs, since the proofs reflect the extensional properties of programs which are likely to be independent of the chosen evaluation strategy.

More specific ties to parallel functional programming are provided by the process model of lazy streams and its links to general process algebra. A

4.10 Conclusion

second link is given by the combinatorial style of FP or the Bird-Meertens formalism, in which laws expressing equivalences between extensionally equal programs can be given an intensional meaning as transformations which improve efficiency or increase parallelism.

5. Realisations for Strict Languages

Werner Kluge[1]

5.1 Introduction

The *Church-Rosser property* shows that functional program terms that are not contained in each other may be evaluated (rewritten) in any order without affecting the determinacy of results. Thus they can also be evaluated non-sequentially[2], under the control of individual *processes* (or *tasks*), in a system of several processing sites. All it takes to do so are some means to partition a program into concurrently executable (sub-)terms, and to compose, in reverse order, an evaluated program from evaluated (sub-)terms.

With some simple rules to this effect, a compiler or a pre-processor could identify syntactical constructs (terms) in a functional program that appear to be good candidates for concurrent evaluation, and insert into the compiled program code the instruction sequences which at run-time create, synchronise and terminate the respective processes (tasks). Ideally, high-level source programs would then look the same irrespective of whether or not they were being executed non-sequentially. Process scheduling, the allocation of memory and the placement of data structures therein may, to some extent, also be figured out by the compiler, and dynamically by the system, based on actual program behaviour and on the availability of resources.

However, in reality things are not that simple. Automated program analysis, specifically in the case of lazy languages, may simply fail to identify large chunks of work that could be done concurrently (see also Chapter 1 and [329]). Also, the dynamic behaviour of non-trivial programs is generally hard to predict as it usually depends on actual input parameters which determine the course of action taken. This, in turn, influences *workload partitioning* and *balancing*, which directly affect performance gains compared with sequential execution.

There is generally no alternative but to lay some of the responsibilities of planning non-sequential program execution in the hands of the programmer in the form of *program annotations*, even though this may contradict the purists' idea of functional programming. However, to compromise the functional style as little as possible, these annotations ought to specify just *what* is to be computed non-sequentially and to what extent (see Chapters 1 and 3 and for instance [476], [571]), whereas the *where* and *when* to compute should be decided by the run-time system, (although there are proposals to include

---

[1] University of Kiel, Germany.
[2] In this chapter, the term *non-sequential* refers to executing *in any order* several threads of control. It will be used synonymously with *concurrent* execution and instead of parallel execution.

annotations that specify the scheduling of tasks on specific virtual or real processing sites as well [476]). The annotations could be based on some good intuition as to how a program is likely to behave, or on extensive run-time profiling with representative input parameters (see Chapter 10).

Program annotations that identify concurrently executable parts are more or less mandatory in concurrent versions of so-called *function-based languages* such as ML or Scheme [403], [182] which also permit side-effecting operations to overcome some of the efficiency problems of purely functional languages. Since long-range side-effects are extremely hard to detect by automated program analysis, it inevitably becomes the programmer's chore to identify *large pieces* of truly concurrent code either by annotations (see Chapter 3) or by explicit specifications of processes and communication channels [140], [494], [32], [566].

Executing functional (or function-based) programs non-sequentially is usually based on the conservative approach of evaluating only those program terms which are bound to contribute to the final result, or are *mandatory*. However, if processing sites are available in abundance, a more aggressive *speculative* (or *eager-beaver*) evaluation strategy may be employed as well. The idea is to evaluate alternative program terms concurrently, without knowing in advance which terms will eventually come up with the needed result. With some luck, this strategy may arrive at problem solutions faster than with sequential processing, though considerable processing power may be wasted on useless computations.

Another important issue for concurrent processing is machine and system architectures. With the emergence of the functional paradigm considerable work was carried out to develop dedicated machinery that met the specific needs of term rewriting (or reduction) [46], [342], [375], [543], [412], [512], [335], [585]. However, it was soon recognised that it was more effective to compile functional languages to conventional machinery, using various abstract machines as intermediate levels of code generation [574], [117], [142], [316], [189], [476], [207] to take advantage of the rapid progress made in conventional processor and compiler (code generation) technology.

Similar considerations apply to suitable machinery for multiprocessing as well. At the level of processes and process interaction it makes little difference whether computations are specified in a functional or imperative style. As process scheduling, memory management policies (garbage collection) and communication mechanisms basically remain the same, it makes good sense to use existing system (software) support as much as possible.

As for the hardware platforms there is a basic choice between shared- and distributed-memory systems (see also Chapter 1). The former have advantages as far as the sharing of code and data structures, memory management and process scheduling are concerned, but memory bandwidth limits the number of processors that can effectively be supported. The latter allow for decidedly more processing sites as all of them are equipped with their own private memories, but here memory limitations recur in just another form. There are increased latencies to deal with when non-local memories need to be accessed and, depending on network topologies, latencies may also increase with distances between sites. Creating new tasks in other sites may require communicating at least data structures, if not pieces of code. The overhead inflicted by these operations must be carefully balanced against expected performance gains. Usually, this cannot be achieved without repeatedly going through cycles of extensive run-time profiling of workload distribution and memory access (communication) patterns, and of subsequent reprogramming and fine-tuning in order to identify and remove performance bottlenecks.

The remainder of this chapter is organised as follows. The next section introduces basic principles of concurrent program execution, including task interaction and task management, under both mandatory and speculative evaluation strategies. Typical realisations are described in Section 5.3. This is followed, in Section 5.4, by an overview of systems that support the non-sequential execution of strict functional and function-based languages, among them implementations of a fully-fledged applied λ-calculus, of a concurrent Lisp dialect, and of several concurrent ML versions.

5.2 Concurrent Program Execution

The basic principles of execution of functional programs non-sequentially derive directly from the evaluation of applications under an *applicative order* (or *strict*) regime (see Section 2.3). For applications of the general form $(f\ e\_1 \ldots e\_n)$ it is recursively defined as:

EVAL $[\ (f\ e\_1 \ldots e\_n)\ ] =$
EVAL $[\ (\ $EVAL $[f]\ $ EVAL $[e_1] \ldots $ EVAL $[e_n])] $,

(with EVAL $[e] = e$ if e is a constant term). The recursive nesting of EVALs in fact defines a hierarchy of *abstract evaluator instances*, (or of *abstract machines* of which those that are not in a parent-child relationship with each other can safely be executed *in any order*. Every evaluator instance may (or may not) be realised as an individual *task* as the basic unit of computation. Thus, a task that evaluates the application $(f\ e\_1 \ldots e\_n)$ may create concurrently executable child tasks for any subset of its terms, and evaluate the remaining terms under its own control. The creation of further child tasks may continue recursively in this manner, possibly until some upper bound which saturates the processing capacity of the system is reached.

5.2.1 Task Interaction

A typical *interaction scheme* between parent and child tasks is depicted in Figure 5.1. It applies to the conservative approach of *mandatory evaluation*, under which program terms are set up for non-sequential execution if, and only if, their values are known to be needed. In this scheme, a task is essentially specified by a triple $<p, t, e>$, with:

- p identifying the parent task by which the task under consideration was created and to which it must eventually return the value of the term e;
- t denoting a unique place-holder which identifies, in the term that remains under the control of the parent task p, the syntactical position to which the value of e must be returned;
- e denoting the term to be evaluated under the control of the task.

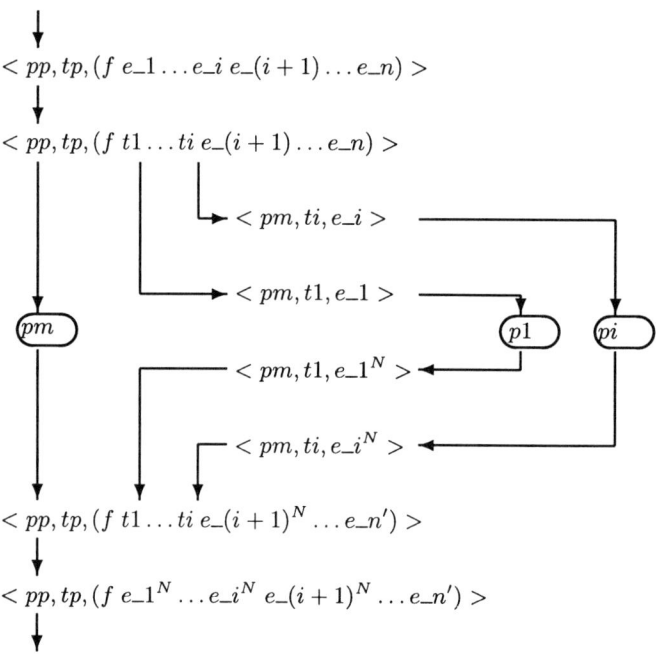

Figure 5.1. The task interaction scheme

The figure shows a parent task pm which originates from yet another task pp. In the course of evaluating the application $(f\ e\_1\ldots e\_n)$, it creates child tasks $p1,\ldots,pi$ for the argument terms $e\_1,\ldots,e\_i$ in that it extracts them from their syntactical positions and replaces them with place-holders $t1,\ldots ti$, respectively. These place-holders are also carried along with the respective child task triples.

The tasks pm and $p1,\ldots pi$ can now proceed concurrently. The parent task pm which evaluates the term f and the remaining arguments synchronises with the child tasks $p1,\ldots,pi$ upon their termination with (weak) normal forms, denoted as $e\_1^N,\ldots,e\_i^N$. Synchronisation includes the substitution of the place-holders in the application left under the control of the parent task by the terms returning from the child tasks. The parent task pm may then continue to evaluate the application thus completed.

Communication in this interaction scheme is of *short range* and extremely simple: there is just one communication of the term to be evaluated from parent to child (which coincides with the creation of the child) and one communication of the evaluated term in the opposite direction (which coincides with the termination of the child and its synchronisation with the parent).

All tasks of a multi-level hierarchy can be scheduled for processing non-preemptively and in any order. Neither different priorities nor fairness aspects need be considered. However, to make efficient use of this task interaction scheme, some additional "rules of the game" need to be established.

Creating, initialising and managing a task is known to be fairly costly in terms of instruction cycles expended. Nevertheless, to achieve acceptable performance gains, it is imperative that the program terms assigned to tasks constitute self-contained pieces of work whose computational complexities outweigh this overhead by around one order of magnitude.

In functional programs, applications of user-defined functions are the natural entities of concurrent computations. *Graph reduction* being the standard execution model, functions (abstractions) must be internally represented in some closed form that prevents name clashes when substituting formal by actual parameters (see Chapter 6). To this effect, most graph reduction systems transform open functions (λ-abstractions) into so-called *supercombinators* [291], [316], [289].

Supercombinator applications are perfect candidates for concurrent processing. They are fully self-contained program terms (graphs) which may start executing on abstract machines (evaluators) of the SECD machine variety (see Section 2.4), with just the application graphs in their heap memories and with pointers to these graphs in their code (C) structures (or in some dedicated graph pointer registers), whereas all other run-time structures may be empty. Upon termination, the run-time structures, other than those for the registers that hold pointers to the resulting graphs, are then empty again. Creating and terminating tasks that run such machines, besides allocating and de-allocating task control blocks and space for the run-time structures, primarily involves passing graph pointers in and out, particularly if the heap can be shared among all tasks (machines). Otherwise, complete graphs may have to be moved as well, either piecemeal or entirely, in and out of task-specific heap sections.

5.2.2 Task Management

As many application problems suited for concurrent processing are highly recursive, the ensuing task hierarchies tend to unfold to considerable depths, with bounds set only by actual program parameters. However, creating tasks far in excess of the number of processing sites inflicts overhead, without further performance gains, and may also exhaust memory. It is therefore imperative that task creation be throttled once the system approaches some degree of saturation.

A simple system-supported measure to this effect consists in controlling the creation of tasks by means of a finite number of *concessions* which, in the form of *tokens* representing available resources, are held in some system-wide reservoir [340], [94]. Potential instances of creating new tasks can then be made to succeed if, and only if, tokens can be allocated (and thereby removed) from the reservoir, otherwise the parent tasks simply evaluate the respective terms by themselves. Terminating tasks return their tokens to the reservoir for further use. Thus, the total number of tasks can never exceed the number of tokens with which the reservoir was initialised. Tokens may simply be allocated on a first come/first served basis and under complete system control. Though the shapes of the task hierarchies that actually develop cannot be fully anticipated, they can, to some extent, be influenced by program annotations which favour the creation of tasks with reasonably high work load.

Concessions can be elegantly integrated into the task interaction scheme of Figure 5.1 which so far lacks a source for the place-holder variables. All there is to do here is to assign unique name tags to the concession tokens since there are just as many place-holders needed as there can be tasks in the system, i.e. the token reservoir can serve both purposes.

The interaction scheme itself may be used as a standard *template*, into which programs with concurrently executable parts may be transformed. Constructing and executing such templates takes four so-called *pseudo-functions* which merely serve organisational purposes but have no effect on the program's semantics.

Let $e = \ldots * e\_1 \ldots * e\_n \ldots$ denote a program term in which some n syntactically disjunct subterms $e\_1, \ldots, e\_n$ are earmarked by the symbol $*$ for concurrent processing[3], it then takes a pseudo-function ABSTRACT to turn this term into: $(\text{ABSTRACT } e) \rightarrow (\overline{\lambda} v_1 \ldots v_n.\overline{e} \, (\text{ FORK } e\_1) \ldots (\text{FORK } e\_n))$ where $\overline{\lambda} v_1 \ldots v_n.\overline{e}$ denotes another pseudo-function, with $\overline{e}$ resulting from e by replacing, for all $i \in \{1, \ldots, n\}$, the term e_i with the variable v_i [4]. The applications of the pseudo-function FORK are to create new child tasks for the evaluation of the terms lifted out of e. They evaluate as follows:

Let T_0 and $T \subseteq T_0$ respectively denote the initial and some actual set (or pool) of concessions, and let P denote the actual set of tasks that participate in executing a program concurrently, then:

---

[3] These marks may be introduced by some pre-processor or by the compiler based on program annotations or on some automated rules for identifying terms which can be expected to generate sufficient workload, e.g. by strictness analysis.

[4] The abstraction described here is in fact similar to the concept of *serial combinators* as introduced in [289], except that what are being abstracted are not necessarily maximally free subterms. In an annotated high-level program this abstraction would be directly specified as `letpar` $v_1 = e_1 \ldots v_n = e_n$ `in` $\overline{e}$.

5.2 Concurrent Program Execution

$$(\text{FORK } e) \rightarrow \begin{cases} (\text{JOIN } t) & \text{if } (T \neq \emptyset) \wedge (t \in T) \\ & \text{side} - \text{effects}: \\ & T \rightarrow T \setminus \{t\} \\ & P \rightarrow P \cup \{<pm, t, e>\} \\ e & \text{otherwise} \end{cases},$$

with pm denoting the task under which the application is reduced. Thus, if a token can be withdrawn from the pool T, FORK evaluates to the application of a pseudo-function JOIN to this token, and as a side-effect creates a new task for the term e that is added to the set P; otherwise it simply returns e as it is in order to have it evaluated by the task pm itself.

Applications of JOIN are to re-insert in evaluated form the terms extracted by FORKs, upon termination of the respective tasks. Assuming that terminated tasks become members of a distinct subset $P_t \subseteq P$, usually called the *zombie state*, the rewrite rule for JOIN is:

$$(\text{JOIN } t) \rightarrow \begin{cases} e^N & \text{if } (\exists p \in P_t)(p = <pm, t, e^N>) \\ & \text{side} - \text{effects}: \\ & T \rightarrow T \cup \{t\} \\ & P_t \rightarrow P_t \setminus \{<pm, t, e^N>\} \\ (\text{JOIN } t) & \text{otherwise} \end{cases},$$

Note that JOIN also returns to the pool T the token t held in possession by the terminated task, which may be immediately recycled to create another task.

Finally, evaluating applications of $\overline{\lambda}$-abstractions is defined as:
$(\overline{\lambda} v_1 \ldots v_n . \overline{e} \; a\_1 \ldots a\_n)$

$$\rightarrow \begin{cases} \overline{e}[v_1 \leftarrow a\_1, \ldots, v_n \leftarrow a\_n] & \text{if } (\forall \; i \in \{1, \ldots, n\}) \\ & (a\_i \neq (\text{FORK } e)|(\text{JOIN } t)) \\ (\overline{\lambda} v_1 \ldots v_n . \overline{e} \; a\_1 \ldots a\_n) & \text{otherwise} \end{cases}$$

with $\overline{e}[\ldots, v_i \leftarrow a\_i, \ldots]$ denoting naive substitution of v_i in $\overline{e}$ by a_i. These substitutions may be thought of as taking place in one conceptual step if, and only if, all argument terms have been stripped of FORKs and JOINs, i.e. after all children have terminated and returned their values. Thus, the rule defines a very conservative synchronisation mechanism between parent and child tasks which in actual system implementations may, of course, be relaxed. For instance, in dynamic data flow systems or in concurrent Lisp implementations the equivalent of the (*join t*) constructs are simply treated as *future contracts* to eventually deliver values not yet computed, and to continue with the evaluation of the terms that contain these futures until values are actually needed [21], [241], [19].

This token game realises a so-called *eager task creation policy*. Program execution sets out with a single task which fairly quickly splits up into a hierarchy of rather small subtasks until all tokens are taken. Once this state is reached, lengthy periods of computations can be expected in all leaves of the tasks tree, provided the respective terms are sufficiently complex. The immediate recycling of tokens released by terminating tasks ensures that a near maximal number of them remain committed as long as applications of FORK remain to be reduced. Since tasks with short run-times also return their tokens early to be picked up where needed more urgently, it can be expected that even the workload of relatively unbalanced computational trees can be fairly evenly distributed over the processing sites. However, since there are decidedly more opportunities for executing FORKs deeper down in a computational tree than there are closer to its root, eager task creation also tends to favour the creation of tasks with decreasing computational work as the computation proceeds. Though this tendency generally has no dramatic effects on performance, it may hurt with programs that produce many FORKs in succession with little to compute in between.

5.2.3 Speculative Evaluation

With processing sites in generous supply, it may pay for some applications to take the more aggressive approach of evaluating several alternative program terms concurrently on a speculative basis, particularly in the area of symbolic computations where many problems are of a trial-and-error nature and thus inherently np-complete. Though only one of them is usually expected (or required) to eventually produce some desired value, there may be a good chance to compute this value much faster than with sequential execution, at the expense of considerable redundancy in terms of processing power expended [460], [450], [442], [449], [380], [123], [520].

Selector Terms. A simple, though usually not very rewarding, form of speculative evaluation applies to selections among several alternative terms which are of the general form

$$(\ case\ s\_e\ e\_1 \ldots e\_n\ )$$

and evaluate as follows:

$$eval[\ (\ case\ s\_e\ e\_1 \ldots e\_n\ )\ ] \rightarrow \begin{cases} eval[\ e\_i\ ] \text{ if } eval[\ s\_e\ ] = i \in [1..n] \\ \text{undefined otherwise} \end{cases}$$

Using a conservative interpretation, the selector term s_e must be evaluated first and, assuming that it returns an index value $i \in [1..n]$, the term e_i next, i.e. it prescribes a sequential execution order.

However, since all subterms of the CASE are syntactically independent, nothing goes wrong if they *are* computed concurrently. Of course, the evaluation of the terms $e\_1, \ldots, e\_n$ can only be of a speculative nature until the evaluation of the selector term s_e terminates with a legitimate index value. From this point on, all computations other than that of the selected term ought to be aborted and all resources they hold in possession should be reclaimed.

To organise this evaluation in an orderly form, the system must:

5.2 Concurrent Program Execution

- Distinguish between *vital tasks* whose results are bound to contribute to the problem solution and *speculative tasks* whose results may or may not be required;
- Treat vital tasks with higher priority than speculative tasks, and possibly distinguish several priority levels among the latter, to prevent the monopolisation of the system with computations of which many are known to be superfluous;
- Apply a fair scheduling discipline to all speculative tasks belonging to the same CASE to ensure that all of them make progress at about the same pace (assuming that the outcome of evaluating the selector term cannot be anticipated), as otherwise all the resources could be committed to a subset of speculative computations which may turn out to be useless, while those which would produce solutions eventually stay behind (or *starve*).

A simple, yet effective, scheduler would run all executable vital tasks with top priority and non-preemptively. Fairness among speculative tasks running on processing sites that are not claimed by vital tasks may be enforced by a preemptive scheduling discipline which maintains a certain *synchronic distance* measured, say, in terms of reduction steps by which individual tasks can at most get ahead of each other. Depending on the outcome of computing by means of a vital task the value of the selector term, speculative tasks may either be aborted or become vital.

Since CASE terms may be recursively nested, the attributes *vital*, *speculative* and *aborted* must be inherited in a task hierarchy from top to bottom and some of them also passed along from the bottom up:

- A vital parent task may have vital and speculative child tasks;
- A speculative parent task may have only speculative child tasks;
- A vital child task which computes a selector value must communicate with its (vital) parent task to have it change the status of the selected speculative child task to vital and to abort all other speculative children;
- A status change from speculative to vital may have to be passed down in a task hierarchy, turning some of the subtasks vital while others remain speculative, possibly at a higher priority though, likewise, aborting a speculative task applies to all its subtasks.

As communication thus goes up and down a task hierarchy, the child tasks must not only know their parent tasks to return results, but the parent tasks must also know their speculative children in order to effect status changes.

Fair progress among speculative tasks belonging to the same CASE may be enforced by the following *barrier synchronisation*: each task is permitted to perform, at most, some q reduction steps after which it must wait until all others have caught up (i.e. have also performed their quantum of q reduction steps). All tasks may then be rescheduled for another quantum of q reduction steps, with q being the chosen synchronic distance. This cycle is repeated until the vital task returns the selector value. States of temporary suspension while waiting at the barrier may be conveniently used to abort speculative tasks or to change their status to vital[5].

Deterministic and Non-Deterministic Choices. More interesting with respect to speculative evaluation are applications of the general form:

(choice $e\_1 \ldots e\_i \ldots e\_n$)

which specify choices among alternative terms which may either be deterministic as, for instance, in pattern matching, or non-deterministic as in search problems.

Assuming that each of the terms e_i, $i \in \{1, \ldots, n\}$ evaluates to either some useful value or to the special value FAIL, the value of a deterministic CHOICE application is defined as:

$$eval[(choice\ e\_1 \ldots e\_i \ldots e\_n)] = \begin{cases} eval[\ e\_i\ ] \text{ if } \quad eval[\ e\_i\ ] \neq fail \\ \qquad\qquad \text{and for all } j \in [1 .. i-1] \\ \qquad\qquad\qquad eval[\ e\_j\ ] = fail \\ \text{undefined otherwise} \end{cases}$$

This definition demands that for the term e_i to *succeed* as the value of the application, it must be made certain that all the preceding terms $e\_1, \ldots, e\_(i-1)$ have *failed*. Thus, when evaluating the components of the application concurrently, it is good practice to start with a vital task for the term e_1 and with speculative tasks for the terms with indices $i > 1$ in monotonically increasing order, possibly with less than the full set (depending on the availability of concessions), and to proceed as follows:

- A speculative task whose term *fails* is aborted, and its concession token immediately re-cycled to create a new speculative task for the next term in sequence (if one is left);
- As soon as it can be decided that some speculative task with index i is bound to produce a value other than FAIL it remains speculative but aborts all speculative tasks with indices $j > i$;
- If the vital task *fails*, it terminates and changes the status of the speculative task with the next higher index to vital; the token may be then recycled to create another speculative task;
- If the vital task is bound to produce a useful value, it continues until orderly termination; all remaining speculative tasks are aborted.

It is important to note that fairness in the case of a deterministic CHOICE is fully compatible with the concept of limited concessions for task creation. Since the semantics of CHOICE demand that the argument terms be evaluated from left to right (which in fact defines a *priority order*), in order to make

---

[5] In actual implementations the barrier synchronisation may be relaxed to some extent so that some speculative task arriving at a barrier i may pass without delay if all other speculative tasks belonging to the same construct (or priority level) have passed the preceding barrier $i - 1$.

sure that all terms preceding the one that succeeds have failed, it suffices to run just as many speculative tasks as concessions can be claimed, as long as these tasks process the terms with the lowest indices among those that still need to be evaluated speculatively.

Organising the speculative evaluation of a non-deterministic CHOICE (also referred to as a *"parallel" OR*) appears to be decidedly simpler. As with the CASE, speculative tasks need to be started for *all* argument terms. The first of these tasks that is bound to succeed is the one that survives and turns vital, whereas all other speculative tasks are subsequently aborted[6]. As a nice sideeffect of the fairness regulation, this scheme is also bound to terminate if there exists at least one problem solution. This cannot be guaranteed for deterministic CHOICES: even if one of the speculative tasks terminates with a value, the preceding tasks may not. This being the case, it is not possible to decide whether or not a solution that may be found is the correct one.

Unfortunately, the non-deterministic CHOICE (and the CASE as well) causes a conflict between fairness among speculative tasks and limited concessions. Since there is no upper bound on the number of terms that may have to be evaluated speculatively, there can be no upper bound on the number of tasks either. Otherwise, processing power (and time) could be completely wasted on terms that never succeed (and may not even terminate), while the terms that would produce solutions make no progress.

The way out of this dilemma is to resort to so-called *order-based speculative evaluation*. They reconcile the demand for fairness among unbounded numbers of speculative tasks with resource constraints (or, more rigorously, with limited concessions). The idea is to arrange the terms to be evaluated speculatively, in an order of priority which can be expected to produce the most likely solutions with the least average execution times (if, as in the case of the deterministic CHOICE, only a subset of them can be processed at the same time) [442]. Evaluation commences with the subset of tasks that have the highest priorities and moves towards tasks with lower priorities, as executing tasks produce FAILs and are aborted or have their priorities dynamically downgraded to a level where the scheduler decides to temporarily de-allocate processors (see also Section 5.4.2).

5.3 System Architectures

The basic principles of concurrent processing, as outlined in Section 5.2, are more or less invariant against the configuration of the underlying multiprocessor machinery, which may be a shared- or a distributed-memory system, and also against evaluation orders, which may be *strict* or *lazy*.

---

[6] Note that if the CHOICE application is itself evaluated by a speculative task, the surviving subtask may simply upgrade its priority level but stays speculative.

5.3.1 Shared-Memory Systems

Concurrent graph reduction can be most conveniently implemented on shared-memory platforms. They typically consist of some large main memory which holds their program code and the graph, i.e. the parts that may be shared among several concurrent tasks, and some k processors, each being equipped with some fast local memory (a cache) that may hold task-specific run-time structures (e.g. stacks) as well as pieces of the graph and of the code which constitute the actual focus of activity.

The main memory also needs to accommodate a small operating system kernel which includes the *task scheduler* and the *garbage collector*. The data structures typically employed by the task scheduler are schematically shown in Figure 5.2. They are arranged around a *task-table* which accommodates some finite number of slots for *task context blocks*. These slots may also be used as the concession tokens for task creation as introduced in Section 5.2. A new task can only be created if a free slot can be claimed from this table for initialisation with a new context, and if a terminating task also releases its slot. All other data structures hold pointers to slots[7]. In particular, there is a:

- READY-queue for executable tasks lined up for the allocation of one of the processors;
- SLEEP-queue for tasks that are temporarily suspended while waiting for the synchronisation with child tasks;
- RELEASE(ed)-queue which contains pointers to free task table slots;
- FORK-queue for (pointers to) graphs set up by FORKs for concurrent processing and for waiting for the allocation of free task table slots;
- RETURN-queue for (pointers to) evaluated graphs that need to be re-JOINed with the graphs under the control of the respective parent tasks.

Since these queues need to be shared among all processors, they must be operated on in a mutually exclusive manner in order to keep their contents consistent. This may be accomplished either by protecting them individually with *locks*, or, more conservatively, by implementing the entire task scheduler as a *monitor*.

This machinery may be operated as a back-end system which executes one program at a time, downloaded from a front-end machine which creates the initial task from where the computation spreads out.

The initial task claims the first task table slot from the RELEASE-queue and immediately starts executing on one of the processors. Upon encountering FORKs in the program code, running tasks place the respective graph pointers into the FORK-queue (also referred to as the *spark pool*) and continue their computations until nothing can be done but wait for synchronisation with child tasks, in which case the tasks are put in the SLEEP-queue. Program

---

[7] Note that this is a somewhat idealised picture as there are many other ways of implementing these data structures, e.g. as (doubly) linked lists etc.

5.3 System Architectures

terms held in the FORK-queue get slots allocated from the RELEASE-queue as long as they are available, and the newly created tasks are appended to the back-end of the READY-queue. Processors looking for work take tasks from the front-end of this queue. Sleeping tasks are awakened again upon synchronisation with child tasks and lined up in the READY-queue to have the respective JOINs executed. The pointers to the evaluated graphs can be found in the RETURN-queue where they have been placed by the terminating children.

In cases of temporary exhaustion of slots, tasks with nothing else left to do may inspect the FORK-queue for terms they have deposited there but which have not yet led to the creation of new tasks, reclaim them and execute them under their own control.

This task scheduling scheme basically looks the same irrespective of whether programs are evaluated under a mandatory regime or speculatively. Mandatory tasks, other than for phases of suspension while waiting for synchronisation with children, may be scheduled non-preemptively, as fairness is of no major concern, though experience shows that preemptive scheduling

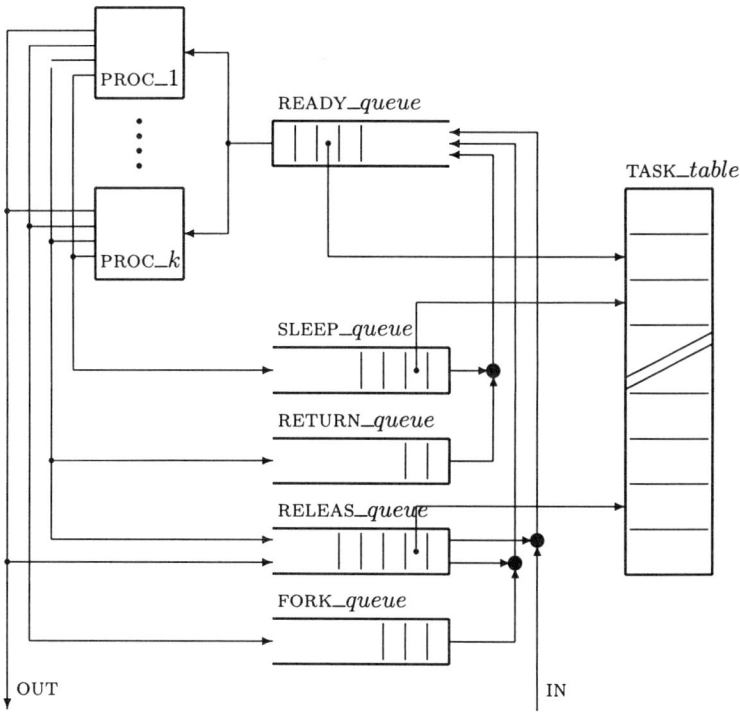

Figure 5.2. Task scheduling scheme

helps to avoid undue delays of sleeping tasks [25]. Speculative tasks require preemptive scheduling to enforce fairness (see Section 5.2.3). To do so, the scheduler must be able to distinguish between tasks of different priorities, either by providing additional FORK- and READY-queues or simply by adding appropriate tags to the task context blocks.

A good choice for the number of task table slots is roughly three times the number of processors in the system. This ensures that all processors can be kept busy, with some tasks held back in the READY-queue to immediately replace terminating tasks, and it even allows for several tasks to be in the SLEEPing state [605].

There are several alternatives to this task scheduling scheme. For instance, each processor could be equipped with a private set of queues, together with a copy of the scheduler's code in its local memory and with permission to fetch tasks from the READY-queues of other processors if its own READY-queues are empty. New tasks may be deposited only in the READY-queues of the processors on which the parent tasks are running. The number of tasks may be limited by distributing concessions evenly over all the processing sites. This scheduling scheme has roughly the same effects on task granularities and workload distribution, except that it removes, at the expense of replication, the bottleneck of sharing a single set of queues among several processors requesting scheduler services.

Another, less strict, method of throttling task creation consists of applying an *unfair* scheduling discipline which selects tasks for execution on a *youngest first* rather than an *oldest first* basis. This can easily be realised by operating the READY-queue(s) as stack(s) [241] or, depending on the actual workload, both ways, i.e. as FIFO-queue(s) until all processing sites are busy, and otherwise as LIFO-queue(s) [238].

Things are slightly more complicated under a lazy regime. Here, several tasks may attempt to reduce a piece of graph at about the same time. Though no harm would be done since all of them would eventually overwrite it with the same normal form (referential transparency), all but one of these computations would be superfluous. To prevent multiple evaluations, the first task to get hold of a shared piece of graph must set a lock which blocks out further tasks. Blocked tasks go to sleep until the task that evaluates the graph terminates and unlocks again (see also Chapter 6).

5.3.2 Distributed-Memory Systems

The organisational problems involved in executing functional programs non-sequentially in a distributed memory system, specifically those of getting the entire workload fairly evenly distributed and of coordinating the interactions among tasks running in different sites, are more formidable.

Processing sites need to be equipped with their own local task schedulers (which have to serve just one processor) and with communication facilities. Rather than just communicating graph pointers between tasks, it may be-

5.3 System Architectures

come necessary to communicate the full structures that are referenced by them. The sites are usually connected to only a limited number of adjacent sites, which may cause considerable communication latencies with remote sites.

Tasks may be distributed over the processing sites in one of two ways. Each processing site has (a limited number of) concessions:

- Either to transfer to its adjacent sites workload held in its own fork pool, which is also called *offloading*;
- Or to request workload from the fork (spark) pools of its neighbors, which is also referred to as *stealing* work.

Program execution typically sets out by downloading copies of the entire program code into the local memories of all processing sites and by starting an initial task in some unique site. This eventually also returns the result of the program run. If all sites have the same connectivity and the same number of concessions per connection to transfer work, then the tasks are evenly distributed over all sites, after exhaustion of all concessions. As concessions are incessantly recycled, a reasonably balanced workload distribution can be sustained until the entire computation tails off, provided the program yields sufficient concurrency in between and the number of processing sites is not too large. Otherwise it takes too much time to spread the computation out over all sites, the tasks tend to become too small, inflicting too many overheads relative to useful computations, and workload balancing becomes less than satisfactory [94].

Other difficulties arise with references to graphs residing in non-local memories. These graphs may have to be copied into the processing sites of the tasks that need them. However, if under a lazy regime an unevaluated graph were to be referenced by several tasks executing in different sites, then copying would result in multiple reductions and also be rather wasteful if only small pieces of the graph were actually required. In either case it is more efficient to have the reductions done in the site of the graph and to have only the result shipped somewhere else.

There is also a complexity problem involved in moving a graph to some other site. If the processors of the sending and receiving sites are directly involved in the move, e.g. by writing the graph into or reading it from special communication buffers, then noteworthy performance gain can only be expected if the complexity of reducing a graph of some n nodes is decidedly larger than $O(n)$, which is the complexity (or the cost) of shipping the graph. Otherwise, the overheads involved in communicating it consumes about the same processing time as the computation itself, i.e. the effort of moving would be completely wasted.

5.4 Systems Supporting Strict Languages

This section gives an overview of typical functional and function-based systems which implement the basic principles of non-sequential program execution as outlined in the preceding sections. Interestingly, the majority of systems described in the literature support lazy languages, even though identifying concurrently executable program parts is much more difficult, whereas there are only few systems based on strict languages, primarily dataflow systems [16], [19], [238], [602], [171], [11], [10], number-crunching systems [113], [115], [239], [61], [312], [515], [236], and systems supporting concurrent versions of Lisp and of ML [241], [408], [494], [140], [566], [32].

Since concurrency is usually abundantly available in strict functional programs, the dominating organisational problems primarily concern the choice of suitable task granularities, load distribution, task scheduling, memory management, and throttling mechanisms which prevent the creation of concurrent tasks far in excess of the available processing capacity.

5.4.1 The π-RED$^+$ System

π-RED$^+$ is an applicative order graph reducer which directly and completely realises the reduction semantics of a *full-fledged λ-calculus* [514], [207]. Its appearance to the user is that of a system which truly performs *high-level program transformations*. It supports a stepwise execution mode which allows the inspection and modification of intermediate program terms in high-level notation. Programs are reduced to *full normal forms*, i.e. partial function applications are converted into functions of lesser arities and returned in intelligible form as results. Naming conflicts are correctly resolved by an indexing scheme similar to de Bruijn's nameless dummies which preserves the original variable names [169]. The high-level language supported by π-RED$^+$ is KiR — a syntactically sugared version of an applied λ-calculus with a rich set of primitive arithmetic, logical, relational and list processing functions, and with powerful pattern matching facilities [341].

The implementation of π-RED$^+$ is based on an abstract stack machine ASM which serves as an intermediate level of code generation. It employs four stacks named A, W, T and R to accommodate the run-time environment for function calls. Stacks A and W hold argument and workspace frames, stack T holds frames for instantiations of non-local variables, and R stores return addresses. As compared to a one-stack machine, this stack system facilitates compilation to intermediate code, code optimisations, and decompilation into high-level programs of intermediate machine states resulting from stepwise code execution [207].

A Distributed Memory Implementation. A concurrent version of π-RED$^+$ was implemented as an experimental test bed on an nCUBE/2 hardware platform [94]. This implementation fully complies with the systems out-

5.4 Systems Supporting Strict Languages

lined in Sections 5.2 and 5.3, other than for some minor modifications necessary to adapt it to the specific needs of a distributed-memory system and to the particularities of the underlying machinery.

The nCUBE/2 system comprises 32 processing sites, each of which is equipped with an nCUBE/2 processor and 16 MBytes of memory. The processors also include autonomous network communication units which may serve up to 14 communication channels per site. Each channel transmits data bidirectionally at a rate of 5 Mbits/sec. Each site runs a small operating system kernel nCX.

The implementation of π-RED$^+$ on this platform requires, on each site, a single nCX master process to run the ASM-code interpreter, a local task scheduler, a heap manager, and, optionally, a task monitoring system for run-time profiling purposes. The tasks of the reduction system are realised as *threads* of this master process. The communication units interface with the master process through dedicated I/O buffers. Program terms (graphs) arriving at some site through the communication channels are written into an input buffer, from where the nCX process copies them into its own address space. Conversely, terms that must be shipped to some other site must be written by the nCX process into an output buffer, from where the communication unit takes over.

Other than serving just one processor, the task scheduler is essentially the same as the one depicted in Figure 5.2. Workload distribution being based on offloading, each site maintains a separate local pool for concessions to create tasks in adjacent sites. The number of concessions in each pool can be chosen to be some $k * n$, where n denotes the connectivity of the cube (which is the same for all processing sites) and k specifies the number of concessions to create tasks in each adjacent site, with $n \in [2,..,5]$ and $k \in [1,..,4]$. Since each site, in turn, may receive up to k jobs from its neighbours, each task table must provide $k * n$ slots for context blocks. Thus, say, with $n = 4$ and $k = 2$, each site may accommodate up to eight tasks, of which one is executing, some of the remainder are typically sleeping, waiting for synchronisation with their children, and the rest are ready for execution, so that a running task that terminates can be immediately replaced.

Each task realises an ASM which, however, shares its heap with all other tasks set up in the same site. When executing a FORK application, the task places the argument term into the local FORK queue, and continues. As soon as a token can be picked up from the local pool of concessions, the term is shipped to the adjacent site selected by the particular token assignment, where it is guaranteed to find a task table slot for the creation of a task. Conversely, a terminating task has its resultant term shipped back to the site of the parent task, where it is placed in the RETURN-queue. After synchronisation with the parent, the token is put back in the local concession pool.

Tasks that run out of work may inspect the local FORK-queue for terms that have been deposited there but, due to temporary exhaustion of tokens, have not yet been shipped somewhere else, reclaim and evaluate them under their own control.

The terms that are typically shipped to other sites for processing are closures representing defined function applications. Each of these closures contains a pointer to the function code, the function's arguments, and a copy of the actual environment of the application (the topmost frame of the parent's T-stack). These components initialise the ASM of the child task to be created. Since the ASM reduces programs to full normal forms, these closures may even contain partial applications of significant complexity.

Some Observations on Performance. The main objective of this implementation was to test, experiment with and validate the basic concepts outlined in Section 5.2 and the organisational problems of concurrently executing functional programs in a distributed-memory system. Absolute performance figures taken from a number of small benchmark programs (Fibonacci numbers, the towers of Hanoi, quicksorting a list of numbers, the eight queens problem, Mandelbrot and some other small number-crunching programs.) are not very conclusive insofar as they were obtained by abstract code interpretation. However, introspective performance measurement indicated that:

- The overriding factor in achieving performance gains that grow linearly with the number of processing sites involved is the ratio between the complexity of the algorithm, measured, say, in numbers of recursion steps necessary to process a data structure, and the complexity of shipping the structure from one site to another. If this ratio is only marginally greater than one, no performance gains can be expected;
- Relative speedups degrade with increasing numbers of processing sites since it takes too much time and overhead to get all processing sites involved in the computation, and workload tends to spread out unevenly and too thinly;
- Choices between hypercubes and fully connected system topologies generally have only a marginal effect on performance if load distribution is completely left to the system. The most dramatic effects on performance gains can be achieved by adapting the system topology to the structure of the problem, provided it partitions fairly evenly. Hypercubes and fully connected topologies in conjunction with fully dynamic load distribution do decidedly better with applications that are unbalanced or whose dynamic behaviour cannot be anticipated.

Somewhat surprising is the observation that performance noticeably improves with increasing numbers of concessions per connection, and thus with finer task granularities. Here one would expect the opposite effect, since creating tasks far in excess of processing sites means more overheads at the expense of useful computations. However, workload distribution and balancing also

5.4 Systems Supporting Strict Languages

improve at the same time, as there are generally more opportunities to immediately replace terminating tasks with others that are ready to run, and task granularities tend to become finer, helping to distribute workload more evenly.

Some Results on Speculative Evaluation. With some minor extensions of the compiler and the task scheduler, the π-RED$^+$ implementation on the nCUBE/2 system could be upgraded to support speculative evaluation as outlined in Section 5.2 and [520].

An interesting application is the problem of finding a path from the centre of a maze to one of several possible exits. A naive implementation of this search process uses a spider which crawls in small steps along the aisles of the maze, represented as a matrix of some $n * m$ grid points in which walls are marked by 1's and the spaces between them by 0's, and after each step checks whether it can go up | down | left | right. The search branches out if at some grid point the spider can move in more than one direction and fails if there is no other alternative but to go backwards. Processing all branches of the unfolding search tree simultaneously remains speculative until they either fail or an exit can be found.

Performance gains of concurrent speculative searches versus sequential searches for an exit critically depend on the one hand on the size and internal structure of the maze, and on the other hand on the synchronic distance between barrier synchronisations of the speculative threads, which in distributed-memory systems incur a considerable overhead.

Typical performance figures can be obtained from a maze structure in which *sequential* searches for one of four possible exits, of which only one is actually opened per program run, differ significantly with respect to the time it takes to find them. This contrasts with *concurrent speculative* searches, which for each of the four exits take about the same time. In one case this time is slightly inferior to the respective sequential search, in the other three cases performance varies from marginally to significantly better, but even in the best case the overall performance is not very impressive relative to the number of processing sites that were engaged in the computation.

These observations are quite characteristic for speculative evaluation in general. Depending on the structure of the problem, it may very well happen that sequential evaluation is faster, and even if speculative evaluation cuts down on total execution times, it comes at the expense of involving processing power far in excess of what is actually gained.

5.4.2 MultiLisp Systems

Lisp and its descendants are function-based languages that are in widespread use in the area of symbolic computations. Since there are many complex application problems programmed in these languages, substantial reductions of execution times by concurrent processing (in some cases of up to several hours on sequential machines) are highly desirable.

Most prominent amongst several other approaches (see [300]) is Multi-Lisp — an extension of Scheme by constructs which make concurrency explicit [241]. As MultiLisp inherits mutable variables from Scheme, it also provides low-level synchronisation mechanisms of the test-and-set variety to enforce mutual exclusion of accesses to data that are shared among several tasks, and the means for data encapsulation in an object-oriented style, keeping side-effects locally confined.

Sharing mutable variables amongst several tasks makes implementation of MultiLisp on shared-memory machinery the natural choice.

Exposing Concurrency in MultiLisp. MultiLisp requires annotations, since long-range side-effects due to mutable variables cannot be reliably detected by automated means. This, in turn, renders it impossible for a compiler or pre-processor to identify program terms of reasonable computational complexity that can be executed truly concurrently in the sense that the (partial) results they produce are invariant against execution orders (the Church Rosser property)[8]. If side-effects are intended, then accesses to the respective mutable variable must at least be made mutually exclusive in order to ensure orderly updates.

The most important form of expressing concurrency in MultiLisp is provided by the construct

$$(e\_0 \ (\texttt{future} \ e\_1 \ ) \ ) \ .$$

The application (future e_1), very much like the FORK of Section 5.2, returns a place-holder token as a promise to deliver the value of e_1 eventually (or in the future). This place-holder serves as a synchronisation mechanism which allows the computation of e_0 (and of the context in which the application is embedded) — the so-called *continuation* of the future[9] — to proceed concurrently with the computation of e_1 up to the point where the value of e_1 is actually needed. Evaluating the continuation beyond this point is suspended until the value of e_1 becomes available.

The interpretation of the future leaves a choice between three different courses of actions. A parent task evaluating the entire application (e_0 (future e_1)) may create a child task for e_1 and concurrently evaluate the continuation e_0; alternatively the parent may evaluate e_1 while the child task works on the continuation. Depending on actual workload, the future may also be completely ignored and the computation of e_1 may be inlined with the task that evaluates (e_0 (future e_1)), very similar to the rule given in Section 5.2 for the evaluation of FORK applications.

---

[8] Creating tasks for fairly complex program terms is essential for substantial performance gains, as it increases the ratio of useful computations versus the fixed overhead that must be devoted to task management.

[9] A continuation of some term is said to be a function which applies to the value of this term and then continues to compute the remainder of the program.

5.4 Systems Supporting Strict Languages

Futures resemble lazy evaluation insofar as computations may proceed beyond the availability of actual argument values, i.e. they may be used to implement non-strict functions. However, the arguments of futures are evaluated eagerly (in applicative order) regardless of whether or not they are actually needed. Thus it remains the programmer's chore to make sure that futures are only used where values are needed and evaluation terminates. To delay the evaluation of a term until its value is required, MultiLisp provides the construct (delay e) which works exactly as (future e), except that it starts evaluating e only if it becomes the argument of a strict function.

A MultiLisp Implementation. A first implementation of MultiLisp an experimental shared-memory multiprocessor system called Concert was described in [241]. It had 32 MC68000 microprocessors connected through a shared bus to 20 MBytes of main memory. Each processor was equipped with some local memory for fast access to frequently used objects. MultiLisp programs were compiled to an intermediate machine language called MCode which, in turn, was interpreted by some 3000 lines of C code. A copy of the interpreter was downloaded into each of the processor's local memories.

Since MultiLisp inherits lexical variable scoping from Scheme, it requires a conventional environment stack in which frames are statically linked, so that parameters can be accessed in the environment in which they are defined. If several concurrent tasks participate in the execution of a program, the environment assumes the shape of a tree, also referred to as a *cactus stack*, in which child tasks originating from the same parent task share the same environments.

Both the compiled program code and the environment structure are held in the main memory as they need to be shared amongst all tasks. The actual state of program execution in each task, besides register contents and some status information, is essentially defined by a pointer to the code, to the top of the task-specific environment, and to some task-specific workspace stack.

A new task is created by an MCode instruction future which carries the pointer to the code as a parameter; the environment pointer is taken over from the parent task. The workspace stack is initialised with just a pointer to a mailbox where the task eventually deposits the value of the future.

Task Creation and Task Scheduling. A unique feature of this implementation is the task creation and scheduling policy. This prevents task creation beyond processor saturation and at the same time keeps computations locally bound. To this end, each processor maintains a *pending stack* which realises an *unfair* scheduling discipline for tasks ready to be executed. An active task executing on some processor which encounters a term (future e) creates a new task to evaluate e, keeps this task active on the same processor, suspends the parent task (which evaluates the continuation) and moves it to the processor's pending stack. Upon termination of the active task, the processor continues with the topmost task it finds on its own pending stack. If empty, the processor inspects the pending stacks of other processors and steals a task from the first non-empty stack it comes across.

Thus, when all processors are saturated, continuations are stacked up on the local pending stacks in much the same order as if the program had been executed sequentially, i.e. the futures, other than for the overhead of task creation, are in fact inlined. This has the two fold advantage of keeping fairly long threads of computation bound to the same processors, and of preventing the explosion of tasks that would otherwise occur with divide-and-conquer computations.

The creation of tasks may be further throttled by limiting the depths of the pending stacks. If the stacks are filled to capacity, the futures encountered by the active tasks are simply inlined without task creation, which has the same effect as the token-based scheduling scheme described in Sections 5.2 and 5.3.

Task creation is basically *eager* insofar as, up to the point of exhausting the capacities of the pending stacks, all *futures* are turned into new tasks regardless of whether or not this increases the number of *active* tasks.

Deviation from this LIFO discipline of stacking and unstacking continuation tasks is only necessary if an active task must be suspended to wait, say, for synchronisation with an as yet unresolved future, in which case the processor must fetch another task either out of order from its own pending stack or from somewhere else. However, these situations rarely occur in a saturated system where tasks that evaluate futures are usually the ones that are active, whilst the tasks that compute the respective continuations are the ones that are kept waiting in the topmost positions of the pending stacks.

To evaluate the efficiency of this scheduling policy, extensive performance measurements were made on an eight processor subsystem of the Concert machinery with two versions of a quicksort program which differed with respect to the futures used. They showed speedups growing linearly with the number of processors, and they also confirmed that the number of continuation tasks actually waiting for the completion of futures was far less than the total number of futures created. However, performance generally degraded with increasing numbers of futures, since their execution took about four times as much time as procedure calls and also inflicted a greater burden on memory (heap) management, specifically on garbage collection [241].

A Lazy Task Creation Policy. Though eager task creation seems to work well for many programs, it carries with it the overhead of inlining tasks (rather than code) and of creating more tasks than are necessary to keep all processors busy. It also tends to prefer smaller rather than larger subterms for task creation, since divide-and-conquer computations feature more *futures* deeper down in the unfolding computational tree than closer to the root, and tasks are moved to other processors from the tops of the pending stacks, where those with the lesser workload are usually found.

5.4 Systems Supporting Strict Languages

Moreover, if task creation is unevenly distributed within a program, processors may occasionally run out of work. Such situations come about when inlining futures on some processors prevents other processors which are looking for work from stealing their continuations. The problem is that inlining, once decided, cannot be undone to separate the execution of a future from its continuation.

These deficiencies have led to the concept of *lazy task creation* [408]. The basic idea here is to have the future in (e_0 (future e_1)) evaluated by the same task that evaluates the entire term, but to take measures that enable another processor to steal the continuation. This policy creates new tasks only if absolutely necessary to supply idling processors with work, i.e. at any given time there are, at most, as many tasks as there are processors in the system.

In order to have tasks execute fairly large chunks of computational work, lazy task creation may be combined with a mechanism which steals future continuations on an *oldest first* basis, i.e. those which are closest to the top of the computational tree.

A simple implementation of this concept centres around task-specific queues whose entries represent future continuations which may be taken over by other tasks. To this effect, these *lazy task queues* contain pointers into the respective task-specific environment stacks where they point to the frames associated with these continuations.

A task T that executes a term (e_0 (future e_1)) pushes a new frame for the continuation e_0 onto the stack, appends a pointer to this frame at the front end of the queue , and then computes e_1. If the future thus inlined returns the value of e_1 before any stealing occurs, the continuation pointer is again removed from the front of the lazy task queue, and the task continues to compute e_0 itself.

A processor attempting to steal a continuation takes the pointer off the back of the queue and turns it over as the stack top pointer to the new task, say T'. Conceptually, this is equivalent to pulling the bottom part out from underneath the stack of task T. It also requires creating a mailbox through which task T communicates the value of e_1 to the task T' which now computes the continuation e_0.

Performance measurements with simple benchmark programs and a more realistic speech processing program, all of the divide-and-conquer variety, show that in comparison to eager task creation (with or without bounds), the number of task creations can be reduced by factors ranging from 3 to 200, depending on how much needs to be computed between future calls. Relative speedups are decidedly more moderate, ranging from 1.5 to 3 for the simple programs, but are almost non-existent for the speech processing program; the reason being that the tasks contain large enough chunks of work to render the overhead negligible, even for eager task creation. Relative speedups grow almost linearly with the number of processing sites (up to

16) for the simple programs, but somewhat less than linearly for the speech program.

A Note on Speculative Evaluation of MultiLisp Programs. As many real-life symbolic computations relate to complex search problems, supporting speculative evaluation in a MultiLisp environment appears to be a particularly attractive concept to reduce raw program execution times. However, as search applications tend to explode rapidly in space and time when executed speculatively, economy of resource utilisation becomes an issue of foremost concern. The allocation of resources to speculative computations requires careful control, beyond the rather simple scheduling scheme described in Section 5.2.3. Task priorities may have to be dynamically changed as program execution progresses and more information about possible future courses of action becomes available to pursue the most promising tasks with top priority.

Other Lisp-specific difficulties arise from side-effects. Decisions as to whether some computation is relevant or not cannot be made as safely as in purely functional programs, since some program terms may have to be executed for their effects, e.g. setting or unsetting a lock, rather than for their values. There are also the problems of what to do with side-effects caused by aborted computations and of getting the correct values of mutable variables shared, say, between the two branches of a conditional expression that have each been evaluated speculatively.

An interesting concept of dealing with these problems has been proposed in [442]. It combines some language extension of MultiLisp with a rather elaborate *task sponsoring* scheme which dynamically controls task priorities and thereby execution orders.

The language extensions include constructs such as (spec_future e p) which designate terms e for speculative evaluation and assign initial (or source) priorities p to them. Other constructs demote or promote tasks by lowering or raising their priority levels, or take tasks completely out of circulation either temporarily or forever.

The basic idea of the sponsor scheme is to control the allocation of resources to tasks by *attributes*, basically priorities, *sponsored* by other sources which may be external (the programmer), tasks requesting values (so-called *toucher sponsors*), parent tasks sponsoring their children, and *controller sponsors* which receive sponsorship from elsewhere and distribute it among the tasks of a particular domain. *Effective task priorities* are computed by some formula from the priorities contributed by each of the sponsors. They may dynamically change as task priorities are directly raised or lowered, sponsors added or deleted by the program itself, and priority changes of a particular task propagated to all tasks sponsored by it. All vital (or mandatory) tasks (those created by ordinary futures) have top priority which never changes[10].

The system always runs the tasks that have the highest effective priorities. All vital tasks are scheduled non-preemptively and all speculative tasks

---

[10] futures inside spec_futures receive the priorities of the latter.

5.4 Systems Supporting Strict Languages

may be preempted, assuming the state *stayed*, by tasks of higher effective priorities. Stayed tasks may be resumed later on unless all references to them are deleted and they become garbage collected. Stayed tasks which produce side-effects for others remain accessible until they deliver. Stayed tasks include those whose effective priorities are down to zero, meaning that they have no sponsors and are therefore (temporarily) not executable.

Within the same conceptual framework, speculative evaluation using priority sponsoring effectively takes care of order-based fair task scheduling and of early reclamation of resources held by tasks that are unlikely to succeed. The system will dynamically adapt the number of speculative tasks to suit the idle processing sites that are available.

The performance measurements for several search problems reported in [442] stress the proper ordering of speculative computations as the single most important factor in achieving noticeable or even substantial speedups relative to lazy or eager evaluation.

5.4.3 Concurrent Implementations of Standard ML

Standard ML (SML) is another widely used strict, lexically scoped and — in contrast to Lisp — also strongly typed language. It is considered largely functional though it allows for some side-effecting operations. It also comes with a sophisticated module system for large-scale real life programming [403]. The more prominent approaches to concurrent ML programming such as CML, paraML or Facile are based on language extensions either with threads (lightweight processes) that communicate through shared mutable variables or with explicit specifications of processes and process communication through channels [494], [140], [566], [31]. They allow the construction of complex networks of cooperating processes whose structures may be decidedly more complex than those of divide_and_conquer computations derived from annotated functional (or MultiLisp) programs. The ensuing programming style is mainly process-oriented rather than functional, requiring some deep understanding of concurrency issues in order to write non-trivial applications.

The idea behind these language extensions is primarily to support concurrent computations as they typically occur in *interactive systems* or in truly *distributed systems*. User interaction (reaction to external events), services to multiple clients, updating displays, etc. all play a dominating role in the former cases. Handling requests for services provided by remote nodes, keeping track of outstanding interactions, managing distributed resources, maintaining the consistency of distributed data (bases) etc. are the main issues in the latter.

Thread-Based Concurrency. The basic extensions necessary to specify concurrent computations in SML are captured in the language CML (for *concurrent ML*) [494]. These include functions to dynamically create *threads* *of control* and (typed) *channels* for message passing, together with *send* and *accept* primitives. In addition, CML provides what are called *first class synchronous operations*. These are based on the notion of *events* as a first class data type which comprises functions that produce *base event values* and combinators to combine event values into more complex (higher-order) operations. The base event producing functions include `transmit` and `receive`, which realise a synchronous message transfer through a channel and `wait` which synchronises with a terminating thread. The combinators `wrap` and `choose` respectively are to bind some action to an event value and to select non-deterministically one out of a list of events. There is also a `sync` operation which, when applied to an event, checks whether one of the base events has occurred and, if so, executes the respective synchronisation operation; otherwise the thread that executes the `sync` simply blocks.

A thread package tailored to the needs of concurrent computations on shared memory multiprocessors which includes such low-level operations is described in [140]. It comprises:

- A function `fork` to create a new thread and a function `exit` to terminate it. Values can be communicated only through shared mutable variables;
- Locks of type `mutex` together with `acquire` and `release` operations to provide mutually exclusive access to shared variables;
- Various synchronisation primitives to create and operate on *condition variables* and to signal and wait for occurrences of *events* (not to be confused with the CML notion of event values).

These SML extensions are sufficient to build more complex concurrency constructs such as the `futures` of MultiLisp, communication buffers of finite capacities, guarded commands, rendezvous mechanisms, or the synchronous events of CML.

SML, complemented by this thread package, has been implemented on a Mach operating system platform which provides a number of primitives to control thread creation and thread management within a UNIX process. Thread creation commences with the allocation of a fixed stack partition from the stack segment of the UNIX process and of a private heap partition (to avoid the overhead of sharing), the Mach `thread_create` routine is then called, followed by other Mach routines which prepare the thread to run the SML code and finally schedule the thread for execution. Special C routines have been added to the SML run-time system to support the locking and synchronisation mechanisms.

However, implementing the thread package with only minor add-ons to the SML system turned out to be unsatisfactory in terms of performance. Inefficiencies were primarily due to the need to context-switch back and forth between SML and C code execution whenever one of the thread routines was called. Incorporating these operations into the language and into the SML compiler would eliminate these problems and also provide opportunities for code inlining. Another problem seems to have been the fixed number of

5.4 Systems Supporting Strict Languages

threads which, due to the predefined partitioning of the stack segment, could be accommodated by a UNIX process.

A full description of CML with examples is contained in Chapter 17.

The Facile System. Facile comprises both an SML-based process specification language and a UNIX-based run-time system [566] (for more details on the language see also Chapter 3). It has been developed at ECRC in Munich, Germany, with large application programs running on distributed memory systems in mind, specifically on *local* or *wide area networks*.

Facile extends SML by various constructs for concurrent processing, for synchronous communication through typed channels, and for workload distribution. A Facile system consists of a set of *nodes* (or *virtual machines*) which may accommodate several Facile processes as the basic units of sequential computations. Nodes are realised as UNIX processes, and Facile processes are *threads*, of which several may run under a UNIX process, sharing its address space. Nodes may reside on the same, or on different, machines within a network, and Facile processes belonging to the same, or to different, nodes may freely communicate via channels.

Creating a Facile system requires the installation of a UNIX process called the *node server* on some network computer, which also creates a special *run directory*. Under this directory, the first Facile node may be started and further nodes may be created from within Facile nodes or from UNIX shells. A Facile system may be shared by several users.

The computations to be performed by Facile processes need to be specified as objects called *scripts*. They consist of pieces of SML code and of so-called *behavioural terms* which differentiate between the (static) composition of complex and simpler scripts. The SML code may include communication constructs (sends and receives) as well as channel and process generation constructs. Processes do not return values but produce (side-) effects.

Process communication via channels is synchronous, i.e. both the sending and the receiving process block until the communication is completed. Channels may be used in both directions and by all processes to which they are known.

Both scripts and channels (but not processes) are first class citizens of the language: they may be passed as parameters to functions and processes, returned as values, communicated through channels and bound to names. This provides considerable freedom in building complex scripts dynamically from simpler ones. Process systems which fully exploit these features may expand dynamically, or collapse and reconfigure themselves to adapt, say, to changing input or to parameter values computed at run-time.

Unfortunately, this *process-oriented* programming style leaves no room for directly exploiting divide-and-conquer concurrency that may be implicitly contained in scripts. There is no other way but to specify the respective recursive functions as processes, to define channels, and to use explicit sends and receives in the scripts to pass argument and result values via channels between parent and child process instances, which — in contrast to program annotations like futures — complicates matters considerably, rendering even simple programs rather incomprehensible.

An Overview of paraML. paraML is another process-based extension of SML primarily designed to specify coarse-grain concurrent computations for distributed-memory machinery [31]. Except for a more flexible asynchronous communication mechanism, it is similar to Facile. The items added to SML are *processes* and *ports* (replacing the Facile channels) together with operations to create and manipulate them.

Processes may receive messages (values) only from the ports they have created, but may send messages to all ports whose names they know. Process and port names may be communicated to other processes via ports, as may all other legitimate values of the language. The ports are in fact queues, of which each delivers messages to a single receiving process in their order of arrival from one or several sending processes.

Two more features have been added to paraML which allow for finer-grain concurrency [33]. One concerns the integration of CML primitives to create concurrent threads within paraML processes which share the same environments. The other concerns support for so-called *data parallelism*. To this effect, paraML provides a library of routines for some canonical operations such as map, filter, reduce and generate (a collection of data).

There is also a library of *algorithmic skeletons* which provides optimised paraML solutions for frequently used patterns of structuring concurrent computations, e.g. worker farms or divide-and-conquer skeletons.

paraML has been implemented on a Fujitsu AP1000 cellular array processor — a distributed-memory system scalable (in increments of 2^k) from 64 to 1024 cells, each comprising a SPARC processor, 16 MBytes of local memory and a message controller, which are connected through high speed networks [32]. There is a front-end machine attached to this system where so-called *process forms* can be defined and subsequently instantiated either by the user or by other processes. A process instance is an ML object which includes both the ML code to be executed and the port description. This object is communicated to some destination cell where it starts executing. To do so, each cell has the complete paraML run-time system installed. Communication between processes is handled by the AP1000 message passing network.

Performance data reported so far indicate good speedups versus sequential execution for a variety of applications, particularly for "data parallel" operations whose efficiency improves significantly with the size of the data collections, and for a large scientific application (the black hole image processing problem) which achieves about a 60% utilisation of the entire processing capacity over a wide range of grid sizes [31], [32].

6. Realisations for Non-Strict Languages

Chris Clack[1]

6.1 Introduction

Parallel implementations of non-strict functional languages using graph reduction are all based on the following model:

1. The graph is held in one or more large heap memories (see below);
2. There are a number of processing agents each of which uses one or more (slightly modified) sequential abstract machines to execute a thread in order to evaluate some part of the graph to WHNF;
3. Threads that are not currently being executed reside in one or more thread pools — if they have not yet started evaluation, they are often called *sparks* (see below) and may reside in one or more separate spark pools;
4. Synchronisation is required whenever a thread requires the value of an expression that is currently being evaluated by another thread.

6.1.1 Sparking

Most non-strict parallel graph reduction implementations use the *sparking* mechanism [135] for generating threads. This model assumes that all possible parallel partitions have been detected statically and annotations or instructions have been inserted into the code to indicate when threads could be generated. When such an annotation or instruction is encountered, the parallel run-time system generally places an appropriate descriptor (a spark) in a spark pool. The descriptor may be no more than a pointer to the thunk which has been identified as a suitable independent thread.

Sparks may either be viewed as mandatory or advisory; in the former case, they will always cause a new thread to be generated, whereas in the latter case they may be discarded if the machine is heavily loaded. Some systems, such as the HDG Machine and the ν—STG Machine [293] use both kinds of sparks.

6.1.2 Departures from the Standard Model

Differences between the various parallel abstract machines occur as follows:

1. Representations of objects in the heap, and the manner in which the agent executes the task, depend on the sequential abstract machine technology

---

[1] Department of Computer Science, University College London, UK.

that is used in the agents. The technology may be coarsely categorised as:
   a) stack-based (e.g. a parallel G-Machine [23], [429]) or
   b) packet-based (e.g. ALICE [163], the $<\nu, G>$ Machine [25]).
The Tim machine [189] marked a radical departure from previous stack-based approaches by using heap-allocated frames to collect together all the arguments in a function application. This frame-based architecture is seductively simple in definition, yet in practice garbage collection is problematic because a frame is treated as an indivisible unit even though some components may no longer be required[2]. A further problem arises with distributed-memory parallel graph reduction, since the sharing of frames appears to hinder efficient distribution of computation;
2. For a shared-memory or virtual shared-memory architecture (SM or VSM), the heap and task pool are both shared, whereas for a distributed-memory architecture (DM), each agent will have a local heap and a local task pool;
3. Mechanisms for blocking and resuming tasks, scheduling, task distribution and load management may differ.

In particular, we note that most parallel implementations are based on sequential lazy implementation technology. This is primarily due to the increasing performance of sequential processor technology and sequential compiler technology: since the purpose of a parallel system is to outperform a sequential system, it is essential to be able to take advantage of the latest sequential technology[3]. However, parallel implementations must also address many issues (such as load balancing, context-switching overheads, communications latencies and garbage collection)[4] that are absent from the sequential context.

6.2 Worked Example: the G-Machine

In this section we provide a worked example of a typical parallel abstract machine for non-strict graph reduction. Our example is based on the G-Machine [316], [24], which uses stack-based evaluation.

---

[2] Though to some extent this problem can be extenuated through the use of "frame-stubbing" which allows individual frame items to be collected (in a similar way to stack-stubbing in the STGM [461]).

[3] This is despite the fact that fast sequential implementations tend to keep a lot of local state which can be expensive in a parallel environment (especially where dynamic load-balancing requires migration of active tasks).

[4] Each of these issues is far more acute in a distributed-memory rather than shared-memory system.

6.2 Worked Example: the G-Machine

6.2.1 The Sequential G-Machine

The G-Machine [316], [24] uses stack-based evaluation to reduce an expression graph to WHNF. The three key technical advances of the G-Machine over previous graph reduction mechanisms are:

1. Lambda lifting was specifically designed for the G-Machine: it transforms the program into a collection of supercombinators which provide larger granularity than SK-combinators and therefore better performance;
2. The G-Machine was the first to show how graph-manipulation code (in preference to interpretive traversal and copying of graphs) could be generated for the supercombinators whose definitions (and therefore code) changes from program to program — previous work had either been purely interpretive [135] or had generated graph-manipulation instructions in the context of small, fixed-definition, SK-combinators [142];
3. Rather than generate native code directly for each supercombinator, the G-Machine introduced the notion of a small fixed set of graph manipulation instructions (*G-code*): supercombinators were compiled into G-code, and the operation of the G-Machine could be expressed (and formally verified) in terms of a set of transition rules for these instructions. This also facilitated portability and implementation via interpretation or compilation to native code.

The G-Machine compiler compiles each supercombinator that has been generated by lambda lifting into a fixed sequence of G-code instructions (similar to the way in which the CAM [142] creates code for SK-combinators); thus, template instantiation entails the (fast) execution of these instructions in order to construct an instance of the supercombinator body rather than a (slow) node-by-node copy of a graph template. Furthermore, this process facilitates many further optimisations to restrict the amount of graph that is built and thereby improve efficiency — there are many such optimisations in the G-Machine (e.g. tail-call optimisation) that we ignore in this presentation.

G-code is an intermediate code which may either be compiled further to native code for a given architecture or may be interpreted at run-time (in this respect it bears some similarity to the rôle played by Java byte-code, which was developed some eight years later [234]). Details of the G-code instructions are not given here (see [316] for the full details), though a few examples are presented below.

The compilation rules take a program comprising a set of supercombinator definitions and an expression to be evaluated: the result is a G-code program which comprises (i) some code to initialise the run-time system and start the evaluation of the primary expression, and (ii) a collection of G-code segments corresponding to each supercombinator definition. The code for each segment expects to find pointers to the arguments (as well as a pointer to the root node of the application) on the S stack (see below).

6. Realisations for Non-Strict Languages

The G-Machine is a stack-based abstract machine, with instructions to construct and manipulate graphs. A state in the abstract G-Machine is given by the 6-tuple $< C, S, V, G, E, D >$ (for this presentation, we ignore the output, O) where:

- C is the G-code sequence currently being executed;
- S is a stack of pointers to graph nodes;
- V is a stack of basic values (used for primitive operations such as addition);
- G is a graph of nodes;
- E is a global environment which maps supercombinator names to (arity, code) pairs;
- D is a dump of (C, S) pairs used for evaluation of strict arguments and for recursive calls.

The operation of the G-Machine is directed by inspection of the tag of a node, which determines its type. A node in the graph may be one of the following five types:

1. A primitive value node (e.g. $INT\ i$);
2. A constructor node for constructor number k, having m arguments ($CONSTR\ k\ n_1\ \ldots\ n_m$);
3. A binary application node with pointers to function and operator, respectively ($AP\ n_1\ n_2$);
4. A function node for the function named f ($FUN\ f$);
5. A place-holder node to be filled in later with a value, used while constructing cycles ($HOLE$).

Reduction is started by executing the G-code **EVAL** instruction which evaluates the graph pointed to from the top of the S stack. The G-Machine transition rules determine the changes to be made to the state tuple given above, according to the current state.

Example. For example, consider the following program:

```
let
    main x   = f (i x)
    f    x   = (k x) x
    k    x y = x
    i    x   = x
in
main 3
```

Execution of the above program can be thought of as consecutively constructing the following graphs (each conceptually overwriting the previous), as illustrated in Figure 6.1.

To illustrate the operation of the G-Machine, we take the third of the above graphs and show, through the use of transition rules, how the G-Machine

6.2 Worked Example: the G-Machine

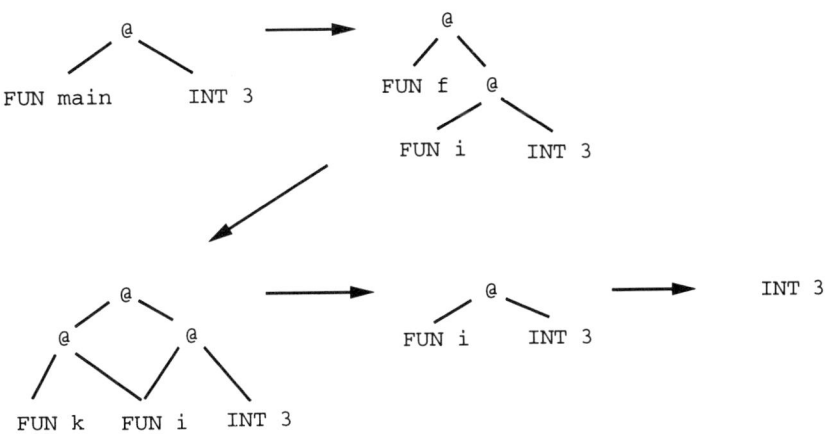

Figure 6.1. Example of graph rewriting

would evaluate it. A transition rule is a mapping from one machine state to another:

$$< C, S, V, G, E, D > \longrightarrow < C', S', V', G', E', D' >$$

We denote pointers to nodes, giving explicit node contents where necessary, using a colon; for example, $\{n : AP \ n_1 \ n_2\}$ denotes an application node containing operator n_1 and operand n_2, together with a pointer n to that node. As before, the graph G is viewed as a set of nodes which may be augmented using set union: $G \cup \{n : AP n_1 n_2\}$. The stacks S and V are denoted using () for an empty stack and a dot (.) for a push. A pair of items (C, S) pushed onto the dump D is denoted $(C, S).D$. For example, here is the transition rule for EVAL:

$$< (EVAL.C), \quad n.S, \quad V, \quad \{n : AP \ n_1 \ n_2\} \cup G, \quad E, \quad D >$$
$$\longrightarrow$$
$$< UNWIND.(), \quad n.(), \quad V, \quad \{n : AP \ n_1 \ n_2\} \cup G, \quad E, \quad (C, S).D >$$

We follow the operation of the abstract machine after EVAL is applied to node 1 of Figure 6.2 (which must be on the top of the stack). The essential difference between the EVAL and UNWIND instructions is that EVAL saves the current state (also known as the "continuation") to the dump (which is essential for the evaluation of strict arguments to primitive operators, and for recursive calls) whereas UNWIND effects the normal order graph traversal. After the call to EVAL, the graph and stack appear as shown in Figure 6.2:

1. EVAL saves the current (C, S) pair (the current code stream and the current stack, which together represent the continuation) onto the dump (D) and resets the stack S to contain only the previous top-of-stack

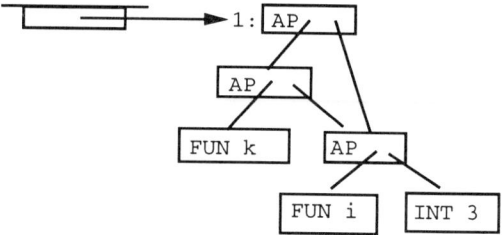

Figure 6.2. Example graph and stack

node (the pointer to node 1 in this case). EVAL then jumps to the UNWIND instruction. The transition rule for EVAL is given above;

2. The UNWIND instruction recursively calls itself to copy the outermost-leftmost spine and its arguments onto the stack. It stops when there are no more AP nodes on the spine. The transition rule for UNWIND while it is traversing down the spine is:

$<UNWIND.(), \quad n.S, \quad V, \quad \{n:AP \quad n_1 \quad n_2\} \cup G, \quad E, \quad D>$
$\longrightarrow$
$<UNWIND.(), \quad (n_1.n_2.n.S), \quad V, \quad \{n:AP \quad n_1 \quad n_2\} \cup G, \quad E, \quad D>$

In our example, after unwinding the whole of the spine, the stack and graph will appear as illustrated in Figure 6.3.

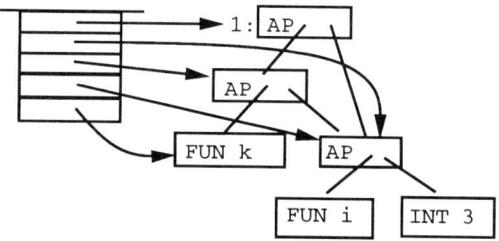

Figure 6.3. After unwinding the spine

3. When a FUN node is encountered by UNWIND, the arity and code for that function are retrieved from the environment E. The arity is used to ensure that enough arguments exist for a reduction to take place, and to identify the appropriate root node for this reduction. If this is a partial application, the saved (C, S) values are restored from D and the bottom

6.2 Worked Example: the G-Machine

node pointer is pushed onto the restored stack: for a full application, the stack is unchanged and a jump is made to the code for the supercombinator. Here is the transition rule:

$$< UNWIND.(), \quad (n_1 \ldots n_k.()), \quad V,$$
$$\{n_1 : FUN f\} \cup G, \{f : (a, c')\} \cup E, (c'', s'').D >$$

$\longrightarrow$ *if full application (check arity a)*
$$< c', \quad (n_1 \ldots n_k.()), \quad V,$$
$$\{n_1 : FUN f\} \cup G, \quad \{f : (a, c')\} \cup E, \quad (c'', s''). \quad D >$$

$\longrightarrow$ *if partial application*
$$< c'', \quad n_k.s'', \quad V, \quad \{n_1 : FUN f\} \cup G, \quad \{f : (a, c')\} \cup E, D >$$

In our example there is a full application, so the stack is unchanged and a jump is made to the code for k.

4. The code for a supercombinator rearranges the S stack (using a series of PUSH m instructions) so that pointers to the graphs for each of the arguments occur at the top of the stack, with a pointer to the root node of the application next on the stack; in our example, the code for k which rearranges the stack is:

    PUSH 4
    PUSH 4
    PUSH 3

Following this rearrangement, the stack and graph appear as depicted in Figure 6.4.

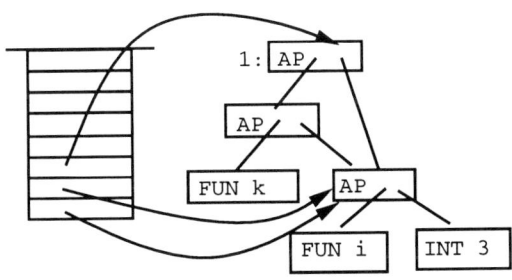

Figure 6.4. After rearranging the spine (shows new pointers only)

Next the function-specific code is evaluated. In general, the function-specific G-code effects a supercombinator instantiation by constructing graph, including pointers to the argument graphs as necessary, updating the root node of the application, and popping all the argument pointers from the S stack: this leaves a pointer to the overwritten result node on the top of the stack.

In our example, the code for k does not need to construct any graph (it is a projection function), so it arranges for a pointer to the first argument to appear at the top of the stack (this requires no instruction — the correct pointer is already there!) and then calls the UPDATE 2 instruction to indicate that the node pointed to by the third item on the stack (counting starts at 0) should be overwritten with[5] the node pointed to by the item on the top of the stack (which is popped). Finally, the RET 1 instruction pops the remaining arguments (used by this reduction) from the stack: see Figure 6.5.

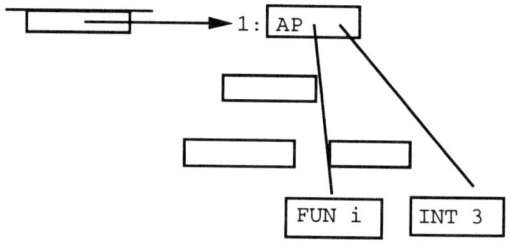

Figure 6.5. After update

5. In general, if the result of the reduction is a basic value, the (C, S) values are restored from D: otherwise, the machine UNWINDs into the graph that has just been constructed. In this example, the machine would UNWIND into FUN i and evaluate the application of FUN i to INT 3.

The sequential G-Machine as presented above actually performs quite poorly and several optimisations are required to achieve efficient operation. Essentially, the inefficiencies are due to building, traversing and copying graph unnecessarily. The development of the Spineless G-Machine and the Spineless Tagless G-Machine provided significant performance increases (see Sections 6.3.2 and 6.3.7). Poor sequential performance notwithstanding, for this worked example we shall use the above sequential machine as the basis for a parallel graph reduction system.

---

[5] For simplicity, we ignore indirections in this presentation, yet the observations given previously regarding the need for indirections still apply.

6.2.2 The Parallel G-Machine

For simplicity, we shall assume a shared-memory parallel architecture which contains several co-operating sequential G-Machines, a shared graph and a shared task pool (see Figure 6.6). Further, we shall assume that the shared graph and the shared task pool are implemented as autonomous, intelligent objects which receive read and write requests and guarantee exclusive access whilst each single request is being fulfilled, including indivisible test-and-set operations. Given these assumptions, we shall describe an abstract parallel G-Machine.

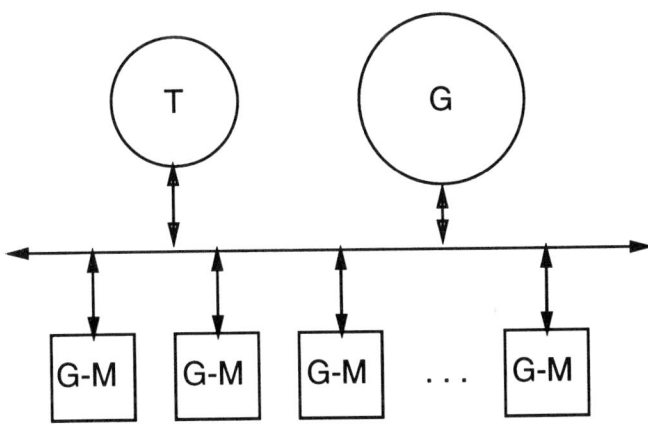

Figure 6.6. Architecture with shared memory and shared task pool

We describe the parallel G-Machine in terms of the individual sequential G-Machines, where the state for each sequential G-Machine is augmented with a task pool T. The graph G and the task pool T are shared amongst all the sequential G-Machines. We represent individual tasks as 5-tuples $< C, S, V, E, D >$, this being the entire non-shared state of a task. Thus, the entire state of the system is given by:

$$< \ <C, S, V, E, D>_{i=1..n}, \quad G, T >$$

This simple exposition exploits a key design feature which is the hallmark of many modern parallel graph reduction architectures; there are no explicit communication channels! Instead, the graph G and the task pool T are both shared structures and all communication between the sequential G-Machines is mediated via these shared structures. The placing of a task descriptor (a "spark") in the task pool immediately makes this spark available to all other G-Machines, and the communication of intermediate results between G-Machines is achieved by overwriting graph nodes in place: thus, it is vitally important that these structures support indivisible test-and-set operations. This approach to communication is part of the "evaluate-and-die" model [135], [467].

A program is loaded as follows:

1. By constructing the graph of the primary expression in the heap G;
2. By placing a single task t in the task pool; and
3. By loading each G-Machine with an initial state which contains the G-code definitions for all the supercombinators in the program:

$$< \; <(),(),(),E,() >_{i=1..n} \quad G, t.() \quad >$$

The operation of each G-Machine is extended so that if the code C is empty a task is fetched from the task pool T: if both C and T are empty then the machine waits before trying again to fetch a task from the task pool.

When a task is first sparked, S contains just a single pointer to the node that requires evaluation, C contains the EVAL instruction, E contains the G-code for all the supercombinator definitions, and all other elements are empty: $< EVAL.(), s.(), (), E, () >^6$. The following transactions illustrate the polling of the task pool for work:

$$< \quad \{\ldots < (), S, V, E, D >_i \ldots\}, G, (c, s, v, e, d).T \quad >$$
$$\longrightarrow$$
$$< \quad \{\ldots < c, s, v, e, d >_i \ldots\}, G, T \quad >$$

$$< \quad \{\ldots < (), S, V, E, D >_i \ldots\}, G, () \quad >$$
$$\longrightarrow$$
$$< \quad \{\ldots < WAIT.(), S, V, E, D >_i \ldots\}, G, () \quad >$$

$$< \quad \{\ldots < WAIT.C, S, V, E, D >_i \ldots\}, G, T \quad >$$
$$\longrightarrow$$
$$< \quad \{\ldots < C, S, V, E, D >_i \ldots\}, G, T \quad > \quad \textit{(implied delay)}$$

When a program is loaded, all G-Machines race to access the task pool first — whichever wins gets the task and all the others execute WAIT instructions until another task becomes available in the task pool. It is worth re-emphasising that testing the task pool for the existence of a task and retrieving that task is an indivisible operation (i.e. at program start, only one G-Machine will see that a task exists in the task pool).

---

[6] Giving each task an entire copy of environment E may seem profligate, but it has the advantage of simplicity for this worked example. In a real implementation many threads on the same processor may share access to a single environment.

6.2 Worked Example: the G-Machine

Detecting Parallelism and Sparking Tasks. The machine described above only places a single task in the task pool; it would therefore evaluate a program sequentially, i.e. using a single G-Machine to execute a single task. For parallel evaluation, it is necessary for additional tasks to be identified and *sparked* (i.e. placed in the global task pool) so that they may be evaluated by the other G-Machines. This involves both partitioning (deciding which parts of the program could potentially be evaluated in parallel without compromising the non-strict semantics) and placement (exporting the responsibility for evaluating part of the graph to another processor — in this case, another G-Machine). We assume that the compiler has already partitioned the program and that this information is communicated via new SPARK instructions embedded in the G-code for each supercombinator as appropriate. We also assume a task-stealing [135], [225] approach to placement — sparks are deposited in the task pool and G-Machines "steal" these tasks when idle. Thus, the operation of the abstract machine only has to be extended with one new transition rule:

$$< \ \{\ldots < SPARK.C, s.S, V, E, D >_i \ldots\}, G, T \ >$$
$$\longrightarrow$$
$$< \ \{\ldots < C, s.S, V, E, D >_i \ldots\}, G, (EVAL.(), s.(), (), E, ()).T \ >$$

The pointer to the argument that is sparked is *not* popped from the argument stack: this is because the current task should be allowed to evaluate the argument itself if another task has not yet started to evaluate the argument (the "evaluate-and-die" model). If the sparked task is executed at some later time, it will find the graph node already in WHNF and will immediately terminate.

Task Suspension and Resumption. The final requirement for our worked example of a non-strict parallel G-Machine is that duplication of work should be avoided. Thus, where a subgraph is shared it is important to ensure that two or more tasks do not attempt to evaluate it at the same time. This is achieved by locking the non-WHNF graph nodes that belong to a subgraph that is currently being evaluated (there is no need to lock the WHNF nodes since they can never change). If another task attempts to evaluate a locked node, it is suspended by placing it (including its current state) back into the task pool. This is achieved with a simple extension to the UNWIND instruction (see below).

The implementation of blocking also requires a modification to the representation of any graph node that is not in WHNF; in our system, only the AP node may not be in WHNF (a $HOLE$ node may be overwritten with an AP, but before it is overwritten it cannot be shared by two separate tasks). We therefore modify AP nodes to support two versions AP (unlocked) and LAP (locked):

- A binary application node with pointers to function and operator, respectively ($APn_1 \quad n_2$);

- A locked binary application node with pointers to function and operator ($LAP n_1 \ n_2$).

The transition rules for UNWIND (when UNWINDing into an AP or LAP node) are now modified as follows:

$< \{\ldots < \text{UNWIND}.(), n.S, V, E, D >_i \ldots\}, \{n : \text{AP } n_1 \ n_2\} \cup G, T >$

$\longrightarrow$

$< \{\ldots < \text{UNWIND}.(), n_1.n_2.n.S, V, E, D >_i \ldots\},$

$\{n : \text{LAP } n_1 \ n_2\} \cup G, T >$

$< \{\ldots < \text{UNWIND}.(), n.S, V, E, D >_i \ldots\}, \{n : \text{LAP } n_1 \ n_2\} \cup G, T >$

$\longrightarrow$

$< \{\ldots < (), (), (), E, () >_i \ldots\}, \{n : \text{LAP } n_1 \ n_2\} \cup G,$

$(\text{UNWIND}.(), n.S, V, E, D).T >$

Though the above modifications may appear to be sufficient for UNWIND, there is one other case to consider; when UNWIND discovers a partial application it normally jumps to the continuation held on the dump, but now it must first unlock all the nodes on the spine that it has just traversed (using the subsidiary function unlock):

$< \{\ldots < \text{UNWIND}.(), \quad (n_1 \ldots n_k.()), V, \{f : (a, c')\} \cup E,$

$(c'', s'').D >_i \ldots\}, \{n_1 : FUNf\} \cup G, T >$

$\longrightarrow$ *if partial application*

$< \{\ldots < c'', \quad n_k.s'', \quad V, \{f : (a, c')\} \cup E, D >_i \ldots\},$

$\{n_1 : FUNf\} \cup G[unlock(n_1 \ldots n_k)], T >$

There is one further instruction that must be modified; the UPDATE instruction overwrites the root of a redex with its result, and must now also be modified to release any locked application nodes on the original spine of the redex that is being updated.

$< \{\ldots < UPDATEk.C, s.s_1 \ldots s_k.S, V, E, D >_i \ldots\},$

$\{s_k : \text{LAP } n_1 \quad n_2\} \cup G, T >$

$\longrightarrow$

$< \{\ldots < C, s_1 \ldots s_k.S, V, E, D >_i \ldots\},$

$\{s_k : \text{IND } s\} \cup G[unlock(s, s_1 \ldots s_k)], T >$

6.2 Worked Example: the G-Machine

Termination: Deadlock and Livelock. All designers of parallel systems need to reason about livelock and deadlock — it happens to be easier for parallel purely functional programming systems because termination proofs of the parallel system can be based on the theoretical termination proofs of the individual sequential systems (for proofs of the G-Machine see [359], [360]). However, we are not aware of any published proofs of parallel functional programming systems and so this should still be viewed as a research area.

Informally, the termination properties of the parallel G-Machine rely on the standard termination properties of graph rewriting plus the additional observations:

1. A conservative sparking strategy ensures that no task will evaluate an expression unless the value of that expression is essential to the evaluated result of the program;
2. The blocking mechanism ensures that no expression is evaluated more than once;
3. Since every task executes a normal (sequential) graph rewrite strategy, all tasks are guaranteed to terminate *unless* either the program specifies a non-terminating computation or the task is blocked as the result of accessing a locked cell;
4. When a task terminates, it always removes the locks on all cells that it has locked;
5. One or more tasks cannot block on themselves.

Observations 1 and 2 assure us that the parallel system does *no more work* than the sequential system (thus, livelock is avoided), whereas Observations 4 and 5 tell us that no task can block indefinitely (thus, deadlock is avoided). Observation 3 links into the standard guarantee of termination for normal order evaluation. Of course, deadlock *may* still occur if the programmer has specified that it will occur (for example, by defining an expression which relies on its own value).

Example Implementations. Nocker and Plasmeijer [429] reported experiments on a simulated parallel machine which used multiple G-Machine evaluators operating on a shared graph in a shared-memory environment. They used serial combinators, including simple complexity and strictness analysis, to identify coarse-grained parallelism, together with extensions to the G-Machine to support the spawning of parallel tasks. Communication between the sequential G-Machines was mediated entirely via the shared graph. A reservation system was used so that multiple tasks did not waste effort evaluating the same subgraph and new instructions were added to support task suspension. Thus, the parallel G-Machine state was represented as $< G, E, T, < O, C, S, V, D >_{i=1..n} >$, though individual G-Machine tasks followed transition rules based on $< O, C, S, V, G, E, D >$ as usual. They reported that the performance was encouraging and attributed much of the success to the use of serial combinators.

However, Nocker and Plasmeijer's parallel G-Machine incurred heavy overheads in terms of locking and unlocking graph nodes during reduction steps, as did the similar systems implemented by Augustsson [23] and Raber et al [482], [483]. The solution to this problem was found in the further development of the G-Machine; the Spineless G-Machine (see Section 6.3.2).

6.3 Analecta of Abstract Machines

We briefly describe a representative selection of abstract machines. In each case we present the published descriptions of the technology — invariably, these are simplified versions which are subject to significant optimisation in a real implementation.

6.3.1 The Four-Stroke Reduction Engine

The Four-Stroke Reduction Engine (4SRE) [135] was one of the earliest abstract machines for parallel graph reduction and was the first abstract machine to be implemented on the GRIP [465] and DIGRESS [133], [131] parallel systems. The machine operated by interpreting a graph of tagged binary application cells (using four interpretive "strokes" of the spine to reduce primitive function applications and two strokes to reduce applications of user functions), and was therefore slow by modern standards. However, it was a true supercombinator reducer and the progenitor of several novel features that are found in modern parallel functional programming systems:

- The "evaluate-and-die" model for transparent communication of results from child to parent tasks (though the term "evaluate-and-die" was not used until several years later — for example, in [460]);
- The encoding of the dump in the heap, rather than being held as an explicit stack (this technique is used in the $<\nu, G>$-Machine, the HDG machine, and DREAM, for example);
- Several novel concepts for throttling parallelism in the system, including the notion of *discardable sparks* and the preferential scheduling of resumed tasks;
- The transparent management of parallel tasks (including scheduling, and synchronisation such as blocking and resumption), with no explicit communication between tasks;
- The optimisation of holding suspended tasks in the heap, in a blocking-queue attached to a heap node, *without* incurring the space overhead of an additional field in every heap cell (by reusing the backwards pointer) — this technique has since been used in the $<\nu, G>$-Machine and the STGM, for example;

- A mechanism (involving the tagging of both function abstractions and application nodes) by which strictness information can be used to provide both static and dynamic partitioning;
- The expression of data structures using a sum-of-products representation (similar to the STGM) [129].

The 4SRE is a general mechanism that does not prescribe the representation of the supercombinators, nor the details of how a supercombinator application is instantiated. The arguments to a supercombinator application are made available on an argument stack, and the supercombinator bodies may be expressed as G-code sequences; it is therefore possible to devise a version of the 4SRE that is similar in many respects to a parallel G-Machine. The primary differences are that the 4SRE does not use a traversal stack, and that it encodes the dump in the heap (which is an optimisation that was not applied to the G-Machine until the development of the $<\nu, G>$-Machine and the HDG Machine several years later).

6.3.2 The Spineless G-Machine

The optimisations introduced in the G-Machine tend to be limited to improving the efficiency of individual reductions. By contrast, the Spineless G-Machine [102] extends the G-Machine by optimising the construction of graph between reductions. The resulting mechanism substantially reduces heap allocation and movement of data (and has many similarities with the Tim abstract machine — see below). The specific advance made by the Spineless G-Machine is that it only updates the graph when there is a risk that sharing might be lost if the update is not made. However, this requires a prior analysis by the compiler to detect which nodes are definitely not shared and which nodes may be shared. Though the Spineless G-Machine was sequential, it formed the basis for several parallel machines including the HDG Machine, PAM and the parallel STGM.

Consider the final action of the G-Machine after the root node of an application has been updated: if the result is a piece of graph, rather than a basic value, the machine UNWINDs into the graph that has just been constructed. This has two disadvantages:

1. The newly-created graph may immediately be entirely overwritten by yet more new graph as the result of the next reduction;
2. Furthermore, the G-Machine reads back onto the stack the graph that it has just created!

It is highly inefficient to construct graph only to overwrite it immediately, but it is an essential step to retain sharing (which is essential for efficient normal order reduction). This is because it is possible that the root node of an application is shared; if an update is not performed then there is a risk that the reduction might be performed more than once.

In a system where allocating nodes in the heap is much more expensive than allocation on the stack or in registers (this includes most architectures, since heap cells are almost always much bigger than stack objects), it would be more efficient to keep short-lived nodes on the stack. The Spineless G-Machine achieves this in three ways:

1. A (safe) compile-time analysis of the program detects sharing and adds a tag to those nodes that are (possibly) both shared and reducible (these are known as the possibly-updatable nodes). The analysis cannot provide an exact detection of sharing, but it can guarantee that those nodes without the tag are not updatable. This requires the G-Machine to be extended so that the graph can support "shared application" (SAP) nodes as well as application (AP) nodes[7];
2. A modification to the G-Machine compilation rules so that new instructions (such as those illustrated below) are generated;
3. A modification to the G-Machine instructions and transition rules so that the root node of an application is only updated if it is a SAP node.

The Spineless G-Machine provides a large performance improvement over the standard G-Machine, but there is still room for further improvement, for example, in the representation of heap objects and the run-time testing of tags.

6.3.3 Tim

Prompted by the poor performance of (an independently-developed variant of) the G-Machine which was initially used in the implementation of the Ponder compiler [188], Fairbairn and Wray introduced a three instruction abstract machine called "Tim" [189] which would evaluate supercombinators more efficiently than the G-Machine.

The motivation for Tim is similar to that which prompted the development of the Spineless G-Machine, i.e. that the G-Machine spends much of its time unnecessarily building and interpreting graph. Just like the Spineless G-Machine, Tim replaces interpretive graph construction and traversal with pointers to code which computes the desired result (whilst taking care to make updates in only those cases where an application is shared); thus, the spine of an application is held on the stack (Tim is "spineless") with similar performance advantages to the Spineless G-Machine. Tim and the Spineless G-Machine were developed independently at about the same time and with almost identical motivation; it is therefore not surprising that, despite a different approach, the two machines are very similar and indeed Burn et al. [102] show how the Spineless G-Machine can easily be converted into Tim and vice versa.

---

[7] Implementations of the G-Machine often additionally support a CAF tag for supercombinators with no arguments; in this case, the implementation would also need to be extended with a SCAF tag.

6.3 Analecta of Abstract Machines

Uniform Representation. Tim requires that the source program be transformed into a collection of supercombinators; a set of compilation rules (not discussed here) produces Tim code for each of the supercombinators to be executed by the Tim abstract machine. Perhaps the most important contribution of Tim is the fact that these compilation rules embody the idea that all objects, both unevaluated suspensions and (weak) head normal forms (including basic data values), have a uniform representation. The machine represents everything as a (code pointer, frame pointer) pair:

- For an unevaluated suspension, the code pointer points to the code for the supercombinator and the frame pointer points to a frame holding all the arguments for that supercombinator;
- A (weak) head normal form is is either a partial application or a basic data value:
  - A partial application is represented identically to an unevaluated suspension (see above) — the only difference is that it cannot be further reduced;
  - Basic data values use a code pointer to the special instruction Self, with the frame pointer providing the data. The Self instruction simply places the raw data value in a special register and then jumps to the continuation (which is held on the stack).

Disadvantages of Tim. The Tim concept of uniform representation had a decisive impact on abstract machine design, as can be seen in the STGM. However, despite an elegant design, Tim has many disadvantages, some of which are outlined below (some of these are provided by Fairbairn and Wray in their description of the machine):

Strictness: Tim is unable to accrue significant advantage from using strictness analysis to evaluate arguments early — this is because it would require new stack markers to be introduced to manage the early reduction of these arguments. Note that, this is despite its being a problem with the G-Machine that Tim was meant to solve! However, the Tim compiler is able to take advantage of strictness analysis to generate strict code for arguments in strict position, even if the application occurs in a lazy context.

Garbage collection: another disadvantage of Tim (one that it shares with most modern abstract machines for graph reduction) is that the garbage collector must be able to handle variable length objects (the frames). Furthermore, there is an added risk of space leaks, since the garbage collector may treat the frame as an atomic reference to all arguments in the frame, whereas in fact many of the arguments may not be required (though this could be ameliorated through the use of "frame-stubbing" — similar to the "stack-stubbing" used in the STGM [461]). However, two or more functions may share a frame pointer, and it is not clear which parts of the frame are used by which function.

Performance: not only do frames potentially waste space, but they also waste time as the frame is copied to the stack and back.

Indirections: in Tim, pushing an application onto the stack risks losing sharing. Thus, indirections cannot be performed through manipulation of pointers on the stack (as in the G-Machine) rather, Tim must push an instruction to enter the argument. If the same argument is pushed several times, a chain of indirections may be built up.

Parallel Evaluation: in a parallel setting, because the frame may contain far more arguments than are needed by a particular task, the familiar problem of shipping the transitive closure of the graph of the arguments becomes much worse. Furthermore, in a distributed-memory parallel setting, the usual problem of having to export pointers (make them pointers to remote objects) is also exacerbated.

In Tim, the dump contains update addresses and the stack contains continuation addresses: in the Spineless G-Machine, the update addresses are on the stack and the continuation addresses are on the dump. Tim's approach fits well with the idea of data-as-function (if a data item is a function, then it would expect to find its argument — the continuation — on the stack!).

6.3.4 The $<\nu, G>$-Machine

A more advanced version of the G-Machine has been specifically designed for non-sequential program execution — the $<\nu, G>$-Machine [25]. In particular, the $<\nu, G>$-Machine uses a packet-based approach to reduction, where the standard G-Machine stack is split into separate stack frames (one for each supercombinator application) and each stack frame is held in a packet in the heap; these packets[8] are essentially vector application nodes which have been extended with additional space for "temporaries" (which of course includes the aforementioned stack frame).

Holding the stack in the heap confers the great advantage that it is no longer necessary to flush the stack to the heap when a task blocks. Furthermore, data movement (of arguments and results) between the heap and the stack is reduced. The $<\nu, G>$-Machine restricts the size of each packet (similar to the HDG Machine); however, the $<\nu, G>$-Machine only uses a partial static analysis to determine the maximum stack depth (and therefore packet size) for a VAP node. Thus, unlike the HDG Machine, the $<\nu, G>$-Machine must sometimes create a bigger packet when the existing packet no longer has sufficient space.

Each packet contains a tag, a pointer to the supercombinator code, a dynamically updated "link" field, pointers to the argument graphs, and space for temporaries (including the stack). The "link" field is only active if control

---

[8] The $<\nu, G>$-Machine papers refer to these packets as "frames", yet they bear more resemblance to the packets of ALICE and Flagship than to frames of the Tim machine and so we prefer to use the term "packet".

6.3 Analecta of Abstract Machines

has arrived at the node, in which case it contains a pointer to the previously-visited packet. Thus, the backwards-pointing links define a stack of visited packets, of which the topmost is the packet where computation is currently taking place. This stack of visited packets is in fact a fragmented dump which is kept in the heap rather than in a contiguous stack.

Consider, as an example, the nested application (f (g e_1 e_2) e_3 e_4). The $<\nu, G>$-Machine graph for this example is given in Figure 6.7. The focus of control is moved about this graph structure in the usual leftmost outermost sequence.

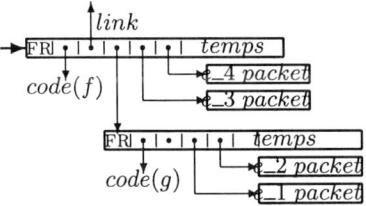

Figure 6.7. $<\nu,G>$ graph representation of f (g e_1 e_2) e_3 e_4

The state of a single machine is defined by the tuple $<\nu, G>$ (hence the name), where G is the graph that is being reduced and ν is the focus of control (the pointer to the packet that is being executed).

The packet tags hold various status flags, e.g. whether a packet is already reduced (in normal form) or is about to be reduced, or whether it has tasks waiting for its normal form, with the link pointer pointing to the first of these tasks.

The parallel version of the system is a collection of such $<\nu, G>$-Machines which share the graph, i.e. feature a shared memory. Program annotations for parallelism compile to instructions which place pointers to the relevant subgraphs into a task pool. Idle processors poll the task pool for work. Blocking and resumption is achieved as for the parallel G-Machine described previously, with a list of blocked tasks attached to a packet via the backwards link pointer.

There is no mutual exclusion with respect to accesses to the task pool itself, i.e. frame node pointers may get lost or be duplicated. However, neither of these are harmful as in the former case the graph is evaluated by the parent task, and in the latter case the locking mechanism prevents duplication of work. Although the published abstract machine places no upper bound on the number of tasks, an implementation would restrict the size of the task pool by discarding sparks as appropriate.

6.3.5 PAM

The Parallel Abstract Machine (PAM) [369] focused on message passing distributed-memory compiled graph reduction. Monomorphic functional programs were compiled into serial combinators, with evaluation transformers being used both to detect sites for parallel evaluation and to control the extent of evaluation for each task. Thus, this abstract machine was very close in design to the HDG Machine (see below). PAM was implemented in Occam on Transputers, with function code that was similar to G-code. Unfortunately, the overhead of interpreting this G-code led to poor absolute performance. However (or, perhaps, therefore) scalability/speedup results were good.

Each task was a complete serial combinator application represented as a tagged VAP plus additional task status information (a 7-tuple). The notification (rather than the evaluate-and-die) model of task communication was used, with the use of special indirection nodes containing a list of places to be notified when an exported task had been successfully evaluated by a remote processor. Unlike a parallel G-Machine, PAM constructed both local ("let") expressions and higher-order applications outside of the graph.

6.3.6 The HDG Machine

The HDG Machine [99], [337] is based on the Spineless G-Machine and has features in common with both the ABC Machine, PAM and the STGM. It uses evaluation transformers [98], [100] to determine which parts of the program can be evaluated concurrently. Activation records are kept in the heap rather than on the stack (i.e. it is a stackless architecture); this minimises task state, so that context switching is fast. It uses VAPs (Variable APplication nodes) to implement function calls; these VAPs have extended tags which include, in addition to the usual tag, (i) the evaluator, (ii) the pending list and (iii) a "being evaluated" flag.

Rather than test the LSB of the tag to determine whether a node is in WHNF before proceeding with further evaluation (this is the route taken by the $<\nu, G>$-Machine), the HDG Machine takes the approach of the STGM and simply jumps through the tag regardless (the "evaluator" part of the tag is always a code pointer). Despite causing two, rather than one, pipeline breaks, this produces more concise code without affecting performance on traditional hardware.

A specific contribution of the HDG Machine is its use of different evaluators so that evaluation to WHNF is not the only strategy that may be employed — this is the evaluation transformer model of parallel execution [98]. Furthermore, expressions only need to have their "being evaluated" tag set once and reset once — this is in contrast to other (previous) parallel reduction machines which require the tags of all the nodes on a spine to be set/reset; this advantage accrues directly from the use of VAPs.

The HDG machine differs from PAM in that:

6.3 Analecta of Abstract Machines   169

- An HDG task is created to evaluate an expression on the processor on which it resides, rather than sending all the task information to a communications processor which decides where the task should be evaluated;
- Compilation is to Transputer machine code, whereas PAM uses an Occam program to interpret abstract machine instructions (the use of Occam means that the heap cannot be shared amongst several threads and so must be implemented as part of the reduction processor);
- The HDG Machine requires no special cell type to deal with higher-order functions.

The HDG Machine was first specified in a functional language [361]; this specification was then used as a basis for a Transputer machine code implementation [337]. In the implementation, the source language is compiled into G-code, which is then macro-expanded into Transputer machine code.

6.3.7 The Spineless Tagless G-Machine

The Spineless Tagless G-Machine (STGM) [469], [461] builds on both the Spineless G-Machine, in that it constructs graph preferentially on the stack rather than in the heap, and Tim, in that it exploits the benefits of uniform representation for both functions and data. Thus, the key contributions of the STGM are:

1. That each closure (including data values) is represented uniformly, and therefore only one operation need be supported on closures regardless of their type or status — they may be entered via a jump to their code;
2. A detailed extension of this uniform representation to support user-defined data structures via vectored updates.

The above contributions are achieved through the use of a "tagless" representation for closures. Rather than reading the (small integer) tag of a node and using this to index a multi-way jump table, all tags are extended to be (normally 32-bit) pointers — now the evaluator simply jumps on the tag! The pointer can be updated dynamically to provide different code for the node once it has been evaluated to WHNF, or to provide variants for different parallel behaviour.

For data structures, the function which needs the value of the structure first sets up a table of code pointers (one continuation for each variant), loads a pointer to this vector onto the dump, and jumps to the code for the data structure — the data structure evaluates itself and jumps to the appropriate continuation.

The benefits of taglessness include:

- Cheap indirections are available (and are useful when performing updates) — they cost nothing when they are not present, and can be eliminated during garbage collection;

- Other exceptional conditions (such as detecting infinite loops and synchronising concurrent threads) can be handled in the same way;
- A variety of return conventions for constructors are possible, including vectored returns (explained above), and returning the components of the constructor in registers — the latter means that data values may not be allocated in the heap at all.

The main cost of taglessness is that in the common case (when an object turns out to be already evaluated), the STGM takes two forced jumps (the first being to an unknown destination) whereas the traditional G-Machine takes only one (conditional) jump^9.

Representation. In the STGM, all off-spine closures are VAPs (auxiliary functions are generated by the code generator in order to ensure uniformity). Every VAP has a single tag that is a code pointer, and data structures are functions (similar to Tim). This gives very fast case analysis and unshared objects need not be allocated in the heap. Furthermore, all base values are also represented as functions *with no loss of efficiency* — this means that all other enumeration types are handled efficiently.

In order to reduce the movement of values from the heap to the stack, the STGM keeps a closure's free variables in the heap and the function arguments on the stack. The STGM uses a segmented stack model and thus occupies a halfway position between the use of a single contiguous stack (like the G-Machine) and the use of heap-allocated stack frames (like the HDG and $<\nu, G>$-Machines). The free variables are identified through the use of the lambda lifting analysis, but rather than construct new functions the existing functions are extended with the additional information of their free variables through the use of a new lambda form. Functions may have embedded lambda expressions. However, name-capture problems do not occur, since the free-variable analysis allows all objects to be accessed via offsets into the free-variable list rather than via name lookup. This approach allows the STGM to benefit from some of the advantages of linked activation records, whilst also benefitting from some of the advantages of a contiguous stack. To our knowledge there has as yet been no systematic investigation of the tradeoffs involved.

The STGM has evolved over many years and in the most recent version the code pointer for a node is referred to as an "info pointer", since it points to (the address after the last item of) a table of alternative pointers for the different actions that might be performed on a node. This table is called the "info table" and immediately precedes the standard entry code (for evaluation of the node). Other actions which might be performed on a node include (i) the two garbage collection operations of evacuation and scavenging, (ii) debugging information, and (iii) flushing the closure into global memory (for a parallel implementation — specifically on GRIP). In some respects, the info

---
[9] Though vectored returns may save a jump.

6.3 Analecta of Abstract Machines

table is similar to the G-Machine, which attaches a tag to each heap cell and uses this tag to index a table of code pointers. However, the STGM generates a new info table for each binding in the program — this essentially eliminates the interpretive unwind used by the G-Machine.

STGM Machinery. The STGM was originally defined as:

- *The Heap:* a collection of VAP nodes, each being a closure (updatable nodes have at least 2 arguments, whereas WHNF nodes have at least 1 argument); *The Stacks:* as follows:
  - *The ArgStack:* which holds the arguments of the current function application (these are pointers into the heap);
  - *The VStack:* which holds unboxed basic values;
  - *The Dump:* which holds update information and return addresses for data objects;
- *The Registers:* as follows:
  - *HP:* The Heap pointer;
  - *SP:* The ArgStack pointer;
  - *SB:* The ArgStack base pointer (used to compute saturation of an application);
  - *DSP:* The Dump pointer;
  - *VSP:* The VStack pointer;
  - *RTag:* A temporary register (used to hold the constructor number);
  - *Node:* A temporary register (used to hold the pointer to the heap node under construction).

However, the definition of the STGM has evolved over time and later publications describe different policies for the usage of the three stacks (for example, which stack should hold basic values, which should hold update frames, etc.). As a result of such policy changes, the three stacks have also been renamed as the ArgStack, the Return stack, and the Update stack. In a concrete implementation, the latter two stacks may even be merged into one, to provide greater performance.

The STGM uses copying garbage collection, with an overflow check on entry to each basic block of code. Garbage collection is, however, quite tricky. For example, definitions (code) for both supercombinators and constant applicative forms (CAFs) are held outside the heap — CAFs may not be in WHNF and therefore may be overwritten with an indirection to point to an updated version in the heap. Unfortunately, it is difficult to detect pointers to CAFs if they occur within code. Thus, the STGM also keeps additional information with each node which details which supercombinators and CAFs are referenced by the node. The supercombinators and the CAFs are then evacuated along with the node (the supercombinators must be evacuated because they too might point to CAFs).

The Parallel STGM. Parallel operation of the STGM is much the same as any other parallel graph reduction system, in that the STGM abstract machinery only affects the sequential evaluation. See, for example, the GRIP implementation of the STGM [461], and Hwang et al.'s ν-STG Machine [293]. However, there is one feature of the STGM that can be co-opted rather elegantly for parallel evaluation, as follows.

When a closure is entered, its code pointer is overwritten with a "black hole" code pointer. In a sequential context, this is used to detect an infinite loop (any attempt to evaluate a "black hole" must mean that a closure is attempting to evaluate itself, which is one example of an infinite loop). In a parallel context, this mechanism can be used to (i) synchronise threads (the "black hole" code instead queues tasks on the node that is currently being evaluated), and (ii) implement indirections to closures on remote processors.

Another aspect of the STGM provides a challenge for parallel evaluation: STGM threads carry a significant amount of state, which increases the overhead of context switching suspended thread, and of thread migration. Furthermore, the amount of state held by an STGM thread varies during its lifetime. This complicates the business of thread management and the overall husbandry of the parallel machine, since either the migration of threads must be entirely outlawed or run-time decisions must be made based on knowledge of the amount of state carried by each thread.

It is, of course, possible to arrange complex schemes whereby a task that is transferred to another processor does not carry with it all of its state, but only, perhaps, the top stack frame of its state. The idea here is that if the older portions of state become necessary in order for evaluation to proceed they can be transferred at a later time. Such schemes can become arbitrarily complex and it is not at all clear how well they would work in practice, especially since a task may be suspended several times during its lifetime and since, at each resumption, it may be transferred to yet another different processor.

Some thought has been given to the possibility of reducing the amount of thread state that needs to be saved, for example by placing function arguments and temporaries in each VAP node (this would lead to a packet-based design, similar to the HDG Machine). However, this has not yet been achieved for the following reasons:

- The STGM is primarily aimed at supporting large applications using the Glasgow Haskell compiler — many such applications use separate compilation, and it is not yet clear how to do the required stacklessness analysis in the case of mutual recursion between separately compiled modules;
- Garbage collection is tricky, since it is necessary to know which items in the frame are pointers, and which are values.

6.3.8 The ABC Machine

The ABC Machine [345], [584], [430], [431], [334] was developed as part of the Dutch Parallel Reduction Machine project [36], [93], [587]. It is a stack-based

6.3 Analecta of Abstract Machines

abstract machine, similar in many respects to the STGM. Its name derives from its three stacks — the A stack (for arguments), the B stack (for basic values), and the C stack (for return addresses — this is essentially the dump). The A and B stacks are used for evaluating or building expressions, and for passing arguments to (or results from) functions.

In the ABC Machine, the heap contains a collection of nodes. Each node comprises two parts: (i) a fixed size header, which contains (amongst other things) a pointer to (ii) a variable size collection of arguments. In this way, variable size nodes may be overwritten without the need for indirections when the result turns out to be bigger than the original node. The disadvantage with this approach is that the arguments always have to be fetched via an indirection.

As well as the pointer to the arguments, the header contains a descriptor (so that different kinds of node can be distinguished — for example, partial applications can be distinguished from full applications) and a code pointer which contains the instructions for evaluating the node. During reduction, the code pointer can be changed, for example to implement "black holing" to detect infinite loops (see the STGM for an explanation of black holing).

The ABC Machine is defined [345], [431] as the eight-tuple:

$$< A, B, C, G, D, PC, PS, IO >$$

where:

- A is the Argument stack, used to reference nodes in the graph;
- B is the Basic value stack, used for efficient processing of basic values (also, keeping basic values separate from pointers significantly speeds garbage collection);
- C is the Control stack, to store and retrieve return addresses;
- G is the graph store containing the graph to be rewritten;
- D is the descriptor store, containing information about the symbols used;
- PC is the program counter;
- PS is the program store, containing the instruction sequence to be executed;
- IO is the input/output channel.

The ABC Machine has exhibited impressive performance [334], much of which can be attributed to the use of programmer annotations and compile-time information (such as type and strictness information) in order to generate efficient native code (simple macro-expansion is eschewed for this purpose). Furthermore, the stack-based architecture is both amenable to optimisation and fits well with conventional processor architectures.

In [345], Koopman et al. present outstanding results for the sequential ABC Machine, peaking at over 1M nfibs per second on a Mac IIfx. In a more extensive study using a T800 Transputer, Kesseler [334] compares the ABC machine to some other abstract machines:

- PAM (using a 20MHz T800) runs at 1.3K nfibs/second (interpreted);

- HDG (using a 25MHz T800) runs at 27K nfibs/second (macro-expanded);
- CCOZ (using a 20MHz T800) runs at 223K nfibs/second (true code generation);
- ABC (using a 25MHz T800) runs at 221K nfibs/second (true code generation).

Note, however, that the HDG Machine performs much better for larger programs that do not rely exclusively on stack manipulation (because the HDG Machine's stack is held in the heap).

The Parallel ABC Machine. The Parallel ABC (PABC) Machine is based on the sequential ABC Machine. It adopts a distributed-memory model and assumes that each processor (i) has its own local memory and (ii) can execute a variant of the sequential machine (or perhaps several such machines, to support multiple local threads). The graph is therefore distributed over a set of local heaps, with interconnection provided by a communication mechanism.

New threads are created through the use of {|P|} or {|I|} annotations in the source code. The former starts a remote thread, whereas the latter starts a local thread. Each local thread has its own ABC stacks, though threads on the same processor share a common heap. Blocking is achieved by overwriting the code pointer for a node with new code to manage the blocking queues. Communication between remote threads is achieved through the use of special *channel* nodes — evaluating a channel node causes a message to be sent to a remote processor and the result is returned as soon as it is available in head normal form (the requesting thread, meanwhile, suspends itself).

6.3.9 Eden, Pearl and DREAM

DREAM (Distributed Eden Abstract Machine) [84] provides distributed-memory parallel evaluation for programs written in the Eden language. DREAM is a variant of the STGM, with explicit processes and implicit communication channels. DREAM reuses several parts of the GUM (Graph reduction for a Unified Machine model) run-time system [573] for Glasgow parallel Haskell programs.

Eden is a variant of Haskell, with explicit coordination facilities for granularity and communication topology (though communication remains implicit, via head-strict lazy streams), plus support for non-deterministic merge and dynamic channel creation. Eden enables the programmer to express systems consisting of processes and interconnecting channels. In contrast to most other parallel systems based on lazy functional languages, message data is evaluated and transmitted eagerly in Eden.

Eden is translated into the Pearl intermediate language (a variant of the STG Language). The compiler technology is very closely based on the Glasgow Haskell Compiler, in order to benefit from optimised code. Run-time communications are achieved explicitly through MPI library calls. DREAM uses a combination of speculative and conservative evaluation — the language has all the hallmarks of laziness (e.g. infinite data structures), yet the implementation uses strict evaluation in order to achieve higher performance. The evaluation of Eden processes is driven by the evaluation of the outport expressions, for which there is always demand. This rule overrides normal lazy evaluation in favour of parallelism. There will be a separate concurrent thread of execution for each outport channel. Furthermore, each process immediately evaluates all *top level* process instantiations. This may lead to speculative parallelism and again overrules lazy evaluation to some extent, but speeds up the generation of new processes and the distribution of the computation.

DREAM supports processes with multiple inputs and multiple outputs, with one-to-one communication between outputs and inputs. Multithreading with a fair scheduler is used to support the concurrent computation of the multiple outputs for each process. Processes are closed entities and there is no need to support VSM for communication between processes — all such communication is explicit. This greatly simplifies global memory management.

The state of a DREAM process includes information common to all threads and the states of the threads. The shared part includes the heap and an inport table, because input is shared among all threads. The state of a thread comprises the state of a sequential abstract machine and a specification of the associated outport referencing the connected inport. The interface of a process is visible in the following way: the outports are associated to threads (runnable or blocked) and the inports are enumerated in the inport table.

Though the Eden/DREAM system currently runs in parallel for simple examples, no experimental results have yet been published.

6.4 Realisations of the Technology

The inefficiency of the early SK-combinator reduction machines was initially ascribed to a mismatch between the execution model of combinators and the execution model of conventional microprocessors. As a result, attempts were made to construct special-purpose hardware to execute these combinators — the microcoded SKIM and SKIM II systems [137], [550], both built at Cambridge, being prime examples.

Unfortunately, SK-combinator reduction proved to be very inefficient due to the small granularity of the reduction steps and the size of the programs when expressed in SK-combinator form (despite increasing the number and complexity of the primitive combinator set).

In this section we briefly introduce a selection of implementations of graph reduction that have been followed through to fully-working (though often prototype) systems on which real programs have been evaluated in parallel. We call these "realisations".

6.4.1 ALICE

The Applicative Language Idealised Computing Engine (ALICE) multiprocessor [163], [146], [490], built at Imperial College, London, is probably the first genuine parallel graph reduction machine. The graph is held in a global memory connected to the processors by a switching network, and scheduling is on the basis of individual reduction steps.

ALICE uses a packet-reduction model (which is similar in some respects to the $<\nu,G>$-Machine and HDG Machine which were developed much later) where the entire graph is represented by packets residing in one of a number of packet pool segments which comprise the global packet pool. Each packet is identified by its address and includes (i) a function to be executed, (ii) a variable number of function arguments (which may be pointers to other packets), and (iii) some control information (a status field, a reference count for reference-count garbage collection, and a signal list).

ALICE supports both an applicative order and a non-strict evaluation regime; the choice between the two can either be made by program annotations, or by taking non-strictness as the default option and generating applicative order annotations in the course of program transformations.

The ALICE abstract machine consists of:

1. A global packet pool comprising several packet pool segments;
2. Several processing agents;
3. An interconnection network.

Free agents select executable packets from the pool, test whether all required arguments have been evaluated and either request the reduction of the arguments or apply the respective reduction rules to construct the graphs for their right-hand sides.

To request that an argument be reduced, a demanding packet writes its identifier into the signal list of the argument packet(s) and the number of arguments it is waiting for into its own status field. Upon successful reduction, argument packets send signals to this effect to all packets listed in their signal list, and waiting packets become active again after having received as many such signals as specified in their status field. Thus, ALICE implements the *notification model*.

A prototype implementation of ALICE used 40 Transputers to realise the processing agents and the packet pools. They were connected by a fast multistage switching network to emulate a globally addressable packet memory with reasonable efficiency. The processors and memory units are built from Transputers running Occam, which imposes a layer of interpretation on many operations. As a result of these factors the machine is quite slow, but a lot has been learned from it [259].

In [490], Reeve reports performance figures of 16,000 nfibs per second at the maximum configuration of 42 boards (16 agent boards and 26 store

6.4 Realisations of the Technology

boards, giving a total of 32 processors). These results are for a *prototype* system where Transputers (interpreting Occam code) were used to emulate an ideal concrete architecture; nevertheless, this is a very disappointing figure (about four times slower than `nfib` running on a single sequential Transputer!). The poor performance of ALICE is probably also attributable to the very small granularity of the packets, and the consequently very high percentage overhead of communication and task management.

However, ALICE laid the foundations for the DACTL and Flagship projects, and ICL's investment in ALICE, GRIP and Flagship was eventually to culminate in a commercial product — the *Goldrush* parallel database engine.

Flagship. The Flagship project [593], [594] built upon earlier work on ALICE and the Manchester Dataflow machine [238]. A set of processor/memory pairs were interconnected by a delta network. Part of the project involved the architecture and organisation of the parallel graph reduction machine itself. Unlike GRIP (for example) the Flagship architecture provides a flat address space; Flagship is clearly targeted at a scalable architecture, and so the issues of scheduling and locality are of crucial importance. One aspect of this is that Flagship has a rather sophisticated mechanism for distributing work through the machine.

6.4.2 ZAPP

The Zero Assignment Parallel Processor machine (ZAPP) [383], developed at the University of East Anglia, comprises a network of Transputers connected as a virtual tree. Programmed in Occam, it utilises a simple divide-and-conquer method to obtain near-linear speedups.

ZAPP [105], [383], [385] was designed to exploit a process-tree interpretation of divide-and-conquer parallelism on a distributed-memory parallel architecture.

ZAPP consists of multiple communicating ZAPP elements, each consisting of a conventional processor with private memory. There is no shared memory: all communication between elements is by message passing (though sharing via pointers may be used within an element). Each element executes a ZAPP kernel (originally designed by Warren Burton [105]) which supports process creation and load balancing using local load information. At initialisation, the user program is broadcast to all elements and then the initial problem and data is injected into a single element. During execution, each element maintains three task pools (Pending, Fixed and Blocked); only tasks in the Pending pool may be offloaded (on request) to an element that is an immediate neighbour. Offloading a task requires that a complete descriptor of the task is copied from one element to another.

In 1987 McBurney and Sleep [383] demonstrated an implementation of ZAPP using Transputer arrays; however, this early implementation required modifications to be made to the ZAPP kernel for each new application. This early work was then extended to a more programmable form in collaboration with the Dutch Parallel Reduction Machine project [93], [587], the aim being to integrate the Clean language (later, Concurrent Clean) with the ZAPP architecture. In this new configuration (CCOZ), a ZAPP reducer implements an abstract machine similar to the G-Machine, though the ZAPP model uses a single stack and heap rather than the three stacks and one heap of, for example, the G-Machine and the PABC Machine. CCOZ uses Transputer process instructions to support concurrent graph rewriting directly. The Transputer's scheduling and communications mechanisms can therefore be used to synchronise reduction tasks. Dynamic control of parallelism is achieved through a mixture of localising fine-grain tasks and throttling task creation according to run-time load information. CCOZ adds two further forms of throttling: (i) two versions of code (parallel and sequential) are generated for each rule group and the appropriate versions chosen at run-time according to whether more or less parallelism is required; (ii) the scheduling of a new task is avoided if it can be in-lined by an existing task.

In [384], McBurney and Sleep report nfib performance on a Transputer implementation of ZAPP — nfib 35 exhibits a speedup of 39.8 on 40 processors, with an absolute speed of 1,017,924 nfibs per second. For comparison, a sequential implementation on a single Transputer has a performance of between 69,390 and 94,577 nfibs per second; thus, a 40-processor ZAPP is providing an absolute performance advantage of about 12 times normal sequential execution. Figures are also reported for matrix multiplication (relative speedups of between 18 and 26 for a 32-processor system), an heuristic search problem (which exhibited superlinear relative speedups for 12 processors), and a knapsack problem (which exhibited relative speedups which were roughly linear for 5 processors).

6.4.3 GRIP

GRIP (Graph Reduction In Parallel) [463], [135], [465], [136], [464], [251], [252], [250], [246], [130], [505] was a virtual shared memory (VSM) multiprocessor developed (initially at University College London, in collaboration with ICL and High Level Hardware Ltd.) specifically to execute functional languages using parallel supercombinator graph reduction. It consisted of up to 20 printed circuit boards, each of which contained four MC68020 processors (each with 1MByte RAM), an Intelligent Memory Unit (the IMU, containing 1M words each of 40 bits, plus a microprogrammable controller), and an asynchronous Bus Interface Processor (BIP), all connected by a fast local bus. The boards were interconnected by a very fast packet-switched bus (an IEEE P896 Futurebus). The (micro-)programmability of the IMUs enabled them to support complex operations rather than merely reads and writes (for example, they were used to support a task pool and associated operations).

6.4 Realisations of the Technology

Whilst at UCL, GRIP initially implemented the Four-Stroke Reduction Engine (4SRE). However, it was subsequently used to support developments in parallel G-Machine technology, culminating in the STGM. GRIP moved to Glasgow University in 1989, where the system software was further improved and GRIP was used for the execution of substantial applications. UCL's partnership with ICL facilitated interaction between the GRIP, DACTL and Flagship projects.

In [128], Clack reports a speedup of 17 with 20 processors running the simple `nfib` 33 benchmark, with absolute speed on a single processor being equivalent to a Sun 3/50 and a peak performance with 20 processors of 306,485 nfibs per second (roughly 2.7M reductions per second). In [251], Hammond provides performance graphs which (given that each tick on the graph represents 0.6 msec) demonstrate performance at that early stage of about 300K nfibs for 6 processors; this compared well with the contemporary sequential LML compiler's performance of about 50K nfibs. Further results may be found in [250], where a ray tracing application exhibited a speedup of 13 on 16 processors (absolute time was 105 seconds for a single processor). Later results on a ray tracing application studied by the FLARE project [505] show almost identical speedups but with markedly improved absolute performance (about three times faster). Hanna and Howells [254] report a speedup of 15 on 16 processors for a parallel theorem-prover, though Zhang et al. [604] report disappointing results for a parallel computational fluid dynamics problem, where a 17-processor configuration only gave a speedup of 3 and where absolute times were four times slower than on a conventional SPARC uniprocessor machine.

The attempts by the FLARE project to parallelise real applications motivated the use of simulation tools and the development of techniques for more precise control of parallelism within the machine.

6.4.4 Alfalfa and Buckwheat

The Alfalfa and Buckwheat systems, built at Yale University by Ben Goldberg [224], were implementations of compiled parallel graph reduction on an Intel Hypercube distributed-memory multicomputer (the iPSC, utilising 32 80286 processors) and an Encore Multimax bus-based shared-memory multiprocessor (utilising 12 10MHz NS32032 processors) respectively.

These two systems were broadly similar to GRIP, but differed in many details. Three key differences were:

- Task creation was decided at compile-time and therefore spawned tasks were *mandatory*;
- Children used explicit notification to reawaken their parents;
- Alfalfa used a distributed-memory model of computation (whereas GRIP used virtual shared memory).

Each graph node carried quite large amounts of administration information, so these two systems paid a fairly heavy overhead for parallelism regardless of whether the machine had capacity to exploit it.

Performance results were much more encouraging for the shared-memory Buckwheat implementation than for Alfalfa, with good relative speedups being obtained for all test programs. Five programs were used in the benchmark suite: pfac, queens, matmult, quad and quicksort. Buckwheat exhibited the following performance:

- pfac: increased from about 1.7 seconds on 1 processor to about 300 milliseconds on 12 processors (a speedup of 5.7);
- queens: increased from about 1.5 seconds on 1 processor to about 200 milliseconds on 12 processors (a speedup of 7.5);
- matmult: increased from about 1.5 seconds on 1 processor to about 200 milliseconds on 12 processors (a speedup of 7.5);
- quad: increased from about 2.6 seconds on 1 processor to about 400 milliseconds on 12 processors (a speedup of 6.5);
- quicksort: increased from about 4 seconds on 1 processor to about 2.25 seconds on 6 processors (a speedup of 6.5) and about 2.7 seconds on 12 processors (speedups of 1.8 and 1.5 respectively).

However, absolute speeds were slow — Vrancken [586] observes that they were about 10 times slower (at best) than C programs on an MC68000 home computer.

6.4.5 The $<\nu,G>$-Machine

The $<\nu,G>$-Machine has been implemented on a sixteen-node Sequent Symmetry [25]. The Symmetry is a bus-based coherent-cache multiprocessor with hardware support for shared memory. The $<\nu,G>$-Machine is well matched to this multiprocessor, since the processors have no explicitly addressable local memories and so could not efficiently support local run-time stacks.

Both local and global task pools were implemented; sparked tasks being added to the local pool, and propagated to the global pool if the system load were low. Idle processors would search the local pool first, otherwise the global pool. This implementation used a preemptive scheduling discipline based on time slicing to ensure that all tasks would proceed at about the same speed. To avoid contentions with respect to the allocation of heap space, all processors had control of their own memory area from which they would allocate as demand arose. A simple garbage collector was originally used, but a concurrent real-time copying collector was added later [501].

Performance measurements for three small benchmark programs showed the following performance gains on 15 processors:

- The Fibonacci numbers exhibited a relative speedup of about 8;

6.4 Realisations of the Technology

- The 10-queens problem exhibited a relative speedup of about 9.5;
- The Euler function for the first 1000 numbers exhibited a relative speedup of about 14.

Compared with the sequential G-Machine in the LML compiler, speedups for the above benchmarks are reported as 5, 6 and 11 respectively. The absolute time taken for nfib on a single processor (using the entire parallel machinery, including sparking) was 62.1 seconds (the sequential G-Machine in the LML compiler took 36.8 seconds).

Following further clarification from the author, we know that the timings above were for nfib 30. Thus we can calculate the following results:

- 26,796 nfibs/second on a single processor;
- 214,368 nfibs/second on 15 processors.

At full stretch that's 14,291 nfibs/second per PE, which is remarkably similar to the HDG Machine (58,689 nfibs/sec on 4 PEs) and early results for GRIP (306,485 nfibs/sec on 20 PEs). However, it should be noted that the $<\nu, G>$-Machine figures are for a system with no throttling — if throttling were to be introduced, the performance would improve substantially. Furthermore, nfib is a very unkind benchmark for packet-based machines such as the $<\nu, G>$-Machine, since nfib evaluation is primarily stack-based.

The deviation from linear speedup is likely to be due to (i) the overhead caused by mutual exclusions and process management, and (ii) bus saturation. Since the former is less than 10%, the latter is cited as a primary cause. The system may also have suffered from cache consistency problems as a consequence of storing and executing the frames directly in the heap.

6.4.6 FAST

The FAST project (1989–92) was a collaboration between Imperial College and Southampton University (with close links also to the University of Amsterdam), whose objective was to produce a highly-optimising compiler for a lazy functional language and to use this sequential compiler technology to exploit distributed-memory parallel computers using explicit control over process placement and partitioning.

The FAST system used Caliban [331] as a coordination language to provide partitioning and placement information in terms of a process network. FAST was primarily aimed at exploiting the static process networks so described [145].

The target architecture for the FAST system was the Meiko Computing Surface, containing 32 Inmos T800 Transputers. The individual processes identified by the programmer using Caliban were mapped 1:1 onto the available Transputers, with conventional sequential compilation and run-time support for each process. Each process was restricted with regard to its input and output configuration, so that these separate sequential processes could be connected to one another (using the topology specified using Caliban) and a single final result could be returned.

6.4.7 The HDG Machine

Kingdon et al. [337] describe a 4-processor Transputer implementation of the HDG machine. The hardware configuration was a network of four fully-connected T800-25 Transputer boards each with 16 MByte DRAM (an unusually large amount for T800 boards).

Three task pools were kept, as follows:

- *Active task pool:* tasks which may not be migrated;
- *Migratable task pool:* which is a double-linked list (tasks are exported from one end — oldest first — and made active from the other end — youngest first);
- *Blocked task pool:* which is distributed across the graph rather than being a separate pool (blocked tasks are attached to the nodes which caused them to block).

Processors which had no executable tasks polled their neighbours for work — if a remote task were found, it was immediately placed in the active task pool (to prevent nomadic tasks).

The system was garbage collected using Lester's distributed collector. This used copying collection locally and weighted reference counting globally (reference counting was not used locally because it cannot collect cycles and because it is perceived to be slower than copying collection where heap occupancy is low — the former takes time proportional to the number of free cells, whereas the latter takes time proportional to the number of live cells). However, interprocessor cycles were not collected.

Basic results were reported for small problems (only) as follows. All results were for four processors, and there was no lower bound on the granularity of tasks (if a lower bound were to be implemented, the results would be improved):

- *nfib:* 58,689 nfibs per second; relative to the parallel code on a single processor (1.284 seconds for `nfib 20` — 17,049 nfibs), the speedup was 3.4 with an efficiency of 86%;
- *tak:* relative to a single-processor time of 5.215 seconds, the speedup for `tak 18 12 6` was 3.6, with an efficiency of 91%.
- *queens:* `queens 4` gives a speedup of only 1.3, whereas `queens 6` gives a speedup of 2.8 (relative to single-processor times of 0.012 and 0.210 seconds respectively).

6.4.8 DIGRESS

DIGRESS (Distributed Graph Reduction Experiment Support System) [133], [131] is a distributed-memory parallel graph reduction system that utilises

6.4 Realisations of the Technology

a network of heterogeneous UNIX workstations. The aim of this work was to provide a component-based system that could be used as a research tool, specifically to support comparative investigations of run-time system components. Areas for investigation included abstract machine design, locality, multiprogramming, heterogeneity and integration with standard operating system services.

In order to achieve the reuse required of a component-based system, DIGRESS was coded (in C++) using an object-oriented approach; in particular, a robust class inheritance hierarchy was utilised. A major engineering effort in DIGRESS was the development of techniques to pack and ship graph and tasks between processors so that they could be unpacked by the receiver with their original type information preserved. Furthermore, these techniques were required to work reliably in a heterogeneous environment (both in terms of CPU architecture and in terms of the version of UNIX being used at each workstation). The success of this approach is evidenced by the ease with which the evaluation mechanism component was upgraded from the initial interpretive prototype (a distributed version of the 4SRE) to a version of the $<\nu,G>$-Machine.

DIGRESS was designed as a general purpose experiment support system and is therefore not aligned to any particular functional language. It was originally designed to accept FLIC (Functional Language Intermediate Code) [467], which is converted into CGF [448]; any required static analysis and optimisation is achieved as a CGF to CGF translation and the result passed to the DIGRESS loader. The system was instrumented with a parallelised version of Lexical Profiling [132] which collected and reported information in real-time (rather than collecting information for post-mortem analysis).

Absolute speeds for the initial prototype were slow (high performance was not a stated design aim): a single-processor system utilising an interpretive reducer ran at about the same speed as Miranda (and about 30 times slower with all debugging and profiling messages turned on). To demonstrate the benefits of a component-based system, the interpretive reducer was replaced with a $<\nu,G>$-Machine, but no absolute performance figures are available.

Despite (or, perhaps, as a result of) the poor absolute performance, good real speedups were reported for simple benchmarks (for example, `pfac` is reported to exhibit a speedup of 1.5 on two workstations and a speedup of 2 on three workstations). These speedups were obtained whilst full UNIX operating systems (including network traffic) were running on all workstations, with the DIGRESS processes being scheduled as normal (heavyweight) UNIX processes.

6.4.9 GUM and GranSim

GUM (Graph reduction for a Unified Machine model) [573] was designed and built with similar motivations to DIGRESS: to make parallel graph reduction more accessible to the wider community, and of more practical use. However, whereas DIGRESS aimed to be a component-based system for research, GUM aims to provide high performance. Furthermore, in order to achieve the aim of high performance, GUM is closely linked to the Glasgow Haskell compiler (GHC). GUM is augmented by the GranSim simulator (see below).

GUM is a highly portable parallel run-time system for GHC which uses an abstract message passing implementation, originally built around the widely available PVM communications harness, but which has recently been ported to MPI by Rita Loogen's group at Marburg, Germany, and which is capable of being ported easily to other systems as appropriate. This implementation has been used to obtain real speedups on both shared-memory machines and networks of distributed workstations. The system has also been used by researchers at Los Alamos National Labs., USA, to yield results for the 1,000-processor CM-5 massively parallel machine.

In GUM, the units of computation are called threads. Each thread evaluates an expression to weak head normal form. A thread is represented by a Thread State Object (TSO) containing slots for the thread's registers and a pointer to heap-allocated Stack Objects (SO). Each processor element (PE) has a pool of runnable threads.

In order to transfer a subgraph from one PE to another, GUM uses sophisticated packing and unpacking algorithms, which guarantee that all the links back to the original graph are maintained and that the duplication of work is avoided. GUM uses a passive work distribution scheme, where PEs looking for work send out requests for work.

An integral part of the GUM parallel program development strategy, which has been tested on several medium and large scale applications, is the use of an accurate, tunable simulator: GranSim [247]. The simulator can work at several levels of abstraction, from highly idealised to a quite accurate simulation of a real architecture, having been calibrated against GRIP and other real parallel machines. Since it uses exactly the same compiler and run-time technology (indeed, shares much of the same code) as the actual GUM system, the results are highly credible, and exploit all optimisations that apply in the real parallel system. The simulator deliberately abstracts the communication system, allowing simulation of a wide range of parallel machines. Simulation results have been used not only to develop applications, but also to guide the development of the GUM run-time system. This system has been used at various institutions, including Durham University, York University, the University of Tasmania, Australia, and the Universities of Tokyo and Kyoto, Japan.

The advantage of using a simulator is three fold: firstly, it allows a range of parallel machine configurations to be explored, including ones not yet designed or built; secondly, it allows the use of robust visualisation and performance analysis tools on commonly available workstation environments; thirdly, statistics can be gathered, and interesting phenomena investigated, without the risk of perturbing the systems that are under investigation. This

6.4 Realisations of the Technology

is important since parallel behaviour can be time critical. The availability of the portable GUM implementation allows us to check these simulation results against real parallel behaviour on a variety of systems ranging from shared-memory multiprocessors to distributed networks of workstations.

GranSim has a number of unusual characteristics that make it especially suitable as a test instrument. It has been designed to model execution and communication in an accurate way without being tied to a particular computer architecture: both communication and processing costs are tunable to allow different architectures. Furthermore, since it instruments the same machine code that is output by the GUM parallel machine rather than simulating evaluation, there is no danger of obtaining unrealistic results due to unanticipated compiler optimisations or other artefacts. GranSim costs are for code which is identical to that which would be run on the real parallel machine. The GranSim run-time system also accurately emulates the corresponding GUM system. The primary difference between GUM and GranSim is that in the latter, communication is simulated using an event-driven virtual message passing system, which interacts directly with a scheduler built on the Glasgow Concurrent Haskell kernel.

6.4.10 The Parallel ABC Machine

Kesseler [334] reports a Transputer implementation of Concurrent Clean utilising the PABC Machine. In Kesseler's version of the PABC Machine, speculative parallelism is supported such that the resources allocated to speculative tasks are controlled with a counter which decreases according to the resources used by the task — when the limit of resources allocated to the task is reached, the task is terminated with the subgraph left in a partially reduced state (whose reduction may be completed at a later time if the subgraph turns out to be needed).

Reported performance on a single T800 processor is 221K nfibs/second, with speedups of 8 and 11 for 16 and 32 processors respectively (i.e. 1.768M and 2.431M nfibs/second). A range of other small benchmark programs were also tested: absolute performance remained good, but speedups were generally disappointing. This was ascribed to load imbalance.

6.4.11 Tabulated Results

Table 6.1 compares simple nfib ratings for the different realisations, where available. Of course, nfib should *not* be taken as a comprehensive evaluation of system performance. It is especially unkind to abstract machines that keep the stack in the heap (such as the $<\nu, G>$-Machine and the HDG Machine); such machines will exhibit much better comparative performance on larger applications.

Unfortunately, it is not easy to undertake a fair comparison of the different technologies utilised in the different realisations. Clearly, there is often a difference in the underlying computer hardware, which can significantly affect performance. Less obvious is the fact that these realisations have been constructed with varying amounts of funding — often (though not always) high performance is achieved after many months of benchmarking and tuning of an implementation, and the ability to do this depends on the available project funds. Furthermore, the published results are often not directly comparable because of different parameter settings; for example, one system might set a lower bound on task granularity whereas another system might not (ignoring tiny tasks can have an enormous beneficial impact on performance).

Despite the obvious need for an objective assessment of parallel functional programming technology, we know of no systematic attempt to undertake comparative benchmarking. In part, this must be due to the large potential cost of such work.

Table 6.1. Nfib performance comparison — $Knfibs/s$ ($Knfibs/s$ per PE)

PEs: System	4	6	15	20	32	40
ALICE					16 (0.5)	
ZAPP						1,018 (25.4)
GRIP (old)				306 (15)		
GRIP (new)			300 (50)			
$<\nu, G>$-Machine			214 (14)			
HDG Machine	59 (15)					
PABC					2,431 (76)	

6.5 Conclusion

This chapter has addressed the implementation technology for non-strict functional languages, including Wadsworth's *graph reduction* technique, SK combinator reduction, and *supercombinator* reduction. The development of abstract machine technology for both lazy (sequential) and non-strict (parallel) supercombinator reduction has been presented, and the differences between the machines (and the importance of those differences) have been discussed. In particular, various implementation issues have been highlighted,

6.5 Conclusion

such as the management of parallel tasks and the management of data in a parallel system.

A selection of abstract machines has been presented, from the Four-Stroke Reduction Engine, via variations of the G-Machine (the Spineless G-Machine, the $<\nu, G>$-Machine and the Spineless Tagless G-Machine) to the PABC Machine. Finally, a selection of *realisations* of those abstract machines has been presented, together with performance figures where available and a comparison of *nfib* ratings for a subset of those systems.

In the 1980s, there was considerable excitement about the prospect of "painless parallelism" through the use of functional programming languages and the exploitation of explicit parallelism. A decade later, it became clear that whilst the goal might be a painless system for parallel programmers, the achievement of that goal would be far from painless for the researchers who must develop the underlying technology:

- Whereas in the early 1980s it was thought that novel architectures would be required, it became clear that such architectures could never keep pace with the development of conventional chip technology;
- Furthermore, even if it were possible to keep pace with changes in hardware technology, it became clear that novel architectures do not compensate for poor compiler technology;
- Whilst functional programming compiler technology is now mature and offers high performance, and is an essential element of a high-performance parallel processing system, this does not address the fundamental problems of organising parallel computation to achieve the optimum parallel efficiency.

What is now abundantly clear is the following: to take a general purpose program, automatically to partition that program into parallel threads, automatically and dynamically to manage both those threads and their associated data within a parallel system, and to achieve high efficiency from that parallel system, is a significant intellectual challenge. Whilst encouraging results have been achieved, far more work is required to harness the full power of parallel functional programming.

Part II

Current Research Areas

7. Data Parallelism

John O'Donnell[1]

7.1 Introduction

The idea behind data parallel programming is to perform global operations over large data structures, where the individual operations on singleton elements of the data structure are performed simultaneously. In the simplest case, for example, this means that a loop over an array is replaced by a constant-time aggregate operation. In order to introduce parallelism, the programmer thinks about the organisation of data structures rather than the organisation of processes. This leads directly to two of the most appealing benefits of data parallelism:

- The program can be quite explicit about parallelism , through the choice of suitable data structure operations, while at the same time it is structured like an ordinary sequential program. Thus data parallelism allows efficient usage of a parallel machine's resources, while providing a straightforward programming style that avoids many of the difficulties of task-oriented concurrent programming.
- The parallelism can be scaled up simply by increasing the data structure size, without needing to reorganise the algorithm. Typical data parallel programs can use far greater numbers of processors than typical task parallel programs.

The most popular data parallel languages are based on Fortran and C. It is necessary to add special support for data parallelism, leading to dialects such as High Performance Fortran (HPF) . However, functional languages such as Haskell are more suitable, for several reasons that will become clear later in this chapter. One interesting advantage is that data parallel programs can be written directly in Haskell without making any modifications to the language, although special purpose functional data parallel languages also exist. In this chapter, Haskell will be used to specify algorithms, to implement them, and to reason about them.

A typical data parallel operation that doubles each element of a vector might be expressed functionally by:

$ys\ =\ map\ (2*)\ xs$

This would be expressed in imperative languages with a loop that performs the computation explicitly on every element of the data structure:

---

[1] Department of Computing Science, Glasgow University, UK.

for $i := 1$ **to** n **do**
$\quad y[i] := 2 * x[i]$

The crucial difference between these program fragments is that the first one expresses an *aggregate* computation, while the second one performs *word-at-a-time* computations on the individual elements of the data structure. The data parallel style corresponds more closely to the programmer's intuition of "doubling all the elements", making it more concise and easier to read. In particular, the data parallel version does not rely on explicit indices, which account for most of the complexity of the conventional program.

The *map* program is already inherently parallel, but the **for** loop program specifies irrelevant sequencing which the compiler must remove before the computation can be parallelised. This sequencing is not inherent in the problem, and it doesn't make the program easier to write, read or understand; it is there simply because traditional languages have no other way of expressing aggregate computations. Many of the "optimisations" of compilers for scientific computation amount to nothing more than removing irrelevant sequencing forced on the programmer by inexpressive languages.

7.2 Data Parallel Combinators

The essence of data parallel computing is to apply a basic operation f to all the elements of an aggregate data structure. This is exactly the kind of computation that higher-order functions are good at expressing; it is possible to express the data parallel operations with a fixed set of built-in language features, but higher-order functions offer several advantages :

- A wide variety of parallel operations can be expressed using just the one language mechanism of higher-order functions, so the same programming language can be used for different architectures;
- The user can define new higher-level parallel data structures and operations, which may simplify algorithms. The higher level operations are used in exactly the same way as the primitive ones (if any);
- All the normal tools for reasoning about functions can be applied to data parallel programs; special methods are not required.

The simplest parallel data structure is the *finite sequence*, which corresponds to a vector, array or list whose elements are distributed across the processors of a distributed-memory multiprocessor. A variety of combinators will be defined to perform aggregate computations over all the elements of a finite sequence in parallel.

A finite sequence xs of length k is written as $[x_0, x_1, \ldots, x_{k-1}]$. Assuming that we have at least k processors, the data structure is represented by placing x_i in the memory of processor P_i; it is *not* represented as a linked list with pointers. If $k < N$ then we must place N/k data elements in each

7.2 Data Parallel Combinators

processor, and the algorithms will be slowed down by that factor. Another way of looking at it is to say that with a fixed number of processors N, we get a speedup of only N, but with an unlimited number of processors the speedup is proportional to the data structure size k. It is straightforward to handle cases where $k > N$, so for simplicity we will assume here that $k = N$.

Since functional languages provide good support for lists, it is common practice to uses the built in list type to represent finite sequences. When doing that, however, it is important to remember that such lists must have finite length, do not allow sharing of sublists, and will be computed strictly. It is also possible to use conventional lists for data parallel computing.

7.2.1 The Nearest Neighbour Network

The simplest data parallel operation is to apply a function f on each element x_i of a finite sequence xs, resulting in a new finite sequence ys. This is the most characteristic machine operation provided by SIMD computers, and we express it in a program with the equation:

$$ys = map \ f \ xs$$

The meaning of map is the same as the corresponding Haskell function:

$$\begin{aligned} & map \ :: \ (a \to b) \to [a] \to [b] \\ & map \ f \ [\,] \ = \ [\,] \\ & map \ f \ (x:xs) \ = \ f \ x \ : \ map \ f \ xs \end{aligned} \qquad (7.1)$$

This standard definition suggests a sequential implementation, which traverses the list and performs the $f \ x$ applications one at a time. However, the data parallel map is *not* implemented by a recursive list traversal; indeed, the finite sequences xs and ys are not represented as ordinary lists—with boxes and pointers—at all. For data parallel programming, we view this definition only as a specification of the semantics, not as an implementation. and it is best to think of map as a primitive function implemented by the parallel architecture, like $+$. Thus we will use the definition for equational reasoning but we will not be compiling it with GHC or some other Haskell compiler and then running the object code on a parallel machine.

The processors in a parallel computer are connected by an interconnection network which makes certain patterns of communication particularly efficient. Our aim is to define combinators reflecting the architecture's capabilities, allowing the programmer easy access to the hardware. The simplest SIMD architectures provide a linear array of processors with nearest-neighbour communication, giving each processor a direct connection to its left and right neighbour. Communications in such an architecture are called shifts. The simplest case is a unidirectional communication. When the system shifts information to the right, each processor must read a value from its left neighbour, while sending its own state to its right neighbour. The shiftr combinator describes the result:

$$\begin{aligned}&\textit{shiftr} \;::\; a \rightarrow [a] \rightarrow ([a], a)\\&\textit{shiftr}\; a\; [\,] \;=\; ([\,], a)\\&\textit{shiftr}\; a\; (x:xs) \;=\; (a:xs',\; x')\\&\quad\textbf{where}\; (xs', x') \;=\; \textit{shiftr}\; x\; xs\end{aligned} \qquad (7.2)$$

The most general communication operation supported by the nearest neighbour topology over finite sequences is the bidirectional shift operation. Each processor starts out with a pair (xa,xb) in its local state; it sends xa to its right neighbour and xb to its left neighbour. Meanwhile, the processor also receives incoming messages from its neighbours which it stores locally as a pair. Boundary inputs must be supplied so that the leftmost processor has a left input, and the rightmost processor has a right input. The type of left-to-right messages is a, while right-to-left messages have type b.

$$\begin{aligned}&\textit{shift} \;::\; a \rightarrow b \rightarrow [(a,b)] \rightarrow (a,\; b,\; [(a,b)])\\&\textit{shift}\; a\; b\; [\,] \;=\; (a, b, [\,])\\&\textit{shift}\; a\; b\; ((xa, xb):xs) \;=\;\\&\quad \textbf{let}\; (a', b', xs') \;=\; \textit{shift}\; xa\; b\; xs\\&\quad \textbf{in}\; (a',\; xb,\; (a, b'):xs')\end{aligned} \qquad (7.3)$$

For example, if there are two processors containing (1,2) and (3,4), then a shift with boundary inputs of 0 and 100 is computed as follows:

$$\textit{shift}\; 0\; 100\; [(1,2), (3,4)] \;\Longrightarrow\; (3,\; 2,\; [(0,4), (1,100)]) \qquad (7.4)$$

7.2.2 Example: The Heat Equation

A simple example of data parallel computation, which requires only the map and shift combinators, is the parallel solution of the one-dimensional heat equation [439]:

$$\frac{\partial u}{\partial t} = \frac{\partial^2 u}{\partial x^2}, \quad \text{for } x \in (0,1) \text{ and } \; t > 0.$$

The numerical solution represents the continuous interval as a linear sequence of n discrete gridpoints u_i, for $1 \leq i < n$. The solution proceeds in discrete timesteps, taking the old u vector and boundary inputs u_0 and u_n, and computing the new u' vector at the next timestep using the equation:

$$u'_i = u_i + k/h^2[u_{i-1} - 2u_i + u_{i+1}].$$

The chief point to notice about this equation is that the new value u'_i at position i depends on the values at the previous timestep of position i and the neighbouring positions $i-1$ and $i+1$. The boundary conditions specify the left input to gridpoint 1 and the right input to gridpoint $n-1$. In order to compute

7.2 Data Parallel Combinators

the vector at the next timestep, we will first perform a `shift` operation so that each processor obtains the current u values of its neighbours; then we will perform a `map` operation to compute the new gridpoint values locally. Both the communication step and the computation step take constant time.

$$
\begin{aligned}
&step \;::\; Float \to Float \to [Float] \to [Float] \\
&step\ a\ b\ xs\ = \\
&\quad \textbf{let}\ ps\ =\ map\ f\ xs \\
&\qquad f\ x\ =\ (x, x) \\
&\qquad (a', b', qs)\ =\ shift\ a\ b\ ys \\
&\qquad rs\ =\ map2\ g\ xs\ zs \\
&\qquad g\ (x, (a, b))\ =\ (k/(h*h))*(a - 2*x + b) \\
&\quad \textbf{in}\ rs
\end{aligned}
\qquad (7.5)
$$

The program starts with an initial value for the spatial grid vector `xs`, and it iterates the `step` function in order to compute the changing state of the grid over time. With an unlimited number of processors, each `step` takes a small fixed amount of time. This is not an unreasonable assumption, since small processors suffice for the map and shift operations, for example, both the MPP and CM-200 systems used very simple processors, so that many of them would fit on a single chip. Typical CM-200 installations had from 16k to 64k processors, providing ideal support for fine-grain, data parallel, scientific computations.

7.2.3 Combining Computation with Communication

The simple combinators we have considered so far make a complete separation between computation (the map functions) and communication (the shift functions). A more interesting class of combinators combines computation with communication. This section introduces the simplest such combinators—the family of fold and scan functions—and the following section shows one way to parallelise them.

The fold functions defined in Section 2.2.3 combine all the elements in a finite sequence in order to produce a singleton result, using an operator f which combines just two arguments. There are several ways to organise this computation. When performed sequentially, one can work from the left using `foldl` or from the right using `foldr`. Furthermore, we can require that the finite sequence contains at least one element (`foldl1` and `foldr1`) or we can provide a boundary input (`foldl` and `foldr`). These functions are part of the standard repertory of functional programming, and they appear in the Haskell Standard Prelude.

$$
\begin{aligned}
&foldl\;::\;(a \to b \to a) \to a \to [b] \to a \\
&foldl\ f\ a\ []\ =\ a \\
&foldl\ f\ a\ (x:xs)\ =\ foldl\ f\ (f\ a\ x)\ xs
\end{aligned}
\qquad (7.6)
$$

$$foldl1 :: (a \rightarrow a \rightarrow a) \rightarrow [a] \rightarrow a$$
$$foldl1 \ f \ (x : xs) = foldl \ f \ x \ xs \qquad (7.7)$$

While folding a function over a list, using any of the sequential definitions above, a sequence of intermediate results is computed. For example to fold the function ($\oplus$) (which is written as an infix operator, to make the expressions more readable) over the sequence $[x_0, x_1, x_2, x_3]$, starting from the left with boundary value a, the `foldr` function works as follows:

$$\begin{aligned}
& foldl \ f \ a \ [x_0, x_1, x_2, x_3] \\
& = foldl \ f \ (a \oplus x_0) \ [x_1, x_2, x_3] \\
& = foldl \ f \ (a \oplus x_0 \oplus x_1) \ [x_2, x_3] \\
& = foldl \ f \ (a \oplus x_0 \oplus x_1 \oplus x_2) \ [x_3] \\
& = foldl \ f \ (a \oplus x_0 \oplus x_1 \oplus x_2 \oplus x_3) \ [] \\
& = a \oplus x_0 \oplus x_1 \oplus x_2 \oplus x_3
\end{aligned}$$

Sometimes it is useful to obtain these intermediate results and put them into a finite sequence. This is the purpose of the `scanl` function:

$$\begin{aligned}
& scanl \ (\oplus) \ a \ [x_0, x_1, x_2, x_3] \\
& = [a, \quad a \oplus x_0, \quad a \oplus x_0 \oplus x_1, \quad a \oplus x_0 \oplus x_1 \oplus x_2]
\end{aligned} \qquad (7.8)$$

The `scanl` function takes the same arguments as `foldl`, but returns a list of results rather than a singleton result. It returns a list of partial `foldl` results over a sequence of prefixes of the argument `xs`, where the lengths of the prefixes increase starting from 0.

$$\begin{aligned}
& scanl :: (a \rightarrow b \rightarrow a) \rightarrow a \rightarrow [b] \rightarrow [a] \\
& scanl \ f \ a \ xs = \\
& \quad [foldl \ f \ a \ (take \ i \ xs) \ | \ i \leftarrow [0 \ .. \ length \ xs - 1]]
\end{aligned} \qquad (7.9)$$

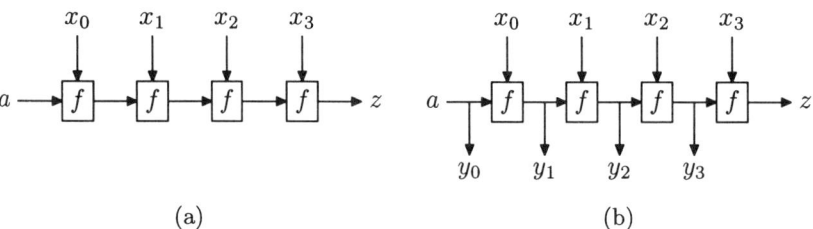

(a)   (b)

Figure 7.1. *scanfoldl f a xs*

There are many alternative formulations of `scanl`. The version that appears in the Haskell Standard Prelude tacks on the complete `foldl` result

7.2 Data Parallel Combinators

at the end. This definition is inimical to data parallel programming, for two reasons: (1) realistic data parallel programs will repeatedly perform parallel operations over finite sequences, so it is simpler if the operations preserve the sequence length; (2) practical parallel implementations of these functions sometimes end up with the complete fold result in a different part of the machine than the elements of the scan result. Another variant of scanl preserves the sequence length, like the definition given here, but it omits the boundary input a at the beginning of the sequence, including instead the complete fold result at the end. That variant is inferior on both theoretical and practical grounds.

$$\begin{aligned}& scanfoldl \ :: \ (a \to a) \to a \to [b] \to [a] \\ & scanfoldl \ f \ a \ xs \ = \ (foldl \ f \ a \ xs, scanl \ f \ a \ xs)\end{aligned} \quad (7.10)$$

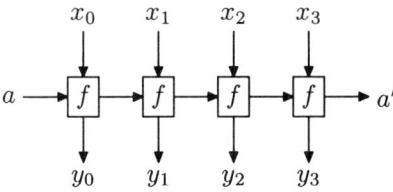

Figure 7.2. Recursive definition of *mscanl*

All the "from-left" functions defined above have duals that transmit information across the sequence from the right. The foldr and foldr1 functions are standard, and the scanr function is analogous to scanl.

$$\begin{aligned}& foldr \ :: \ (b \to a \to a) \to a \to [b] \to a \\ & foldr \ f \ a \ [\,] \ = \ a \\ & foldr \ f \ a \ (x : xs) \ = \ f \ x \ (foldr \ f \ a \ xs)\end{aligned} \quad (7.11)$$

$$\begin{aligned}& foldr1 \ :: \ (a \to a \to a) \to [a] \to a \\ & foldr1 \ f \ (x : xs) \ = \ foldr \ f \ x \ xs\end{aligned} \quad (7.12)$$

$$\begin{aligned}& scanr \ :: \ (b \to a \to a) \to a \to [b] \to a \\ & scanr \ f \ a \ xs = \\ & \quad [foldr \ f \ a \ (drop \ (i+1) \ xs) \quad | \quad i \leftarrow [0\mathbin{..} length \ xs \ - \ 1]]\end{aligned} \quad (7.13)$$

In ordinary functional programming, where the lists are really lazy lists with sharing, there are subtle performance tradeoffs between foldl and foldr. Sometimes foldl is faster, sometimes foldr is faster, and sometimes it makes no difference. Figuring out which is the case in a non-strict language requires a good understanding of graph reduction and lazy evaluation, and this is a notoriously tricky problem for beginners in functional programming.

In data parallel programming, where the lists are really strict finite sequences without shared substructures, there is no performance difference between the from-left and from-right functions. Sometimes the problem specification will require one or the other; if not, the programmer can use whichever seems clearer.

Just as the bidirectional shift combinator generalises the unidirectional shiftr and shiftl operations, there are bidirectional versions of the fold and scan families. Rather than presenting the entire (rather large) family of fold and scan functions, we will just give the most commonly useful one: mscan, the bidirectional mapping scan. This combinator combines left-to-right and right-to-left communications with local computation.

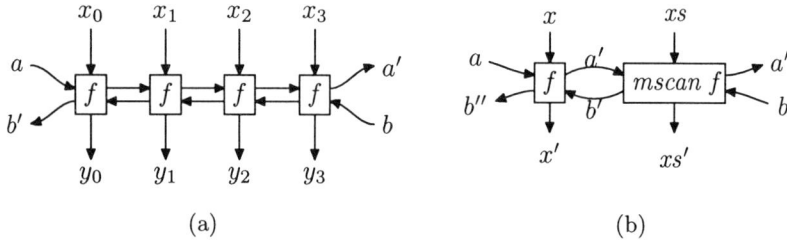

Figure 7.3. *mscan f a xs*

The mscan operation causes each processor to read a message from each of its input ports, to compute a new local state, and to send a message to each of its output ports. The first argument to mshift is the processor behaviour function f; the next two arguments are the boundary input messages; the last argument is the finite sequence of processor states; and the result contains the boundary output messages as well as the finite sequence of new processor states.

The types of left-to-right and right-to left messages are a and b respectively, c is the type of a processor state before the mshift operation is executed, and d is the type of the resultant processor state after the operation has completed. During the mshift, each processor uses the same behaviour function f, which takes three arguments (the two incoming messages of types a and b, and the local state of type c), and it produces the new local result of type d.

```
mscan :: (a->b->c->(a,b,d)) -> a -> b -> [c] -> (a,b,[d])
mscan f a b [] = (a,b,[])
mscan f a b (x:xs) =
  let (a',b'',x')  = f a b' x
      (a'',b',xs') = mscan f a' b xs
  in  (a'',b'',x':xs')
```

7.2.4 Example: Maximum Segment Sum

Published examples of the fold and scan functions are often trivial; for example, you can find the maximum of a sequence of numbers xs by computing fold max xs, and you can sum up the sequence with fold (+) xs. However, such examples are quite misleading; the scan functions achieve their full potential only with more complex sequence types and base functions. Examples of substantive algorithms using scans include parallel list manipulation [435], the comb communication algorithm [437], carry lookahead [440] and ESF arrays [436]. Here we present only an easy example: a solution to the maximum segment sum problem. We will emphasise the conceptual question—how to write the program—rather than the formal question—how to derive it or prove its correctness.

The problem is to take a list of numbers, and to find the largest possible sum over any segment of contiguous numbers within the list. If all the numbers are non-negative, then the problem is trivial: just take the sum of all the numbers. However, if a run of positive numbers is fenced in by negative ones, what should we do? Sometimes including the negative endpoints just makes the result worse, as in:

$$[-500, 1, 2, 3, -500, 4, 5, 6, -500]$$

Here, the maximum segment sum is $4 + 5 + 6$ because inclusion of either -500 makes the sum smaller, and the other segment sum $1 + 2 + 3$ is also smaller. However, sometimes a segment sum can be improved by including some negative numbers, which allows you to get through to some positive numbers. For example, consider this sequence:

$$[-500, 3, 4, 5, 6, -9, -8, 10, 20, 30, -9, 1, 2]$$

Here, the basic sum $10 + 20 + 30$ cannot be improved to the right, because the $1 + 2$ cannot overcome the -9. To the left, however, we can increase the sum by $3 + 4 + 5 + 6 = 18$ at the cost of adding in $-9 - 8 = -17$. Hence the maximum segment sum is $3 + 4 + 5 + 6 + -9 + -8 + 10 + 20 + 30 = 61$.

The examples given above were solved by random fiddling, but how can we solve the problem systematically? Let's approach the problem top down. First we define the sequence of maximum segment sums *centred on* each list element. That is, for each i where $0 \leq i < n$, let p_i be the maximum segment sum which is constrained to contain x_i, and let ps be the list of all the p_i. Then the maximum segment sum for the entire list is just fold max ps.

Notice that we have split the problem in half with the concept of centred sums, for there are now two subproblems: (1) does x_i appear in the solution? and (2) assuming it does, how far to the left and right should we go to get the best result? The answer to the first question is solved by computing fold max ps, and we need only answer the second question.

Perhaps the most obvious way to proceed is to start with an arbitrary sequence element x_i and work out to the left and right, but this is a bad idea for two reasons: (1) it is not clear how far to the left and right we should look—this approach does not actually solve the problem; and (2) this approach would not be implementable with a parallel scan. What we should do instead is to start from each endpoint of the entire sequence, moving toward x_i while calculating the best possible contribution to the sum which is obtainable from the left and from the right. This insight is the key to the problem.

A productive way to think about scan problems is to imagine traversing the list, starting at the left (or right) boundary with the initial boundary input, and to consider what information is available when the next list element is encountered. The value that is transmitted from one list element to the next (moving left to right) is the best possible contribution from the left. If the elements to the left of some x_j produce a contribution a, then those elements together with x_j will produce a net contribution of $a + x$. However, the contribution must never become negative; if we had a net negative contribution from the left, then we should simply omit all elements to the left from the segment. Therefore, given a contribution from the left of x_j of a, the contribution which should be sent to x_{j+1} is $max\ 0(a+x)$. Similarly, the best possible contribution moving from right to left is $max\ 0(b+x)$, and the starting boundary values on both sides are 0. Finally, the maximum segment sum centred on an arbitrary element x_i, with best possible contributions from the left of a and from the right of b, is simply $a + b + x$.

Now we can compute all the centred sums together, with one mscan, and the final result is obtained by picking the largest one. The following function returns the list of centred sums as well as the result.

$$mss\ ::\ [Int] \rightarrow (Int, [Int])$$
$$mss\ xs =$$
$$\quad let\ (a', b', ps) = mscan\ g\ 0\ 0\ xs$$
$$\qquad g\ a\ b\ x = (max\ 0\ (a+x),\ max\ 0\ (b+x),\ a+b+x) \qquad (7.14)$$
$$\qquad z = fold\ max\ ps$$
$$\quad in\ (z,\ ps)$$

Here are some examples of the mss function:

$mss[-500, 1, 2, 3, -500, 4, 5, 6, -500]$
$\implies\quad (15, [-494, 6, 6, 6, -479, 15, 15, 15, -485])$
$mss[-500, 3, 4, 5, 6, -9, -8, 10, 20, 30, -9, 1, 2]$
$\implies\quad (61, [-439, 61, 61, 61, 61, 61, 61, 61, 61, 55, 55, 55])$

7.2.5 Recursive Doubling

The nearest-neighbour network is capable of implementing $scan\ f\ a\ xs$ for arbitrary f, but it takes time $O(n)$, where n is the length of xs. There are

7.3 Active Data Structures

two methods for reducing this to $O(\log n)$ in cases where f is associative: recursive doubling and a tree network.

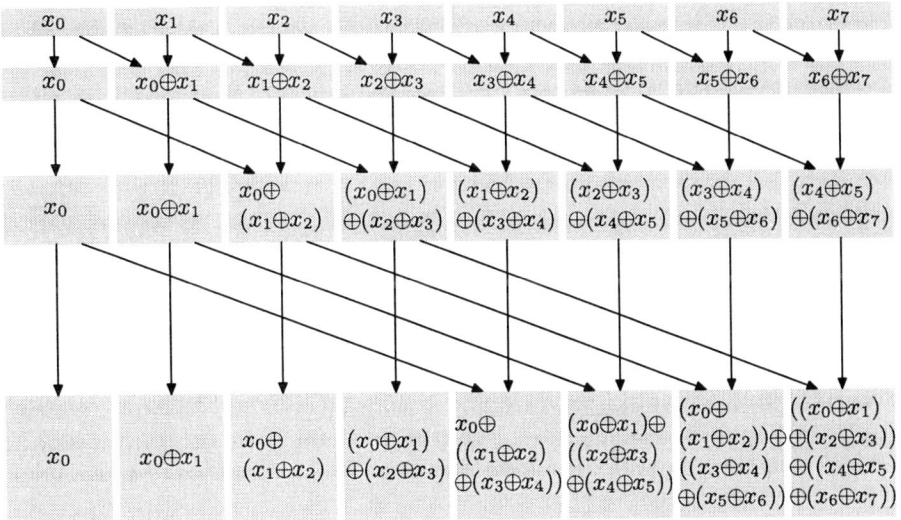

Figure 7.4. Recursive doubling implementation of parallel scan

Figure 7.4 shows the structure of the recursive doubling network, and also illustrates how it can perform a scan in $O(\log n)$ time. The network consists of $\log n$ stages, where each stage is a row of n processing elements. Each PE has two input and two output ports; in every case one input and one output is vertical—connecting to the corresponding PE in an adjacent stage—and the other output is diagonal, connecting to a more distant PE in an adjacent stage. The distance travelled by the diagonal connections doubles at each stage.

7.3 Active Data Structures

Data parallelism can do more than just speeding up loops over arrays: it leads to a distinctive class of *active data structures*. When executed on fine-grain parallel machines, such algorithms may achieve a significant speedup even if they appear to perform more calculations than a sequential program. The study of active data structures is a rich and largely unexplored subject in algorithmics. Hillis and Steele survey some early results in this field [281].

This section introduces the flavour of active data structures by presenting one example, a sorting algorithm using an active data structure representation called *index intervals*. An earlier version of this algorithm appeared in [434].

7.3.1 Index Intervals

Imperative programmers are accustomed to defining the elements of an array completely and strictly, but lazy functional programmers are comfortable with the idea that array elements might be evaluated lazily. This could result in representations of an array where there is only partial knowledge of the values of the elements.

Interval arithmetic provides a different way to represent partial information about numeric data: instead of representing an imprecisely known value x by a floating point approximation, it can be represented by a pair $[a, b]$ representing the set $\{x \mid a \leq x \leq b\}$ of all real numbers between a and b. This is useful for keeping track of the "error bars" on data, which may be caused both by imprecise experimental measurements of physical quantities and by inexact computations inside the computer.

The idea of interval representations can be extended to array indices as well as array elements, resulting in data structures where there is only partial knowledge about the *location* of an element within an array. An index interval is an approximation to an index i, written as $\langle a, b \rangle$, which denotes the set of indices between a and b. An index interval will be represented in Haskell by a type XI consisting of a pair of integers.

```
type XI = (Int,Int)
```

If an index interval has the form $\langle a, a \rangle$ then it contains only one index a, and is said to be precise. A precise index interval is equivalent to a conventional index.

```
precise :: XI -> Bool
precise (a,b) = a==b
```

Index intervals are useful for algorithms that move data around within an array, particularly when the algorithm gradually refines its knowledge of the exact final location of a piece of data. The following section presents an example.

7.3.2 Index Interval Sort

Suppose we need to sort the vector $x = [x_0, x_1, \ldots, x_{n-1}]$. The result y will be a permutation of x that assigns a new index to each value x_i; thus y_i will be the ith smallest element of x. We can notate this by writing the index below each value in the vector y. Since the index corresponding to each value is written explicitly, the entries in the array can be written in any order. If we choose arbitrarily to store the elements in order of increasing index, then the input array $x = [40, 70, 10, 20, 80, 30, 90, 50]$ would be represented as follows:

$$x = \begin{bmatrix} 40, & 70, & 10, & 20, & 80, & 30, & 90, & 50 \\ [0] & [1] & [2] & [3] & [4] & [5] & [6] & [7] \end{bmatrix}$$

7.3 Active Data Structures

The array can be sorted simply by modifying the index values; there is no need to move the data physically. Thus the final result we are aiming for would be represented as:

$$y = \begin{bmatrix} 40, & 70, & 10, & 20, & 80, & 30, & 90, & 50 \\ [3] & [5] & [0] & [1] & [6] & [2] & [7] & [4] \end{bmatrix}$$

This says that $y_0 = 10$, $y_1 = 20$, $y_2 = 30$ and so on. The actual data values, however, still reside in the same memory locations.

The algorithm begins by constructing an initial representation with completely imprecise index intervals, reflecting the total absence of knowledge about the final resting place of each element in the result. All that is known is that every element has an index interval of $\langle 0, 7 \rangle$, so the initial representation is:

$$\begin{bmatrix} 40, & 70, & 10, & 20, & 80, & 30, & 90, & 50 \\ \langle 0, 7 \rangle & \langle 0, 7 \rangle & \langle 0, 7 \rangle & \langle 0, 7 \rangle & \langle 0, 7 \rangle & \langle 0, 7 \rangle & \langle 0, 7 \rangle & \langle 0, 7 \rangle \end{bmatrix}$$

As it proceeds, the algorithm gradually narrows the index intervals. When they are all precise the sort is finished, with the following result:

$$\begin{bmatrix} 40, & 70, & 10, & 20, & 80, & 30, & 90, & 50 \\ \langle 3, 3 \rangle & \langle 5, 5 \rangle & \langle 0, 0 \rangle & \langle 1, 1 \rangle & \langle 6, 6 \rangle & \langle 2, 2 \rangle & \langle 7, 7 \rangle & \langle 4, 4 \rangle \end{bmatrix}$$

Each data value is represented in a cell (abstract processor) that contains the array element value, its index interval, and a *select* flag used for associative searches [199].

```
data Cell = Cell {select::Bool, value::Int, interval::XI}
```

The first step in the sorting algorithm is to construct the initial state by annotating each data element with a fully imprecise index interval $\langle 0, n-1 \rangle$, where n is the size of the data vector. For simplicity, we will assume that the number of cells is also n, so that every processor holds exactly one data element. We could assume that n is known in advance; alternatively, it could be computed by adding up a 1 for every cell in the memory, using a parallel fold. Once n is known, the initial index intervals are constructed by a parallel map. The fold requires time $O(\log n)$ and the map requires time $O(1)$, where n is the number of cells.

Although we will not define in this chapter all the details of the data parallel operations, or the monadic form of the top level algorithm, we will give some code extracts from the algorithm, expressed in Haskell, in order to give the reader a feel for this style of programming. The first step of the algorithm is a monadic fold to count the number of processors; the singleton result is bound to n. The second step uses a map to construct the totally-imprecise initial representation. The argument to the map is the old state of the set of processing elements, and the effect of the map is to perform a local computation in each processing element, and to store the result locally.

Since a monadic style is used to enforce the single threading of the state, we need special versions of fold and map functions that use the state rather than taking explicit arguments.

```
n <- dpt_fold (\x -> 1) (+)
dpt_map (\x -> x {xi=(0,n-1)})
```

The sort now begins by searching associatively for an imprecise interval $\langle p, q \rangle$ to work on. If there are several imprecise intervals, it does not matter which we pick (the others can wait for later), so an associative *fetch* operation is used to select arbitrarily the leftmost imprecise interval it finds. The operation returns a value of type Maybe Cell; the result is Nothing if all the index intervals are precise (which would mean the sort is finished), and otherwise it will return the contents of an arbitrarily chosen cell containing an imprecise interval.

```
dpt_map (\x -> x {select = not (precise (xi x))})
r <- fetch select id
```

If the result r is *Nothing* then we are finished, because all the data elements have precise index intervals. Otherwise r has the form $Just\,(s, x, (p, q))$, where $\langle p, q \rangle$ is an imprecise index interval that needs refinement, and x is a splitter that can be used to refine it. In this example, the first element is imprecise, so the associative search will yield a cell with value 40 and index interval $\langle 0, 7 \rangle$.

```
case r of
    Nothing ->    ... finish up ...
    Cell c ->     ... count, split and continue ...
```

Assuming that r is of the form *Cell c*, the algorithm needs to consider all the cells with the same index interval as the splitting cell (the associative *select* flag is used to disable all other cells during the ensuing computation). A fold operation is used to obtain two counts: i the number of cells whose value is less than the value in c, while j is the number of cells whose value is greater.

```
let sp = value c
let xi = interval c
(i,j) <- dpt_fold (xiCompare sp xi) addPair
```

The first argument to the fold is a function *xiCompare* which is executed simultaneously in each cell, producing the (i, j) value just for that cell. This is computed by comparing the local value with the broadcast value ($value\ x$) of the splitter.

```
xiCompare :: Int -> XI -> Cell -> (Int,Int)
xiCompare sp ii x =
```

7.3 Active Data Structures

```
        if interval x = ii
          then (oneif (value x < sp), oneif (value x > sp))
          else (0,0)

oneif :: Bool -> Int
oneif True = 1
oneif False = 0
```

The fold uses the *addPair* function to sum up the pairs.

```
addPair :: (Int,Int) -> (Int,Int) -> (Int,Int)
addPair (a,b) (c,d) = (a+c,b+d)
```

In our example, the splitter has value 40 and index interval $\langle 0, 7 \rangle$. The count considers all the cells, since at this point they all still have the same index interval. There are 3 values less than the splitter and 4 values greater than the splitter, so $(i, j) = (3, 4)$.

The count is now finished, and the next step is to perform the split. This means narrowing the index intervals of those cells whose index interval matches xi. Define $\langle p, q \rangle = xi$ (i.e. we are naming the bounds of the index interval to be p and q). For each cell, there are three cases:

- If $(value < sp)$ then the interval becomes $\langle p, p + i - 1 \rangle$;
- If $(value = sp)$ then the interval becomes $\langle p + i, p + i \rangle$;
- If $(value > sp)$ then the interval becomes $\langle q - j + 1, q \rangle$.

This definition allows for the possibility that several cells have the same value as the splitter; this will result in several array elements with the same rank order. The splitting is a local operation performed by a data parallel map:

```
dpt_map (xiSplit sp xi (i,j))
```

In our running example, cells with a small value will have their interval narrowed from $\langle 0, 7 \rangle$ to $\langle 0, 2 \rangle$. There happens to be only one cell—the splitter itself—whose value is equal to the splitter, and its new interval is $\langle 3, 3 \rangle$. The cells with large splitter have interval $\langle 4, 7 \rangle$. This results in the following representation:

$$\begin{bmatrix} 40, & 70, & 10, & 20, & 80, & 30, & 90, & 50 \\ \langle 3, 3 \rangle & \langle 4, 7 \rangle & \langle 0, 2 \rangle & \langle 0, 2 \rangle & \langle 4, 7 \rangle & \langle 0, 2 \rangle & \langle 4, 7 \rangle & \langle 4, 7 \rangle \end{bmatrix}$$

This finishes the main loop of the sorting algorithm. It searches again for a splitting cell with an imprecise index interval to work on. This happens to be the cell containing 70, and the count/split produces the following result:

$$\begin{bmatrix} 40, & 70, & 10, & 20, & 80, & 30, & 90, & 50 \\ \langle 3, 3 \rangle & \langle 5, 5 \rangle & \langle 0, 2 \rangle & \langle 0, 2 \rangle & \langle 6, 7 \rangle & \langle 0, 2 \rangle & \langle 6, 7 \rangle & \langle 4, 4 \rangle \end{bmatrix}$$

After all index intervals have become precise, the representation is in the final state:

$$\begin{bmatrix} 40, & 70, & 10, & 20, & 80, & 30, & 90, & 50 \\ \langle 3,3 \rangle & \langle 5,5 \rangle & \langle 0,0 \rangle & \langle 1,1 \rangle & \langle 6,6 \rangle & \langle 2,2 \rangle & \langle 7,7 \rangle & \langle 4,4 \rangle \end{bmatrix}$$

7.3.3 Discussion

The entire Index Interval Sort algorithm consists of data parallel maps and folds. Assuming that each array element is stored in a separate processing element, all of the maps can be executed in unit time. All of the folds use associative functions, and can be executed in time $\log(n)$, where n is the number of processing elements. The complete sorting algorithm requires average time $O(n)$.

This algorithm combines some of the characteristics of quicksort and selection sort. Indeed, it is trivial to modify it into a selection algorithm: to find the ith largest element of the array, we simply change the main loop so that it narrows only those intervals $\langle p, q \rangle$ such that $p \leq i \leq q$. When a selection is performed, the index intervals of many cells are narrowed as a side-effect, causing subsequent selections to be faster.

We have just used sorting as an example of what can be achieved with active data structures. This is not the only application: several other more intriguing algorithms are known, although they are more complicated.

There are no clear dividing lines that separate parallel algorithms into neat categories like data parallel versus task parallel. It is possible to model task parallelism within data parallelism, and vice versa. It is also possible to combine both data and task parallelism within the same program. The TwoL model [486] provides an effective way to organise this combination in the context of parallel scientific programs with irregular structure. Evaluation Strategies [571] allow data parallel algorithms to be expressed in a functional language using conventional function argument parallelism. Data parallelism is thus not a sharply defined programming style suitable only for SIMD architectures; it is a useful programming paradigm that is applicable in a wide variety of algorithms and architectures.

8. Cost Modelling

David Skillicorn[1]

8.1 Why Model Costs?

A number of different aspects of parallel programming could be considered as costs, but we will restrict our attention to cost as total execution time. This cost is a function of a program's structure, properties of the target architecture that is used to execute the program, and the interactions between them. Many of the issues we will discuss apply equally well to other kinds of costs.

The question of why the cost of parallel programs should be modelled is often misunderstood. A common misconception is that the purpose of a cost model is to be able to find out how long a particular program will take on a particular parallel computer. Such a cost model is of limited interest, since the question can be easily answered by running the program. It does allow the resource implications of starting long-running programs to be appreciated, but beyond that not much can be learned from such models.

It is much more interesting to be able to determine the cost of a program for a range of possible parallel computers. In other words, the cost of the program is an expression with parameters that depend on the target architecture. Such a cost model is now more useful – it can be used to choose among possible target computers before execution. For example, a program whose cost expression shows that it computes heavily but communicates only rarely can be executed on a computer with a low-bandwidth interconnection network, while a program with heavy communication demands can be executed on a computer with a much higher bandwidth interconnection network. Such cost models can also guide buying decisions for new computing resources if a typical mix of programs is known.

It is even more interesting to be able to determine the cost of a program based on the structure of the program in the abstract as well as the range of possible target architectures. The cost is an expression with architectural parameters, and information derived from the program's structure, or perhaps even its specification. Such cost information can be used for *design*. It becomes possible to choose one algorithm over another, or one data structure over another as the program is being built, based on the impact these choices will have on the eventual cost of execution.

Of course, an important input to any cost model is the size, and sometimes the content, of the data that the program uses. We will take the standard route of assuming that only the size of the data affects the cost, although the

---

[1] Queen's University, Kingston, Canada.

values of the input data may be relevant more often than in the sequential case.

In sequential programming, a single cost model dominates. It is based on instruction counts and order analysis, and is often called the von Neumann cost model or the RAM model. It is so pervasive that every programmer uses it without thinking. Even papers on programming by transformation exhibit derivations without bothering to mention that the underlying notion of improvement comes from this cost model. It adapts easily to a functional setting, where the added rigour of the programming model makes some automatic analysis possible [509].

Parallel programs are inherently more complex than their sequential counterparts, because there is a new dimension — space. The work must be divided among the processors, and points where communication or synchronisation are required must be decided. This complexity seems tractable only within some software development methodology, and a workable, but accurate, cost model is essential to such a methodology in practice. Finding such cost models is an active research area, and some interesting results are known, but an industrial-strength cost model is still some distance away.

In the next section, we discuss why parallel cost models are hard to build. In Section 8.3, we present some of the simpler cost models, which allow the cost of a single program piece to be determined. Section 8.4 presents an example of a little-known transformation whose usefulness can be demonstrated within several practical cost models. In Section 8.5, we show how hard it is to make cost models compositional and present some approaches that are partially successful. Finally, we categorise cost models by the kind of transformation system they induce.

8.2 Why is Cost Modelling Hard?

No matter how a parallel program is represented textually, it can be naturally regarded as a collection of actions, with dependencies between them. In other words, a program's behaviour looks like a dataflow graph. Of course, a program really describes a family of such graphs, the precise member depending on the size of the program's inputs, and, perhaps, on their values as well, but it is a useful way to think about program structure from the point of view of cost.

Such graphs have a long history in the management of complex projects, for example, where they are sometimes called PERT charts. If each node of the graph (each action) is labelled with the time it will take, then it is possible to find the path from beginning to end of the graph that will take the longest time (the *critical path*). This path determines the overall time that the project will take. Other useful cost measures can also be computed from this representation: for example, the maximum number of employees required is related to the maximal width of the graph.

8.2 Why is Cost Modelling Hard?

There are two reasons why this simple insight does not lead to neat cost models for parallel programs:

1. While a large project can hire employees as required to meet the demands of the shortest schedule, a parallel computer has a fixed number of processors. The width of the graph representing a program captures the maximal required parallelism, but the executing computer will often not be so parallel. Thus, the graph width must be reduced, usually by increasing its length. (Note also that any alteration to the graph changes the path that has the greatest length; the critical path is not a fixed object.)

   A related issue is the best way to schedule actions. Given unlimited width, starting each action as soon as possible (that is, as soon as the actions on which it depends have finished) is the optimal way to minimise the overall completion time. When the graph must have bounded width, this strategy is no longer necessarily the best. A greedy schedule may delay actions on the critical path behind actions whose deadlines have a lot of slack, and leave a long, thin "tail" of actions at the end. This is illustrated in Figure 8.1, where the first graph shows a greedy schedule, and the second graph in which actions are not scheduled greedily.

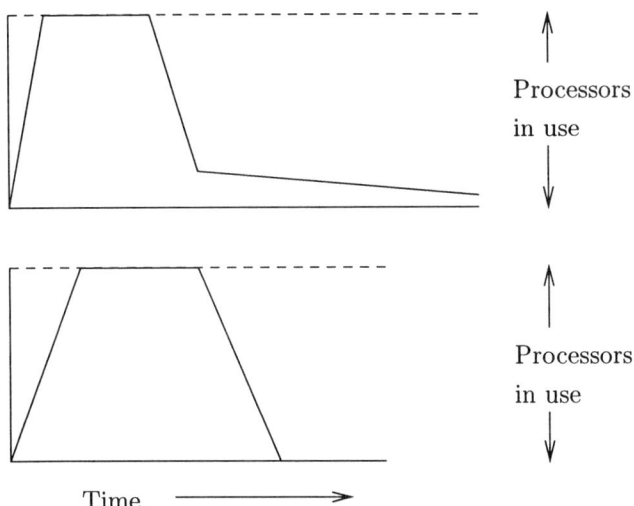

Figure 8.1. Two schedules for a dataflow graph. The first uses greedy scheduling while the second does not.

   Furthermore, the actions in the graph must execute on particular processors, and only one action can be executing at a time. The arrangement of the graph must take this into account, that is the graph must not only be of a particular width, but must be properly arranged in "columns", each representing those actions that one processor will handle.

It is, of course, possible to find the optimal schedule for a graph with a given width restriction, but this computation has exponential complexity, so it is not useful in practice. There is a vast literature on automatic scheduling, searching for simplifications that make the problem tractable [185], [322].

2. In a dataflow graph, actions are independent, and the dependencies between them, even though they may convey data, are independent as well. However, this is not the case once the graph has been mapped to a parallel computer. The flow of data along edges of the graph must share the communication links that connect processors (and possibly memories). The interaction that this causes is the hardest part of cost modelling. Suppose that the applied load on a particular communication link could be modelled as a Poisson process and that the size of data transferred as a result of each communication was similarly distributed (both already strong assumptions). Then the communication link can be modelled as an M/M/1 queueing system. Such systems have the property that, at high load (above 80% of capacity) congestion is both large and variable [344]. In other words, performance is non-linear. So modelling even a single link is a complex process.

No simple "trick", such as modelling the edges of the original graph as new actions with durations attached to them, will work because the time each communication takes depends on all the other communications that are taking place at the same time and this in turn depends on exactly how the program graph is mapped to the parallel computer, *and* what happened to the communications that occurred before the present moment. Finding solutions for the overall cost is intractable for all but the smallest or most regular cases.

Fundamentally, cost modelling is hard because determining the cost of a general program mapped to an architecture requires detailed global knowledge of both. It is not possible to separate the cost into orthogonal terms arising from different aspects.

All of this discussion assumes that we have access to a complete program (and information about its inputs). Even if a well-behaved cost model could be found for this setting, it would still not be adequate as a basis for design, for each program would have to be entirely built before its cost could be known. This makes it a practical impossibility to explore the design space, since the development costs for each exploration step are large.

To achieve the more interesting goal of a cost model that can be used at the design stage, some simplifications will be required, and the question becomes: how much accuracy and flexibility must be given up if practical cost models are to be found?

8.3 Easy Cost Modelling

We now consider some existing cost models, beginning with those that ignore communication costs (which makes the problem a great deal easier) and then looking at some approaches that control communication modelling by restricting the form of parallel programs.

Suppose that a program graph has already been transformed to a particular maximum width, say p. Then it is easy to see that it can be further transformed to some smaller width, say p', by taking "rows" where it is too wide, dividing them into sections of length p', and then executing those sections sequentially. No dependencies are violated, since there could not have been any dependencies *within* a row of the original graph. The overall time to execute the graph will have increased because of the added rows, and may now be larger by a factor of, at most, p/p'. This transformation is shown in Figure 8.2 and is known as Brent's theorem [87]. It is also clear that the converse transformation is not possible in general, because successive rows might have a dependency.

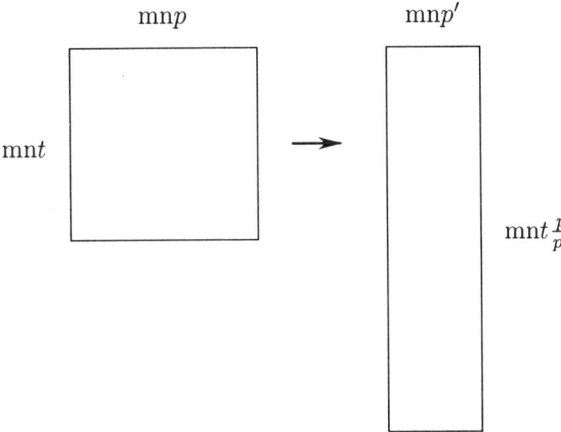

Figure 8.2. Any program may be transformed to use less parallelism and take more time.

The existence of this transformation suggests that a good strategy for developing parallel programs is to express all of the available parallelism as late as possible in development. Brent's theorem can then be used to match the program's parallelism to the available parallelism of the target computer at the end. Note that the transformation preserves the work complexity (the product of time taken and processors used): this is often the strongest property that a transformation can have.

The most common cost model for parallel computing is the PRAM model [198]. It is based directly on an abstract machine in the same way as the ordinary sequential cost model is based on the von Neumann machine. An edifice of complexity theory has been built on the PRAM model. Unfortunately, very little of it is directly applicable to practical parallel computing.

The PRAM abstract machine consists of a set of processors, and a shared memory. Any location can be accessed by a processor in unit time (that is, in a single instruction time). The same memory location may not be accessed on the same step by more than one processor, and it is the programmer's responsibility to ensure this (so programmers must understand the global state of the program at each moment).

The assumption of unit time access to memory is the weak point of the PRAM model, since it cannot be satisfied in a scalable, and hence cost-effective, way. Essentially, the model assumes that dependencies in an abstract program graph have no cost. We have already seen that this assumption avoids the hard part of the modelling task, but also fails to model terms that can alter the cost of real programs by large magnitudes. There is no straightforward way to add communication costs into the model and convert PRAM costs to real costs, because the discrepancy between the two depends on the precise arrangement of memory, and the communication that is induced by it.

A more realistic model has been developed by Blelloch [59], [65]. It divides the cost of a parallel program into a vector cost, corresponding to the maximum width of the dataflow graph of the program, and a step cost, corresponding to the maximum depth of the graph. As we have seen, such costs are both natural and easy to manipulate. Blelloch has also developed an algorithm, called *flattening*, for transforming data parallel programs on arbitrarily-nested lists into a load-balanced form for which cost expressions can be derived [65]. This cost model is more abstract than the PRAM, but it still fails to account for communication costs. In my view, its major drawback is that this omission encourages load-balancing at the deepest level of nesting in the list structure, even though this can create arbitrarily large amounts of communication. Thus the cost model not only underestimates the cost of programs, it encourages transformations that are likely to make performance worse in practice.

There are two parallel programming models for which realistic, but simple, cost models have been developed. The first is Bulk Synchronous Parallelism (BSP) ([581], [389], [386] and Chapter 12) in which communication is treated as an aggregate action of entire programs and architectures. The second is the skeleton approach ([156], [139] and Chapter 13), in which programs are based around predefined building blocks. An implementation is constructed once and for all for each block on each architecture, so the precise arrangement of each necessary communication is known and can be used to provide a cost for that block.

8.3 Easy Cost Modelling

BSP programs are based on *supersteps*, which occupy the full width of a parallel computer, and are divided sequentially into three phases. In the first phase, each processor computes using local values. In the second phase, processors transmit data to other processors. In the third phase, the whole machine does a barrier synchronisation, after which any transmitted data becomes visible in the local memory of its destination processor [540].

Communication in the BSP model is a global activity of the machine, rather than just the combination of individual point-to-point communications between individual threads. Thus it can be globally controlled, and optimised, by the BSP run-time system. There exist methods for doing this in which the time taken to complete the global communication phase depends only on the volume of data leaving or entering individual processors and a *single* architectural parameter, g [278], [540].

Let w be the maximum time for the computation phases in any of the processors, and h be the maximum (over processors) of the data entering or leaving. The time to complete a superstep is

$$w + hg + l$$

where l is an architectural parameter measuring the time required for the barrier synchronisation. Both g and l are functions of the number of processors, p, in the target architecture.

The BSP programming model is rather low-level, in the sense that programs must be matched closely to the target architecture, but its simple and accurate cost model compensates for this to a large extent.

The skeleton model of parallel computation is based on a set of building blocks, called skeletons, from which all programs are constructed. Skeletons raise the level of abstraction of parallel programming by capturing common patterns. They can be divided into two families. *Algorithmic skeletons* use building blocks that capture common algorithms, or algorithm fragments [139]. *Data skeletons* encapsulate data types and morphisms on them [534].

While skeletons make it easy to write parallel programs, an implementation of each skeleton for each target architecture must be built. The saving comes because this need only be done once for each skeleton, rather than once for each program. Thus skeletons can be seen as a structured form of code reuse. Because skeleton implementations are only done once, they can be designed by specialists who understand the intricacies of each target architecture and can exploit them for performance. The cost of each skeleton can then be calculated, typically as a function of p, and made available at the software level.

Data skeletons are particularly attractive for parallel programming because the communication pattern required to evaluate morphisms on them is directly related to the structure of the data type they encapsulate. It is thus possible to determine the interconnection network that a target architecture must have to ensure that all of the required communication is local. When this is achieved, implementations can once again ignore the cost of communication, and hence generate simple, but realistic, cost models. This idea has been extensively explored in the context of *homomorphic skeletons* [534] based on the Bird-Meertens formalism [47], [392]. We will return to it in the context of compositionality.

8.4 An Example

To illustrate many of these issues, let us examine alternative implementations of a broadcast when the object to be broadcast is itself large and can be divided into pieces.

Let us define the following three slightly-specialised operations, all of which have been discussed earlier.

$$\text{scatter}_p : List(A) \longrightarrow List_p(List(A))$$
$$\text{broadcast}_p : List(A) \longrightarrow List_p(List(A))$$
$$\mathbb{X}_p(f) : List_p(A) \longrightarrow List_p(B)$$

where $f : List(A) \to B$. Scatter divides a list into p pieces and places one piece on each processor; broadcast replicates the list onto each processor, while total exchange sends each piece to each processor, and then applies f to the resulting lists. Thus we have the trivial identity:

$$\mathbb{X}_p(f) = Map(f) \cdot \mathbb{X}_p(Reduce(+))$$

Now consider the identity:

$$broadcast = \mathbb{X}(Reduce(+)) \cdot scatter \qquad (8.1)$$

and three different cost models: a locality-based cost model in the style of [538], a pipelined version of this, and the BSP cost model. Figure 8.3 gives the costs of each of these operations under the various cost models. The (higher-order terms) of the costs of the left- and right-hand sides are given in Figure 8.4. It can be seen that the right-hand side implementation is always to be preferred because the scatter and the total exchange always move data of size m/p. Even for total exchange implemented on a tree-like topology, the smaller size of the data being moved translates into overall reduced communication times.

8.5 Hard Cost Modelling

We have seen that there are several viable ways to choose the implementation of a single piece of program using cost information. This is not enough for a workable cost model, however, for two reasons. First, programs involve compositions of program pieces *in time*, and costs do not behave well with respect to such sequential compositions. Second, programs are normally built

8.5 Hard Cost Modelling

Locality			
C(scatter)	=	$m/2 + m/4 + \ldots$ $= \mathcal{O}(m)$ (log p terms)	broadcast with message size halving
C(tot)	=	$2.m/p.p = \mathcal{O}(m)$	reduction with message size doubling
C(broadcast)	=	$m.\log p$	message of size m pushed down tree
Pipelined			
C(scatter)	=	$\max(m/2, \log p)$	depends on whether entire message is in flight
C(⋈)	=	$3m/p \log p$	pipeline messages up and down tree
C(broadcast)	=	$m + \log p$	start-up plus pipeline depth
BSP			
C(scatter)	=	mg	each sends msg. of size m/p to p others
C(⋈)	=	mg	each sends msg. of size m/p to p others
C(broadcast)	=	mpg	one sends msg. of size m to p others

Figure 8.3. Costs of each operation for three cost models

Technique →	Locality	Pipelined	BSP
⋈ · scatter = RHS	$3m$	$3m/p \log p$	$2mg$
broadcast = LHS	$m \log p$	$m + \log p$	mpg

Figure 8.4. Comparative costs for distributing a list of length m under three cost models

by more than one person or group, and this requires composition of program pieces that are constructed separately. Again, it is hard to build cost models that are well-behaved with respect to composition in space.

The two requirements of compositionality in time and space are fulfilled by models with the following property: a cost model is said to be *convex* if it is not possible to reduce the cost of a composition by increasing the cost of an element of the composition. Cost convexity makes piecewise construction possible because it defines a sensible design strategy for each piece. If each piece is designed with minimal cost, then the entire program will have minimal cost.

To see why convexity is such an important property, consider some situations in which it fails. Two program pieces are shown in Figure 8.5. Clearly, composing them sequentially allows some of the work to overlap in time, so that processors that complete the first piece early may begin work on the second. Thus the cost of the composition is smaller than expected from the costs of the pieces. Trying to reduce the length of the longest path in the first piece at the expense of the shortest path appears to be sensible when only that piece is considered, but is clearly bad in the larger context.

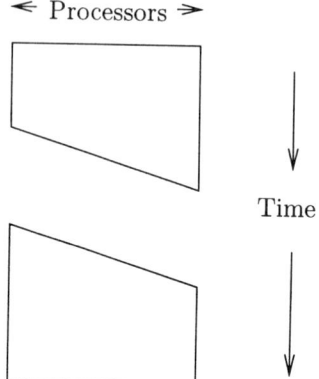

Figure 8.5. Two program pieces whose sequential composition is cheaper than expected

Composing pieces constructed independently is likely to cause cost errors when they execute concurrently. For example, if one piece assumes a certain amount of communication bandwidth is available, and so does the second, the costs of both will be wrong because the delivered bandwidth will be (less than) half of that expected. Indeed, this is precisely the weakness of programming models that allow point-to-point message passing: the designer can never know what else is happening in the interconnection network at the moment that the message begins transmission.

Two approaches to cost modelling with respect to composition have been suggested. There are typically several different implementations of each program piece with the same functional behaviour, but with different costs, especially different costs in different contexts. One strategy is to optimise over the entire program, using standard linear programming techniques. This guarantees minimal cost, but is computationally expensive. The approach can only be applied to entire programs, so it does not help at design time. Details of one approach can be found in [485]. A more efficient approach that works for the BSP cost model can be found in [539].

A second approach is outlined in [537], [538] for a homomorphic skeleton system equipped with an equational transformation system. Such skeletons are higher-order functions, with each skeleton parameterised by function arguments. The method requires that the cost of these higher-order functions are monotonic in the costs of the argument functions, but this is neither difficult nor surprising.

8.5 Hard Cost Modelling

First consider the set of equations in the transformation system. Whenever an equality has different costs on each side, say $A \cdot B = C \cdot D$, define a new skeleton E, and replace the original equation by two: $A \cdot B = E$ and $C \cdot D = E$. One of these equations is now cost-reducing left to right, while the other is cost neutral. Now consider the set of single skeletons, and form all compositions of length 2. If the cost of any composition is less than the sum of its components, define a new skeleton to represent this new composition and add a defining equation to the equation set. Continue with compositions of length 3, and so on. This procedure builds a set of equations that can now be viewed as rewrite rules; and the rewriting system is confluent and terminating, with length providing a well-founded ordering. It does not guarantee minimal cost programs because the process of generating new skeletons need not terminate. However, it does allow arbitrary approximations to minimality and, in practice, does not seem to require many new skeleton definitions, at least for the sets of skeletons so far proposed.

Cost modelling with respect to spatial composition is more difficult because of the interaction between communication referred to above. Consider two program pieces developed independently but executing at the same time. Their communications, even if they only take place within the respective pieces, will interfere with each other, causing performance reductions or improvements that are context-dependent. This effect can be ignored for skeleton approaches in which the implementation of each piece ensures that only communication paths within the section of computer on which it executes are used. However, even this is hard to guarantee on computers that use adaptive routing – it is easy to demonstrate that data travels outside the allocated submachine on a Cray T3D for example (Jonathan Hill, personal communication).

BSP has attractive properties from the point of view of spatial composition. Present implementations of BSP are SPMD and programs occupy all the processors of a target machine. However, there is no intrinsic reason why this need be so. If different pieces of a BSP program are allocated to disjoint sets of processors, then their computations do not affect each other, and nor do their communications, since the communication cost is based on the fan-in and fan-out at each individual processor. (Simultaneously executing BSP program fragments each require their own mechanism for barrier synchronisation, however, so this is not true for architectures that provide a single hardware mechanism for it.)

These cost models are the first steps towards models that are compositional, but they must be characterised more as attempts to understand the problem than as solutions. Much remains to be done.

8.6 Summary

Since transformation and cost models are deeply connected, it is instructive to examine what is known and possible in cost-directed transformation. We have seen that a cost model has the effect of turning a transformation system into a rewriting system, because any transformation either reduces the cost in one direction or the other, or is cost-neutral. The induced system may have one of the following four properties:

1. The rewriting system may be confluent (global optimisation is possible);
2. The rewriting system may be simple confluent, that is, it is confluent for simple programs, but not across certain constructors (local optimisation is possible);
3. The rewriting system is not confluent, but directed rewriting rules exist (local improvement is possible);
4. The effect of transformation rules on costs is not known.

We can also further classify cost models by whether or not they are convex.

If we use a symbol such as **1C** to indicate a cost model with property 1 that is also convex, then interesting combinations of these properties are:

- **1C**: Such a cost model would be very flexible and powerful. These requirements are strong and it seems unlikely that such a system could exist for a practical and general-purpose programming model.
- **2C**: This seems to be a plausible target for research, and is flexible enough to form the underpinning for a software development methodology. Multi-programmed BSP models provide cost models that are close to this, but the programming style required appears restrictive at present.
- **3C**: This level of cost modelling exists for homomorphic skeleton models [538], [536]. It is useful in practice, and several novel algorithms have been developed using it.

Note that class **4C** cannot exist since there is no global way to define a direction for "improvement", and hence no way to define convexity.

Conventional sequential compiler technology is only in Class 3. A great deal of the work in performance modelling is in Class 4, that is, fine-tuning parallel programs by executing them, collecting profiling data, and using it to alter programs in ways that may improve their cost. Some progress has been made in relating run-time behaviour to the program structures responsible for it [295], but it remains something of a black art.

Cost modelling is critical to successful parallel software construction precisely because intuition is not to be relied on in the parallel context. Designing and implementing effective programs depends on using algorithms and data structures whose behaviour is good in practice, not in some abstraction that does not map to real parallel computers. Deciding what to model, and which level of abstraction to use has proven difficult, but progress has been made. Many interesting problems, however, remain.

9. Shaping Distributions

C. Barry Jay[1]

9.1 Introduction

Knowledge of the shapes of data structures can be used to improve memory management, which in turn has an impact on programming style, error detection and optimisation. While the FISH language [196] shows that significant benefits accrue in the sequential setting, an even greater impact is anticipated in parallel, as shape theory is able to address some of the key issues exposed in earlier chapters. Let us consider these issues first, before getting down to details.

This book features over a hundred references to list data types, and about an equal number of references to arrays and sequences. Other data types are barely considered. Very roughly, lists predominate when programs are the focus, and arrays are dominant in implementations, with sequences occupying an intermediate position. This is natural if one views lists as supporting strong reasoning principles, and arrays as a means of improving performance, but there is a tendency to treat these types interchangeably, which is perhaps the rationale for "sequences".

In fact, completely separate techniques have been developed for distributing lists and arrays. Regular arrays, especially matrices, support an elaborate suite of distributions, such as block-cyclic distribution in High Performance Fortran [172]. Conversely, nested lists, or irregular arrays, are commonly flattened as in NESL [61]. Of course, neither approach is satisfactory when irregular structures contain pockets of regularity, as in trees of arrays [600]. Let us consider these two approaches on regular data.

Flattening produces a single data distribution strategy, good load balancing, and a decent cost model, but is far from optimal on regular data. In this case, load balancing is not a major problem, but flattening breaks up sub-structures, e.g. matrix rows, in random places, which generates rather high communication costs.

This diversity of distributions for regular data impacts on the design and implementation of parallel languages. Each of the fundamental second-order functions, such as scan, must be able to interact with data in a variety of forms. Further, evaluation must be able to incorporate any of the strategies for combining the results from the individual processors, as outlined in Chapter 12. Clearly, there is too much detail here for an ordinary programmer to cope with, and even when the right decision has been made for a particular application, the resulting code is not reusable in practice. The alternative is to have the compiler choose, on the basis of a cost model (see Chapter 8).

---

[1] University of Technology, Sydney, Australia.

Chapter 12 provides a representative analysis of scan in which the algorithm is chosen to minimise costs as a function of the BSP hardware parameters. This has proved to be enormously effective, but contains three implicit assumptions. First, the data must be regular, i.e. an array, to enable uniform costing. Second, and more significant, the cost of the function being applied must be known. The function cost is easily determined if it is a primitive operation, e.g. addition, but in general, it must be inferred, and will depend on the nature of the array entries. For example, if the operation is the pointwise addition of two vectors then its cost is linear in the length of the entries. Third, the size of the array is known.

This simple example shows that the cost model must take into account the size and shape of the arguments, and it must be higher-order, i.e. able to handle the cost function of the function to be scanned above.

Such shape information is often assumed to be freely available. For example, the size, n, of a data structure is typically treated as a parameter having the same status as the number, p, of processors. But practical programs typically contain many intermediate data structures whose shape must be somehow inferred. For example, the matrix parenthesisation algorithm determines the right parenthesisation of a product of many matrices to minimise the work. This, in turn, determines the shapes of the intermediate matrices produced, so that the shapes necessary to cost the program are themselves the result of a complex algorithm beyond the reach of the programmer.

In addition to the challenge of optimising a single parallel function, composition of programs introduces additional, non-local issues. In particular, data redistribution may be required to patch programs together. These are comparatively expensive, and must be taken into account when costing.

All of these problems can be addressed by giving due consideration to the shapes of data structures.

Shape theory [304] provides a semantic framework in which to distinguish nested lists from regular arrays, and, more generally, the regular and irregular data types. Let us first establish some terminology. From now on, an *array* is always regular and a one-dimensional array is a *vector*. The key to resolving the ambiguity between lists and vectors lies in the following

Definition. *A vector is a list whose entries all have the same shape.*

This distinction only becomes meaningful when the entries may have internal structure. For example, the entries in a vector of vectors must all have the same length, so that the whole corresponds to a matrix, not an arbitrary list of lists. The same approach generalises to arbitrary numbers of array dimensions or levels of list nesting.

A shape-based approach holds out the prospect of supporting all the natural data structures, with appropriate reasoning tools and implementations throughout. For example, the standard array distributions become total functions on arrays, instead of partial functions on lists of lists. Also, vectors support formal proofs of correctness, e.g. of the fast Fourier transform [303].

9.1 Introduction

Most of the work is still ahead of us, but some of the benefits of acknowledging regularity can be illustrated immediately.

Consider the implementation of foldleft, i.e. `foldl` f x ys on a uniprocessor. In general, each of the intermediate values will have a different shape, and so have distinct storage requirements, as when folding append. On the other hand, the most common case is that all the intermediate values have the same shape, as when folding some arithmetic operation. Then a single location can store all the intermediate values using a *reduction* algorithm. Unfortunately, if ys is a list then the shape of each intermediate value must be checked separately before a reduction is safe. However, if ys is a vector then one check, using the common shape of the entries, suffices.

As before, it would be better to automate this decision than to foist it on the programmer. In FISH notation, the required check becomes:

$$\#f \ \#x \ sh \ \#= \ \#x$$

where $\#$ is the shape combinator, $\#=$ is shape equality, and sh is the common shape of the entries of ys. This can be checked by shape analysis during compilation. Thus FISH only requires a single combinator to handle both cases.

Turning to the parallel scan discussed above, we see that shape analysis is able to confirm the regularity of the arrays, and determine the shapes of both the function and the argument. It remains to extend the analysis with cost information. This can be done by augmenting the shape analysis with cost information using a *cost monad* [310]. This will enable costing to take into account both hardware and shape parameters in a very flexible framework. Once costs are available, they can be used to drive the application of equational laws, as explained in Chapter 8. Note, however, that even when the hardware parameters are fixed, a single equation may be driven in either direction depending on the shape parameters. For example, a small structure will be best left on a single processor while a large one should be distributed. Shape-based costing is easily able to handle such granularity issues.

All of this analysis is conducted in a compositional framework. By making data distributions explicit, the difficulties of composition can be reduced to a search for an optimal solution within a set of correct composites.

The structure of the chapter is as follows. Section 9.2 reviews some essential shape theory. Section 9.3 reviews the FISH programming language — a sequential, higher-order language for array programming that supports static shape analysis. Many of the issues of parallel programming are resolved at this level. Also, FISH programs execute at a speed comparable to native code in, say, C. Section 9.4 discusses aspects of the design of the data parallel variant of FISH called GOLDFISH. In particular, Section 9.5 looks at data distribution, and Section 9.6 covers the shape-based cost model. Section 9.7 draws conclusions.

9.2 Shape Theory

Shape theory [305] provides a well-grounded technique for separating computation of data (e.g. numbers) from that of the structures, or *shapes* (e.g. the size of a matrix) that store them. Semantically, this decomposition can be represented by a commuting square (actually, a pullback). For example, a matrix type MA whose entries are in A can be represented by:

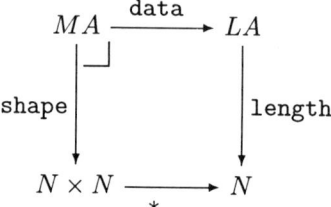

where N is the natural numbers, used to represent the number of rows and columns of the matrix, and the length of the entry list [304].

Observe that we can identify $N \times N$ with $M1$, the matrices whose entries are of unit type, and N with $L1$, the lists of unit type. Generalising, from M to some unknown type constructor, or functor F we obtain the following pullback:

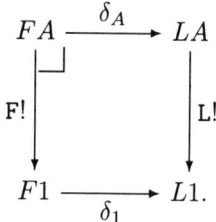

Such functors F are called *shapely over lists* [304]. Quantification over such functors leads to *shape polymorphic* [309] or *polytypic* programming [393], [302] which also connects to work on design patterns [444].

Returning to arrays, note that we can represent arrays in three or more dimensions in the same style as the matrices, by using ever longer tuples of numbers in their shapes. An alternative is to view these higher-dimensional array types as iterations of a single, vector construction, so that a matrix is a vector of vectors. This is not the same as a list of lists, as the latter need not be *regular*. The point is that the inner vectors in a vector of vectors must all have the same length. Similarly, the inner matrices in a vector of matrices must all have the same numbers of rows and columns, i.e. the same shape. Thus, regularity itself can be defined using shape theory, provided we are prepared to make the shapes explicit.

Represent a type by a function $a : A \to I$ where A represents the actual values, and I their shapes. Then we can define the vector of a by:

9.3 The FISH Language

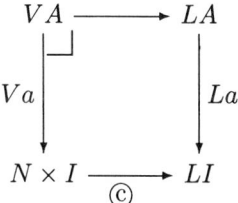

where ⓒ takes a number n and a shape i and produces a list of length n whose entries are all i. Note that the shape of a vector includes its length. Hence a vector of vectors is a matrix. The mathematics of this approach are worked out in [303].

This approach can be extended to interpret matrices (as above). More generally, k-dimensional arrays have shapes that include k-tuples of sizes. Furthermore, arrays of arbitrary finite dimension can be shaped by lists of sizes. The corresponding diagram is:

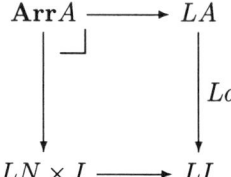

where the base arrow multiplies all the entries in the number list, and then applies ⓒ. *Polydimensionality* is the ability to write programs which are polymorphic with respect to such a type of finite-dimensional arrays.

The shape theoretic account of arrays provides a semantic distinction between lists and vectors that has been missing till now. The common distinctions are operational rather than denotational; that arrays have constant access time, or mutable entries. While this ambiguity has been fruitful, allowing parallel programmers to exploit the combinators of the Bird-Meertens Formalism (BMF) for mapping and folding, etc. it suffers from the various limitations outlined in the introduction.

Equally important, function types are not shapely either. The shape of a function is itself a function (of shapes), not a structure with a finite number of "holes" for storing data. Again, to create a vector of functions would require that the entries all have the same shape, but function types do not generally support decidable equality.

9.3 The FISH Language

The FISH language [311], [306], [307] is a new, higher-order, polymorphic language that supports polydimensional array programming. It also compiles into simple, imperative code, equivalent to hand-coded C, which runs several times faster (on typical array problems) than the best of the existing functional languages [308]. This combination is achieved by basing the language on shape theory, which supports abstractions for the shape of arrays, i.e. their size in each dimension, and their use by the compiler.

FISH is a higher-order, polymorphic programming language, and so satisfies the key criteria for supporting the functional programming style, as laid out in Section 1.2. However, it gives equal weight to imperative features and a central place to the study of shapes, and these concerns produce a novel mix of language features.

Although functions are "first class phrases" that can be passed as parameters or returned as results, they are not "first class data" as they cannot be stored in arrays. This is captured in the type system by distinguishing the *data types*, such as arrays, which are storable, from the *phrase types*, such as functions, used to represent meaningful program fragments. This division, and indeed the whole language framework, is adapted from that of Algol-like languages [496], [441]. Having made the distinction between data and phrases, it is natural to allow a phrase type comm of commands, too. Function evaluation (β-reduction) is call-by-name, to ensure that commands are executed where used, rather than where called. This is a common hallmark of purity in functional programming, but note that evaluation of FISH expressions may indeed have side-effects.

Polymorphism in the data and phrase types is captured by supporting corresponding type variables, and their quantification in type schemes. The full type system is given in Figure 9.1.

$$\begin{aligned}
\delta &::= \text{int} \mid \text{bool} \mid \text{float} \mid \ldots & \text{shp } U &= \#U \\
\alpha &::= X \mid \delta \mid [\alpha] & \text{shp } (\#U) &= \#U \\
\sigma &::= \tilde{\ }\delta \mid \#\alpha & \text{shp } (\text{exp } \alpha) &= \text{exp } \#\alpha \\
\tau &::= \alpha \mid \sigma & \text{shp } (\text{exp } \sigma) &= \text{exp } \sigma \\
\theta &::= U \mid \#U \mid \text{exp } \tau & \text{shp } (\text{var } \alpha) &= \text{exp } \#\alpha \\
&\mid \text{comm} \mid \theta \to \theta & \text{shp comm} &= \text{exp fact} \\
\phi &::= \theta \mid \forall_\alpha X.\phi \mid \forall_\theta U.\phi & \text{shp } (\theta \to \theta') &= \text{shp } \theta \to \text{shp } \theta'
\end{aligned}$$

Figure 9.1. The FISH types and their shapes.

The *datum types* δ represent the usual atomic types of integers, booleans, floats, etc. *Array types* α are generated by array type variables X, datum types and closed under the array type constructor $[-]$. The type $[\alpha]$ represents regular, finite-dimensional arrays with entries of type α. *Shape types* σ include a type of the form $\tilde{\ }\delta$ for each datum type δ (used to represent static constants) and a type of shapes $\#\alpha$ for each array type α. It is important not to confuse ˜int, otherwise called size, with #int. The former is used to represent the size of arrays, while the latter has only a single value int_shape

9.3 The FISH Language

which represents the common shape of all integers. Together, the array and shape types constitute the *data types* τ, i.e. types whose values can be stored.

Programs are typed using *phrase types* θ. These are generated by the *phrase type variables* U and their *shapes* $\#U$, *expression types* exp τ for each data type τ, and *variable types* var α for each array type α, and a type comm of *commands*. Terms of type var α can be assigned to, while expressions may not. For example, if x : var α and e : exp α then $x := e$: comm is a command. There are no types of the form var σ as the shape of an array is fixed at creation. The phrase types are also closed under function formation $\theta_0 \to \theta_1$. Function types are used to represent both the usual functional programs, but also procedures, of type var $\alpha \to$ comm, etc.

Hindley-Milner style polymorphism is obtained by quantifying phrase types by array and phrase type variables.

Each term $t : \theta$ has a *shape* obtained by applying the combinator $\# : \theta \to \text{shp}(\theta)$ where shp is defined in the figure above. We usually abuse notation and write $\#\theta$ for $\text{shp}(\theta)$.

The FISH terms form a simply-typed λ-calculus with constants. The FISH constants include some basic datum operations, read and write operations for arrays, some shape constants for building array shapes, and the basic commands, such as conditionals, for-loops and while loops. Some key points will be presented here, but a complete description of the FISH constants is beyond the scope of this chapter. See the formal language definition [307] for details.

The shape-data decomposition of arrays, and their regularity, is reflected in the fill ...with ... syntax for constructing arrays, e.g.:

```
>-|> let mat = fill {~2,~3:int_shape} with [0,1,2,3,4,5];;
mat : [int]
#mat = { ~2,~3 : int_shape }
>-|> %run mat;;
fill { ~2,~3 : int_shape }
with [
  0,1,2,
  3,4,5
]
```

The text within the curly braces is the shape, given by a list of sizes, e.g. ~2 : size paired with the common shape int_shape of the entries. Thus mat is a 2×3 matrix of integers. After with comes a list of entries, given by outer dimension first, here in row order. Note that both the type and shape of mat are determined by the compiler. The instruction %run mat executes the program which evaluates the entries as you see.

The regularity of arrays is maintained by checking that arrays, sub-arrays and entries are updated by arrays of the same shape. That is, every assignment x:= e generates a shape check, that x and #e agree. This check is performed by the compiler as part of shape analysis, which computes the shape of every program fragment, detecting all shape errors, and guiding memory allocation. Note, too, that #e is not only internal to the compiler, but can be used by the programmer to make checks or control optimisation.

FISH is able to distinguish a vector of vectors from a matrix, e.g.:

```
>-|> let vecvec = fill{~2:~3:int_shape} with [0,1,2,3,4,5];;
vecvec : [[int]]
#vecvec = { ~2 : ~3 : int_shape }
```

Note the change in shape compared to mat. This is important for operations like the mapping of an array function across an array, e.g.:

```
>-|> let sum_int = reduce plus_int 0;;
sum_int : [int] -> int
>-|> let vec = map sum_int vecvec;;
vec : [int]
#vec = { ~2 : int_shape }
>-|> %run vec;;
fill { ~2 : int_shape }
with [
   3,12
]
```

FISH supports all of the usual BMF constants, such as reduce, and also operations for block decomposition, etc. as array functions. Furthermore, these operations are *polydimensional*, i.e. able to act on arguments of arbitrary finite dimension. A fundamental example is the defined function:

```
doall : (a -> comm) -> [a] -> comm
```

When given a procedure and a k-dimensional array it is converted to k nested for-loops to traverse all of the array dimensions. Detailed descriptions would require a more thorough examination of the language syntax, but some insight can be obtained from consideration of polydimensional reduce.

```
>-|> let accum f z =
   let pr y = z:= f !z !y
   in
      doall pr
;;
accum : (a -> b -> a) -> var a -> var [b] -> comm
>-|> let reduce_pr f x z y =
   (z := x ;
   accum f z y)
;;
reduce_pr : (a -> b -> a) -> a -> var a -> var [b] -> comm
>-|> let reduce_sh fsh xsh ysh =
   check (equal (fsh xsh (zeroShape ysh))
```

```
    xsh )
  xsh
  ;;
  reduce_sh : (#a -> #b -> #a) -> #a -> #[b] -> #a
  let reduce f x =
    proc2fun (reduce_pr f x) (reduce_sh #f #x)
  ;;
  reduce : (a -> b -> a) -> a -> [b] -> a
```

accum f z y performs a reduction of the variable y into the variable z. reduce_pr f x z y is the same except that a separate variable z is used for the accumulation. reduce_sh is the shape function that checks the side-condition for reduction, that the shape of the accumulation parameter never changes, and returns that shape as its result. The imperative procedure reduce_pr and the shape function reduce_sh are combined using proc2fun to produce a higher-order function reduce. This technique for producing higher-order functions from imperative procedures and shape functions is central to the FISH ethos, producing the slogan that names the language:

$$\boxed{\text{Functional} = \text{Imperative} + \text{Shape}}$$

9.4 Aspects of the Design of GOLDFISH

FISH shows that many of the problems confronting parallel programming arise from fundamental limitations of existing programming styles, which can be overcome by taking due account of shapes. This section will examine the application of these ideas to the design of a data parallel language GOLDFISH. Although the design is well in hand, it should be stressed that no details have been fixed at this stage. The purpose here is to consider the underlying principles, to give some flavour of what we expect to achieve.

GOLDFISH will be derived from FISH in three steps:

1. Add some parallel combinators (or skeletons) for parallel work, e.g. map and fold and data distribution, e.g. block decomposition of arrays;
2. Restrict the function arguments to these combinators so that side-effects remain local to the processor that triggers them;
3. Introduce a shape-based cost model.

The implementation of the parallel combinators will adapt to changes of machine architecture or problem granularity by using an accurate cost model to choose between alternative implementations. (While fully automatic, the programmer may enforce decisions by explicit programming.) Hence, it will be both fully portable and fully polymorphic. Fragments of GOLDFISH programs assigned to individual processors are treated as FISH programs and compiled into simple, efficient, imperative code, e.g. C or Fortran, so that inclusion of existing sequential programs is easy. Hence, GOLDFISH acts as a coordination language, but with a very transparent interface. This approach is feasible because of FISH's efficient execution.

Point 2, above, is necessary to support effective parallelisation of combinators like map. However, GOLDFISH will still support user-defined functions of arbitrarily high order, and also assignment, provided that the constraint above is not violated. This is important to achieve in-place update of distributed arrays. Also assignment to a distributed array can achieve a data redistribution which places data in existing storage, instead of allocating afresh. The rest of this section will address the other two points.

9.5 Distributions

The hardest part of designing a skeleton-based language is not the basic BMF combinators, such as fold, but the data distributions. Often these are described in terms of processor identities, or by using an intermediate language that is hidden from the user. These additions to the basic BMF approach create a tension between the user language and the implementation which is problematical. GOLDFISH will handle all issues within the source language, using nested, polydimensional arrays to represent distributed data. For example, a block decomposition of a matrix can be considered as a matrix of matrices, where the outer matrix structure represents an array of virtual processors. Such decompositions can be represented in GOLDFISH as a function:

    [a] -> [[a]]

where the outer array structure represents the virtual array of processors, and the inner array structure represents the blocks. Indeed, such distributions can be defined to act uniformly on vectors, matrices, and all higher-dimensional arrays. This is a crucial step in describing distributions, as it eliminates the need for separate consideration of processors, which become merely the outermost level of data structure. Communication between processors becomes one of data alignment, which is achieved by matching shapes. Thus, all distribution decisions can be described within the source language, which becomes the setting for all cost and optimisation decisions. This simplification has several advantages. In particular, it simplifies the task of compiler construction and allows the programmer to address distributions at any level of detail. Let us consider some possible choices of distribution primitives.

9.5.1 Basic Distributions

Here are some examples of some operations for gathering and distributing data. This is not intended to be an exhaustive list, but to illustrate the potential of this approach. First, here are some operations that arise directly from shape theory.

9.5 Distributions

```
implode_type  : [[a]] -> [a]
explode_type  : size -> [a] -> [[a]]
implode_shape : [a] -> [a]
explode_shape : #[a] -> [a] -> [a]
```

implode_type x removes the distinction between the inner and outer array levels. For example, implode_type vecvec = mat above. explode_type is its partial inverse. explode_type k x treats the outermost k dimensions of x as belonging to the outer array, and the remainder to the inner array structure. For example, explode_type ~1 mat= vecvec. Note that these operations change the type of the array but not the total number of dimensions.

By contrast, implode_shape converts a multi-dimensional array into a one-dimensional array, leaving the type unchanged. It converts mat into a vector of length ~6. Its partial inverse explode_shape takes a shape sh and an array x and produces an array of shape sh with entries from x. It returns an error unless x contains exactly the right amount of data.

9.5.2 Block Decomposition

Although these operations are powerful enough to express many, perhaps all, of the data distributions one can envisage, it is important that compound distributions be executed with the minimum number of data movements. One of the most common distributions is the block decomposition and its inverse:

```
unblock : [[a]] -> [a]
block   : #[a] -> [b] -> [[b]] .
```

unblock x requires that the number of dimensions of x equal the number of dimensions of its entries, e.g. that x be a vector of vectors, or a matrix of matrices. It treats the entries as blocks of a larger array, and recombines them. For example, if:

```
#x = {~2,~3:~4,~5:int_shape}
```

then:

```
#(unblock x) = {~8,~15:int_shape}
```

block is its partial inverse. It takes an array shape (ignoring the shape of the entries) representing the array of blocks, and an array of the same dimensionality, and produces a block decomposition. For example, if:

```
#x = {~4,~4:int_shape}
```

then:

```
#(block {2,2 :int_shape} x) = {~2,~2 :~2,~2 :int_shape}
```

It is not yet clear what should happen if the array sizes are not exact multiples of the number of blocks in each dimension. The result could be an error, null values (i.e. values with a shape but no data) could be used to fill the gaps, or the programmer could be required to supply default values.

9.5.3 Stencilling

Stencilling is used to create arrays of neighbourhoods. This is particularly important in scientific applications where neighbouring particles or fields interact, and is given prominence in some parallel systems, such as ZPL [578]. Stencils can also be seen as a fundamental example of a cover [552]. A basic issue is to decide what happens on the boundaries of the array where the necessary values are missing. Essentially, one can either supply additional boundary values (an outer stencil) or drop those entries where there is insufficient information (an inner stencil). Here is the type of an inner stencil.

```
inner_stencil : #[a] -> #[b] -> [c] -> [[c]] .
```

The first two arguments are used to describe the size of the neighbourhood, as measured from the centre. The third argument is the source array. Here is an example:

```
>-|> let v = fill {3,3:int_shape} with [0,1,2,3,4,5,6,7,8];;
v : [int]
#v = { ~3,~3 : int_shape }
>-|> %run v;;
fill { ~3,~3 : int_shape }
with [
  0,1,2,
  3,4,5,
  6,7,8
]
>-|> let w = stencil {1,0:int_shape} {0,1:int_shape} v;;
w : [[int]]
#w = { ~2,~2 : ~2,~2 : int_shape }
>-|> %run w;;
fill { ~2,~2 : ~2,~2 : int_shape }
with [
  0,1,  1,2,
  3,4,  4,5,

  3,4,  4,5,
  6,7,  7,8
]
```

(The layout of w has been modified to improve readability.) Here, the neighbourhood takes one row above and one column to the right, so that the neighbourhood of the entry 3 has entries 0,1,3 and 4. Of course, some entries of the source do not have a neighbourhood of the desired shape, so that the result of stencilling is typically an array of smaller size than the original. In our example the neighbourhoods are 2×2 so that the overall array is reduced by $2-1$ in each dimension.

Stencilling can be used to solve difference equations, and hence differential equations, such as arise in scientific programming. FISH (and eventually GOLDFISH) supports a generic difference equation solver, of type:

```
>-|> diff_solver : ([a] -> a) -> (a -> a) ->
                   (bool -> [a] -> [a] -> bool) -> [a] -> [a]
```

whose arguments are accounted for by:

```
>-|> let diff_solver
         diff_eqn   // acts on stencils to produce new values
         boundary   // computes new boundary values
         converged  // criterion for termination
         initial    // initial conditions.
```

The solver is completely polymorphic in the number of dimensions, the size in each dimension, the type of the array entries, the size of the stencils and and the equation to be solved.

9.6 Cost Modelling

The GOLDFISH parallel combinators naturally support a BSP approach to implementation and costing. Once the program is in final form, ready to execute, its combinators will either represent work to be performed on individual processors, e.g. mapping of functions across processor arrays, or distribution and gathering operations, to be performed during global communication steps.

Further, exact knowledge of the shapes of the arrays being distributed, and of the hardware characteristics, e.g. number of processors, means that more accurate cost estimates will be possible than before.

Costs are represented by functions in $C = H \to T$ from hardware parameters H (as in BSP) to time T but which also depend on the shapes of the data structures. This is captured by augmenting the usual shape analysis with cost information. The shape of a function $f : X \to Y$ is given by a function $\#f : \#X \to \#Y$. Cost information is added by replacing $\#f$ by:

$$\mathsf{cost}(f) : \#X \to C \times \#Y$$

a function which returns both shape and cost information. The action $MY = C \times Y$ is that of a monad, which is augmented with the ability to add costs, making it a *cost monad* [310]. The cost of a composite program is given by the usual rules for monadic composition [407], [588]. Note that the particular choice of H and T does not affect the overall structure, so that the choice of hardware parameters can be varied to include cache size or other parameters chosen by the manufacturer willing to adopt this framework. Similarly, the costs can be extended to account for other factors such as space or access to expensive hardware.

For example, consider the cost of a mapping map f x. The cost of evaluating f and x will be added automatically using the cost monad, so we need only focus on the actual mapping itself. In the BSP model this is given by the cost of the local mapping plus a barrier synchronisation. The former can be estimated by multiplying the number of entries in the block by the average time to perform f on one entry of x. Note that the shape of the entries of x is known, which makes the latter estimate much more robust.

In general, the complexity of the cost analysis will reflect the complexity of the possible implementation. For example, the cost of a parallel fold must take into account whether a reduction is possible, and the various choices of communication strategy, plus any redistribution that may be required once the final data structure is completed. While some care will be required here, the effort will be strictly local to the implementation of the combinator. All interactions between components will be handled by the monad structure.

9.7 Conclusion

Shape theory gives a clean account of the differences between regular data types, such as arrays, and the irregular ones, such as trees. This distinction has a number of consequences for programming, and especially the treatment of data distributions.

The FISH language uses shapes and their analysis to support the introduction of regular arrays to functional programming. This allows many of the standard array programs and distributions to be defined, programs which only imperfectly captured, if at all, in a list-oriented setting. Also, FISH supports polydimensional programming, so that block decompositions, etc. can be described uniformly over any number of dimensions. Future versions of FISH are expected to represent irregular data types as well, and their mixtures, such as M-trees [600].

GOLDFISH will extend FISH with some parallel primitives and a monadic cost model that can be adapted to new algorithms, new choices of hardware parameters, and new notions of cost. A moderately successful search strategy should enable the compiler to take full responsibility for all distribution decisions, so that GOLDFISH will become a fully portable, implicitly parallel language.

10. Performance Monitoring

Nathan Charles[1] and Colin Runciman[1]

10.1 Introduction

The full details of a parallel computation can be very complex. For example, many run-time systems employ a number of strategies to ensure best use of available hardware. Most parallel functional languages hide this information from the programmer, providing very simple annotations to control the parallelism in a program [476], [288], [573], [104]. Some, such as Hudak's *para-functional* programming [288], allow the programmer to describe the mapping of tasks onto processors [404], [432], [331], [560], whilst the more recent GUM system [573] only requires the programmer to annotate possible expressions that can be evaluated in parallel.

When a parallel program does not achieve the level of performance that the programmer expected they naturally ask why. To aid this analysis, the programmer is often equipped with parallel profiling tools [504], [248]. The aim of these tools is to provide a bridge between the high-level view of the parallel computation held by the programmer, and the low-level details of exactly what happened during the execution of the parallel program.

The model of concurrent evaluation used by the tools is typically left implicit. It usually lies on some intermediate point between the naïve programmers view and the technical details of the computation. The aim of this chapter is to make explicit the models used by different tools. We do this by using standard data modelling techniques. This process helps to improve our understanding of the different models and allows us to ask questions about them.

Section 10.2 analyses a parallel execution using a current set of profiling tools and highlights some of their weaknesses. Section 10.3 presents a framework for developing future tools using data modelling techniques.

10.2 Analysing an Example Using Current Tools

Figure 10.1 shows a parallel Haskell program, based on an example by Augustsson and Johnsson [25], that calculates the sum of the results of applying a naïvely defined Euler totient function to the numbers from one to nine. The program introduces parallelism using the par and seq combinators [500] (see Chapter 3). In this example the placing of combinators has been determined using a simple scheme based on strictness analysis.

---
[1] Department of Computer Science, University of York, UK.

Parallelism is introduced in four places:

1. Within sumEuler there is a parallel annotation to evaluate numbers, the list from 1 to n;
2. within euler there is also a parallel annotation to evaluate numbers;
3. The sumEuler function applies parList, a function which evaluates all the members of a list in parallel, to the list of euler applications from euler 1 to euler n;
4. The euler function evaluates the spine of the list of relative primes in parallel with the calculation of the result.

```
main = (print . show . sumEuler) 9

sumEuler :: Int -> Int
sumEuler n
   = let eulerList = let numbers = [1..n]
                     in par numbers (map euler numbers)
     in seq (parList eulerList) (sum eulerList)

euler :: Int -> Int
euler n
   = let relPrimes = let numbers = [1..(n-1)]
                     in par numbers (filter (relprime n) numbers)
     in par (spine relPrimes) (length relPrimes)

parList :: [Int] -> ()
parList = foldr par ()

spine :: [Int] -> ()
spine []     = ()
spine (_:xs) = spine xs

hcf :: Int -> Int -> Int
hcf x 0 = x
hcf x y = hcf y (rem x y)

relprime :: Int -> Int -> Bool
relprime x y = (hcf x y==1)
```

Figure 10.1. Source code for SumEuler program.

In the rest of this section we analyse this example using one of the current sets of parallel profiling tools. We choose GranSim [248], [363], [365] as it is the most developed parallel profiling system for Haskell [457].

GranSim is a parallel simulator built on top of the Glasgow Haskell compiler. A program is compiled for GranSim to generate an executable. When this executable is run, a record of various events related to each parallel

10.2 Analysing an Example Using Current Tools

thread's life time, such as the start and end time of a thread, is dumped to a log-file. This log-file can then be processed to produce graphs using the various visualisation tools that accompany GranSim.

GranSim is highly configurable and it is possible to test the performance of a program on imaginary machines with different characteristics. For the purpose of illustration, we configure GranSim to simulate a three-processor machine with no latency and no communication costs. Figure 10.2 shows the activity profile for the program. The bars show the numbers of running (dark grey), runnable (light grey) and blocked (black) threads during the execution of the program. We have also identified seven regions where at least one processor is idle. This is indicated on the graph by our own annotations.

Analysing the whole example in detail is a lengthy process. Here we limit the analysis to reasoning why there are idle processors within the first three regions.

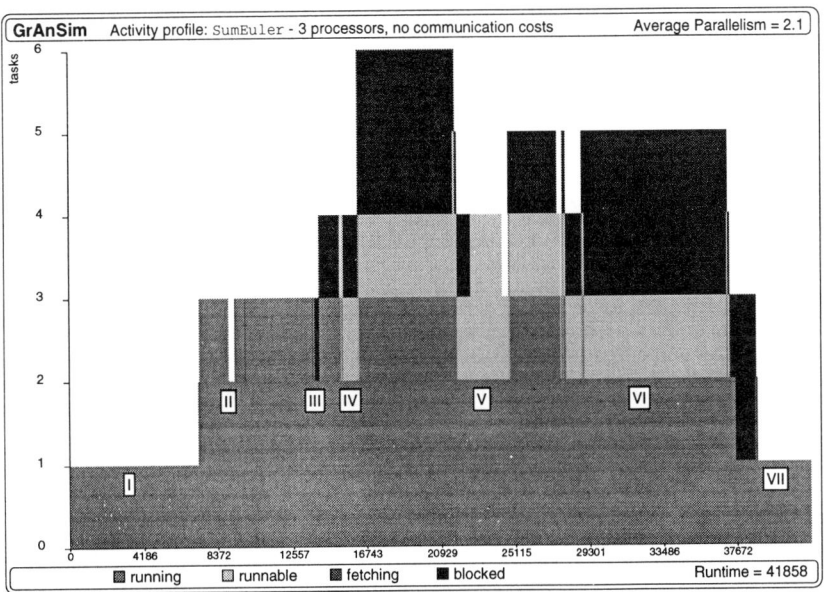

Figure 10.2. Activity graph for SumEuler 9, with annotations for regions where at least one processor is idle added by hand.

10.2.1 Region (I)

Every parallel computation has an initial start-up period: it takes time to execute the code that creates the parallelism. The lack of parallelism in region (I) could be because no par application has been evaluated yet, or because threads have not been distributed onto other processors, or because the expressions to be evaluated by the sparks created within this region are already evaluated. It is not clear from the activity graph which of these explanations is correct. It is necessary to look at the beginning of the log-file:

```
PE  Time     Event      Thread Id   Node/Spark Id   Optionals
0   [0]:     START      0           0xbe420         [SiteName: Main]
0   [4994]:  SPARK                  0x309368        [sparks 0]
0   [5197]:  PRUNED                 0x309368        [sparks 1]
0   [5755]:  SPARK                  0x309398        [sparks 0]
0   [6788]:  SPARK                  0x3093e8        [sparks 1]
0   [7263]:  EXPORTED               0x309398        [sparks 2]
1   [7263]:  ACQUIRED               0x309398        [sparks 0]
0   [7291]:  EXPORTED               0x3093e8        [sparks 1]
1   [7263]:  USED                   0x309398        [sparks 1]
1   [7263]:  START      1           0x309398        [SiteName: parList]
```

In order to understand this portion of the log-file it is necessary to understand the distinction GranSim makes between a spark and a thread. A *spark* is a task created by an evaluation of a par statement and may either be turned into a *thread* and begin running, or else may be pruned and discarded, see Chapter 6.

The log-file shows that three sparks are created before threads begin to run. Two are turned into threads (i.e. start to run) soon after being sparked but one of the sparks is pruned. The log-file does not record the par-site that created the pruned spark. However, from a simple analysis of the evaluation order, the pruned spark is created by the par-site inside euler. This par-site causes the evaluation of numbers, which takes less than 1/140th of total run-time to evaluate, so it is likely that before the spark had chance to turn into a thread, the node had already been evaluated to normal form. This would cause the spark to be pruned. After this pruning two further sparks are created, exported onto different processors, and the parallelism begins. This confirms that the lack of parallelism in region (I) is due to the time taken to execute the code that produces parallel threads.

Using the standard version of GranSim the only way to make this confirmation is to look at the logfile, as we have done. An alternative approach would be to use the parallel cost centre profiler GranCC [249] (GranSim augmented with the cost centre mechanism [510]). This can produce graphical views similar to the Activity graph but with the work broken down into associated cost centres. It should be possible to use these graphs to verify that the expression being evaluated during region (I) is the code that creates the parallelism.

10.2.2 Region (II)

Within this region only two threads are running concurrently. From Figure 10.2 it is not clear why one processor is idle. A fuller insight can be gained by looking at the per-thread graph (Figure 10.3), which shows the activity of each thread, rather than the number of running threads. The thick

10.2 Analysing an Example Using Current Tools

grey lines show when the thread is running. The medium-width black lines show when the thread is runnable and the breaks in the bars show when a thread is blocked. The x-scale and extra annotations match the ones given in the activity profile.

This graph shows that the lull starts immediately after a thread has finished. No other thread begins running at the point at which the thread finishes, suggesting that there are no unused sparks or runnable threads. The current graphs produced by GranSim do not convey enough information to confirm this. To help our understanding of this example we produced an annotated version of the per-thread profile which we call the per-thread spark and block profile (Figure 10.4). This profile contains a lot more information, most of which can be extracted from current log-files[2]. In this graph the following extra annotations have been introduced:

- *Thread labels* – each thread is labelled on the y-axis with the `par`-site that created the thread;
- *Processor numbers* – the number of the processor on which the thread is running is recorded at the beginning of the first bar for the thread (there is no thread migration so there are no numbers on subsequent bars);
- *Spark lines* – for each spark that is turned into a thread, the spark creation time and thread that created the spark are shown. These are indicated by the straight lines on the graph. The vertical lines point to the thread that creates the spark and the horizontal lines point to the thread the spark turns into;
- *Pruned spark lines* – for each spark that is pruned, a horizontal line is placed on the thread that created the spark, indicating its creation and pruning time. A spark is pruned when its closure is evaluated by another thread;
- *Block lines* – where a thread blocks, an arc connects the blocked thread (blockee) to the thread evaluating the closure that the blockee is awaiting the value of (blocker). The line is curved to remind us that the blocker is not necessarily evaluating the node at the current time.

From this graph we can extract more information about the computation. For example, it is clear that the `euler` spark site produces considerably shorter computations than the `parList` spark site.

Within region (2) we see that although there are suitable sparks they are not residing on processor one, which is idle. A spark is soon exported from processor zero. When this arrives on processor one (immediately, as there are no communication costs) the idle processor has some more work to do and so the level of parallelism picks up. It is not surprising that processor one ran out of sparks. Following the work trail of processor one, we see that all the tasks exported to it are rather small (compared to the tasks exported to

---

[2] Current log-files do not contain enough information to establish a link between the blockee and corresponding blocker. Also, the construction of the spark lines is only possible for some examples using the current log-files.

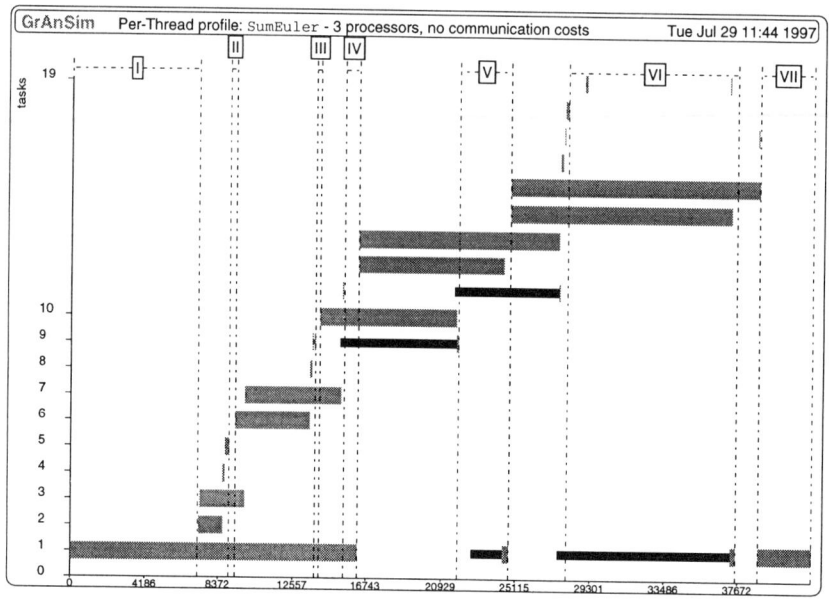

Figure 10.3. Per-thread graph for SumEuler 9, with annotations for regions where at least one processor is idle added by hand

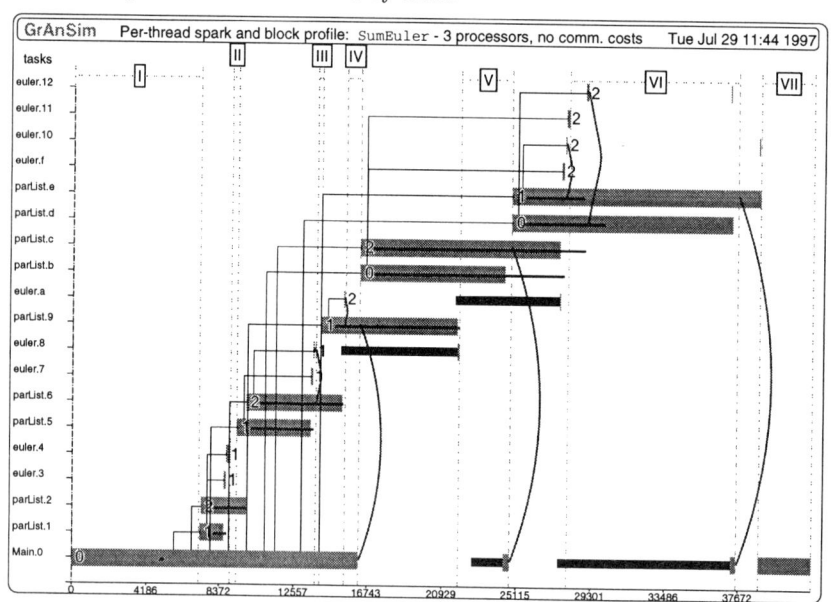

Figure 10.4. Per-thread spark and block graph for SumEuler 9 with annotations identical to those in Figure 10.3

the other processors) and so the processor used up all its sparks before any other sparks were exported to it. In the optimal situation each processor has approximately the same amount of work as the other processors throughout execution.

10.2.3 Region (III)

This region differs from region (II) because, although there are no runnable threads, there is a blocked thread waiting to be evaluated. Again it is only the per-thread spark and block profile that reveal what is happening. This graph clearly shows that the blocked thread is being blocked by the thread that created it. The computation attempted by the blocked thread has already begun. If we look at the code we see that this is because the function `euler` (evaluated by the blockee) and function `parList` (evaluated by the blocker) will attempt the evaluation of the same computation at one point, namely, the spine of `relPrimes` for a given `euler` function application. The per-thread spark and block profile confirm that the processor is idle during this period as it has no sparks or runnable threads. As soon as a spark is imported from another processor the parallelism starts up again.

10.2.4 Conclusions from the Example

Although this is a very small example, a lot of manual analysis of the logfile and source code is necessary in order to answer only a few questions. The activity graphs are able to give a very general view of the computation but do not contain enough information to answer some questions. The per-thread spark and block profiles convey a lot more information than can be produced with current tools and it would not be too hard to develop a tool to produce these profiling graphs automatically. However, most examples have far more threads with far more activities, so the bars on a per-thread spark and block profile would be much too dense and unreadable — a scalability problem. The same is true for the normal per-thread graphs. The profiles could be split on to multiple pages but this is unlikely to make them any more understandable and the compactness of a single page profile is lost. The crux of the problem is that large quantities of information can be obtained from a parallel computation, whether it is held in a log-file or a graph. We need a way of allowing the programmer to process the data to extract information as they require it.

In the next section we present a framework for implementing a more general profiling tool.

10.3 Data Modelling Parallelism

In the previous section we highlighted some inadequacies of current parallel profiling tools. One reason why tools are deficient is that no formal data modelling was done when developing the tool. There is a big difference between what the log-files record and what the graphs show. In this section we give various data models for parallel graph reduction. An explicit data model makes clear to the developer of the profiling tool the information that needs to be recorded, and to the user of the tool what the underlying model is.

There are a number of ways to carry out conceptual data modelling. We use the most common, the Entity-Relationship (E-R) approach [598], [186], [346]. This does not provide the mathematical rigour of specification languages such as Z [547] but does give a simple diagrammatic way of specifying a data model, convenient for both users and developers.

The aim of this section is to show how to make explicit the data model a profiling tool uses. For purposes of illustration we build up an explicit model for GranSim. We do this by starting with a simple model and then introduce extra entities and relationships to reflect different parts of GranSim's data model. We are not saying the GranSim model is the right one. Indeed, one reason to make the model explicit is in order to judge its merits. Although we comment on the differences between different tools we do not attempt to synthesise an 'ideal' model.

10.3.1 A Simple Parallel Graph Reduction Model

Probably the simplest view of parallel graph reduction is one where there is one main thread which creates threads which, in turn, may create further threads. This is a simple model that abstracts away from details of resources such as processors and memory. It is the model of a naïve programmer who places **par** annotations anywhere in their program hoping for parallelism. This model is naturally represented as an E-R diagram (see Model 10.0). In this diagram there is one entity which represents the threads. The arc labelled *sparks*, represents thread creation. A thread optionally sparks other threads; this is indicted by one direction of the arc being dashed. The spark relationship is one-to-many as a thread may spark many threads but a single thread can only be sparked by one thread.[3]

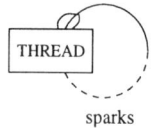
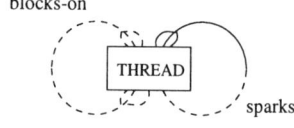

Model 10.0. A naïve view of concurrent graph reduction

Model 10.1. Introducing blocking

---

[3] The main thread is not really created by another thread so we take Main to be the unique fixed point of the relation *sparked by* (inverse of *spark* relation).

10.3 Data Modelling Parallelism

When a thread tries to evaluate a shared data structure that is already being evaluated, the thread *blocks* until another thread has finished evaluating the expression. Using Model 10.0 it is not possible to ask any questions related to blocking or even to establish whether a thread blocks at all. A slight refinement of the original model is required to store this information, see Model 10.1. The *blocks-on* relation is used to represent when a thread tries to evaluate an expression already being evaluated by another thread. One side of the relation is the thread that blocks (blockee) and the other side is the thread that evaluates the expression that the blockee tries to evaluate (the blocker).

If one of the attributes of the entity THREAD is the **par**-site that created the thread (i.e. a reference to the source code) it is possible to ask questions such as "Does **par**-site p always create threads that block on thread t?". This type of information can be used to identify bottlenecks in the code. Runciman and Wakeling [504], [506] required information similar to this when profiling the soda program.

Although we use the **par**-site as a reference to the source code for the THREAD entity some parallel profilers use other methods. GranCC [249], the parallel cost centre profiler, uses cost centres [510] to reference the source code. Cost centres are annotations to sections of code that can be assigned independently of the **par**-site, giving the programmer more control over what portion of the source code to associate with each thread. GranSP [336] is a profiler for programs using evaluation strategies [571] (see Chapter 3) to create parallelism. It allows the programmer to mark strategies with annotations which could be used as an attribute of THREAD. For strategic code these annotations may be better references to the source code than cost centres because they correspond directly to the division of work that the programmer has specified.

10.3.2 Introducing Time

Current profiling tools place a lot of emphasis on the order and duration of events. The log-file typically records a time-stamp for each event recorded and one of the dimensions of a graph is usually time. Already in Model 10.1 there is an implicit record of time: a thread must be sparked before it can be blocked, and a thread can only spark a new thread when it has been sparked itself. Although this may be useful for determining the order in which threads are created, it is too high a level of abstraction to establish the duration of events. Knowledge of the duration of events is useful: for example, it helps to identify **par**-sites that create threads doing very little work. These **par** applications can in turn be removed in the hope of increasing the granularity of threads.

Model 10.2 incorporates a notion of time. In this model a thread can have many activities, where each activity is either *running* or *blocked* on the thread evaluating a shared expression. The horizontal bar under the ACTIVITY entity specifies that RUN and BLOCK are subtypes of ACTIVITY: they have all the attributes of ACTIVITY, plus some extra ones.

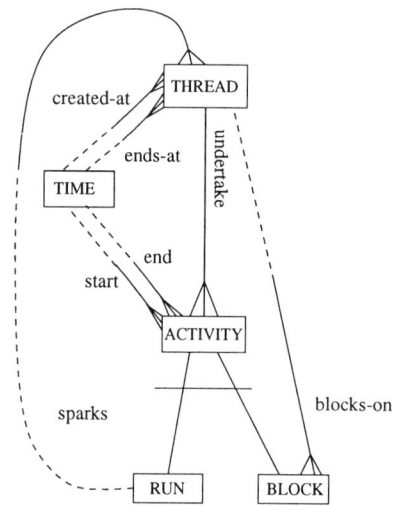

Model 10.2. Introducing time

Model 10.3. Limiting the number of concurrently executing threads

Model 10.2 is used both by HBC-PP [504], with an unbounded number of processors, and by GranSim-light[4]. However, the unit of time they use is different. GranSim-light records time as an internal clock and HBC-PP as the number of reduction counts. These two methods of recording times can lead to very different results for exactly the same computation. So, even though HBC-PP and GranSim-light both fit the above data model, we cannot expect the same results when the same program is run on both systems. It is also important to realise that even if they did have the same measure of time they still may give totally different results because the data model is only abstract and the concrete implementation details (e.g. scheduling policies) may be very different.

Making underlying models explicit for two different tools, it is possible to compare the differences between what data is implicit in the model, what is stored in the log-files and what is currently accessible through use of the visualisation tools. HBC-PP records all the information in Model 10.2. GranSim-light does not record the data for the *blocks-on* relationship. None of the visualisation tools that accompany GranSim or HBC-PP are able to show the *sparks* relationship or the *blocks-on* relationship. This highlights the gap between the data model used and the information that can be extracted us-

---

[4] A simplified version GranSim with no processor limit and no communication costs.

10.3 Data Modelling Parallelism

ing the high-level graphs. The per-thread spark and block profile is designed to display as much information as possible, so, unsurprisingly, it is able to display all the information in Model 10.2.

10.3.3 Introducing Processors

Model 10.2 does not model a limit on the number of concurrent threads that can be evaluated at one time. A third activity, *queue*, needs to be incorporated to model this behaviour. A thread queues when it is not blocked but because the limit on the number of running threads has been reached it cannot run. This queue is often called the queue of runnable threads. A slight refinement is made to Model 10.2 to incorporate this new state (see Model 10.3). In this model, a thread may run, block or queue during a single activity period.

This is the model used by HBC-PP, where the number of processors can be limited. Again, all the information required to answer any of the queries is recorded in the log-file but the visualisation tools do not present the sparks or blocks-on relationship in any way.

A limit on the number of concurrent running threads is one simple way to model a limited number of *processors*. This is particularly suited to a thread-oriented view of the computation. Another way to view the computation is processor-oriented. Model 10.4 extends the previous model to include an explicit representation of processors. The advantage of doing this is that it is now possible to ask questions about processor load and how well the sparks and threads are distributed across the processors.

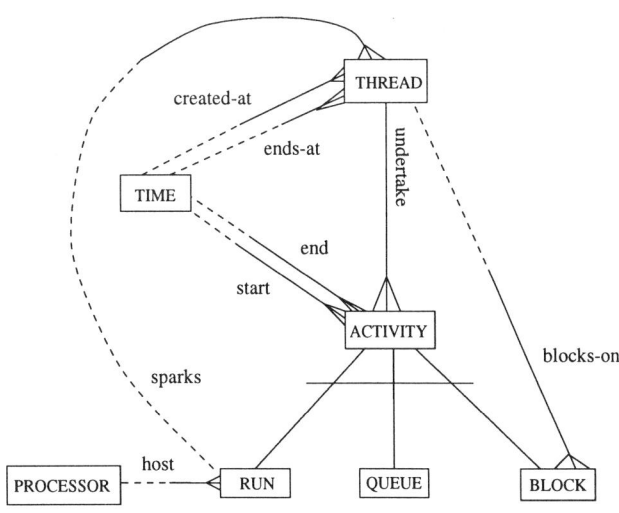

Model 10.4. Introducing processors

10.3.4 Introducing Nodes

None of the models so far distinguish between blockers that evaluate a *tiny* subexpression that other threads also want to evaluate, and those where the *whole* expression evaluated by the thread is required by other threads. Theoretically it is possible to record this distinction with the addition of an extra entity, NODE (see Model 10.5), which records the subexpression that the threads are trying to evaluate when they block. To record this type of information we enter the realm of tracing [546]. In practice this would be too costly to integrate into a parallel profiling system. One compromise between recording full expressions that cause threads to block and just the par-site of the blocker is to record the cost centre [249] of the expression being evaluated.

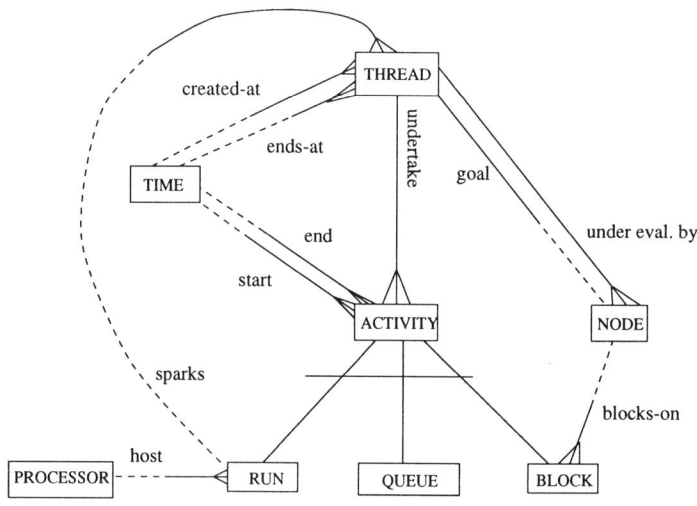

Model 10.5. Introducing graph nodes

10.3.5 GranSim

GranSim is highly configurable. Its implicit data model depends on the options selected. We model:

- Spark/thread distinction;
- Spark migration;
- Thread migration;
- Fetching nodes;

in addition to the properties modelled in the previous models, see Model 10.6.

10.3 Data Modelling Parallelism

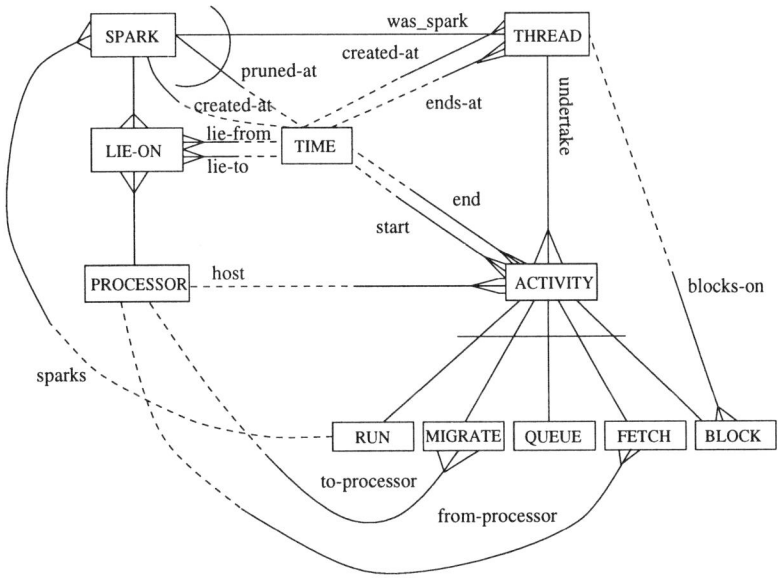

Model 10.6. Introducing spark/thread distinction, thread migration, fetching

GranSim uses an *evaluate-and-die* mechanism (similar to *lazy thread creation* [408]), described in Chapter 3, to help increase the granularity of threads. *Sparks* and *threads* are different objects. A spark is created by a thread and joins the spark pool on the processor evaluating the thread. This spark may then be pruned, if its associated closure has already been evaluated. Alternatively the spark is turned into a thread, which evaluates its associated expression. During the time the task is a spark it may be exported to other processors. This is essential: if this did not happen there would be no parallelism! The time when a task is only a spark could be considered as an activity of a thread, and modelled in a similar way to the running, runnable and blocked states. However, the sparking period always happens at the start of a task's lifetime and to reflect this we treat sparking differently, as shown in the model.

Sometimes it is necessary for threads, as well as, sparks to migrate between processors [252]. Also GranSim explicitly fetches graph nodes from different processors when the current processor does not have access to the required node. Both of these actions are represented in Model 10.6 as new states of activity.

Model 10.6 is more complex than the previous E-R models, allowing more complex queries. GranSim does not record all this information in its log-file (it only dumps a selected portion of the information it records internally). In particular it does not record the *was_spark* relation or the *blocks_on* relation. The absence of these relations reduces the class of queries that can be formed.

For example, it is not possible to determine which thread created which thread. Further, the current visualisation tools do not even display some of the information that *is* recorded in the log-file. For example, none of the graphical charts display anything about sparks.

10.4 Conclusions and Future Work

Summary. Section 10.2 details some of the weaknesses of current tools for parallel Haskell programming. Sometimes it is not possible to retrieve all the information required to analyse a program without delving into the log-file. Moreover, because of the large amount of information that can be obtained from a parallel computation it is not really practical to show all the information on a single graph. Section 10.3 contains a number of conceptual data models for concurrent graph reduction. This modelling process has given us a clearer understanding of the implicit assumptions behind current tools.

Applications. Making explicit the data models used by profiling tools is useful for both programmers and implementors. Programmers can use this high-level information to understand what happens when executing their programs without knowing the full low-level implementation details. Implementors can identify inconsistencies between the implicit model their tools use, the data recorded in the log-file, and the information displayed by visualisation tools.

We have begun work on a *database query* system based on Model 10.6 that allows the programmer to ask questions about the execution of a parallel program. So far we have a promising prototype that allows the user to:

1. View graphs similar to those produced by GranSim;
2. Ask questions about parallel execution using queries;
3. Interact with graphs to help fill in queries;
4. Use queries to filter the information displayed in a graph.

For further information see [121].

Future Work. An important extension to the data modelling process that we are currently investigating [120] is the issue of *refinement*. We have presented a number of successive models but have provided little theoretical justification for the implicit claim that the model is enriched at each stage. Precise definitions of the refinement transformations are required. Batini et al. [41] present a library of primitives to describe schema transformations. We are currently implementing a tool which, given a source schema and refinements written using the primitives, produces *relational views* [187]. This will be integrated into our database query system so that the views can be used to pose queries based on an abstract model, to extract information from a database based on a more concrete model. The data modelling process presented in this chapter is not restricted to parallel profiling and could equally be applied to other forms of profiling. We plan to substantiate this claim by extending our tool to handle at least one other form of profiling.

11. Memory Performance of Dataflow Programs

A.P. Willem Böhm[1] and Jeffrey P. Hammes[1]

11.1 Introduction

This chapter reports on the experience of writing numeric, scientific algorithms in a mostly functional style. One-dimensional FFT, three-dimensional FFT, Eigensolvers, and a Monte Carlo Photon Transport code are studied. While the functional paradigm is effective in the expression of these problems, their memory space use is poor as compared with imperative implementations. The focus is on the programming language Id and its Monsoon Dataflow Machine implementation, and the Id codes are sometimes compared to Haskell or SISAL versions. Each algorithm is informally described, and its performance is treated in a qualitative fashion. These studies show that there continue to be serious problems in the performance of functional languages, especially with respect to space use. (For work on profiling space use in functional language implementations, see Chapter 10. The designers of Id have recognised this problem and have proposed non-functional extensions to enhance the efficiency and expressiveness of the language. Such extensions do improve performance, but they exact a programming cost due to the very low-level, explicit parallel programming that is required.

11.2 The Dataflow Model of Computation

In an imperative execution model, memory cells are read and written in an unpredictable order, often making parallelisation difficult because of the data dependencies involved. The dataflow model of computation, in its basic form, avoids this problem by precluding mutable global memory. This results in an elegant and simple data-driven graph model of parallel computation, where nodes are operations and edges are data paths that connect them. A node can execute when data "tokens" are available on all its inputs.

Structured data, such as arrays, can be represented in a variety of ways. The most straightforward approach represents an entire array as one "mega" token that travels on the graph edges just as scalar tokens do. A structured token becomes available only when all its constituents are available, giving rise to a strict data structure model. Implementation of this approach is impractical, motivating a modification in which data structures are allocated from a separate store, and the structure tokens are pointers to the structures

---

[1] Colorado State University, USA.

themselves. As in the "mega" token model, the only necessary form of synchronisation is the arrival of the token at a node, and data structures are again strict. The third approach, accepted by many dataflow machine designers, stores data structures in a memory, called a *structure store*, where each storage cell is given two *tag* bits, a *presence bit* and a *defer bit*, to allow for non-strict data structures with element level synchronisation. The instruction architecture now includes two special structure store access operations. A *read* checks the presence bit, and if it is set the datum is read and sent to the successors of the read instruction. If the presence bit is not set, the defer bit is set and the read operation is enqueued at the memory cell, until a write operation fills it. A *write* operation checks the presence bit, and an error occurs if it is set, thus preventing destructive writes. If the presence bit is not set, the write operation fills the memory cell, satisfies all deferred memory requests, resets the defer bit and sets the presence bit.

The above storage model implements deterministic, parallel, asynchronous memory access, which is the standard mode of operation for dataflow programs. In some situations, truly updatable memory is necessary. This can occur in state-based run-time system routines such as I/O and garbage collection operations, or in explicit program operations such as a global updatable "best-solution-so-far" variable in a parallel search. Updatable memory may also be necessary for efficiency reasons. For instance, if a list element must be updated, a pure functional language requires a new list to be built up to the point of the changed element, incurring a sometimes serious loss of efficiency.

Deterministic *read* and *write* operations are sufficient to implement pure functional programs, but two new operations are introduced to implement impure language extensions. The *get* operation reads a value from a storage cell and resets the presence bit, in effect *extracting* the value from the store. As in the deterministic read, the *get* operation will be blocked and enqueued if the cell is empty. The *put* operation writes a value in a storage cell, and if there are deferred *gets* it will allow *one* of them to extract the value. The rest of the deferred *gets* will continue to see an empty cell and must wait for subsequent *puts* to occur. As in the deterministic write, a *put* to a cell whose presence bit is set causes a run-time error. *Put* and *get* together allow for the efficient implementation of locks, data buffers, and global shared variables, but can make a computation *indeterminate*, or time dependent.

The abstract or *idealised* execution of a dataflow program assumes infinite parallel resources, i.e. that each operation can be executed as soon as its inputs have arrived. It also assumes that each instruction takes one clock tick or time step to execute. There are two commonly used time measures that derive from an idealised execution: S_1 is the total number of instructions executed. S_∞, also called the *critical path*, is the number of parallel time steps required. A *parallelism profile* plots the number of instructions executed in each time step. The *average parallelism* is defined as $\pi = \lfloor S_1/S_\infty \rfloor$.

11.3 Programming Languages

Because of the single assignment nature of the dataflow model, functional languages are a natural choice for dataflow programming. The fine-grain dataflow graph, combined with the word-level storage synchronisation model, allows a straightforward mapping of non-strict functional languages onto dataflow machines. The Id (Irvine Dataflow) programming language, designed by Arvind and his colleagues at Irvine and later at MIT [425], maps one-to-one onto the dataflow model of computation, with inherent expression, loop, and function call parallelism, and executes on the MIT/Motorola Monsoon Dataflow Machine [270]. Id has three language layers. The inner layer (F) is purely functional with non-strict, eager, data-driven semantics. Arrays in this functional kernel are created using monolithic constructors called *array comprehensions*, very much like Haskell's list comprehensions. Elements of an array comprehension can depend on each other in a dynamic fashion. Such dependencies could cause an execution to block if a fixed evaluation order were chosen, but Id's concurrent execution model, combined with the non-strictness of data structures, avoids this.

Functional arrays in Id are implemented using structure store *read* and *write* operations. In [20] Arvind and others introduced I-structures (Incomplete Structures with write-once, read-often semantics) to model the behaviour of the dataflow structure store. In the same paper, it is argued that functional arrays created with array comprehensions are not sufficiently expressive, and that for certain problems it is useful to expose I-structure operations at the language level. The I-structure layer (I) of Id allows explicit declaration of initially empty I-structures, which subsequently can be defined on an element by element basis using an imperative assignment statement of the form $A[i] = expr$. A definition of an I-structure element can occur anywhere in the program, with multiple assignments to an element giving rise to a run-time error.

Because of its single assignment nature, an I-layer program is deterministic, but referential transparency is lost. For example, two declarations of an I-structure of the same type and size do not refer to the same object, hence:

```
typeof A = I_Vector(F); A = I_Vector(1,n);
typeof B = I_Vector(F); B = I_Vector(1,n);
```

declares two distinct empty I-arrays and is not the same as:

```
typeof X = I_Vector(F); X = I_Vector(1,n);
A = X; B = X;
```

which creates just one empty array. An I-level program, if it terminates without run-time error, will always produce a consistent result; in that sense I-level programs are determinate. However, if a program produces a run-time error, any results already produced are potentially erroneous. For example, consider:

```
def f A i j = {
typeof A = Vector(F); A[i] = Expr1; A[j] = Expr2
in (A[i], A[j])
};
```

If $i = j$, an error will occur, but it can manifest itself in different ways. The error will not occur until both write statements have executed, but non-strictness allows elements of the result to be returned before the function has completed. Thus, depending on the time ordering of the concurrent operations, the function can produce a $(value, error)$ pair, an $(error, value)$ pair, or an $(error, error)$ pair. All parts of the execution that depend on either of the return values will be erroneous.

In the previous section, and much more extensively in [40], it is argued that for certain problems I-structures are still not sufficiently powerful. The M-layer of Id allows the declaration of M-structures, which are not bound by the single-assignment restriction. M-structures use the previously described structure store *put* and *get* operations to express destructive updates and potentially non-deterministic phenomena. Because time ordering in M-structures can affect the computed result, *barriers* generally must be used to enforce proper access order to these memory elements. Barriers are also important in memory reclamation, since in Id the programmer is responsible for deallocating data structures and function closures. This adds considerable complication to the writing of Id programs that otherwise could be written cleanly in the F- or I-layers.

The SISAL (Streams and Iteration in a Single Assignment Language) programming language [391] was designed by McGraw and others in an attempt to create a general purpose, implicitly parallel programming language that could be implemented easily and efficiently on a variety of parallel architectures. SISAL indeed has been implemented on dataflow [72], vector, and shared-memory machines [114]. In order to keep the detection of parallelism simple, the language is purely functional and thus enforces a single-assignment restriction but it goes quite a step further in that it allows no circular definitions, e.g. no array elements can be defined in terms of elements of the same array. An array is created in a monolithic style, as in an array comprehension, but in a simpler way using a loop structure. To ensure that every array element is defined exactly once, SISAL dictates that loop body $(i_1, ..., i_n)$, of an n-deep nested loop, defines elements $(i_1, ..., i_n)$ of an n-dimensional array. This property allows efficient array allocation and partitioning, but with a loss of expressiveness. Because data and control structures are non-circular, SISAL allows a strict implementation that, in turn ,allows for easy, automatic resource management, both in terms of process scheduling (because processes cannot be mutually dependent,) and data management (because data structures can be automatically deallocated using reference counting schemes.)

The functional language Haskell is described in detail elsewhere in this book.

11.4 Programming Issues

The two essential issues in the programming process, *expressiveness* and *efficiency*, are influenced by the features available in a programming language.

(Non-)Strictness.. There is no "silver bullet" in the choice of strictness versus non-strictness. Strictness, as in SISAL with its strict loop-order creation of arrays, can make expressing certain algorithms, such as the Jacobi Eigensolver, hard, or can cause a loss of parallelism, as in the stream-oriented version of MCP-Functional [244]. The non-strict implementation of data structures in Haskell can lead to serious inefficiencies, as in the three-dimensional FFT in the NAS FT benchmark. At the same time, the Dongarra-Sorensen Eigensolver demonstrates that non-strictness allows for overlapping producer-consumer parallelism.

(Im)Purity.. In [192], Felleissen argues that there are *essential* and *non-essential* language features. The non-essential features can be systematically replaced, in a macro expansion style, by other language constructs, whereas the absence of an essential feature forces a complete restructuring of a program. *Destructive update* is such an essential feature. In [473] Pippenger shows that the absence of destructive update can cause an order of magnitude increase in the complexity of some programs. These two theoretical results are strongly reinforced by practical experience. As an example, in the three-dimensional FFT, an Id program with destructive updates allows an eight-fold increase in the problem size that can be run on a Monsoon machine compared to a purely functional version of the code.

Data Structure Components.. When dealing with a multi-dimensional array, it is often necessary to manipulate lower-dimensional components as if they were independent data structures. As an example, a three-dimensional FFT is composed of many one-dimensional FFTs. In this case, it is useful to be able to select and target one-dimensional "slices" of a three-dimensional array. It turns out that none of the three languages studied here have a truly satisfactory way of expressing this.

The combination of the particular design choices made with regard to the above features seriously affects programming style and efficiency.

11.5 The Benchmarks

In this section, four benchmark problems, written in Id, are introduced. Some comparisons of the Id codes with SISAL and Haskell are also available. Each algorithm is informally described, and its performance is treated in a qualitative fashion.

11.5.1 One-dimensional Fast Fourier Transform (FFT)

Quantitative studies of parallelism, with time and space complexities of Id versions, are described in [69], [70]. Also see Barry Jay's chapter on FFTs (Chapter 9). The FFT algorithm transforms a function from one representational domain to another. Engineers often think of the FFT in terms of a "frequency" and "time" domain, but here the FFT is introduced in terms of a "coefficient" and "point" domain. An n-th degree polynomial $P(x)$ can be represented by the $n + 1$ coefficients of its terms, as well as by $n + 1$ pairs $(x_i, P(x_i))$. A straightforward transformation of a polynomial, from coefficient to point representation, requires $n + 1$ polynomial evaluations, each requiring $O(n)$ operations and yielding a complexity of $O(n^2)$. However, because it is possible to choose freely the evaluation points of the polynomial, the complexity can be reduced to $O(n.log(n))$ by evaluating at the *complex roots of unity*, exploiting simple relations between the n-th roots of unity and the $n/2$-th roots of unity. To achieve this, the array of coefficients is "unshuffled" into two arrays containing the odd and even coefficients, the *fft* function is recursively applied to the two arrays, and the resulting arrays are recombined.

```
def  unshuffle  V  = {
(_,SizeV)  = bounds  V  ;  Mid  = SizeV / 2  in
({ array(1, Mid)  |  [i]  = V[(i*2)-1]  ||  i <- 1 to Mid };
 { array(1, Mid)  |  [i]  = V[(i*2)]    ||  i <- 1 to Mid })
};

def fft  v  = {
(_,SizeV)  =  bounds   V in
if (SizeV == 1)  then   V else {
  (OddV,EvenV)  =  unshuffle  V ;

  fft0   = fft OddV;   fftE  = fft EvenV;
  Mid    = SizeV / 2;  X     = TwoPi / SizeV;
  Xi     = X * (i-1);

  Coeff  = { array(1,Mid)  |  [i] = Cmplx (cos(Xi) (-sin(Xi))
                              ||  i <- 1 to Mid };

  Prod   = { array(1,Mid)  |  [i] = Cmplx_Mul Coeff[i] fftE[i]
                              ||  i <- 1 to Mid }

  in {array(1,SizeV)
       | [i]      = Cmplx_Add fft0[i] Prod[i] ||  i <- 1 to Mid
       | [Mid+i]  = Cmplx_Sub fft0[i] Prod[i] ||  i <- 1 to Mid }
}};
```

The divide-and-conquer nature of this function, with its inherent parallelism, is clear from the two recursive calls on the odd and even components. The computation proceeds in $log(n)$ stages, each allocating k arrays of size n/k. For each allocated array element it takes a constant amount of work

11.5 The Benchmarks

to calculate its value, so there is $O(n.log(n))$ total work. In a parallel implementation one would expect a critical path length $S_\infty = O(log(n))$ and an average parallelism $\pi = O(n)$, since all elements of the array can be shuffled into place in parallel and, in the recombination step, each pair of elements of the resulting array depend on a pair of elements from the previous stage. The

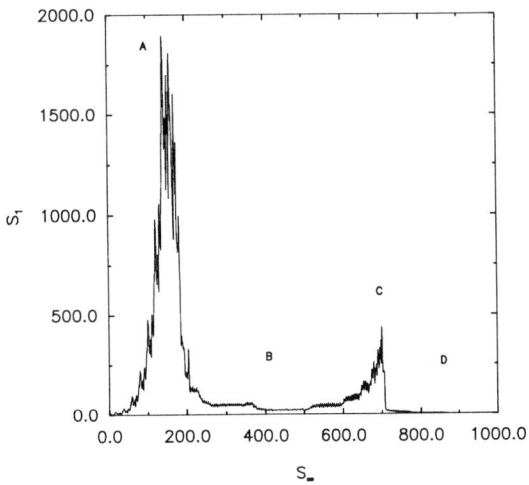

Figure 11.1. Parallelism profile for fft, SizeV = 128

parallelism profile in Figure 11.1 is the result of running *fft* for $SizeV = 128$, and differs significantly from what is expected based on the complexity measures discussed above. Remember that S_1 refers to the number of instructions executed, along the critical path, indicated by S_∞. First, there is explosive divide-and-conquer parallelism (A), in which the dynamic dataflow graph is unfolded, followed by a stretch of low parallelism (B). Then comes a second burst of parallelism (C), which dies down to an almost sequential tail (D). As the problem size increases, the B and D segments become more dominant. They are caused by array comprehensions that are translated into loops, and there is a sequential cost in the critical path for spawning loop bodies (in this case, five time steps per iteration.) The last body of the first loop is executed at time-step 640 (5*128), after which divide-and-conquer parallelism becomes dominant (C). The production of the final results causes the "mouse tail" (D) in the parallelism profile. These sequential bottlenecks can be avoided by explicitly strip-mining the loops, i.e. turning array comprehensions into doubly nested loops that perform assignments to I-structure elements. This eliminates the (B) and (D) segments in Figure 11.1, reducing the critical path length threefold for $SizeV = 128$ and more for larger problems.

Recursive and iterative FFTs written in the I-layer of Id are compared, both with and without explicit storage management, in [69]. These experiments demonstrate that the space use of iterative algorithms is about half that of their recursive counterparts because they avoid the intermediate unshuffle arrays. They also show that *k-bounding* loops [148] can reduce space use even further by limiting the amount of parallelism. Even so, these programs use at least ten times the amount of space required by an explicit parallel von Neumann algorithm. Finally, these experiments demonstrate that use of an implicit parallel programming language does not free the programmer from thinking deeply about parallelism and ways to achieve it.

11.5.2 NAS Benchmark FT

This section discusses F-, I-, and M-layer Id implementations of NAS FT, and compares them to a Haskell implementation[556], [243]. NAS benchmark *FT* [29] solves a three-dimensional heat equation by transforming it using a three-dimensional FFT, solving the transformed equations directly, and transforming it back using an inverse three-dimensional FFT.

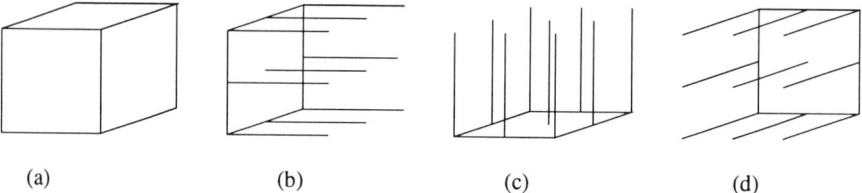

Figure 11.2. Steps in performing a three-dimensional FFT

A three-dimensional (inverse) FFT takes a complex array of size $n_1 \times n_2 \times n_3$ and performs $n_2 \times n_3$ n_1-point one-dimensional (inverse) FFTs in the n_1 direction, followed by $n_3 \times n_1$ n_2-point one-dimensional FFTs in the n_2 direction, followed by $n_1 \times n_2$ n_3-point one-dimensional FFTs in the n_3 direction. Figure 11.2 sketches the steps and the orientations of the intermediate one-dimensional FFTs. Hence the main issue centers on finding a representation of the three-dimensional object such that one-dimensional slices can be *selected* (read) and *targeted* (written) in any of the three directions. A slice becomes the input and output of a one-dimensional *fft* function, as described earlier.

In the Id F-layer it is not possible to target a slice in a multi-dimensional array, so the straightforward three-dimensional representation does not work. Hence the favoured representation for the intermediate cubes in Id is a matrix

11.5 The Benchmarks

of vectors. There are two pure functional approaches to selecting a slice. The first simply creates a copy of the slice and passes this as a parameter to a one-dimensional *fft* function. The second dynamically creates a *selection function* and passes it as a parameter to a higher-order version of the one-dimensional *fft* function. The selection function is designed to take a single index parameter and return an array element from the slice in the three-dimensional object. In a sense, the selection function plays the role of a copy, but makes the actual copy unnecessary.

With explicit deallocation, both the selection function and the slice copying versions of the Id codes (with iterative one-dimensional FFTs) use approximately 10 M-bytes of space for a size 32^3 problem, roughly ten times the amount needed by an imperative code. Using M-structures, it is possible to run a size 64^3 problem in the 4 M-word memory of the Monsoon machine. This is comparable to the amount of space an imperative code would use.

Haskell's approach to array creation differs from that of Id. In Haskell, an array is specified by a list of associations, though creating this through the use of a list comprehension yields a form that looks much like an Id array comprehension. An association is an index-value pair $(i_1, ..., i_n) := v$, where the index in an n-dimensional array is represented by an n-tuple. Even though the array-creating semantics involves the association list, a Haskell programmer reasonably expects the compiler to store an array in a contiguous block of memory and to avoid creating the association list where possible. Slice selection in Haskell can be implemented just as it was in Id, using a selection function passed to an appropriately defined higher-order one-dimensional *fft*. Such a slice selection function, and an *fft* function designed to use it, would have the following type signatures and corresponding function call:

```
-- user-defined type for slice function
type Sel_Slice_Func = (Int -> Element)

-- a 1d array of Element, indexed by Int
type Vector = Array Int Element

-- type signature of 'fft' function
fft :: Sel_Slice_Func ... -> Vector
...
let f i = x!(i,j,k) in fft f ...
```

Haskell uses the infix operator "!" to reference an array element. It is important to note that both the slice selection function and the *fft* function that uses it are general with regard to the dimensionality of the source array: the type signatures do not expose the array's dimensions, making it possible to use one function that can take slices from arrays of any dimensionality. Only the body of a particular instance of the selection function deals with the array's dimensions but an attempt to *target* (write, define) slices, using a similar higher-order technique, cannot hide the particulars of the target array. Because Haskell's arrays are created from association lists, slice targeting means creating a list of associations that eventually, along with other slices, will be transformed into a three-dimensional array. The type signatures of the target function and the *fft* show that they are specific to the target array's dimensionality:

```
type Three_D_Assoc = ((Int,Int,Int),Element)
type Target_Slice_Func = Int -> Element -> Three_D_Assoc
fft :: Target_Slice_Func  ... -> [Three_D_Assoc]
...
let f i v = ((i,j,k),v) in fft f ...
```

It appears to be impossible to create a general target-slice-producing *fft* function, because array indexing is done through *tuples* and the type system distinguishes among different tuple sizes. Since a general solution to target slicing is not apparent, the *fft* function in the Haskell experiments produces a vector, as in the selection function type signature above, and the intermediate arrays are represented as matrices of vectors.

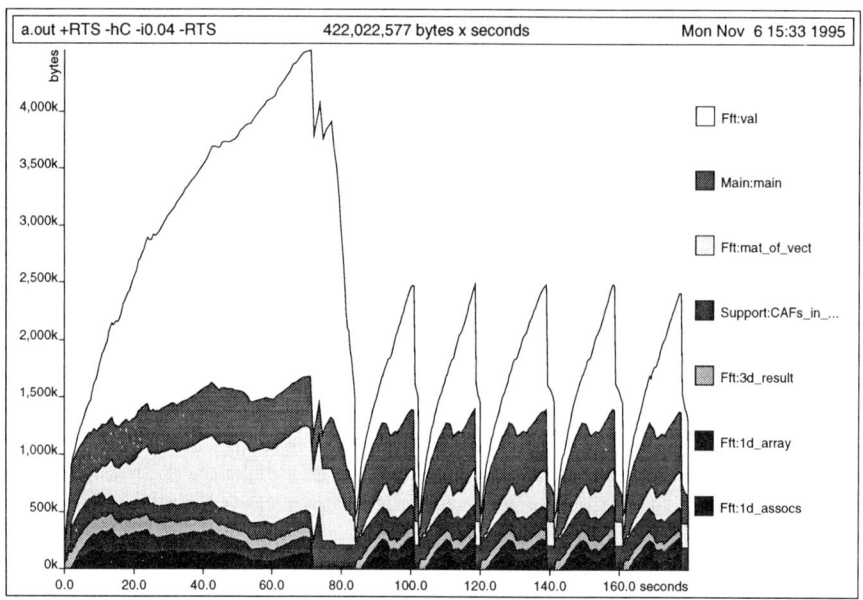

Figure 11.3. Heap profile for 16^3 lazy, copying, recursive version

Figure 11.3 shows the heap profile for the 16^3 copy-recursion code, run sequentially on a SUN workstation. The large white areas are caused by the non-strictness of array elements. To measure the effects of strict arrays, versions of these codes were created in which the value in every array association is given a strictness annotation; this reduced the peak heap requirements by

11.5 The Benchmarks

as much as 80% over the lazy versions, and made it feasible to run the 32^3 problem, which had consumed too much heap space in the non-strict version. With strict arrays, it takes approximately 6 Mbytes to run a 32^3 problem, or roughly six times more than an imperative code would require. Clearly, this example shows that there continue to be serious problems in the space use of functional languages.

11.5.3 Eigensolvers for Symmetric Matrices

Given a symmetric $\mathbf{N} \times \mathbf{N}$ matrix $\mathbf{A}$, the eigenvalue problem is the determination of eigenvectors $\mathbf{x}$ and eigenvalues λ defined by $Ax = \lambda x$. Standard references on numerical methods [479] provide several methods for determining the solution to this problem.

The Jacobi Eigensolver: Strictness versus Non-Strictness for Expressiveness. The Jacobi algorithm uses two-dimensional rotations applied successively to each off-diagonal element of the matrix $\mathbf{A}$. When the rotations are done systematically, $\mathbf{A}$ converges to a diagonal matrix, thereby producing both the eigenvectors and the corresponding eigenvalues. The "plane" or Jacobi rotation is described by an "orthogonal" transformation matrix $\mathbf{R}_{pq}$, in which all diagonal elements are unity except for the two elements c located at $\mathbf{R}_{pp}$ and $\mathbf{R}_{qq}$, and all off-diagonal elements are zero except for s and $-s$ located at $\mathbf{R}_{pq}$ and $\mathbf{R}_{qp}$, respectively. The rotation is defined by the values c (cosine) and s (sine) with respect to a free angular parameter ϕ. A rotation is performed by the matrix product $\mathbf{A}' = \mathbf{R}^T_{pq} \mathbf{A} \mathbf{R}_{pq}$.

A sequential implementation of Jacobi's algorithm performs *sweeps* of rotations around points in the upper triangle in row major order, until the sum of the absolute values of the upper triangle of the matrix is sufficiently small. A rotation zeroing element (p, q) updates the array elements on rows and columns p and q. As an example, the pattern of element updates as induced by the rotation zeroing element $(3, 5)$ is depicted below. The updated elements are denoted by a'.

$$\begin{bmatrix} . & . & a' & . & a' & . & . & . \\ . & . & a' & . & a' & . & . & . \\ a' & a' & 0 & a' & a' & a' & & \\ . & . & a' & . & . & . & & \\ & & a' & a' & a' & a' & & \\ & & . & . & . & & & \\ & & . & . & & & & \end{bmatrix}$$

When elements are zeroed in a strict cyclic order, the convergence of this method is quadratic for non-degenerate eigenvalues (i.e. eigenvalues that are not identical). Because the matrix $\mathbf{A}$ is symmetric, one *sweep* of the Jacobi method is applied to $n(n-1)/2$ distinct off-diagonal elements. Furthermore, each rotation requires $O(n)$ operations, so that the total computational complexity is of order n^3 for each sweep.

A pure functional Id implementation is based on array comprehensions and closely follows the mathematics of the Jacobi transformation, allowing a natural exploitation of parallelism. Unfortunately this algorithm is space inefficient: each rotation, coded as an array comprehension, updates $O(n)$ elements in A, and copies the rest. Since a sweep involves $O(n^2)$ rotations, the functional implementation of a sweep takes $O(n^4)$ operations, which is one order of magnitude higher than should be necessary. A non-functional solution to this copying problem would be to use updatable M-structures.

A more parallel, and at the same time more space efficient, implementation of the Jacobi algorithm allows several rotations to be performed concurrently [71]. A *group of rotations* $(p_1, q_1) \ldots (p_k, q_k)$ is *valid* if each point (p_i, q_i) occupies its own row and column in the upper triangle of A. Clearly there cannot be more than $\lfloor n/2 \rfloor$ rotation points in a group. In a parallel rotation based on all rotation points of such a group, each element in the resulting matrix is affected by at most two rotation points. A set of groups *partitions* the upper triangle of a matrix if every point in the upper triangle is a member of exactly one group. In [508], Sameh defines a minimal number of $2n - 1$ groups of maximal size $\lfloor n/2 \rfloor$. These groups form anti-diagonals that wrap around the matrix boundaries. The following are Sameh's groups for n=5:

$$\begin{bmatrix} . & 2 & 4 & 1 & 3 \\ & . & 1 & 3 & 5 \\ & & . & 5 & 2 \\ & & & . & 4 \\ & & & & . \end{bmatrix}$$

Sameh's group definition can be directly translated into the following I-layer Id function *MakePQs*:

```
def MakePQs n =
{ m = floor( float (n+1)/2.0 );
  PQs = 2D_I_array ((1,2*m-1),(1,n)) in
  { for k <- 1 to 2*m-1 do
    if k <= (m-1)
    then {for q <- (m-k+1) to (n-k) do
             p = if ( ((m-k+1) <= q)   and  (q <= (2*m-2*k)) )
                 then ((2*m-2*k+1)-q)
                 else if (((2*m-2*k) < q) and (q<=(2*m-k-1)) )
                      then ((4*m-2*k)-q)
                      else n;
          (i,j) = if p < q then (p,q) else (q,p);
          PQs[k,i] = (i,j);  PQs[k,j] = (i,j) }
    else {for q <- (4*m-n-k) to (3*m-k-1) do
             p = if ( q < (2*m-k+1) )
                 then n
```

11.5 The Benchmarks

```
                  else if ( ((2*m-k+1) <= q) and (q<=(4*m-2*k-1)) )
                      then ((4*m-2*k)-q)
                      else ((6*m-2*k-1)-q);
            (i,j) = if p < q then (p,q) else (q,p);
            PQs[k,i] = (i,j);  PQs[k,j] = (i,j)};
    {for i <- n to 2*m-1 do PQs[k,2*m-k] = (0,0)}
    finally PQs
} };
```

The table *PQs* can be used to drive the parallel Jacobi Eigensolver, thereby performing $S_1 = O(n^3)$ operations with $\pi = O(n^2)$ average parallelism. The above code shows the power of non-strict I-structure definitions. The elements of *PQs* are computed in a non-linear order, and the I-layer allows it to be written in exactly that way. This approach is not possible in SISAL, with its strict index ordering, because the loop computes the array target index. This forced a redesign of the *MakePQs* function, which turns out to be simpler than the original *MakePQs* and much more efficient than an implementation that builds an intermediate array with unordered rows and reorders these in a separate sweep. Writing this in SISAL was a useful and interesting programming problem[2], but, in general, forcing a program to create arrays in index order can reduce programming productivity.

The Dongarra-Sorensen Eigensolver: Non-Strictness for Expressiveness and Efficiency. A different, more efficient, approach composes an Eigensolver from three components: a tridiagonalisation function, a tridiagonal solver, and a matrix multiplication. In a study of the effectiveness of non-strict functional computation, the Householder tridiagonalisation function [479] and the Dongarra and Sorensen [180] tridiagonal solver were implemented in Id [555]. Dongarra and Sorensen mention the possibility of exploiting producer-consumer parallelism between the tridiagonalisation function and their tridiagonal solver, and state that "an efficient implementation of this scheme is difficult". In [555] it is shown that in a non-strict functional execution environment, the Dongarra-Sorensen algorithm can run completely in parallel with the Householder tridiagonalisation function. Moreover, this is achieved without any change in the code components. Expressing this producer-consumer parallelism was easy in Id, as the non-strict data structures that interface the modules allowed a natural and implicit exploitation of fine-grain parallelism [292].

11.5.4 Monte Carlo Photon Transport

The Monte Carlo particle transport problem involves tracking many particles (photons, neutrons, or electrons) in a user-specified simulated physical system, and gathering statistical information about the locations, energies, etc. of the particles [597]. The photon transport code, written in Id, Haskell and

---
[2] and is left as an exercise

SISAL, is called MCP-Functional, and is based on a large Fortran code, called MCNP, which originated in, and is still maintained at, Los Alamos National Laboratory [88]. MCP-Functional does not duplicate all of MCNPs capabilities, but it does capture the essence of its particle transport simulation behaviour [244]. MCP-Functional is much larger than the other benchmarks discussed here.

The program can be considered at two levels. At the lower level there is photon tracking, through a set of functions that describe the physics of the particles as they collide with the nuclei of various atoms in the simulated materials. These routines include such activities as table lookup and interpolation, random number generation, weighted decisions based on random values, photon splitting, and three-dimensional geometry calculations with cell crossings. This low-level code is entered through the function *track*, which takes as its argument a photon (with all its attributes such as location, direction, energy, etc.) and returns a list of *events* that fully describe the history of that photon. The tracking function is complicated by the fact that photons can split into multiple photons, each of which must be individually tracked. The lifetimes of photons can vary greatly: a photon can "die" at any arbitrary point in its track due to its location or energy level, which, in turn, are functions of its history. This results in an irregular execution tree for each source photon.

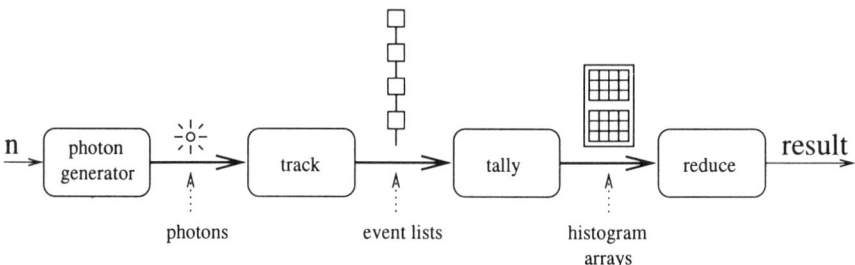

Figure 11.4. High level view of MCP-Functional

At its upper level (see Figure 11.4) MCP-Functional generates photons with appropriately weighted random energies and directions, calls the *track* function on each, and gets back an event list for each photon. Each event list must be traversed to gather user-specified information (called *tallies*) into histograms. Similar histograms containing the squares of these values are also created. The histograms are then summed across all photons, producing mean and standard deviation values of specified tally information, such as photon flux across a surface, binned by specified energy bands.

Each answer that comes from a Monte Carlo simulation is not a discrete value, but rather a range that represents a given confidence level. Quadrupling the number of source particles cuts the range in half, and a real-world user of such a program may need to simulate millions of source particles to get sufficiently narrow result ranges. MCP-Functional is an "embarrassingly parallel" application, since each source particle's track is completely independent of the others. Thus the implementation challenge lies not in finding parallelism, but in managing it so that system resources are not overwhelmed. The MCP-Functional implementations in the three functional languages are all structured identically in the *track* function and the routines below it. The interesting programming decisions occur at the upper level, where source photons are created, tracked and tallied.

Programming issues. Functional languages express the particle transport problem very cleanly. The core problem in coding the upper-level part of MCP-Functional relates to accumulating histograms, and this happens in two levels. The lower of the two involves traversing an event list (returned from the tracking of a single source photon) and creating, for each user tally, a histogram that is usually a small two-dimensional array. A typical example of a tally is photon flux across a selected set of surfaces, and binned according to energy bands; the histogram is indexed by surface number in one dimension and energy band in the other dimension. During the event list traversal, any event that involves a surface crossing must add that photon's flux contribution to the histogram entry for that surface and the energy band corresponding to the photon's energy in that event. When the traversal is complete, the histogram represents that photon's flux across the specified surfaces. Note that a single source photon may contribute multiple times to a given tally. This can happen in two ways: first, back scatter may cause the photon to cross a surface more than once, second, photons can split and any of the daughter photons may cross the surface and make a tally contribution.

An upper-level accumulation of these histograms must take place to determine the mean and standard deviation, on an array element-by-element basis, of the tallies for all the source photons. The mean requires summing the histograms, and the standard deviation requires also summing the squares of the histograms. The value in a given cell of the final 2D histogram, and the sum of the squares, allows the mean and standard deviation across that specific surface caused by all photons in the specific energy range to be computed and reported to the user.

Creating the first functional code was very difficult: it is necessary to run large numbers of photons in order to get meaningful results for assessing program correctness. Thus space deallocation issues had to be dealt with from the start of the development process. The first version was done in Id, using M-structures for the accumulated tally arrays. The upper-level approach was essentially imperative in nature: a k-bounded loop spawned the photons, and each event list, returned from the photon's *track* call, was immediately traversed to extract the tallies, which were summed into M-structure arrays. As soon as a list's traversal was complete, the histogram was summed into the upper level M-structure histogram for that tally, and its squares were summed into the second M-structure histogram. Then the event list and its accumulator array were deallocated. The k-bounding of the loop ensured that space use would be constrained. Once the first implementation was complete, the other functional codes were easily created: the low-level routines remained unchanged, and by using the same random number generator algorithm in all three languages, all the codes could be expected to give precisely identical answers.

Two approaches to the upper-level code structure were explored in the pure functional realm. The first essentially duplicates the approach used in the development code, but uses functional, rather than M-structure, arrays for the accumulations. A top-level loop (or its recursive equivalent) is used, where each iteration spawns a source photon, tracks it, reduces its event list to histograms, and sums those histograms into the accumulators. Histograms present challenges in pure functional contexts because a naive implementation requires array copying every time a value is added in. Both the Id and Haskell languages have array accumulation functions that were included specifically for the histogram problem, but they must be applied to a "complete" structure. Thus they work well for the lower-level reduction of an event list to a histogram array. However, there is no way to use accumulator array functions in a top-level loop that must sum a photon's histogram into an upper-level accumulating histogram on an iteration by iteration basis. Thus the loop-based approach requires explicit array copying.

A second approach to code structuring takes a producer-consumer, stream-oriented view of the problem. The start of the pipeline is a generator that creates the data structures of the source photons, each with its own initial random seed. These are consumed by the *track* function, which produces a stream of event lists. These lists in turn are consumed by the tally functions, which produce the histograms, and finally these histograms are reduced to the output result. This is an attractive way to view the problem, and it is especially natural for functional programmers since such a pipeline is easily formed by function composition. It also exposes pipeline parallelism, and allows the use of accumulator array functions in the final stage, thereby eliminating array copying. In Id and Haskell the "streams" can be lists, whereas SISAL has explicit stream data structures in the language.

Performance. Space problems can be deadly for Monte Carlo simulations since users must run very large problems, and any space use that grows with problem size is unacceptable. So the crucial matter of importance in MCP-Functional relates to the space use of the programs.

Id. As mentioned, the first implementation was done in Id with M-structures and explicit space deallocation, resulting in a code that runs in constant heap space. A 20,000,000-photon simulation on an eight-processor Monsoon executed correctly, taking about 50 hours. It is useful to note that the top-level loop has loop-carried dependencies in two places. The first is in the sequence

11.5 The Benchmarks

of random seeds that are given to the source photons, where each photon uses a subsequence of the random number sequence; each seed depends on its predecessor. The second is in the accumulator histogram arrays. Nevertheless Id's non-strictness allows loop iterations to overlap, and since the time spent in seed generation and array summing is dwarfed by the time spent in the tracking function, useful parallelism is achieved. Parallel speedups of seven are typical for this code on the eight-processor machine. However, pure functional Id implementations without explicit deallocation become unusable for more than a few thousand photons, due to heap memory exhaustion.

Haskell. Laziness plays a crucial role in the space use of the Haskell codes, even though the Haskell systems have automatic garbage collection. The problem centres on the sharing of large data structures by two or more consumers. One obvious example of this occurs when a user specifies more than one tally. The execution begins by demanding the first part of the result, i.e. the first tally's histogram. This, in turn, causes (by backward-rippling demands) the generation and tracking of all photons, creating the event lists. As the first tally traverses the event lists, none of these lists can be garbage collected because a second tally has yet to use them. Thus *all* events, possibly numbering in the billions, must exist simultaneously at some point in the run. The extensive space use is a consequence of the program's evaluation order; the space use could be reduced through careful placement of strictness annotations.

SISAL. Surprisingly, though SISAL emphasises the stream data structure in its name, a stream version of the MCP code cannot run large problems due to space use. The SISAL compiler implements streams as strict data structures, meaning that a producer generates an entire stream before a consumer begins to use it. Thus, the entire stream of event lists must exist at some point in the run, just as occurs in the Haskell implementation, but for a different reason. This problem was circumvented by creating a loop version of the code [242]. This SISAL implementation has achieved what the other MCP-Functional codes have not: a pure functional code that runs large problems in a constant and very moderate amount of space (approximately 54 K-bytes in the benchmark problem.)

Parallelism experiments were performed on the SISAL loop code, run on a four-processor Sun SuperSPARC workstation. In spite of the massive parallelism available in the problem, no parallel speedup occurred. The reason centres on the two loop-carried dependencies in the top-level loop, described earlier in the Id code description. The dependencies cause the compiler to implement the loop sequentially, without the overlap that Id's non-strictness allowed. Thus one iteration will not start until the previous one is complete.

For this reason an explicitly strip-mined code was created. A new loop was put around the main loop, to spawn multiple chunks of work. For n-fold parallelism the main loop is executed n times. Each chunk of work proceeds independently, accumulating its own histograms. Finally, the histograms are combined into the end result. This code exhibited a two-fold speedup for four processors on the Sun, surprisingly poor for a code with large, seemingly independent chunks of work. The reason for this performance has been traced to the memory deallocation mechanism: SISAL uses a reference count field on each data structure. This count is appropriately adjusted as the structure is handed to different parts of the computation and as those parts eventually finish using it. Since the Sun is a shared-memory machine, the reference count fields must be protected by locks. With four processors there is considerable contention on the locks for the read-only lookup tables that are referenced frequently by the low-level tracking routines. The counts are manipulated because the SISAL run-time system tries to deallocate these arrays, and it cannot infer that they will exist through virtually the entire program execution and are not worth trying to reclaim.

11.6 Conclusions and Future Work

The functional algorithm research described here supports the claim that (non-strict) functional languages allow a natural separation of programs into modules, while still exploiting inter- and intra-module parallelism [292]. Non-strict data structures glue the modules together and support fine-grain element-level synchronisation of producers and consumers. Moreover, a fundamental strength of functional languages is their ability to express the implementation of parallel algorithms in ways that closely follow their mathematical formulations, in a machine-independent fashion. This, combined with their ability to express parallelism at the function, loop, and instruction levels, provides a strong argument for the use of functional languages and the development of functional algorithms for parallel computing.

In spite of this, functional languages have not been embraced by the parallel programming community at large, in good part because there are still serious performance problems, in time and space, with functional languages. The excessive space use of these codes is a more serious problem than the time inefficiency, because executions on realistic problems can sometimes fail to produce answers.

There is often a difference in programming a first version of a parallel code, which closely resembles the specification of the abstract algorithm, and writing an efficient version of that code. Functional languages prove to be very helpful in writing an initial code because functional languages are implicit: they do not refer to machine resources, but an efficient code must exploit the computational characteristics of the algorithm and explicitly express these in architectural terms. When optimising a functional language code, it can be difficult to get sufficient control over resources exactly because of the implicit nature of the language. Also, parallelism in the abstract algorithm does not necessarily lead to parallelism in the execution of the functional program.

11.6 Conclusions and Future Work

In some cases, the only way to achieve performance is to step outside of the pure functional paradigm and introduce explicit machine-level constructs such as M-structures, barriers and explicit deallocations. Currently it seems that a parallel functional programmer has to choose between two extremes: the pure functional paradigm, without enough control over machine resource use; or a paradigm that reintroduces imperative, machine-level constructs. Practical programming requires something in between: a higher-level way of expressing lower-level concerns. A good example of this is Id's [425] *accumulator array*, where the efficiencies of M-structures are exploited without such structures being exposed at the programming language level.

For increasing numbers of applications, performance considerations are becoming less important due to ongoing improvements in computer hardware. Philip Wadler rejects the idea that the poor reception given to functional languages by the programming community at large is due to performance problems [589]. Nevertheless, interest in parallel computing is driven by the need for greatly improved performance, especially for large scientific problems. Here, space performance may be more critical than time performance since the penalty may be *no* results rather than merely *slow* results. Among the items Wadler considers mandatory for a useful functional programming system is a profiler. We would extend this to include not only user feedback but language mechanisms that will allow the programmer to deal with performance-related issues.

12. Portability of Performance in the BSP Model

Jonathan Hill[1]

12.1 Introduction

The usefulness of any programming model depends upon whether there is a simple mathematical description of the model, and if it is possible to clearly express useful computations in that model. This chapter describes the Bulk Synchronous Parallel (BSP) model [580], [389], [540], and presents algorithms and associated cost formulae for a parallel scan and sorting algorithm. A growing number of researchers have found that BSP provides a realistic programming model, at a sufficiently high-level of abstraction, for the development of scalable parallel applications [96], [498], [411], [489], [181], [147], [399], [443], [97], [417], as well as research into numerical algorithms [287], [286], [388], [111], [141], [92], [55], [54], [347], [56], sorting and searching [217], [219], [217], [274], [42], simulation [109], [376], [378], communication [218], [323], [177], [458], parallel data structures [377], [216], [221], [220], and parallel programming in general [539], [68], [184], [110], [43], [108], [34]. Whilst having a tractable cost calculus is not the only prerequisite for the development of portable scalable parallel applications, we argue that without a cost calculus there will be no *portability of performance*.

An objective of this chapter is to show that the BSP cost calculus provides the right foundations upon which practical variants of parallel functional languages could be developed. This is particularly timely, as the majority of research into BSP has concentrated upon low-level communications libraries that are used from C or Fortran [277], [235], [398]. As BSP is paradigm neutral, there is great potential for raising the level of abstraction of the programming language used to express BSP algorithms.

12.2 The BSP Programming Model

The BSP model [582], [580], [389], [540] views a parallel machine as a set of processor-memory pairs, with a global communication network that delivers messages in a point-to-point manner among the processors, and a mechanism for globally synchronising all processors by means of a barrier. Unlike some of the parallel functional languages described in Chapter 3, in which the creation of processes can be highly dynamic, it is normal for BSP programs to be written in a Single Program Multiple Data (SPMD) style in which

---
[1] Sychron Ltd, Oxford, UK.

a fixed number of processes, each of which executes the same program, is created at program start-up. Also, the model has no concept of processor locality or the topology of the underlying network; both of which have been successfully used to provide impressive performance results in domains for which locality is critical, for example low-level image processing. For these types of applications BSP may not be the best choice.

These limitations not withstanding, with the emergence of parallel machines that have powerful communication interconnects and use, for example, two-phase random routing [579], the abstraction is surprisingly efficient [175], [278]. The distinguishing feature of the model is that it decouples the two fundamental aspects of parallel computation: communication and synchronisation. This separation is the key to:

- A simple and accurate cost model that can be used to analyse and guide the design of parallel algorithms. The use of the cost model, and its applicability to the analysis of parallel functional programs is one of the focuses of this chapter (see Section 12.5);
- Achieving universal applicability across a wide range of parallel architectures, from shared-memory multiprocessors [279] to tightly-coupled distributed-memory machines [278] or networks of workstations [178], [179], [531], [175].

BSP programs consist of a sequence of parallel *supersteps* which are global operations of the entire machine. Each superstep is semantically subdivided into three ordered phases consisting of: (1) simultaneous local computation in each process, using only values stored in the memory of its processor; (2) communication actions amongst the processes, causing transfers of data between processors; and (3) a barrier synchronisation, which waits for all of the communication actions to complete, and which then makes any data transferred visible in the local memories of the destination processes. Although it was originally envisaged that BSP programs would be written using BSP languages [387], [390], the model has actually been realised in terms of programming libraries [277], [398], [235], [73].

In the next section we motivate the advantages of BSP, by contrasting it with the advantages of functional programming. In Section 12.4 we describe the various ways in which BSP algorithms can be expressed. Section 12.5 provides an introduction to the BSP cost model, which is used to analyse a scan (Section 12.6) and sorting algorithm (Section 12.7). Both these examples are provided as an example of the usefulness of accurate cost modelling, and we describe in the conclusions how this style of cost analysis is applicable to parallel functional programming in general.

12.3 Simplicity by Restriction

Functional programming languages provide a high-level programming abstraction for both the sequential von Neumann programming model, *and* a variety of parallel models: dataflow, graph reduction, and data parallelism. From a programming perspective, the two advantages of non-strict functional languages are that they do not require the programmer to explicitly encode evaluation order into their algorithms, and there is an absence of side-effects. These two properties ensure that the value denoted by a fragment of program depends solely upon a small amount of contextual information, and therefore functional languages are amenable to equational reasoning [48]. Although it would seem that equational reasoning comes at the price of no explicit state in non-strict languages, this omission can be considered an advantage [292] in the same way that the omission of goto statements in structured programming languages can also be considered an advantage—*with unrestricted freedom comes chaos*.

The message passing programming model provided by communications libraries such as PVM [212] or MPI [395] have been the dominant model for scientific and commercial parallel applications for the last decade. The BSP model [580], [389], [540] provides an alternative parallel model that is based upon a restricted style of communication. As with non-strict languages, the benefits of this restrictive style can be yet again considered in terms of the structured programming analogy. Pair-wise communication in message passing systems provide a general mechanism for exchanging data between processors. However, unrestricted use of pair-wise message passing primitives can result in a "spaghetti" of matching sender-receiver pairs which can be difficult to reason about, and may lead to problems of deadlock or livelock. As an aside, the spaghetti of matching pairs can be time dependent, as receivers may use wild-cards to specify from which process to receive data.

In contrast to the generality of pair-wise messaging, the BSP model provides a *structured communication* model in which communication is treated as a bulk action of a program, rather than as the aggregate of a set of individual, point-to-point messages. Communications in BSP take effect at barrier synchronisations that involve all processors. Therefore, although full participation in barriers may be restrictive, getting past the barrier allows a process to deduce, locally, that the whole group has reached a common, global state. Barriers are common in data parallel languages, and therefore BSP shares many of the features of such languages, such as an absence of deadlock and livelock. However, whilst all the systems described so far provide software developers with a mechanism for writing portable software that will run unchanged on a wide range of parallel architectures, only BSP provides a simple framework for parallel algorithm design in which there are anticipated levels of performance across parallel machines. This *portability of performance* is the subject of this chapter. We discuss the problems of the lack of any anticipated levels of performance for parallel functional languages, which are even more acute than the predictability of MPI or PVM programs.

12.4 BSP Programming

The BSP model shares many similarities with the more general data parallel model, although BSP takes cost analysis more seriously. As with data parallel languages, there are two alternative viewpoints that can be adopted [80]: either a *macroscopic* or *microscopic* view of the language.

The *macroscopic* view, realised by data parallel programming languages such as HPF [271], adopts a centralised programming model which enriches the standard sequential Von Neumann model with parallel arrays or collections that can be manipulated by data parallel primitives in a monolithic manner. In this macroscopic view, parallel computation arises from the use of *map*-like operations that apply arbitrary functions to each element of the collection in parallel. Communication occurs by the wholesale rearrangement of the elements of the collection. For example, a permutation can be applied by using an index-set that specifies how each element in the collection should be rearranged.

The alternative *microscopic* view usually corresponds to the SPMD (Single Program Multiple Data) programming model that is used by programming libraries. In the SPMD view of data parallelism, there are multiple instances of the same program running on a fixed number of p processors. The task of writing an SPMD program will typically involve mapping a problem that manipulates a *notional global* data structure of size n into p instances of a program that each manipulate n/p sized *physical* data structures that are local to each processor. The role of communication in a SPMD model is to provide the infrastructure required for the *user* (or compiler) to take care of the data distribution, and any implied communication necessary to manipulate parts of the data structure that are on a remote process. This ensures that an illusion of a single monolithic global data structure of size n can be maintained.

When BSP was first presented [580], there were two programming styles proposed that mirrored the macroscopic and microscopic view of data parallelism:

- Automatic mode BSP where programs are written in a high-level language that hides the low level details of the data distribution, and any required communication amongst the processes;
- Direct mode BSP where the programmer has to explicitly control the data distribution, and any communication amongst the processes.

The automatic style of programming has been realised in terms of macroscopic data parallel [553], [554] and PRAM (Parallel Random Access Machine) [198], [394], [257] programming styles [567], [357], [9], [356]. In the macroscopic data parallel framework, collection types such as sets and sequences are distributed amongst the processes, and an interface of operations such as map, filter, fold, and scan provide the mechanism for achieving parallelism in a program. An alternative PRAM style of programming uses a SPMD style programming model, but the distributed memory abstraction of such a model is enriched with a shared-memory abstraction. This has been implemented in the distributed-memory framework of BSP by using a hashing technique to distribute memory cells among processes. This style of programming is only really appropriate when there is no data locality in an algorithm, for example, in problems such as list contraction [220] or sparse matrix computations [567].

To date, the direct mode of programming has been the main focus of programming in a BSP style. *BSPlib* [277] is a communications library that provides a small number of communication primitives for BSP programming in an SPMD manner. The library uses a static allocation of processes at program start-up, and does not provide any mechanism for the dynamic allocation of processes during program execution. The main features of *BSPlib* are two modes of communication:

- One-sided direct remote memory access where a process can copy contiguous regions of memory directly into the memory of another process, without the active participation of the remote process (at least at the level of the programming model). Writes into remote memory are visible after the barrier synchronisation that marks the end of a superstep;
- Bulk synchronous message passing where a non-blocking send operation delivers messages to a system buffer associated with the destination process. The message is guaranteed to be in the destination buffer at the beginning of the subsequent superstep, and can be accessed by the destination process only during that superstep. If the message is not accessed during that superstep it is removed from the buffer.

Although it is possible to program in a BSP style in message passing libraries such as MPI, it has been found that such systems are rarely optimised for the small number of primitives that are necessary for BSP programming. However, *BSPlib* is not just an alternative communications library. As we shall see in the following sections, the benefit of using BSP over existing parallel programming models is its simple and intuitive cost calculus.

12.5 The BSP Cost Calculus

The standard way of analysing the cost of a parallel algorithm is to use simple asymptotic cost analysis to provide estimates of performance. For example, a logarithmic combining technique can be used to calculate the sum of n values in time $\mathcal{O}(\log n)$ on n processors (see Chapter 7). The purpose of the BSP cost model is to refine such cost analysis by: (1) decoupling the asymptotic analysis of the problem size n, from the potentially modest number of processes p; (2) costing communication as well as computation; and (3) introducing constants of proportionality that capture the communication performance of a machine, so that the *comparative* performance of an algorithm can be analysed across machines.

The BSP cost calculus is straightforward because of the superstep structure of programs. As the barrier synchronisation involves all processes, then the cost of a sequence of supersteps is simply the sum of the costs of the separate supersteps. As an individual superstep contains three *ordered* phases of computation, communication, and synchronisation, it is natural to express the cost of a superstep by a formula that has the structure:

$$\text{cost of a superstep} = \underset{\text{processes}}{\text{MAX}} w_i + \underset{\text{processes}}{\text{MAX}} h_i\, g + l$$

where i ranges over the processes. Intuitively, the cost of a superstep is the execution time of the process that performs the largest local computation (denoted by MAX w_i), plus the communication time of the process that performs the largest communication (MAX $h_i g$), plus a constant cost l that arises from the barrier synchronisation and other one-time costs associated with the superstep, such as the overhead of initiating communication. If $h = $ MAX h_i, then such a communication pattern is called an *h-relation*. Note that an h-relation may involve transferring a total volume of data ranging from h (all but one h_i are 0) to ph (all of the h_i are equal). Hence the BSP cost model is implicitly asserting that communication performance is determined by the time taken to get data into and out of the network, and not by congestion inside it. The costs given by this model are not theoretical costs, but closely match the observed execution times over a wide variety of applications and target architectures (for example, [147], [489]).

The g and l parameters of the cost model depend on the performance of the underlying architecture. For example, g depends on: (1) the bisection bandwidth of the communication network topology; (2) the protocols used to interface with and within the communication network; (3) buffer management by both the processors and the communication network; and (4) the routing strategy used in the communication network. The l parameter also depends on these properties of the architecture, as well as specialised barrier synchronisation hardware, if this exists.

However, the BSP run-time system also makes an important contribution to the value of these parameters, by acting to improve the effective value of g and l by the way it uses the architectural facilities. The key to the performance improvement is to exploit the extra information implicit in structured communication. In particular, because communication is patterned, each process learns something about the global state whenever it receives a message. This information can be used to modify the processes' own behaviour to improve collective use of the communication system. For example, we have

12.5 The BSP Cost Calculus

Table 12.1. The BSP cost parameters for a variety of shared-memory and distributed-memory parallel machines

Machine	s	p	l flops	l/s μs	g flops/word	g/s μs/word
Origin 2000	101	2	804	7.9	8.26	0.08
		4	1789	17.9	10.24	0.10
		8	3914	39.8	15.10	0.15
		16	15961	158.5	44.9	0.45
400Mhz Pentium NOW 100Mbps Ethernet switch, 3C905B	88	2	5654	64.2	33.5	0.38
		4	11759	133.6	31.5	0.36
		8	18347	208.5	30.9	0.35
PowerChallenge	74	2	1132	15.3	10.2	0.14
		4	1902	25.7	9.3	0.13
266Mhz Pentium NOW 10Mbps Ethernet hub, TCP/IP	61	2	52745	870.4	484.5	8.00
		4	139981	2309.9	1128.5	18.62
		8	826054	13631.3	2436.3	32.91
Cray T3E	47	2	269	5.7	2.14	0.05
		4	357	7.6	1.77	0.04
		8	506	10.8	1.64	0.03
		16	751	16.0	1.66	0.04
IBM Sp2	26	2	1903	73.2	7.8	0.30
		4	3583	137.8	8.0	0.31
		8	5412	208.2	11.4	0.43
Cray T3D	12	2	164	5.6	0.3	0.02
		8	175	14.4	0.8	0.07
		64	148	12.3	1.7	0.14
		128	301	24.9	1.8	0.15
		256	387	32.1	2.4	0.20

shown [278]how orders of magnitude improvements in g can be obtained, for architectures using point-to-point connections, by packing messages before transmission, and by altering the order of transmission to avoid contention at receivers. In shared media networks such as Ethernet, BSP's global perspective on communication allows each processor to pace its transmission to maximise throughput of the system as a whole [176]. Similarly, [175], [178] shows how both implicit and explicit global information can be used to design improved error recovery techniques, reduce acknowledgement packet traffic by using expected traffic information, and reduce acknowledgement packet traffic further by using BSP's superstep structure. Table 12.1 shows the values for l and g for a variety of parallel machines (the benchmarks used to calculate these constants are described in [275]). It is particularly interesting to contrast the row *200Mhz Pentium NOW TCP/IP* and *400Mhz Pentium NOW 3C905B*. The former uses a network of workstations communicating with a TCP/IP implementation of *BSPlib* over shared 10Mbps Ethernet, whilst the later implementation uses switched 100Mbps Ethernet, and a BSP device driver dedicated for a 3Com 3C905B Ethernet network interface card that re-implements the entire communication protocol stack of the machine. When $p = 8$, g measures the communication performance when all processors are simultaneously communicating. If g is recast into the percentage of the achievable bandwidth, then the switched 100Mbps Ethernet and dedicated protocol stack is 94 times more powerful than shared 10Mbps Ethernet and TCP/IP. i.e.

- 10 Mbps, TCP/IP *BSPlib* $32.91\mu s/word$ which is equivalent to $32/32.91 = 0.972 Mbps$ on each of the eight links, which equates to a global bandwidth of $8 \times 0.972 = 7.778 Mbps$, or 77.8% efficiency of the hub;
- 100 Mbps, 3C905B *BSPlib* $0.35\mu s/word$ which is equivalent to $32/0.35 = 91.428 Mbps$ on each of the eight links, which equates to a global bandwidth of $8 \times 91.428 = 731.428 Mbps$, or 91.4% efficiency of the switch.

These large performance improvements ensure that BSP on a commodity cluster of PCs can give identical performance to tightly-coupled parallel machines such as the IBM SP2, and ball-park performance to an Origin 2000 [175], [179].

12.5.1 An Example Cost Formula

Returning to the problem of summing n values posed in the start of this section, it is natural to distribute the data amongst the processes in n/p sized chunks, when $n > p$. The sum of the n values can then be calculated in two stages where each of the processes sequentially sums the values in their possession in time $\mathcal{O}(n/p)$, and then a parallel sum of the resulting p values can be obtained using the logarithmic technique in time $\mathcal{O}(\log p)$. The cost of the logarithmic summation can be refined into the BSP cost calculus by considering the computation and communication costs of a single stage of the logarithmic algorithm. During the ith iteration of the algorithm, 2^{i-1} processes send a single data item to one other process; where no process receives more than a single item. This communication pattern realises a 1-relation, and the communication cost of the superstep will therefore be $1 \times g + l$. As the computational cost in each of the stages will just be one flop, because at most one addition of local and communicated values occurs in each process, then the total cost of summing p values is $\log p\, (1 + g + l)$. By combining the cost of locally summing each processes n/p sized chunk of data with the cost of the summation of p values gives a total cost of summing n values on p processes as $n/p + \log p\, (1 + g + l)$.

It is clear from this cost formula, and from the values of l and g in Table 12.1, that the logarithmic number of barrier synchronisations used in this algorithm will form the dominant cost, unless $n > p \log p\, (1 + g + l)$. From this formula, and the values of l and g, then, for a network of eight workstations running over TCP/IP n should be greater than $20,000,000$ elements for the computation time to start to dominate communication time; for an eight-processor BSP cluster (100 Mbps switch and 3C905B device driver), n should be greater than $441,000$; whereas for an eight-processor Cray T3D, n should be greater than $4,200$. In summary, although the logarithmic reduction minimises the computational complexity of summing p values, it places a great burden on the communication performance. Without a cost calculus that models both the computation and communication complexity of an algorithm, unrealistic implementations of parallel algorithms, such as the one above, will continue to proliferate the parallel programming literature. This has been the case in the parallel functional programming community, as both the design of parallel algorithms, and the implementation techniques used in parallel functional languages have suffered from this problem. In the following sections, we introduce parallel scan (i.e. a similar problem to summation) and sorting algorithms that overcome the computation/communication tradeoff in algorithm design.

12.6 BSP Design: Parallel Scan

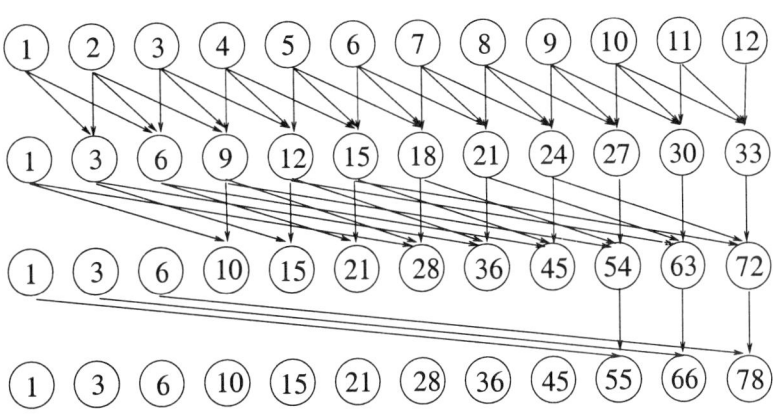

Figure 12.1. Generalised parallel prefix, with $d = 3$

Consider the parallel scan algorithm specified in Chapter 7, in which an associative operator $\oplus$ is used to calculate the running totals of p values, such that the result in process i (where $0 \leq i < p$) is $x_0 \oplus \cdots \oplus x_i$. As the algorithm is parameterised by $\oplus$, the following cost formulae are parameterised upon n, the size of data held in each process, and c_n, the cost in flops of applying the associative binary operator to a pair of values of size n (i.e. for addition, $n = 1$ and $c_n = 1$).

```
void bsp_scan(int d,
    void (*fun)(void *res,void *left,void *right ,int *len),
    void *src, void *dst, int nbytes) {
  int i, i_pow_d,j, src_pid, no_buckets, nprocs, pid;
  char *incoming_data, *result_so_far;

  nprocs        = bsp_nprocs();
  pid           = bsp_pid();
  incoming_data = calloc(d,nbytes);
  result_so_far = malloc(nbytes);
  if (!incoming_data || !result_so_far)
    bsp_abort("{bsp_scan} failed to allocate %d bytes",
              (d+1)*nbytes);
  bsp_push_reg(result_so_far,nbytes);
  bsp_sync();

  memcpy(result_so_far,src,nbytes);
  for((i=1,i_pow_d=1);i_pow_d<nprocs;(i++,i_pow_d*=d)) {
    for((no_buckets=0,j=d-1);j>=0;j--) {
      src_pid = pid - (i_pow_d*j);
      if (src_pid>=0)
        bsp_get(src_pid,result_so_far,0,
                &incoming_data[(no_buckets++)*nbytes],nbytes);
    }
    bsp_sync();

    if (pid>=i_pow_d) {
      memcpy(result_so_far,incoming_data,nbytes);
      for (j=1;j<no_buckets;j++) {
        fun(dst,result_so_far,&incoming_data[nbytes*j],&nbytes);
        memcpy(result_so_far,dst,nbytes);
      }
    }
  }
  bsp_pop_reg(result_so_far);
  free(incoming_data);free(result_so_far);
}
```

Figure 12.2. d−ary tree scan in C with *BSPlib* communications

The $\mathcal{O}(\log p)$ complexity parallel prefix technique [351] has the following BSP cost and memory requirements:

$$BSP\ cost = \log_2 p\ (c_n + ng + l)$$

memory per process $= n$

Although the algorithm is work optimal, in that it reduces $\mathcal{O}(n)$ addition operations to $\mathcal{O}(\log n)$ parallel steps, as with the summation algorithm in the last section, high synchronisation costs can make the algorithm unsuitable on many parallel architectures. An alternative algorithm can be realised in a single superstep, where each process sends the data value in its possession to all processes that require that element, and then a linear number of $\oplus$ operations are performed locally on the received values. As the bottleneck for the communication pattern is process $p-1$ because there are $p-1$ data items of size n entering that process, then the superstep realises a $(p-1)n$ relation with cost $(p-1)ng + l$. The BSP cost and memory requirements of this algorithm are:

$$BSP\ cost = (p-1)c_n + (p-1)ng + l$$
$$memory\ per\ process = (p-1)n$$

Although this algorithm minimises communication, it does so at the expense of computation and memory requirements. When p is large, this makes this algorithm also unsuitable. Surprisingly, these two algorithms form two extremes of a generalised parallel prefix algorithm that operates upon d-ary trees. For example, Figure 12.1 shows a 3-ary tree that calculates the running sums of twelve integers in three supersteps. When $d = 2$, the generalised algorithm is the same as the parallel prefix technique; when $d = p$, it is the single superstep algorithm. The BSP cost formula for this generalised algorithm is:

$$BSP\ cost = \log_d p\ ((d-1)c_n + (d-1)ng + l)$$
$$memory = (d-1)n$$

The purpose of this generalised formula is that an implementation of scan can tailor the value of d, and hence the algorithm, to a particular architecture depending upon p, l, g, and $\oplus$. This approach of encapsulating parallelism within higher-order functions has the same goals as the Skeletal approach to architecture independent parallelism (see Chapter 13). Figure 12.2 shows an implementation of the generalised algorithm using C and *BSPlib* [277]. The function requires as arguments an associative operator expressed as a C function, a source data structure of size nbytes, and a resulting data structure dst which is updated with the partial results of applying the associative operator to all data held in processes with a process-id less than the calling process. The function uses a bsp_get() [277] operation to perform a remote memory copy from data result_so_far held on a remote process, into the calling process.

12.7 BSP Design: Sample Sorting

A functional implementation of Hoare's $\mathcal{O}(n \log n)$ complexity quicksort [282] can be implemented on either a graph reduction machine, or by using a divide-and-conquer skeleton, in parallel time $\mathcal{O}(\log n)$ on n processors. At first sight, quicksort seems amenable to parallel execution as each of the logarithmic number of phases in the algorithm can be performed independently, and in parallel. However, the $\mathcal{O}(\log n)$ computational complexity of the algorithm ignores: (1) the cost of dynamically allocating threads, if a dynamic allocation of processes to partitions of the data is used; and (2) the implicit communication requirements of the algorithm.

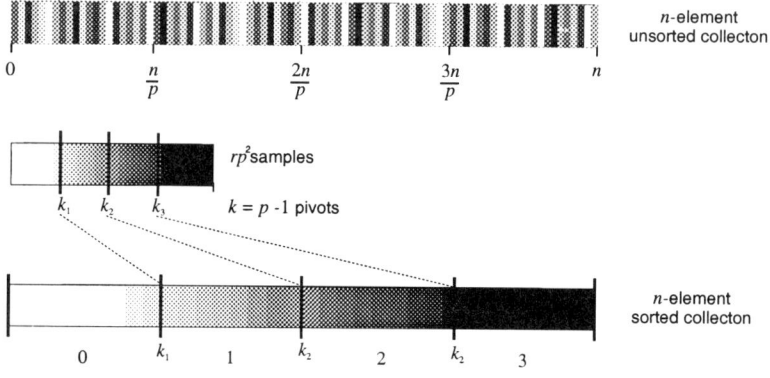

Figure 12.3. Parallel samplesort

The objective of a parallel sorting algorithm is to rearrange a data structure that contains n elements that are distributed among p processes[2], so that on termination of the algorithm, each process contains approximately n/p elements which are monotonically increasing in value among the p processors.

The sequential predecessor to the algorithm is sequential samplesort [203], proposed by Frazer and McKellar as a refinement of quicksort. The fact that the sampling approach could be useful for splitting keys in a balanced manner over a number of processors was discussed in the work of Huang and Chow [285] and Reif and Valiant [491]. Its use was first analysed in a BSP context by Gerbessiotis and Valiant [221].

Samplesort shares many similarities with parallel merge sort, such that the algorithm contains the following local sort then merge steps: (1) each process sorts the n/p elements in its own possession using a sequential sorting algorithm; and (2) the p sorted sequences are then merged to attain the desired effect of a global sort throughout all the processes. Naively, the merge can be implemented by sending all the data to a single process, a sequential merge [343] can then be performed in time $\mathcal{O}(n \log p)$, and finally the data elements are distributed among all the processes. The limitation of this approach is that it requires communication and per-process memory requirements of $\mathcal{O}(n)$. In contrast, parallel samplesort uses a regular sampling technique to reduce the computation, communication, and memory requirements of the

---

[2] The upper-bounds on the analysis that follows assumes an input distribution of p chunks of size n/p. However, the algorithm works correctly for any distribution.

12.7 BSP Design: Sample Sorting

merge by a factor of p. Samplesort therefore provides the *basis* of a scalable sorting algorithm.

The ideas behind samplesorting can be best understood by analogy with the processes involved in the election of a political party. The purpose of an election is to determine the percentage of the electorate which voted for each political party. During the run-up to the election, organisations such as Mori or Gallup perform polls on a subset of the electorate to predict the outcome of the election. Neither of these organisations go to the trouble of polling the entire electorate (that is the point of the election), but if a large enough, representative, subset of the population is polled, then the outcome of the election can be predicted.

Sample sorting uses a similar technique to Mori polling, whereby a property of the entire dataset is obtained by analysing only a subset of the data. The algorithm is best explained by working backwards. Consider the *sorted collection* of n elements shown in Figure 12.3, where each process contains approximately n/p elements. The data elements at the start (or, alternatively at, the end) of each process' local n/p chunk of data is termed a pivot element, such that there are p pivots, one per process in total. The essence of the samplesort algorithm is the calculation of these pivot elements, *without actually sorting the data*. By analogy with polling, Mori do not want to sample the entire electorate when performing a mini-poll. Therefore, if it is possible to calculate the pivot elements from the unsorted data set, then global sorting can be achieved as follows: (1) locally sort each process' n/p elements in parallel; (2) the pivots are copied onto each process and used to partition the local data into p blocks of size n/p^2; (3) each process sends its partition i to process i; and finally (4) a local merge of the sorted partitions produces the desired effect of a global sort.

The selection of pivots that define approximately equal-sized partitions is a crucial issue. Given n elements, then the $p-1$ pivots shown in Figure 12.3 will be at regular n/p intervals in the globally sorted array. If the original data set contained a uniform random distribution of data values throughout all processes, then choosing p values from the global *sorted* data set is exactly the same as choosing p values from an n/p sized subset of sorted data. Therefore, if each process chooses rp pivots at regular intervals from the sorted sequence of n/p values in its possession (where r is an oversampling ratio), then these pivots will be a good approximation to a global choice of pivots. By gathering each process' choice of rp pivots onto one process, sorting the rp^2 samples, and then choosing $p-1$ real pivots from this sample, problems of data skew, or non-random data in each process are minimised. By choosing a large enough oversampling ratio, it can be shown, with high probability, that no partition in the sorted output will contain many more than n/p elements on average [285].

The following table summarises the BSP cost of each of the steps in the sample sorting algorithm:

1. Locally sort n/p chunks in parallel; $\qquad \frac{n}{p}\log\frac{n}{p}$
2. Gather rp^2 samples from p processors; $\qquad rp^2 g + l$
3. Sort rp^2 samples and pick p pivots; $\qquad rp^2 \log rp^2$
4. Broadcast p pivots; $\qquad p^2 g + l$
5. The pivots are used to break each processes n/p block into p chunks of size $\approx \frac{n}{p^2}$; $\qquad \approx 0$
6. Each of the p blocks are then distributed to p processes; $\qquad \frac{npg}{p^2} + l$
7. Locally merge p $\frac{n}{p^2}$ chunks using a sequential logarithmic merging technique: $\qquad \frac{np}{p^2}\log p$

$$Sorting\ cost = \frac{n}{p}\log n + \boxed{rp^2 \log rp^2 + rp^2 g + p^2 g} + \frac{ng}{p} + 3l \qquad (12.1)$$

From this analysis, it is clear that when large data sets are used on a machine with a small number of processors, then the dominant cost in the algorithm will be the local sort and merging steps in the algorithm which cost $(n/p)\log(n/p) + (n/p)\log p$ which simplifies to $(n/p)\log n$. This prediction is reflected in Table 12.2 which shows experimental results[3] on a shared-memory multiprocessor (SMP). The table shows timings for two sequential quicksort algorithms:

1. The sequential Unix library function qsort, which provides a yardstick by which our work can be compared with others. The function is a general purpose higher-order sorting function that takes a comparator function as one of its arguments.
2. An iterative integer quicksort algorithm. This algorithm is used in the sequential substep of our parallel sample sorting algorithm. All parallel speedups that follow are given with respect to this optimal implementation of sequential quicksort.

Comparing the absolute performance of the different machines in Tables 12.2, 12.3 and 12.4, shows that for sorting one million elements, at $p = 4$ on all machines, the BSP cluster is 2.7 times faster than the T3D, and 2.2 faster than the SGI shared-memory multiprocessor.

When sorting one million elements, an approximately linear speedup is achieved. However, as the size of data to be sorted decreases in size, the communication costs start to dominate, and linear speedup is not achieved. This limit on performance is clearly visible in the Cray T3D results shown in Table 12.3 and Figure 12.4. This data shows that for a modest number of processes, super-linear speedup is possible. This is caused by the effective size of the combined primary caches (the Cray T3D does not have a secondary

---

[3] All the results use an oversampling ratio of $r = 1$.

12.7 BSP Design: Sample Sorting

Table 12.2. Experimental results on a four-processor SGI PowerChallenge

n	Algorithm	p	Time (sec)	Speedup
1,000,000	Unix qsort	1	9.492	0.28
	C quicksort	1	2.715	1.00
	Samplesort	2	1.301	2.09
		3	0.917	2.96
		4	0.713	3.81
100,000	Unix qsort	1	0.789	0.30
	C quicksort	1	0.240	1.00
	Samplesort	2	0.112	2.14
		3	0.083	2.89
		4	0.067	3.58
10,000	Unix qsort	1	0.075	0.29
	C quicksort	1	0.022	1.00
	Samplesort	2	0.011	1.98
		3	0.010	2.12
		4	0.009	2.37

cache) of a group of processors which is larger than any individual cache. In contrast, the effect is not as pronounced in the results on the shared-memory multiprocessor, as the machine has a unified secondary cache, which means that the effective cache size remains constant as the number of processors is scaled.

Cache effects aside, Figure 12.4 also shows that as the number of processors increases, there is an obvious decrease in the efficiency of the algorithm. Figure 12.5 quantifies this decrease in performance by comparing the experimental results with the analytical cost model. The curve labelled "predicted T3D speedup" plots p against the expected speedup of the samplesort algorithm, calculated by dividing $n \log n$ by Equation 12.1. The curve labelled "predicted (ignoring sample)" gives the predicted speedup if the computation and communication requirements of calculating the p pivots are ignored (i.e, the terms in the box in Equation 12.1 are omitted from the analysis).

These results show the importance of modelling communication, and what would be expected to be the leading order terms. Even when the perceived computation and communication bottlenecks in the program are modelled (i.e. predicted cost ignoring sample), the important computation and communication requirements of calculating the samples are ignored when p is

Table 12.3. Experimental results on the Cray T3D

n	Algorithm	p	Time (sec)	Speedup
1,000,000	Unix qsort	1	26.211	0.16
	C quicksort	1	4.330	1.00
	Samplesort	2	1.632	2.65
		4	0.874	4.95
		8	0.462	9.37
		16	0.240	18.04
		32	0.137	31.60
100,000	Unix qsort	1	2.306	0.16
	C quicksort	1	0.383	1.00
	Samplesort	2	0.141	2.71
		4	0.071	5.33
		8	0.039	9.66
		16	0.023	15.99
		32	0.025	15.31
10,000	Unix qsort	1	0.283	0.14
	C quicksort	1	0.040	1.00
	Samplesort	2	0.011	3.36
		4	0.007	5.70
		8	0.004	8.46
		16	0.005	7.83
		32	0.015	2.67

large. The purpose of BSP cost analysis is to provide a framework for the *design* and analysis of parallel algorithms. Therefore, although the experimental results do not exhibit linear scalability above fifty processors on the T3D when n is one million, *the cost model shows that the experimental limitations on the scalability of the algorithm are accountable.* This result can either be interpreted as highlighting the advantages of accurate cost modelling, or alternatively the validity of the BSP cost calculus.

The prediction curve labelled "predicted (ignoring sample)" provides a hard lower bound on the improvements in performance that are achievable if the sampling technique were modified. Possible improvements to the sampling are:

12.8 BSP and Functional Programming

Table 12.4. Experimental results on an eight-processor BSP cluster

n	Algorithm	p	Time (sec)	Speedup
1,000,000	Unix `qsort`	1	2.591	0.45
	C quicksort	1	1.171	1.00
	Samplesort	2	0.597	1.96
		4	0.323	3.62
		8	0.168	6.96
100,000	Unix `qsort`	1	0.252	0.37
	C quicksort	1	0.095	1.00
	Samplesort	2	0.053	1.79
		4	0.029	3.26
		8	0.017	5.43
10,000	Unix `qsort`	1	0.0439	0.38
	C quicksort	1	0.0091	1.00
	Samplesort	2	0.0052	1.76
		4	0.0047	1.92
		8	0.0039	2.31

1. The sorting of the $rp^2 \log rp^2$ samples can be replaced by a merging of the samples to reduce the cost to $rp^2 \log p$;
2. The $p^2 g + l$ cost broadcast can be substituted with a two-phase broadcasting technique [276], [323], [39] that can be realised in time $2pg + 2l$;
3. Alternatively, the centralised sampling scheme outlined here can be replaced by a distributed sampling scheme which sorts and then selects $p-1$ pivots from the rp^2 samples. Gerbessiotis and Sinniolakis [217] provide such a refinement to the sampling technique that uses a sub-optimal parallel sorting algorithm, such as Batcher's bitonic sorter, to sort and select the pivots in a distributed fashion.

12.8 BSP and Functional Programming

Any data parallel language that uses the *macroscopic* view of data parallelism can adopt the BSP cost calculus to model computation and communication costs. Therefore, the BSP cost model can be used to analyse algorithms developed in any of the data parallel functional languages that emerged in the late 1980's such as NESL [59], the Paralation Model [507], CM-Lisp [548],

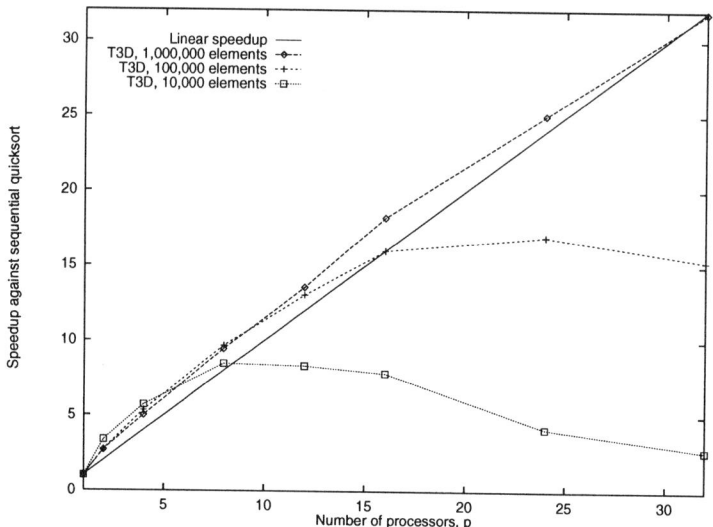

Figure 12.4. Parallel speedup of samplesort on a Cray T3D

FX [558] and DPHaskell [273, 272]. This approach is also applicable to some of the work on skeletons [139], [81], [156], although any skeleton that explicitly utilises the topology of the parallel machine such as a mesh or pipeline skeleton may not readily fit within the BSP framework. Of the skeletal approach to parallelism, the recent work of Gorlatch [229], [231] has adopted a BSP-style cost model in the analysis and transformation of programs. This approach has been successfully used to transform general specifications of an FFT algorithm into an implementation that is competitive with a hand-optimised version of the algorithm.

There has been some work on expressing microscopic SPMD data parallel programs within a functional framework. The work of Serot [521], described in Chapter 18, provides access to some of the MPI message passing constructs from within ML. Similar work on Caml-Flight [197] and BSML [370] have incorporated the one-sided communications of BSP within ML. Although these systems provide ways of expressing SPMD computations within ML, they fall into a category of "bolting" on features into existing languages. A more radical approach of incorporating BSP and functional programming is exemplified by the work of Hains on CDS [371] and $BS\lambda$ [372] which enriches the lambda calculus with rules that allow macroscopic style BSP operations to be expressed.

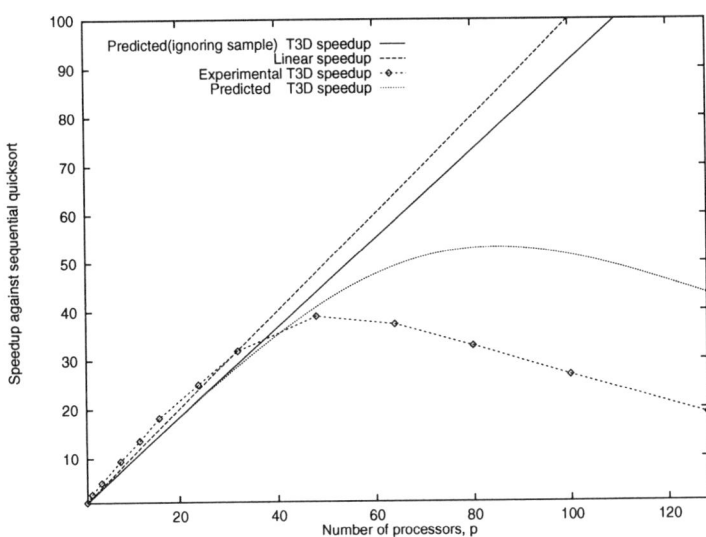

Figure 12.5. Predicted versus actual speedup on the Cray T3D

12.9 Conclusion

For high-level languages to succeed, the gap between high-level programming abstraction and efficient execution must be bridged. In Section 12.4 the *macroscopic* and *microscopic* (SPMD) views of data parallelism were described. It is generally accepted that programs written using languages that adopt the macroscopic view are easier to understand than SPMD programs, as they bear a closer resemblance to sequential programs, and the user does not have to consider the distribution of data. Many researchers have considered integrating macroscopic data parallelism into a functional language, however, for it to be tenable the gap to efficient execution has to be bridged by the compiler. When the work in this area was initially started, SIMD architectures, such as the DAP [447] or early Connection Machines [280], provided a natural execution environment for programs written in a macroscopic style. However, due to the commercial failure of SIMD machines, this implementation path is no longer available.

Today the market is dominated by shared- and distributed-memory architectures. On these machines, compilers for HPF-like languages attempt to provide the user with an illusion of macroscopic data parallelism, whilst generating code that is targeted to the underlying shared- or distributed-memory architecture. On shared-memory architectures the compilers have been moderately successful, as data-distribution can be handled by the underlying shared-memory abstraction. However, on distributed memory machines, this problem needs to be solved by the compiler, which usually results in the user requiring a detailed understanding of the data-distribution techniques used by the compiler for adequate levels of performance.

The problem with this parallelisation approach is that data-distribution is implicit within the language, whilst effective performance requires explicit control. Similarly, extolling the virtues of implicitly parallel functional programming is misleading, if performance requires annotations that explicitly control the parallelism within the language. It would seem that the problem arises when the programmer uses one programming model, and the implementation uses another.

Unfortunately, these conclusions are not encouraging for the parallel functional programming community as they also have to bridge the orthogonal gap between high-level programming abstraction and the sequential microprocessor—it is unclear if both of these gaps are a *bridge too far*.

Table 12.5. A communications hierarchy

System	Communication actions	Data distribution	Cost analysis
MPI	direct	direct	poor
BSPlib	direct	direct	good
BSP PRAM	direct	automatic	good when p is large
HPF	automatic	direct	poor
Shared-memory	automatic	automatic	non-existent

Table 12.5 attempts to characterise the different parallel programming models and languages in terms of the way in which communication actions are expressed, and the policy used to distribute data amongst the processors. A system that uses a *direct* style of communication requires the programmer to insert explicitly communication primitives into their parallel program, for example, in *BSPlib* or MPI. Alternatively, systems such as HPF try to hide the low-level details of communications, and *automatically* perform communications between processors when they are needed as a result of a dependence between data structures used in the language.

A system that adopts a direct data-distribution policy will require the programmer to explicitly deal with the data-distribution in their program. Alternatively, an automatic system will control the distribution within the run-time system.

It is clear that a fully direct system places burdens on the programmer as they have to explicitly deal with all aspects of communication. Because

12.9 Conclusion

of the creativity of programmers, it is has traditionally been these systems that have provided impressive levels of performance. As more components of the communication system are controlled by the system, then typically the performance of automatic systems suffer. For example, data parallel languages such as HPF have never been able to match the performance of fully direct systems in the hands of creative programmers. However, maybe there is an opportunity for a middle ground, and we believe the key to such systems will be that cost analysis is not sacrificed in the quest for high levels of abstraction.

The BSP model was designed to provide the user with a bridging model between high-level programming abstraction and real parallel machines. BSP programs can be viewed as occupying the middle ground between the microscopic and macroscopic view of data parallelism: algorithms are *designed* in the global macroscopic view, but realised as efficient SPMD programs that execute in the microscopic view. This balance between the two has been particularly effective in the scientific community, as demonstrated by some recent performance results from the NAS parallel benchmarks: a $15,000 BSP cluster of commodity PCs outperforms MPI implementations of the benchmarks on a Origin 2000 (a machine that is an order of magnitude more expensive) [179].

However, BSP does have its limitations, in particular not all programs fit into the superstep structure, and the static arrangement of processes to processors in the current generation of programming tools is too restrictive. Some initial work has investigated extending BSP to dynamic groups of processors [535], whilst retaining the simple approach to cost analysis that BSP promotes. This dynamic style of programming is more in line with existing parallel approaches to parallel functional programming, and therefore provides foundations upon which BSP variants of functional languages could be developed.

13. Algorithmic Skeletons

Murray Cole[1]

13.1 Introduction

Over the past ten years a number of parallel programming research projects, both inside and outside the functional programming community, have investigated the exploitation of "algorithmic skeletons". In this chapter, we introduce the central concept involved, outline the research issues which arise and investigate the two projects which have made most progress towards practical realisation.

13.2 Patterns of Parallel Computation

As with many good ideas, the underpinning observation is, in retrospect, "obvious": within the existing body of parallel algorithms a number of patterns recur frequently. These patterns are composed of computations and the interactions between them and can be conceptually abstracted from the detail of the activities they control. Such abstractions have come to be known as *algorithmic skeletons* or simply as *skeletons*. To the functional programmer, they have a natural concrete expression as higher (usually second) order functions (see Chapter 2). Thus, to the parallel functional programmer, a skeleton is a higher-order function, drawn from a system defined set, which will (or may, in the case of implementations which attempt structural optimisation) invoke its associated parallel evaluation strategy.

Sequential algorithm designers have long recognised that a small number of generic problem-solving strategies can be specialised to produce algorithms in a wide range of application areas - any decent algorithms text will include coverage of the principles of "divide-and-conquer", "dynamic programming", "branch-and-bound" and so on. Ongoing work within the Algebra of Programs group at Oxford [53] addresses the task of formalising these concepts and analysing their structure.

In the parallel context, the most commonly discussed technique is "divide-and-conquer" (d&c). A general formulation is illustrated below:

```
d&c :: (a->bool)->(a->b)->(a->[a])->([b]->b))->a->b
d&c trivial solve divide conquer P =
  if (trivial P) then (solve P)
    else conquer (map (d&c trivial solve divide conquer) (divide P))
```

---

[1] University of Edinburgh, UK.

Other variants may fix or limit the number of subproblems at each `divide`, or otherwise restrict the operations allowed in the various components. Parallelism emerges naturally from the tree of computations produced by the combination of recursion and a `divide` function which generates more than one subproblem. Many well known parallel algorithms can therefore be expressed as instantiations of d&c, with no explicit reference to the intended parallelism. For example, a classic mergesort simply requires the programmer to express a "sorted merge of two sorted lists" function to play the role of `conquer`. More interestingly, the skeletal approach can simplify the expression of programs in which parallelism exists at several conceptual levels. For example, [414] discusses a three-level rendition of the well known bitonic sorting algorithm, in which the outer layer is essentially as for mergesort, the second layer, within the `merge` step is itself, a d&c (or more precisely, really just a `divide`) within which the innermost layer maps a simple "compare-and-exchange" building block across a list of pairs.

As we shall see, many other such paradigms have been suggested. Three intriguing questions arise.

- Can such a methodology provide the applications programmer with a more appealing handle on parallelism than direct low-level methods?
- Can the implementation mechanisms (both at compile- and run-time) use the structural information implied by skeletons to marshal better the available resources?
- Can this compact abstraction of complex operational structure facilitate formal reasoning about the semantic and temporal properties of parallel programs?

13.3 Challenges in Skeletal Programming

13.3.1 Choice of Skeletons

Brinch-Hansen, in an essay on programming language design [90], quotes Simon [530] thus:

> "How complex or simple a structure is depends critically upon the way in which we describe it. Most of the complex structures found in the world are enormously redundant, and we can use this redundancy to simplify their description. But to use it, to achieve the simplification, we must find the right representation."

The message is relevant. Consider first the aim of conceptual simplification. Just what are the patterns to which we have alluded? This is a tricky question because, of course, there is no correct answer but rather a variety of shades of opinion ([112] attempts a classification). One person's skeleton is another's composition of more fundamental skeletons. If the skeletons become

13.3 Challenges in Skeletal Programming

too simple then they may lose their simplifying power, too complex and they may lose applicability. In any case, is it realistic to expect to find a universal set of skeletons? Might application area-specific sets be more fruitful? The structured programming movement argued successfully that good sequential programming boils down to a small number of primitive concepts. Can skeletons be the structured programming of parallelism, or is such parsimony inappropriate in the parallel case?

Turning to the issue of concrete representation we must find a suitable language framework. As noted above, a functional presentation seems the natural choice. On the other hand, the conservative world of parallel programming may feel more at home with an imperative style. Investigations of both have begun, as have attempts to integrate imperative building blocks into a functional, skeletal superstructure.

13.3.2 Implementation Mechanisms

Skeletons allow the programmer to give the compiler explicit information on the dynamic evolution of a parallel computation. This information would be difficult, or even impossible to extract by static analysis of a lower-level specification of the same algorithm. The challenge to the implementation mechanism is to make full use of it with respect to the underlying architecture. In general, implementation of any single skeleton is unproblematic. The associated dynamic structure is built into the compiler's repertoire of implementation templates and appropriate code is generated. The task becomes more demanding when arbitrary composition and nesting of skeletons is permitted. For architectures in which data placement is significant, composition introduces the possibility that the distribution expected of the input to one template does not match that produced by the output of its predecessor. For schemes in which each skeleton may have several possible implementations, a significant combinatorial optimisation arises across both templates and data reorganising "glue". Nesting of skeletons raises the issue of efficient nesting of implementations in program dependent combinations. What are conceptually single nodes in the upper levels are instantiated with complex parallel structures at lower levels. The clarity and conciseness with which the computation is expressed will only be affordable if the compiler and run-time system can cooperate to reproduce the dynamic behaviour of the more conventionally expressed "flat" program. The question of whether the ability to nest is actually important pragmatically remains open. The bulk of existing parallel applications seem to exhibit relatively simple, flat behaviour but this may reflect the difficulty of structuring more complex algorithms in ill-suited languages.

In the functional programming framework, it is clear that the skeletal approach is somewhat at odds with traditional implementation methods, and in particular with parallel graph reduction, where the focus on dynamically determining and scheduling unpredictable parallelism contrasts with the skeletal world of predistributed computational structure. Satisfactory resolution may lie in hybrid schemes in which skeletal solutions provide short-cuts to good distribution for those parts of a program which are statically determined, with the full dynamic mechanism reserved for the unpredictable remainder.

13.3.3 A Formal Framework

The suitability of pure functional languages as vehicles for work on derivation and transformation of programs is well known. Given care over the treatment of possible non-termination, skeletons can be defined semantically in pure functional terms and so benefit from work in these areas. An intriguing aspect here is that skeletons package up significant pieces of computation, often the key structural components of whole algorithms. This means that transformation sequences which significantly alter that high-level computational structure become feasible with semi-automated support, in contrast to the pragmatically intractable task of performing corresponding manipulations of an equivalent low-level program. The bulk of work in this area is rooted in the "program calculation" methodology of Bird and Meertens [47], which has more recently been applied in the parallel context, notably by Skillicorn (see Chapter 8) and Gorlatch and Lengauer [230], [233]. Pepper and Südholt [551], [455] introduce and apply the concept of a "cover" of a data structure, indicating its potentially overlapping partition, for subsequent skeletal manipulation. Further work in Lengauer's group pursues a comprehensive formal analysis of the structure and implementation of divide-and-conquer [268], [595]. Other work on formal transformation of skeletal programs includes [209], while the flattening of nested parallelism as an implementation level optimisation is pursued in [60], [162], [330]. Jay's concept of "shape" encourages the exploitation of skeleton-like static analysis by restricting the form of programs and promises benefits in the parallel context (see Chapter 9).

13.4 From Theory into Practice

The skeleton concept has spawned a substantial body of work addressing the questions raised above in various combinations. Since it would be impossible to do justice to all within a single chapter, we choose to focus on the two projects which have produced the most substantial practical realisations. Work at Imperial College has concentrated on the functional route, latterly moving into functional-imperative hybrids. In contrast, the Pisa team have taken an imperative view from the outset, while resorting to the functional perspective to present concise semantics. The section opens with a short review of earlier related work and concludes with a brief survey of other projects.

13.4 From Theory into Practice

13.4.1 Skeletons in the Cupboard

While the term *algorithmic skeleton* is coined in [138], a number of earlier papers proclaim the benefits of working with classes of parallel algorithms. Divide-and-conquer was particularly prominent [456], [45], [383], [478], [414]. Other classes were typically less precisely specified. Jamieson's paper [301] included among its motivational questions:

> "To what extent should the design of new architectures and languages be based on models of classes of algorithms?"

Two of the collected papers respond with observations which are "skeletal" in spirit if not detail. Nelson and Snyder [416] present three "parallel programming paradigms", compute-aggregate-broadcast, systolic and d&c. In a manner reminiscent of algorithms textbooks, these are described in a deliberately informal style, with the intention that precise details of structure will be allowed to vary from one application to another. They observe:

> "Finally, there is a cautionary remark to be made on precision: it is difficult to define paradigms precisely. We know of no adequate and convenient formulation that can be used. Paradigms are not algorithms, so one does not present them in a programming language, *nor are they algorithmic schemata which could be presented in some meta-language.*"

Similarly, Finkel [195] notes the existence of loosely defined classes (generate and solve, iterative relaxation, passive data pool and systolic) but declines to define these more precisely.

A common theme linking many of these papers is the prominence given to architectural rather than algorithmic structure. This is particularly evident in [350], in which the bulk of the classification is made explicitly and directly in terms of the implementing network. Similarly, the popular classification into "algorithmic", "geometric" and "processor farm" parallelism [480] illustrated a concern for the form of the actual implementation over the semantics of the computation. In contrast, the "problem heap" paradigm [410] is presented operationally but for a relatively abstract computational model.

It is clear that the concept was gaining acceptance by the mid to late 1980s. The main contribution of [139] was to draw these strands together and propose the deliberate creation of a parallel programming model in which tightly specified, potentially parallel (and in one case explicitly parallel) program forms, the "algorithmic skeletons" themselves, provided the *only* means of introducing parallelism within a computation. Four example skeletons were introduced, together with implementation sketches and asymptotic costings for a mesh architecture. In contrast to later developments, it is interesting to note that these original skeletons were intended as one-per-program constructs, completely characterising the parallel structure of a complete computation.

13.4.2 Skeletal Programming at Imperial College

The most substantial body of work in functional skeletal programming has been amassed by the group working with Darlington at Imperial College (see also Chapter 14).

In their early work (for example [156]), the Imperial team present a skeletal framework featuring two key developments. Firstly, the notion of skeleton is refined to encompass multiple levels of abstraction, from the abstract specification of computations which may have no obvious parallel implementation, to machine oriented skeletons which match the architectural capabilities of real machines fairly directly (but still in the functional framework). Secondly, the use of program development by transformation *at the level of skeletons* is advocated. This is a powerful technique. If skeletons represent algorithmic structure, then transformations at this level can represent substantial reorganisations of computations (a striking example of such a methodology in action is presented in [260], where the d&c structure is transformed to a pipeline).

The skeletons presented are d&c (of course!), pipe, a direct representation of pipelined computation:

```
pipe :: [a->a] -> (a -> a)
pipe = fold (o)
```

(where o represents functional composition), farm, a task farm with a common static environment

```
farm :: (a->b->c) -> b -> ([a] -> [c])
farm f e = map g
           where g x = f x e
```

and at the more abstract level, ramp (for "reduce-and-map-over-pairs") which captures the essence of a step in computations (such as a simple "n-body" calculation) which iteratively consider all pairwise interactions among some collection of objects, combining these into new state information for each object:

```
ramp :: (a->a->b) -> (b->b->b) -> [a] -> [b]
ramp f g xs = map h xs
              where h x = fold g (map (f x) xs)
```

Finally, the "catch-all" skeleton dmpa (for "dynamic-message-passing-architecture") encapsulated the ability to describe arbitrary patterns of message passing (and is arguably scarcely a skeleton at all). The paper also advocates the use of skeletal performance models, presenting a conventional model of d&c by way of example.

The suggested skeletons are applied in [158] where a ray tracing algorithm is expressed as an instantiation of ramp. Structural transformations then produce two equivalent programs, one exploiting farm, the other pipe. These

13.4 From Theory into Practice

were expressed in Hope$^+$ and implemented in C on a Meiko Computing Surface. The results are compared with those predicted by detailed performance models. The d&c model is developed under similar assumptions on regularity as [139] but mapped directly to a matching binary tree processor network. The farm model assumes regularity (in execution time) of farmed tasks and a simple, topology-independent model of communication cost, while the pipe model similarly assumes regularity of computation and communication time across both stages and items in the pipelined sequence. The pipe and farm models are instantiated with the performance parameters of the available machine (and refined slightly to account for the implementation overhead of garbage collection in this completely functional implementation). Actual performance is impressive. Perhaps more interestingly, the match between predicted and actual performance is good (particularly for the farm), with discrepancies in the pipe time being attributed to poor modelling of garbage collection.

The Imperial College Group's philosophy is reiterated in [164], where an interesting diversion is made into the area of application-specific skeletons, with the observation that

> "The skeletons methodology can be further refined by observing that many specific applications domains have characteristic data and control structures."

The possibility is explored in the context of solid modelling, using Constructive Solid Geometry (CSG). A data type is introduced for CSG trees, which represent solids as collections of simple solids (blocks, spheres and so on) composed with conventional set operations. The two standard generic CSG operations are then presented as skeletons. transformCSG is analogous to map over trees, applying a given transformation to each primitive solid.

```
transformCSG :: (PrimitiveInstance->PrimitiveInstance)->CSGtree
                ->CSGtree

transformCSG primF NullSolid = NullSolid

transformCSG primF (Primitive primInst) = Primitive (primF primInst)

transformCSG primF (Composite s1 op s2)
 = Composite (transformCSG primF s1) op (transformCSG primF s2)
```

Similarly, reduceCSG is analogous to fold.

```
reduceCSG :: a -> (PrimitiveInstance->a) -> (SetOp->a->a->a) ->
             -> CSGTree -> a

reduceCSG base primF compF NullSolid = base

reduceCSG base primF compF (Primitive primInst) = primF primInst
```

```
reduceCSG base primF compF (Composite s1 op s2)
  = compF op r1 r2
    where r1 = reduceCSG base primF compF s1
          r2 = reduceCSG base primF compF s2
```

An excursion into skeleton transformation is motivated by the observation that while the CSG tree is conceptually convenient, a competing representation, the octree, is more easily amenable to efficient processing. Analogous skeletons are defined on octrees, and a transformation (now including data type transformation [258]) is introduced which allows programs to be expressed on CSG trees but implemented on octrees.

More recently (for example [159]) the Imperial group present SCL (Structured Coordination Language). The emphasis is again on a layered skeletal approach with the conventional strict division between the structures which introduce parallelism and the other arbitrary sequential code.

> "The upper layer SCL language abstracts all the relevant aspects of a program's parallel behaviour, *including partitioning, data placement, data movement* and control flow, whilst the lower level expresses sequential computation through procedures written in any sequential base language. SCL skeletons can be freely composed and eventually instantiated with base language components, but the base language cannot call any of the SCL primitives."

The italicised text highlights one of the novel features of SCL, its concern for a lower level of detailed control than hitherto envisaged in skeletal systems. In contrast to [156], where skeletons were specified as operations on conventional data types such as lists and sets, SCL introduces a new, explicitly distributed type, the ParArray (and notes that the idea could be generalised to other types), upon which all the skeletons operate. ParArrays have an index type (typically tuples of int) and an element type. They are constructed by partitioning conventional (functional) sequential arrays (of type SeqArray) through application of one of the lowest level "skeletons", partition:

```
partition :: Partition_pattern -> SeqArray index a ->
             ParArray index (SeqArray index a)
```

The partition pattern determines the mapping of items from the SeqArray into the SeqArray items of the ParArray and it is envisaged that standard distributions (row-block, column-cyclic and so on) will be predefined. A corresponding gather skeleton reconstructs a SeqArray from a ParArray. If we think of a partition as distributing a SeqArray across an abstract array of processors, then the align operator indicates that two such distributions (with the same index type) should be co-located (and can be thought of abstractly as a zip with makepair).

```
align :: ParArray index a -> ParArray index b ->
         ParArray index (a,b)
```

13.4 From Theory into Practice

The concern for this abstract level of control of data distribution is reminiscent of the directives of High Performance Fortran (and indeed, this link is noted explicitly in the paper).

At its higher levels, SCL makes an explicit conceptual distinction between *elementary skeletons* which abstract data parallel computations across ParArrays and *computational skeletons* which abstract parallel control flows. In the former category, we find the expected maps, fold and scan now typed to operate on distributed data:

```
map  :: (a->b) -> ParArray index a -> ParArray index b

imap :: (index->a->b) -> ParArray index a -> ParArray index b

fold :: (a -> a -> a) -> ParArray index a -> a

scan :: (a -> a -> a) -> ParArray index a -> ParArray index a
```

(where the function argument of imap expects an item's index as its own first argument), together with a collection of *communication skeletons*, allowing data to be shuffled around within a ParArray, in the usual data parallel patterns, rotate-row, rotate-col and so on. Meanwhile, the computational skeletons described are farm (familiar from earlier work, but now applied to ParArrays):

```
farm :: (a->b->c) -> a -> ParArray index b -> ParArray index c
farm f e = map (f e)
```

and SPMD:

```
SPMD :: [(ParArray index a -> ParArray index a, index->a->a)] ->
        ParArray index a -> ParArray index a
SPMD [] = id
SPMD (gf, lf): fs = (SPMD fs) o (gf o (imap lf))
```

which abstracts the "Single-Program-Multiple-Data" paradigm as a sequence of phases, each involving a local step followed by a global step, with step details variable from phase to phase. Finally, sequential iteration is captured by iterUntil:

```
iterUntil :: (a->a) -> (a->b) -> (a->bool) -> a -> b
iterUntil iterSolve finalSolve con x
  = if con x then finalSolve x
      else iterUntil iterSolve finalSolve con (iterSolve x)
```

A noteworthy point here is that iterSolve is defined without reference to any parallel constructs or data. It can only contribute to the SCL layer of parallel control structures because it is explicitly accorded "skeleton" status. Of course, it introduces no new parallelism itself, but allows other parallel steps (when presented as the first three arguments) to be iterated. SCL is applied to the description of hyperquicksort [481] and a genuinely layered, skeletal program emerges. This is transformed into a flattened form to facilitate implementation by hand, in the absence of a completed SCL compiler, through composition of calls to a library of skeleton implementations.

The flattening process is of particular interest here, in that it addresses one of the main compilation challenges for skeletal programming, namely the handling of nested skeletons. In this example, the key transformation allows nested SPMD computation to be flattened. Suppose split be a partitioning function which operates upon already distributed data:

```
split :: Partition_pattern -> ParArray index a ->
         ParArray index (ParArray index a)
```

then the transformation rule notes that:

```
SPMD [(gf0, SPMD [(gf1, lf)])] o (split P) = SPMD [(sgf, lf)]
    where sgf = gf0 o map gf1 o (split P)
```

It is interesting to speculate upon the extent to which similar flattening transformations might be applicable to skeletons with more complex internal structures.

Further developments of the SCL approach are described in [162]. Two textbook matrix multiplication algorithms are developed, both employing an iterated SPMD structure at the skeletal level, differing in their data distributions and flow but exploiting the same sequential matrix multiplication function at the base level. The natural next step is to abstract the common structure as a "generic matrix multiplication" skeleton which takes details of the distribution and redistribution strategies as arguments. This is a pleasing illustration of the conceptual power of the SCL framework. At a more pragmatic level, the paper introduces "Fortran-S", a prototype instantiation of the methodology, using Fortran as the base language, and includes a discussion of the issues to be addressed at the resulting imperative-functional interface. Most obviously, the imperative base code, must behave with referential transparency with respect to the superstructure in order that powerful transformations can be applied at the functional level. Similarly, the semantics of the calling interface and related type information must be handled carefully, as the language boundary is crossed. Good performance is reported for the matrix algorithms (speedup of 70 on a 100 processor Fujitsu AP-1000). Fortran-S is also examined in [160], where a Gaussian elimination program is expressed as an iterated map and broadcast (another of the "elementary" skeletons from SCL's data parallel layer).

To's thesis [568] investigates the implementation of programs combining several skeletons. An SCL-like language is described, with simple skeletons introduced as operations on "Parallel Abstract Data Types" (here, variations of lists and arrays) which are distinguished by the fact that no conventional piecewise constructors are available. As in the SCL work, a clear separation is intended between the skeletal (and hence potentially parallel) levels of a program, and the sequential base level code. The specification of what is permissible at the upper level is made concrete by a definition of "well-formedness" for skeletal programs. Essentially this is a restriction on the compositions and combinations which may be expressed, in order to prohibit the description of programs which "would imply that process networks can be generated at run-time". The bulk of the thesis considers the description and combination of skeleton behaviours with particular concern for systems in which each skeleton may have several possible implementations. Complexity is managed by the introduction of "behaviour signatures" for data structures. These characterise the intended abstract scheme for each input data structure as explicit annotations by the programmer. A "behaviour inference" algorithm is presented which allows signatures to be deduced for intermediate structures.

13.4.3 The Pisa Parallel Programming Language

The Pisa Parallel Programming Language (P3L) [453] group led by Pelagatti and Danelutto has been similarly active for a number of years. Three significant contrasts may be drawn with the work at Imperial.

- At a conceptual level, constructs are deliberately chosen and expressed in such a way that the intended parallelism is quite explicit. The P3L programmer understands that a parallel program is being written, and is simply choosing the forms of parallelism to be exploited and expressing their composition. In return, the P3L system takes responsibility for filling out and composing the details of the chosen structures in terms of the lower-level parallel language of the machine to hand, and for addressing scheduling issues in the final mapping of process network to machine;
- With respect to implementation philosophy, P3L adopts a default strategy of sequentialised stream-based transmission of implicitly parallel data between composed and nested skeletons, in contrast to SCL's explicitly distributed data types;
- At a more pragmatic level, P3L has always used imperative code (typically C) to define base-level computations, in contrast to the Imperial flirtation with functional programming at all levels (although recent developments in SCL have brought the groups closer together in this respect).

P3L has undergone several revisions. Here we will focus on its most recent incarnation [453], which has seven constructs. These must be used to express the high-level structure of the program and are the only means of introducing potential parallelism. As in SCL, they cannot be called from within sections of base-level sequential code (in other words, the same two-level program structure is enforced syntactically). Each construct instance defines a "module", which can be thought of as a stream processor. Data elements in the stream can be simple data items (integers, reals and so on), potentially parallel compound items (arrays or structures) or collections of these. While the internal construction of a module may employ parallelism of different forms, the operational interface involves sequentialised streams, accepted through an input channel and returned through an output channel. Gluing together of channels provides the implementation mechanism for the composition and nesting of constructs.

The `sequential` construct allows the introduction of arbitrary sequential code at the leaves of a program's construct tree. As with all the constructs, its syntactic formulation is in the imperative style. Here is an example in which the generated module accepts a stream of integer vectors and returns a stream of integers, consisting of the sums of the vectors.

```
sum_vect in(int v[n]) out(int c)
  ${ int i;
     c = 0;
     for (i=0; i<n; i++)
        c = c + v[i];
  }$
end
```

In the example, `in` and `out` are keywords introducing the types of the corresponding streams (the input stream is passed by value), the `${` and `}$` parenthesise a fragment of base level code. The stream notation allows lists of types to be specified as both inputs and outputs.

The `farm` construct allows the specification of a "task farmed" module, in which successive items from the input stream are "farmed" out to a collection of identical worker modules according to a demand-driven distribution strategy. The worker modules may be internally sequential, or be constructed from further parallel construct instances. The implementation is responsible for ensuring that the stream of results is emitted in the same order as the corresponding inputs, in spite of the internal non-determinism. Here is an example in which the vector summing module defined above is applied in farmed style to a stream of vectors.

```
farm farm_vsum in(int x[n]) out(int y)
   sum_vect in(x) out(y)
end farm
```

The same effect could have been achieved by explicitly providing the sequential code for vector summation as the body of the farm. Notice that the `farm` construct is purely an annotation, expressing the intended choice of implementation structure. It has no inherent computational content and its functional semantics are effectively those of the identity function on stream processors, in other words, in a more abstract form:

```
farm f = f
```

(the same applies to the sequential construct). The number of "workers" to be constructed is not specified, since the P3L philosophy dictates that this detail should be handled by the implementation, which allocates the available

13.4 From Theory into Practice

resources to the various constructs in a program on the basis of cost-modelled predictions of load.

The pipe construct directs the use of a pipelined implementation, in which the output stream from one module becomes the input stream of another. Syntactically, the language allows the introduction of temporary stream variables to express the flow between internal stages of a pipeline. Here is an example in which r and y play this role:

```
pipe blah in(int v[]) out (int x)
   s1 in(v) out(real r)
   s2 in(r) out(int y)
   s3 in(y) out(x)
end pipe
```

where s1, s2 and s3, are appropriately typed constructs. A static check ensures that the specified ins and outs do not violate the intended simple pipeline structure.

While sharing the name of a familiar functional paradigm, the map construct in fact denotes a powerful facility for data parallelism, incorporating the ability to gather, replicate, compute and redistribute across arrays. Items of the input stream are tuples containing at least one array. The output stream contains arrays. Conceptually, the input items are partitioned across a set of virtual processors (where the partition can involve replication) which each apply the same given function to the data they receive. The results of these independent operations are recombined as the output stream item. A concise and powerful indexing notation allows the expression of complex patterns of data distribution, replication and collection. To give a flavour of the construct, here is an example in which a pre-defined inner_product function is used to express a matrix multiplication program.

```
map mat_mul in(int a[n][n], b[n][n]) out(int c[n][n])
   inner_product in(a[*i][], b[][*j]) out(c[*i][*j])
end map
```

The * notation indicates P3L "free variables", a mechanism used to specify data array distributions across a corresponding array of virtual processors. The example constructs an $n \times n$ virtual processor array onto which elements of c are mapped one to one in the obvious way. Rows and, respectively, columns of a and b are broadcast across the corresponding rows and columns of the virtual processor array.

The reduce construct expresses reduction of an array with an associative, commutative binary operator (which must be expressed sequentially). As with map, an indexing notation expresses the dimensions which are to be reduced.

The loop construct allows iteration of a computation, either in a bounded form in which the number of iterations is specified, or an unbounded form in which iteration proceeds until some condition is met. Its formulation allows a distinction to be made between those parts of the result of an iteration which are fed back to the next iteration and those which are output as the result of an instantiation of the whole construct.

Finally, the comp construct allows the expression of compositions of data parallel steps. Conceptually, this means that "the same" virtual processors are executing a sequence of data parallel operations. This can be contrasted with a functionally equivalent, but operationally quite distinct, use of pipelining to achieve composition. As with farm and the sequential construct, the presence of two functionally similar but operationally diverse mechanisms illustrates the P3L principle that the programmer is explicitly in control of the form of parallelism chosen.

P3L has been implemented for a number of platforms, with results reported in [452], [453] for applications such as optical character recognition (OCR), ray tracing, circuit test generation and volumetric visualisation. Early implementations on machines such the Meiko CS-1 and subsequent ports to networks of workstations and the Cray T3D exhibit encouraging performance. Transparent portability of the parallel aspects of the applications was achieved, with the only stumbling blocks resulting from low-level architecture-specific dependencies within blocks of sequential code! The OCR example provides a pleasing case-study, in that while an initial "obvious" parallelisation (as a four stage pipeline consisting of segmentation, thinning, vectorisation and feature level analysis) proved disappointing (barely speeding up at all on four processors), the combination of profiling tools available and high level restructuring facilitated by the language allowed rapid development of two refined programs (in which the pipeline bottleneck of vectorisation was itself attacked with map parallelism, and finally the remaining lightweight stages were combined) culminating in a 40-fold speedup on 50 processors. The compilation philosophy employs templates for each construct, targeting the P3L abstract machine, a distributed-memory, message passing model with options for either full or mesh connectivity. The template library includes both parametric process graphs and corresponding performance models for each template. The middle-end of the compiler implements a complex optimisation process involving the selected templates, techniques for composition and actual performance parameters of the eventual hardware and generates an abstract process graph for the program. Many decisions are guided by the use of profiling information gathered sequentially and plugged into the template performance models. Transformations of the program's construct tree are considered automatically. The back-end simply compiles the result down to the low-level specifics of the real machine.

13.4.4 Related Projects

A number of other projects have investigated skeletal parallelism in practice. Here we merely touch on papers which will lead the interested reader to the more extensive work of each group. An on-line bibliography of skeletal parallelism[2] provides a comprehensive overview. Rabhi [484] has investigated a purely functional realisation of the "static iterative transformation" skeleton, a powerful generalisation of the "iterative combination" skeleton discussed earlier. The Clean project (see Chapter 15) has exploited the concept to provide skeletal I/O templates among others, while data parallel languages in which the operations such as "map" and "fold" are properly second-order are closely related [60]. Brinch-Hansen [89] presents a number of independent imperative skeletal case-studies, while the "Skil" language [76] mixes functional and imperative features. The Heriot-Watt group [81], [396] have extracted and exploited skeletal parallelism within Standard ML programs, and have investigated the use of skeletal prototyping of vision algorithms. Further skeletal work based on ML is discussed in Chapter 18 and in [30], [240]. Work at Leeds [168] has concentrated on developing application-specific functional skeletons for CSG.

13.5 The Way Ahead

Skeletal parallel programming is at a crossroads. While the manifesto is proclaimed and its application developed by the immediate research community, more widespread acceptance remains elusive. Contemporary developments in the *de facto* standards of the parallel programming world indicate a growing awareness of the benefits of imposing structure (for example, MPI's collective operations and the notion of partitionable communication contexts). Proponents of skeletal parallelism would do well to respond to and harness these trends before the various *ad hoc* fixes become a new standard. To do so successfully may require considerable creativity and compromise in both superficial matters of syntactic presentation and, perhaps also, underlying principle. While difficult to quantify precisely, more direct validation of the claimed "productivity without performance loss" with respect to direct approaches in competitor systems would strengthen the case.

---

[2] http://hypatia.dcs.qmw.ac.uk/SEL-HPC/Articles/SkeletonArchive.html

14. Coordination Languages

Paul Kelly[1] and Frank Taylor[1]

14.1 Introduction

The power of functional programming derives not just from simple expressive power, but from the ease with which software components can be reused. When these components are parallel computations, composition carries with it the need to coordinate process placement, communications and resource allocation. We call this the parallel component composition problem.

This chapter concerns languages and language mechanisms which allow the programmer to specify explicitly how composed parallel programs are to be coordinated to yield efficient code for distributed-memory multicomputers. A powerful general language called Caliban, is presented as a common framework in which different approaches to composing parallel functional components can be expressed and compared.

14.2 Caliban: A Common Framework

Caliban was introduced in [331], and has been refined, implemented and redesigned by Frank Taylor [560]. It is Taylor's version of the language that is presented here.

The goals were:

1. To allow partitioning to be expressed declaratively;
2. To make the full power of the functional language available for specifying how parallelism is to be exploited;
3. To allow the operators used to implement the application to be reused in coordination; and
4. To allow coordination to be separated from configuration, as discussed above.

The resulting language achieves all these objectives, but there remain quite serious problems, and one of the purposes of this chapter is to elaborate on the experience gained.

14.2.1 Underlying Principle: Static Process Networks

Caliban is an annotation mechanism which specifies how a Haskell program is executed in parallel. It specifies how the computation is partitioned and

---

[1] Department of Computing, Imperial College, London, UK.

allocated *statically* to processors (we discuss extending Caliban to handle more dynamic mapping in Section 14.6). The processors form a task graph, linked by communication channels carrying streams of messages.

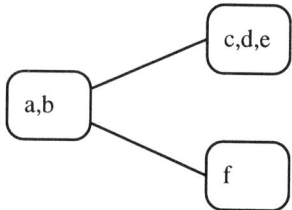

Figure 14.1. Example task graph; expressions a and b are on one processor, c, d and e on another, and f on a third. The arcs indicate where some communication (in either direction) is expected.

Annotations are introduced by the **moreover** keyword; annotations consist simply of a declarative description of the graph; for example, the task graph shown in Figure 14.1 is expressed as:

Bundle [a,b] And Bundle [c,d,e] And Bundle [f] And
(Arc a d) And (Arc a f)

The Bundle assertions specify that the expressions named a and b are allocated to the same processor, c, d and e to the same, presumably different processor, and f to a third. The Arc a d assertion specifies a link in the task graph, either because a consumes d or *vice versa*.

14.2.2 Processes, Streams and Strictness

- Placed expressions such as f must be of list type. Our implementation serialises such lists by evaluating and sending each element, in its entirety, in turn.

Caliban is based on the model of a static network of processes communicating via streams of messages. To support this, we require that in an annotation such as Bundle f, the name f should refer to an object which can be transmitted as a stream of messages.

Note that this compromises Haskell's semantics: all the elements are evaluated in sequence, regardless of which parts are used by the consumer.

Output Channels and Compute-ahead.

- Evaluation proceeds in anticipation of demand, so that the producer of a stream can operate in parallel with its consumer. This "compute-ahead" is restricted by the availability of buffer space in the consumer.

14.2 Caliban: A Common Framework

Note that this is not, in itself, inconsistent with lazy evaluation: even if a producer commits itself to computing a value which is not actually needed, the consumer can proceed freely.

14.2.3 The Process Placement Rule

The **moreover** assertion specifies the placement of named expressions onto the task graph. The "process placement rule" (analogous to "owner computes" in HPF) specifies where the computation of these expressions takes place:

- In the absence of any annotations, *every* processor executes the *entire* program. Some arbitrarily-chosen processor's result expression is output;
- The expression Bundle [x] asserts that x is computed on one processor only, and all non-local references to x involve communication.

14.2.4 Threads: Co-locating Tasks by "Bundling"

- In an assertion such as Bundle [a,b], two expressions are assigned to the same processor. We create a thread for each expression, each charged with computing elements ahead of demand and sending the values to each of the consumer processors.

In principle, these threads should be preemptively and fairly scheduled, so that evaluation of all the expressions allocated to a processor proceeds even if one of the threads loops or blocks.

In practice preemption does not appear to be necessary. Although, in principle, this simplification raises a further compromise to Haskell's strictness semantics, and could be a performance problem, preemption incurs performance overheads (primarily due to locking) which make it unattractive.

14.2.5 Parallel Composition using And

- Given two annotations a_1 and a_2, the annotation a_1 And a_2 describes a process network in which a_1 and a_2 run in parallel;
- In a_1 And a_2, a_1 and a_2 run on disjoint groups of processors except where Bundle is used to specify that the same processor is used.

14.2.6 Sequential Composition using With

- Given two annotations a_1 and a_2, the annotation a_1 With a_2 describes a process network in which a_1 and a_2 are assigned to the same set of processors. A heuristic algorithm is used to map the two process networks in order to minimise communications.

NoPlace	Null assertion
Bundle [x,y]	Place x and y on the same processor
Annot x	x's annotation
Arc a b	Document a data dependency between a and b
a And b	Join annotations a and b
a With b	Phase subnets a and b

Figure 14.2. Caliban assertions and connectives

14.2.7 Finding the Placement of an Expression: Annot

- The Annot operator extracts the placement asserted for an expression. Thus, given two expressions e_1 and e_2:

  (Annot e_1) With (Annot e_2)

  describes a process network in which e_1 and e_2 are assigned to the same set of processors.

Annot is only needed in conjunction with With because And is assumed unless otherwise specified. Annot should not normally be used outside a Moreover annotation.

14.2.8 Documenting Communications: Arc

- The need for communication between the processors responsible for the two expressions is easily inferred by the compiler automatically. The programmer's assertion a Arc b is checked and if no dependence actually occurs, or if dependence occurs where no Arc assertion has been made, a warning is generated.

14.2.9 Language Summary

Figure 14.2 shows the complete set of assertions and connectives available in Caliban. Figure 14.3 shows some equivalences which may help in understanding the language.

14.3 Simple Example: Ray Tracing

A simple, non-recursive ray tracer can be reduced to the following Haskell program:

14.3 Simple Example: Ray Tracing

$$
\begin{array}{rcl}
\text{a And NoPlace} & \equiv & \text{a} \\
\text{a And b} & \equiv & \text{b And a} \\
\text{a With b} & \equiv & \text{b With a} \\
\text{(a And b) And c} & \equiv & \text{a And (b And c)} \\
\text{(a With b) With c} & \equiv & \text{a With (b With c)} \\
\text{a Arc b} & \equiv & \text{b Arc a} \\
\text{Bundle [x,y]} & \equiv & \text{Bundle [y,x]} \\
\text{Bundle [x,y] And Bundle [y,z]} & \equiv & \text{Bundle [x,y,z]} \\
\text{Bundle [x,y] With Bundle [y,z]} & \equiv & \text{Bundle [x,y,z]} \\
\text{Bundle [x] And Bundle [x]} & \equiv & \text{Bundle [x]} \\
\end{array}
$$

Figure 14.3. Equivalences in Caliban assertions

```
rayTrace scene viewpoint =
         map impact rays
         where
         rays = generate_rays viewpoint
         impact ray = fold earlier impacts
                      where
                      impacts = map (hit ray) scene
```

The function `impact` takes a ray and generates an impact description (either the object name and impact location or the fact that no impact has occurred) for each object in the scene database by mapping `hit` over `scene`. From the list of impacts the program finds the closest one to the viewpoint using `fold earlier` (i.e. the one that will colour the output pixel).

Although very simple, this captures the essence of volume rendering by ray casting. In many application areas much more sophisticated approaches are applicable, but an example of a real application with essentially this structure is rendering human tomography data in the MPIRE [313] project (http://mpire.sdsc.edu).

To provide a simple illustration of Caliban at work, we present two different parallel implementations.

14.3.1 Ray Tracing Using a Processor Farm

The first parallel implementation focuses on the first `map` operator, and exploits data parallelism by decomposing the list of `rays`. Figure 14.4 shows the process network.

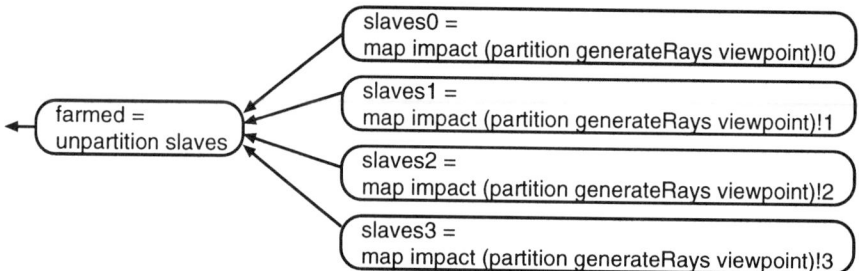

Figure 14.4. Process network for ray tracing using a processor farm

Network Forming Operators. The diagram shows an instance of a common communications pattern, a fan of arcs. We can define a Haskell function to generate an assertion which captures this:

```
fan :: Stream → [Stream] → Placement
fan s [] = NoPlace
fan s (a:as) = (Bundle [a]) And (Arc a s) And (fan s as)
```

The function `fan` is an example of a "network forming operator". For example, the expression `fan farmed [slave0, slave1, slave2, slave3]` yields the annotation

(Bundle [slave0]) And (Arc slave0 farmed) And
(Bundle [slave1]) And (Arc slave1 farmed) And
(Bundle [slave2]) And (Arc slave2 farmed) And
(Bundle [slave3]) And (Arc slave3 farmed)

Skeletons. We can define a reusable function which encapsulates the processor farm behaviour as follows; we use the `fan` operator to build its annotation:

```
farm :: (a→a) → [a] → [a]
farm func input = farmed moreover fan farmed input
                  where
                  farmed = map func input
```

The assertion is evaluated by the compiler (so the parameter must be known at compile time), to yield an annotation which places each of the `farmed` expressions on a separate processor.

The Parallel Implementation. The processor farm implementation is shown in Figure 14.5. The only change from the original sequential code is that `map` has been replaced by `farm`. In Section 14.5.1, we modify this example to work on blocks of objects and blocks of rays, and show performance results.

14.4 Implementing Caliban

```
rayTrace scene viewpoint =
            farm N impact rays
            where
            rays = generateRays viewpoint
            impact ray = fold earlier impacts
                          where
                          impacts = map (hit ray) scene
```

Figure 14.5. Farmed raytracing in Caliban

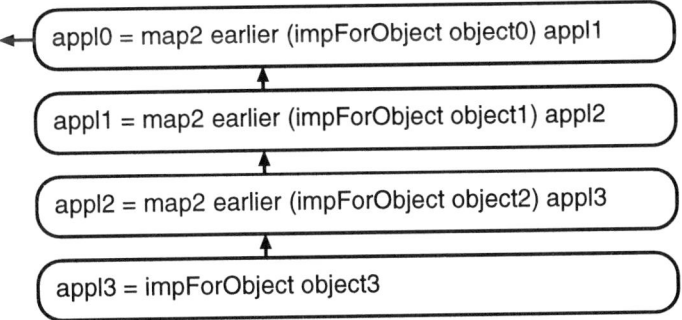

Figure 14.6. Process network for ray tracing using a pipeline

14.3.2 Ray Tracing Using a Pipeline

Although unlikely to be faster than the straightforward approach above, we consider a more interesting way to parallelise the ray tracer. Figure 14.6 shows the process network. The idea is that each processor tests all the rays against the subset of objects in the scene that it holds. Each processor forwards the earliest impact it finds down the pipeline; each stage selects either its locally-computed candidate or the candidate impact received from its neighbour, whichever is the earlier. We discuss the performance of this example, and how it can be improved, in Section 14.5.2.

14.4 Implementing Caliban

Implementing Caliban has proven fairly challenging. Frank Taylor's compiler [560] is structured as follows:

- Standard Haskell front-end (moreover is defined as an infix operator in a special prelude);
- Symbolic evaluation to propagate annotations up to top level call with function return values.

```
rayTrace scene viewpoint =
        parInsert (map2 earlier) llimps
        where
        llimps = map impForObject scene
        impForObject obj = map (λray . hit ray obj) rays
        rays = generateRays viewpoint
parInsert :: ([a]→[a]) → [[a]] → [a]
parInsert f [s] = s moreover Bundle [s]
parInsert f (s:ss) =
        appl moreover Bundle [appl] And Arc appl next
        where
        appl = f s next
        next = parInsert f ss
```

Figure 14.7. A pipeline ray tracer in Caliban

A function like farm in the ray tracer example above carries a moreover annotation. This must be integrated with the annotations of its calling context. We do this by marking where such "nested moreovers" occur, and then symbolically evaluating the marked source code using a modified interpreter which carries annotations along with return values. This fails if a call to a function carrying annotations is conditional on values available only at run-time, or if elaboration of the annotation fails to terminate;

- Symbolic execution to evaluate placement annotations.
  Annotations may still be in the form of unevaluated Haskell expressions (such as an application of the fan function in the ray tracer example). We use another modified symbolic interpreter to reduce annotation expressions to expose the static process network stucture. Again, this may fail if computing the annotation takes too much time or space, or needs run-time input;
- Dependence analysis of placed expressions to find where inter-processor communication has to be introduced (and to validate Arc assertions);
- Mapping of virtual processors to physical processors;
- Synthesis of a call to run-time communication management functions (setup and connect) giving details of which expression should be executed on each processor, and the wiring list to route communication streams between them;
- Optimisation and code generation, using a standard optimising Haskell compiler back-end;
- Run-time system: evaluation threads, communication channels, garbage collection.

The Caliban compiler was built on top of the FAST project Haskell⁻ front-end (a Haskell subset implementation developed at Imperial College), a pre-

14.4 Implementing Caliban

existing interpreter, and Koen Langendoen's FCG back-end [354]. Communication was implemented using MPI [544].

14.4.1 Run-Time System

Each processor is responsible for evaluating a given set of stream-valued expressions – the set of expressions "Bundled" together in the moreover clause. Each of these expressions is then sent on the appropriate channels to the processors where the value is used (it may have to be copied to several different destinations).

The connect run-time system function call (which is synthesised during the Caliban compilation phases outlined above) creates the communication channels, creates a closure representing each remote stream reference, and issues an asynchronous MPI receive on each channel so that it is ready for the data which will be sent.

The setup function, also generated by the Caliban compiler, creates a separate thread for each expression. This thread manages an output buffer for each of the remote processors to which the expression's value is to be sent. Whenever any of these buffers becomes empty (i.e. after successful message transmission) the thread becomes runnable; it then evaluates the next element of the stream, copies it (recursively, in fully-evaluated form) ready for contiguous message transfer, and initiates the message send to the waiting channel(s) using MPI.

During evaluation, a thread may encounter a closure representing a value which should be computed remotely. The code activated when the closure is executed checks whether the value has yet been received. If not, the thread blocks. On receipt, the message (the next stream element) is unpacked and rebuilt as a local, fully-evaluated heap structure. Before returning, the thread reposts the MPI receive call so that delivery of the next stream element can be overlapped with computation.

When a thread blocks waiting for input, the thread scheduler switches to another runnable thread, if one exists.

Thread Scheduling. In our current implementation, threads are not preempted — thread switching occurs only when a thread blocks or outputs a value. As mentioned in Section 14.2.4, this is somewhat unsatisfactory. Evaluation of a needed value could be prevented or delayed because it has been bundled with an expression which takes a very long time to relinquish the processor. In our experience this is rarely a practical problem. Implementing preemptive scheduling would incur a small overhead on all execution due to the need for locks to ensure heap updates are atomic, which are not otherwise needed on a uniprocessor.

Garbage Collection. Because all inter-processor references are explicit, garbage collection within each node can proceed independently. We use a standard two-space collector. Inter-processor garbage collection occurs when a remote reference to an expression on another processor is freed during local collection. We use what is, in effect, a reference counting scheme; the sender is informed that the reference is dead. The sender frees the channel buffer structure and thereby removes its reference from the sender's heap root set. If all the channels referring to a given stream are deleted, the thread itself is collected. Reference counting fails to collect inter-processor reference cycles, which in Caliban arise from cyclic data flow networks. This has not yet proven a problem.

14.5 Performance and Performance Tuning

Having introduced Caliban and explained how it has been implemented, we present some performance results using the ray tracer example used in the introduction. As is very common in parallel computing, some adjustments have to be made to improve performance, and we show how this can be done in Caliban.

14.5.1 Ray Tracer Performance: Farm Implementation

Partitioning the Work. To make the implementation shown earlier in Figure 14.5 realistic, we need to modify it so that the large set of rays to be traced is partitioned onto a fixed number of processors. We modify farm as follows:

```
farm :: Int → (a→a) → [a] → [a]
farm n func input = farmed moreover fan farmed slaves
                    where
                    farmed = unblock slaves
                    slaves = map (map func) jobs
                    jobs = blockOnto n input
```

We assume the existence of functions blockOnto and unblock to divide the list into n chunks and reassemble it. The number of virtual processors used is determined by n, which can be chosen to match the number of physical processors available.

Blocking by Rays. Impacts are small structures and there are many of them, which give very poor performance if they are collected from the slaves one-by-one. Instead of writing:

```
rayTrace scene viewpoint = farm N impact rays
```

we need to process the rays in blocks of size M, to amortise the message passing overheads:

14.5 Performance and Performance Tuning

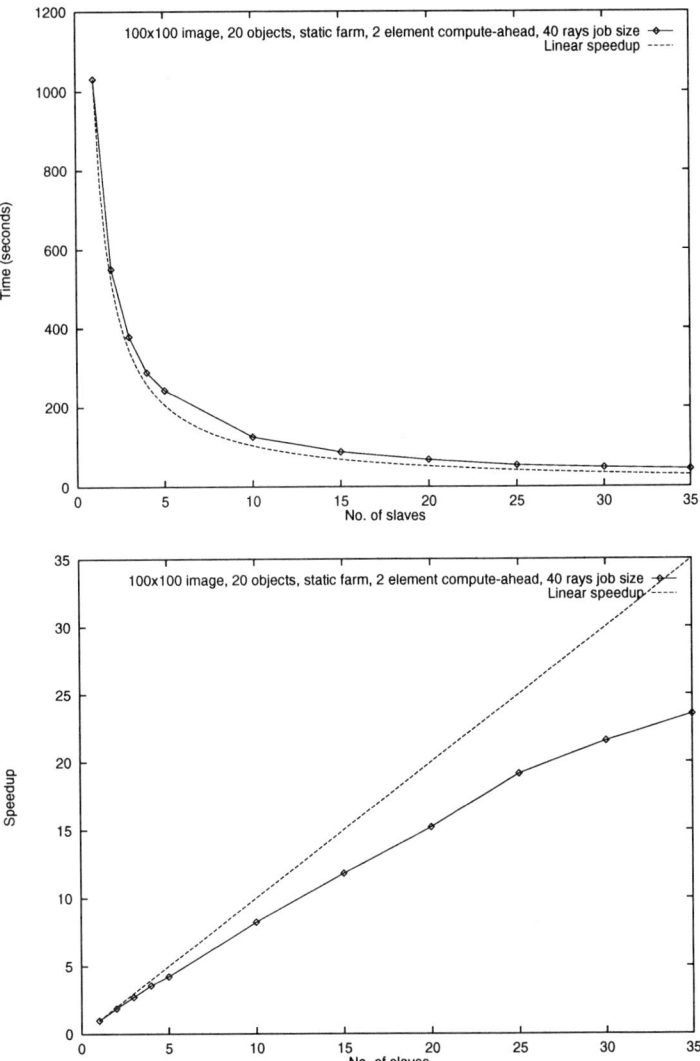

Figure 14.8. Execution time, and speedup relative to single-processor Caliban performance, for the task farm ray tracer implementation. 100×100 rays were traced, rendering a scene consisting of 20 cubes. Rays/impacts were collected in blocks of 40, which proved the optimum balance between load balance and overheads. A stream compute-ahead factor of 2 proved adequate. Results are from the 128-processor Fujitsu AP1000 at Imperial College, which has 25MHz Sparc processors and a 25MB/s mesh interconnect.

```
rayTracescene viewpoint = impacts
    where
        impacts = parInsert (map2 earlier) llimps
        llimps = map (rayTrace rays) subScenes
        rayTrace rs ss = map (λr. fold earlier (map (hit r) ss)) rs
        subScenes = block N scene
        rays = generateRays viewpoint
```

Figure 14.9. Pipeline farm with control over the number of stages

```
rayTrace scene viewpoint =
    unblock (farm N impact' (blockInto M rays))
```

where impact' rays = map impact rays. The function blockInto divides the list of rays into a list of blocks of rays of length M.

Performance. The performance achieved using the farm is shown in Figure 14.8. The actual code executed for these experiments incorporates some minor adjustments as discussed in Section 14.5.3, where it is listed in full in Figure 14.12.

14.5.2 Ray Tracer Performance: Pipeline Implementation

Blocking Over Objects. Figure 14.9 shows a version of the pipelined ray tracer shown earlier, modified to use a given number of processors with a number of objects assigned to each stage. As each stage can now render more than one object it is necessary for impact data for each ray to be folded to produce the single best impact for that ray. This means that impact selection now happens in two places, once at the very top level of the program where impacts from each pipeline stage are merged, and once on each pipeline stage where the best impact for that objects on that stage is produced.

Blocking Over Rays. As with the farm version of the ray tracer, grain size can be an issue due to message handling overheads. Figure 14.10 shows a new version where the rays are passed from processor to processor in packets of M. Too large a value for M leads to a loss of parallelism due to pipeline start-up delay. We found that blocks of 10 to 20 rays worked best.

Figure 14.11 shows the performance. Speedup is far from linear because computations in a pipeline are tightly coupled to each other. A delay in one part of the pipeline causes delays elsewhere: a pipeline runs at the speed of its slowest stage. The pipelined approach is probably only of interest if processors do not have enough memory to store all the objects.

14.5 Performance and Performance Tuning   317

```
blockedRayTrace scene viewpoint =
       unblock bImpacts
       where
       bImpacts = parInsert (map2 blockedEarlier) llimps
       blockedEarlier a b = map2 earlier a b
       llimps = map (map rayTrace rayBlocks) subScenes
       rayTrace rs ss = map (λr. fold earlier (map (hit r) ss)) rs
       rayBlocks = block M rays
       subScenes = block N scene
       rays = generateRays viewpoint
```

Figure 14.10. The pipeline ray tracer with grain size control

14.5.3 Subtleties and Complications

Avoiding Unwanted Compile-Time Computation. An intriguing (and annoying) problem arises with the farm version of the ray tracer presented in Section 14.5.1. The Caliban annotation simplifier has to evaluate each Bundled expression in order to check whether it is distinct from other Bundled expressions (the annotation could, for example, involve indexed selection of several expressions from a list). Evaluation stops at weak head normal form (WHNF), or when a run-time parameter is encountered.

The problem is that the farm's moreover annotation Bundles each block of rays - so the compiler ends up calling block, which, in turn, calls generateRays. Unless blocked by encountering a run-time parameter, the first N blocks of rays are calculated at compile-time. Although this may improve the run-time execution time, it is not satisfactory.

Figure 14.12 shows how this problem was overcome. We simply add a dummy element to each list of blocks of rays. This provides a simple normal form for Caliban's simplifier to find. It is this code which produced the performance results shown in Figure 14.8.

Blocking Using Annotations Only. In Section 14.5.1, we showed a version of farm which partitions the work evenly over a given number of processors:

```
farm :: (a→a) → [a] → [a]
farm func input = farmed moreover fan farmed slaves
                where
                farmed = unblock slaves
                slaves = map (map func) jobs
                jobs = blockOnto n input
```

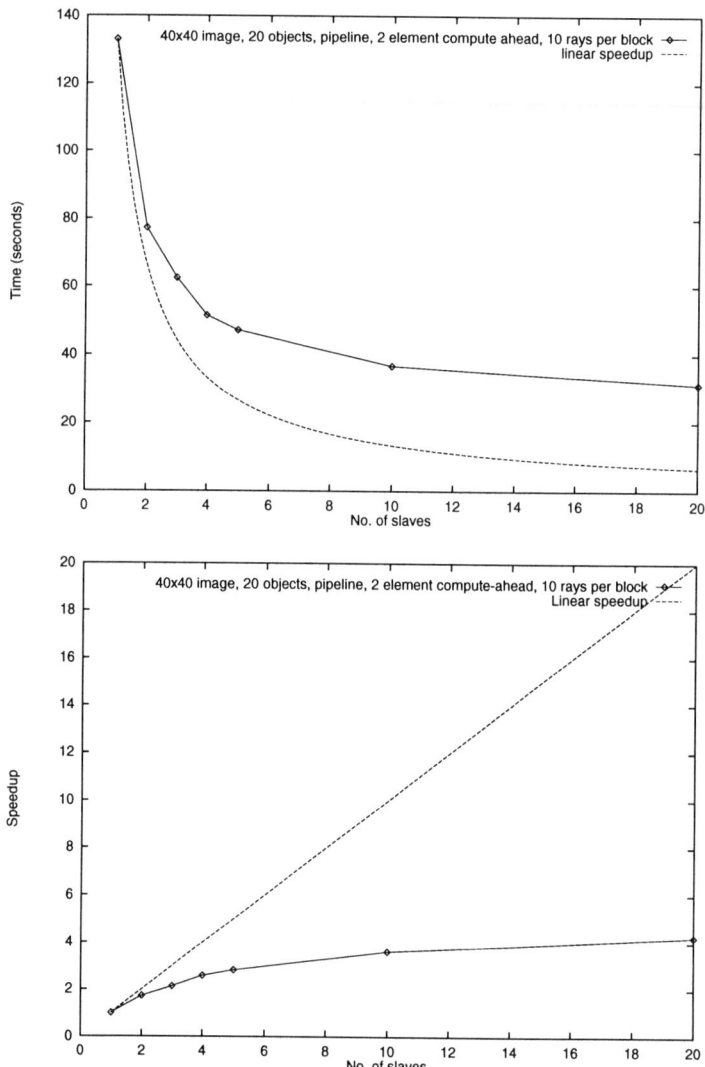

Figure 14.11. Pipeline ray tracer performance with 40×40 rays, a 20-cube scene, compute ahead of two and block size of 10. Again, results are from the 128-processor Fujitsu AP1000 at Imperial College

14.5 Performance and Performance Tuning

```
rayTrace scene viewpoint =
        unblock results
        where
        results = farm N impact' (block M rays)
        rays = generateRays viewpoint
        impact' rays = map impact rays
        impact ray = fold earlier impacts
                     where
                     impacts = map (hit ray) scene

farm :: Int → (a→a) → [a] → [a]
farm n func input = farmed moreover fan farmed slaves
                    where
                    farmed = unpartition (map unred slaves)
                    slaves = map red (map (map func) jobs)
                    jobs = partition n input

red :: Stream → Stream
red s = (CHAR '!') : s

unred :: Stream → Stream
unred = tail
```

Figure 14.12. Final task farm ray tracer implementation. Each of the N tasks in the farm operates on its share of the rays. The results are gathered in chunks of M rays to reduce message passing overheads. The function red (meaning "stop") adds a dummy element to a stream to prevent excess compile-time execution; unred removes it.

It would have been much more satisfactory to separate the partitioning from the computation, confining this performance optimisation to a moreover clause. This is very straightforward to do:

```
farm :: Int → (a→a) → [a] → [a]
farm n func input = farmed
        moreover fan farmed
                  (map Bundle (blockOnto n input))
        where
        farmed = map func input
```

To see what this does, consider a small example:

```
farm 3 f [e0, e1, e2, e3, e4, e5] = farmed
        moreover fan farmed
                  (map Bundle [[e0, e1], [e2, e3], [e4, e5]])
        where
        farmed = map f [e0, e1, e2, e3, e4, e5]
```

Evaluating the annotation gives:

```
fan farmed [Bundle [e0, e1], Bundle [e2, e3], Bundle [e4, e5]]
 = Bundle [e0, e1] And Arc [e0, e1] farmed
   Bundle [e2, e3] And Arc [e2, e3] farmed
   Bundle [e4, e5] And Arc [e4, e5] farmed
```

This expresses the desired partitioning, but unfortunately:

- The compiler has to evaluate the list of expressions e0...e5. This involves doing a lot of work at compile-time – which might be blocked if producing the list requires a run-time parameter.;
- The compiler generates a separate thread for each e0...e5;
- Each of the streams e0...e5 is communicated via a separate channel. Messages are not aggregated.

It might be possible to overcome some of these problems with a much more sophisticated compiler, but it seems unlikely that the problem is solvable in any but trivial examples. Note, in particular, that to send corresponding elements of e0 and e1 in a single message (as specified explicitly in the code given in Figure 14.12), requires strictness analysis.

14.6 Discussion

Caliban was designed to enable the pragmatic details of how a parallel functional program is mapped onto a distributed-memory parallel machine to be given as an annotation which is:

1. Separate from the functional description of the computation itself;
2. Declarative: the process network is specified by describing its structure, rather than as a side-effect of executing the program.

In the time since Caliban was first proposed (1987), some progress has been made and the design goals for a coordination language have been refined. In particular researchers have recognised

- The importance of linking resource allocation with a model of the resulting performance;
- The need to characterise the resource requirements and structural constraints of each parallel component in a generic but tractable form;
- The value of formulating the problem of managing data partitioning, computation and communication as a mathematical optimisation problem.

14.7 Future Directions

We plan to build on our experience with Caliban by designing software tools for run-time manipulation and optimisation of software components. We will

14.7 Future Directions

construct metadata for each component, describing its (predicted or measured) characteristics and optimisation/restructuring alternatives.

We will then be able to construct an optimised execution plan, which applies partitioning, resource allocation and scheduling, and perhaps loop fusion, tiling etc. In many ways this is a generalisation of ideas present in the database query optimisation community [166].

This framework could also enable the programmer to invoke partial evaluation [154] at run-time, so that a component can be specialised using knowledge of some of its run-time parameters.

This research programme is intended to experiment with explicit control over optimisation at run-time, using high-level semantic information about the software components. It is intended to exploit more powerful partial evaluation techniques than used in Caliban.

Caliban's objective of separating performance tuning annotations from the functional source code of the application has much in common with the goals of aspect-oriented programming. An example, which includes user-controlled cross-component optimisations such as loop fusion, is Irwin, Loingtier, Gilbert and Kiczale's work on optimising sparse matrix code [296].

15. Parallel and Distributed Programming in Concurrent Clean

Rinus Plasmeijer[1], Marko van Eekelen[1], Marco Pil[1], and Pascal Serrarens[1]

15.1 Introduction

Clean is a state-of-the-art lazy pure functional language which offers:

- Higher order functions and currying
- Lazy evaluation and (cyclic) sharing
- Lambda expressions and local definitions (where and let)
- Guards and case expressions, patterns, and list and array comprehensions
- Strong typing with Milner/Mycroft type inference (with polymorphic types, abstract types, algebraic types, synonym types) extended with existentially quantified types, overloading via type classes and type constructor classes
- Predefined types and type constructors (integers, reals, booleans, characters, files, lists, tuples, records, arrays)
- strictness annotations in (function and data) type definitions
- Separate compilation of modules (with implementation and definition modules with implicit or explicit imports).

Haskell [457] and Clean [93], [432], [476] developed independently as descendants of the language Miranda [575] and influenced by the language Gofer [319] (type classes for overloading). The most important differences between Clean and Haskell are that Clean has graph rewriting semantics, offers uniqueness typing, and has a sophisticated library for defining window based interactions.

15.2 Parallel Programming in Clean

Concurrent Clean has *concurrency* annotations to create functions which can be executed in *parallel* [476], [332]. The annotations allow the creation of *arbitrary process topologies* using a communication mechanism based upon the *lazy-copy concept* [37], [476]. Communication takes place automatically when one function on one processor demands the result being calculated on another. The concurrency primitives influence the order of evaluation and the execution speed of programs. They do not affect the outcome since everything remains pure.

---

[1] Computer Science Institute, University of Nijmegen, The Netherlands.

Data parallelism, working on e.g. distributed arrays, can be dealt with efficiently in Clean without introducing new language constructions. Distributed arrays have the elements distributed over a number of processors. This can be achieved via remote values, a special data structure in which a value at a remote processor is associated with its location. Distributed arrays have the same flexibility as standard arrays in Clean and can be updated destructively using uniqueness typing. In the matrix-vector multiplication example below, we show that distributed arrays are well suited to implement parallel algorithms with little overhead.

15.2.1 Basic Annotations for Explicit Parallelism

The following basic annotations are available in Clean to control concurrent evaluation of expressions:

- {| **I** |} This annotation starts up a new process on the current processor. It will reduce the annotated expression to *R*oot *N*ormal *F*orm (RNF). No communication takes place; instead, the new process shares nodes in the same heap with other processes. Processes on the same processor will run *interleaved* and scheduling is fair;
- {| **P** |} This annotation starts up a new process at some other remote processor (if one exists) that will reduce the annotated expression in *parallel* to RNF. Only the annotated function will be evaluated at the remote processor. The arguments will always be evaluated locally and transportation of arguments will always take place after evaluation. If they are strict, they will be evaluated before starting the new process; otherwise they will be evaluated lazily when (and if) the new process needs its arguments;
- {| **P at** processor |}: This is the same as {| **P** |}, only now the expression "processor" evaluates to a processor-id and the new process will be started at the given processor. Basically, all annotations are some form of the {| **P at** ... |} annotation.

All communications take place implicitly, except for those implied by the annotations above. All objects are represented by graphs. If a function needs an object that is stored on another processor, the graph for that object will be automatically transported to the function. In order to achieve this, a graph copying mechanism is used that copies as much of the graph as possible at once. However, only the evaluated parts of the graph will be transported directly. If a function needs a structure that has not yet been reduced, it will not be shipped immediately. Instead, a new lazy process will be started to evaluate the structure and it will be transported only after it has been reduced to root normal form (RNF – equivalent to head normal form), to the extent that it has been reduced. The effect is to permit only normal forms to travel implicitly between processors; closures are always evaluated before copying and act as "copy-stoppers". This "Lazy Normal

15.2 Parallel Programming in Clean

Form Copying" [334] provides the concept of distributed processes, which all reduce lazily to normal form, although in reality each process only reduces to RNF. Amongst other advantages, work is never copied implicitly and the programmer can easily determine what is to be copied by inspecting the type of a function.

Specifying Process Structures. The fact that Concurrent Clean is a graph rewriting language is clearly an advantage for the specification of process topologies. The graph structure can be used to define explicitly the required process topology. This makes, for instance, the creation of cyclic process structures much easier to understand. To illustrate the use of graph rewriting in specifying process topologies, several Concurrent Clean examples are given below.

A Hierarchical Process Topology. Divide-and-conquer parallelism is expressed with hierarchical process topologies. They have a straightforward process behaviour.

```
Fib :: !Int → Int
Fib 0 = 1
Fib 1 = 1
Fib n
  | n > Threshold = {| P |}left + {| P |}right
  | n > 2         =       left +       right
  | otherwise     = abort "Fib called with a negative value"
  where
    left  = Fib (n - 1)
    right = Fib (n - 2)
```

Both calls of `Fib` can be evaluated in parallel on another processor. First (n-1) and (n-2) are evaluated, forced by the local strict annotations because these annotations are put on subgraphs of the graphs on which the process annotations are put. Next, two parallel processes are created on lazy copies of `right` and `left` respectively. The parent process continues with the addition, but it has to wait until the arguments are evaluated and have been lazily copied back. A more efficient solution would be to create a child process for just one of the arguments. The parent process will then automatically calculate the other.

A Pipeline of Processes. The sieve of Eratosthenes is a classic example in which parallel sieving processes are created dynamically in a pipeline. This can be defined in Clean in the following way:

```
Primes :: [Int]
Primes = Sieve ({| P |}gen 2)
where
  gen n = [ n : {| I |}gen (n + 1) ]
```

```
Sieve :: [Int] → [Int]
Sieve [ ]   = [ ]
Sieve [p:s] =
    [ p : {| P |} Sieve ( {| I |} [ e \\ e ← s | e <> p ] ) ]
```

A parallel process is created for the initial generation of the list of numbers [2..]. For each sieve a separate parallel process is created which will stop as soon as a RNF is reached. The head of a list (a Cons node) is in RNF. However, in this case a process such as gen should not stop as soon as the head element has been evaluated but should continue evaluating the tail of a list. This effect can be achieved by creating an interleaved process for the tail.

Cyclic Process Topologies with Location Directives. The following toy example creates a cyclic parallel process structure. A pipeline is created between five processes in a cycle. When the next number in the pipeline list is received from the left neighbour, it is incremented by one and, in turn, passed to the right neighbour. This continues indefinitely. In a similar way, cyclic process structures can be explicitly specified in more elaborate examples obtaining speedups, e.g. for the Sieve algorithm (see [7]).

```
Start :: [Int]
Start = cycle
where
   cycle     = CreateCyclicProcs NrOfProcs cycle
   NrOfProcs = 5

CreateCyclicProcs :: Int [Int] → [Int]
CreateCyclicProcs pid left
   | pid == 1 = NewProcess 1 left
   | otherwise = CreateCyclicProcs (pid − 1)
                              ({| P |}NewProcess pid left)

NewProcess :: Int [Int] → [Int]
NewProcess n [hd:tl] = [ n : {| I |}NewProcess (n + hd) tl ]
```

CreateCyclicProcs is initially called with a reference to itself, thus forming a cyclic process structure of length one. CreateCyclicProcs recursively creates new processes NewProcess. Each NewProcess has a process number. CreateCyclicProcs will finally form the first NewProcess in the cycle with process number 1. Each NewProcess is connected to the next one, i.e. the one with the next processor-id number, by means of a channel. During the creation of the processes this channel is passed as a parameter: left.

Defining Skeletons. With the help of the basic Clean annotations, more powerful primitives can be defined. In particular higher-order functions may be used. For instance, the following function ParMap is a parallel version of map

15.2 Parallel Programming in Clean

in which the function to be mapped over the elements of the list is evaluated in parallel.

```
ParMap :: (a → b) [a] → [b]
ParMap f [ ]    = [ ]
ParMap f [x:xs] = [ {| P |}f x : {| I |}ParMap f xs ]
```

By using function definitions, local sets of skeletons can be defined for commonly occurring kinds of parallelism.

15.2.2 Data Parallelism

For an efficient implementation of distributed arrays some administration is needed, in which a pointer to a remote value is stored together with its actual location ([333], [524]).

The R constructor (being in RNF) protects the remote graph x from being accessed directly.

```
:: Remote x = R x ProcId
```

The program has to ensure that the physical location of the remote graph corresponds with the administered location ProcId which is stored in the data type. This can be accomplished by making Remote an abstract data type and providing a set of functions on it, each of which fulfills the property above.

Moving Data and Information. The first three functions to be introduced respectively copy data to, from and between processors:

```
putRemote :: ProcId a → Remote a
putRemote p x = R y p
where
   y = {| P at p |} x

getRemote :: (Remote a) → a
getRemote (R x p) = x

locationOf :: (Remote a) → ProcId
locationOf (R x p) = p

copyTo :: ProcId (Remote a) → Remote a
copyTo p2 (R x p1) = R y p2
where
   y = {| P at p2 |} x
```

The last function is important. Clean provides implicit communication: when a graph is needed at a different processor, the run-time system copies the graph to the new location. However, many parallel algorithms describe in detail how and when data is moved between processors, to ensure that the communication overhead is as small as possible. Therefore, a function is provided for explicitly moving data between processors which, together with locationOf, can be used to align data on the same processor.

Sending Work. The key functions on remote graphs are the apply-like functions which send a function to the remote graph and apply it there. When applying a binary function, the result may be left at the location of either argument, depending on the situation. Therefore two functions are provided: rap2_1 and rap2_2 which leave the result on the location of their first and second argument respectively.

```
rap :: (a → b) (Remote a) → Remote b
rap f (R x p) = R y p
where
    u = {| P at p |} f x

rap2_1 :: (a b → c) (Remote a) (Remote b) → Remote c
rap2_1 f (R x p1) (R y p2) = R z p1
where
    z = {| P at p1 |} f x y

rap2_2 :: (a b → c) (Remote a) (Remote b) → Remote c
rap2_2 f (R x p1) (R y p2) = R z p2
where
    z = {| P at p2 |} f x y
```

Distributed Arrays. Using the remote values from the previous section an array can be built with elements located on remote processors. A distributed array is simply a type synonym for an array of remote values:

```
:: DArray a :== { Remote a }
```

Operations on Distributed Arrays. Distributed arrays are created by combining two arrays: an array containing the elements and an array containing the locations of those elements. These two arrays are combined with putRemote:

```
createDArray :: { ProcId } { a } → DArray a
createDArray ps a = { putRemote p e \\ e ← : a & p ← : ps }
```

Many functions on distributed arrays are straightforward since they are basically normal array manipulations. Implementations are provided to map a function over a distributed array and to zip the elements of two distributed arrays together using a specified function. Likewise, variants of fold can also be produced [524].

15.2 Parallel Programming in Clean

```
mapDArray :: (a → b) (DArray a) → DArray b
mapDArray f dx = { rap f rx \\ rx ← : dx }

zipwithDArray1 :: (a b → c) (DArray a) (DArray b) → DArray c
zipwithDArray1 f dx dy =
    { rap2_1 f rx ry \\ rx ← : dx & ry ← : dy }
```

In the same way as with the functions `rap2_1` and `rap2_2` from Section 15.2.2, there are two variants of `zipWith`: `zipwithDArray1/2`. The subarrays can be rotated across the processors using the `lRotateDArray` function:

```
lRotateDArray :: Int (DArray a) → DArray a
lRotateDArray s dx =
    { copyTo (locationOf dx.[i]) dx.[(i + s) mod n]
        \\ i ← [0 .. n − 1] }
    where
        n = size dx
```

An Example: Matrix-Vector Multiplication. As an example, consider Kumar et al.'s matrix-vector multiplication algorithm [349]. The algorithm assumes a mesh-shaped processor network. The matrix is distributed blockwise over the network, while the vector is distributed blockwise over the rightmost column of the network. In this algorithm, the vector is first distributed over the processors, then all processors perform a local matrix-vector multiplication and at the end the local results are summed, leaving the result vector in the rightmost column of the processor network.

Two kinds of distributed structures are required: a distributed matrix and a distributed vector, with types:

```
:: DMatrix :== {{ Remote Matrix }}
:: DVector :== { Remote Vector }
```

In order to minimise communication overhead for the broadcast of the vector, the algorithm prescribes a two-step mechanism. In the the first step the vector is copied to the diagonal of the network:

```
copyToDiagonal :: DVector DMatrix → DVector
copyToDiagonal dv dm =
    { copyTo (locationOf dm.[i,i]) dv.[i]
        \\ i ← [0 .. size dv − 1] }
```

Table 15.1. Performance measurements for the matrix-vector multiplication. $t =$ running time in seconds, $s =$ speedup compared to sequential code

matrix size	sequential	4 processors		16 processors		64 processors	
	t	t	s	t	s	t	s
512^2	6.2	1.7	3.7	0.7	8.8	1.2	5.2
2048^2	97.6	24.7	3.9	6.7	14.6	3.0	33.0
8192^2	1555.5	390.1	4.0	98.9	15.7	27.1	57.5

In the second step the vector is broadcast over the columns. The result of this step is a distributed vector for each row of processors:

```
distributeVector :: DVector DMatrix → { DVector }
distributeVector dv dm =
  {{ copyTo (locationOf dm.[r,c]) dv.[c]
    \\ c ← [0..nc−1] } \\ r ← [0..nr−1] }
  where
    nr = size dm
    nc = size dm.[0]
```

Next, every processor evaluates its own local matrix-vector multiplication, using `zipwith2DArray1`, a 2-dimensional variant of `zipwithDArray1`:

```
localMatMulVec :: DMatrix { DVector } → { DVector }
localMatMulVec dm dv = zipwith2DArray1 matVecMult dm dv
```

Every row of the distributed vector is summed from left to right, with the result ending up in the rightmost column, for every row in the array. We assume that the addition operator (+) is defined for vectors:

```
accumSums :: { DVector } → DVector
accumSums dv = { foldlrDArray (+) row \\ row ← : dv }
```

Performance Measurements. This implementation of the matrix-vector multiplication was tested on a 64-node Transputer network. The code was compared against sequential code with no overheads for parallelism. Table 15.1 shows good speedups, because the local matrix-vector multiplications take most of the time.

Another test case is the conjugate gradient algorithm. The sequential version compared well to C and Haskell [523]. The parallel implementation ran on a network of 4 Macintosh II computers connected by Localtalk and Ethernet. Using many map-like operations, there is lots of communication, so worse speedups could be expected, but Table 15.2 shows that the results were encouraging. These times can be further improved by using broadcasting as described in [525].

Table 15.2. Performance measurements for the conjugate gradient algorithm

matrix size	sequential	4 Localtalk		4 Ethernet	
	t	t	s	t	s
400^2	22.1	67.9	0.3	25.5	0.9
1600^2	175.9	152.7	1.2	83.1	2.1
3600^2	590.9	306.9	1.9	200.7	2.9
6400^2	1386.9	552.7	2.5	416.1	3.3

15.3 Distributed Programming in Clean

The kind of parallelism discussed so far is generally used to speed up the execution of programs. We now turn our attention to concurrency for reactive window-based applications.

Although there is a direct Clean interface to TCP/IP, the advantages of functional programming can be better exploited with communication primitives at a higher level of abstraction, such as offered by the Clean Object I/O library for lightweight processes. The sequential Object I/O message passing primitives can also be extended to handle communication between a number of distributed running applications.

Since fully distributed applications are now no longer part of a single Clean program source, static type checking is impossible. Clean currently offers a hybrid type system with both static and dynamic types [471]. Messages passed between programs can now be checked at run-time (see Section 15.3.2). Programs can communicate any data structure and any function (!) in a typesafe manner. This also enables the system to type check the contents of files. Data as well as code can be stored and retrieved, with one function call.

15.3.1 Message Passing Primitives for Distributed Applications

Communication between Programs. In Clean there are channels which are split into a sending and a receiving part: the send channel and the receive channel (in the spirit of Broadcasting Sequential Processes [210], which is based on CSP [283]).

```
:: SChannel a      // a send channel
:: RChannel a      // a receive channel
```

Sending can only happen on a send channel, while receiving is only allowed on receive channels. This is very convenient: it is always clear in which direction the messages go. As send and receive channels are first-class citizens, they can be shared and be sent on other channels, enabling flexible communication patterns.

A message sent on a send channel will be sent to all locations which possess the corresponding receive channels, where they will be queued until needed. A receive channel represents the list of messages in the order in which they are sent using the send channels. The ordering between messages from two independent send channels is indeterminate and depends on the environment in which the message is received.

It is guaranteed that all messages which are sent on a send channel will be received on a receive channel, so messages cannot be lost. This simplifies reasoning about these channels greatly, but has the consequence of complicating the implementation.

Dynamic typing is normally used for flexible, type-safe, inter-program communication (see Section 15.3.2), but in this section we assume that the messages between programs are of fixed type Int.

```
:: ChName :== String

:: Maybe a = Just a | Nothing

createRChannel :: ChName *World → (Maybe (RChannel a), *World)

findSChannel   :: ChName *World → (SChannel a, *World)

newChannel     :: *World → (SChannel a, RChannel a, *World)
```

With createRChannel a new channel is created with the given name which is stored in a table on the local network. If the name already exists, it will fail and return Nothing; otherwise it will return the receive side of the channel.

The send side of the channel can be retrieved from the table multiple times: the same send channel is returned. One way to obtain a send channel is by using findSChannel. This will wait until a channel with the given name is available in the local table and return the send side when it is. Channels for local use can be created using newChannel. This returns both the send- and receive side of a new channel. Other variants (e.g. non-blocking) of the given primitives are also available [526].

Primitives for Sending and Receiving. send sends the message argument to all locations of the receive sides of the channel. It will return immediately, as it is an asynchronous channel. The message is sent using lazy normal form copying [332], which enables the sending of infinite structures. Strictness annotations can be used to force the message to be in (root) normal form when it is sent.

```
send    :: a (SChannel a) *World → *World
receive :: (RChannel a)    *World → (a, RChannel a, *World)
```

15.3 Distributed Programming in Clean

The `receive` function retrieves one message from the buffer. The rest of the messages are returned as a new receive channel. This function is blocking, so when there are no messages available, it will wait until one arrives. This blocking behaviour can be avoided using the function `available`, which returns a boolean stating whether a message is available for reception.

Example: Producer–Consumer. In the next example, there are two programs: one being a producer, sending the numbers 1 to 10 on a send channel which it has found using the name "Consumer". The other program consumes 10 messages on the channel it created under the name "Consumer" and computes the sum of the received numbers:

(The keyword # indicates a let-expression which can be defined before a guard. It introduces a new lexical scope, while the right-hand side identifiers can be reused on the left-hand side; they are internally tagged with a number.)

Program 1, the producer:

```
Start :: *World → *World
Start w
  # (sc, w) = findSChannel "Consumer" w
  = produce sc 10 1 w

produce :: (SChannel Int) Int Int *World → *World
produce sc n i w
  | n == 0
    = w
  | otherwise
    # w = send i sc w
    = produce sc (n - 1) (i + 1) w
```

Program 2, the consumer:

```
Start :: *World → (Int, *World)
Start w
  # (maybe_rc, w) = createRChannel "Consumer" w
  = case maybe_rc of
      Nothing → abort "channel already exists"
      Just rc → consume rc 10 0 w

consume :: (RChannel Int) Int Int *World → (Int, *World)
consume rc n r w
  | n == 0
    = (r, w)
  | otherwise
    # (i, rc, w) = receive rc w
    = consumer rc (n - 1) (r + i) w
```

Table 15.3. The performance of message passing within (internal) and between (external) processors for various message sizes

msg. size	4 bytes	40 bytes	400 bytes	4000 bytes
internal	413 kb/s	4,444 kb/s	32 Mb/s	421 Mb/s
external	720 b/s	7,020 b/s	64 kb/s	241 kb/s

To make a producer-consumer variant for lightweight processes the same code can be used, only the types would be slightly different. In this case, sending unique graphs can be useful, for example, where there are two threads within one program running on the same processor where both threads manipulate the same data structure in turn. Uniqueness typing can ensure that only one process at a time can access the data structure.

Performance. A simple producer-consumer benchmark which communicates a large number of integers demonstrated good basic communication speed (Table 15.3).

15.3.2 Communicating Data and Code Using Dynamic Typing

When distributed programs communicate with each other, it would be advantageous to guarantee the type safety of the messages. Distributed applications are generally not developed at the same time so the consistency of the messages communicated between them cannot therefore be checked statically by inspecting the source code. As a consequence, in practice messages have a fixed standard type, e.g. a byte stream (it can be a string or an array of characters or a list of characters). This is also needed when performing file I/O where characters are read from, or written into, a file.

A disadvantage of the fixed type approach is that all data structures have to be converted to, for example, a string before they can be communicated (written). When reading from a file or when receiving a message, it is necessary to parse the input to test for correctness and to translate the string back to an internal data structure. A significant part of the source code of an applications is needed to handle these types of data conversions. This is rather primitive, error prone and limited: for example, it is not usually possible to transfer code in this way.

Clean's Hybrid Type System. These disadvantages may be avoided by using a dynamic type system where types are checked at run-time. But we do not want the entire Clean language to become dynamically typed. Statically typed programming languages allow compile-time error checking, and generation of more efficient object code than languages where all type consistency checks have to be performed at run-time. Therefore a hybrid type system is needed in which some parts of a program are type checked dynamically, while the largest part is still checked statically.

15.3 Distributed Programming in Clean

The concept of *objects with dynamic types*, or *dynamics* for short, as introduced by Abadi et al. [1], can provide such an interface [471]. We distinguish between objects (terms) on which only static type checks are performed (*Statics*) and objects on which dynamic type checks are performed (*Dynamics*). Values of this Dynamic type are, roughly speaking, pairs of a value and a type, such that the value component can be typed with the type component.

From a static point of view all dynamics belong to the same static type: the type Dynamic. Applications involving dynamics are no longer checked statically, but type checks are deferred until run-time. Objects, values, expressions and terms can be explicitly projected from the static into the dynamic world and vice versa.

Converting Statics into Dynamics. The projection from the static to the dynamic world is done by pairing an expression with an encoding of its type. The expression is *wrapped* into a container. The type of the expression is hidden from the static world and the container receives the static type Dynamic.

Definition 15.3.1. *A dynamic can be created using the keyword* **dynamic**:

dynamic < *expression* > :: < *type* >

The <*type*> *may contain variables. If a variable (say* a*) does not occur anywhere but in this type, a quantifier is presumed to precede the type:* $\forall$a.<*type*>. *In this way, a polymorphic expression can be wrapped with an appropriate type.*

It can be checked statically that the "*expression*" is indeed of that static "*type*".

The "*expression*" lives in the dynamic world. It is contained in a dynamic, which has the static type Dynamic.

Example 15.3.1. Examples of dynamics are:

dynamic True :: Bool
dynamic fib :: Int $\rightarrow$ Int
dynamic reverse :: [a] $\rightarrow$ [a]

All three expressions have the static type Dynamic. Note that reverse is a polymorphic function that has been stored as such in its dynamic.

Converting Dynamics to Statics. To complement projection into the dynamic world, a mechanism is required to get objects back to the static world. Otherwise little could be done with objects once they had been packed in dynamics.

Uncontrolled use of objects in dynamics may be unsafe, since their types are no longer known at compile-time. Therefore, access to an object of type Dynamic has been limited. The value can only be accessed if its type matches a specific statically determined type. For this purpose the pattern match mechanism of Clean has been extended to describe matching on types.

Dynamics can thus only be inspected using a pattern match in a function. If the type of a dynamic matches the statically specified type of a pattern, then the value of the dynamic can safely be used in the right hand side expression. This can be checked statically, since the type pattern is known statically.

Example 15.3.2. An example of a dynamic pattern match is:

```
f :: Dynamic → Int
f (x :: Int)            = x
f (g :: Int → Int)      = g 5
f _                     = 0
```

It can be checked statically that if the dynamic contains an integer then this can safely be accessed as the result of f. If the dynamic contains a function from Int to Int, then this function can safely be applied to 5 and the result is indeed of type Int.

Type Pattern Variables. The type patterns need not fully specify the demanded type: they may include *type pattern variables*, which match any subexpression of the dynamic's type. If such a match has been successful, the subexpressions are bound to the type pattern variables they have matched. A full-blown run-time unification is used during matching of dynamics. A successful unification leads to a substitution for the type pattern variables and possibly for the (polymorphic) variables of the actual type.

Example 15.3.3. The following function is polymorphic in the types of its arguments (and its result). It checks whether its first argument is a function and whether the type of its second argument matches the input type of that function:

```
dynamicApply :: Dynamic Dynamic → Dynamic
dynamicApply (f :: a → b) (x :: a) = dynamic (f x) :: b
dynamicApply  df           dx      = dynamic "Error" :: String
```

Now

```
Start = dynamicApply (dynamic fib :: Int → Int)
(dynamic 7 :: Int)
```

will reduce to dynamic 21 :: Int,

```
Start = dynamicApply (dynamic reverse :: [a] → [a])
(dynamic [1,2,3] :: [Int])
```

will reduce to dynamic [3,2,1] :: [Int], and

15.3 Distributed Programming in Clean

```
Start = dynamicApply (dynamic reverse :: [a] → [a])
                    (dynamic 7 :: Int)
```

will reduce to dynamic "Error" :: String.

Pil [472] has shown that matchable type patterns can be generalised using a special kind of overloading such that type restrictions that are imposed on a dynamic type can be determined by the static context in which the function is used (so called *type dependent functions*). Type dependent functions allow abstraction over types of dynamics beyond the scope of a function, just as type pattern variables let us abstract over these types within one function alternative.

Communicating Dynamics. Dynamics are very useful for communication between distributed programs. Using dynamics, any data structure or function can be communicated over a single channel. The receiving site has to test the actual type stored in the dynamic.

In the producer-consumer program, the producer has to pack all static messages into a Dynamic type, which have to be unpacked by the consumer using a pattern match.

Program 1, the producer:

```
    Start :: *World → *World
    Start w
      # (sc, w) = findSChannel "Consumer" w
      = produce sc 10 1 w

    produce :: (SChannel Dynamic) Int Int *World → *World
    produce sc n i w
      | n == 0
          = w
      | otherwise
          # w = send (dynamic i :: Int) sc w
          = produce sc (n - 1) (i + 1) w
```

Program 2, the consumer:

```
    Start :: *World → (Int, *World)
    Start w
      # (maybe_rc, w) = createRChannel "Consumer" w
      = case maybe_rc of
          Nothing → abort "channel already exists"
          Just rc → consume rc 10 0 w

    consume :: (RChannel Dynamic) Int Int *World → (Int,*World)
```

```
consume rc n r w
  | n == 0
    = (r, w)
  | otherwise
    # (dyn_i, rc, w) = receive rc w
      i               = unpack dyn_i
    = case dyn_i of
        (i :: Int) → consume rc (n - 1) (r + i) w
                   → abort "No integer was received"
```

Implementation. Dynamics are very convenient for the programmer, but hard to implement, in particular in a heterogeneous distributed environment.

Since a dynamic can contain functions as well, both the dynamic and the corresponding program code have to be communicated. This code might depend on the type of processor the application is running on so code has to be transmitted in a platform independent way.

ABC-code (see Section 6.3.8) is platform independent and well suited for this purpose. Like JAVA byte-code, ABC-code can be just-in-time compiled to platform dependent object code which is dynamicaly linked into the receiving application when it accepts the dynamic. A version management control is also included.

15.4 Conclusion

This chapter has introduced the Concurrent Clean language, showing how it can be used to develop a variety of parallel programs using concurrency annotations. It has also introduced the use of explicit channel annotations and dynamic types for concurrent applications. These concepts are revisited in the chapter on Concurrent ML (Chapter 17).

16. Functional Process Modelling

Ali Abdallah[1]

16.1 Introduction

In order to develop generic skeleton solutions for general parallel architectures, it is necessary to formulate the design within a concurrency framework such as CSP [284]. Often parallel functional programs [505] show peculiar behaviours which are only understandable in the sole terms of concurrency rather than relying on hidden implementation details.

The formalisation in CSP of the parallel behaviour of operational interpretations of skeletons not only leads to better understanding but also allows accurate analysis of correctness and performance issues. In addition, the establishment of refinement concepts between functional and concurrent behaviours may allow systematic generation of parallel implementations for various architectures such as array processors, MIMD, pipelined, and systolic machines.

Throughout this chapter, we will use the functional notation and calculus developed by Bird and Meertens [47], [50], [51] for specifying algorithmics and reasoning about them and will use the CSP notation and its calculus developed by Hoare [284] for specifying processes and reasoning about them. We also use the standard `map`, `filter`, `fold` and `scan` functions defined in Section 2.2.6.

16.1.1 CSP Processes

CSP is a process algebra introduced by Hoare [284] for studying concurrency. CSP provides a concise notation for describing communicating systems and a theoretical framework for reasoning about their behaviours. CSP's operational semantics is based on a collection of firing rules described in Roscoe's recent textbook [502]. The operational behaviour is congruent to the denotational semantics.

Primitive Processes.

$STOP$	does nothing because of deadlock
$SKIP$	does nothing because of successful termination
$CHAOS$	behaves in the most unpredictable way!

---

[1] Department of Computer Science, Reading University, UK.

Communications Events.

$c?x$ inputs *any* value v from channel c and binds it to the variable x.

$c!e$ outputs the value of the expression e to channel c.

CSP conventions stipulate that communications take place over channels in a synchronous way; a channel links two processes, one is used for input and the other for output. When communication takes place, the value of the output message is instantly received by the inputting process and is bound to the input variable.

Summary of CSP Operators.

$a \to P$	does the event a and then behaves as P (associates to the right).
$\mu X.F(X)$	recursion; solution to the equation $P = F(P)$.
$P \triangleleft b \triangleright Q$	infix conditional; P if b is true else Q.
$a \to P \mid b \to Q$	behaves as P if a is chosen and as Q if b is chosen.
$P; Q$	sequential composition
$P \parallel Q$	parallel composition
$P \gg Q$	process piping
$P \sqcap Q$	non-deterministic composition
$P \setminus A$	hiding events of the set A from the behaviour of P.

In general, we use identifiers with lower case letters to name functional values and identifiers with upper case letters to name processes or types. In CSP, the notation $P \triangleleft b \triangleright Q$ is just an infix form for the traditional selection construct **if** b **then** P **else** Q.

We find it convenient to use pattern matching conventions as in the following definition:

$$P = left?\text{``}a\text{''} \to Q$$
$$\mid$$
$$left?(x, y) \to R(x, y)$$

to mean:

$$P = left?z \to (Q \triangleleft z = a \triangleright R(\textit{fst } z, \textit{snd } z))$$

For example, a process $CAT2$ which takes a list of pairs from channel $left$ and outputs on channel $right$ the result of their concatenation can be written as:

$$CAT2 = \mu X \bullet\ left?\text{``}eot\text{''} \to right!eot \to SKIP$$
$$|$$
$$left?(x, y) \to right!x \to right!y \to X$$

instead of:

$$CAT2 = \mu X \bullet\ left?x \to (\ right!eot\ \{\!\!\{x = eot\}\!\!\}$$
$$right!(fst\ x) \to right!(snd\ x) \to X\ )$$

16.1.2 Networks of Processes

In order to concisely describe structured networks of processes, we find it very convenient to use, in addition to the CSP notation, functions which return processes and functional operators such as map ('map') and fold (/). For example, if F is a function which returns processes, $\oplus$ is an associative CSP operator and $[a_1, a_2, \ldots, a_n]$ is a list of values, we have:

$$F\ \text{'map'}\ [a_1, a_2, \ldots, a_2] = [F(a_1), F(a_2), \ldots, F(a_n)]$$
$$fold\ (\oplus)\ F\ \text{'map'}\ [a_1, a_2, \ldots, a_n] = F(a_1) \oplus F(a_2) \oplus \cdots \oplus F(a_n)$$

For example, a bounded buffer of size n, designed as a chain of n identical $COPY$ processes, can be concisely captured as:

$$fold\ (\gg)\ (const\ COPY)\ \text{'map'}\ [1 \ldots n]$$

where $const$ is the constant function defined as $const\ x\ y\ = x$.

Occasionally, we will underline a symbol, such as $\underline{F}$, in order to emphasise the fact that it is a function which returns processes. We will also use the notation $F(x)$ instead of $(\underline{F}\ x)$ to denote the process obtained by applying the function $\underline{F}$ to the value x. When parsing expressions, we assume that functional application has the highest precedence and associates to the left, but all other functional operators have equal precedence and associate to the right. For example, the expression F 'map' $s \mathbin{+\!\!+} t$ means F 'map' $(s \mathbin{+\!\!+} t)$ and not $(F$ 'map' $s) \mathbin{+\!\!+} t$.

A number of tools have been developed to support CSP. They include FDR [502] which supports the formal verification of properties of processes and *VisualNets* [4] which supports the visualisation and animations of networks of communicating CSP processes.

16.2 Modelling Functions as Processes

The refinement from functions to CSP processes is based on the formal treatment given in [2], [4]. In general, a function $f :: [A] \to [B]$ is viewed as an abstract specification of a process which consumes a stream of values (argument) on an input channel and produces a stream of values (result) on an output channel. By convention, the end of each stream is denoted by eot, a special symbol to indicate "end of transmission". A CSP pipe process Q is said to refine a function $f :: [A] \rightarrow [B]$, written as $(f \prec Q)$, iff whenever a stream of values $s + [eot]$ is injected into the input channel of Q and provided that the list s is drawn from the domain of the f, the stream $f(s) + [eot]$ is produced on the output channel of Q. This concept is clearly illustrated in Figure 16.1

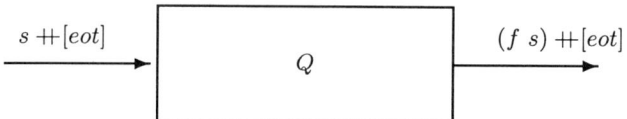

Figure 16.1. A process Q refining a function f

Formally, a pipe process Q is a refinement of a function $f :: [\alpha] \rightarrow [\beta]$, written as $(f \prec Q)$, iff the following condition holds:

$$\forall s \in \text{dom } f \bullet Prd(s) \triangleright Q = Prd(f\ s)$$

The operator $\triangleright$ (see [2], [4]) is similar to the CSP piping operator $\gg$ except that the left operand of $\triangleright$ is a producer (a process which can only output). The producers EOT and $Prd(s)$, for all lists s, are defined as follows:

$EOT \qquad\qquad\quad = !eot \rightarrow SKIP$

$Prd\ [a_1, a_2, \cdots, a_n] = !a_1 \rightarrow !a_2 \rightarrow \cdots !a_n \rightarrow EOT$

There are usually several, and possibly infinite, semantically different sequential processes which refine (or correctly implement) a given function. Care must be taken when refining a function into a sequential process which is to be placed as a node in a network of communicating processes. Although all implementations of the function lead to correct networks, the performances of these networks are not identical and may show dramatic differences. The proof that a process Q refines a function f, that is $(f \prec Q)$, is usually established by a simple inductive argument using the algebraic definition of $\triangleright$ and CSP algebraic laws. We find it convenient to describe transformation rules and specification refinement using the conventions from the CIP transformation project [126]). Hence, the notation

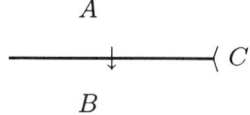

16.2 Modelling Functions as Processes

means that the program template A is a valid refinement of the program template B, provided that the condition C holds.

16.2.1 Examples of Refinements into Sequential Processes

We consider several useful functions and present a typical refinement of each of these functions as a sequential CSP process. The resulting processes will be the basic building blocks for the construction of several parallel algorithms which will be encountered later. The refinement proofs and how CSP definitions are systematically synthesised from the functional definitions can be found in [4].

The Identity Function id_L. The process $COPY$ is a refinement of the identity function $id_{[A]} :: [A] \to [A]$ over lists of values.

$$COPY = \mu X \bullet ?x \to !x \to (SKIP \triangleleft x = eot \triangleright X)$$

It can be shown that all bounded buffer processes are correct refinements of $id_{[A]}$, despite the fact that they are all semantically different in CSP.

The Function map. For any function $f :: A \to B$, the function f 'map' $:: [A] \to [B]$ can be refined by the process:

$$MAP(f) = \mu X \bullet ?x \to (EOT \triangleleft x = eot \triangleright !(f\ x) \to X)$$

The Function filter. For any predicate $p :: A \to bool$, the filter function $(p \triangleleft) :: [A] \to [A]$ can be refined by the process:

$$FILTER(p) = \mu X \bullet ?x \to (EOT \triangleleft x = eot \triangleright !x \to X \triangleleft p\ x \triangleright X)$$

The Function accumulate. The accumulation function acc is recursively defined as:

$$acc\ (\oplus)\ e\ [] \quad = [e]$$
$$acc\ (\oplus)\ e\ (a:s) = e: (acc\ (\oplus)\ (e \oplus a)\ s)$$

this function can be refined into the following sequential CSP process:

$$ACC(\oplus, e) = ?x \to !e \to (EOT \triangleleft x = eot \triangleright ACC(\oplus, e \oplus x))$$

Another satisfactory sequential implementation of acc which is semantically different from the one above is:

$$ACC'(\oplus, e) = !e \to ?x \to (EOT \triangleleft x = eot \triangleright ACC'(\oplus, e \oplus x))$$

The Function insert. For all values a, the function $(insert\ a) :: [A] \rightarrow [A]$, inserts a at the correct position of a sorted list.

$$insert\ a\ [\,]\quad = [a]$$
$$insert\ a\ (x\!:\!s) = x\!:\!insert\ a\ s,\ \text{if}\quad x < a$$
$$= a\!:\!x\!:\!s,\qquad \text{otherwise}$$

This function can be refined by the CSP process:

$$INSERT(a) = \mu X \bullet ?x \rightarrow\ (\,!a \rightarrow !eot \rightarrow SKIP \quad \{\!x = eot\!\}$$
$$!x \rightarrow X \qquad\qquad\qquad \{\!x < a\!\}$$
$$!a \rightarrow !x \rightarrow COPY\ )$$

Another valid refinement of the function $insert(a)$ is the following pipe process $INSERT'(a)$ which insists on consuming the whole input stream before producing any output.

$$INSERT'(a)\qquad = INS(a, [\,], [\,])$$
$$INS(a, less, greater) = ?x \rightarrow$$
$$(prd(less +\!\!+[a] +\!\!+ greater) \quad \{\!x = eot\!\}$$
$$INS(a, less +\!\!+[x], greater) \quad \{\!x < a\!\}$$
$$INS(a, less, greater +\!\!+[x]))$$

16.3 Decomposition Strategies for Pipelined Parallelism

Pipelined parallelism is a very effective means for achieving efficiency in numerous algorithms. It is generally much harder to detect than data parallelism. The *function decomposition* strategy aims at exhibiting pipelined parallelism in functional programs. The fundamental objective of this strategy is to transform a given algorithmic expression into a new form in which the dominant term is a composition of several functions. To fully appreciate the usefulness of this transformation, we will appeal to a basic result, shown in [2], that the composition of functions is naturally refined in CSP by the piping operator as follows:

$$f :: [A] \rightarrow [B];\ g :: [B] \rightarrow [C]$$
$$\cfrac{g \cdot f}{F \gg G}\ \{\!f \prec F \wedge g \prec G\!\}$$

16.4 Parallel Decomposition of Map

By an inductive argument, using the associativity of $\gg$, this result can be generalised so that the composition of any finite list of functions, say $[f_1, f_2, .., f_{n-1}, f_n]$, is refined by piping the list $[F_n, F_{n-1}, .., F_2, F_1]$ of processes where for each index i, $1 \leq i \leq n$, the process F_i is a refinement of the function f_i. Finally, we introduce one more general refinement law which will be frequently used:

$h :: T \to ([A] \to [A]); \underline{H} :: T \to PROC; \ s :: [T]$

$$\dfrac{fold \ (\cdot) \ (map \ h \ s)}{fold \ (\gg) \ (map \ \underline{H} \ (reverse \ s))} \ \langle h \prec \underline{H}$$

16.4 Parallel Decomposition of Map

In this section we present several algebraic laws which allow the decomposition of $(map \ f)$ to be directly derived from the decomposition of f. We also consider the decomposition of $(map \ f)$ when the function f is described as a right reduction or recursively defined over a list of values. To achieve this, it is necessary to introduce a new data-tupling transformation technique which leads to the decomposition of h into several simpler functions. The whole derivation is later encapsulated as a compact transformation rule which allows the whole synthesis of the parallel implementation to be done in a single transformation step. We show how the generic decomposition of $(map \ f)$ can be realised in CSP as an efficient pipelined network of processes. Finally, we show several examples of applying this rule.

16.4.1 Map Decomposition Laws

The first decomposition law is captured by the distributivity property of the *map* function over function composition $(\cdot)$. We have:

(map DC1) $map \ (g \cdot f) = (map \ g) \cdot (map \ f)$

By a simple inductive argument the above law can be generalised to any finite composition of functions. Hence, this generalisation allows the decomposition of the function h 'map' to be directly derived from the decomposition of h by the following law:

(map DC2) $map \ (fold \ (\cdot) \ fs) = fold \ (\cdot) \ (map \ (map) \ fs)$

It is often the case that all the functions in the list fs of the above law are just different instances of a single function h with two arguments. The instances are obtained by initialising the first argument of h to values drawn from a given list s. This leads to a yet more general map decomposition law.

(map DC3) $map\ (fold\ (\cdot)\ (map\ h\ s)) = fold\ (\cdot)\ (map\ (map \cdot h)\ s)$

As we shall see in subsequent examples, this law map DC3 will be used most frequently. An informal justification for this law is as follows:

$$
\begin{aligned}
&map\ (fold\ (\cdot)\ (map\ f\ [a_0, a_1, \cdots a_p])) \\
&= map\ (fold\ (\cdot)\ [f\ a_0, \cdots, f\ a_p]) &&\{\ \text{DEF. } map\ f\ \} \\
&= map\ (fold\ (\cdot)\ map)\ [f\ a_0, \cdots, f\ a_p] &&\{\ \text{map DC2}\ \} \\
&= fold\ (\cdot)\ [map\ (f\ a_0), \cdots, map\ (f\ a_p)] &&\{\ \text{DEF. } (map)\ \} \\
&= fold\ (\cdot)\ [(map \cdot f)\ a_0, \cdots, (map \cdot f)\ a_p] &&\{\ \text{DEF. } (\cdot)\ \} \\
&= fold\ (\cdot)\ (map\ (map \cdot f)\ [a_0, \cdots, a_p]) &&\{\ \text{DEF. } (map)\ \}
\end{aligned}
$$

16.4.2 Map Decomposition for Recursively Defined Arguments

Starting Specification. Now we turn to investigate a more powerful map decomposition rule. We consider the decomposition of $map\ (h\ m)$ where m is a given list of values and the function h is recursively defined as follows:

$$
\begin{aligned}
&h\ [\ ]\ x &&= e \\
&h\ (a\colon s)\ x &&= f\ a\ x\ (h\ s\ x)
\end{aligned}
$$

This definition of h will be referred to as *tail recursion with shared data* because the value of x is "shared" among all the recursive calls of h. An alternative definition of h can be described in terms of the `foldl` function:

$$h\ s\ a = foldl\ \oplus_a\ e\ s$$

$$\text{where } x \oplus_a y = f\ a\ x\ y$$

An Example. Two lists of words ws, representing a document, and ks, representing a list of keywords, are given. Consider the problem of counting the number of occurrences in the document ws of each word in the keywords list ks. A straightforward specification of this problem is captured as follows:

$$
\begin{aligned}
&wordcount\ ws\ ks = map\ (count\ ws)\ ks \\
&count\ s\ a \qquad = foldl\ \oplus_a\ 0\ s \\
&\qquad\qquad \text{where } x \oplus_a n = \quad \text{if } x = a \text{ then } n+1 \text{ else } n
\end{aligned}
$$

The function *count* is obviously an instance of h. Typical instances of h will also be encountered in the context of polynomial evaluation (at the end of this section) and spell checking (next section).

16.4 Parallel Decomposition of Map

Decomposition. We propose to generalise the function h into a new function, say th, that returns a pair of values, or a tuple in the more general case. The first component of the pair is the value of the relevant shared data whereas the second component of the pair is the required computational result. Hence, we suggest the following definition:

(**D3**) $\quad th\ s\ x = (x,\ h\ s\ x)$

Our first task is to redefine h as an instance of th. By definition we have:

$h\ s = \mathit{final} \cdot (th\ s)$

where the function *final* returns the second element of a pair. The second task is to synthesise a new definition for th which does not involve shared parameters. For the base case, we have:

$$\begin{aligned}
th\ [\,]\ x &= (x,\ h\ [\,]\ x) &&\{\ \text{INSTANTIATION}\ \} \\
&= (x,\ e) &&\{\ \text{UNFOLDING}\ \}
\end{aligned}$$

and in the general case, we reason as follows:

$$\begin{aligned}
th\ (a\!:\!s)\ x &= (x,\ h\ (a\!:\!s)\ x) &&\{\ \text{INSTANTIATION}\ \} \\
&= (x,\ f\ a\ x\ (h\ s\ x)) &&\{\ \text{UNFOLDING}\ \} \\
&= f'\ a\ (x,\ h\ s\ x) &&\{\ \text{ABSTRACTION}\ \} \\
&= f'\ a\ (th\ s\ x) &&\{\ \text{FOLDING}\ \} \\
&= ((f'\ a) \cdot (th\ s))\ x &&\{\ \text{DEF. OF}\ (\cdot)\ \}
\end{aligned}$$

where the subsidiary function f' is defined as follows:

(**D4**) $\quad f'\ a\ (x,\ y) = (x,\ f\ a\ x\ y)$

By defining the function *initial* as:

(**D5**) $\quad \mathit{initial}\ x = (x,\ e)$

we can, therefore, redefine th as follows:

(**RD3**) $\quad th\ [\,] \quad = \mathit{initial}$
$\phantom{(\mathbf{RD3})\quad}th\ (a\!:\!s) = (f'\ a) \cdot (th\ s)$

The important point is that the new specification is also in inductive form but this time without shared data. It can be directly decomposed as follows:

$th\ s = \mathit{fold}\ (\cdot)\ (\mathit{map}\ f'\ (s \mathbin{+\!\!+} [\mathit{initial}]))$

The above detailed derivations can be encapsulated in a single transformation rule as follows:

(DC-SD-R1)

$spec :: A \to B; \ h :: [T] \to A \to B; \ m :: [T]; \ e :: B;$

$f :: T \to A \to B \to B$

(D1) $spec \quad = h \ m$

(D2) $h \ [] \ x \quad = e$

$h \ (a : s) \ x = f \ a \ x \ (h \ s \ x)$

(RD1) $spec \quad = fold \ (\cdot) \ [final] \ +\!\!+ (map \ f' \ m) \ +\!\!+ [initial]$

(D3) $f' \ a \ (x, \ y) \ = (x, \ f \ a \ x \ y)$

(D4) $initial \ x \quad = (x, \ e)$

(D5) $final \ (x, \ y) = y$

Using the above rule, the function $(h \ m)$ can be decomposed as follows:

$h \ m \quad = fold \ (\cdot) \ [final] \ +\!\!+ (map \ f' \ m) \ +\!\!+ [initial]$

$f' \ a \ (x, \ y) = (x, \ f \ a \ x \ y)$

$initial \ x \quad = (x, \ e)$

$final \ (x, \ y) = y$

By applying the map decomposition law map DC3 and using some elementary properties of the operator $(fold \ (\cdot))$, we get:

$map \ (h \ m) = fold \ (\cdot) \ ([map \ final] \ +\!\!+ (map \ (map \cdot f') \ m)$
$\qquad\qquad\qquad +\!\!+ [map \ initial])$

This completes the decomposition of $map(h \ m)$ and, therefore, the whole derivation can be encapsulated in the following compact transformation rule:

16.4 Parallel Decomposition of Map

(DC-MAP-R1)

$spec :: [A] \rightarrow [B]; \ h :: [T] \rightarrow A \rightarrow B; \ m :: [T]; \ e :: B;$

$f :: T \rightarrow A \rightarrow B \rightarrow B$

(D0) $spec \quad = map \ (h \ m)$

(D1) $h \ [] \ x \quad = e$

         $h \ (a : s) \ x = f \ a \ x \ (h \ s \ x)$

───────────────────────────⟨

(RD0) $spec \quad = fold \ (\cdot) \ ([map \ final] + \!\!+ (map \ (map \cdot f') \ m)$

                        $+ \!\!+ [map \ initial])$

(D2) $f' \ a \ (x, \ y) \ = \ (x, \ f \ a \ x \ y)$

(D3) $initial \ x \quad = \ (x, \ e)$

(D4) $final \ (x, \ y) = y$

Thus we have shown how to transform $map \ (h \ m)$ into a new functional form which exhibits a high degree of pipelined parallelism. The degree of parallelism of the new version depends on the size of the parameter m. For example, the above rule expresses $map \ (h \ [a_1, a_2, \cdots, a_n])$ as a composition of $(n+2)$ simpler functions:

$h \ [a_1, a_2, \cdots, a_n] = fold \ (\cdot) \ [map \ final, map \ (f \ a_1), map \ (f \ a_2), \cdots$

                       $map \ (f \ a_n), map \ initial]$

As we already know, this form can be implemented in CSP as a pipelined network of $(n+2)$ processes. What remains to be shown is how the behaviour of the individual processes in the pipe can be synthesised. We will deal with this in the next section.

Transformation to CSP. For any function $f : A \rightarrow B$, the function f 'map' can be refined into the process $MAP(f)$. Hence, we get:

(P1) $(map \ initial) \prec MAP(initial)$

(P2) $(map \ final) \prec MAP(final)$

and by applying the following refinement rule [2], [4]:

$fold \ (\cdot) \ (map \ (f \cdot g) \ s)$

─────────────────⟨ $f \prec$ F

$fold \ (\gg) \ (map \ (\underline{F} \cdot g) \ (reverse \ s))$

we get:

(P3) $fold\ (\cdot)\ (map\ (map \cdot f')\ m) \quad \preceq$
$fold\ (\gg)\ (map\ (MAP \cdot f')\ (reverse\ m))$

This allows $map\ (h\ m)$ to be simply refined as follows:

$map\ (h\ m) = \quad \{\ \text{RD0}\ \}$
$\qquad fold\ (\cdot)\ ([map\ final] \mathbin{+\!\!+} (map\ (map \cdot f')\ m)$
$\qquad \mathbin{+\!\!+} [map\ initial])$
$\quad \preceq \quad \{\ \text{P1, P2, P3}\ \}$
$\qquad fold\ (\gg)\ ([MAP(initial)] \mathbin{+\!\!+} (map\ (MAP \cdot f')\ (reverse\ m))$
$\qquad \mathbin{+\!\!+} [MAP(final)])$

Therefore, the pipelined network of CSP processes $SPEC$, which refines the functional specification $map\ (h\ m)$ is synthesised as follows:

$SPEC\ =$
$\quad fold\ (\gg)\ ([MAP(initial)] \mathbin{+\!\!+} (map\ (MAP \cdot f')\ (reverse\ m))$
$\quad \mathbin{+\!\!+} [MAP(final)])$

and hence, by unfolding f in the definition of $MAP(f)$, the complete behaviour of the processes involved in the pipe can be directly obtained as follows:

$MAP(initial) = \mu Z \bullet left?\text{``}eot\text{''} \rightarrow right!eot \rightarrow SKIP$
$\qquad\qquad\qquad\qquad |$
$\qquad\qquad\qquad\qquad left?x \rightarrow right!(x,\ e) \rightarrow Z$

$(MAP \cdot f')\ (a) = MAP(f'\ a)$
$\qquad\qquad\quad = \mu Z \bullet left?\text{``}eot\text{''} \rightarrow right!eot \rightarrow SKIP$
$\qquad\qquad\qquad\qquad |$
$\qquad\qquad\qquad\qquad left?\ (x,\ y) \rightarrow right!\ (x,\ f\ a\ x\ y) \rightarrow Z$

$MAP(final) = \mu Z \bullet left?\text{``}eot\text{''} \rightarrow right!eot \rightarrow SKIP$
$\qquad\qquad\qquad\quad |$
$\qquad\qquad\qquad\quad left?\ (x,\ y) \rightarrow right!y \rightarrow Z$

The above network can be depicted as follows:

16.4 Parallel Decomposition of Map

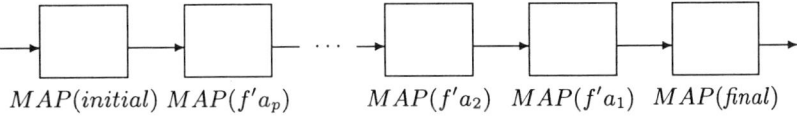

Figure 16.2. The decomposition of map as a pipe network of CSP processes

16.4.3 Example: Polynomial Evaluation

Consider the construction of a process $POLYS$ to translate each number in its input stream to the corresponding value of the following polynomial in x:

$$a_0 + a_1 x + a_2 x^2 + \cdots + a_p x^p$$

where the polynomial coefficients $a_0, a_1, a_2, \cdots, a_p$, are given constants. A clear functional specification of the process $POLYS$ is captured by

$polys :: [num] \rightarrow [num]$

$polys\ xs = map\ (poly\ [a_0, a_1, \cdots, a_p])\ xs$

where the function *poly* takes a list of polynomial coefficients *as* and a value x and returns the value of the corresponding polynomial at x. That is, we have:

$poly :: [num] \rightarrow (num \rightarrow num)$

$poly\ [a_0, a_1, \cdots, a_n]\ x = a_0 + a_1 x + a_2 x^2 + \cdots + a_n x^n$

Using Horner's method we can inductively define *poly* as follows:

$poly\ []\ x \quad = 0$

$poly\ (a:s)\ x = a + x \times (poly\ s\ x)$

The above definition of *poly* is already expressed in an inductive form with shared parameters. More precisely, we have:

$poly\ (a:s)\ x = f\ a\ x\ (poly\ s\ x)$

$f\ a\ x\ y \quad = a + (x \times y)$

Therefore, by a straightforward application of the DC-MAP-R1, we obtain:

$polys \quad = fold\ (\cdot)\ ([map\ final] +\!\!+ (map\ (map \cdot f')\ [a_0, a_1, \cdots, a_p])$
$\qquad\qquad +\!\!+ [map\ initial])$

$f'\ a\ (x,\ y)\ =\ (x,\ f\ a\ x\ y)$

$initial\ x \quad = (x,\ poly\ []\ x)$

$final\ (x, y) = y$

and by simply unfolding the above definitions we get:

$$polys = fold\ (\cdot)\ ([map\ final] +\!\!+(map\ (map\cdot f')\ [a_0, a_1, \cdots, a_p])$$
$$+\!\!+[initial\ map])$$
$$f'\ a\ (x, y) = (x, a + x \times y)$$
$$initial\ x = (x, 0)$$
$$final\ (x, y) = y$$

Finally, as we have already shown, the above specification can be efficiently implemented as a network of CSP processes as follows:

$$POLYS =$$
$$fold\ (\gg)\ ([MAP(initial)] +\!\!+ (map\ (MAP \cdot f')\ [a_p, a_{p-1}, \cdots, a_0])$$
$$+\!\!+[MAP(final)])$$

$$MAP(initial) = \mu Z \bullet\ left?\text{``eot''} \rightarrow right!eot \rightarrow SKIP$$
$$|$$
$$left?x \rightarrow right!\,(x, 0) \rightarrow Z$$
$$MAP(f'\ a) = \mu Z \bullet\ left?\text{``eot''} \rightarrow right!eot \rightarrow SKIP$$
$$|$$
$$left?\,(x, y) \rightarrow right!\,(x, a + x \times y) \rightarrow Z$$
$$MAP(final) = \mu Z \bullet\ left?\text{``eot''} \rightarrow right!eot \rightarrow SKIP$$
$$|$$
$$left?\,(x, y) \rightarrow right!y \rightarrow Z$$

16.5 Parallel Decomposition of Directed Reductions

Much research effort has been devoted towards investigating the data parallelism that is inherent in the general reduction operator (*fold*). Most existing data parallel implementations rely on two facts. The binary operator for the reduction must, firstly, be associative and, secondly, be computed in constant time. However, there are numerous applications where these assumptions may not hold [47]. Fortunately, neither of the directed reduction operators relies on either assumption.

16.5 Parallel Decomposition of Directed Reductions

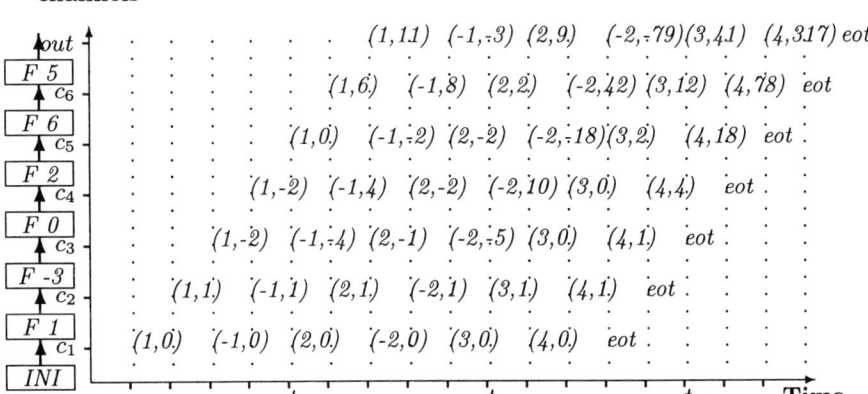

Figure 16.3. Timing diagram depicting the parallel computation of the polynomial $X^5 - 3X^4 + 2X^2 + 6X + 5$ for the input stream $[1, -1, 2, -2, 3, 4, eot]$

16.5.1 Parallel Decomposition of Right Reduce

The right reduction operator captures a general pattern of computation which can informally be described as:

$$foldr\ (\oplus)\ e\ [a_1, a_2, \cdots, a_n] = a_1 \oplus (a_2 \oplus (\cdots \oplus (a_n \oplus e) \cdots))$$

An alternative formulation of this pattern is given by the following recursive definition of the higher-order function $foldr$:

$$foldr :: (\alpha \to [\beta] \to [\beta]) \to [\beta] \to ([\alpha] \to [\beta])$$
$$foldr \oplus e\ [] \quad\ \ = e$$
$$foldr \oplus e\ (a : s) = a \oplus (foldr \oplus e\ s)$$

Right reduction captures the computation of those functions which can be defined using *tail recursion*. This pattern has a high degree of implicit parallelism. The parallelism can be clearly exhibited by using the function decomposition strategy. All we need is to transform $(foldr\ f\ e\ s)$ into an expression in which the dominant term is of the form $fold\ (\cdot)\ fs$, for some list of functions fs. This is achieved by using the following decomposition rule:

(Right Reduction Decomposition)

$foldr :: (\alpha \to [\beta] \to [\beta]) \to [\beta] \to ([\alpha] \to [\beta])$

$foldr\ f\ e\ [\,] = e$

$foldr\ f\ e\ (a\colon s) = f\ a\ (foldr\ f\ e\ s)$

$$\updownarrow\mathrel{\reflectbox{$\prec$}}$$

$foldr\ f\ e\ s = (fold\ (\cdot)\ (map\ f\ s))\ e$

The informal justification for this transformation is as follows:

$foldr\ f\ e\ [a_1, a_2, \ldots, a_n]$
$= f\ a_1\ (foldr\ f\ e\ [a_2, a_3, \ldots, a_n])$
$= f\ a_1\ (f\ a_2\ (foldr\ f\ e\ [a_3, \ldots, a_n]))$
$= (f\ a_1 \cdot f\ a_2)\ (foldr\ f\ e\ [a_3, \ldots, a_n])$
$= (f\ a_1 \cdot f\ a_2 \cdot \cdots \cdot f\ a_n)\ (foldr\ f\ e\ [\,])$
$= (fold\ (\cdot)\ (map\ f\ [a_1, a_2, \ldots, a_n]))\ e$
$= (fold\ (\cdot)\ (map\ f\ s))\ e$

A formal proof of this rule is straightforward by induction. Now provided that for all values $a \in A$, the function $(f\ a)$ is refined into a pipe process $F(a)$, that is $f \prec F$, then $(foldr\ f\ e\ s)$ can be refined into the following network of communicating processes:

$$FOLDR(f, e, s) = Prd(e) \triangleright fold\ (\gg)\ (map\ \underline{F}\ (reverse\ s))$$

The proof of this result directly follows from the refinement of function composition and the refinement of function application [2], [4].

The network
$FOLDR(f, e, [a_1, a_2, \ldots, a_n])$, can be pictured as depicted in Figure 16.4.

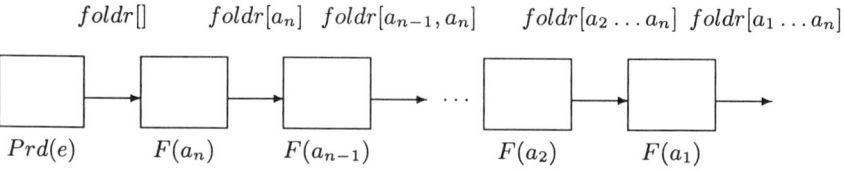

Figure 16.4. $FOLDR(f, e, [a_1, a_2, \ldots, a_n])$

16.5 Parallel Decomposition of Directed Reductions

Several parallel algorithms for list processing were derived by directly applying the above refinement technique [2], [3]. It is shown that the application of this transformation strategy leads to linear time parallel algorithms with linear number of processes from quadratic time sequential programs. However, it is important to note that in order to ensure efficiency of the network $SPEC([a_1, a_2, \ldots, a_n])$, the function f must have an on-line implementation (that is, repeatedly consumes some input and produces some output until it terminates).

16.5.2 Parallel Insertion Sort

The insertion sort algorithm, *isort*, which is usually defined by tail recursion, can be formulated as an instance of the right reduction operator as follows:

$isort :: [\alpha] \to [\alpha];$

$isort\ s = (insert\ foldl\ [])\ s$

where the function *insert* is defined as:

$insert :: \alpha \to [\alpha] \to [\alpha]$

$insert\ a\ [] \quad = [a]$

$insert\ a\ (x: s) = x: insert\ a\ s, \text{ if } \quad x < a$

$\qquad\qquad\qquad = a: x: s, \qquad \text{otherwise}$

For all values a, the function $(insert\ a)$ can be refined into the following process $INSERT(a)$:

$INSERT(a) = \mu X \bullet ?x \to \ (\ !a \to !eot \to SKIP \quad \{x = eot\}$

$\qquad\qquad\qquad\qquad\qquad\quad !x \to X \qquad\qquad\qquad \{x < a\}$

$\qquad\qquad\qquad\qquad\qquad\quad !a \to !x \to COPY\ )$

Hence, for all lists s, $isort(s)$ can be refined into the following network of communicating processes :

$ISORT(s) = FOLDR(insert, [], s)$

$\qquad\qquad = EOT \triangleright (fold\ (\gg)\ (map\ \underline{INSERT}\ (reverse\ s)))$

Figure 16.5 depicts how the network $ISORT([5, 4, 8, 9, 3, 5, 8])$ may evolve with time by illustrating the timed behaviour of the individual processes in the network. Note that the input stream for each process in the network is displayed on the horizontal line below it and its output stream is displayed on the line above it. Communications can only take place between neighbouring processes in a synchronised fashion, that is, the output of each process is simultaneously input to the process above it.

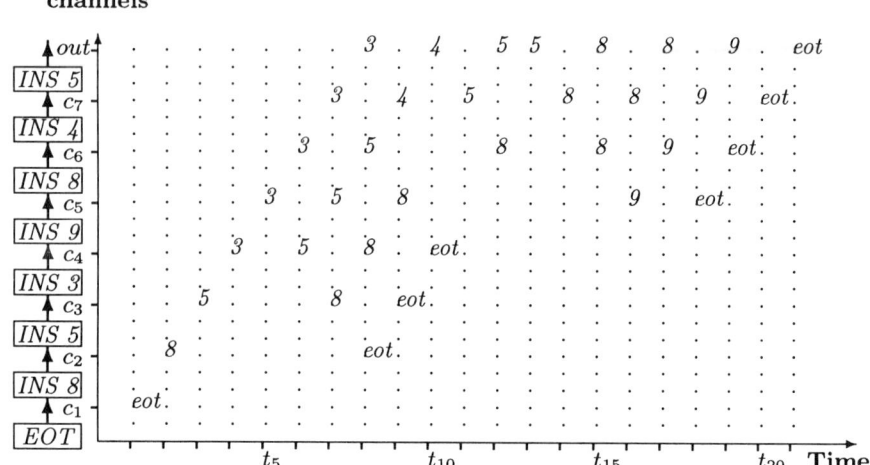

Figure 16.5. Time diagram depicting the pipelined computation of $ISORT([5,4,8,9,3,5,8])$.

For a list s whose length is n, the sequential implementation of $isort(s)$ requires $O(n^2)$ steps but the parallel implementation is linear.

16.5.3 Parallel Decomposition of Left Reduce

The left reduction operator $foldl\ (\oplus)\ e$ is informally described as:

$$foldl\ (\oplus)\ e\ [a_1, a_2, \cdots, a_n] = (\cdots((e \oplus a_1) \oplus a_2) \oplus \cdots) \oplus a_n$$

This captures a general pattern for the computation of a class of functions which are usually defined recursively using the well-known technique of *parameter accumulation*. A function is usually defined using an additional parameter for accumulating the result after each recursive call. Typically, the computation of a list of values starts from the first element of the list and proceeds towards the last. This is in contrast with tail recursion where computation starts from the last element of the list and proceeds towards the first. The left reduction operator $foldl$ which is used for this purpose is formally defined as follows:

$$foldl :: ([\beta] \to \alpha \to [\beta]) \to [\beta] \to ([\alpha] \to [\beta])$$
$$foldl \oplus t\ []\quad = t$$
$$foldl \oplus t\ (a:s) = foldl\ \oplus\ (t \oplus a)\ s$$

Our objective is to show how the above pattern can be transformed into a highly parallel network of communicating processes. We aim to achieve

16.5 Parallel Decomposition of Directed Reductions

this by transforming *foldl* into an instance of the right reduce operator *foldr* and then applying the decomposition result of Section 16.5.1. To do so, we appeal to the following algebraic law [47] which closely relates both directed reduction operators.

$$foldr \ (\oplus) \ e \ s = (foldl \ (\widetilde{\oplus}) \ e) \ (reverse \ s)$$

where the binary operator $\widetilde{\oplus}$ is defined as $x \widetilde{\oplus} y = y \oplus x$. Therefore, by using the *foldr* decomposition rule, we get the following decomposition rule for *foldl*:

(Left reduction decomposition)

$$foldl \ (\oplus) \ e \ s = (fold \ (\cdot) \ (map \ (\widetilde{\oplus}) \ (reverse \ s))) \ e$$

Finally, the refinement of the CSP network of processes corresponding to the above decomposition of $foldl \ (\oplus) \ e \ s$ is synthesised as follows:

$$FOLDL(\oplus, e, s) = Prd(e) \triangleright (fold \ (\gg) \ (map \ ADD \ s))$$

where for all values of a, the process $ADD(a)$ refines the function $(a \ \widetilde{\oplus}) = (\oplus a)$.

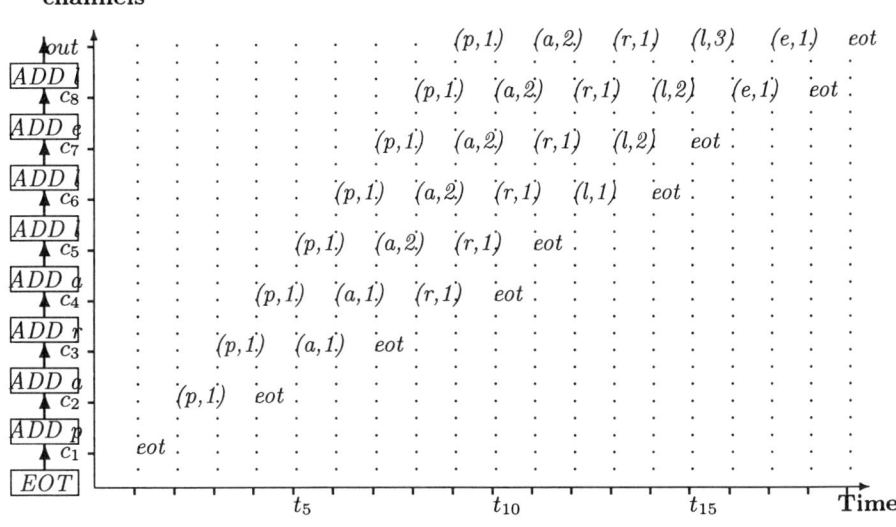

Figure 16.6. Parallel computation of $MKBAG(\text{"parallel"})$

16.5.4 Parallel Conversion of Lists to Bags

The function $mkbag$ converts a list into a bag. For any list xs, $(mkbag\ xs)$ is a list of pairs. Each pair has the form (x, i) where x is an element of xs and i is a positive number indicating the count of occurrences of x in the list xs. For example, we have:

$$mkbag\ \text{``parallel''} = [(p, 1), (a, 2), (r, 1), (l, 3), (e, 1)]$$

The function $mkbag$ can be defined recursively as follows:

$mkbag :: [\alpha] \rightarrow [(\alpha, num)]$

$mkbag\ s \qquad\qquad = mkbag'\ [\,]\ s$

$mkbag'\ t\ [\,] \qquad = t$

$mkbag'\ t\ (x\!:\!s) = mkbag'\ (t \uplus x)\ s$

where the operator $\uplus$ is defined as:

$\uplus :: [(\alpha, num)] \rightarrow \alpha \rightarrow [(\alpha, num)]$

$[\,] \quad \uplus\ x \quad = [(x, 1)]$

$((y, i)\!:\!ys) \uplus\ x = (y, i)\!:\ (ys \uplus x),\ \text{if}\ x \neq y$

$\qquad\qquad\qquad\ = (y, i+1)\!:\!ys, \quad \text{otherwise}$

The function $mkbag$ is clearly an instance of left reduction in which we have $mkbag\ s = (\uplus\!\not\!\rightarrow [\,])\ s$. Therefore, provided that the process $ADD(x)$ correctly implements the function $(\uplus\ x)$, $mkbag\ s$ can be refined into the following pipelined network of processes:

$MKBAG(s) = FOLDL(\uplus, [\,], s)$

$\qquad\qquad\ \ = Prd([\,]) \triangleright fold\ (\gg)\ (map\ \underline{ADD}\ s)$

For all values x, the process $ADD(x)$ is defined as follows:

$ADD(x) = \mu X \bullet ?z \rightarrow (\ !(x, 1) \rightarrow EOT \qquad \{\!\{z = eot\}\!\}$

$\qquad\qquad\qquad\qquad\ \ !(x, i+1) \rightarrow COPY\ \ \{\!\!\{\ x = y\ \}\!\!\}$

$\qquad\qquad\qquad\qquad\ \ !z \rightarrow X$

$\qquad\qquad\qquad\text{where}\ \ z = (y, i) \qquad)$

The timed behaviour of the network $MKBAG(\text{``parallel''})$ can be pictured as in Figure 16.6. Assuming that the length of the list s is n, the sequential implementation of $mkbag(s)$ requires $O(n^2)$ steps but the parallel implementation runs in linear time.

16.6 Related work

This chapter has been profoundly influenced by the work of many computer scientists on transformational programming [47], [50], [53], [52], [126], [155], [317], [373], in particular the work of Bird and Meertens on their calculus for algorithmic manipulation which has been used here extensively.

Many researchers have proposed the use of functional notations and formalisms for programming parallel machines. In contrast with the work described in this chapter, the focus has, however, mainly been on exploiting data parallelism rather than pipelined or MIMD parallelism. For example, Skillicorn [533], [534] argued the benefits of using the Bird-Meertens formalism as a coherent approach to data parallel programming. Misra [405] elegantly described many functional (divide-and-conquer) data parallel algorithms using a data structure called *powerlist* together with its algebra. Darlington, Field, Harrison, and Kelly [156], [331], Cole [139], Mou and Hudak [603], Blelloch [58], Harrison and Gúzman [294] Runciman and Wakeling [505], Partsch and Pepper [454], Lengauer and Gorlatch [232], [228] to name but a few, have also all used functional notations and algebraic laws to develop parallel functional programs. On a hardware level, Sheeran, Jones, and Luk [373], [317] have developed a relational algebra for deriving regular synchronous circuits from their specifications. Although this algebra greatly facilitates the description of circuits with complex configurations, the resulting algorithms are globally synchronized. In contrast, the algorithms presented in this chapter require only local synchronization.

This chapter has mainly focused on exploiting implicit MIMD and pipeline parallelism in functional programs. It develops this by refining the resulting implicitly parallel functional version into networks of CSP processes using a formal transformation based approach. This allows us to address performance issues and reason about the parallel implementation within a proper framework of concurrency in which these phenomena can be clearly understood.

16.7 Conclusion

In this chapter we have presented a calculus for parallel programs derivation based on the Bird-Meertens Formalism. The calculus consists of algebraic laws which allow functional decomposition of the higher order functions *map*, *filter*, *foldl* and *foldr* to be derived from the decomposition of their arguments. We have also shown, in each case, how to refine the derived functional algorithmic form into a massively pipelined network of communicating CSP processes. We have applied this calculus for the derivation of several highly parallel algorithms drawn from a broad range of examples.

The compact transformation rules which have been established in this chapter are important for three reasons. Firstly, they involve functional templates which are frequently encountered in program derivation. Secondly, they concisely embody new interesting parallel programming techniques. Thirdly, their underlying derivations are either skillful or quite lengthy. Consequently, whenever a problem is expressed as an instance of the initial template of one of these rules it is not necessary to repeat the entire expensive derivation process. A highly parallel implementation of the problem automatically follows in a single transformation step by taking the corresponding instance of the derived template of the rule.

The underlying ideas behind the transformation rules vary in depth. The succinctness of the Bird-Meertens notation and the large repertoire of laws relating expressions in this notation were important not only for deriving deep and complex results from simple ones, but also for deriving them quickly using only a few transformation steps.

17. Validating Programs in Concurrent ML

Flemming Nielson[1]

17.1 Introduction

Interactive and embedded applications often require an ability to deal with concurrent operations. In this chapter we give an overview of one way to extend a functional language with concurrency primitives. Unfortunately, the presence of concurrency may make programs harder to reason about because the flow of control is less perspicuous (as is the case when imperative features are present). This calls for the use of automatic techniques to extract the flow of control in a more readable and succinct form so as to validate the overall structure of communication taking place in the program. In this chapter, we show how type and effect systems can be extended with a notion of causal behaviour (in the manner of process algebras) that makes this possible.

17.2 Program Analysis

Static analysis of programs allows us the prediction of a variety of properties holding for all dynamic executions. Many of the issues studied ultimately involve the halting problem and are therefore formally undecidable; to solve this dichotomy, static analysis only provides approximate information that always *errs on the safe side* — typically by producing sets of abstract values that might be too large but never too small. Thus, in the worst case, an analysis will analyse a difficult legal program by merely pretending that all information can reach everywhere; for the analysis to be useful this should of course happen very rarely.

Traditionally, static analysis has been used in the context of compiler development. This naturally leads to demanding that *all* legal programs can be analysed — simply because a compiler is expected to be able to compile all legal programs. What constitutes a legal program is normally expressed by means of a context-free grammar; it is frequently augmented with a collection of static well-formedness conditions that must be fulfilled for a program to be legal; in some approaches static well-formedness takes the form of a fully-fledged type system in the manner of the Hindley/Milner system for polymorphism as found in Standard ML [403], [255] and several other functional languages. This can then be used to demonstrate that certain dynamic errors (like adding integers and booleans) never take place.

An increasingly popular approach to static analysis is based on annotating type systems by properties or effects that express further intensional aspects

---
[1] DAIMI, Århus, Denmark.

of the computation being performed [419]. It is normally required that the resulting effect system must be a *conservative extension* of the original type system: this means that if a program has an ordinary type then the type can be annotated so as to produce a type for the program in the effect system, and that if a program has a type in the effect system then one can remove the annotations so as to produce a type for the program in the ordinary type system. In other words, the demand of conservative extension is very analogous to the demand that all programs can be analysed.

Recently, static analysis has been used for *validating* that the program under consideration adheres to certain safety or security policies. Normally this means that the analysis will be used to reject certain programs that are otherwise regarded as being legal: we may reject purchasing a software system if we find it too risky to use it, or we may reject installing a web tool on a server if we fear that perhaps it could lead to a breach of security or safety. For the analysis to be useful it should accept a large class of valid programs that actually guarantee the safety policies. However, by the very nature of static analysis we must accept that certain programs are rejected even though they would never give rise to a breach of security (e.g. because the "dangerous code" could never be reached with "dangerous data").

It is interesting to note that the validation aspect somewhat weakens the demands on static analysis. While it is still desirable that all programs can be analysed, it is no longer essential to be able to deal with the most obscure facets of a language or the most obscure programming styles, because the failure of the analysis can be masked as a rejection of the program. Naturally, for the analysis to be useful it should still accept a large proportion of those valid programs that actually guarantee the safety policies.

In this chapter we discuss how static analysis can be used to validate software dealing with concurrency, communication and mobility. We begin by reviewing Concurrent ML that adds concurrency and communication primitives to Standard ML. We then devise a type and effect system for tracking the concurrency and communication taking place; the effects are called behaviours and have the appearance of terms in a process algebra that has been defined so as to suit the primitives of Concurrent ML; indeed, the type and effect system allows extension of the type inference algorithm by automatically extracting the behaviour of a given program. We then discuss a case study where behaviours have been used to pinpoint the failure of a control program (developed by researchers outside of our group for the Karlsruhe Production Cell) to fulfill all of the safety conditions of the specification. Finally, we turn to some recent developments, expressed at the level of process algebras, for validating that programs maintain a secure distinction between public and secret information, and for rejecting firewalls that might contain a trapdoor.

17.3 Concurrent ML

The language Concurrent ML (or CML) [445], [495] is based on Standard ML (or SML) [255], [403]; another language from the same "design space" is Facile [565]. A language widely used in the area of telecommunications that shares many of the same characteristics is Erlang, whereas Concurrent Haskell is based on a lazy functional language.

As a simple example of a program in SML consider the following program:

```
fun map f [] = []
  | map f (x::xs) = (f x) :: (map f xs)
```

for mapping a function down the list supplied as an argument. As an example, `map (fn x => x>3) [1,3,5]` yields `[false,false,true]`.

The type system will report the polymorphic type:

map: ('a -> 'b) -> ('a list -> 'b list)

where 'a -> 'b is determined by the type of the function f, 'a list is the type of the argument to map f, and 'b list is the type of the resulting list.

In CML, a program gives rise to a number of threads (or computations or processes); the main program gives rise to the initial thread. Intuitively, the threads execute in parallel but most implementations will implement all threads on a uniprocessor using preemptive scheduling taking care of critical regions related to input/output operations. It is the intention that the threads do not use imperative constructs to update shared data so as to avoid inter-thread interference; instead, CML offers a selection of first-class operations for synchronous communication.

We shall begin by introducing the most most basic of the concurrency primitives that are added by CML [445]:

- spawn is a function that when called upon some function creates a new parallel thread (or computation) to be executed in parallel with all other computations; upon creation the thread begins evaluating the function on the argument (); upon termination the thread merely becomes idle. The type of spawn is (unit -> unit) -> thread_id where the result type is the type of so-called thread identifiers that uniquely name the thread created;
- channel is a function that when applied to () returns a new channel over which values can be sent and received. The polymorphic type of channel is () -> 'a chan where 'a chan denotes the type of a channel over which values of type 'a can be passed; this is somewhat analogous to the reference type 'a ref of SML;
- recv is a function that when applied to a channel returns a value sent over that channel; the communication is *synchronous* and hence the operation blocks until some other thread (possibly the main program) sends a value. The polymorphic type of recv is 'a chan -> 'a;

- `send` is a function that when applied to a pair consisting of a channel and a value actually sends the value over the channel; the communication is *synchronous* and hence the operation blocks until some other thread (possibly the main program) receives a value. The polymorphic type of `send` is `('a chan * 'a) -> unit`.

Let us consider a given channel `ch`. Each communication over `ch` involves exactly one thread performing a send over `ch` and exactly one other thread performing a receive over `ch`. If more than one thread is willing to send over `ch`, or more than one thread is willing to receive over `ch`, a single sender and a single receiver is chosen; in the abstract semantics this choice is non-deterministic but in the implementation it is realised using a structure of queues so that fairness can be imposed. If no thread is willing to send over `ch` then any threads willing to receive over `ch` are blocked until a sender becomes available, and, similarly, if no thread is willing to receive over `ch` then any threads willing to send over `ch` are blocked until a sender becomes available.

With these primitives we can code two variants of the `map` function that make use of communication; the idea is that if more than one processor is available then the spawned threads may be allocated on different processors thereby giving rise to true parallelism.

The first function is `mappar` defined as follows:

```
fun mappar f [] = []
  | mappar f (x::xs) = let ch = channel () in
                       spawn (fn () => send (ch, (f x)));
                       let ys = mappar f xs in
                       (recv ch) :: ys
```

The second function is `parmap` defined as follows:

```
fun parmap f [] = []
  | parmap f (x::xs) = let ch = channel () in
                       spawn (fn () => send (ch, parmap f xs));
                       (f x) :: (recv ch)
```

Both functions have the type `('a -> 'b) -> ('a list -> 'b list)` also possessed by `map`. The difference between the two functions is that `mappar` spawns threads to apply the function to elements of the list, whereas `parmap` spawns threads to unwind the list.

17.3.1 Event-Based Communication

The four primitives introduced above are quite useful on their own but they do not allow programs to wait for information on more than one channel and to choose the communication that first becomes possible. It is not feasible to do so based on the `recv` and `send` primitives introduced above (unless the semantics of SML is changed in major ways) and CML therefore introduces non-blocking versions of the operations as well as ways of combining them:

17.3 Concurrent ML

- `recvEvt` is the non-blocking version of `recv`. It has the polymorphic type (`'a chan`) -> (`'a event`) where `'a event` is the type of a communication that may be synchronised so as to produce a value of type `'a`;
- `sendEvt` is the non-blocking version of `send`. It has the polymorphic type (`'a chan * 'a`) -> (`unit event`) where `unit event` is the type of a communication that may be synchronised so as to send a value over the channel;
- `sync` is the primitive for synchronising a non-blocking operation. In short, the functional composition (`sync o recvEvt`) is equivalent to the function `recv`, and the functional composition (`sync o sendEvt`) is equivalent to the function `send`. The polymorphic type of `sync` is `'a event -> 'a`;
- `choose` is a non-blocking operation for choosing a non-blocking communication from a list of candidate events. When synchronising on a choose-construct, the system chooses one of the candidate events as soon as that event is able to synchronise, and then that event is synchronised upon; if the list is empty this means blocking forever. The polymorphic type of `choose` is ((`'a event`) `list`) -> (`'a event`);
- `select` is a blocking version of `choose` and is equivalent to the functional composition (`sync o choose`). It has the polymorphic type ((`'a event`) `list`) -> `'a`;
- `wrap` allows the modification of the value returned by a non-blocking operation once it has been synchronised. The expression `sync(wrap(recvEvt ch, f))` applies the function `f` to the value received over `ch` and is equivalent to the expression `f (recv ch)`. The polymorphic type of `wrap` is ((`'a event`) * (`'a -> 'b`)) -> (`'b event`).

Events are used to suspend the actual communications in such a way that the suspended communications can be passed around as first-class citizens; they can be forced (using `sync`) or they can be used to construct other delayed communications (using `choose` or `wrap`). One may therefore view events as analogues of the "thunks" (or procedures taking only a dummy parameter) used for encoding lazy features in an eager functional language. So `recvEvt ch` is somewhat analogous to `fn () => recv ch`, and `sync e` is somewhat analogous to `e ()`.

As a simple example of how to use some of these more advanced primitives, consider the following sensor function that is always willing to receive measurements on the channel `measurement` as well as to communicate the average of the last 10 measurements received on the channel `average`:

```
val ms = ref [0,0,0,0,0,0,0,0,0,0];

fun sensor () =
        select [wrap (recvEvt measurement,
                       fn m => ms := take(m::!ms, 10) ),
                sendEvt (average, sum(!ms)/10) ];
        sensor ()
```

It uses a reference cell ms of type int ref which is initialised to a list of ten 0's to compute the required average whenever requested.

17.4 Behaviours

The CML type system conveys useful information about the *functionality* of a program but does not express information about the *pattern of communication*. This is potentially troublesome because the presence of concurrency may make programs harder to reason about because the flow of control is less perspicuous (as is also the case when imperative features are present).

This motivates extending the type system with *behaviours* (or effects) that describe what communications may take place at various points. The behaviours will provide information about what channels are used for communication and we choose to identify a channel with a *region* indicating the set of program points where it might have been created. (A similar approach could have been taken for the reference cells of SML and is in fact used in the region-inference approach to implementing SML without using a heap.)

Consider a function type of the form t_1 -> t_2. We shall now modify the notation used for functions to be of the form t_1 ->^{b} t_2 where in place of b we will be writing a behaviour that expresses the communications that might take place when the function executes. Next consider a channel type of the form t chan that will now be written t chan r where in place of r we will be writing a region that expresses where the channel might have been created. Finally consider the event type of the form t event that is now written t event b to indicate the behaviour b that may be unleashed whenever the event is being synchronised. The remaining type constructors of CML do not have to be changed.

The syntax of behaviours is motivated by process algebras such as CCS, CSP and the π-calculus but the primitives have been chosen so that they more closely mimic the concurrency primitives found in CML. A behaviour, b, may take one of the following forms:

- A behaviour variable '1, '2, etc. in analogy with type variables (like 'a or ''a);
- The silent behaviour S indicating that no communication, creation of channels or spawning of threads can take place;
- A sequential composition $b_1;b_2$ that expresses that first the behaviour b_1 and then the behaviour b_2 takes place (in the manner of concatenating regular expressions);
- A choice operator b_1+b_2 indicating that one of b_1 or b_2 may take place (in the manner of summing regular expressions) and where we do not distinguish between internal non-determinism due to conditionals and external non-determinism due to communication;
- SP(b) that expresses that a thread with behaviour b may be spawned;

17.4 Behaviours

- $t\,\mathrm{CH}\,r$ indicating that a channel might be created at a program point indicated by the region r and that it might be used for communicating values of type t;
- $t\,??\,r$ that expresses that a value of type t may be received along a channel that was created at one of the program points indicated by the region r;
- $t\,!!\,r$ that expresses that a value of type t may be sent along a channel that was created at one of the program points indicated by the region r;
- REC('i) b that is used to denote the recursive behaviour b where all occurrences of 'i themselves stand for b.

The purpose of regions is simply to indicate the program points where a channel could have been created. One possibility is for a region to take the form of a region variable ''1, ''2, etc. in analogy with behaviour variables. Another possibility is that it is some (unspecified) notation for a concrete program point — this may take the form of line numbers, pointers into the parse tree or explicit annotations also being added to the syntax of the program (like point3 in channel$_{\mathrm{point3}}$) . The possibility of expressing more than one program point is partly due to the sum operator r_1+r_2 indicating the union of the program points expressed by r_1 and r_2, and partly due to the region # that stands for all program points whatsoever. In the remainder of Section 17.4 we shall mainly use the region # and therefore do not go deeper into the syntax of regions.

17.4.1 Example Behaviours

Let us return to the map, mappar and parmap functions introduced earlier; before adding behaviours they all shared the polymorphic type ('a -> 'b) -> ('a list -> 'b list). Having added behaviours, the types are now all different because they all have different communication structures. It should come as no surprise that map is intended to have the type:

   map : ('a ->^{S} 'b) ->^{S} ('a list ->^{S} 'b list)

but in fact one can assign it the even more general type

   map : ('a ->$^{'1}$ 'b) ->^{S} ('a list ->^{b} 'b list)
   for $b \equiv$ REC('2)(S+('1;'2))

taking care of the situation where the argument function to map is performing some communication in order to compute its value. The behaviour b amounts to an explicit recursive definition of the Kleene closure of the string '1 and thus stands for arbitrarily long sequences of the behaviour '1; however, we are not able to express that there are as many occurrences of '1 as there are elements in the argument list (of type 'a list).

The type of mappar is:

   mappar : ('a ->$^{'1}$ 'b) ->^{S} ('a list ->^{b} 'b list)
   for $b \equiv$ REC('2)(S+('bCH#; SP('1; 'b!!#); '2; ('b??#)))

and the type of parmap is:

    parmap : ('a ->'¹ 'b) ->ˢ ('a list ->ᵇ 'b list)
    for b ≡ REC('2)(S+(('b list)CH#; SP('2; ('b list)!!#);
                      '1; ('b list)??#))

(In both cases we could have dealt more generally with regions.)

Note that the behaviours clearly show that mappar f xs and parmap f xs both intend to fully exploit the parallelism that may be possible: mappar f xs spawns processes for applying the function f to each element of the list xs, whereas parmap f xs spawns processes to recurse down the spine of the list xs. As a consequence, mappar would seem to be preferable because it only communicates elements of lists on the channels as opposed to parmap that communicates rather larger lists; this latter insight could also have been gained by inspecting the "internal type" of the channel ch created.

The following example shows that behaviours add insights that cannot be obtained merely by inspecting "internal types." Consider the following variation seqmap of parmap:

```
fun seqmap f [] = []
  | seqmap f (x::xs) = let y = f x in
                       let ch = channel () in
                       spawn (fn () => send (ch, seqmap f xs));
                       let ys = recv ch in
                       y :: ys
```

When inspecting the type and behaviour:

    seqmap : ('a ->'¹ 'b) ->ˢ ('a list ->ᵇ 'b list)
    for b ≡ REC('2)(S+('1; ('b list)CH#; SP('2;('b list)!!#);
                       ('b list)??#))

one may note that the computation incurred by f actually delays the spawning of a new process for performing the recursive call down the spine of the list: the '1 occurs before SP('2; ···). Thus, the behaviours express in a clear way aspects of the communication behaviour that may be buried in the code and thus lead to a better understanding of the code produced. They are therefore a useful tool when deciding between which implementation to use for a given task.

17.4.2 Causal Type and Effect System

We now present the ideas behind some of the rules given in [12] for assigning annotated types to CML expressions (inspired by the developments in [318], [423], [542], [559]). *Judgements* take the form:

$$C, A \vdash e : t \& b$$

Such a judgement states that the CML expression e has type t and that the evaluation of e gives rise to visible actions as indicated by b, assuming that:

17.4 Behaviours

- The *type environment* A contains type information about the identifiers occurring free in e;
- The relation between the various type, behaviour and region variables in t and b is given by the *constraint set* C.

Conditional. The type of a conditional is determined by the rule:

$$\begin{array}{ll} \text{if} & C, A \vdash e_0 \,:\, \texttt{bool}\,\&\,b_0 \\ \text{and} & C, A \vdash e_1 \,:\, t\,\&\,b_1 \\ \text{and} & C, A \vdash e_2 \,:\, t\,\&\,b_2 \\ \text{then} & C, A \vdash \texttt{if}\ e_0\ \texttt{then}\ e_1\ \texttt{else}\ e_2 \,:\, t\,\&\,b_0\,;(b_1{+}b_2) \end{array}$$

where the use of the choice operator $b_1{+}b_2$ reflects that we cannot predict which branch will be taken (due to "internal non-determinism" as the analysis does not attempt to determine the values of conditions).

Function Application. The type of a function application is determined by the rule:

$$\begin{array}{ll} \text{if} & C, A \vdash e_1 \,:\, t_2 \text{ ->}^b\, t_1\,\&\,b_1 \\ \text{and} & C, A \vdash e_2 \,:\, t_2\,\&\,b_2 \\ \text{then} & C, A \vdash e_1\ e_2 \,:\, t_1\,\&\,(b_1\,;b_2\,;b) \end{array}$$

where the behaviour $b_1\,;b_2\,;b$ clearly states that CML employs a call-by-value evaluation strategy: first the function e_1 is evaluated, then its argument e_2 is evaluated, and finally the function is applied enacting the latent behaviour on the function arrow.

Function Abstraction. The type of a function abstraction is determined by the rule:

$$\begin{array}{ll} \text{if} & C, A[x : t_x] \vdash e \,:\, t\,\&\,b \\ \text{then} & C, A \vdash \texttt{fn}\ x\ \texttt{=>}\ e \,:\, (t_x \text{ ->}^b\, t)\,\&\,\textsf{S} \end{array}$$

where the body e is analysed in an environment binding x to t_x, with its behaviour b becoming latent in the resulting function type; the overall behaviour is silent because creating a function does not involve any communication.

Subeffecting. As stated earlier, we must ensure that the causal type and effect system is a conservative extension of the CML type system. This does not hold automatically because whenever the type system demands two functions to have the same type we now also demand that they have the same internal communication structure which might very well fail. The simplest remedy is to introduce the following rule for subeffecting:

if $C, A \vdash e : t \& b$ and $C \vdash b \subseteq b'$

then $C, A \vdash e : t \& b'$

Here the behaviour ordering $C \vdash b_1 \subseteq b_2$ states that b_1 is a more precise behaviour than b_2 (relative to the assumptions listed in C); this means that whenever b_1 describes the behaviour of some expression then b_2 does also. We do not have the space to provide the details of how to define the ordering or to study its theoretical properties; however, we should mention that sequential composition ";" is associative with S as neutral element, that "$\subseteq$" is a congruence with respect to the various behaviour constructors, and that "+" is the least upper bound operator with respect to $\subseteq$. (For a fuller treatment, we refer to [12] and also to [422] where a syntactically defined ordering on behaviours is shown to be a decidable subset of the undecidable simulation ordering, induced by an operational semantics for behaviours.)

Subtyping. Subeffecting solves the problem of obtaining a conservative extension of the standard type system for CML by coarsening the behaviours as *early* as possible. An alternative is to coarsen the behaviours as *late* as possible and for this the following rule for subtyping is useful:

if $C, A \vdash e : t \& b$ and $C \vdash t \subseteq t'$

then $C, A \vdash e : t' \& b$

Here, the subtype relation $C \vdash t_1 \subseteq t_2$ states that t_1 is a more precise type than t_2 (relative to the assumptions listed in C); it is induced by the subeffecting relation and *only* allows to change the behaviour annotations occurring in types. As is to be expected, the ordering is contravariant in the argument position of a function type:

if $C \vdash t_1' \subseteq t_1$ and $C \vdash b \subseteq b'$ and $C \vdash t_2 \subseteq t_2'$

then $C \vdash t_1 \rightarrow^b t_2 \subseteq t_1' \rightarrow^{b'} t_2'$

Since the type of a channel is used covariantly when receiving a value (by means of `recv`) and contravariantly when sending a value (by means of `send`) we only allow to change channel types to equivalent types:

if $C \vdash t \subseteq t'$ and $C \vdash t' \subseteq t$

and $C \vdash r \subseteq r'$

then $C \vdash t$ chan $r \subseteq t'$ chan r'

Primitives of CML. The following table summarises the causal type schemes assigned to the primitives of CML:

17.4 Behaviours

CML function	Causal type scheme for the CML function
spawn	(unit ->$^{'1}$ unit) ->$^{SP('1)}$ thread_id
channel	unit ->$^{'a\ CH\ ''1}$ ('a chan ''1)
recv	'a chan '1 ->$^{'a\ ??\ ''1}$ 'a
send	(('a chan '1) * 'a) ->$^{'a\ !!\ ''1}$ unit
recvEvt	'a chan '1 ->^{S} 'a event ('a ?? ''1)
sendEvt	(('a chan '1) * 'a) ->^{S} unit event ('a !! ''1)
sync	('a event '1) ->$^{'1}$ 'a
choose	('a event '1) list ->^{S} 'a event '1
select	('a event '1) list ->$^{'1}$ 'a
wrap	('a event '1) * ('a ->$^{'2}$ 'b) ->^{S} 'b event ('1;'2)

The types make it clear that sendEvt is a non-committing version of send and similarly for recvEvt versus recv and choose versus select. Perhaps the most interesting case is that of sync that clearly shows how one commits to the latent behaviour of an event by placing it on the arrow of the function type.

Polymorphic Instantiation. To use a CML function one needs to instantiate the type variables, behaviour variables and region variables with other types, behaviours and regions (respectively). So far a type scheme σ has taken the form t of a type and we have tacitly assumed that the set $FV(t)$ of all type, behaviour and region variables occurring in t could be instantiated. This is not the case, in general, when dealing with programmer defined polymorphic entities. There a type scheme σ takes the form $[C - V]\,t$ and only type, behaviour and annotation variables occurring in $FV(t)\setminus V$ can be instantiated and the instantiated version of the constraint set C must be derivable from the overall constraint set. In this notation the type scheme for recv takes the form:

$$\text{recv} : [\emptyset - \emptyset]\ ('a\ \text{chan}\ '1\ \to^{'a\ ??\ ''1}\ 'a)$$

and similarly for the other primitives. Omitting the details of instantiation (but see [12]), we can then use the following rule for using polymorphic constants in CML:

if   the CML function c has type scheme $[C' - V']\,t'$ and

     the type t is an instance of $[C' - V']\,t'$ relative to C

then $C, A \vdash c : t\,\&\,b$

A somewhat similar rule can be used to instantiate the type scheme assigned to polymorphic functions and other polymorphically defined entities.

Polymorphic Definition. As an example of polymorphic definitions let us consider the let-construct. Here, `let x = `e_1` in `e_2 allows us to use x polymorphically in e_2 (whereas any occurrences of x in e_1 refer to a previously defined x). The typing rule has the following general form:

if $\quad C \cup C_1, A \vdash e_1 : t_1 \,\&\, b_1$ and

$\quad\quad C, A[x : [C_1 - V_1] \, t_1] \vdash e_2 : t_2 \,\&\, b_2$ and

$\quad\quad (FV(t_1) \setminus V_1) \cap FV(C_1, A, b_1) = \emptyset \,\wedge\, \cdots$

then $\quad C, A \vdash$ `let x = `e_1` in `$e_2 : t_2 \,\&\, (b_1 ; b_2)$

We refer to [12] for additional conditions that need to be imposed upon the type scheme $[C_1 - V_1]\, t_1$; they can be viewed as further restricting the set C_1 of constraints but will be trivially satisfied in case $C_1 = \emptyset$. Note that we do not allow to generalise over type, behaviour and region variables in $FV(A)$, as is customary in SML, nor over those occurring in $FV(b_1, C_1)$, as is customary in effect systems; this is essential for the type system to be semantically sound.

17.5 A Case Study

We now study a CML program for the Production Cell [362] developed by FZI, in Karlsruhe, as a benchmark for the development of verified software for embedded systems. The Production Cell is designed to process metal blanks in a press and operates as follows. The work pieces (metal blanks) enter the system on a feed belt and are then transferred one at a time to a rotating table; the table is then lifted and rotated such that one of two robot arms can take the work piece and place it in the press. After processing the work piece, the other robot arm will take it out of the press and deliver it to a deposit belt. For testing purposes, a crane has been added to move the work pieces from the deposit belt back to the feed belt (in order to have a closed system that can run forever).

The CML program was developed outside of our group and has been developed using systematic design methods [499]: its functionality has been specified in CSP and many of its safety conditions have been formally verified; furthermore, it has been combined with the FZI simulator to a working prototype that has subsequently been tested. The CML program consists of 7 processes; they communicate with the simulator using 63 channels and they communicate internally using 16 channels.

17.5 A Case Study

```
fun table () =
let
   fun clockwise (a) =
      (* rotate clockwise until degree a *)

      let val x = recv(table_angle)
      in (send(table_right,());
          while (recv(new_table_angle); recv(table_angle)) < a
          do ();
          send(table_stop_h,()) )
      end;

   fun counterclockwise (a) =
      (* rotate counterclockwise until degree a *)

      let val x = recv(table_angle)
      in (send(table_left,());
          while (recv(new_table_angle); recv(table_angle)) > a
          do ();
          send(table_stop_h,()) )
       end;

   fun main () =
      (recv(belt1_transmit_ready); recv(belt1_transmit_done);
       clockwise(50);
       send(table_upward,());
       recv(table_is_top);
       send(table_stop_v,());
       send(table_transmit_ready,()); recv(table_transmit_done,());
       send(table_downward,());
       recv(table_is_bottom);
       send(table_stop_v,());
       counterclockwise(0);
       main())
in
   spawn(fn () => main())
end;
```

Figure 17.1. CML program for the table

$b = \text{SP}(b_0)$
$b_0 = \texttt{unit??\{belt1\_transmit\_ready\}; unit??\{belt1\_transmit\_done\};}$
     $\texttt{int??\{table\_angle\}; unit!!\{table\_right\};}$ b_1;
       $\texttt{unit!!\{table\_stop\_h\};}$
     $\texttt{unit!!\{table\_upward\}; unit??\{table\_is\_top\};}$
       $\texttt{unit!!\{table\_stop\_v\};}$
     $\texttt{unit!!\{table\_transmit\_ready\}; unit!!\{table\_transmit\_done\};}$
     $\texttt{unit!!\{table\_downward\}; unit??\{table\_is\_bottom\};}$
       $\texttt{unit!!\{table\_stop\_v\};}$
     $\texttt{int??\{table\_angle\}; unit!!\{table\_left\};}$ b_1;
       $\texttt{unit!!\{table\_stop\_h\};}$
     b_0
$b_1 = \texttt{unit??\{new\_table\_angle\}; int??\{table\_angle\}; (S +}$ b_1)

Figure 17.2. Behaviour for the table (in the notation of the system)

The Table. The part of the program dealing with the table is shown in Figure 17.1; it uses the following channels for communicating with the simulator:

```
(* actuator channels *)
val table_left      = channel(): unit chan;
val table_stop_h    = channel(): unit chan;
val table_right     = channel(): unit chan;
val table_upward    = channel(): unit chan;
val table_stop_v    = channel(): unit chan;
val table_downward  = channel(): unit chan;

(* sensor channels *)
val table_is_bottom     = channel(): unit chan;
val table_is_not_bottom = channel(): unit chan;
val table_is_top        = channel(): unit chan;
val table_is_not_top    = channel(): unit chan;
val table_angle         = channel(): int  chan;
val new_table_angle     = channel(): unit chan;
```

Internally, the table synchronises its movements with the feed belt and the robot and for this it uses the following channels:

```
val belt1_transmit_ready = channel(): unit chan;
val belt1_transmit_done  = channel(): unit chan;

val table_transmit_ready = channel(): unit chan;
val table_transmit_done  = channel(): unit chan;
```

Behaviour Analysis. The analysis to be surveyed here was described in [421] and is based on the type and behaviour reconstruction system described in [13]; the system has been implemented in Moscow ML and is available on

17.5 A Case Study

the web. For the part of the program corresponding to Figure 17.1, the algorithm will determine the type unit $\to^b$ thread_id where b is the behaviour of Figure 17.2; here we have followed the system in using the names of channels as substitutes for regions, and in using equation systems for behaviours rather than explicit uses of the REC(···) ··· behaviour (as this would detract from readability).

Safety Conditions. The table can be in one of two vertical positions and it can be rotated clockwise as well as counterclockwise. The Production Cell [362] imposes the following safety conditions as far as the table is concerned:

1. The table must not be moved downward if it is in its lower position, and it must not be moved upward if it is in its upper position.
2. The table must not be rotated clockwise if it is in the position required for transferring work pieces to the robot, and it must not be rotated counterclockwise if it is in the position to receive work pieces from the feed belt.
3. There can only be one work piece at the table at any time.

We deal here with condition 3 that can be validated for Figures 17.1 and 17.2, and condition 1 that can be shown *not* to be validated for Figures 17.1 and 17.2; we refer to [421] for a discussion of condition 2 since it demands more powerful techniques that those present in the type and effect system of Section 17.4.

Condition 1. Validation of this condition relies on some assumptions about the environment: the vertical movement of the table can only be initiated by communicating on the two channels table_upward and table_downward. Information about the table's vertical position can only be obtained from table_is_bottom, table_is_not_bottom, table_is_top and table_is_not_top.

With respect to these six channels the system allows to simplify the behaviour of Figure 17.2 to take the form:

$b_0 \approx$ unit!!{table_upward}; unit??{table_is_top};
    unit!!{table_downward}; unit??{table_is_bottom};
    b_0

Thus we see that all communications on table_downward are preceded by a communication on table_is_top. By unfolding the behaviour is is also easy to see that, except for the initial case, all communications on table_upward are preceded by a communication on table_is_bottom.

However, this is not the case for the initial communication on table_upward. The behaviour will *never* allow a communication on any of the four channels giving information about the vertical position of the table before the initial communication on the channel table_upward. It follows that the

CML program will never be able to do that either. Hence the analysis has shown that the CML program does *not* fulfill Condition 1! (This problem never arose during simulation because the simulator always commenced with the table in the lower position although this is not part of the specification of the system.)

Condition 3. This condition is concerned about the synchronisation between the individual processes of the system and hence its validation will depend on properties of the other processes, in particular those for the feed belt and the robot. The table is the passive part in both of these synchronisations. The channels belt1_transmit_ready and belt1_transmit_done are used to synchronise with the feed belt; between these two communications it is the responsibility of the feed belt to place a work piece on the table. The channels table_transmit_ready and table_transmit_done are used to synchronise with the robot; between these two communications it is the responsibility of the robot to remove a work piece from the table.

The analysis of the table will therefore need to make some assumptions about the feed belt and the robot. These assumptions will later have to be validated by analysing the behaviour of the program fragments for the respective processes. The assumptions are:

a) Whenever the feed belt leaves the critical region specified by the two channels belt1_transmit_ready and belt1_transmit_done it will have moved one (and only one) work piece to the table.;
b) Whenever the robot leaves the critical region specified by the two channels table_transmit_ready and table_transmit_done it will have emptied the table.

Under these assumptions we can now validate Condition 3.

We shall concentrate on the four channels specifying the critical regions and we obtain the following simplified behaviour for the table:

$b_0 \approx$ unit??{belt1_transmit_ready}; unit??{belt1_transmit_done};
  unit!!{table_transmit_ready}; unit!!{table_transmit_done};
  b_0

Clearly this shows that the two pairs of communications alternate. Also it shows that the synchronisation with the feed belt happens first and by assumption (a) a work piece is placed on the table. The simplified behaviour shows that subsequently there will be a synchronisation with the robot and by assumption (b) the work piece will be removed from the table. Hence, Condition 3 has been validated with respect to the assumptions.

17.6 Conclusion

The case study shows that a system may have been developed using formal methods but still have bugs. Advanced proof techniques may have been used to show that the specification fulfills certain safety and liveness properties, but there is always the risk that the formalisation does not fully correspond to the informal description (or even a formal description in another framework) and there is the risk that the code written does not fully correspond to the specification. On top of this there is the risk of human mistakes (like those that may be introduced when manually editing the program text) and malicious intent (like a subcontractor cutting corners to increase profit).

Program analysis is clearly no substitute for a careful system development, where one formally reasons about key components of the system, but it is an indispensable addition to the repertoire of techniques for development (including formal verification) and testing (on an extensive test suite). This view will become more pervasive as the trend intensifies to construct systems from components that are downloaded from the Internet or purchased from subcontractors. Each time a new version of a component is procured one then has to repeat all of the validation activities; these had better be automatic and program analysis is generally better than testing in identifying undesirable internal behaviour and is surely much better than testing in pointing out where they could arise from (as is important when the final system misbehaves and the inadequate component needs to be identified).

These validation problems can be studied directly on programs using type and effect systems or some of the more classical approaches to program analysis (like data flow analysis, control flow analysis and abstract interpretation). Alternatively, one can take a phased approach where first a system of behaviours is extracted from a program and the behaviours are further analysed by other techniques. Clearly the behaviours constitute a process algebra in the manner of CCS, CSP, the π-calculus and the Mobile Ambients calculus. Recently we have pursued this approach for processes written directly in the π-calculus and the Mobile Ambients calculus and we are confident that the development carries over to the CML behaviours as well.

The general approach has been to devise a control flow analysis for determining what channels or ambients could reach what points in the program; presumably a type and effect system could have been used instead. In [66] we showed that a security policy for maintaining a distinction between private and public data was maintained. In [67] we showed that a security policy for Bell and LaPadula's no-read-up and no-write-down was maintained. In [420] we have devised a polynomial time test for determining whether or not a proposed firewall is indeed protective in the sense that attackers not knowing the required passwords cannot enter (even though the firewall sends out probes to guide agents inside). The next step in this work is to consider how these approaches scale up to programs of more realistic size.

Acknowledgements

Much of the work reported here was initiated by the LOMAPS project (funded by ESPRIT BRA); I am indebted to Hanne Riis Nielson and Torben Amtoft for working with me on this project.

18. Explicit Parallelism

Jocelyn Sérot[1]

18.1 Motivations

Following the broad classification given in Section 1.2.4, *fully explicit* parallelism will refer to the programmer (rather than the compiler) being responsible for (almost) every aspect of the parallelisation problem, including the partitioning of the program into processes, the mapping of these processes onto the processors and their synchronisation (in a broad sense). At first sight, the resulting approaches to parallelism do not blend gracefully into the functional framework of this book; after all, functional programming is mainly concerned with *abstraction* and according to,for instance, Skillicorn and Talia's definition of *full explicitness* [541], explicitly parallel programs expose too much of their operational semantics (through low-level constructs such as message transfers or shared-memory access) to be viewed as illustrations of abstraction at work. There are some *pragmatic* reasons, however, for which one may wish to reconcile explicit parallelism with functional programming.

Performance. Reducing the gap between specification and implementation has always been a straightforward means of improving performance. This is precisely what explicit approaches allow (at the cost of increasing the programmer's burden, of course!), by making possible a better match between software and hardware/OS level constructs.

Expressiveness. As stated in Section 3.5, some distributed systems and algorithms cannot be expressed without some constructs for building arbitrary process networks and explicitly handling their communications. This is especially true of a large class of parallel algorithms described in the literature which are tailored to a specific network topology (for example, Gentleman's algorithm [215] for matrix multiplication, which is specifically designed to operate efficiently on torus-shaped topologies). For these algorithms, efficiency is obtained using data distributions and clever communication schedules. For example, the very high latency of LAN-based architectures is traditionally hidden by the judicious use of asynchronous communications. Except in very specific contexts, it is not realistic to assume that an implicitly parallel compiler can reinvent them. This remark extends to some more generic program structures that have been recognised as useful parallel constructs such as master/workers farms or client/server(s) networks;

---

[1] Université Blaise Pascal, Clermont-Ferrand, France.

Relying on existing software technology. In the imperative mainstream, a great deal of work has been devoted to the development of portable tools for building and monitoring parallel programs, including communication libraries such as PVM and MPI. Evidently, any approach allowing the direct reuse of this technology would be of great practical interest. Whilst such a layered approach to parallel system building can advantageously form the basis of implicit approaches — as evidenced by the GUM [573] parallel Haskell compiler, built upon a PVM layer — the possible benefits resulting from the integration of these tools are more easily obtained when both the tools and the source program share the same abstraction level. To state it in a rather exaggerated way, what help could an *upshot* profile of underlying `PVM_sends` be to a GUM programmer dealing only with `par` annotations ?

Of course, relying on low-level explicit models for parallelism has well-known costs: increased programmer's burden, high potential for run-time errors such as deadlocks, much more difficult debugging due to possible non-determinism, etc. These costs, alas, are not lessened in a functional framework[2]. Therefore, it must be emphasised that the point here was *not* to develop new algorithms or techniques using a low-level explicit model. Instead, we wanted to see how existing and matured low-level algorithms and techniques taken from the imperative mainstream could be *reformulated* within a functional language, and if any benefit could be drawn from such a formulation. Anticipating Section 18.2 slightly and quoting Peyton-Jones et al. in a recent paper dealing with a similar problem [468], we wanted to prove that interfacing a functional language with an existing message passing library was not only *possible* but also *desirable*.

18.2 Design Choices

Exploring the various *practical* issues resulting from the integration of imperative parallel programming techniques into a functional framework clearly required the building of some kind of experimental system. This in turn involved making some design choices, not least for keeping the development effort within our available resources. These choices (the visible *programming model*, the underlying *execution model* and the functional *host language*) are detailed in Sections 18.2.1, 18.2.2 and 18.2.3. It is important, however, to first underline the main concerns which guided these choices. These concerns, which were essentially of a pragmatic nature, can be summarised in three words: performance, portability and compatibility.

Performance. Here the emphasis is effectively put on parallelism rather than on concurrency, in the sense given in Section 1.1.2. Our primary goal was to

---

[2] Although some facilities traditionally available in functional languages, such as polymorphic strong typing and exception handling, may help in building reliable programs

18.2 Design Choices

deliver significant absolute speedups (relative to the current sequential compiler technology) for large, realistic applications to be run on multiprocessors. This should be contrasted with most previous comparable experiences in explicit functional parallelism (CML, Facile), in which explicit extensions have been used to increase the expressiveness of the language rather than to speed up computations.

Compatibility. This requires the ability to reuse existing sequential code (C, Fortran). We believe that it is not realistic to try to demonstrate the benefits of functional programming by obliging programmers to entirely recode their sequential applications in ML, Haskell, etc.

Portability. This can be practically achieved by building on *off-the-shelf*, portable software components. We particularly wanted to avoid the design and implementation of complex run-time systems (RTS) which are the hallmark of more implicit approaches. The development of such RTS — and, later on, their portage to new target machines and/or OS — has always been hindered by the specialist knowledge of compilation techniques and target hardware architecture required.

18.2.1 A Message Passing Programming Model

The first design choice was to rely on a Message Passing programming model for explicit parallelism. Let us recall the basic underlying model of message passing (MP), which is that of a collection of processes connected by some kind of network and explicitly exchanging messages (synchronisation is viewed as a special case of message exchange) using **send** and **recv** instructions. Despite its low-level orientation — it has sometimes been called the "assembly language" of parallel programming — MP has become a mature, if not comfortable, technique within the imperative mainstream, with many applications running, including industrial-strength code. As a matter of fact, several communication libraries supporting the MP model are available today, both in the public and commercial domains: NX, p4 [106], Express, PVM (Parallel Virtual Machine) [212], MPI (Message Passing Interface) [395]. Amongst these, MPI has become a de facto standard, enjoying sizeable success in both academia and industry, and we decided to rely on it to provide a portable communication harness for a message-based programming model. One motivation for this choice was the very large number of platforms on which MPI is available (more than 50 machine/OS combinations in 1998[3]), including both shared-memory multiprocessors and distributed-memory architectures. In the latter case, the ability to use a LAN of workstations as a parallel machine is an advantage which cannot be underestimated. Another reason for the success of MPI is the ease with which existing, computationally-intensive sequential code (written in C or Fortran) can be reused for parallelisation, using basic data parallel SPMD techniques (see next section).

---

[3] Source: http://www.mpi.nd.edu/MPI/

Technically speaking, MPI provides a large number[4] of message passing primitives, including a rich subset of point-to-point communication routines (by far the richest of any library to date) and a large subset of collective communication routines for communicating and synchronising between groups of processes. Moreover, and from a system programmer's point of view, the MPI concept of *communication context* (a group of related processes) provides a natural support for the design of safe parallel libraries. On the other hand, the MPI-1 standard (released in 1994) does not make provision for dynamic process creation (this feature was added in MPI-2) and this clearly influenced our original design.

Our choice of MPI, in any case, should not be viewed as critical. In fact, any comparable communication library, such as PVM, would have provided a perfectly suitable communication harness. The GUM [573] parallel Haskell compiler, for instance, uses PVM (though in a semi-implicit context). For a comparative study discussing the relative merits and flaws of PVM and MPI, the interested reader may consult [213]. Moreover, and as underlined in [573], should the overhead of the MPI or the PVM layer become unbearable on a particular architecture, a machine-specific communication substrate could be readily substituted.

18.2.2 An SPMD Execution Model

The second design choice was to rely on a static SPMD (Single Program Multiple Data) execution model. In this model, parallelism is achieved by replicated copies of a single program executing asynchronously on several processors and synchronising explicitly through message passing. All processes are created at the beginning of program execution and remain active until the end of computation. Each copy gets a unique *address* (the so-called *process-id*) which is used firstly to specialise its behaviour (by taking actions according to its value) and secondly to identify senders and receivers when exchanging messages.

Despite sounding restrictive, compared to a true MPMD (Multiple Program Multiple Data, in which each processor runs a distinct program) the SPMD model clearly had significant advantages, both at the user and the system level, in the light of our pragmatic concerns.

For the application programmer, SPMD fits naturally within the *data parallel* programming style, which focuses on operations to be done in parallel on large distributed data structures, rather than on independent expressions to be evaluated in parallel (as in most of the *control-based* implicit approaches). The advantages of the data parallel programming model are discussed in Chapter 7. For us, it has two attractive features. The first lies in its ability to offer *scalable* performances, since the amount of parallelism is proportional to the size of the processed data. This property is of crucial importance for the

---
[4] More than 150 in version 1

large-scale applications, such as numerical applications or n-dimensional signal processing, which represent a large proportion of the parallel computer's consumption. The second attractive feature is that — under the SPMD assumption — data parallel programs can often be derived from working sequential ones; they are essentially obtained by distributing data structures and replicating behaviours. This property favours the reusability of existing code and helps program management (the sequential version can serve as a reference for profiling or debugging, for instance). This can explain why, although MPI or PVM do not strictly impose a SPMD programming style, it is actually a widely used programming technique[5]. Another interpretation of this fact is that, by de facto limiting the number of ways processes can interact (and thus the number of ways they can go wrong !), SPMD helps in building more structured and manageable applications.

For the system designer, one most attractive feature of the static SPMD model is that it does not require any support for dynamic process creation. This should be contrasted with most other explicitly parallel functional languages cited in Section 18.6, which classically provide some facilities to dynamically `fork` (`spawn`) new processes at run-time and, of course, with all the more implicit approaches focusing on independent expressions to be evaluated in parallel by separate tasks, which therefore require the creation of some kind of dynamic process at the implementation level. From our "off-the-shelf" system-building point of view, this means in practice that the run-time system running on each processor can be generated using any existing *sequential* compiler. All that is needed is the ability to make calls to the message passing routines. Apart from the code for these "primitives", the (replicated) run-time systems are exactly the same as the one used by sequential programs[6]. Finally, let us emphasise that since message passing is the sole means of exchanging data, each process has its own purely local environment. Therefore, there is no need for a distributed garbage collecting scheme, a well-known effort-focusing point in most distributed implementations of functional languages.

18.2.3 The Functional Host Language

Our last design choice concerned the functional host language. Insofar as parallelism is provided by explicit message passing, *strict* languages (see Section 1.2.2) have a definite advantage over non-strict ones: they make execution order predictable. This point is of crucial importance, since any MP system using explicit `send`/`recv` calls intrinsically relies on side-effects (this point is

---

[5] For MPI, the lack of really *portable* OS-level facilities to launch true MPMD applications on many parallel platforms (especially distributed networks of workstations) cannot be underestimated, however

[6] Technically speaking, they will simply be built by linking the native code produced by the sequential Caml compiler with the `libmpi.a` C library

evidenced by the return type signature of the send function, which is typically unit - see Section 18.3). It must be emphasised that the presence of side-effects at the send level automatically makes the host language *impure*, as defined in Section 1.2.3. In reality, this means that side-effects are not incompatible in a parallel setting; they only force the programmer to be *explicit* about program decomposition and communication scheduling.

These considerations led us to select a functional host language from the ML family. The Objective Caml system [143], developed and freely distributed by INRIA, has many features that — in addition to purely personal taste — matched our design choices very well. Firstly, Caml is highly portable: it can generate native code for most modern CISC and RISC processors and the system runs on virtually any UNIX box with the help of an ANSI-compliant C compiler. Secondly, Caml generates very efficient sequential native code, with performances reportedly on a par with (and sometimes better than) those of some C compilers. Thirdly, the latest version of Caml (version 1.6) comes with a built-in *marshaller* and *unmarshaller*, allowing *serialisation* of arbitrary data structures. By serialisation we mean the conversion of any ML object (including function closures[7]) into a finite one-dimensional stream of bytes for transmission along an untyped communication channel. Such a facility is essential for polymorphic message passing (see Section 18.3.1). Finally, the Objective Caml system features a powerful module system which allows clean encapsulation of functionalities as separately compiled modules and/or libraries.

From an application programmer's point of view, let us emphasise that the choice of a functional host language for writing message passing programs does not prevent the coordinated functions being written in an imperative sequential language, such as C or Fortran, as long as as a decent foreign language interface is provided[8]. This point is of crucial practical importance given the concern for compatibility expressed at the beginning of Section 18.2.

18.2.4 Explicitness

Given all the above-mentioned points, our definition of *explicitness* can now be refined, in terms of Skillicorn and Talia's criteria [541]:

- **Decomposition** is explicit: there will be exactly n threads, one per processor;
- **Mapping** is explicit: each processor runs the same process (but process behaviour can be specialised according to processor number);
- **Communication** is explicit: using the MPI layer;
- **Synchronisation** is explicit: both synchronous and asynchronous sends and recvs must be paired.

---

[7] Though this facility is not used in our design
[8] Caml provides a full, easy-to-use C interface

18.3 A Caml Interface to MPI

The design choices detailed in the previous section resulted in the definition and implementation of the Scampi library. Scampi simply (Simple Caml interface to MPI) provides some MPI bindings to the Objective Caml language (referred to as Caml from now on). These bindings are provided in a single Caml module, which basically defines a few MPI related data types (pid, tag, ...), interfaces to blocking and non-blocking communication routines and a very simple wrapping mechanism for turning a Caml *function* into a (set of) MPI *process*(es). An excerpt of the signature of this module is given in Figure 18.1. The types pid and tag are for process-ids and message tags.

```
type pid = int
type tag = int
type status = { source : int; tag: tag }
type request
val comm_size : unit -> int
val comm_rank : unit -> pid
val ssend : 'a -> pid -> tag -> unit
val recv : pid option -> tag option -> 'a * status
val issend : 'a -> pid -> tag -> request
val wait : request -> status
val run : (unit -> unit) -> unit
```

Figure 18.1. An excerpt of the Scampi module signature

The type (opaque) request represents communication handles returned by asynchronous communication functions such as issend. The (manifest) type status records the information wrapped by MPI around all messages (the so-called communication *envelop*). Comm_size returns the number of processes actually running (this number is fixed, and specified at launch time). Comm_rank returns the id of the calling process. Ssend msg dst tag makes a synchronous, blocking send of the message msg to process with the id dst, with the tag tag. Recv (Some src) (Some tag) waits (blocking) for a message with the tag tag coming from the process with the pid src. Wildcard can be specified for the source process and/or tag using None instead of Some x. Recv returns the communication status with the actual message received. Issend msg dst tag makes a synchronous, non-blocking send of the message msg to process with the id dst, with the tag tag. It returns a communication request on which the process can block later on using the wait function. Run is a global wrapper by which Caml functions are turned into MPI processes. It creates a new MPI context, evaluates the given function f within this context and terminates MPI. Any uncaught ML exception (including those raised by the communicating functions on failure of the underlying MPI routines) coming from f calls MPI_Abort and terminates program.

The Scampi model is based upon the static SPMD execution model: all the processes are created at launch time and remain active until the end of the computation (there is no process creation at run-time). Running a Scampi program on n processors simply produces n similar processes giving n times the same answer. The *process-id* (as returned by the comm_rank function is used to distinguish processes (it ranges from 0 to $n-1$ where n, the actual number of running processes, is obtained with comm_size).

A basic program for exchanging a string between two processes will therefore look like this:

```
let main () =
  let np = Scampi.comm_size ()
  and id = Scampi.comm_rank () in
  match id with
  | 0 -> Scampi.ssend "Hello" 1 0
  | 1 -> let msg, stat = Scampi.recv (Some 0) None in
         print_string msg

let _ = Scampi.run main
```

Figure 18.2. A small SPMD program in Caml

The next example (Figure 18.3) is a Scampi program for computing the global sum of a bunch of values distributed on a set of processors. This program is admittedly not a good illustration of "massive data parallelism". It was chosen only to illustrate the style of programming offered by the Scampi layer. The program works by shifting and locally accumulating the values among the processors, using a ring-like addressing scheme, so that, after np steps, each process gets the global sum. The deadlock-free shifting communication pattern is implemented by pairing non-blocking isend instructions with blocking recvs. The default numbering of processes in MPI communicators being linear (from 0 to np-1), the ring topology is encoded using arithmetic on integers. This technique can be used to encode any kind of logical topology, regardless of the underlying physical topology. Such a scheme promotes portability, but the performances, of course, depend on the actual mapping of the former onto the latter. This point is typically addressed by MPI topology-related functions (MPI_Cart_create, ...).

18.3.1 Some Implementation Issues

Polymorphism. The reader will have noticed, from the signatures appearing in Figure 18.1 that the Scampi send and recv functions are polymorphic

18.3 A Caml Interface to MPI

```
let rsum x =
 let id = Scampi.comm_rank ()
 and np = Scampi.comm_size () in
 let left = if id = 0 then np-1 else id-1
 and right = if id = np-1 then 0 else id+1 in
 let rec loop acc x = function
  | 0 -> acc            (* Returns final accumulator after n steps *)
  | n -> let acc' = acc +. x in          (* Update accumulator *)
         (* Initiate send of local value to left neighbour ... *)
         (*    ... while receiving value from right neighbour *)
         let rq = Scampi.issend x left 0 in
         let x', _ = Scampi.recv (Some right) (Some 0) in
                (* Waits for completion of asynchronous send *)
         let _ = Scampi.wait rq in
         loop (acc') x' (n-1) in             (* Loops *)
 loop 0 x np

let main () =
 (* These are the initial values to sum on each processor *)
 let x = ... in
 let s = rsum x in
 Printf.printf "P%d: sum = %d\n" (Scampi.comm_rank()) s

let _ = Scampi.run main
```

Figure 18.3. A small SPMD program in Caml

in their "message" argument and result respectively. This is the only way to avoid the definition of a pair of send/recv functions for *any* valid ML type. At the implementation level, such polymorphism requires the existence of generic *serialisation* and *deserialisation* functions to transform (non-functional) ML values into blocks of bytes[9]. From a performance standpoint, these functions inevitably incur a certain penalty, since some kind of local buffering is generally required. This can be seen as the price to pay for genericity and can be solved, anyway, by providing specialised, monomorphic functions for basic types such as int, float, int arrays, float array, etc[10]. From a semantic standpoint, polymorphic send/recv functions raise a much more tricky problem, since they are known to destroy the type safety of functional programs, as illustrated in the following Scampi program:

```
let _ = Scampi.run (function () ->
  match (Scampi.comm_rank ()) with
   | 0 -> Scampi.ssend "Hello" 1 0
   | 1 -> let msg, _ = Scampi.recv (Some 0) None
          in print_float msg)
```

---

[9] These functions are provided by the Marshall module in Objective Caml v1.06
[10] This is precisely what Scampi offers

The above program is accepted by the type checker but actually crashes at run-time. This is because, since the received msg is passed to the print_float function, the type checker instantiates its statically declared generic type 'a to float, causing the run-time system to misinterpret the sent string value. Apart from requiring the programmer to "manually" check send/recv pairs for type mismatch, there are two "classical" solutions to this problem: resorting to dynamic type checking or introducing new abstractions such as Reppy's *typed channels* [492]. We did not apply these solutions, since they require specific RTS facilities, and hence contradict the "off-the-shelf" approach exposed in Section 18.1. Instead, we believe that most of the typing hazards resulting from polymorphic message passing can be avoided by designing and systematically reusing higher-order communication functions instead of raw, atomic send and recv calls. For example, the previous example could be rewritten using the following remote function:

```
val remote: 'a -> pid -> pid -> ('a -> unit) -> unit
let remote msg src dst f =
  if id = src then Scampi.ssend msg dst 0 else
  if id = dst then let msg, _ = Scampi.recv src None in f msg else
  ()
let _ = Scampi.run (function () -> remote "Hello" 0 1 print_float)
```

Note the *declared signature* of the remote function automatically forces the sent and received messages to have the same type. In the same vein, the communication pattern used in the rsum function in the previous example can be *encapsulated* within the following higher-order function:

```
val shift : 'a -> pid -> pid -> 'a
let shift x left right =
  let rq = Scampi.issend x left 0 in
  let x', _ = Scampi.recv (Some right) (Some 0) in
  let _ = Scampi.wait rq in
  x'
```

so that the second matching clause of this function can be rewritten in a rather more readable manner:

```
let rsum x =
  ...
  | n -> let acc' = acc +. x in
         let x' = shift x left right in
         loop (acc') x' (n-1) in
  ...
```

The full consequences of such an *abstraction* mechanism will be analysed in Section 18.5.

Error Handling. Just like their imperative counterparts, Scampi programs can suffer from two dynamic errors related to their message passing activity.

The first class of errors are those caused by bad usage of message passing primitives, for example, an invalid process-id if in a send call. These errors

18.3 A Caml Interface to MPI

are detected by the Scampi layer, which in turn raises a corresponding Caml exception (BadPid in the previous example).

The second class of errors represent a failure in the global state of the process set, for example, a process blocked on a recv without a matching send, or a deadlock. These errors, reflecting a "logical" misconception, cannot be detected by the Scampi layer, nor by the Caml run-time system. They are clearly the price to pay for explicitness.

Selective Communication. By selective communication we mean the situation in which the source process in a communication cannot be determined by the receiver until run-time. This is typically the equivalent of the Occam ALT construct. Such a scheme necessarily involves some kind of non-determinism, since it must encompass the case where several senders are eligible for communication. It is essential for the implementation of dynamic protocols such as master/workers or clients/server. In CML[492], for instance, it is handled by the choose and wrap language level constructs. With Scampi, this behaviour can be emulated using MPI *wildcards* as recv arguments. This is illustrated in the following program fragment which is taken from an master/workers (farming) application:

```
let main f xs =
  let np = Scampi.comm_size () and id = Scampi.comm_rank () in
  if id = 0 then (************ FARMER ****************************)
    let rec farmer = function               (* Core looping process: *)
    | [] -> []                               (* No more work *)

                (* Still some work. Wait for the result from a worker *)

    | z::zs ->
        let y, st = Scampi.recv None (Some t_result) in

        (* Find which worker, and load it again *)
        let w = st.src in
        let _ = Scampi.ssend z st.Scampi.source t_work in
        ... in
    farmer xs
  else       (***************** WORKERS *******************************)
    let rec worker () =                     (* Core looping process *)
      let x, st = Scampi.recv (Some 0) None in    (* Wait for msg *)
      let _ = Scampi.ssend (f x) 0 t_result in    (* Send result *)
    in worker ()
```

Profiling. The need for profiling tools to understand (and optimise) the run-time behaviour of parallel programs is explained in Chapter 10. This is especially true for programs based on an explicit message passing model, for which the latency of the communication network can easily destroy any potential speedup. The "off-the-shelf" approach advocated in Section 18.2 turned out to be of great practical interest in this context, since it allowed a direct reuse of the existing monitoring and visualisation tools provided with most of the available MPI software. The initial Scampi design was therefore augmented with a set of bindings to various monitoring and logging functions taken from the MPE library[11]. Here is another excerpt of the Scampi module signature, showing a few MPE-related functions:

```
val init_log: unit -> unit (* Initialises MPE logging system *)

val finish_log: string -> unit
  (* Send all collected log data to root process, who dumps it
   * to the specified file in alog format, for visualisation
   * with the upshot program *)

val register_log_states: (string * string) list -> unit
  (* Register a list of log state descriptions.
   * Each state is defined by a name and a couple of colours
   * for displaying its state *)

val log_start_state : string -> unit

val log_end_state : string -> unit
  (* Records a registered state as active/inactive
   * in the current log-file *)
```

The profiling information generated by these functions can be analysed by visualisation tools such as the (n)upshot utility. This is illustrated in Figure 18.4 with a profiled version of the rsum program in which two states corresponding to the local computations and global communications have been registered[12].

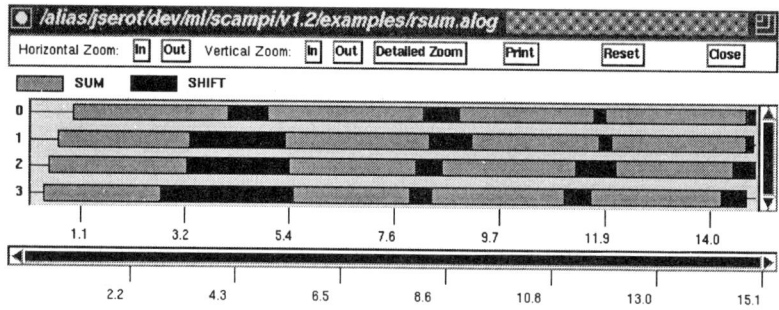

Figure 18.4. An execution profile viewed by the MPICH *upshot* utility

---

[11] Distributed with the MPICH public implementation of MPI
[12] For the sake of readability, the addition has been artificially slowed down in this version

18.4 An Example

In order to evaluate both the usability and the performance of the Scampi model, we considered the implementation of a parallel matrix multiplication algorithm. Matrix-multiplication is a "classical" data parallel problem, which has been extensively studied and implemented in many architectures. Moreover, and because most of the existing solutions rely on sophisticated data distribution and/or communication schedule strategies, it naturally calls for an *explicit* parallel approach.

We consider the multiplication of two $n \times n$ matrices A and B on a ring of p processors. We will, classically, assume that processor number k starts with a subblock A_k of rows of A and a subblock B_k of columns of B. The computation requires p steps, where each step involves a local computation followed by a global communication phase. The local phase computes the product $A_k \times B_k$ (in parallel on each processor), leading a square subblock $C_{k,p}$ (of size $n/p \times n/p$) of the result. Then the subblocks B_k are shifted in a ring-like manner, so that on each processor $B_{(k+1) mod p}$ replaces B_k. After p steps, each processor p holds a block C_k of n/p rows of $C = A \times B$. The Scampi program is given in Figure 18.5. The computation of the local subproducts is performed by the smmul sequential function, whose definition is not reproduced here[13]. Note that, for obvious efficiency reasons, this smmul function actually operates by side-effect[14], so that, on each processor, the result is built incrementally, by successive updates to the c matrix.

The measured execution times (in seconds), for various values of n and p, on a network of Sun IPC(tm) workstations are shown in Table 18.6 (compiler is ocaml-2.00 native compiler). Table 18.7 gives the corresponding timings on the same platform for an equivalent program written in C[15] (compiler is gcc 2.6.0).

Both versions provide an near-linear speedup for sufficiently large input matrices. The measured run-times are comparable to those reported in [348] for a similar algorithm[16] implemented in C and DPFL — an explicit data parallel functional language — and running on a torus of T800 Transputers (with a factor of 2.6 in favour of their C version and a factor of 1.3 in favour of our Caml version). These results are not surprising since Scampi and DPFL programs essentially exhibit the same level of explicitness, though DPFL provides specific language-level constructs (skeletons) for dealing with

---

[13] In the experiment reported here, this function was written directly in Caml but it could be also be implemented in C, or even imported from an existing BLAS package, provided some "stub code" performs the conversion between the C and Caml data representations

[14] Its signature is: `val smmul: int -> float array -> float array -> float array -> unit`

[15] The Scampi program was actually obtained by converting this preexisting C program.

[16] Gentleman's algorithm [215], based upon a *2D* block decomposition of matrices

```
let main () =
  let p = Scampi.comm_size ()
  and k = Scampi.comm_rank () in
  let n, a, b = get_matrices ()   (* Get (sub)matrices Ak and Bk *)
  let nr = n / np                 (* Number of rows for Ak (columns for Bk *)
  and c = create_matrix nr n in                 (* Allocate result *)

  (* Left and right neighbours *)
  let left = if k = 0 then np-1 else k-1
  and right = if k = np-1 then 0 else k+1 in
  let rec step a b c i =           (* OPERATION AT STEP i *)
    if i < np then begin

                                                 (* COMPUTE phase *)
      (* Each step computes a [nr*nr] subblock of [c] starting    *)
      (* at row [k*nr] and column [((k+i)*nr) mod n] by calling   *)
                          (* the sequential [smmul] function *)

      let offset = ((k + i) * nr ) mod n in
      smmul k i a b c offset;

                                              (* COMMUNICATION phase *)
                  (* Shift [b] blocks in a ring-like manner *)

      let rq = Scampi.issend sb left 0 in
      let b', _ = Scampi.recv (Some right) None in
      let _ = Scampi.wait rq in
      step a b' c (step+1)                     (* Next step *)
    end in
  step a b c 0;
  ...                                        (* Result is now in c *)

let _ = Scampi.run main
```

Figure 18.5. Scampi program for matrix multiplication

p , n	32	64	128	256
1	0.17	1.40	11.98	102.00
2	0.15	0.88	6.83	50.12
4	0.15	0.68	3.72	27.69

Figure 18.6. Execution times for Caml+MPI matrix multiplication program

p , n	32	64	128	256
1	0.19	1.57	13.85	112.130
2	0.14	0.89	7.15	58.43
4	0.14	0.59	3.82	29.43

Figure 18.7. Execution times for C+MPI matrix multiplication program

distributed arrays. More noticeable is the fact that our Scampi implementation does not perform any worse than the original C program (it is even slightly more efficient for large matrices!). A careful analysis of the execution profiles shows that this can be attributed to the quality of the sequential code generated by the Objective Caml native code compiler, and this is despite the higher communication costs observed in the Scampi version[17].

18.5 Lessons and Perspectives

The experimental results reported in the previous section show that, at least for coarse-grain, regular, data parallel algorithms, Caml+MPI programs can be as efficient as their C+MPI counterparts. This can be viewed as the direct result of our design choices. Firstly, the SPMD execution model leaves the choice of the right granularity, and hence of the optimal balance between communication and processing, in the hands of the programmer, who has complete (if not easy) control on the final efficiency. Secondly, the message passing programming style allows well-tried parallel programming techniques and paradigms to be directly reused, which would be impossible for an implicit compiler to handle. On the other hand, because Scampi programs expose almost as many details about parallelism to the programmer as their imperative counterparts, they are probably almost as hard to write and debug. It is therefore legitimate to ask whether the game is worth playing or, to state it more explicitly, what benefits can be drawn from *reformulating* imperative MPI programs in (Ca)ML. Various experiments with the Scampi system (including the development of realistic image processing applications [521]) led to the identification of both *technical* and *conceptual* benefits. The technical benefits are those drawn more generally from a functional framework: automatic buffer management (thanks to the garbage collector), the ability to transfer messages of arbitrary type without the added complexity of building and registering MPI *user-defined data types*, implicit error-handling code via the general exception mechanism, etc. These benefits mainly result, however,

---

[17] Mainly because of the marshalling of float arrays involved in the polymorphic **send** and **recv** functions

in the removal of some tedious book keeping declarations and operations, and thus could hardly be seen as sole justification for the work presented here. The conceptual benefits are of much more significant importance, since they refer to one of the most advocated features of FP languages, namely abstraction. Indeed, we have found the ability to "capture" specific parallel patterns of communication/computation — such as the ones described in Section 16.2 — within higher-order functions to be of crucial importance both at system and user level. At system level, we have already mentioned that it can solve most of the typing problems resulting from the unstructured use of polymorphic send/recv functions. At user level, these higher-order functions significantly reduce the burden of the programmer by providing her with a set of well-tried building-blocks from which to compose. For instance, the abstraction process which led to the definition of the shift function in Section 16.2 can be be pushed further to give the following HOF:

```
val rotate : ('a -> 'b -> 'a) -> 'a -> 'b -> 'a
let rotate f z x =
  let id, np, left, right = ... (* Just like in rsum *)
  let rec loop acc = function
  | 0 -> acc
  | n -> let acc' = f acc x in
         let rq = Scampi.issend x left 0 in
         let x', _ = Scampi.recv (Some right) (Some 0) in
         let _ = Scampi.wait rq in
         loop acc' (n-1) in
  loop z x np
```

So that the previous rsum function can be readily rewritten as:

```
let rsum = rotate (+.) 0.0
```

It is now straightforward to reuse the rotate function for computing the global maximum of the initial values:

```
let maxv = rotate (fun x y -> if x>y then x else y) min_int
```

the histogram of these values:

```
let histogram =
  rotate (fun h i -> h.(i) <- h.(i) + 1)
         (Array.create maxv 0)
```

or even the matrix multiplication algorithm of Section 18.4:

```
...
let step offset b = smmul offset a b c; (offset+nr) mod nc
and offset_init = k * nr in
let _ = rotate step offset_init b in
...
```

It must be said that the approach illustrated in the above examples can be emulated — to a limited extent — using an imperative language such as C, by means of some MPI *collective* routines such as MPI_Reduce or MPI_Scan. These routines, however, only offer the possibility of abstracting over the reduction *operator* [18], not over the communication pattern. By contrast, the embedding of MPI calls within Caml HOFs really brings a new dimension to message passing programming, which promotes a truly constructive approach to parallel program development trough the design and systematic reuse of *higher-order communication abstractions*.

This last point has, of course, fruitful connections with the so-called "skeletal" approach to parallel programming described in Chapter 13. This led us to the conclusion that, as far as parallelism (as opposed to concurrency) is concerned, a fully explicit programming model such as Scampi should be viewed as an intermediate (and highly portable) *system-level* layer for building skeletons, rather than as a user-level programming layer.

18.6 Related Work

There have been several propositions for adding explicitly parallel extensions to existing functional languages. For the reasons given in Section 18.2, most of these languages are strict.

CML [492] and Facile [565] have been covered in Section 3.5 and Chapter 17. Others that can be cited include Distributed ML and paraML [33] and, more recently, the MP extensions to Clean [526]. In all these dialects, the emphasis is put on concurrency rather than on parallelism. CML, for instance, supports the notion of *first class events*, allowing users to write sophisticated protocols. Most of them also require specific run-time systems which are hard to implement efficiently on DM machines.

The DPFL (Data Parallel Functional) language [348] puts the emphasis on data parallelism by providing a set of primitives for manipulating *distributed arrays*. Communications remain implicit, thus disabling problems such as deadlock, but preventing the programmer from creating new communication abstractions.

The Caml-Flight experiment [197] shares many motivations and design choices with our model. The emphasis is put on data parallelism and it relies on a static SPMD execution model. It has a solid theoretical basis, based upon the DPCAM abstract model [240]. It is a "low-level" language, with explicit placement and communication. The use of a get-based communication protocol, together with the concept of *communication waves*, is advocated as a way of structuring programs that mantain a "mostly deterministic" behaviour (as opposed to those that are unstructured and intrinsically non-deterministic send/recv-based programs). The authors of the Caml-Flight

---

[18] By means of a rather restricting "operator registration" mechanism

experiment reached a similar conclusion to ourselves regarding the applicability of the resulting programming layer, presenting it as an *intermediate* language for implementing higher-level parallel functional compilers.

Very recently, and independently of our project, X. Leroy also released OCamlMPI, a much larger subset of MPI bindings for OCaml than Scampi.

18.7 Conclusion

This chapter has tried to demonstrate how building on existing tools — such as the widely used Objective Caml compiler and the de facto standard MPI message passing library — can be a very practical way of producing, with a minimum amount of work, an extensible and highly portable parallel programming environment. In contrast to most of the related work described or cited in this book [492] [33] [197] [573] we deliberately did not seek theoretical soundness but quick and smooth integration of pre-existing concepts and software components. This clearly resulted in a programming style in which parallelism essentially takes place at an imperative level (with, for instance, explicit scheduling of communications), but which benefits from the functional language superset. Experimental results shows that this shift need not be at the expense of performance.

Replacing the imperative host language by a functional one also opened the door for a typically functional abstraction process, by which many parallel programming techniques and paradigms well-tried in the imperative mainstream could be readily incorporated into functional programs.

Furthermore, this approach could have fruitful implications for building and embedding distributed applications, relying on complex protocols encapsulated as higher-order communication protocols, but we did not investigate this.

On the other hand, insofar as (data) parallelism — as opposed to concurrency — is concerned, our conclusion is that the Scampi programming model should be better viewed as an intermediate, system-level layer for building efficient and portable skeleton implementations.

The work described here is largely experimental and could be extended in many ways. For instance, the addition of dynamic process creation capabilities, as offered by the recent MPI-2 standard, could remove the necessity of writing SPMD programs, although it is not clear whether the expressivity thus gained is really needed and, more pragmatically, whether this could be done without destroying the simplicity and portability of the run-time system. From the standpoint of skeletons, support for MPI topology-related functions should improve the usability of the library for building more accurate performance models.

Part III

Conclusion

19. Large Scale Functional Applications

Philip W. Trinder[1], Hans-Wolfgang Loidl[1] and Kevin Hammond[2]

19.1 Introduction

This chapter describes applications that have been written using parallel functional language technology. While the majority of these applications have been produced as part of a computer science research project aimed at testing the limits of the technology, others such as those written by Ericsson in Erlang, are being used in real commercial products. Furthermore, projects such as Compaq's Smart Kiosk application written using the dataflow inspired Stampede system [428] represent serious trial uses of the technology by commercial organisations.

Functional programming is a wide-spectrum, general purpose paradigm, and the applications therefore cover a wide area, including high-performance numerical applications, symbolic applications, data-intensive applications and computer vision. Some of these areas present hard problems for traditional parallel approaches, which are usually best suited to regular computation patterns and regular data structures. Symbolic or irregular applications that are described here include compilers, theorem provers, computer algebra and natural language processing.

It is a common misconception that functional programming can only be applied to small scale programs, or that parallelism has only been obtained for toy examples. This chapter describes several real parallel applications that are large in absolute terms, e.g. the 230000-line Erlang mobility server from Section 19.5.3, or the 47000-line Lolita natural language parser from Section 19.3.2. Since functional programs are often a factor of 5-10 shorter than the equivalent C or Fortran, these represent serious, and realistic bases for assessing the quality of a parallel language and its development environment.

Although, as the preceding chapters have shown, there is still much research to be done, parallel functional programming technology has been maturing rapidly, and many large parallel functional applications have been produced in recent years. Although this chapter aims to be reasonably comprehensive, it is therefore necessarily selective in the applications that are covered. We are particularly heartened by results from systems such as SAC [518] and SISAL [391], which are not merely competitive with the performance of C, but have actually exceeded the performance of equivalent Fortran pro-

---

[1] Department of Computing and Electronic Engineering, Heriot-Watt University, UK.
[2] School of Computer Science, University of St Andrews, UK.

grams compiled using high-quality parallelising compilers. These results are reported in Section 19.2.1.

The chapter uses the taxonomy that was introduced in Chapter 3. Implicit, semi-explicit, coordination, explicit and derivational approaches are each covered in separate sections. Within those sections, applications are covered by area. Ideally we would like to report a consistent set of program and parallel platform characteristics, and performance figures for each application. In the absence of a standard set of parallel benchmarks, such results are currently unobtainable. Results are therefore given using either absolute or relative speedup figures as recorded by the authors of the research papers on particular parallel architectures.

19.2 Purely Implicit Parallel Applications

19.2.1 Numerical Applications

Some of the most successful parallel functional applications have been numerical programs. In addition to the benefits of much higher-level coding, which include shorter, simpler (and hopefully more maintainable) code, several SISAL [391] applications not only approach the speed of "slow" imperative implementations such as C, but even exceed the performance produced by the fastest Fortran compilers! Significantly, these results are often achieved without requiring any changes to the source code.

SISAL. A good example of the use of functional languages to improve parallel performance is the Australian *weather prediction model*. This is a 10,000 line Fortran program for short-term (36-hour) weather forecasting [358]. Egan reimplemented the kernel of this application as a 500-line SISAL [114] program [183] that can be called from the original Fortran shell.

For the SISAL version, Egan achieved a speedup of 3.7 on a 4-processor Cray-90. This represented a performance improvement of 34% over the sequential Fortran code (the parallelising Fortran compiler was unable to find any performance improvement here). Subsequent work on the compiler has improved the performance of SISAL relative to Fortran, to the extent that it is now possible to achieve a relative speedup of 6.1 on an 8-processor Cray Y-MP/864 (20 iterations), representing a speedup of 5.8 over the equivalent Fortran program running on a single processor [114], [355].

Mitrovic and Trobina have implemented some components of a *computer vision* system in SISAL [406], using a purely implicit approach: specifically the Gaussian smoothing and Canny edge detector algorithms (cf. Michaelson and Scaife's system in Section 19.3.1). The SISAL program was about 300 lines, compared with 600 for the C version, and took 2 days to write, compared with about a week for the C program. The final stage of the vision system (image compilation) was however slightly larger than the corresponding C

19.2 Purely Implicit Parallel Applications

Table 19.1. Implicitly-parallel applications summary

Application Area	Language	Program
Numerical	SISAL	Weather Prediction
		Computer Vision
		MCNP: Photon Transport
		NAS Benchmark MG
		Several Fourier Transforms (FFT)s
	Id	GCM: Global Climate Modelling
		Hydrodynamics: `simple`
		MCNP: Photon Transport
		Eigen-Solver
		NAS Benchmark MG
		Photon Trajectory: `gamteb`
	NESL	n-Body Problem
		Delaunay Triangulation
		Support Tree Preconditioners
	SAC	Jacobi Relaxation
Symbolic	SISAL	Sky-Scanning
	Visual Haskell	Digital Signal Processing
	Id	Boyer-Moore Theorem Prover
		Paraffins
	ParLisp	Boyer-Moore Theorem Prover
Data-Intensive	AGNA	Wisconsin Benchmark

program (600 lines versus 500). Overall the SISAL program ran 10% faster than the C program when run sequentially and achieved a relative speedup of 3.1 on a 4-processor shared-memory SGI machine, without requiring further coding effort. This is clearly a very creditable performance gain for such modest programmer effort.

NESL. The first-order nested data parallel language NESL [60] has also delivered good parallel performance on a range of supercomputer multiprocessors [62].

For example, in order to solve sparse, linear systems of partial differential equations a new class of preconditioners have been implemented in NESL [237]. This class of *support tree preconditioners* is based on the connectivity of the graphs corresponding to the coefficient matrices of the linear systems. These new preconditioners have the advantage of being well-structured for parallel implementation, both in construction and in evaluation. Performance measurements on a Cray C-90 show that these support tree preconditioners have similar convergence properties as Cholesky preconditioners. Furthermore, support tree preconditioners require less overall storage, less work per iteration, and yield better parallel performance than incomplete Cholesky preconditioners. Other NESL applications include a *Delaunay triangulation* algorithm [63] and several algorithms for solving the *n-body problem* [64].

Computational Fluid Dynamics.

Id. The 1000-line Id program *simple* simulates hydrodynamics and heat conduction, generating highly irregular parallelism. The core of this program is an iterative solution of a set of partial differential equations. On an 8-processor Monsoon — a novel dataflow machine produced in collaboration with Motorola, Hicks et al. [270] report a speedup of 6.3 for 100 iterations of a 100×100 grid of nodes containing information about position and velocity, over a series of zones with different fluid characteristics. The same program achieves a speedup of roughly 18 on a 64 processor CM-5 running the TAM abstract dataflow machine [150]. Three quarters of the overhead in the TAM version are attributed to message handling. The `simple` application has also been implemented in SISAL, where researchers achieved relative speedups of 4.3 on an 8-processor Cray Y-MP/864 and 13.9 on a 20-processor Sequent Symmetry for 62 iterations [355]. In both cases the SISAL version was significantly faster than the single-processor Fortran code, representing speedups over Fortran of 4.1 and 13.7 respectively.

Another large computational fluid dynamics application that has been extensively studied is the *Global Ocean Circulation Model*. The core of the several thousand lines Fortran code has been converted to Id and tuned on the parallel Monsoon dataflow architecture [529]. The core of the whole application, and therefore a central part in the Id code, is a preconditioned conjugate gradient solver, which requires about 80% of the total run-time. In common with many scientific applications this program has a regular control structure, centred around a triply nested loop, but an irregular data structure, namely an adaptive mesh. The application was tuned for parallel execution on Monsoon using loop unrolling and the introduction of k-bounded

19.2 Purely Implicit Parallel Applications

loops [19] loops to throttle excess parallelism. Performance results for realistic data sets, measured in machine independent cycles per required floating point operations, showed that the 8-processor Id/Monsoon application was between 2 times slower and 2 times faster than the equivalent 128-processor CM Fortran/CM-5 version.

The experience with various constructs for tuning the performance of parallel programs in Id has been rather two sided. On the one hand, quite dramatic improvements in performance can be achieved by choosing appropriate loop bounds, and thereby tuning the granularity of the generated threads [148]. However, in practice the correct choice for loop bounds requires knowledge of the total amount of parallelism at a particular point in the computation. Since the parallelism in Id is, by design, dynamic in nature, the best loop bounds are very hard to predict and so far no compiler techniques for choosing loop bounds have been developed. Furthermore, these decisions cannot be made in a modular way, complicating the performance tuning of large applications.

Several numerical applications have been implemented by the same group in different parallel functional languages in order to also assess the suitability of these languages for numerical applications. For example, the *NAS benchmark MG*, which solves a 3-dimensional partial differential equation using forward and inverse Fast Fourier Transformations, is the core of a simulation of heat propagation. The program has been implemented in both Id [556] and in SISAL [71]. Results for this application show space consumption problems that are similar to those reported in Chapter 11 for both the Monte Carlo Photon Transport Application [244] and the Dongarra-Sorensen algorithm for solving Eigenvectors [180], but which can be alleviated in the same way using M-structures. The Dongarra-Sorensen algorithm is especially interesting in that it demonstrates the automatic pipelining that can be achieved using non-strict languages.

The 750-line Id program *Gamteb* was written by researchers from Los Alamos National Laboratories to simulate the trajectory of photons through a carbon rod that has been divided into a number of cells of a given geometry. Each photon can be tested independently. On the 8-processor prototype Monsoon dataflow machine, this highly parallel application achieved a speedup of 7.35 for a problem containing 40,000 particles [270]. The same program achieved a speedup of roughly 34 on a 64-processor CM-5 running the TAM abstract dataflow machine [150]. In the TAM version about half of the overhead is attributed to message handling.

SAC. The strict, purely functional language SAC (Single Assignment C) [516] uses a familiar C-like syntax. Importantly for numerical applications, SAC provides both dimension-invariant array computations and a set of high-level array operations which can be optimised for both sequential and parallel execution [517]. The current parallel implementation of SAC focuses on the so-called With-loop construct for extracting implicit parallelism, yielding data parallelism across arrays.

A sequential implementation of the *NAS benchmark MG* in SAC [518] demonstrates its high single-processor performance. With all optimisations enabled, and assisted by type inference over the dimensions of the grid, the SAC version is between 5% and 10% faster than an optimised Fortran version, and between 50% and 80% faster than the SISAL version. Performance measurements for a 2-dimensional *Jacobi relaxation* on two Sun Ultra Enterprise multiprocessor workstations show good relative speedups of 3.71 on 4 processors and 8.83 on 12 processors [236].

19.2.2 Symbolic Applications

Theorem Provers. There have been several implementations of the well-known *Boyer-Moore theorem prover*. For example, Sodan and Bock's automatically parallelising Lisp system, ParLisp, has achieved a simulated speedup of between 5.1 and 29.5 on an idealised configuration of the MANNA machine containing an infinite number of processors [545]. The same system has also been implemented in Id as part of the Impala benchmark suite [528], but no performance results are available. Semi-explicit approaches are described in Section 19.3.2.

Molecular Biology.

Id. The *Paraffins* program enumerates all possible paraffin molecules constructed from carbon and hydrogen atoms [270]. With about 300 lines of Id it is a rather small program, but it is interesting for its crucial use of non-strictness and cyclic data structures, resulting in a very natural description of wavefront parallelism. On a 8-processor Monsoon machine this program achieved a speedup of 7.25.

19.2.3 Data-Intensive Applications

AGNA. Data-intensive applications are primarily concerned with manipulating large amounts of data, which usually persists in files or a database. For example, the AGNA parallel persistent object system uses list comprehensions to structure read-only queries over an on-disk database [269]. Since each lookup is independent of the results of any other lookup, parallelisation is straightforward and very high parallelism can be achieved with a good prospect of scalability. Heytens and Nikhil implemented the *Wisconsin database benchmark suite* [57], and report a speedup of 31 on a 32-processor distributed-memory machine for non-indexed lookup. Indexed lookup is much faster, but speedup is limited to a factor of 8, due to overheads associated with task creation and result construction.

19.2.4 Summary

Implicit parallel programming offers the prospect of a "free lunch". Programs can be written at a high level, without needing to consider how parallelism is to be introduced or managed. Programs are therefore easily written, highly portable, and maintainable. The challenge is to achieve high performance whilst retaining these benefits.

This section has shown that good implicit parallel performance can be achieved for the right applications using functional languages such as SISAL, SAC or NESL running on stock parallel supercomputers. This performance can be as good as, or even better than, the best performance that can be obtained using optimising compilers for conventional languages such as Fortran, even in the area of numerical applications.

In order to achieve this result, language designers have generally restricted the features offered by their languages. For example, SISAL is first-order and monomorphic, as is SAC. Of the languages discussed in this section, only Id is non-strict. It may be that such a tradeoff in power is essential in order to obtain high performance from an implicitly parallel system.

A number of challenges remain: performance tuning may still be necessary, but is difficult to achieve without any direct control; performance models can be hard to produce due to the gap between the program and its implementation; incorporating features such as polymorphism or non-strictness may compromise performance; and both languages and implementations may need to be adapted to better support data-intensive and symbolic applications, especially those with irregular structures. Implicit approaches do, however, appear to work well now in the domain of regular numerical applications, and can hopefully be extended to other domains in the near future.

19.3 Semi-Explicit Parallelism

19.3.1 Numerical Applications

DPFL. DPFL is a data parallel functional language that uses Haskell-like syntax and annotations for partitioning and distributing arrays. Dimov et al. have studied two versions of a Monte Carlo algorithm for solving boundary value problems for *elliptic differential equations* [174]: the grid-walk algorithm is based on partitioning the problem into a number of distinct grids; the grid-free algorithm uses an integral representation of the problem. Measurements show near-linear speedup on a 64-processor Transputer-based machine for both algorithms. The unoptimised DPFL implementation of both algorithms is, however, about 2 to 6 times slower than the corresponding parallel C implementation, though simple hand optimisations can recover a factor of 2 performance. Other programs that have been implemented in DPFL and parallel C include Gaussian elimination and FFT.

Table 19.2. Semi-explicit applications summary

Application Area	Language	Program
Numerical	DFPL	Elliptic Differential Equations
	Skil	Multigrid Algorithms
		Helmholtz Equation
	Dutch Parallel Reduction Machine	Tidal Prediction
Symbolic	Skeleton ML	Computer Vision
		Image processing
	SkelML	Ray Tracer
	Concurrent Clean	Ray Tracer
	Hope+	Constructive Solid Geometry
	GpH	Naira: Compiler
		Lolita Nat. Lang. Processor
		Theorem Prover
	MultiLisp	Parser Generator
		Nucleic Acid Structure
	pD	Linear Equation Solver
Data-Intensive	GpH	Transaction-Processing
		Complex Database Queries

Skil. Skil [77] is a C-like imperative language that includes functional features such as higher-order functions, partial applications, and polymorphism. Compile-time instantiation of higher-order and polymorphic code yields performance that is between 3% and 40% slower than equivalent hand-coded C

19.3 Semi-Explicit Parallelism

programs [78]. Skil uses skeletons for parallelism (introduced in Chapter 13), including specialised support for numerical applications.

Multigrid methods are the fastest known algorithms for the solution of discretised (elliptical) partial differential equations. Several (non-adaptive) *multigrid algorithms* have been implemented in Skil [75], using application-specific multigrid skeletons. These skeletons use a finite difference discretisation of the continuous domain, and are parameterised with the method used for relaxation. They can be classified into constructors or destructors of a grid hierarchy, operators on a single grid, and map-like or fold-like skeletons. The same skeletons can be used for a variety of multigrid applications including the Barnes-Hut algorithm for the n-body problem

Using these skeletons, the solution of a Poisson equation with Dirichlet boundary conditions (several hundred lines of Skil) gave a speedup of 24 on 32 processors and an estimated speedup of 175 on 256 processors, on a 1024-processor Parsytec multiprocessor [74]. Similar results were achieved for a solution of the *Helmholtz equation* on a 2-dimensional domain with Dirichlet boundary conditions, yielding measured speedup of 87 on 128 processors and 143 on 256 processors. The Skil program source was approximately a factor of ten shorter than the original source (a few thousand lines of C).

These results demonstrate both high absolute performance and good scalability of these programs on large parallel machines for seriously sized applications. The use of "overlap domains" contributed to this good performance. Section 19.6 covers similar techniques used for derivational approaches.

Dutch Parallel Reduction Machine. The Dutch Parallel Reduction Machine Project [36] implemented a 560-line Miranda program for *tidal prediction* in the North Sea. The program uses an iterative wavefront method to approximate the solution to a set of partial differential equation, using a tile representation for the grid. The program was parallelised using a special divide-and-conquer "sandwich" skeleton [261] plus "communication lifting" transformations to expose pipelining.

Relative speedup was 2.5 on a 4-processor shared-memory machine, though the application should scale to larger shared-memory systems. Absolute performance was, however, poor compared with sequential C, a consequence of poorly developed compiler technology and the cost of dynamic memory allocation.

19.3.2 Symbolic Applications

Computer Vision. Graphical applications offer many opportunities for parallelism. While imperative parallel graphics applications generally depend on partitioning (updatable) arrays, more sophisticated data structures may simplify the partitioning process and offer better long-term opportunities for parallelism. Applications have been produced in several parallel languages to perform complex graphical manipulations. These include ray tracing to determine the intensity of light that falls on an object, as discussed in Section 19.4, and the computer vision applications prototyped by Michaelson and Scaife in Standard ML.

SML with Skeletons. Michaelson and Scaife [397] describe the implementation of several components of a *parallel vision system*. The overall purpose of the system is to recognise 3D objects in a 2D scene by using information about the relative intensity of light throughout the scene. The parallel algorithms are prototyped using a skeleton-based SML implementation, before being translated to Occam and executed on a distributed-memory Meiko machine (based on Transputers). The SML prototype required 1,700 lines against the 3,000 lines of the final OCCAM implementation.

The primary algorithm used in this application is the Hough transform for solving sets of underdetermined equations. This is parallelised in a data-oriented fashion using a farm skeleton to realise a parallel map over a nested list. Performance was optimised by splitting the data into more sets of equations, so introducing more small tasks which can be managed more efficiently to improve the overall load balance. This confirms other observations concerning task granularity as well as theoretical analyses: finer-grained programs are much easier to manage dynamically, and result in much better balanced computation. Overall, Michaelson and Scaife achieve an absolute speedup of 10.5 on a 30-processor Meiko. This performance was less than hoped for, possibly as a consequence of poor load balancing and/or high communication costs that may arise from the nature of the farm skeleton, which will tend to introduce communication bottlenecks at the farming processor.

Unrelated to the work above, a programming environment for prototyping parallel *image processing* applications is discussed in [522]. One concrete application implemented on a 4-processor Transputer network is a connected component labelling algorithm [223]. It is implemented in ML and uses a set of data parallel skeletons for introducing parallelism. The overall speedup obtained in this setup was 2.7 on a 4-processor machine.

SkelML. SkelML is an automatically parallelising skeleton-based compiler for SML that has been used to study a simple *ray tracer* [82]. A simulated annealing approach based on structured operational semantics is used to obtain a good static schedule and initial resource allocation. Performance predicted in this way is usually within 10% of the actual value.

For the ray tracer, SkelML identifies a map function as a source of parallelism and chooses a processor farm as a parallel implementation. Results show a speedup up to 9.5 on 22 Transputers for the largest example that was tried. Results for a similar program using a coordination approach are given in Section 19.4.1.

Concurrent Clean. In an interesting comparison, Kesseler has also used the same *ray tracer* as a benchmark for a skeleton-based implementation of Concurrent Clean [333], [334] on the Transputer. Concurrent Clean (see Chapters 3 and 15) is a Haskell-like lazy functional language, with annotations similar to GpH for parallelism.

The single processor Concurrent Clean program is significantly faster than the SkelML program (almost 4 times faster). Kesseler also reports speedup of 10 on 16 processors, rising to 33.5 on 64 processors, where he is clearly encountering some performance bound, perhaps due to static process allocation giving poor distribution at this size of problem.

GpH. The simple *ray tracer* that was originally developed in Kelly's thesis for the Caliban coordination language [331] has formed the basis for a number of subsequent studies, including one for the FLARE project. This demonstrated good speedup for this application on GRIP, achieving an absolute speedup of 10.5 on 17 processors, with no evidence of a software performance bound [250]. Relative speedup for the same configuration was a factor of 14.

Hope$^+$. Another application of the skeletons approach to parallel functional programming is the *Constructive Solid Geometry* (CSG) library developed in Hope$^+$ at the University of Leeds [168]. This library mainly uses a divide-and-conquer skeleton to introduce parallelism, reflecting the tree structure generated when modelling a solid object out of a small class of primitives. The main algorithm implemented in this project is point membership classification, which tests whether a point lies inside a given solid object. Simulation results of the algorithm predict a speedup of about 51 on a 64-processor machine.

Compilers and Rule-Based Systems.

GpH: Naira Compiler. Naira [320], [321] is a 5000-line parallelising compiler for a subset of Haskell, which was written using GpH. The compiler itself has been parallelised using pipeline parallelism between the stages of the compiler, data parallelism over individual functions of the input program, and an internally parallelised type checking phase. It has been measured on several simulated architectures as well as on a network of workstations. The maximum absolute speedup of 2.46 was reported for a network of 5 Sun SPARC/4 machines.

GpH: Lolita Natural Language Processor. Evaluation strategies [571] are coordination functions, written in GpH, that specify evaluation order, evaluation degree, and parallelism of a pure Haskell function. Hence, the sequential and parallel combinators of GpH are only used within evaluation strategies, and the rest of the program is purely declarative. A special using function applies an evaluation strategy to a pure Haskell function.

Another GpH application is the *Lolita natural language engineering system* comprising more than 47000 lines of GpH and a few thousand lines of C [367]. By using data-oriented parallelism over non-strict data structures most of the parallelisation has been done in the top level module without changing sub modules. Simulation results of the parallel code exhibited speedups between 2.4 and 3.1 on 4 processors, with wallclock speedups being limited by the overall heap consumption of the application. The experiences with various symbolic applications written in GpH with evaluation strategies are summarised in [368].

MultiLisp. In an unusual application, Boucher and Feeley have constructed a parallel implementation of an LR(0) *parser generator* [79] in MultiLisp [241]. Parallelism was introduced using lazy "future" annotations (similar to the par combinators in GpH and Concurrent Clean) to create all reachable states in parallel. Simple explicit locks are used in place of the sequential hash table to prevent several tasks working on the same state simultaneously, and to ensure atomic update for each state. These rather low-level programming constructs are reminiscent of the use of M-structures [40] in Id and pH (see Chapter 11), and similarly sacrifice referential transparency for direct control.

Overall, the parser generator achieves an absolute speedup of 10.4 on 32 processors. The parallel overhead was particularly serious for this system, generating a slowdown of a factor of 3 on one parallel processor, so this represents an impressive superlinear relative speedup (a factor of 33.6 on 32 processors). The super-linearity is claimed to reflect decreased garbage collection costs in the parallel implementation.

Theorem Provers.

GpH. In addition to the theorem provers already covered in Section 19.2.2, Hanna and Howell parallelised the 8500-line tautology checker that forms the core of the Veritas theorem prover as one of several realistic applications developed by the FLARE project [505]. Individual propositions were parallelised using a divide-and-conquer approach, with thresholding on the size of subpropositions controlling task granularity. Performance results for the novel GRIP multiprocessor [251] gave an absolute speedup of 18 on 20 processors.

Since this work predated the development of evaluation strategies [571], only basic par annotations were used. Experience showed that the parallelisation was generally much easier than for an equivalent imperative version. Placing annotations in crucial subfunctions of the code did, however, require a deep understanding of its behaviour. This application therefore motivated the subsequent development of evaluation strategies. A direct comparison of pre-strategy with strategic code for a linear system solver is given in [364].

Molecular Biology.

MultiLisp. Feeley et al. have worked on a parallel application for *determining the three-dimensional structure of nucleic acids* [191]. This application involves solving a set of constraints that collectively define all legal 3D structures that can be built from the input set of nucleotides.

Each nucleotide contains one free variable describing its three-dimensional position relative to other nucleotides. This position constrains the placement of other nucleotides in the structure. The parallel implementation of the algorithm involves checking each possible solution for a nucleotide's position in parallel. The application is written as a 3500-line MultiLisp program and uses lazy task creation [409], [299] to introduce parallel tasks.

This application has been tested on two interesting data sets. For the larger of the two data sets, *pseudoknot*, it is possible to achieve a maximum absolute speedup of 13.7 on 24 processors. This represents the limit of parallelism — additional processors result in lower speedups due to added contention. While the parallel overhead is a quite reasonable 21%, the single processor parallel case is still 2.4 times slower than sequential C. The smaller data set, *anticodon* displays good absolute speedup of 49 on 64 processors.

Computer Algebra.

pD. Schreiner has applied his small strict para-functional language *pD* to a number of problems taken from *computer algebra:* a linear equation solver, using a modular approach and Cramer's rule; two programs to compute multivariate polynomial resultants; and part of a polynomial factorisation algorithm.

Highly significantly, Schreiner's performance results show that good absolute speedup can be achieved using a para-functional approach [519]. Compared with sequential C, Schreiner achieved performance of 14 on a 16-processor shared-memory system for the linear equation solver (his best result). Sequential performance is also broadly in line with that obtained for the corresponding C programs. Although these applications are small, they do suggest that parallel symbolic computation is amenable to exploitation by functional programming techniques.

19.3.3 Data Intensive Applications

GpH. Another application investigated by the FLARE project was *database transaction processing*. Transactions involve not simply queries, as with AGNA (see Section 19.2.3), but also update operations that may introduce dependencies with subsequent database transactions [8]. The results show that acceptable parallel performance can be achieved through the use of techniques to reduce the "hot spot" that arises from contention on the root of the B-tree data structure that forms the index to the on-disk database. Overall, an absolute speedup of 12.6 on 15 GRIP processors was achieved for in-memory copies of the database with simulated disk accesses. Larger data sets gave better performance than smaller ones, so it seems likely that these results could be scaled to larger systems with higher throughput.

The later Parade project investigated more complex database queries, including the standard *parts explosion*, or *bill of materials* problem. A similar, but more challenging, program analyses police road traffic accident reports to discover accident blackspots, i.e. places where several accidents have occurred [572]. There are several conditions under which accidents are identified as occurring in the same place, and the problem amounts to partitioning the set of accidents under all of the conditions. Alternative parallelisations were investigated, and a coarse partitioning of the data into geographical areas proved the most effective.

By exploiting the architecture-independence of GpH, the accident blackspot database program has been measured on a number of different architectures. The best result to date is an absolute speedup of 10 (relative speedup of 12) on a network of 16 workstations. *Scaleup* measures the increase in run-time as data is increased in line with processing elements. This is an important measure for parallel data intensive programs. The best scaleup results were also achieved on the workstation network: an increase of 40% in run-time when increasing the volume of data, and processing elements, by a factor of 16.

19.3.4 Summary

Semi-explicit approaches are more broadly applicable than implicit approaches: in contrast with the applications covered in Section 19.2, the applications covered in this section are more symbolic and less regular, though regular numerical applications have also been successfully parallelised. In contrast with most of the fully implicit approaches described earlier, semi-explicit languages are usually fully featured, offering polymorphism and higher-order functions. Non-strictness is also more common.

As we have seen for implicit parallelism, performance tuning is problematic if there are no control mechanisms that can be used to influence parallel behaviour. Exposing parallelism restores some element of control that may be important for this purpose. Two ways to expose parallelism without introducing explicit control constructs are annotation-based approaches and skeleton approaches.

Annotation-based approaches have generally achieved better performance results, and appear to be more portable. For large applications, however, they can introduce serious clutter, because the algorithm is obscured by the litter of annotations describing the parallel behaviour. The result is a program that is hard to understand — the very opposite of what parallel functional languages aim to provide. Reducing this clutter is the major challenge facing annotation-based approaches. One solution to the problem that we have experimented with is to use evaluation strategies to provide a separation of functional specification from coordination.

Skeleton approaches are, in principle, more desirable if the skeletons can be automatically extracted from the program and mapped to a variety of architectures. Overly restrictive skeletons may, however, constrict programming style and require extensive rewriting of the source either to expose parallelism, or to provide alternative skeletons for different architectures.

19.4 Coordination Languages

As seen in Chapter 14, functional coordination approaches can be divided into two categories. The first category of languages combine a functional computation language with a coordination language, for example Caliban [331]. The other category of functional coordination languages use a functional coordination language to control a host language taken from some other paradigm, such as P3L [27] or SPF [161]. The latter have mainly been applied to numerical applications, whereas the former have generally targeted symbolic applications.

Table 19.3. Coordination-language applications summary

Application Area	Language	Program
Numerical	SCL	n-Body Problem
		Gauss-Jordan Solver
		Conjugate Gradient Solver
	P3L	Circuit Fault List Analysis
		Radiological Image Analysis
		Delaunay Triangulation
		Ray Tracer
	PCN	Climate Modelling
Symbolic	SCL	Data Mining
	Caliban	Ray Tracer

19.4.1 Numerical Computation

SCL. Structured Parallel Programming, SPP(X) [162], aims to use skeletons for compositional parallel programming. It is structured in two layers: the upper layer, called Structured Coordination Language (SCL), specifies the program's parallel behaviour via skeletons, whereas the lower layer describes sequential computation in a sequential base language. This approach allows good performance prediction: for a parallel *conjugate gradient algorithm* predicted performance is within 10% of the observed value on a Fujitsu AP1000 distributed-memory machine [157].

Structured Parallel Fortran, SPF [161], is an instance of SPP(X) that uses Fortran as the sequential "host" language. It extends SPP(X) by adding support for irregular data structure via parallel abstract data types [165]. This is particularly useful for more symbolic or data-intensive applications, e.g. in data mining, as suggested by Chattratichat et al. [122].

The most successful SPF application to date is a standard *Gauss-Jordan algorithm* for linear system solving, which achieves speedups on the AP1000 of up to 25 on 64 processors using a prototype SPF compiler [601][Section 6.7]. Yang has also implemented the *Barnes-Hut algorithm*, for the n-body problem (see Section 19.2, but performance results are unavailable.

P3L. The P3L system [27] takes a similar approach to SPF, but using C as the host. An important difference is that P3L adopts greater abstraction in specifying data distribution, alignment, and processor allocation. These must all be specified explicitly in SPF, whereas P3L only requires the specification of dependencies between the data and the parallel activities.

One interesting application that has been implemented in P3L is a *circuit fault list analysis* package used in testing electronic chips for defects [26]. This application generates test patterns from a circuit layout and a list of likely faults. The two main components of the application are an automatic test pattern generator and a simulator that tests whether a test pattern detects more than one fault. Test patterns have to be generated until all likely faults are covered. The parallel version of the algorithm uses data parallelism over the list of faults and pipeline parallelism between test pattern generation and simulation. Performance measurements on a Transputer-based Meiko multi-processor showed wall-clock speedups compared to single processor versions run on much faster workstations. Similar results were achieved for computer vision applications.

PCN. The Program Composition Notation, PCN [201], [200], is a general coordination language, influenced by the parallel declarative language Strand [202], a guarded Horn clause language. PCNs major features show its heritage from parallel declarative languages: compositionality, determinism, implicit synchronisation, higher-order functions via program templates, non-strict lists as streams used for communication.

The most prominent of the numerous scientific applications of PCN (see also [124], [256]) is the *Icosahedral Climate Modelling Code* (ICMC) [124], which implements a standard numerical method for studying atmospheric circulation. The program is data parallel over an irregular data structure with a fairly regular computation structure. Communication is mainly performed via streams. In total the program comprises 1,400 lines of Fortran (called via PCNs foreign language interface), 870 lines of C, and 750 lines of PCN. On a 528-node i860-based Intel Touchstone Delta the PCN version is between 40% faster to 20% slower than an equivalent parallel Fortran implementation.

19.4 Coordination Languages

Data Mining.

SCL. Chattratichat et al. have implemented several parallel SPP(X) algorithms for *data mining* on a Fujitsu AP1000 [122]. These classification algorithms find a set of rules that classifies a given data item into one of a set of predefined classes. The algorithms take a training set of data items with their correct classification as input and are based on two approaches: tree induction and neural networks. The tree induction algorithm generates a decision tree as a result and uses either task parallelism, for generating subtrees in parallel, or data parallelism, over the distributed training set. Due to the small training sets, the best variant achieved only moderate speedups of up to a factor of 2.2 on 15 processors. The second algorithm uses a multi-layer, feed forward neural network, and exploits task parallelism with a distributed neural network in the error back-propagation stage. The measurements achieved a speedup of up to 3.6 on 6 processors, with the size of the network imposing a limit on the scalability of this approach.

Computer Vision.

Caliban. Caliban/Advanced Caliban is a declarative coordination language that is used to describe static parallel process networks for a functional language [331], [560]. Process descriptions are combined with the functional program via a moreover clause, similar to the GpH using function. A more detailed discussion of Caliban and Advanced Caliban [560] can be found in Section 14.2.

In his thesis [560], Taylor studies this same *ray tracer* in the context of Advanced Caliban. Advanced Caliban extends the Caliban coordination language in a number of new and interesting ways that parallel the development of GpH evaluation strategies (for example, the use of nested moreover clauses to control placement is similar to the use of strategies to describe process structures). Unlike evaluation strategies, however, Caliban remains firmly routed in a static model of process placement, and the target architecture is restricted to a distributed, closely-coupled parallel machine (in Taylor's case, the 48-node AP1000 at the Imperial College Parallel Centre, London). Using a static process farm, with limited speculative evaluation, Taylor achieves a relative speedup of 17 on 35 processors for this implementation of the ray tracer. With the introduction of manual granularity control, performance can be boosted to a relative speedup of 24 on 35 processors.

19.4.2 Summary

The use of functional coordination to control tasks written in some host language promises to offer the dual advantages of a high level of abstraction for the coordination component with high performance for the sequential component. Higher-order functions are especially useful in this context, since they can be used to "glue" together independent computations in a dynamic manner. This is the approach taken by both SCL and P3L, with some success. There is evidence from the use of the declarative coordination languages PCN (for numerical applications) and Strand (for symbolic applications) that such an approach can be highly effective.

Compared with annotation-based semi-explicit approaches, coordination languages overcome the problem of embedded control by offering a clean separation of control and evaluation concerns. The cost is in needing to deal with a separate (and maybe separated) coordination language. This separation may introduce complex semantic or interfacing issues. A more elegant approach is to use the same language to express both coordination and computation, as with Caliban.

The results given here generally indicate that it is much easier to deal with static process networks for regular problems than with dynamic networks or irregular problems. Consequently, one of the major research challenges in this area is the smooth nesting and composition of coordination constructs: it is frequently the case that two locally optimal constructs will not yield a good composition.

19.5 Explicit Parallelism

Explicit languages such as Concurrent Haskell, CML, Erlang, or Facile frequently use concurrent algorithms that were originally developed for operating systems use. Many of the large applications that have been written in these languages are therefore distributed, rather than parallel.

19.5.1 Numerical Computation

The FFTW system. FFTW (Fastest Fourier Transform in the West) is claimed to be the fastest existing multidimensional discrete Fourier transformation algorithm [206]. It has three main components: the codelet generator, the planner and the executor. The codelet generator automatically produces a number of highly optimised C code fragments (codelets) that calculate the FFT using the Cooley-Tukey FFT algorithm. The planner determines, at run-time, an efficient way of composing the codelets. Finally, the executor runs the codelets.

FFTW exploits many functional ideas. The codelet generator [205] is written in Caml Light, and optimises the abstract syntax tree of the sequential C code, in a similar way to optimising functional compilers [462]. The simplifier is written using memoisation and monads, both of which are common functional notions. Finally, the FFTW system uses a dynamic self-optimising approach, in which the planner automatically adapts the behaviour of the parallel algorithm to the characteristics of the underlying parallel machine. In this sense, the planner closely resembles the run-time system in an implicit or semi-explicit functional system.

19.5 Explicit Parallelism

Table 19.4. Explicitly-parallel applications summary

Application Area	Language	Program
Numerical	Caml Light & C	FFTW: Fast Fourier Transforms
	paraML	Black Hole Imaging
	Stampede	Smart Kiosk
Symbolic	Concurrent Haskell	UniForM: Formal Development Environment
	CML	User Interface Toolkit
Data-Intensive	Erlang	Mnesia: a Distributed Database Management System
		Mobility Server
	Facile	Calumet
		Mobile Service Agents

paraML. Like CML, paraML is an extension of ML with explicit threads and dynamically created, typed communication ports for explicit message passing synchronisation. In contrast to CML, however, paraML uses a logically distributed address space, and the design of processes and ports is modelled after the π-calculus [402].

The paraML system has been used to implement a Schwarzschild black hole imaging system [33]. This uses ray tracing techniques to determine how the appearance of an object is distorted when its photons are deviated near the vicinity of the black hole.

The Bulirsch-Stoer method has been parallelised in paraML to solve the two first-order ordinary differential equations which describe the photon trajectories. The application achieves the impressive absolute speedup of 76 on a 126 processor Fujitsu AP1000 compared with the same program compiled sequentially using the optimised SML/NJ compiler.

Computer Vision.

Stampede. Like FFTW, Compaq's Smart Kiosk system exploits the use of functional language ideas and technology in more conventional languages, in this case Stampede [428]. The Smart Kiosk aims to act as an on-line advisor dispensing information to consumers. In order to do this effectively, it must interpret user expressions and gestures to obtain feedback on the responses that are provided, or to provide contextual information about queries. It is therefore critical to provide fast image recognition and tracking. This is achieved using a network of Compaq Alpha-based SMPs. Preliminary results suggest that the performance goals can be met by this system.

19.5.2 Symbolic applications

Concurrent ML. Concurrent ML [492], [493] was introduced in Chapter 17. It has been used for several applications, the most substantial of which is a *user interface toolkit* [208] that can be used for software development environments.

Concurrent Haskell. The largest Concurrent Haskell [466] application is the *UniForM Concurrency Toolkit* [327], [325], which comprises 50000 lines of Concurrent Haskell plus a few thousand lines of C. UniForM is a tool integration framework for formal Software Development Environments. Concurrent Haskell is used to integrate different tools, possibly written in different languages, into an environment. Given that the tools are provably correct, it is then possible to produce correctness proofs for complete systems that are built in this way.

UniForM has itself been used to implement a Graphical User Interface on top of the Tk library [326], an encapsulation of a relational database manager [328], and a workbench for specification and proof in Z (5000 lines of Haskell), using Isabelle as the underlying theorem proofer [374].

19.5.3 Data-intensive Applications

Erlang. The Erlang [15] language is used by the telecommunications giant Ericsson for a number of important commercial applications [14]. Like CML, it is a concurrent language with explicit process control and impure features. It differs from CML in that it is not typed.

In real-world use, Erlang has been found to produce applications that are both "fast enough" for commercial use and that consume less memory than their C/C++ counterparts. The applications can also be written more quickly and maintained more easily.

One of the most interesting applications of Erlang is *Mnesia*, a multiuser distributed database management system (DBMS) especially designed for industrial telecommunications applications [381]. These applications require a range of important features, implemented in Mnesia, but not usually found in traditional DBMSs: high fault-tolerance, complicated non-real-time queries (mainly for operation and maintenance), dynamic reconfiguration, complex objects and the usage of a shared address space for the DBMS and its applications. In total, Mnesia comprises about 15000 lines of Erlang. Mnesia uses

Erlang as a very powerful database programming language, underlining the usefulness of functional languages for data-intensive applications.

Other significant telecommunications applications include the 230000 line *Mobility Server*, which acts as an intelligent call routing system linked to an internal telephone exchange, and which is in widespread use.

Facile. Several prototypes of telecommunication applications have been implemented in the SML-based Facile language [222], [566], which supports both process descriptions and channels as first-class objects. For example, the *Calumet* system [557] is a cooperative application for teleconferencing, supporting remote presentation of virtual documents, similar to overhead slides, over a network of conventional workstations with a built-in audio interface. The Calumet prototype has been used internally by ECRC. Another application implements *Mobile Service Agents*, self-contained pieces of software that can move between computers on a network. These agents form an autonomous, intelligent interface to various information services on the world wide web. It possesses information about the structure of data provided by certain services, in order to interpret them, and it is tailored to the needs of mobile users.

19.5.4 Summary

Unlike the applications that have been encountered in previous sections, the target of explicitly parallel functional programs is generally concurrent execution rather than performance. Notable exceptions are the FFTW program, the Schwarzschild black hole imaging system and Compaq's Smart Kiosk system. The first two systems achieve very creditable performance, while the third is still under development but has developed good preliminary results. The FFTW and Smart Kiosk applications are especially interesting in showing how functional ideas can be used to advantage in more conventional settings.

The remaining applications are either symbolic or data-intensive. In the first case, they exploit the strong symbol manipulation capabilities of functional languages and ease of constructing (type safe) distributed programs. In the second, they also exploit the good software engineering properties of functional languages, as observed by Ericsson.

19.6 Derivational Approaches

The development of parallel algorithms can also be seen as a process of program derivation, where the programmer starts with an abstract program specification and refines this specification until a concrete program has been developed. In contrast to conventional program derivation, as the program becomes more concrete, more and more coordination directives are included.

This approach is described in detail in Chapter 7. In addition to the possibility of deriving provably correct programs, in the context of parallel programming this approach offers a high degree of reusability of the intermediate steps of the derivation process. For example, a parallel program developed for a shared-memory machine does not have to be developed from scratch when generating a distributed-memory version. Only a few design decisions in the derivation process have to be changed.

The development of many parallel functional programs has a derivational element, for example the communication lifting transformation in the tidal prediction application of Section 19.3.1 is derivational. This section, however, focuses on approaches where the program development model is entirely derivational.

Table 19.5. Derivational applications summary

Application Area	Derivation Methodology	Program
Numerical	TwoL	Runge-Kutta Algorithm
	Pepper et al.	Wang's Algorithm
		Simulation of Cell Receptive Fields in the Visual Cortex
		Multigrid Algorithms
	Gorlatch, Lengauer et al.	FFT
		Polynomial Multiplication Algorithm
Symbolic	Formal Haskell	Heat Equation
		Simulator for Parallel Hardware
		Hierarchical Radiosity Algorithm

19.6.1 Numerical Computation

TwoL. The TwoL model [487] distinguishes two levels of parallelism: high-level, irregular *method parallelism* which is inherent in the algorithm; and low-level, *regular system* parallelism, which addresses aspects such as task granularity. This approach is tailored to a hierarchical group-SPMD model of parallelism, with groups of regular SPMD-style computations clustered into an irregular higher level. The TwoL model starts with a specification that exposes the maximal parallelism in the algorithm, and refines it in several stages

19.6 Derivational Approaches

to yield a concrete parallel program. The early stages in this refinement process are parallel functional programs – essentially executable specifications of the parallel algorithm with some level of refinement added. The final outcome is not paradigm-specific, however, and may be either functional, imperative or object-oriented.

Most of the applications of the TwoL model perform numerical computations such as the *Runge-Kutta algorithm* for the solution of initial value problems of ordinary differential equations [487]. These algorithms are in turn used in the simulation of collision-less electron plasma and a chemical reactor-diffusion system.

Skeleton-based Derivation. A derivational methodology for developing parallel functional programs, using a skeletons approach is described in [454]. The derivation methodology places particular emphasis on data distribution, and necessary redistributions when combining skeletons that require different data distributions. An abstract description of the distribution of data structures is defined in the form of a number of overlapping covers ("halos") [551]. The kernels of these covers form a partition of the original data structure. The edges of these covers contain neighbouring data in order to minimise communication. The central parallel tasks that have to be specified in this methodology are: the data distribution; the local computations operating on individual covers; and the global interaction between the processors. At this level, this approach has strong similarities with the BSP/SPMD approaches, and it should be fairly easy to adapt the derivation to generate such programs.

Pepper and Südholt have used this technique to derive a parallel functional program that computes *Wang's Algorithm* for the solution of tridiagonal systems of linear equations [455]. The underlying data structure in this case is a 2-dimensional matrix. The skeletons used in this algorithm are mostly basic, rather than application-specific skeletons: *map*, *zip*, and *fold* skeletons proved to be most useful.

More complex applications using the same derivation methodology include a *simulation for the development of simple cell receptive fields in the visual cortex* [552]. The core of this application, which has been derived from a large scale neural network simulation, is the numeric integration of a difference equation, which specifies the learning process of this neural network. This integration can be implemented via the solution of a system of ordinary differential equations using convolutions and Fast Fourier transformations. In common with many other applications in neuroscience, this algorithm involves a huge number of neurons and lends itself for a large-scale data parallel implementation.

Compared with an existing hand-written implementation in the imperative data parallel language C*, the derived parallel functional program was found to be more flexible in how data is distributed (a vital characteristic for such an algorithm).

BMF and Skeletons. Gorlatch, Lengauer, et al. use a similar methodology based on BMF-style program specification and formal derivation, in order to derive parallel programs with skeletons. In [231], [230] skeletons for a special class of data parallel algorithms, called distributed homomorphisms, are used to derive a generic SPMD algorithm for the *FFT*. The skeleton uses two subsequent steps of computation and group-wise communication, resembling a BSP-style of parallel computation, in this case implemented via MPI. Performance prediction, usually within 15% of the actual computation time, is used to allocate resources. Measurements of the derived parallel program on a Transputer-based 64-node Parsytec GCel64 yielded speedups of up 34.

Another example of using such an approach starting with a BMF-style specification is a parallel, SPMD-style *polynomial multiplication algorithm* discussed in [227]. The main tools used in order to guide the derivation are formal type analysis and performance prediction. The decisions made in the derivation cover the extraction of parallelism, data partitioning and distribution, processor topology, and scheduling of computation and communication.

19.6.2 Symbolic Computation

Closely related to the TwoL approach is a strand of work using equational reasoning to derive programs from mathematics, via Haskell to a range of implementations, including digital circuits and C with MPI. The approach is rigorous, rather than formal, and emphasises reuse of parts of the derivation to produce alternative implementations.

There are several examples of the approach, including the following. The derivation of a program to solve the *heat equation*, a partial differential equation is given in [439]. A *simulator for parallel hardware* expressed in C with MPI has also been derived. A very complex numerical algorithm is the *hierarchical radiosity algorithm*. A Haskell version of this algorithm, using subroutines of an existing C-implementation, is presented in [438]. Although, this algorithm is not yet parallel, its parallelisation is discussed in the aforementioned paper.

19.6.3 Summary

Deriving parallel programs from high-level specifications offers the prospect of systematically developing new parallel algorithms, and of adapting existing derived algorithms for new parallel architectures. The rigorous derivation process gives a high degree of confidence in the correctness of the final algorithm. When coupled with good high-level performance prediction models this approach may also help avoid developing implementations with poor performance properties before they have become too highly developed. Functional languages are exploited to give high-level abstractions of the parallel program which can then be encoded in a more efficient form, if necessary.

Despite these advantages, few large applications yet use a derivational approach. This is probably due to the complex labour-intensive process of deriving a first parallel program, and the low provision of automated support for the derivation process. The approach would appear to be most useful at present for developing novel parallel algorithms, with the attraction that variants of the basic algorithm could easily be derived for different classes of architecture.

19.7 Conclusion

Previous chapters have introduced parallel functional programming technology, and demonstrated the issues that arise in implementing this technology effectively. This chapter has discussed how this technology can be used in practice, covering applications in numerical programming, symbolic computing, computer vision, telephony, and data-intensive programming, some of which are extremely large (e.g. the 230000-line Erlang Mobility Server in Section 19.5.3). The range of applications illustrates the broad spectrum of application areas that are amenable to functional approaches: functional programming is a general purpose paradigm. The range of target architectures is also extremely diverse: because of the high level of abstraction, functional implementations and applications can often be made essentially target-independent.

The sheer variety of parallel approaches that have been adopted reflects the suitability of functional languages as vehicles for computer science research. Approaches covered here range from fully implicit to explicit, and including emerging approaches based on rigorous program derivation. Many of these approaches have proven to be capable of delivering good speedups, and in some cases (e.g. SISAL or SAC) they outperform conventional imperative alternatives such as parallel C or Fortran for regular numerical applications on supercomputers. This, however, comes at the expense of sacrificing important language features such as higher-order functions and polymorphism.

Of increasing interest are the emerging parallel symbolic computation applications in multi-media, language processing, computer algebra, etc. In contrast to numerical applications, such systems often exhibit irregular (task) parallelism and operate over complex data structures. Functional languages are appropriate for these applications because they provide good support for manipulating complex, and dynamic data structures, and for abstracting over common computation patterns through the use of higher-order functions. These features, in turn, are increasingly sought for in modern programming languages, in order to facilitate large-scale program design.

Although the applications introduced here use a variety of approaches and cover a range of areas, several common themes emerge.

Programming Model. Many applications reveal how important it is to find the *right level of abstraction* for both computation and coordination in the programming model. At too high a level, important aspects of the application cannot be expressed, and cost modelling may be difficult. At too low a level, the program is cluttered with irrelevant detail. Many of the irregularly-parallel programs use detailed knowledge of the language, or application, to achieve good performance.

Memory Consumption. Generally speaking, much less attention has been paid to memory issues in parallel functional systems than to absolute performance. Many research papers report problems with *large memory consumption*, and some researchers have resorted to the use of impure features in order to overcome such problems. A good example of this is given in Chapter 11. The problem of efficient dynamic allocation is, of course, not unique to functional systems: parallel object-oriented systems also have similar problems. More research into the specific issues associated with dynamic allocation for parallel functional languages would be welcome, however.

Foreign Language Interfacing. Many of the large applications described here use components that are written in a foreign language. These components may be legacy code, shared libraries, or simply components that are better written in some other paradigm. Suitable foreign language interfaces must therefore be provided, whether as a separate mechanism, or by the use of a coordination approach to control components that are written using foreign languages.

Familiar Syntax. Language familiarity, or availability, can be a barrier to the use of new techniques. Several new languages have therefore adopted syntaxes or constructs that are taken from widely-used languages. For example, SISAL uses a Fortran-like syntax, and SAC, Skil and Cilk are all based on C. In a similar vein, coordination languages add a new layer to an existing, familiar language. The advantage is that such languages should be adopted more readily. The cost is usually a loss of code abstraction, or powerful techniques such as higher-order functions, which consequently affects the compactness of code produced in such languages.

Architecture Independence. Many of the systems described here are portable not only in targeting different machine types, but even different classes of architecture. For example, SISAL and GpH are both available on shared-memory and distributed-memory multiprocessors as well as networks of workstations. Using these systems, at least some applications have been produced that run without modification on all three classes of architecture. Such high-level retargetability is important in a setting where the most cost-effective parallel platforms and even architectures change on a regular basis.

19.7.1 Future Directions

Based on the applications that have been surveyed in this chapter, several research directions can be identified.

19.7 Conclusion

Irregular and Symbolic Applications. In recent years new, computationally intensive application areas, such as multi-media programming, have become important. Simultaneously new and affordable parallel hardware, such as symmetric multiprocessors, has emerged. These new applications, as well as more established ones such as compilers and computer vision, are mostly symbolic and often use complex algorithms and data structures exhibiting *irregular parallelism*. Such applications have increased the number of programmers interested in easily-exploited parallelism. Parallel functional languages, with their aforementioned strengths in symbol manipulation, may well represent an appropriate programming paradigm to achieve this goal.

Implementations. There is a strong belief that future parallel functional applications must be based on *stock hardware*: they should not require special hardware. Moreover, few large applications are built in a single language, and so languages must interface with other system components. These requirements generate significant challenges for language implementors. Many implementations of parallel functional languages are novel because they attempt automatically to manage most aspects of the parallel program execution, e.g. load balancing, task synchronisation, data distribution etc. Some key implementation issues revealed by the applications are the need for improved data locality, and for the reduction of heap usage.

Architecture Independence. In the parallel programming community as a whole there is a great deal of interest in constructing *architecture-independent applications*. It appears that the high level of abstraction in functional languages has the potential to ease the movement between parallel platforms [570]. Architecture-independent languages would aid a comparative measurement of implementations of programs using imperative and a range of parallel functional approaches.

Metrics for Parallelism. Although we had hoped to provide a set of comparative measurements covering all of the applications introduced in this chapter, this resolve was thwarted by the lack of standard metrics in the research literature. Assessment of parallel systems and applications would be greatly facilitated by the widespread use of a standard set of program and parallel platform characteristics, and standard performance metrics. There is, of course, no particular reason why such a set of metrics should be restricted to parallel functional programs.

Programming Environments. Both the *development environments* and the *development methodologies* that are currently used for parallel functional programming are at an early stage, and require improvement. The production of new programming environments is essentially an engineering problem, though new kinds of tools may need to be developed. Some of the most developed current environments are *Id World* [413], the GpH [571] and the Dutch Parallel Reduction Machine [36] environments.

New static and dynamic program analyses are also required to guide the development of parallel programs. For example, new cost models covering a wider class of programs are required. Improved profiling and visualisation tools will also aid the development of large programs, regardless of whether these are developed using formal derivation or less formal refinement approaches.

20. Summary

Greg Michaelson[1] and Kevin Hammond[2]

This book has covered the full range of parallel functional programming, providing insight into the challenges and problems that have been overcome, and indicating those that remain. The clean properties of functional languages make them highly suitable for research into all aspects of parallel computation, as well as many aspects of sequential computation, and this has been demonstrated here. Work described in this book ranges from fully implicit purely functional approaches such as Concurrent Clean (Chapter 15) and SAC to approaches controlling task creation and communication through explicit side-effects such as Concurrent ML (Chapter 17) or Scampi (Chapter 18). In between lie a vast range of alternatives. It is too early to say which of these very different approaches will prove most successful, or indeed whether any one approach can be completely suitable for all purposes. The nature of parallel programming is changing rapidly with the introduction of commodity desktop multiprocessor systems. Parallel processing is no longer the sole preserve of specialised high performance computer centres. It is already widely accepted for data intensive computations, it is becoming a technique of choice for high performance computer graphics work and it will become increasingly important to personal computer users. It is vital that efficient portable parallelism can be achieved for all these multifarious application areas, many of which fit the traditional functional programming strengths of very high level of abstraction, ease of programming, modularity, and reliability within a symbolic computation. At the same time, systems like SISAL and SAC show that non-symbolic numeric computations may be performed more efficiently using functional programming techniques than using traditional Fortran-based approaches. Functional programming research clearly has much to offer in terms of assessing different models of parallelism and investigating both performance and usability issues.

Several themes have run through this book. One is the tension between concurrency and parallelism. We have enjoyed many debates among authors and others about the essential meaning of our subject. In this book we have focused on using multiprocessors for enhanced performance, that is, on functional parallelism. There is a large and emerging body of work dealing with multiple processors for programming complex distributed systems, i.e. functional concurrency for reactive systems. This is typified by the commercial language Erlang, which is widely used within the telecommunications giant that is Ericsson as well as elsewhere in the commercial environment. There is also much current interest in work on distributed component-based pro-

---

[1] Department of Computing and Electronic Engineering, Heriot-Watt University, UK.
[2] School of Computer Science, St Andrews University, UK.

gramming geared at the growing market for network solutions. While this is only of peripheral interest to the main focus of the book, this area has been discussed where appropriate. It is a secondary target of systems such as Eden (Chapter 3).

A wide-ranging theme is the model of parallelism that is to be used. Implicit approaches, exemplified by dataflow languages are very attractive in terms of the promise of instant gratification at low programmer cost. In the right circumstances, it is even possible to deliver very high performance. Approaches such as ones based on the skeletons (Chapter 13) or specific models of parallelism such as BSP (Chapter 12) impose some constraints on the programmer, but accept that good parallelism in a general setting cannot be achieved without some thought on the part of the programmer. Controlled and explicit approaches take this philosophy some stages further, as do coordination languages such as Caliban (Chapter 14). The tension is between controllability and usability, and research continues in order to find optimal levels for particular purposes.

It is a matter of interest that architectural issues are not a major issue in the work presented here. In early work on parallelism, hardware issues dominated the discussion, with software results highly dependent on the parallel architecture that was used (and often obtained under extreme duress). Over the last few years, however, it has become generally accepted that a message passing interface, or, less generally accepted, a virtual shared-memory interface, can provide efficient access to a wide class of parallel architecture while enhancing the portability of parallel programs. This is the approach that has been embraced by the GUM system amongst others. Architecture independence is a key property for widespread acceptance of parallel programming and it is easily delivered by the right functional programming technology. In contrast, the distinction between strict realisations (Chapter 5) and non-strict realisations (Chapter 6) is reflected throughout the book.

Another issue that has become blurred in recent years is the distinction between control parallelism and data parallelism. It is now accepted that control parallel systems can be used to program data parallel constructs that can then be implemented using suitably efficient hardware, or to identify parts of a computation that are suitable for data parallelism. It is also accepted that data parallelism can be used for a number of less regular parallel applications, and work is proceeding to enhance the range of such applications. The distinction has become sufficiently blurred that it is, in fact, debatable whether BSP (Chapter 12) and the more recent SPMD (Chapter 18) models represent control or data parallelism, since they possess features of both, especially in nested versions. True exploitation of data parallelism on a massive scale requires a special mindset, however, as shown in Chapter 7. Such an approach can yield high dividends when suitable parallel hardware is available.

The construction of robust parallel programs in functional languages is eased by such languages' roots in formal theories. Formal properties of functional languages provide a sound general basis for program manipulation, as discussed in Chapter 4, and many other chapters draw implicitly upon them. The role of a relatively small set of higher-order functions as a source of parallelism is particularly apparent in the discussions of skeletons (Chapter 13), data parallelism (Chapter 7) and process modelling in CSP (Chapter 16). The latter chapters draw heavily on properties of *map*, *fold* and *compose* for program refinement and transformation.

Performance evaluation is a strong theme in this book. It is obviously crucially important to monitor time performance for a parallel implementation, and Chapter 11 has also stressed the need for good memory performance evaluation. Static cost modelling (Chapter 8) is attractive for predicting parallel performance and is most easily performed for functional languages. Like shape analysis for GOLDFISH (Chapter 9), it is currently most effective for regular forms of parallelism such as BSP/SPMD or skeletons using strict evaluation, and the challenge remains to extend it to less regular parallelism and non-strict evaluation. Cost modelling is complemented by dynamic performance monitoring techniques as introduced in Chapter 10. Until good automated systems can be produced that will treat parallelisation in the same way as other compilation techniques, it is necessary to at least verify that the programmers expectations with respect to parallelism have been successfully implemented, and perhaps to explore the effect of alternative parallelisations. The performance evaluation system described in Chapter 10 extends existing good systems to provide a basis for experimental research.

A problem that remains is the design and use of suitable benchmarks. This was noted in Chapter 6, where the rather trivial benchmark based on Fibonacci numbers was used in an attempt to assess parallel performance for a variety of parallel systems. This benchmark is, unfortunately, not really effective for this purpose since it is extremely (and unrealistically) fine-grained. Several better benchmark suites are, in fact, available for parallel functional programs and a number of common benchmarks have been used by a number of different systems. Examples include the Salishan benchmark suite for SISAL, the suite of implicitly parallel functional programs for Id, the NESL suite of programs, and the parallel nofib suite for GpH. Unfortunately systematic comparison of functional parallelism is hindered by a number of differences at a system level: in order to compare the effectiveness of different parallel implementations, it is necessary to eliminate factors such as architectural differences (including communications systems), differences in compiler technology (e.g. levels of sequential optimisation). It is often also necessary to adapt the benchmarks to suit different parallel languages and techniques. Finally, in order to provide a base line for performance evaluation, there should ideally be equivalent benchmarks written in a standard imperative parallel language. Tackling this is an entirely reasonable challenge that we hope the functional community will rise to in the near future.

As implementations have matured and the limitations on benchmarks have become more apparent, so attention has focused on realistic parallel applications. Chapter 19 has covered the gamut of parallel functional applications by model of parallelism. Many exciting applications have been prototyped in the fields of computer vision, database manipulation, particle physics, natural language processing, telephony, global weather prediction etc. The challenge remains in most cases to take these promising applications out of the laboratory and to find commercial sponsors for this work.

As we head into the 21st century we look forward to an exciting and vibrant research community tackling these research challenges, and others that we are still unable to predict. May we continue to live in interesting times!

References

1. M. Abadi, L. Cardelli, B. Pierce, and G. Plotkin. Dynamic Typing in a Statically Typed Language. *ACM Transactions on Programming Languages and Systems*, 13(2):237–268, 1991.
2. A. E. Abdallah. Derivation of Parallel Algorithms from Functional Specifications to CSP Processes. In B. Moller, editor, *Mathematics of Program Construction*, volume 947 of *Lecture Notes in Computer Science*, pages 67–96. Springer-Verlag, 1995.
3. A. E. Abdallah. Synthesis of Massively Pipelined Algorithms for List Manipulation. In A. M. L. Bouge, P. Fraigniaud and Y. Robert, editors, *Proceedings of the European Conference on Parallel Processing, EuroPar'96*, volume 1024 of *Lecture Notes in Computer Science*, pages 911–920. Springer-Verlag, 1996.
4. A. E. Abdallah. An Algebraic Approach for Refining Functions into CSP Processes. *(Submitted to) Formal Aspects of Computing*, 1999.
5. S. Abramsky. The Lazy Lambda Calculus. In D. A. Turner, editor, *Research Topics in Functional Programming*, pages 65–116. Addison Wesley, 1990.
6. S. Abramsky and C. Hankin. *Abstract Interpretation of Declarative Languages*. Ellis Horwood, Chichester, West Sussex, 1987.
7. P. Achten. Annotations for Load Distribution. In H. Glaser and P. Hartel, editors, *Proceedings of the Workshop on Parallel Implementation of Functional Languages, CSTR 91-07*, pages 247–264, University of Southampton, U.K., 1991.
8. G. Akerholt, K. Hammond, S. L. Peyton Jones, and P. W. Trinder. Processing Transactions on GRIP. In *PARLE'93 — Parallel Languages and Architectures Europe*, Lecture Notes in Computer Science, pages 634–647, Munich, Germany, June 14–18, 1993. Springer-Verlag.
9. A. G. Alexandrakis, A. V. Gerbessiotis, D. S. Lecomber, and C. J. Siniolakis. Bandwidth, Space and Programming: The BSP Approach. In *Proceedings of SUPEUR'96*, Krakow, May 1996.
10. M. Amamiya. Data Flow Computing and Parallel Reduction Machine. *Future Generation Computer Systems*, 4:53–67, 1988.
11. M. Amamiya and R. Hasegawa. Dataflow Computing and Eager and Lazy Evaluation. *New Generation Computing*, 2:105–129, 1984.
12. T. Amtoft, F. Nielson, and H. R. Nielson. *Type and Effect Systems: Behaviours for Concurrency*. Imperial College Press, 1999.
13. T. Amtoft, H. R. Nielson, and F. Nielson. Behaviour Analysis for Validating Communication Patterns. *Software Tools for Technology Transfer*, 2(1):13–28, 1998.
14. J. Armstrong. Erlang — a Survey of the Language and its Industrial Applications. In *INAP'96 — The 9th Exhibitions and Symposium on Industrial Applications of Prolog*, pages 16–18, Hino, Tokyo, Japan, October 1996.

15. J. Armstrong, R. Virding, C. Wikström, and M. Williams. *Concurrent Programming in Erlang, Second Edition*. Prentice-Hall, 1996.
16. Arvind and D. Culler. Dataflow Architectures. *Annual Review of Computer Science*, 1:225–254, 1986.
17. Arvind, V. Kathail, and K. K. Pingali. A Dataflow Architecture with Tagged Tokens. Technical Report LCS Memo TM-174, MIT, 1980.
18. Arvind and R. S. Nikhil. Can Dataflow Subsume von Neumann Computing? Technical Report CSG Memo 292, MIT, November 1988.
19. Arvind and R. S. Nikhil. Executing a Program on the MIT Tagged-Token Dataflow Architecture. *IEEE Transactions on Computers*, 39(3), 1990. Also: CSG Memo 271.
20. Arvind, R. S. Nikhil, and K. K. Pingali. I-structures: Data Structures for Parallel Computing. *ACM Transactions on Programming Languages and Systems*, 11(4):589–632, October 1989.
21. Arvind and R. Thomas. I-Structures : An Efficient Data Type for Functional Languages. Technical Report 178, MIT Laboratory of Computer Science, 1980.
22. C. Assmann. Coordinating Functional Processes using Petri Nets. In Kluge [339].
23. L. Augustsson. A Parallel G-Machine. Technical Report PMG53, Department of Computer Science, Chalmers University of Technology, Gteborg, SE, 1987.
24. L. Augustsson. *Compiling Lazy Functional Languages, Part II*. Phd thesis, Chalmers University of Technology, Gteborg, SE, 1987.
25. L. Augustsson and T. Johnsson. Parallel Graph Reduction with the $<\nu$, G>-Machine. In *Proceedings of the Conference on Functional Programming Languages and Computer Architecture '89, Imperial College, London*, pages 202–213, New York, NY, 1989. ACM.
26. B. Bacci, B. Cantalupo, M. Danelutto, S. Orlando, D. Pasetto, S. Pelagatti, and M. Vanneschi. An Environment for Structured Parallel Programming. In *Advances in High Performance Computing*, pages 219–234. Kluwier, 1997.
27. B. Bacci, M. Danelutto, S. Orlando, S. Pelagatti, and M. Vanneschi. P^3L: A Structured High Level Programming Language and its Structured Support. *Concurrency — Practice and Experience*, 7(3):225–255, May 1995.
28. J. Backus. Can Programming Be Liberated From the Von Neumann Style? *Commuinactions of the ACM*, 21(8):287–307, 1978.
29. D. Bailey and et. al. The NAS Parallel Benchmarks. Technical Report Report RNR-91-002 revision 2, NASA Ames Research Center, 1991.
30. P. Bailey. Algorithmic Skeletons in paraML. TRACS Research Report, Edinburgh Parallel Computing Centre, 1994.
31. P. Bailey and M. Newey. An Extension of ML for Distributed Memory Computers. In *Proceedings of 16th Australian Computer Science Conference, Brisbane, Australia*, pages 387 – 396, 1993.
32. P. Bailey and M. Newey. Implementing ML on Distributed Memory Multicomputers. *ACM SIGPLAN Notices*, 28(1):59 – 63, 1993.
33. P. Bailey, M. Newey, D. Sitsky, and R. Stanton. Supporting Coarse and Fine Grain Parallelism in an Extension of ML. In *CONPAR'94 — Conference on Algorithms and Hardware for Parallel Processing*, volume 854 of *Lecture Notes in Computer Science*, pages 693–704, Linz, Austria, September 1994. Springer-Verlag.
34. M. Bamha and G. Hains. A Self-Balancing Join Algorithm for SN Machines. In *PDCS'98 10th International Conference on Parallel and Distributed Computing Systems*, Las Vegas, 1998.

References

35. H. P. Barendregt. *The Lambda Calculus: its Syntax and Semantics*. North-Holland, 1981.
36. H. P. Barendregt, M. C. J. D. van Eekelen, P. H. Hartel, L. O. Hertzberger, M. J. Plasmeijer, and W. G. Vree. The Dutch Parallel Reduction Machine Project. *Future Generation Computer Systems*, 3(4):261–270, December 1987.
37. E. Barendsen and J. E. W. Smetsers. Extending Graph Rewriting with Copying. In *Graph Transformations in Computer Science*, volume 776 of *Lecture Notes in Computer Science*, pages 51–70, Dagstuhl, Wadern, 1993. Springer-Verlag.
38. G. H. Barnes, R. M. Brown, M. Kato, D. Kuck, D. Slotnick, and R. Stokes. The ILLIAC IV Computer. In C. G. Bell and A. Newell, editors, *Computer Structures: Readings and Examples*, chapter 27. McGraw-Hill, 1971.
39. M. Barnett, D. Payne, R. van de Geijn, and J. Watts. Broadcasting on Meshes with Wormhole Routing. *Journal of Parallel and Distributed Computing*, 35(2):111–122, 1996.
40. P. S. Barth, R. S. Nikhil, and Arvind. M-Structures: Extending a Parallel, Non-Strict, Functional Language with State. In *FPCA'91 — Conference on Functional Programming Languages and Computer Architectures*, volume 523 of *Lecture Notes in Computer Science*, pages 538–568, Harvard, MA, Aug. 1991. Springer-Verlag. Also: CSG Memo 327.
41. C. Batini and G. Battista. A Methodology for Conceptual Documentation and Maintenance. *Information Systems*, 13(3):297–318, 1988.
42. A. Bäumker and W. Dittrich. Fully Dynamic Search Trees for an Extension of the BSP Model. In *SPAA'96: ACM Symposium on Parallel Algorithms and Architectures*, pages 233–242, 1996.
43. A. Bäumker, W. Dittrich, F. Meyer auf der Heide, and I. Rieping. Realistic Parallel Algorithms: Priority Queue Operations and Selection for the BSP* Model. In *EuroPar'96*, number 1124 in Lecture Notes in Computer Science, pages 369–376, Lyon, France, Aug. 1996. Springer-Verlag.
44. H. Ben-Ari. *Principles of Concurrent and Distributed Programming*. Prentice Hall, Englewood Cliffs, 1990.
45. J. L. Bentley. Multi-Dimensional Divide-and-Conquer. *Communications of the ACM*, 23:214–229, 1980.
46. K. Berkling. Reduction Languages for Reduction Machines. In *Proceedings of the 2nd Annual Symposium on Computer Architecture*, pages 133–140. ACM/IEEE, 1975.
47. R. S. Bird. Introduction to the Theory of Lists. In M. Broy, editor, *Logic of Programming and Calculi of Discrete Design*, volume 36 of *NATO ASI Series F*, pages 3–42. Springer-Verlag, 1987.
48. R. S. Bird. Algebraic Identities for Program Calculation. *The Computer Journal*, 32(2):122–126, 1989.
49. R. S. Bird. A Calculus of Functions for Program Derivation. In D. A. Turner, editor, *Research Topics in Functional Programming*, pages 287–308. Addison Wesley, 1990.
50. R. S. Bird. Functional Algorithm Design. *Mathematics of Program Construction*, 947:2–17, 1995.
51. R. S. Bird. *Introduction to Functional Programming Using Haskell*. Prentice-Hall, 2nd edition, 1998.
52. R. S. Bird and O. de Moor. List Partitions. *Formal Aspects of Computing*, 5(1):61–78, 1993.
53. R. S. Bird and O. de Moor. *Algebra of Programming*. Prentice-Hall, 1997.
54. R. H. Bisseling. Sparse Matrix Computations on Bulk Synchronous Parallel Computers. In G. Alefeld, O. Mahrenholtz, and R. Mennicken, editors,

Proceedings ICIAM'95. Issue 1. Numerical Analysis, Scientific Computing, Computer Science, pages 127–130. Akademie Verlag, Berlin, 1996.
55. R. H. Bisseling. Basic Techniques for Numerical Linear Algebra on Bulk Synchronous Parallel Computers. In L. Vulkov, J. Waśniewski, and P. Yalamov, editors, *Proceedings First Workshop on Numerical Analysis and Applications, Rousse, Bulgaria, 1996*, volume 1196 of *Lecture Notes in Computer Science*, pages 46–57. Springer-Verlag, Berlin, 1997.
56. R. H. Bisseling and W. F. McColl. Scientific Computing on Bulk Synchronous Parallel Architectures. In B. Pehrson and I. Simon, editors, *Technology and Foundations: Information Processing '94, Vol. I*, volume 51 of *IFIP Transactions A*, pages 509–514. Elsevier Science Publishers, Amsterdam, 1994.
57. D. Bitton, D. DeWitt, and C. Turbyfill. Benchmarking Database Systems: A Systematic Approach. In *Very Large Database Conference*, 1983.
58. G. E. Blelloch. Scans as Primitive Parallel Operations. *IEEE Transaction on Computers*, 38(11):1526–1538, 1989.
59. G. E. Blelloch. *Vector Models for Data-Parallel Computing*. MIT Press, 1990.
60. G. E. Blelloch. Programming Parallel Algorithms. *Communications of the ACM March 1996*, 39(3):85–97, 1996.
61. G. E. Blelloch, S. Chatterje, J. Hardwick, J. Sipelstein, and M. Zagha. Implementation of a Portable Nested Data–Parallel Language. *Journal of Parallel and Distributed Computing*, 21(1):4 – 14, 1994.
62. G. E. Blelloch and J. Hardwick. A Library of Parallel Algorithms. Web Page, February 1999.
http://www.cs.cmu.edu/~scandal/nesl/algorithms.html.
63. G. E. Blelloch, G. L. Miller, and D. Talmor. Developing a Practical Projection-Based Parallel Delaunay Algorithm. In *12th Annual Symposium on Computational Geometry*. ACM, May 1996.
64. G. E. Blelloch and G. Narlikar. A Practical Comparison of N-Body Algorithms. In *Parallel Algorithms*, volume 30 of *Series in Discrete Mathematics and Theoretical Computer Science*. American Mathematical Society, 1997.
65. G. E. Blelloch and G. Sabot. Compiling Collection-Oriented Languages onto Massively-Parallel Computers. *Journal of Parallel and Distributed Computing*, pages 119–134, 1990.
66. C. Bodei, P. Degano, F. Nielson, and H. R. Nielson. Control Flow Analysis for the π-Calculus. In *Proceedings of CONCUR'98*, number 1466 in Lecture Notes in Computer Science, pages 84–98. Springer-Verlag, 1998.
67. C. Bodei, P. Degano, F. Nielson, and H. R. Nielson. Static Analysis of Processes for No Read-Up No Write-Down. In *Proceedings of FOSSACS'99*, number 1578 in Lecture Notes in Computer Science, pages 120–134. Springer-Verlag, 1999.
68. C. Boeres, V. E. F. Rebello, and D. B. Skillicorn. Static Scheduling Using Task Replication for LogP and BSP Models. In *EuroPar'98*, volume 1470 of *Lecture Notes in Computer Science*, pages 698–708. Springer-Verlag, September 1998.
69. A. P. W. Böhm and R. E. Hiromoto. Dataflow Time and Space Complexity of FFTs. *Journal of Parallel and Distributed Computing*, 18, 1993.
70. A. P. W. Böhm and R. E. Hiromoto. The Dataflow Complexity of Fast Fourier Transforms. In L. Bic, G. R. Gao, and J. L. Gaudiot, editors, *Advanced Topics in Dataflow Computing and Multithreading*. IEEE CS Press, 1995.
71. A. P. W. Böhm and R. E. Hiromoto. Functional Implementations of the Jacobi Eigen-Solver. *Journal of Scientific Programming*, 5:111–120, 1996.
72. A. P. W. Böhm and J. Sargeant. Code Optimisation for Tagged Token Dataflow Machines. *IEEE Transactions on Computers*, 38(1):4–14, January 1989.

References

73. O. Bonorden, B. Juulink, I. von Otto, and I. Rieping. The Paderborn University BSP (PUB) Library—Design, Implementation and Performance. In *13th International Parallel Processing Symposium & 10th Symposium on Parallel and Distributed Processing*, April 1999.
74. G. H. Botorog. *High-Level Parallel Programming and the Efficient Implementation of Numerical Algorithms*. PhD thesis, RWTH-Aachen, Jan. 1998. Also: Technical Report 97-15.
75. G. H. Botorog and H. Kuchen. Algorithmic Skeletons for Adaptive Multigrid Methods. In *Irregular '95*, volume 980 of *Lecture Notes in Computer Science*, pages 27–41, 1995.
76. G. H. Botorog and H. Kuchen. Efficient Parallel Programming with Algorithmic Skeletons. In L. Bouge, P. Fraigniaud, A. Mignotte, and Y. Robert, editors, *Proceedings of EuroPar '96*, volume 1123 of *Lecture Notes in Computer Science*, pages 718–731. Springer-Verlag, 1996.
77. G. H. Botorog and H. Kuchen. Skil: An Imperative Language with Algorithmic Skeletons for Efficient Distributed Programming. In *HPDC'96 — International Symposium on High Performance Distributed Computing*, pages 243–252. IEEE Computer Society Press, 1996.
78. G. H. Botorog and H. Kuchen. Efficient High-Level Parallel Programming. *Theoretical Computer Science*, 196:71–107, 1998.
79. D. Boucher and M. Feeley. Construction Parallèle de l'Automate LR(0): Une Application de MultiLisp à la Compilation. In *6ième Rencontres Francophones du Parallélisme*. Département d'Informatique et R.O., Université de Montréal, June 1994.
80. L. Bougé. The Data-Parallel Programming Model: A Semantic Perspective. In *The Data-Parallel Programming Model*, volume 1132 of *Lecture Notes in Computer Science*, pages 4–26. Springer-Verlag, June 1996.
81. T. A. Bratvold. Parallelising a Functional Program Using a List-Homomorphism Skeleton. In H. Hong, editor, *PASCO'94: First International Symposium on Parallel Symbolic Computation*, pages 44–53. World Scientific Publishing Company, Sept. 1994.
82. T. A. Bratvold. *Skeleton-Based Parallelisation of Functional Programs*. PhD thesis, Department of Computing and Electrical Engineering, Heriot-Watt University, Edinburgh, November 1994.
83. S. Breitinger, U. Klusik, and R. Loogen. From (sequential) Haskell to (parallel) Eden: An Implementation Point of View. In *International Symposium on Programming Languages: Implementations, Logics, Programs (PLILP)*, volume 1490 of *Lecture Notes in Computer Science*. Springer-Verlag, 1998.
84. S. Breitinger, U. Klusik, R. Loogen, Y. Ortega-Mallen, and R. Pena. DREAM: The Distributed Eden Abstract Machine. In Clack et al. [127], pages 250–269.
85. S. Breitinger, R. Loogen, Y. Ortega-Mallén, and R. Peña. Eden — Language Definition and Operational Semantics. Technical Report 10, Philipps-Universitat Marburg, 1996.
86. S. Breitinger, R. Loogen, Y. Ortega-Mallén, and R. Peña. The Eden Coordination Model for Distributed Memory Systems. In *High-Level Parallel Programming Models and Supportive Environments (HIPS)*, volume 1123 of *Lecture Notes in Computer Science*. IEEE Press, 1997.
87. R. Brent. The Parallel Evaluation of General Arithmetic Expressions. *Journal of the ACM*, 21, No.2:201–206, April 1974.
88. J. F. Briesmeister. MCNP–A General Monte Carlo N-Particle Transport Code, Version 4A. Technical Report Report LA-12625-M, Los Alamos National Laboratory, 1993.
89. P. Brinch-Hansen. *Studies in Computational Science*. Prentice-Hall, 1995.

90. P. Brinch-Hansen. *The Search for Simplicity*. IEEE Computer Press, 1996.
91. S. D. Brookes, C. A. R. Hoare, and A. W. Roscoe. A Theory of Communicating Sequential Processes. *Journal of the ACM*, 31(3):560–599, 1984.
92. R. Bru and J. Marin. BSP Cost of the Preconditioned Conjugate Gradient Method. In *Proceedings of the VII Jornadas de Paralelismo*, Santiago de Compostela, Spain, September 1996. Universidad de Santiago de Compostela.
93. T. Brus, M. C. J. D. van Eekelen, M. O. van Leer, and M. J. Plasmeijer. Clean: A Language for Functional Graph Rewriting. In *Third International Conference on Functional Programming Languages and Computer Architecture*, volume 274 of *Lecture Notes in Computer Science*, pages 364–384, Portland, Oregon, USA, 1987. Springer-Verlag.
94. T. Buelck, A. Held, W. Kluge, S. Pantke, C. Rathsack, S.-B. Scholz, and R. Schroeder. Experience with the Implementation of a Concurrent Graph Reduction System on an nCUBE/2 Platform. In *Joint International Conference on Parallel and Vector Processing*, volume 854 of *Lecture Notes in Computer Science*. Springer-Verlag, 1994.
95. W. Burge. *Recursive Programming Techniques*. Addison-Wesley, Reading, MA, 1975.
96. D. A. Burgess, P. I. Crumpton, and M. B. Giles. A Parallel Framework for Unstructured Grid Solvers. In S. Wagner, E. Hirschel, J. Périaux, and R. Piva, editors, *Computational Fluid Dynamics '94. Proceedings of the Second European Computational Fluid Dynamics Conference 5-8 September 1994 Stuttgart, Germany*, pages 391–396. John Wiley & Sons, 1994.
97. D. A. Burgess and M. B. Giles. Renumbering Unstructured Grids to Improve the Performance of Codes on Hierarchical Memory Machines. Technical Report 95/06, Numerical Analysis Group, Oxford University Computing Laboratory, Oxford OX1 3QD, England, May 1995.
98. G. Burn. Evaluation Transformers - A Model for the Parallel Evaluation of Functional Languages. In G. Kahn, editor, *Functional Programming Languages and Computer Architecture*, pages 446–470. Springer-Verlag, Berlin, DE, 1987.
99. G. Burn. A Shared Memory Parallel G-machine Based on the Evaluation Transformer Model of Computation. In T. Johnsson et al., editors, *Aspens Workshop on Implementation of Functional Languages*, pages 301–330. Programming Methodology Group, University of Gteborg and Chalmers University of Technology, 1988.
100. G. Burn. The Evaluation Transformer Model of Reduction and its Correctness. In *TAPSOFT '91*, pages 458–482. Springer-Verlag, New York, NY, 91.
101. G. Burn, C. L. Hankin, and S. Abramsky. Strictness Analysis of Higher Order Functions. *Science of Computer Programming*, 7, 1985.
102. G. Burn, S. L. Peyton Jones, and J. Robson. The Spineless G-machine. In *Proceedings of the 1988 ACM Conference on LISP and Functional Programming, Snowbird, UT*, pages 244–258, New York, NY, 1988. ACM.
103. R. M. Burstall and J. Darlington. A Transformation System for Developing Recursive Programs. *Journal of the ACM*, 24(1):44–67, 1977.
104. F. W. Burton. Functional Programming for Concurrent and Distributed Computing. *Computer Journal*, 30(5):437–450, 1987.
105. F. W. Burton and M. R. Sleep. Executing Functional Programs on a Virtual Tree of Processors. In *Proceedings of the ACM Conference on Functional Programming Languages and Computer Architecture, Portsmouth, NH*, pages 187–194, New York, 1981. ACM.
106. R. Butler and E. Lusk. Users's Guide to the p4 Parallel Programming System. Technical Report ANL-92/17, Mathematics and Computer Science Division,

Argonne National Laboratory, Oct 92.
107. C. J. Caeser. *Commentarii de Bello Gallico*. Rome, 46 BC. http://harvest.ablah.twsu.edu/caesar/gallic/.
108. E. Caceres, F. Dehne, A. Ferreira, P. Flocchini, I. Rieping, A. Roncato, N. Santoro, and S. W. Song. Efficient Parallel Graph Algorithms for Coarse Grained Multicomputers and BSP. In *24th International Colloquium on Automata, Languages and Programming (ICALP'97)*, volume 1256 of *Lecture Notes in Computer Science*, pages 390–400, Bologna, Italy, 1997. Springer-Verlag.
109. R. Calinescu. Bulk Synchronous Parallel Algorithms for Conservative Discrete Event Simulation. *Parallel Algorithms and Applications*, 9:15–38, 1996. A preliminary version of this paper appeared as Technical Report PRG-TR-16-95, Programming Research Group, Oxford University Computing Laboratory, April 1995.
110. R. Calinescu. A BSP Approach to the Scheduling of Tightly-Nested Loops. In *nternational Parallel Processing Symposium (IPPS'97)*, pages 549–553, Geneva, Switzerland,, April 1997. IEEE Computer Society Press.
111. R. Calinescu and D. Evans. Bulk-Synchronous Parallel Algorithms for QR and QZ Matrix Factorisation. *Parallel Algorithms and Applications*, 11:97–112, 1997.
112. D. K. G. Campbell. Towards the Classification of Algorithmic Skeletons. Technical Report YCS 276, Department of Computer Science, University of York, 1996.
113. D. Cann. Compilation Techniques for High Performance Applicative Computation. Technical Report CS-89-108, Lawrence Livermore National Laboratory, LLNL, Livermore, California, 1989.
114. D. Cann. Retire Fortran? A Debate Rekindled. *Communications of the ACM*, 35(8):81–89, August 1992.
115. D. Cann and P. Evripidou. Advanced Array Optimizations for High Performance Functional Languages. *IEEE Transactions on Parallel and Distributed Systems*, 6(3):229–239, 1995.
116. L. Cardelli. ML Under UNIX. *Polymorphism: The ML/LCF/Hope Newsletter*, I(3), December 1983.
117. L. Cardelli and D. McQueen. The Functional Abstract Machine. *The ML/LCF/HOPE Newsletter, AT&T, Bell Labs, Murray Hill, NJ*, 1983.
118. M. Castan, G. Durrieu, B. Lecussan, M. Lematre, A. Contessa, E. Cousin, and P. Ng. Toward the Design of a Parallel Graph Reduction Machine: The MaRS Project. In J. Fasel and R. Keller, editors, *Graph Reduction: Proceedings of a Workshop at Santa Fe, New Mexico*, pages 160–180, New York, NY, 1987. Springer-Verlag. Lecture Notes in Computer Science 279.
119. M. M. Chakravarty. Integrating Multithreading into the Spineless Tagless G-machine. In D. N. Turner, editor, *Glasgow Workshop on Functional Programming*, Workshops in Computing. Springer-Verlag, 1995.
120. N. Charles. *New Tools for Parallelism in Lazy Functional Programs*. D.Phil Thesis, Department of Computer Science, University of York, 1999. Forthcoming.
121. N. Charles and C. Runciman. An interactive approach to profiling parallel functional programs. In Hammond et al. [245], pages 20–37.
122. J. Chattratichat, J. Darlington, M. Ghanem, Y. Guo, H. Hüning, M. Köhler, J. Sutiwaraphun, H. W. To, and D. Yang. Large Scale Data Mining: The Challenges and The Solutions. In *KDD97 — International Conference on Knowledge Discovery and Data Mining*. AAAI Press, August 1997.
123. I. Checkland. *Speculative Concurrent Evaluation in a Lazy Functional Language*. PhD thesis, Department of Computer Science, University of York,

1994.

124. I. Chern and I. Foster. Design and Parallel Implementation of Two Methods for Solving PDEs on the Sphere. In *Conference on Parallel Computational Fluid Dynamics*, pages 83–96, Stuttgart, Germany, 1991. Elsevier Science Publishers.
125. A. Church. *The Calculi of Lambda Conversion*. Princeton University Press, 1941.
126. CIP Language Group. *The Munich Project CIP*, volume 1 of *Lecture Notes in Computer Science*. Springer-Verlag, 1984.
127. In C. Clack, K. Hammond, and T. Davie, editors, *Proceedings of 9th International Workshop on the Implementation of Functional Languages*, volume 1467 of *Lecture Notes in Computer Science*. Springer-Verlag, 1997.
128. C. Clack. GRIP Status Update — 1989. In T. Fountain and M. Shute, editors, *Multiprocessor Computer Architecture*, pages 119–120. North Holland, Amsterdam, 1990.
129. C. Clack. The Implementation of Sum and Product Domain Constructors for the Four-Stroke Reduction Engine. Research Note RN/92/54, Department of Computer Science, University College London, London, UK, 1992.
130. C. Clack. GRIP: the GRIP Multiprocessor. In T. Fountain, editor, *Parallel Computing Principles and Practice*, pages 266–275. Cambridge University Press, 1994.
131. C. Clack. The DIGRESS Project: Final Report. Internal technical report, Athena Systems Design Ltd., London, UK, 1994.
132. C. Clack, S. Clayman, and D. Parrott. Lexical Profiling — Theory and Practice. *Journal of Functional Programming*, 5(2):225–277, 1995.
133. C. Clack and S. Courtenage. An Overview of the UCL DIGRESS Project. Research Note RN/92/55, Department of Computer Science, University College London, London, UK, 1992.
134. C. Clack and S. L. Peyton Jones. Strictness Analysis - A Practical Approach. In J.-P. Jouannaud, editor, *Functional Programming Languages and Computer Architecture*, pages 35–49. Springer-Verlag, Berlin, DE, 1985.
135. C. Clack and S. L. Peyton Jones. The Four-Stroke Reduction Engine. In *Proceedings ACM Conference on Lisp and Functional Programming*, pages 220–232. ACM, 1986.
136. C. Clack, S. L. Peyton Jones, and J. Salkild. Efficient Parallel Graph Reduction on GRIP. Research Note RN/88/29, Department of Computer Science, University College London, London, UK, 1988.
137. T. Clarke, P. Gladstone, C. MacLean, and A. Norman. SKIM - The S,K,I Reduction Machine. In *Conference Record of the 1980 LISP Conference, Stanford University*, 1980.
138. M. I. Cole. *Algorithmic Skeletons: A Structured Approach to the Management of Parallel Computation*. Phd thesis, University of Edinburgh, Computer Science Department, 1988.
139. M. I. Cole. *Algorithmic Skeletons: Structured Management of Parallel Computation*. Research Monographs in Parallel and Distributed Computing. Pitman, 1989.
140. E. Cooper and J. Morrisett. Adding Threads to Standard ML. Technical Report CMU–CS–90–186, School of Computer Science, Carnegie–Mellon University, Pittsburgh, PA 15213, 1990.
141. C. Corral, I. Gimenez, J. Marin, and J. Mas. An M-Step Block Diagonal Multisplitting Preconditioned Conjugate Gradient Method. In *EAMA-97 (International Meeting on Matrix Analysis and Applications)*, September 1997.

References

142. G. Cousineau, P. Curien, and M. Mauny. The Categorial Abstract Machine. *Science of Computer Programming*, 8:173–202, 1987.
143. G. Cousineau and M. Mauny. *The Functional Approach to Programming*. Cambridge University Press, 1998.
144. P. Cousot. Methods and Logics for Proving Programs. In J. van Leeuwen, editor, *Handbook of Theoretical Computer Science, Volume B: Formal Models and Semantics*, pages 814–993. MIT Press/Elsevier, 1990.
145. S. Cox, S.-Y. Huang, P. H. J. Kelly, J. Liu, and F. Taylor. An Implementation of Static Functional Process Networks. In D. Etiemble and J.-C. Syre, editors, *PARLE '92: Proceedings of the 4th International Conference on Parallel Architectures and Languages Europe, Paris*, pages 497–514, Berlin, DE, 1992. Springer-Verlag.
146. M. D. Cripps, J. Darlington, A. J. Field, P. G. Harrison, and M. J. Reeve. The Design and Implementation of ALICE: A Parallel Graph Reduction Machine. In *Proceedings of the Workshop on Graph Reduction*, New York, NY, 1987. Springer-Verlag.
147. P. I. Crumpton and M. B. Giles. Multigrid Aircraft Computations Using the OPlus Parallel Library. In *Parallel Computational Fluid Dynamics: Implementation and Results Using Parallel Computers. Proceedings Parallel CFD'95*, pages 339–346, Pasadena, CA, USA, June 1995. Elsevier/North-Holland.
148. D. Culler. *Managing Parallelism and Resources in Scientific Dataflow Programs*. PhD thesis, Laboratory for Computer Science, M.I.T., June 1989.
149. D. Culler and Arvind. Resource Requirements of Dataflow Programs. In *15th. Annual ACM Symposium on Computer Architecture*, 1988.
150. D. Culler, S. Goldstein, K. Schauser, and T. von Eicken. TAM — A Compiler Controlled Threaded Abstract Machine. *Journal of Parallel and Distributed Computing*, 18:347–370, June 1993.
151. D. E. Culler and J. P. Singh. *Parallel Computer Architecture*. Pitman/MIT Press, 1989.
152. P. L. Curien. *Categorical Combinators, Sequential Algorithms and Functional Programming*. Research Notes in Theoretical Computer Science. Wiley, 1986.
153. H. Curry, W. Craig, and R. Feys. *Combinatory Logic, Volume 1*. North-Holland, Amsterdam, NL, 1958.
154. O. Danvy, R. Glück, and P. Thiemann, editors. *Partial Evaluation*, volume 1110 of *Lecture Notes in Computer Science*. Springer-Verlag, 1996.
155. J. Darlington. A Synthesis of Several Sorting Algorithms. *Acta Informatica*, 11(1), 1978.
156. J. Darlington, A. J. Field, P. G. Harrison, P. H. J. Kelly, D. W. N. Sharp, and Q. Wu. Parallel Programming Using Skeleton Functions. In A. Bode, M. Reeve, and G. Wolf, editors, *Proceedings of PARLE '93*, pages 146–160, 1993.
157. J. Darlington, M. Ghanem, Y. Guo, and H. W. To. Guided Resource Organisation in Heterogeneous Parallel Computing. *Journal of High Performance Computing*, 4(1):13–23, Dec. 1997.
158. J. Darlington, M. Ghanem, and H. To. Structured Parallel Programming. In *Massively Parallel Programming Models Conference*, pages 160–169, Berlin, Sept 1993. IEEE Computer Society Press.
159. J. Darlington, Y. Guo, H. To, and J. Yang. Parallel Skeletons for Structured Composition. In *Proceedings of ACM SIGPLAN Symposium on Principles and Practice of Parallel Programming*, pages 19–28. ACM Press, 1995.
160. J. Darlington, Y. Guo, H. W. To, Q. Wu, J. Yang, and M. Kohler. Fortran-S: A Uniform Functional Interface to Parallel Imperative Languages. In *Proceedings of the Third Parallel Computing Workshop*, Fujitsu Laboratories Ltd,

Kawasaki Japan, 1994.
161. J. Darlington, Y. Guo, H. W. To, and J. Yang. SPF: Structured Parallel Fortran. In *PCW'96 — International Parallel Computing Workshop*, Kawasaki, Japan, November 1996.
162. J. Darlington, Y. K. Guo, H. W. To, and J. Yang. Functional Skeletons for Parallel Coordination. In *EuroPar'95 — European Conference on Parallel Processing*, volume 966 of *Lecture Notes in Computer Science*, pages 55–69, Stockholm, Sweden, August 29–31, Aug. 1995. Springer-Verlag.
163. J. Darlington and M. Reeve. ALICE - A Multi-Processor Reduction Machine for the Parallel Evaluation of Applicative Languages. In *Proceedings of the ACM Conference on Functional Languages and Computer Architecture, Portsmouth, NH*, pages 65–76, 1981.
164. J. Darlington and H. W. To. Building Parallel Applications Without Programming. In *Abstract Machine Models*, Leeds, 1993.
165. J. Darlington and H. W. To. Supporting Irregular Applications in SPF. In *PCW'97 — International Parallel Computing Workshop*, Canberra, Australia, September 1997.
166. D. Das and D. Batory. Prairie: A Rule Specification Framework for Query Optimizers. In *International Conference on Database Engineering*, pages 201–210. IEEE, 1995.
167. A. Davie and D. McNally. CASE - A Lazy Version of an SECD Machine with a Flat Environment. In *Proceedings of the IEEE TENCON '89, Bombay*, New York, NY, 1989. IEEE.
168. J. R. Davy, H. Deldarie, and P. M. Dew. *Constructive Solid Geometry Using Algorithmic Skeletons*. Research Report 96.1, School of Computer Studies, University of Leeds, 1996.
169. N. G. de Bruijn. Lambda–Calculus Notation with Nameless Dummies. A Tool for Automatic Formula Manipulation with Application to the Church–Rosser Theorem. *Indagationes Mathematicae*, 34:484–492, 1972.
170. J. B. Dennis. First Version of a Data-Flow Procedure Language. In B. Robinet, editor, *Proceedings of the Colloque sur la Programmation*, volume 19 of *Lecture Notes in Computer Science*, pages 362–376, Berlin, DE, 1974. Springler-Verlag.
171. J. B. Dennis. Dataflow Computation. In M. Broy, editor, *Control Flow and Data Flow: Concepts of Distributed Programming*, volume 14 of *NATO ASI Series, Series F: Computer and System Sciences*, pages 346–398. Springer-Verlag, 1984.
172. F. Desprez, S. Domas, J. J. Dongarra, A. Petitet, C. Randriamaro, and Y. Robert. More on Scheduling Block-Cyclic Array Redistribution. In *Proceedings of 4th Workshop on Languages, Compilers, and Run-time Systems for Scalable Computers (LCR98)*, volume 1511 of *Lecture Notes in Computer Science*, pages 275–287, Pittsburgh, PA, 1998. Springer-Verlag.
173. D. Deutch. Quantum theory, the Church-Turing Principle and the Universal Quantum Computer. *Proceedings of the Royal Society (London)*, A400:97–117, 1985.
174. I. Dimov, A. Karaivanova, H. Kuchen, and H. Stoltze. Monte Carlo Algorithms for Elliptic Differential Equations — a Data Parallel Functional Approach. *Journal of Parallel Algorithms and Applications*, 9:39–65, 1996.
175. S. R. Donaldson, J. M. D. Hill, and D. B. Skillicorn. BSP Clusters: High Performance, Reliable and Very Low Cost. Technical Report PRG-TR-5-98, Programming Research Group, Oxford University Computing Laboratory, September 1998.
176. S. R. Donaldson, J. M. D. Hill, and D. B. Skillicorn. Predictable Communication on Unpredictable Networks: Implementing BSP over TCP/IP. In

EuroPar'98, Lecture Notes in Computer Science, Southampton, UK, September 1998. Springer-Verlag.
177. S. R. Donaldson, J. M. D. Hill, and D. B. Skillicorn. Communication Performance Optimisation Requires Minimising Variance. *Journal of Future Generation Computer Systems*, April 1999.
178. S. R. Donaldson, J. M. D. Hill, and D. B. Skillicorn. Exploiting Global Structure for Performance on Clusters. In *IPPS/SPDP*, San Juan, Puerto Rico, April 1999. Springer-Verlag.
179. S. R. Donaldson, J. M. D. Hill, and D. B. Skillicorn. Performance Results for a Reliable Low-latency Cluster Communication Protocol. In *PC-NOW '99: International Workshop on Personal Computer based Networks Of Workstations, held in conjunction with IPPS'99*, San Juan, Puerto Rico, April 1999. Springer-Verlag.
180. J. J. Dongarra and D. C. Sorensen. A Fully Parallel Algorithm for the Symmetric Eigenvalue Problem. *SIAM Journal of Scientific and Statistical Computation*, 8:139–154, March 1987.
181. M. C. Dracopoulos, C. Glasgow, K. Parrott, and J. Simkin. Bulk Synchronous Parallelisation of Industrial Electromagnetic Software. *International Journal of Supercomputer Application of High Performance Computing*, 1996.
182. R. Dybvig. *The SCHEME Programming Language*. Prentice-Hall, Englewood Cliffs, NJ, 1987.
183. G. Egan. Implementing the Kernel of the Australian Weather Prediction Model in Sisal. In *Sisal'93 — Sisal Users Conference*, number CONF 9310206 in LLNL Report, pages 11–17, San Diego, CA, Oct. 1993.
184. J. Eisenbiegler, W. Löwe, and W. Zimmermann. BSP, LogP, and Oblivious Programs. In *EuroPar'98*, volume 1470 of *Lecture Notes in Computer Science*, pages 865–874. Springer-Verlag, September 1998.
185. H. El-Rewini and T. Lewis. Scheduling Parallel Programming Tasks onto Arbitrary Target Machines. *Journal of Parallel and Distributed Computing*, 9:138–153, 1989.
186. R. Elmasri and S. B. Navathe, editors. *Fundamentals of Database Systems*. Benjamin/Cummings, second edition, 1994.
187. R. Elmasri and S. B. Navathe. SQL: A relational database language. In *Fundamentals of Database Systems* [186], chapter 7.4, pages 215–219.
188. J. Fairbairn and S. Wray. Code Generation Techniques for Functional Languages. In *Proceedings of the 1986 ACM Conference on LISP and Functional Programming*, pages 94–104, New York, NY, 1986. ACM. Held at MIT, Cambridge, MA.
189. J. Fairbairn and S. Wray. TIM : A Simple Lazy Abstract Machine to Execute Supercombinators. In G. Kahn, editor, *Proceedings of Conference on Functional Programming and Computer Architecture*, volume 274 of *Lecture Notes in Computer Science*, pages 34–45. Springer-Verlag, 1987.
190. W. Farmer, J. Ramsdell, and R. Watro. A Correctness Proof for Combinator Reduction with Cycles. *ACM Transactions on Programming Languages and Systems*, 12(1):123–134, 1990.
191. M. Feeley, M. Turcotte, and G. LaPalme. Using MultiLisp for Solving Constraint Satisfaction Problems: an Application to Nucleic Acid 3D Structure Determination. *Lisp and Symbolic Computation*, 7:231–247, 1994.
192. M. Felleissen. On the Expressive Power of Programming Languages. *Science of Computer Programming*, 17:35–75, 1991.
193. J. Feo, P. Miller, S. Skedzielewski, S. Denton, and C. Solomon. Sisal 90. In A. P. W. Böhm and J. T. Feo, editors, *High Performance Functional Computing*, pages 35–47, Apr. 1995.

194. A. J. Field and P. G. Harrison. *Functional Programming.* Addison-Wesley, 1988.
195. R. A. Finkel. Large Grain Parallelism - Three Case Studies. In L. Jamieson, D. Gannon, and R. Douglass, editors, *Characteristics of Parallel Algorithms*, pages 21–64, 1987.
196. FISh web-site.
   http://www-staff.socs.uts.edu.au/~cbj/FISh.
197. C. Foisy and E. Chailloux. Caml Flight: A Portable SPMD Extension of ML for Distributed Memory Multiprocessors. In A. P. W. Böhm and J. T. Feo, editors, *High Performance Functional Computing*, pages 83–96, April 1995.
198. S. Fortune and J. Wyllie. Parallelism in Random Access Machines. In *Proceedings of the 10th Annual ACM Symposium on Theory of Computing*, pages 114–118, 1978.
199. C. C. Foster. *Content Addressable Parallel Processors.* Van Nostrand Reinhold Co., New York, 1976.
200. I. Foster. Compositional Parallel Programming Languages. *ACM Transactions on Programming Languages and Systems*, 18(4):454–476, 1996.
201. I. Foster, R. Olson, and S. Tuecke. Productive Parallel Programming: The PCN Approach. *Journal of Scientific Programming*, 1(1):51–66, 1992.
202. I. Foster and S. Taylor. *Strand: New Concepts in Parallel Programming.* Prentice-Hall, 1989.
203. W. D. Frazer and A. C. McKellar. Samplesort: A Sampling Approach to Minimal Storage Tree Sorting. *Journal of the ACM*, 17(3):496–507, 1970.
204. D. P. Freidman and D. S. Wise. CONS Should Not Evaluate its Arguments. In S. Michaelson and R. Milner, editors, *Automata, Languages and Programming: 3rd International Colloquium.* Edinburgh University Press, 1976.
205. M. Frigo. A Fast Fourier Transform Compiler. In *PLDI'99 — Conference on Programming Language Design and Implementation*, Atlanta, GA, May 1999. SCM SIGPLAN. To appear.
206. M. Frigo and S. Johnson. The Fastest Fourier Transform in the West. Technical Report MIT-LCS-TR-728, MIT Laboratory for Computer Science, September 1997.
207. D. Gaertner and W. Kluge. π-RED$^+$ – An Interactive Compiling Graph Reduction System for an Applied λ-Calculus. *Journal of Functional Programming*, 6(5):723–757, 1996.
208. E. R. Gansner and J. H. Reppy. A Multithreaded Higher-Order User Interface Toolkit. In *User Interface Software*, volume 1 of *Software Trends*, pages 61–80. John Wiley & Sons, 1993.
209. A. Geerling. Program Transformations and Skeletons: Formal Derivation of Parallel Programs. In N. Mirenkov, editor, *pAs'95 Parallel Algorithm/Architecture Synthesis*, pages 250–256. IEEE Computer Society Press, 1995.
210. N. Gehani. Broadcasting Sequential Processes (BSP). *IEEE Transactions on Software Engineering*, 10(4), July 1984.
211. T. Gehrke and M. Huhn. ProFun - A Language for Executable Specifications. In *PLILP*, volume 1140 of *Lecture Notes in Computer Science*, pages 304 – 318. Springer-Verlag, 1996.
212. G. A. Geist, A. Beguelin, J. J. Dongarra, W. Jiang, R. Menchek, and V. Sunderam. *PVM: Parallel Virtual Machine. A Users' Guide and Tutorial for Networked Parallel Computing.* MIT press, 1994.
213. G. A. Geist, J. A. Kohla, and P. M. Papadopoulos. PVM and MPI: A Comparison of Features. *Calculateurs Paralleles*, 8(2):137–150, 1996.

References

214. D. Gelernter and N. Carriero. Coordination Languages and Their Significance. *Communications of the ACM*, 32(2):97–107, February 1992.
215. W. Gentleman. Some Complexity Results for Matrix Computations on Parallel Processors. *Journal of the ACM*, 25:112–115, 1978.
216. A. V. Gerbessiotis and C. Siniolakis. Selection on the Bulk-Synchronous Parallel Model with Applications to Priority Queues. In *Proceedings of the 1996 International Conference on Parallel and Distributed Processing Techniques and Applications*, August 1996.
217. A. V. Gerbessiotis and C. J. Siniolakis. Deterministic Sorting and Randomized Median Finding on the BSP Model. In *Proceedings of the 8th ACM Symposium on Parallel Algorithms and Archictures*, Padova, Italy, June 1996. ACM Press.
218. A. V. Gerbessiotis and C. J. Siniolakis. Primitive Operations on the BSP Model. Technical Report PRG-TR-23-96, Oxford Unversity Computing Laboratory, October 1996.
219. A. V. Gerbessiotis and C. J. Siniolakis. An Experimental Study of BSP Sorting Algorithms: Theory, Practice and Experience. Technical Report PRG-TR-06-97, Oxford Unversity Computing Laboratory, February 1997.
220. A. V. Gerbessiotis, C. J. Siniolakis, and A. Tiskin. Parallel Priority Queue and List Contraction: The BSP approach. In *Europar'97*, Lecture Notes in Computer Science, pages 409–416, Passau, Germany, 1997. Springer-Verlag.
221. A. V. Gerbessiotis and L. G. Valiant. Direct Bulk-Synchronous Parallel Algorithms. *Journal of Parallel and Distributed Computing*, 22(2):251–267, Aug. 1994.
222. A. Giacolone, P. Mishra, and S. Prasad. Facile: A Symmetric Integration of Concurrent and Functional Programming. *International Journal of Parallel Programming*, 18(2), 1989.
223. D. Ginhac, J. Sérot, and J. Dérutin. Fast Prototyping of Image Processing Applications Using functional Skeletons on MIMD-DM Architecture. In *IAPR Workshop on Machine Vision Applications*, Chiba, Japan, Nov. 1998.
224. B. Goldberg. *Multiprocessor Execution of Functional Programs*. Phd thesis, Yale University, Department of Computer Science, New Haven, CT, 1988.
225. R. G. Goldsmith, D. L. McBurney, and M. R. Sleep. Parallel Execution of Concurrent Clean on ZAPP. In M. R. Sleep, M. J. Plasmeijer, and M. C. J. van Eekelen, editors, *Term Graph Rewriting: Theory and Practice*, pages 283–302. Wiley, Toronto, 1993.
226. A. J. Gordon. *Functional Programming and Input/Output*. British Computer Society Distinguished Dissertations in Computer Science. Cambridge University Press, 1994.
227. S. Gorlatch. From Transformations to Methodology in Parallel Program Development: A Case Study. *Microprocessing and Microprogramming*, 41:571–588, 1996.
228. S. Gorlatch. Systematic Efficient Parallelization of Scan and Other List Homomorphisms. In L. Bouge, P. Fraigniaud, A. Mignotte, and Y. Robert, editors, *Proceedings of the European Conference on Parallel Processing, Euro-Par'96*, volume 1124 of *Lecture Notes in Computer Science*, pages 401–408. Springer-Verlag, 1996.
229. S. Gorlatch. Abstraction and Performance in the Design of Parallel Programs. Technical Report MIP-9803, Universitat Passau, January 1998.
230. S. Gorlatch. Programming with Divide-and-Conquer Skeletons: An Application to FFT. *Journal of Supercomputing*, 12(1–2):85–97, 1998.
231. S. Gorlatch and H. Bischof. A Generic MPI Implementation for a Data-Parallel Skeleton: Formal Derivation and Application to FFT. *Parallel Processing Letters*, 1998.

232. S. Gorlatch and C. Lengauer. Parallelization of Divide-and-Conquer in the Bird-Meertens Formalism. *Formal Aspects of Computing*, 7(6):663–682, 1995.
233. S. Gorlatch and C. Lengauer. (De)Composition Rules for Parallel Scan and Reduction. In *Proceedings of 3rd International Working Conference on Massively Parallel Programming Models (MPPM'97)*, 1998.
234. J. Gosling. Java Intermediate Bytecodes. In *Papers of the ACM SIGPLAN workshop on Intermediate representations*, New York, NY, 1995. ACM.
235. M. W. Goudreau, K. Lang, S. B. Rao, T. Suel, and T. Tsantilas. Towards Efficiency and Portability: Programming with the BSP Model. In *Proceedings of 8th Annual ACM Symposium on Parallel Algorithms and Architectures*, pages 1–12, June 1996.
236. C. Grelck. Shared–Memory Multiprocessor Support for SAC. In Hammond et al. [245], pages 38–54.
237. K. Gremban, G. Miller, and M. Zagha. Performance Evaluation of a New Parallel Preconditioner. Technical Report CMU-CS-94-205, School of Computer Science, Carnegie Mellon University, October 1994.
238. J. R. Gurd, C. C. Kirkham, and I. Watson. The Manchester Prototype Dataflow Computer. *Comm. ACM*, 28(1):34–52, January 1985.
239. M. Haines and A. P. W. Böhm. Task Management, Virtual Shared Memory, and Multithreading in a Distributed Implementation of SISAL. *Lecture Notes in Computer Science*, 694:12 – 23, 1993.
240. G. Hains and C. Foisy. The Data-Parallel Categorical Abstract Machine. In *Parallel Architectures & Languages Europe*, Lecture Notes in Computer Science. Springer-Verlag, 1993.
241. R. H. Halstead, Jr. Multilisp: A Language for Concurrent Symbolic Computation. *ACM Transactions on Programming Languages and Systems*, 7(4):501–538, 1985.
242. J. Hammes and A. P. W. Böhm. Towards a Time and Space Efficient Functional Implementation of a Monte Carlo Photon Transport Code. In *Proceedings of PACT'97*, pages 286–294, 1997.
243. J. Hammes, S. Sur, and A. P. W. Böhm. On the Effectiveness of Functional Language Features: NAS benchmark FT. *Journal of Functional Programming*, 7(1), January 1997.
244. J. P. Hammes, O. Lubeck, and A. P. W. Böhm. Comparing Id and Haskell in a Monte Carlo Photon Transport Code. *Journal of Functional Programming*, 5(3):283–316, July 1995.
245. In K. Hammond, T. Davie, and C. Clack, editors, *Proceedings of 10th International Workshop on the Implementation of Functional Languages*, volume 1595 of *Lecture Notes in Computer Science*. Springer-Verlag, 1998.
246. K. Hammond. Parallel Functional Programming - an Introduction. In *Proceedings PASCO Symposium on Parallel Symbolic Computation*, pages 181–193, 1994.
247. K. Hammond, H.-W. Loidl, and A. S. Partridge. Improving Granularity for Parallel Functional Programs: A Graphical Winnowing System for Haskell. In *Proceedings of the 1995 Conference on High Performance Functional Computing (HPFC'95), Denver, Colorado*, pages 208–221, 1995.
248. K. Hammond, H.-W. Loidl, and A. S. Partridge. Visualising Granularity in Parallel Programs: A Graphical Winnowing System for Haskell. In A. P. W. Böhm and J. T. Feo, editors, *HPFC'95 - High Performance Functional Computing*, pages 208–221, 1995.
249. K. Hammond, H.-W. Loidl, and P. W. Trinder. Parallel cost centre profiling. In *Proc. 1997 Glasgow FP Workshop, Ullapool, Scotland*. Department of Computer Science, University of Glasgow, 1997.

References 445

250. K. Hammond, J. S. Matson, Jr., and S. L. Peyton Jones. Automatic Spark Strategies and Granularity for a Parallel Graph Reducer. In *Proceedings CONPAR'94*, volume 854 of *Lecture Notes in Computer Science*, pages 521–532. Springer-Verlag, 1994.
251. K. Hammond and S. L. Peyton Jones. Some Early Experiments on the GRIP Parallel Reducer. In *IFL'90 — International Workshop on the Parallel Implementation of Functional Languages*, pages 51–72, Nijmegen, The Netherlands, June 1990.
252. K. Hammond and S. L. Peyton Jones. Profiling Strictness Strategies on the Grip Parallel Reducer. Bericht Nr. 92-19, RWTH Aachen, Fachgruppe Informatik, Aachen, DE, 1992. Proceedings of the 4th International Workshop on the Parallel Implementation of Functional Languages.
253. C. Hankin. *Lambda Calculi*. OUP, 1994.
254. F. Hanna and W. Howells. Parallel Theorem-Proving. In Runciman and Wakeling [505].
255. M. R. Hansen and H. Rischel. *Introduction to Programming Using SML*. Addison Wesley Longman, 1999.
256. H. Harrar, H. Keller, D. Lin, and S. Taylor. Parallel Computation of Taylor-Vortex Flows. In *Conference on Parallel Computational Fluid Dynamics*, Stuttgart, Germany, 1991. Elsevier Science Publishers.
257. T. J. Harris. A Survey of PRAM Simulation Techniques. *ACM Computing Surveys*, 26(2):187–206, June 1994.
258. P. Harrison and H. Khoshnevisan. A New Approach to Recursion Removal. *Theoretical Computer Science*, 93:91–113, 1992.
259. P. Harrison and M. Reeve. The Parallel Graph Reduction Machine, Alice. In J. Fasel and R. Keller, editors, *Graph Reduction: Proceedings of a Workshop at Santa F, New Mexico*, pages 181–202, New York, NY, 1987. Springer-Verlag.
260. P. G. Harrison. A Higher-Order Approach to Parallel Algorithms. *Computer Journal*, 35(6):555–566, 1992.
261. P. Hartel, R. Hofman, K. Langendoen, H. Muller, W. Vree, and L. Hertzberger. A Toolkit for Parallel Functional Programming. *Concurrency — Practice and Experience*, 7(8):765–793, 1995.
262. I. J. Hayes and C. B. Jones. Specifications are Not (Necessarily) Executable. *Software Engineering Journal*, 4(6):330–338, 1989.
263. P. Hedqvist. A Parallel and Multithreaded Erlang Implementation. Master's thesis, Uppsala University, 1998.
264. P. Henderson. *Functional Programming: Application and Implementation*. Prentice-Hall, London, UK, 1980.
265. P. Henderson. Functional Geometry. In *Proceedings of the 1982 ACM Symposium on LISP and Functional Programming*. ACM Press, 1982.
266. P. Henderson, G. Jones, and S. Jones. The LispKit Manual. Technical monograph PRG-2, Oxford University Computing Laboratory, 1982. Two volumes.
267. P. Henderson and J. H. Morris. A Lazy Evaluator. In *Proceedings of 3rd ACM Symposium on Principles of Programming Languages*, 1976.
268. C. A. Herrmann and C. Lengauer. Transformation of Divide & Conquer to Nested Parallel Loops. In H. Glaser, P. Hartel, and H. Kuchen, editors, *Programming Languages: Implementation, Logics, and Programs (PLILP'97)*, Lecture Notes in Computer Science 1292, pages 95–109. Springer-Verlag, 1997.
269. M. Heytens and R. S. Nikhil. List Comprehensions in Agna, a Parallel, Persistent Object System. In *FPCA'91 — Conference on Functional Programming Languages and Computer Architectures*, volume 523 of *Lecture Notes in Computer Science*, pages 569–591, Harvard, MA, Aug. 1991. Springer-Verlag.

270. J. Hicks, D. Chiou, B. S. Ang, and Arvind. Performance studies of Id on the Monsoon Dataflow System. *Journal of Parallel and Distributed Computing*, 18(3):273–300, 1993.
271. High Performance Fortran Forum, Houston, Texas. *High Performance Fortran Language Specification*, November 1994. Version 1.1.
272. J. M. D. Hill. The *aim* is Laziness in a Data-Parallel Language. In K. Hammond and J. T. O'Donnell, editors, *Glasgow Functional Programming Workshop*, Workshops in Computing, pages 83–99. Springer-Verlag, 1993.
273. J. M. D. Hill. *Data-Parallel Lazy Functional Programming*. PhD thesis, Departmentof Computer Science, Queen Mary & Westfield College, University of London, Sept. 1994.
274. J. M. D. Hill, S. R. Donaldson, and D. B. Skillicorn. Portability of Performance with the *BSPlib* Communications Library. In *Programming Models for Massively Parallel Computers, (MPPM'97)*, London, November 1997. IEEE Computer Society Press.
275. J. M. D. Hill, S. R. Donaldson, and D. B. Skillicorn. Stability of Communication Performance in Practice: from the Cray T3E to Networks of Workstations. Technical Report PRG-TR-33-97, Programming Research Group, Oxford University Computing Laboratory, October 1997.
276. J. M. D. Hill, S. Jarvis, C. Siniolakis, and V. P. Vasilev. Portable and Architecture Independent Parallel Performance Tuning Using a Call-Graph Profiling Tool. In *6th EuroMicro Workshop on Parallel and Distributed Processing (PDP'98)*, pages 286–292. IEEE Computer Society Press, January 1998.
277. J. M. D. Hill, B. McColl, D. C. Stefanescu, M. W. Goudreau, K. Lang, S. B. Rao, T. Suel, T. Tsantilas, and R. Bisseling. BSPlib: The BSP Programming Library. *Parallel Computing*, to appear 1998. see www.bsp-worldwide.org for more details.
278. J. M. D. Hill and D. B. Skillicorn. Lessons Learned from Implementing BSP. *Journal of Future Generation Computer Systems*, March 1998.
279. J. M. D. Hill and D. B. Skillicorn. Practical Barrier Synchronisation. In *6th EuroMicro Workshop on Parallel and Distributed Processing (PDP'98)*, pages 438–444. IEEE Computer Society Press, January 1998.
280. W. D. Hillis. *The Connection Machine*. MIT Press, 1985.
281. W. D. Hillis and G. L. Steele, Jr. Data Parallel Algorithms. *Communications of the ACM*, 29(12):1170–1183, 1986.
282. C. A. R. Hoare. Quicksort. *Computer Journal*, 5(1):10–15, 1962.
283. C. A. R. Hoare. Communicating Sequential Processes. *Commmunications of the ACM*, 21:666–671, Aug. 1978.
284. C. A. R. Hoare. *Communicating Sequential Processes*. Prentice-Hall International, 1985.
285. J. S. Huang and Y. C. Chow. Parallel Sorting and Data Partitioning by Sampling. In *IEEE Computer Society's Seventh International Computer Software & Applications Conference (COMPSAC'83)*, pages 627–631, Nov. 1983.
286. Y. Huang and W. F. McColl. Analytical Inversion of General Tridiagonal Matrices. *Journal of Physics, A: Mathematics and General.*, 30:7919–7933, November 1997.
287. Y. Huang and W. F. McColl. Two-Way BSP Algorithm for Tridiagonal Systems. *Future Generation Computer Systems*, 13:337–347, March 1998.
288. P. Hudak. Para-functional programming. *IEEE Computer*, 19:60–71, 1986.
289. P. Hudak and B. Goldberg. Serial Combinators: Optimal Grains for Parallelism. In *Proceedings of the Conference on Functional Programming and Computer Architecture*, volume 201 of *Lecture Notes in Computer Science*, pages 382–399. Springer-Verlag, 1985.

290. R. J. M. Hughes. Graph Reduction with Super Combinators. Technical Monograph PRG-28, Oxford University Computer Laboratory, 1982.
291. R. J. M. Hughes. Super-Combinators - A New Implementation Technique for Applicative Languages. In *Proceedings of ACM Conference on LISP and Functional Programming, Pittsburgh, PA*, pages 1 – 19, 1982.
292. R. J. M. Hughes. Why Functional Programming Matters. *The Computer Journal*, 32(2):98–107, 1989.
293. S. Hwang and D. Rushall. The ν-STG Machine: A Parallelized Spineless Tagless Graph Reduction Machine in a Distributed Memory Architecture. Bericht Nr. 92-19, RWTH Aachen, Fachgruppe Informatik, Aachen, DE, 1992.
294. I. P. de Guzman and P.G. Harrison and E. Medina. Pipelines for Divide-and-Conquer Functions. *The Computer Journal*, 36(3), 1993.
295. R. Irvin. *Performance Tool for High-Level Parallel Programming Languages*. PhD thesis, University of Wisconsin-Madison, November 1995.
296. J. Irwin, J.-M. Loingtier, J. R. Gilbert, and G. Kiczales. *Aspect-Oriented Programming of Sparse Matrix Code*, volume 1343 of *Lecture Notes in Computer Science*. Springer-Verlag, 1997.
297. ISO. *Information Processing Systems: Open Systems Interconnection: Estelle: A Formal Description Technique Based on an Extended State Transition Model*. ISO 9074:1989. International Organization for Standards, 1989.
298. ISO. *Information Processing Systems: Open Systems Interconnection: LOTOS: A Formal Description Technique Based on the Temporal Ordering of Observational Behaviour*. ISO 8807:1989(E). International Organization for Standards, 1989.
299. T. Ito. Efficient Evaluation Strategies for Structured Concurrency Constructs in Parallel Scheme Systems. In *PSLS'95 — International Workshop on Parallel Symbolic Languages and Systems*, volume 1068 of *Lecture Notes in Computer Science*, pages 22–52. Springer-Verlag, 1995.
300. T. Ito and R. H. Halstead, editors. *Parallel Lisp: Languages and Systems*, volume 441 of *Lecture Notes in Computer Science*. Springer-Verlag, 1990.
301. L. Jamieson, D. Gannon, and R. Douglass. *The Characteristics of Parallel Algorithms*. MIT Press, 1987.
302. P. Jansson and J. Jeuring. PolyP - a Polytypic Programming Language Extension. In *POPL '97: The 24th ACM SIGPLAN-SIGACT Symposium on Principles of Programming Languages*, pages 470–482. ACM Press, 1997.
303. C. B. Jay. Matrices, Monads and the Fast Fourier Transform. In *Proceedings of the Massey Functional Programming Workshop 1994*, pages 71–80, 1994.
304. C. B. Jay. A Semantics for Shape. *Science of Computer Programming*, 25:251–283, 1995.
305. C. B. Jay. Shape in Computing. *ACM Computing Surveys*, 28(2):355–357, 1996.
306. C. B. Jay. Poly-Dimensional Regular Arrays in FISh, April 1998. superceded.
307. C. B. Jay. The FISh language definition, 1998. http://www-staff.socs.uts.edu.au/~cbj/Publications/fishdef.ps.gz.
308. C. B. Jay. Partial Evaluation of Shaped Programs: Experience With FISh. In O. Danvey, editor, *ACM SIGPLAN Workshop on Partial Evaluation and Semantics-Based Program Manipulation (PEPM '99) San Antonio, Texas, January 22-23, 1999: Proceedings*, pages 147–158. BRICS, 1999.
309. C. B. Jay, G. Bellè, and E. Moggi. Functorial ML. *Journal of Functional Programming*, 1999. to appear.
310. C. B. Jay, M. I. Cole, M. Sekanina, and P. A. Steckler. A Monadic Calculus for Parallel Costing of a Functional Language of Arrays. In C. Lengauer, M. Griebl, and S. Gorlatch, editors, *Euro-Par'97 Parallel Processing*, volume

1300 of *Lecture Notes in Computer Science*, pages 650–661. Springer-Verlag, August 1997.
311. C. B. Jay and P. A. Steckler. The Functional Imperative: Shape! In C. Hankin, editor, *Programming languages and systems: 7th European Symposium on Programming, ESOP'98 Held as Part of the Joint European Conferences on Theory and Practice of Software, ETAPS'98 Lisbon, Portugal, March/April 1998*, volume 1381 of *Lecture Notes in Computer Science*, pages 139–53. Springer-Verlag, 1998.
312. J. I. Jenkins, M. A.; Glagow. A Logic Basis for Nested Array Data Structures. *Computer Languages Journal*, 14(1):35 – 51, 1989.
313. G. Johnson and J. Genetti. Volume Rendering of Large Datasets on the Cray T3D. In *Spring Proceedings (Cray User Group)*, 1996.
314. T. Johnsson. Efficient Compilation of Lazy Evaluation. In *Proceedings of ACM Conference on Compiler Construction*, pages 58–69, Montreal, 1984.
315. T. Johnsson. Lambda Lifting: Transforming Programs to Recursive Equations. In J.-P. Jouannaud, editor, *Functional Programming Languages and Computer Architecture*, pages 190–203. Springer-Verlag, Berlin, DE, 1985.
316. T. Johnsson. *Compiling Lazy Functional Languages*. Phd thesis, Department of Computer Science, Chalmers University of Technology, Göteborg, SE, 1987.
317. G. Jones and M. Sheeran. Circuit Design in Ruby. *Formal Methods in VLSI Design*, pages 13–70, 1990.
318. M. P. Jones. A Theory of Qualified Types. In *Proceedings of ESOP'92*, volume 582 of *Lecture Notes in Computer Science*, pages 287–306. Springer-Verlag, 1992.
319. M. P. Jones. A System of Constructor Classes: Overloading and Implicit Higher- Order Polymorphism. *Journal of Functional Programming*, 5(1):1–37, January 1995.
320. S. Junaidu. *A Parallel Functional Language Compiler for Message Passing Multicomputers*. PhD thesis, School of Mathematical and Computational Sciences, University of St. Andrews, March 1998.
321. S. Junaidu, A. Davie, and K. Hammond. Naira: A Parallel^2 Haskell Compiler. In Clack et al. [127], pages 215–231.
322. H. Jung, L. Kirousis, and P. Spirakis. Lower Bounds and Efficient Algorithms for Multiprocessor Scheduling of DAGs with Communication Delays. In *Proceedings of ACM Symposium on Parallel Architectures and Algorithms*, pages 254–264, 1989.
323. B. H. H. Juurlink and H. A. G. Wijshoff. Communication Primitives for BSP Computers. *Information Processing Letters*, 58:303–310, 1996.
324. G. Kahn and D. MacQueen. Coroutines and Networks of Parallel Processes. In *IFIP 77*. North Holland, 1977.
325. E. Karlsen. The UniForM Concurrency Toolkit and its Extensions to Concurrent Haskell. In *Glasgow Workshop on Functional Programming*, Ullapool, Scotland, September 1997. Department of Computing Science, University of Glasgow.
326. E. Karlsen. The UniForM User Interaction Manager. Technical report, University of Bremen, Germany, March 1998.
327. E. Karlsen. The UniForM WorkBench — a Higher Order Tool Integration Framework. In *AFM'98 — International Workshop on Current Trends in Applied Formal Methods*, Boppard, Germany, October 7–9, 1998.
328. E. Karlsen and S. Westmeier. Using Concurrent Haskell to Develop Views over an Active Repository. In Clack et al. [127], pages 285–303.
329. O. Kaser, C. Ramakrishnan, I. V. Ramakrishnan, and R. C. Sekar. EQUALS – A Fast Parallel Implementation of a Lazy Language. *Journal of Functional*

Programming, 7(2):183 – 217, 1997.
330. G. Keller and M. Simons. A Calculational Approach to Flattening Nested Data Parallelism in Functional Languages. In J. Jaffar and R. H. C. Yap, editors, *Concurrency and Parallelism, Programming, Networking, and Security: Second Asian Computing Science Conference, ASIAN'96*, volume 1179 of *Lecture Notes in Computer Science*, pages 234–243. Springer-Verlag, 1996.
331. P. H. J. Kelly. *Functional Programming for Loosely-coupled Multiprocessors*. Research Monographs in Parallel and Distributed Computing. Pitman, London and MIT Press, Boston, 1989.
332. M. H. G. Kesseler. Uniqueness and Lazy Graph Copying - Copyright for the Unique. In *Proceedings of the 6th International Workshop on the Implementation of Functional Languages*, Norwich, UK, 1994. University of East Anglia.
333. M. H. G. Kesseler. Constructing Skeletons in Clean: the Bare Bones. In *HPFC'95 — Conference on High Performance Functional Computing*, pages 182–192, Denver, CO, April 10–12, 1995. ftp://sisal.llnl.gov/pub/hpfc/papers95/paper30.ps.
334. M. H. G. Kesseler. *The Implementation of Functional Languages on Parallel Machines with Distributed Memory*. PhD thesis, Wiskunde en Informatica, Katholieke Universiteit van Nijmegen, The Netherlands, 1996.
335. R. Kieburtz. Performance Measurements of a G–Machine Implementation. Technical report, Oregon Graduate Center, University of Oregon, 1988.
336. D. King, J. Hall, and P. W. Trinder. A Strategic Profiler for Glasgow Parallel Haskell. In Hammond et al. [245], pages 88–102.
337. H. Kingdon, D. Lester, and G. Burn. The HDG-Machine: A Highly Distributed Graph-Reducer for a Transputer Network. *Computer Journal*, 34(4):290–301, 1991.
338. S. C. Kleene. *Introduction to Metamathematics*. North-Holland, 1952.
339. In W. Kluge, editor, *Proceedings of 8th International Workshop on the Implementation of Functional Languages*, volume 1268 of *Lecture Notes in Computer Science*. Springer-Verlag, 1996.
340. W. Kluge. Cooperating Reduction Machines. *IEEE Transactions on Computers*, C-32(11):1002 – 1012, 1983.
341. W. Kluge. A User's Guide for the Reduction System π-RED. Internal Report 9409, Department of Computer Science, University of Kiel, 1994.
342. W. E. Kluge. The Architecture of a Reduction Language Machine — Hardware Model. Internal Report ISF 79.03, Institut für Informationssystemforschung, Gesellschaft für Mathematik und Datenverarbeitung, St. Augustin, Germany, August 1979.
343. D. E. Knuth. *The Art of Computer Programming. Volume III: Sorting and Searching*. Addison-Wesley, 1973.
344. H. Kobayashi. *Modeling and Analysis: An Introduction to System Performance Evaluation Methodology*. Addison-Wesley, 1978.
345. P. W. M. Koopman, M. C. J. D. van Eekelen, E. G. J. M. H. Nöcker, J. E. W. Smetsers, and M. J. Plasmeijer. The ABC-Machine: A Sequential Stack-based Abstract Machine for Graph Rewriting. Technical Report 90-22, Department of Computer Science, University of Nijmegen, 1990.
346. H. F. Korth and A. Silberschatz. *Database System Concepts*. McGraw-Hill, 1986.
347. J. Koster and R. H. Bisseling. An Improved Algorithm for Parallel Sparse LU Decomposition on a Distributed-Memory Multiprocessor. In J. G. Lewis, editor, *Proceedings of the Fifth SIAM Conference on Applied Linear Algebra*, pages 397–401. SIAM, Philadelphia, PA, 1994.

348. H. Kuchen, R. Plasmeijer, and H. Stoltze. Distributed Implementation of a Data Parallel Functional Language. In *Parallel Architectures & Languages Europe*, volume 817 of *Lecture Notes in Computer Science*, pages 464–477. Springer-Verlag, 1994.
349. V. Kumar, A. Grama, A. Gupta, and G. Karypis. *Introduction to Parallel Computing, Design and Analysis of Algorithms*. The Benjamin/Cummings Publishing Company, Inc., California, 1994.
350. H. Kung. The Structure of Parallel Algorithms. In M. Yovits, editor, *Advances in Computers, Volume 19*, pages 65–112. Academic Press, 1980.
351. R. E. Ladner and M. J. Fischer. Parallel Prefix Computation. *Journal of the ACM*, 27(4):831–838, Oct. 1980.
352. J. Lambek and P. J. Scott. *Introduction to Higher Order Categorical Logic*. Cambridge University Press, 1986.
353. P. Landin. The Mechanical Evaluation of Expressions. *Computer Journal*, 6(4):308–320, January 1964.
354. K. Langendoen and P. H. Hartel. FCG: A Code Generator for Lazy Functional Languages. In U. Kastens and P. Pfahler, editors, *Compiler Construction; 4th International Conference CC'92 Proceedings*, pages 278–296, Berlin, Germany, 1992. Springer-Verlag.
355. Lawrence Livermore National Laboratories. Sisal Performance Data. http://www.llnl.gov/sisal/PerformanceData.html, June 1998.
356. D. S. Lecomber, K. R. Sujithan, and J. M. D. Hill. Architecture-Independent Locality Analysis and Efficient PRAM Simulations. In *High Performance Computing and Networking (HPCN'97)*, volume 1225. Springer-Verlag, April 1997.
357. D. S. Lecomber, K. R. Sujithan, and C. J. Siniolakis. PRAM Programming In Theory and In Practice. In *Concurrency: Practice and Experience*, 1998.
358. L. M. Leslie et al. A High Resolution Primitive Equations NWP Model for Operations and Research. *Australian Metereological Magazine*, 33:11–35, Mar. 1985.
359. D. Lester. The G-Machine as a Representation of Stack Semantics. In G. Kahn, editor, *Functional Programming Languages and Computer Architecture*, pages 47–59. Springer-Verlag, Berlin, DE, 1987. Lecture Notes in Computer Science 274; Proceedings of Conference held at Portland, OR.
360. D. Lester. Combinator Graph Reduction: A Congruence and its Applications. Technical Monograph PRG-73, Oxford University Computing Laboratory, Oxford, UK, 1989. D. Phil Thesis.
361. D. Lester and G. Burn. An Executable Specification of the HDG-Machine. *International Journal of High Speed Computing*, 5(3):327–378, 1993.
362. C. Lewerentz and T. Lindner. *Formal Development of Reactive Systems, Case Study "Production Cell"*, volume 891 of Lecture Notes in Computer Science. Springer-Verlag, 1995.
363. H.-W. Loidl. *GranSim User's Guide*, 1996. http://www.dcs.glasgow.ac.uk/fp/software/gransim/.
364. H.-W. Loidl. LinSolv: A Case Study in Strategic Parallelism. In *Glasgow Workshop on Functional Programming*, Ullapool, Scotland, September 15–17, 1997.
365. H.-W. Loidl. *Granularity in Large-Scale Parallel Functional Programs*. Phd thesis, University of Glasgow, Department of Computing Science, Glasgow, Scotland, 1998.
366. H.-W. Loidl and K. Hammond. Making a Packet: Cost-Effective Communication for a Parallel Graph Reducer. In Kluge [339], pages 184–199.

367. H.-W. Loidl, R. Morgan, P. W. Trinder, S. Poria, C. Cooper, S. L. Peyton Jones, and R. Garigliano. Parallelising a Large Functional Program; Or: Keeping LOLITA Busy. In Clack et al. [127], pages 199–214.
368. H.-W. Loidl, P. W. Trinder, K. Hammond, S. B. Junaidu, R. Morgan, and S. L. Peyton Jones. Engineering Parallel Symbolic Programs in GPH. *Concurrency — Practice and Experience*, 1999. To appear.
369. R. Loogen, H. Kuchen, K. Indermark, and W. Damm. Distributed Implementation of Programmed Graph Reduction. In K. Odijk, M. Rem, and J.-C. Syre, editors, *PARLE '89, Parallel Architectures and Languages Europe, Volume I: Parallel Architectures, Eindhoven, NL*, volume 365 of *Lecture Notes in Computer Science*, pages 136–157. Springer-Verlag, Berlin, DE, 1989.
370. F. Loulergue. BSML : Programmation BSP Purement Fonctionnelle. In *REN-PAR'10, Rencontres Francophones du Paralllisme*. Université de Strasbourg, Juin 1998.
371. F. Loulergue and G. Hains. Parallel Functional Programming with Explicit Processes: Beyond SPMD. In C. Lengauer, M. Griebl, and S. Gorlatch, editors, *EuroPar'97 Parallel Processing*, volume 1300 of *Lecture Notes in Computer Science*, pages 530–537, Passau, Germany, August 1997. Springer-Verlag.
372. F. Loulergue and G. Hains. An Introduction to BSλ. Rapport de Recherche 98-09, Université d'Orléans, LIFO, Orléans, France, september 1998.
373. W. Luk and G. Jones. The Derivation of Regular Synchronous Circuits. In *Proceedings of the International Conference on Systolic Arrays, San Diego*, 1988.
374. C. Lüth, E. Karlsen, Kolyang, S. Westmeier, and B. Wolff. HOL-Z in the UniForM WorkBench — a Case Study in Tool Integration for Z. In *ZUM'98 — 11th International Conference of Z Users*, September 1998.
375. G. Mago. A Network of Multiprocessors to Execute Reduction Languages. *International Journal of Computer and Information Science*, 8(5):349 – 471, 1979.
376. M. Marin. Billiards and Related Systems On The Bulk Synchronous Parallel Model. In *ACM/IEEE/SCS 11th Workshop on Parallel and Distributed Simulation (PADS'97)*, Vienna, Austria, June 1997. IEEE-CS Press.
377. M. Marin. Priority Queue Operations on EREW-PRAM. In *Europar'97*, Lecture Notes in Computer Science, pages 417–420, Passau, Germany, 1997. Springer-Verlag.
378. M. Marin. Asynchronous (Time-Warp) Versus Synchronous (Event-Horizon) Simulation Time Advance in BSP. In *EuroPar'98*, volume 1470 of *Lecture Notes in Computer Science*, pages 897–905. Springer-Verlag, September 1998.
379. P. Martin-Löf. *Intuitionistic Type Theory*. Bibliopolis, Napoli, 1984.
380. J. S. Mattson. An Efficient Speculative Evaluation Technique for Parallel Supercombinator Graph Reduction. PhD thesis, Department of Computer Science and Engineering, University of California at San Diego, 1993.
381. H. Mattsson, H. Nilsson, and C. Wikström. Mnesia — A Distributed Robust DBMS for Telecommunications Applications. In *International Switching Symposium*, Toronto, Canada, 1997.
382. D. McAllester and K. Arkondas. Walther Recursion. In M. Robbie and J. Slaney, editors, *CADE 13*, pages 643–657. Springer-Verlag, 1996.
383. D. McBurney and M. Sleep. Transputer-Based Experiments with the Zapp Architecture. In J. de Bakker, A. Nijman, and P. Treleaven, editors, *PARLE: Parallel Architectures and Languages Europe (Volume 1: Parallel Architectures)*, volume 258 of *Lecture Notes in Computer Science*, pages 242–259. Springer-Verlag, Berlin, DE, 1987.

384. D. McBurney and M. Sleep. Experiments with the ZAPP Virtual Tree Architecture. In T. Fountain and M. Shute, editors, *Multiprocessor Computer Architecture*, pages 83–99. North Holland, Amsterdam, 1990.
385. D. McBurney and M. Sleep. Graph Rewriting as a Computational Model. In A. Yonezawa and T. Ito, editors, *Concurrency: Theory, Language and Architecture*. Springer-Verlag, New York, NY, 1991. Lecture Notes in Computer Science 491.
386. W. F. McColl. General Purpose Parallel Computing. In A. Gibbons and P. Spirakis, editors, *Lectures on Parallel Computation*, Cambridge International Series on Parallel Computation, pages 337–391. Cambridge University Press, Cambridge, 1993.
387. W. F. McColl. BSP Programming . In G. E. Blelloch, K. M. Chandy, and S. Jagannathan, editors, *Specification of Parallel Algorithms. Proceedings of DIMACS Workshop, Princeton, May 9-11, 1994*, volume 18 of *DIMACS Series in Discrete Mathematics and Theoretical Computer Science*, pages 21–35. American Mathematical Society, 1994.
388. W. F. McColl. Scalable Parallel Computing: A Grand Unified Theory and its Practical Development. In *Proceedings of IFIP World Congress*, volume 1, pages 539–546, Hamburg, August 1994.
389. W. F. McColl. Scalable Computing. In J. van Leeuwen, editor, *Computer Science Today: Recent Trends and Developments*, volume 1000 of *Lecture Notes in Computer Science*, pages 46–61. Springer-Verlag, 1995.
390. W. F. McColl and Q. Miller. The GPL Language: Reference Manual . Technical report, ESPRIT GEPPCOM Project, Oxford University Computing Laboratory, Oct. 1995.
391. J. McGraw et al. SISAL: Streams and Iteration in a Single Assignment Language: Reference Manual Version 1.2. Technical Report Memo M-146, Rev. 1, Lawrence Livermore National Laboratory, 1985.
392. L. Meertens. Algorithmics – Towards Programming as a Mathematical Activity. In *Proceedings of CWI Symposium on Mathematics and Computer Science*, pages 289–334. North-Holland, 1986.
393. L. Meertens. Calculate Polytypically! In H. Kuchen and S. Swierstra, editors, *Programming Languages: Implementations, Logics, and Programs: 8th International Symposium, PLILP'96, Proceedings*, volume 1140 of *Lecture Notes in Computer Science*. Springer-Verlag, 1996.
394. K. Mehlhorn and U. Vishkin. Randomized and Deterministic Simulations of PRAMs by Parallel Machines with Restricted Granularity of Parallel Memories. *Acta Informatica*, 21:339–374, 1984.
395. Message Passing Interface Forum. MPI: A Message Passing Interface. In *Proceedings of Supercomputing '93*, pages 878–883. IEEE Computer Society Press, 1993.
396. G. Michaelson, A. Ireland, and P. King. Towards a Skeleton Based Parallelising Compiler for SML. In Clack et al. [127], pages 539–546.
397. G. Michaelson and N. Scaife. Prototyping a Parallel Vision System in Standard ML. *Journal of Functional Programming*, 5(3):345–382, July 1995.
398. R. Miller. A Library for Bulk Synchronous Parallel Programming. In *Proceedings of the BCS Parallel Processing Specialist Group Workshop on General Purpose Parallel Computing*, pages 100–108, December 1993.
399. R. Miller. *Two Approaches to Architecture-Independent Parallel Computation*. D.Phil thesis, Oxford University Computing Laboratory, Wolfson Building, Parks Road, Oxford OX1 3QD, Michaelmas Term 1994.
400. R. Milner. *Communication and Concurrency*. Prentice-Hall, 1989.
401. R. Milner. Calculi for Interaction. *Acta Informatica*, 33:707–737, 1996.

402. R. Milner, J. Parrow, and D. Walker. A Calculus of Mobile Processes I & II. *Information and Computation*, 100(1):1–77, 1992.
403. R. Milner, M. Tofte, and B. Harper. *The Definition of Standard ML*. MIT Press, 1990.
404. R. Mirani and P. Hudak. First-Class Schedules and Virtual Maps. In *Proceedings of FPCA '95, La Jolla, CA*, pages 78–85. ACM Press, June 1995.
405. J. Misra. Powerlist: A Structure for Parallel Recursion. *ACM TOPLAS*, 16(6), 1994.
406. S. Mitrovic and M. Trobina. Computer Vision Algorithms in Sisal. In *Sisal'93 — Sisal Users Conference*, number CONF 9310206 in LLNL Report, pages 114–119, San Diego, CA, Oct. 1993.
407. E. Moggi. Notions of Computation and Monads. *Information and Computation*, 93(1):55–92, 1991.
408. E. Mohr, D. Kranz, and R. H. Halstead, Jr. A technique of increasing the granularity of parallel programs. In *Proceedings of the ACM Conference on Lisp and Functional Programming*, pages 185–197. ACM Press, 1990.
409. E. Mohr, D. A. Kranz, and R. H. Halstead, Jr. Lazy Task Creation: A Technique for Increasing the Granularity of Parallel Programs. *IEEE Transactions on Parallel and Distributed Systems*, 2(3):264–280, July 1991.
410. P. Moller-Nielsen and J. Staunstrup. Problem-Heap: A Paradigm for Multi-Processor Algorithms. *Parallel Computing*, 4:63–74, 1987.
411. P. B. Monk, A. K. Parrott, and P. J. Wesson. A Parallel Finite Element Method for Electro-Magnetic Scattering. In *COMPEL*, volume 13, pages Supp.A:237–242, 1994.
412. D. Moon. The Architecture of the Symbolics 3600. In *Proceedings of 12th International Symposium on Computer Architecture, Boston*, pages 76 – 83, 1985.
413. D. Morais. Id World: An Environment for the Development of Dataflow Programs Written in Id. Technical Report MIT-LCS-TR-365, Laboratory of Computer Science, M.I.T., May 1986.
414. Z. G. Mou and P. Hudak. An Algebraic Model for Divide-and-Conquer and Its Parallelism. *Journal of Supercomputing*, 2:257–278, 1988.
415. A. Mycroft. *Abstract Interpretation and Optimising Transformations for Applicative Programs*. PhD thesis, Departmentof Computer Science, University of Edinburgh, 1981.
416. P. Nelson and L. Snyder. Programming Paradigms for Nonshared Memory Parallel Computers. In L. Jamieson, D. Gannon, and R. Douglass, editors, *Characteristics of Parallel Algorithms*, pages 3–20, 1987.
417. M. Nibhanupudi, C. Norton, and B. Szymanski. Plasma Simulation on Networks of Workstations Using the Bulk Synchronous Parallel Model. In *Proceedings of International Conference on Parallel and Distributed Processing Techniques and Applications*, Athens, GA, November 1995.
418. F. Nielson, editor. *ML with Concurrency: Design, Analysis, Implementation and Application*. Monographs in Computer Science. Springer-Verlag, 1997.
419. F. Nielson, H. R. Nielson, and C. L. Hankin. *Principles of Program Analysis*. Springer-Verlag, 1999.
420. F. Nielson, H. R. Nielson, R. R. Hansen, and J. G. Jensen. Validating Firewalls in Mobile Ambients. In *Proceedings of CONCUR'99*, Lecture Notes in Computer Science. Springer-Verlag, 1999.
421. H. R. Nielson, T. Amtoft, and F. Nielson. Behaviour Analysis and Safety Conditions: A Case Study in CML. In *Proceedings of FASE'98*, number 1382 in Lecture Notes in Computer Science, pages 255–269. Springer-Verlag, 1998.

422. H. R. Nielson and F. Nielson. Communication Analysis for Concurrent ML. In Nielson [418], pages 185–235.
423. H. R. Nielson, F. Nielson, and T. Amtoft. Polymorphic Subtyping for Effect Analysis: The Static Semantics. In M. Dam, editor, *Analysis and Verification of Multiple-Agent Languages*, number 1192 in Lecture Notes in Computer Science, pages 141–171. Springer-Verlag, 1997.
424. R. Nikhil and Arvind. *Implicit Parallel Programming in pH*. John Wiley & Sons, 1999. To appear.
425. R. S. Nikhil. Id (Version 90.1) Reference Manual. Technical Report CSG Memo 284-2, Laboratory for Computer Science, MIT, July 1991.
426. R. S. Nikhil, Arvind, and J. Hicks. pH Language Proposal (Preliminary), 1st. September 1993. Electronic communication on comp.lang.functional.
427. R. S. Nikhil, G. M. Papadopoulos, and Arvind. *T: A Multithreaded Massively Parallel Architecture. In *19th. ACM Annual Symposium on Computer Architecture*, pages 156–167, 1992.
428. R. S. Nikhil, U. Ramachandran, J. M. Rehg, R. H. Halstead, Jr., C. F. Joerg, and L. Kontothanassis. Stampede — A Programming System for Emerging Scalable Interactive Multimedia Applications. Technical Report CRL 98/1, Cambridge Research Laboratory, May 1998.
429. E. G. J. M. H. Nöcker and M. J. Plasmeijer. Combinator Reduction on a Parallel G-Machine. Technical report, Department of Computer Science, University of Nijmegen, 1986.
430. E. G. J. M. H. Nöcker, M. J. Plasmeijer, and J. E. W. Smetsers. The Parallel ABC Machine. In H. Glaser and P. Hartel, editors, *Proceedings of the Workshop on the Parallel Implementation of Functional Languages*, pages 351–382, Southampton, UK, 1991. Department of Electronics and Computer Science, University of Southampton.
431. E. G. J. M. H. Nöcker, J. E. W. Smetsers, M. C. J. D. van Eekelen, and M. J. Plasmeijer. Concurrent Clean. In E. Aarts and J. van Leeuwen, editors, *Parallel Architectures and Languages Europe PARLE91*, volume 505 of *Lecture Notes in Computer Science*, pages 202–219. Springer-Verlag, New York, NY, 1991.
432. E. J. S. Nöcker, M. J. van Eekelen, and M. Plasmeijer. Concurrent clean. In *Proc. PARLE '91 — Parallel Architectures and Reducti on Languages Europe*, volume 505 of *Lecture Notes in Computer Science*, pages 202–220. Springer-Verlag, 1991.
433. B. Nordström, K. Petersson, and J. M. Smith. *Programming in Martin-Löf's Type Theory — An Introduction*. Oxford University Press, 1990.
434. J. O'Donnell. Functional Microprogramming for a Data Parallel Architecture. In *Glasgow Workshop on Functional Programming*, volume 89/R4, pages 124–145. Computing Science Department, University of Glasgow, 1988.
435. J. O'Donnell. MPP Implementation of Abstract Data Parallel Architectures for Declarative Programming Languages. In *Frontiers '88: Proceedings of the Secons Symposium on the Frontiers of Massively Parallel Computation*, pages 629–636. IEEE Computer Society, 1988.
436. J. O'Donnell. Data-Parallel Implementation of Extensible Sparse Functional Arrays. In *Parallel Architectures and Languages Europe*, volume 694 of *Lecture Notes in Computer Science*, pages 68–79. Springer-Verlag, June 1993.
437. J. O'Donnell. The Comb Communication Algorithm for Fine Grain Data Parallel Systems. Technical report, University of Glasgow, 1998.
438. J. O'Donnell and G. Ruenger. A Coordination Level Functional Implementation of the Hierarchical Radiosity Algorithm. In *Glasgow Workshop on Functional Programming*, Ullapool, Scotland, September 1997. Department of

Computing Science, University of Glasgow.
439. J. O'Donnell and G. Rünger. A Case Study in Parallel Program Derivation: the Heat Equation Algorithm. In *Functional Programming, Glasgow 1994*, Workshops in Computing, pages 167–183. Springer-Verlag, 1994.
440. J. O'Donnell and G. Rünger. Formal Derivation of a Parallel Binary Addition Circuit. Technical Report TR-1995-19, University of Glasgow, 1995.
441. P. O'Hearn and R. Tennent, editors. *Algol-Like Languages, Vols I and II*. Progress in Theoretical Computer Science. Birkhauser, 1997.
442. R. B. Osborne. Speculative Computation in Multilisp. In T. Ito and R. H. Halstead, Jr., editors, *Parallel Lisp: Languages and Systems*, volume 441 of *Lecture Notes in Computer Science*, pages 103 – 137. Springer-Verlag, 1990.
443. F. O. Osoba and F. A. Rabhi. A Parallel Multigrid Skeleton Using BSP. In *EuroPar'98*, volume 1470 of *Lecture Notes in Computer Science*, pages 704–708. Springer-Verlag, September 1998.
444. J. Palsberg and C. B. Jay. The Essence of the Visitor Pattern. Technical Report 05, University of Technology, Sydney, 1997. COMPSAC'98, to appear.
445. P. Panangaden and J. H. Reppy. The Essence of Concurrent ML. In Nielson [418], pages 5–29.
446. G. Papadopoulos. Implementation of a General Purpose Dataflow Multiprocessor. Technical Report 432, Laboratory for Computer Science, Massachusetts Institute of Technology, Cambridge, MA, 1988.
447. D. Parkinson and J. Litt, editors. *Massively Parallel Computing with the DAP*. Research Monographs in Parallel and Distributed Computing. Pitman, 1990.
448. D. Parrott and C. Clack. A Common Graphical Form. In J. Darlington and R. Dietrich, editors, *Proceedings of the Phoenix Workshop on Declarative Programming*, number RN/91/27 in Workshops in Computing, pages 224–238. Springer-Verlag, 1992.
449. A. S. Partridge. *Speculative Evaluation in Parallel Implementations of Lazy Functional Languages*. PhD thesis, Department of Computer Science, University of Tasmania, 1991.
450. A. S. Partridge and A. Dekker. Speculative Parallelism in a Distributed Graph Reduction Machine. In *Proceedings of 22nd Anual Hawaii International Conference on System Sciences, Vol. 2*, pages 771 – 779, 1989.
451. L. C. Paulson. *Logic and Computation — Interactive proof with Cambridge LCF*. Cambridge University Press, 1987.
452. S. Pelagatti. Compiling and Supporting Skeletons on MPP. In *Proceedings of MPPM97*. IEEE Computer Society Press, 1997. to appear.
453. S. Pelagatti. *Structured Development of Parallel Programs*. Taylor and Francis, 1998.
454. P. Pepper. Deductive Derivation of Parallel Programs. In *Parallel Algorithm Derivation and Program Transformation*, chapter 1, pages 1–53. Kluwer Academic Publishers, 1993. Also: Technical Report 92-23, Technische Universitat Berlin, July 1992.
455. P. Pepper and M. Südholt. Deriving Parallel Numerical Algorithms Using Data Distribution Algebras: Wang's Algorithm. In *HICSS'97 — 30th Hawaii International Conference on System Sciences*, Hawaii, USA, January 7–10, 1997. IEEE.
456. F. Peters. Tree Machines and Divide and Conquer Algorithms. In *Proceedings CONPAR 81*, volume 111 of *Lecture Notes in Computer Science*, pages 25–36. Springer-Verlag, 1981.
457. J. C. Peterson, J. Hammond, L. Augustsson, B. Boutel, F. W. Burton, J. Fasel, A. D. Gordon, R. J. M. Hughes, P. Hudak, T. Johnsson, M. P. Jones, E. Meijer, S. L. Peyton Jones, A. Reid, and P. L. Wadler. *Report on the Non-Strict*

Funtional Language, Haskell, Version 1.4, 1997.
458. F. Petrini. Total-Exchange on Wormhole K-ary N-Cubes with Adaptive Routing. In *12th International Parallel Processing Symposium & 9th Symposium on Parallel and Distributed Processing*, April 1998.
459. S. L. Peyton Jones. *The Implementation of Functional Programming Languages*. Prentice-Hall, London, UK, 1987.
460. S. L. Peyton Jones. Parallel Implementations of Functional Programming Languages. *The Computer Journal*, 32(2):175–186, 1989.
461. S. L. Peyton Jones. Implementing Lazy Functional Languages on Stock Hardware: The Spineless Tagless G-machine. *Journal of Functional Programming*, 2(2), 1992.
462. S. L. Peyton Jones. Compiling Haskell by Program Transformation: A Report from the Trenches. In *ESOP'96 — European Symposium on Programming*, volume 1058 of *Lecture Notes in Computer Science*, pages 18–44, Linköping, Sweden, April 22–24, 1996. Springer-Verlag.
463. S. L. Peyton Jones, C. Clack, and N. Harris. GRIP: A Parallel Graph Reduction Machine. In *Proceedings Workshop on Implementation of Functional Languages*, pages 59–91, 1985. Technical Report 17.
464. S. L. Peyton Jones, C. Clack, and J. Salkild. High-Performance Parallel Graph Reduction. In K. Odijk, M. Rem, and J.-C. Syre, editors, *PARLE '89: Parallel Languages and Architectures Europe*, volume 1, pages 193–206. Springer-Verlag, New York, NY, 1989.
465. S. L. Peyton Jones, C. Clack, J. Salkild, and M. Hardie. GRIP - A High-Performance Architecture for Parallel Graph Reduction. In G. Kahn, editor, *Functional Programming Languages and Computer Architecture*, pages 98–112. Springer-Verlag, Berlin, DE, 1987.
466. S. L. Peyton Jones, A. Gordon, and S. Finne. Concurrent Haskell. In *POPL'96 — Symposium on Principles of Programming Languages*, pages 295–308, St Petersburg, Florida, January 1996. ACM.
467. S. L. Peyton Jones and M. Joy. FLIC - a Functional Language Intermediate Code. Research Report 148, Department of Computer Science, University of Warwick, Coventry, UK, 1989.
468. S. L. Peyton Jones, E. Meijer, and D. Leijen. Scripting COM Components in Haskell. In *Fifth Intl Conf on Software Reuse*, Jun 1998.
469. S. L. Peyton Jones and J. Salkild. The Spineless Tagless G-Machine. In *Proceedings of the Conference on Functional Programming Languages and Computer Architecture '89, Imperial College, London*, pages 184–201, New York, NY, 1989. ACM.
470. B. C. Pierce and D. N. Turner. Pict: A programming language based on the pi-calculus. In G. Plotkin, C. Stirling, and M. Tofte, editors, *Proof, Language and Interaction: Essays in Honour of Robin Milner.* mit, 1998.
471. M. Pil. First Class File I/O. In Kluge [339], pages 233–246.
472. M. Pil. Dynamic Types and Type Dependent Functions. In Hammond et al. [245], pages 171–188.
473. N. Pippenger. Pure Versus Impure Lisp. *ACM Transactions on Programming Languages and Systems*, 19(2), March 1997.
474. A. M. Pitts. A Co-Induction Principle for Recursively Defined Domains. *Theoretical Computer Science*, 124(2):195–219, 1994.
475. A. M. Pitts and I. D. B. Stark. Operational Reasoning for Functions with Local State. In A. D. Gordon and A. M. Pitts, editors, *Higher Order Operational Techniques in Semantics*, Publications of the Newton Institute, pages 227–273. Cambridge University Press, 1998.

References

476. M. J. Plasmeijer and M. C. J. D. van Eekelen. *Functional Programming and Parallel Graph Rewriting*. Addison-Wesley Publishers Ltd., 1993.
477. E. Poll and S. Thompson. Review of "R. Bird and O. de Moor, Algebra of Programming, Prentice-Hall, 1997". *Journal of Functional Programming*, To appear 1999.
478. F. Preparata and J. Vuillemin. The Cube-Connected Cycles: A Versatile Network for Parallel Computation. *Communications of the ACM*, 24(5):300–309, 1981.
479. W. Press and others. *Numerical Recipes, the Art of Scientific Programming*. Cambridge University Press, 1986.
480. D. Pritchard and others. Practical Parallelism Using Transputer Arrays. In J. de Bakker, editor, *PARLE 87*, volume 258 of *Lecture Notes in Computer Science*. Springer-Verlag, 1987.
481. M. J. Quinn. *Parallel Computing: Theory and Practice*. McGraw-Hill, 1994.
482. M. Raber, T. Remel, E. Hoffman, D. Maurer, F. Muller, H.-G. Oberhauser, and R. Wilhelm. Compiled Graph Reduction on a Processor Network. Technical report, Universitdt des Saarlandes, Saarbrucken, DE, 1987.
483. M. Raber, T. Remel, D. Maurer, F. Muller, H.-G. Oberhauser, and R. Wilhelm. A Concept for a Parallel G-machine. Technical Report SFB 124-C1, Universitdt des Saarlandes, Saarbrucken, DE, 1987.
484. F. A. Rabhi. A Parallel Programming Methodology Based on Paradigms. In P. Nixon, editor, *Transputer and Occam Developments*, pages 239–252. IOS Press, 1995.
485. T. Rauber and G. Rünger. Parallel Numerical Algorithms with Data Distribution Types. Technical Report 95-04, University of Saarbrucken, Sonderforschungsbereich 124, 1995.
486. T. Rauber and G. Rünger. Deriving Structured Parallel Implementations for Numerical Methods. *Microprocessing and Microprogramming*, 41:589–608, 1996.
487. T. Rauber and G. Rünger. The Compiler TwoL for the Design of Parallel Implementations. In *PACT'96 — International Conference on Parallel Architecture and Compilations Techniques*, pages 292–301, Boston, USA, October 1996. IEEE Computer Society Press.
488. C. Reade. *Elements of Functional Programming*. Addison-Wesley, 1989.
489. J. Reed, K. Parrott, and T. Lanfear. Portability, Predictability and Performance for Parallel Computing: BSP in Practice. *Concurrency: Practice and Experience*, 8(10):799–812, December 1996.
490. M. Reeve and S. Wright. The Experimental ALICE Machine. In T. Fountain and M. Shute, editors, *Multiprocessor Computer Architecture*, pages 39–20. North Holland, Amsterdam, 1990.
491. J. H. Reif and L. G. Valiant. A Logarithmic Time Sort for Linear Size Networks. *Journal of the ACM*, 34(1):60–76, 1987.
492. J. H. Reppy. CML: A Higher-Order Concurrent Language. In *PLDI'91 — Programming Languages Design and Implementation*, pages 293–305. ACM Press, June 1991.
493. J. H. Reppy. Concurrent ML: Design, Application and Semantics. In *Programming, Concurrency, Simulation and Automated Reasoning*, volume 693 of *Lecture Notes in Computer Science*. Springer-Verlag, 1992.
494. J. H. Reppy. Higher–Order Concurrency. Tr 92-1852, Department of Computer Science, Cornell University, Ithaca, NY 14853, 1992.
495. J. H. Reppy. *Concurrent Programming in ML*. Cambridge University Press, 1999.

496. J. Reynolds. The Essence of ALGOL. In J. de Bakker and J. van Vliet, editors, *Algorithmic Languages*, pages 345–372. IFIP, North-Holland Publishing Company, 1981.
497. J. C. Reynolds. *Theories of Programming Languages*. Cambridge University Press, 1998.
498. C. P. Riley, R. C. F. McLatchie, R. Janssen, A. Longo, T. Gutiérrez, S. Casado, J. Simkin, P. Brochet, G. Molinari, P. Alotto, J.-F. Lemoine, and G. Drago. Optimisation of Electromagnetic Design Using HPCN. In *HPCN'98: High-Performance Computing and Networking*, volume 1401 of *Lecture Notes in Computer Science*. Springer-Verlag, April 1998.
499. H. Rischel and H. Sun. Design and Prototyping of Real-time Systems Using CSP and CML. In *Proceedings of 9th Euromicro Workshop on Real-Time Systems*, pages 121–127. IEEE Computer Society Press, 1998.
500. P. Roe. *Parallel Programming Using Functional Languages*. PhD thesis, University of Glasgow, UK, 1991.
501. N. Rojemo. A Concurrent Generational Garbage Collector for a Parallel Graph Reducer. In Y. Bekkers and J. Cohen, editors, *Memory Management; International Workshop IWMM 92. Proceedings*, pages 440–453, Berlin, Germany, 1992. Springer-Verlag.
502. W. A. Roscoe. *Theory and Practice of Concurrency*. Prentice-Hall, 1998.
503. C. Ruggiero and J. Sargeant. Control of Parallelism in the Manchester Dataflow Machine. In G. Kahn, editor, *Functional Programming Languages and Computer Architecture*, volume 274 of *Lecture Notes in Computer Science*, pages 1–16. Springer-Verlag, Berlin, DE, 1987.
504. C. Runciman and D. Wakeling. Profiling Parallel Functional Computations (Without Parallel Machines). In *Functional Programming, Glasgow '93*, pages 236–251. Springer-Verlag, 1993.
505. C. Runciman and D. Wakeling, editors. *Applications of Functional Programming*. UCL Press, 1995.
506. C. Runciman and D. Wakeling. A quasi-parallel evaluator. In Runciman and Wakeling [505], chapter 10, pages 161–176.
507. G. Sabot. *The Parallation Model : Architecture Independent SIMD Programming*. MIT Press, 1988.
508. A. H. Sameh. On Jacobi-Like Algorithms for a Parallel Computer. *Mathematical Comput.*, 25:579–590, 1971.
509. D. Sands. *Calculi for Time Analysis of Functional Programs*. PhD thesis, Imperial College, London, September 1990.
510. P. Sansom and S. Peyton Jones. Formally Based Profiling for Higher-Order Functional Languages. *ACM Transactions on Programming Langauges and Systems*, 19(1), 1997.
511. V. Sarkar and J. Hennessy. Partitioning Parallel Programs for Macro-Dataflow. In *ACM Symposium on Lisp and Functional Programming*, pages 202–211, 1986.
512. M. Scheevel. NORMA: A Graph Reduction Processor. In *ACM Conference on LISP and Functional Programming, Cambridge, MA*, pages 109–139, 1986.
513. D. A. Schmidt. Denotational Semantics as a Programming Language. Technical Report CSR-100-82, Department of Computer Science, University of Edinburgh, January 1982.
514. C. Schmittgen, H. Bloedorn, and W. Kluge. π-RED* – A Graph Reducer for a Full-Fledged λ-Calculus. *New Generation Computing, OHMSHA Ltd. and Springer-Verlag*, 10(2):173–195, 1992.
515. S.-B. Scholz. On Programming Scientific Applications in SAC – a Functional Programming Language Extended by a Subsystem for High–Level Array Op-

erations. In Kluge [339], pages 85 – 104.
516. S.-B. Scholz. *Single Assignment C – Entwurf und Implementierung einer funktionalen C-Variante mit spezieller Unterstützung shape-invarianter Array-Operationen (in German)*. PhD thesis, Institut für Informatik und praktische Mathematik, Universitat Kiel, October 1996.
517. S.-B. Scholz. With-Loop-Folding in SAC — Condensing Consecutive Array Operations. In Clack et al. [127], pages 225–242.
518. S.-B. Scholz. A Case Study: Effects of WITH-Loop-Folding on the NAS Benchmark MG in SAC. In Hammond et al. [245], pages 220–231.
519. W. Schreiner. Application of a Para-Functional Language to Problems in Computer Algebra. In *HPFC'95 — Conference on High Performance Functional Computing*, pages 10–24, Denver, CO, April 10–12, 1995.
520. R. Schroeder. Distributed Breadth–First Searches as Speculative Evaluations. In Clack et al. [127], pages 243 – 259.
521. J. Sérot. Embodying Parallel Functional Skeletons: An Experimental Implementation on Top of MPI. In C. Lengauer, M. Griebl, and S. Gorlatch, editors, *EuroPar'97 Parallel Processing*, number 1300 in Lecture Notes in Computer Science, pages 629–633, Passau, Germany, August 1997. Springer-Verlag.
522. J. Sérot, D. Ginhac, and J. Dérutin. SKiPPER: A Skeleton-Based Parallel Programming Environment for Real-Time Image Processing Applications. In *PaCT'99 — International Parallel Computing Technologies Conference*, St-Petersburg, September 6–10, 1999.
523. P. R. Serrarens. Implementing the Conjugate Gradient Algorithm in a Functional Language. In Kluge [339], pages 125–140.
524. P. R. Serrarens. Distributed Arrays in the Functional Language Concurrent Clean. In *Proceedings of the 3rd International Euro-Par Conference*, volume 1300 of *Lecture Notes in Computer Science*, pages 1201–1208, Passau, Germany, August 1997.
525. P. R. Serrarens. Using Multicasting for Optimising Data-Parallelism. In Clack et al. [127], pages 271–285.
526. P. R. Serrarens and M. J. Plasmeijer. Explicit Message Passing for Concurrent Clean. In Hammond et al. [245], pages 229–245.
527. E. Shapiro. The Family of Concurrent Logic Programming Languages. *ACM Computing Surveys*, 21(3), 1989.
528. A. Shaw. Impala – IMplicitly PArallel LAnguage Application Suite. Technical report, MIT Computation Structures Group, June 11th 1998.
529. A. Shaw, Arvind, K.-C. Cho, C. Hill, R. Johnson, and J. Marshall. A Comparison of Implicitly Parallel Multithreaded and Data Parallel Implementations of an Ocean Model. *Journal of Parallel and Distributed Computing*, 48(1):1–51, January 1998.
530. H. Simon. *The Sciences of the Artificial*. MIT Press, 1969.
531. A. Simpson, J. M. D. Hill, and S. R. Donaldson. BSP in CSP: Easy as ABC. In *Workshop on Formal Methods for Parallel Computing, held in conjunction with IPPS/SPDP (IPPS'99)*, San Juan, Puerto Rico, April 1999. Springer-Verlag.
532. S. K. Skedzielewski. Sisal. In Szymanski, editor, *Parallel Functional Languages and Compilers*. ACM Press, 1991.
533. D. B. Skillicorn. Models for Practical Parallel Computation. *International Journal of Parallel Programming*, 20(2):133–158, 1991.
534. D. B. Skillicorn. *Foundations of Parallel Programming*. Number 6 in Cambridge Series in Parallel Computation. Cambridge University Press, 1994.
535. D. B. Skillicorn. miniBSP: A BSP Language and Transformation System. http://www.qucis.queensu.ca/home/skill/mini.ps, November 1996.

536. D. B. Skillicorn. Parallel Implementation of Tree Skeletons. *Journal of Parallel and Distributed Computing*, 39:115–125, 1996.
537. D. B. Skillicorn. Towards a Framework for Cost-Based Transformation. *Journal of Systems and Architectures (the Euromicro Journal)*, 42:331–340, 1996.
538. D. B. Skillicorn and W. Cai. A Cost Calculus for Parallel Functional Programming. *Journal of Parallel and Distributed Computing*, 28(1):65–83, July 1995.
539. D. B. Skillicorn, M. Danelutton, S. Pelagatti, and A. Zavanella. Optimising Data-Parallel Programs Using the BSP Cost Model. In *EuroPar'98*, volume 1470 of *Lecture Notes in Computer Science*, pages 698–708. Springer-Verlag, September 1998.
540. D. B. Skillicorn, J. M. D. Hill, and W. F. McColl. Questions and Answers about BSP. *Scientific Programming*, 6(3):249–274, Fall 1997.
541. D. B. Skillicorn and D. Talia. Models and Languages for Parallel Computation. *ACM Computing Surveys*, 30(2):123–169, 1998.
542. G. S. Smith. Principal Type Schemes for Functional Programs with Overloading and Subtyping. *Science of Computer Programming*, 23:197–226, 1994.
543. S. Smith. The LMI Lambda Technical Summary. Technical report, LMI Inc., Los Angeles, CA, 1984.
544. M. Snir, S. Otto, S. Huss-Lederman, D. Walker, and J. J. Dongarra. *MPI: The Complete Reference*. MIT Press, Cambridge, MA, 1995.
545. A. Sodan and H. Bock. Extracting Characteristics from Functional Programs for Mapping to Massively Parallel Machines. In *HPFC'95 — High Performance Functional Computing*, pages 134–148, Denver, CO, April 10–12, 1995.
546. J. Sparud and C. Runciman. Complete and Partial Redex Trails of Functional Computations. In Clack et al. [127], pages 160–177.
547. M. Spivey. *The Z Notation: A Reference Manual*. Prentice-Hall, 1989.
548. G. L. Steele, Jr. and W. D. Hillis. Connection Machine Lisp : Fine-Grained Parallel Symbolic Processing. In *ACM Conference on Lisp and Functional Programming*, pages 279–297, 1986.
549. J. E. Stoy. *Denotational Semantics: the Scott-Strachey Approach to Programming language theory*. MIT, 1977.
550. W. Stoye. The SKIM II Microprogrammer's Guide. Technical note, Cambridge University Computer Laboratory, 1983.
551. M. Südholt. *The Transformational Derivation of Parallel Programs Using Data-Distribution Algebras and Skeletons*. PhD thesis, Fachbereich 13 Informatik, Technische Universitat Berlin, August 1997.
552. M. Südholt, C. Piepenbrock, K. Obermayer, and P. Pepper. Solving Large Systems of Differential Equations Using Covers and Skeletons. In *50th IFIP WG 2.1 Working Conference on Algorithmic Languages and Calculi*, Strasbourg, France, Feb. 1997. Chapman & Hall.
553. K. R. Sujithan. *Bulk Synchronous Parallelism in Object-Relational Database Systems*. D.Phil. thesis, Oxford University Computing Laboratory, Trinity Term 1997.
554. K. R. Sujithan and J. M. D. Hill. Collection Types for Database Programming in the BSP Model. In *5th EuroMicro Workshop on Parallel and Distributed Processing (PDP'97)*. IEEE Computer Society Press, Jan. 1997.
555. S. Sur and A. P. W. Böhm. Analysis of Non-Strict Functional Implementations of the Dongarra-Sorensen Eigensolver. In *Proceedings of ICS94*, pages 412–418, Manchester, UK, 1994.
556. S. Sur and A. P. W. Böhm. Functional, I-Structure, and M-Structure Implementations of NAS Benchmark FT. In *PACT'94 — International Conference on Parallel Architecture and Compilation Techniques*, pages 47–56, Montreal,

References

Canada, Aug. 1994.
557. J.-P. Talpin. The Calumet Experiment in Facile — A Model for Group Communication and Interaction Control in Cooperative Applications. Technical report ECRC-94-26, ECRC Munich, 1994.
558. J.-P. Talpin and P. Jouvelot. Compiling FX on the CM-2. In *Workshop on Static Analysis*, volume 724 of *Lecture Notes in Computer Science*, 1993.
559. J.-P. Talpin and P. Jouvelot. The Type and Effect Discipline. *Information and Computation*, 111(2):245–296, 1994.
560. F. Taylor. *Parallel Functional Programming by Partitioning*. PhD thesis, Department of Computing, Imperial College of Science, Technology and Medicine, University of London, January 1997.
561. A. Telford and D. Turner. Ensuring Streams Flow. In M. Johnson, editor, *Algebraic Methodology and Software Technology 1997*, pages 509–523. Springer-Verlag, 1997.
562. S. Thompson. *Type Theory and Functional Programming*. Addison Wesley, 1991.
563. S. Thompson. A Logic for Miranda, Revisited. *Formal Aspects of Computing*, 7:412–429, 1995.
564. S. Thompson. *Haskell: The Craft of Functional Programming (2nd Edition)*. Addison-Wesley, 1999.
565. B. Thomsen, L. Leth, and T.-M. Kuo. FACILE — From Toy to Tool. In Nielson [418], pages 97–144.
566. B. Thomsen, L. Leth, S. Prasad, T.-M. Kuo, A. Kramer, F. Knabe, and A. Giacalone. Facile Antigua Release Programming Guide. Technical Report ECRC-93-20, ECRC Munich, 1993.
567. A. Tiskin. The Bulk-Synchronous Parallel Random Access Machine. *Theoretical Computer Science*, 196(1):109–130, 1998.
568. H. W. To. *Optimising the Parallel Behaviour of Combinations of Program Components*. PhD Thesis, Department of Computer Science, Imperial College, 1995.
569. K. Traub, D. Culler, and K. Schauser. Global Analysis for Partitioning Non-Strict Programs into Sequential Threads. In *LFP'92 — Conference on LISP and Functional Programming*, San Francisco, CA, June 1992.
570. P. W. Trinder, E. Barry, Jr., M. K. Davis, K. Hammond, S. B. Junaidu, U. Klusik, H.-W. Loidl, and S. L. Peyton Jones. GPH: An Architecture-Independent Functional Language. *IEEE Transactions on Software Engineering*, 1999. Submitted for publication.
571. P. W. Trinder, K. Hammond, H.-W. Loidl, and S. L. Peyton Jones. Algorithm + Strategy = Parallelism. *Journal of Functional Programming*, 8(1):23–60, January 1998.
572. P. W. Trinder, K. Hammond, H.-W. Loidl, S. L. Peyton Jones, and J. Wu. A Case Study of Data-Intensive Programs in Parallel Haskell. In *Glasgow Workshop on Functional Programming*, Workshops in Computing, Ullapool, Scotland, July 8–10, 1996. Springer-Verlag.
573. P. W. Trinder, K. Hammond, S. L. Peyton Jones, and A. Partridge. GUM: A Portable Parallel Implementation of Haskell. In *Proceedings SIGPLAN Symposium on Programming Language Design and Implementation (PLDI'96)*, 1996.
574. D. A. Turner. A New Implementation Technique for Applicative Languages. *Software - Practice and Experience*, 9:31–49, 1979.
575. D. A. Turner. Miranda: A Non-Strict Functional Language with Polymorpic Types. In J. Jouannaud, editor, *Functional Programming Languages and Computer Architecture*, volume 201 of *Lecture Notes in Computer Science*,

pages 1–16, Nancy, France, 1985. Springer-Verlag.
576. D. A. Turner. An Approach to Functional Operating Systems. In D. A. Turner, editor, *Research Topics in Functional Programming*. Addison Wesley, 1992.
577. D. A. Turner. Elementary Strong Functional Programming. In P. Hartel and R. Plasmeijer, editors, *Functional Programming Languages in Education (FPLE)*, volume 1022 of *Lecture Notes in Computer Science*, pages 1–13. Springer-Verlag, Heidelberg, 1995.
578. University of Washington. ZPL, 1997. http://www.cs.washington.edu/research/zpl/index.html.
579. L. G. Valiant. A Scheme for Fast Parallel Communication. *SIAM Journal of Computing*, 11(2):350–361, May 1982.
580. L. G. Valiant. A Bridging Model for Parallel Computation. *Communications of the ACM*, 33(8):103–111, August 1990.
581. L. G. Valiant. General Purpose Parallel Architectures. In J. van Leeuwen, editor, *Handbook of Theoretical Computer Science, Vol. A*. Elsevier Science Publishers and MIT Press, 1990.
582. L. G. Valiant. Bulk-Synchronous Parallel Computer. U.S. Patent No. 5083265, 1992.
583. M. van Eekelen and M. Plasmeijer. Specification of Reduction Strategies in Term Rewriting Systems. In J. Fasel and R. Keller, editors, *Graph Reduction: Proceedings of a Workshop at Santa F, New Mexico*, pages 215–239, New York, NY, 1987. Springer-Verlag.
584. J. van Groningen. Implementing the ABC-Machine on M680x0 Based Architectures. Master's thesis, University of Nijmegen, 1990.
585. S. R. Vegdahl. A Survey of Proposed Architectures for the Execution of Functional Languages. *IEEE–Transactions on Computers*, C–33(12):1050 – 1071, 1984.
586. J. Vrancken. Reflections on Parallel Functional Languages. In *Proceedings 2nd International Workshop on Implementation of Functional Languages on Parallel Architectures*, 1990.
587. W. Vree. Experiments with Coarse-Grain Parallel Graph Reduction. *Future Generation Computer Systems*, 4:299–306, 1988.
588. P. Wadler. Comprehending Monads. *Mathematical Structures in Computer Science*, 1993. Special issue of selected papers from 6'th Conference on Lisp and Functional Programming, 1992.
589. P. Wadler. Why No One Uses Functional Languages. *ACM SIGPLAN*, 33(8), August 1998.
590. P. Wadler and S. Blott. Type Class Overloading. In *Proceedings of POPL '89 – ACM Symposium on Principles of Programming Languages*, pages ??–??, 1989.
591. C. P. Wadsworth. *Semantics and Pragmatics of the Lambda-Calculus*. PhD thesis, University of Oxford, 1971.
592. C. P. Wadsworth. The Relation Between Computational and Denotational Proerties for Scott's D_∞ Models of the Lambda-Calculus. *SIAM Journal of Computing*, 5, 1976.
593. I. Watson, J. Sargeant, P. Watson, and V. Woods. Flagship Computational Models and Machine Architecture. *ICL Technical Journal*, pages 555–574, 1987.
594. P. Watson and I. Watson. Evaluating Functional Programs on the FLAGSHIP Machine. In G. Kahn, editor, *Functional Programming Languages and Computer Architecture*, pages 80–97. Springer-Verlag, Berlin, DE, 1987.

595. C. Wedler and C. Lengauer. Notes on the Classification of Parallel Implementations of Linearly Recursive Programs. In *Proceedings of GI/ITG FG PARS'95*, PARS Mitteilungen Nr.14, pages 140–147. Gesellschaft für Informatik e.V., 1995.
596. P. Wegner. *Programming Languages, Information Structures and Machine Organization*. McGraw-Hill, 1971.
597. D. J. Whalen, D. E. Hollowell, and J. S. Hendricks. MCNP: Photon Benchmark Problems. Technical Report Report LA-12196, Los Alamos National Laboratory, 1991.
598. R. P. Whittington. *Database Systems Engineeering*. Clarendon Press, Oxford, 1998.
599. G. Winskel. *The Formal Semantics of Programming Languages*. MIT Press, 1993.
600. Q. Wu, A. J. Field, and P. H. J. Kelly. M-Tree: A Parallel Abstract Data Type for Block-Irregular Adaptive Applications. In C. Lengauer, M. Griebl, and S. Gorlatch, editors, *EuroPar'97 — European Conference on Parallel Processing*, volume 1300 of *Lecture Notes in Computer Science*, pages 638–49, Passau, Germany, August 1997. Springer-Verlag.
601. J. Yang. *Co-ordination Based Structured Parallel Programming*. PhD thesis, Department of Computing, Imperial College of Science, Technology and Medicine, University of London, September 1998.
602. T. Yuba, T. Shimada, K. Hiraki, and H. Kashiwagi. SIGMA-1: A Dataflow Computer for Scientific Computations. *Computer Physics Communications*, pages 141–148, 1985.
603. Z.G. Mou, and M. Hudak. An Algebraic Model for Divide-and-Conquer Algorithms and its Parallelism. *Journal of Supercomputing*, 2(3), 1988.
604. X. Zhang, M. Webster, J. Sharp, and P. Grant. Parallel Computational Fluid Dynamics. In Runciman and Wakeling [505].
605. R. Zimmer. *Zur Pragmatik eines Operationalisierten λ-Kalkuels als Basis fuer Interaktive Reduktionssysteme*, volume 192 of *GMD-Bericht*. Oldenbourg, 1991.

Glossary

⊥: See **bottom**.

α-**conversion:** See **alpha conversion**.

β-**reduction:** See **beta reduction**.

δ-**rule:** See **delta rule**.

η-**reduction:** See **eta reduction**.

λ-**calculus:** See **lambda calculus**.

π-**calculus:** See **pi calculus**.

Absolute speedup: The speedup of a program compared with that of the same program optimised for sequential execution. See **relative speedup**.

Abstract interpretation: An interpretation process that aims to determine properties of an expression other than its value. Source expressions are translated into abstract versions that can be evaluated symbolically to yield some interesting property, such as cost, shape or strictness information. A useful introductory text is that by Neilson et al. [419]. See **bottom, strictness** and Chapter 2.

Abstract machine: A set of rules and data abstractions that describe how a program can be evaluated. Data abstractions may include representations for closures, heap, stacks etc. Examples are the SECD machine [353], and the G-Machine [314]. See **evaluation, execution** and Chapters 2, and 5–6.

Alpha conversion, or α-conversion: The process by which names are replaced by alternatives without changing the meaning of an expression [125]. See **beta reduction**, and Chapter 2.

Architecture: The abstract structure of a computer or other system as opposed to its concrete realisation in hardware, software etc.

Asynchronous communication: Communication where the sender does not wait for acknowledgement from the receiver. See **non-blocking, synchronous communication**.

Bandwidth: The limit to the quantity of data that can be transferred across a communication link in a given unit of time. See **latency**.

Barrier Synchronisation: A form of blocking communication among a group of tasks or processors. Having initiated a barrier synchronisation, the next computation step will be processed only when all other members of the group have participated in the synchronisation. See **communication**, **BSP** and Chapter 12

Beta reduction, or β-reduction: The basic evaluation mechanism in the λ-calculus, in which all instances of a named variable in an expression are replaced with some argument expression. See **alpha conversion**, **substitution** and Chapter 2.

Bird-Meertens Formalism: See **BMF**.

Blocking: A synchronisation mechanism involving suspending execution of a task/thread pending the production of a needed result by another task/thread. See **notification**, **resumption**, **non-blocking**.

BMF: The Bird-Meertens Formalism (or BMF) provides a calculus for reasoning about recursive expressions. It has a close correspondence to pure functional languages and is used to formulate and prove functional program transformations. The ability to manipulate composed higher-order functions makes it particularly relevant to parallel functional programming. See Chapters 2 and 4.

Bottom, or ⊥: The value of an undefined expression, represented as ⊥. If the result of a function is ⊥ (undefined) whenever an argument is also ⊥, then the function is *strict* in that argument. This is significant for non-strict languages, since strict arguments may be evaluated in parallel with the evaluation of the function. See **strictness**, **abstract interpretation** and Chapter 2.

Branch-and-bound: A parallel paradigm in which several parallel task are created speculatively to compute the same result, or to search a space of possible results. As soon as any result is obtained, any outstanding tasks are terminated. See **speculative evaluation**.

BSP: Bulk Synchronous Parallelism. An approach to structuring parallel programs as a series of computation steps interspersed with synchronous communications across the entire system. Has the advantage of possessing a strong cost model. See **SPMD** and Chapters 12 and 8.

Cache coherency: The process by which multiple caches are synchronised in order to ensure a globally consistent view of the contents of memory in all caches that contain a copy of the same memory location. See **shared-memory**.

Call-by-name: An early non-strict evaluation mechanism originally used in Algol-60, which implements beta reduction by replacing the argument variable with a call to a *thunk*, a procedure to evaluate the expression to be substituted for that variable. Simpler, but less efficient than lazy evaluation. See **call-by-need**, **lazy evaluation**, **call-by-value**, **eager evaluation**.

Call-by-need: An improved non-strict evaluation mechanism, in which function arguments are evaluated only when needed. Gives equivalent results to call-by-name. The result of evaluating an argument is, however, shared among all uses of the variable. This is often done by using

Glossary

a graph structure to model the reduction process. The basis for modern implementations of non-strict functional languages such as Haskell. See **lazy evaluation, call-by-name, non-strictness**.

Call-by-value: The usual evaluation mechanism used for both strict functional and standard imperative programming languages — arguments to functions are evaluated to yield a value which is then passed to the function, usually using a stack or register. See **eager evaluation, strictness**.

Category: The fundamental concept from category theory, a mathematical theory that can be used to formally model the structure of many objects used in computer science, including computations themselves [352]. Used for semantic modelling, and to gain insight into the structure of computations by applying general theorems.

Closure: A representation for a function together with the bindings for its free variables (its arguments and any other data that is needed to produce its result). See **graph reduction, SECD** and Chapter 2.

Cluster: A cluster is a group of (perhaps heterogeneous) computers acting as a parallel unit. Modern clusters are usually built from standard workstations, though commercial NUMAs (Non-Uniform Memory Architectures) are also a form of cluster. These typically implement some form of distributed shared memory. See **distributed shared memory**.

Combinator: A combinator is a function without any free variables; often one of a fixed set such as S, K or I. See **supercombinator** and Chapter 2.

Communication: The transmission of values between independent agents (whether threads, tasks, or processes). In parallel systems, communication between separate processors will involve the use of some communications network. At one extreme, this may be a high-latency commodity local-area network, while at the other this may be a dedicated low-latency, and usually proprietary, shared-memory system. See **network, asynchronous communication, synchronous communication**.

Concurrency: Processes are concurrent if no order is defined between them (that is they may execute simultaneously). Concurrent processes usually compete for processing and other resources. Concurrency may be simulated on a uni-processor system using time-sharing. See **parallelism, fairness**.

Conservative evaluation: Under a conservative scheme, parallel threads or tasks are only introduced if they are needed to contribute to the result of the program. See **speculative evaluation**.

Control flow: In contrast to dataflow, more conventional control flow systems are driven by control sequences which request data. In particular, they evaluate function arguments when they are needed. See **dataflow, eager evaluation, lazy evaluation**.

Coordination: Parallel coordination languages separate control and computation, typically adding coordination constructs as a separate language to the sequential host language. Examples include Linda [214], Strand [202] and Caliban [214]. See Chapter 14.

Cost model: A system that can be used to predict dynamic execution costs based on static information. Also called a performance model. See **BSP**, **skeleton** and Chapters 12 and 13

Dataflow: Dataflow systems are driven by data items requesting to be processed. Dataflow languages allow function results to be computed once all arguments become available (triggering). This inverts the usual control-flow mechanism, where function arguments are computed when the result of the function is itself needed, allowing a more eager (but still potentially non-strict) evaluation mechanism. See Section 2.6 and Chapter 11.

Data parallelism: This arises from simultaneously applying the same programming construct to all the elements of a collection type, such as a list or tree. This can give rise to massive amounts of parallelism if the data structure is large. Parallelism created in this way is usually cheap to distribute, and easy to identify, but may be excessively fine-grained. See **BSP**, **SPMD** and Chapter 7.

Deadlock: Deadlock occurs when all tasks are prevented from making further progress due to resource starvation, typically as resources required by each are held but not relinquished by other tasks. See **livelock** and Chapter 16.

Decomposition: See **partitioning**.

Delta rule/reduction, or δ-rule: A built-in rule used in λ-calculus for simple arithmetic or similar constructs that can be computed directly, yet which would be complicated to express in the pure λ-calculus. See **lambda calculus, beta reduction**.

Distributed memory: Referring to a parallel architecture in which each processor has its own distinct memory space. Usually characterised by medium to high-latency communication. See **shared memory, distributed shared memory, tightly coupled, distributed system**.

Distributed system: A distributed system is a collection of loosely coupled autonomous (possibly heterogenous) processors. See **loosely coupled, tightly coupled** and **parallel system**.

Distributed shared memory: A parallel architecture in which memory is physically distributed, but where there is a single logical address space. Either hardware or software can be used to map logical memory accesses to physical memory addresses. If remote memory locations are cached, it will be necessary to maintain cache-coherency. Examples are the SGI Origin and Challenge. See **distributed memory, shared memory, virtual shared memory**.

Divide-and-conquer: A well-known paradigm [107] in which a problem is divided into a number of sub-problems that can be executed in parallel. Results from each of the sub-problems are combined to form a complete solution to the problem. The process is repeated recursively until the

Glossary

problem to be solved is simple enough to be solved sequentially. This acts as a mechanism to control task granularity. See also **branch-and-bound**.

Eager evaluation: Involves evaluating all arguments to a function application before evaluating the body of the function using the values of those arguments. Used for strict functions, and implemented using call-by-value. See **evaluation, call by value, lazy evaluation, dataflow, strictness** and Chapter 5.

Efficiency: The proportion of total execution time spent performing useful work. The definition of useful work should (but in the general literature does not always) exclude all overhead costs, including communication, task creation, speculation, scheduling etc. That is, it should be identical to the sequential execution time. See **speedup**.

Eta reduction, or η-reduction: A reduction rule used in some, but not all, variants of the λ-calculus.

$$(\lambda x.ex) = e \text{ if } x \text{ is not free in } e$$

Can be used to simplify functional programs by removing surplus arguments to functions. For example,

```
  g l = map ((+) 1) l
==  g  = map ((+) 1)
```

See also **alpha renaming, beta reduction, delta reduction** and **partial application**.

Evaluation: The process by which the value of an expression is determined. Expressions that are simple values, such as integers, can be evaluated trivially. More complex expressions such as function applications will involve evaluating the body of the function and some or all of the arguments to the application before its value can be determined. Evaluation is thus an abstract mechanism that transforms a symbolic representation of an expression into some other symbolic form. In contrast, execution involves actually realising that symbolic mechanism on some concrete machine, performing real machine instructions that collectively implement evaluation. See **dataflow, control flow, lazy evaluation, eager evaluation, call-by-name, call-by-need, call-by-value, function application**.

Execution: Running a program, typically on a concrete machine. See **evaluation**.

Explicit parallelism: Involves identifying sources of parallelism, communication, etc. in the program source. See **implicit parallelism** and Chapters 3, 17 and 18.

Fairness: *Strong fairness* is the property that requires equal distribution of processing resources among all executable concurrent processes. *Weak fairness* (the variant that is usually implemented) simply requires that each process should execute eventually, so preventing livelock. See **concurrency, livelock** and **deadlock**.

Farm: A parallel paradigm in which work is apportioned to a number of worker tasks, with results collected by a farmer task. See also **branch-and-bound, divide-and-conquer, pipeline**, and Chapter 13.

First-order function: See **higher-order function**.

Fixed point: A fixed point is a function whose result is the same as its argument, so that if f is a fixed point, then f d == d, for all values of d. See **lambda calculus** and Chapter 2.

Fold: Like map and scan, the family of fold functions represent basic patterns of recursion. The expression fold op b s may be thought of as applying a function op between each member of a sequence s, with b representing the base case for the function op. There are two common varieties of folding function: foldl and foldr which begin applying op at the left or right end of the sequence, respectively. See **map, scan, divide-and-conquer** and Chapter 2.

Fork-and-join: A model of control parallelism in which a new task is created using a fork operation, with results being collected at a later point using a join.

Free variable: In λ-calculus, a variable which is not bound by a λ-abstraction.

Function application: A function plus one or more arguments. For example, f 1 2 3 is the application of f to arguments 1, 2 and 3. See **partial application**.

Function composition: The consecutive application of two functions. For example double . sqr is the composition of the two functions double and sqr. The full expression is itself a function whose effect is to first apply sqr to its argument and then to apply double to that result. The composition operator (.) is defined by:

(f . g) x = f (g x)

See **function application**.

Functional language: A language which involves programming using *functionals* — higher-order functions. Functional languages are characterised by the exclusive use of functions (mappings from inputs to an output) to define a set of rules that can be used to give the value of an expression that represents the result of the program. In a purely functional language, functions are devoid of implicit side-effects, and all control. See **pure functional language, impure functional language**.

G-Machine: Quintessential abstract machine supporting a lazy graph reduction model. See **SECD machine, graph reduction, lazy evaluation, abstract machine**.

Graph reduction: An implementation technique that is usually used for *lazy evaluation*, in which the functional program to be evaluated is represented as a graph structure. Sharing is ensured by treating variables as pointers to graph nodes, and by updating each graph node that is evaluated with its (weak head) normal form. In order to achieve *lazy evalu-*

ation, graph nodes must be locked as soon as their evaluation is started. Subsequent attempts to evaluate the same node will then block pending the result of the node. The mechanism is easily adapted for parallel evaluation. It is possible to have several threads, each of which is evaluating an independent piece of subgraph, and which will automatically block whenever a value is needed that is under evaluation by another thread. See **lazy evaluation, call-by-need, locking, blocking**, and Chapter 6.

Head normal form: An expression in head normal form is a function whose body is not a redex. In particular, the body may be a function application where the function position expression is not a redex but the argument position expression is a redex. See **reduction, redex, normal form, weak head normal form** and Chapter 2.

Higher-order function: A function that manipulates other functions, either by using them as arguments, or by returning a result that is a function. A first-order function, by contrast, is one that has no functional arguments and returns a non-functional result. Higher-order functions are extremely powerful, since they effectively allow the introduction of new control constructs. For example,

    twice f x = f (f x)

applies the function f to the argument x twice.

    quad f x = twice twice f x

applies the function `twice` twice, to give a function that takes a function argument `f` and applies `f` to its argument four times. See Chapter 2

Implicit parallelism: In contrast to explicit parallelism, which must be indicated by the programmer, implicit parallelism is obtained directly from the program source. Some systems allow programmer-specified hints that may however be ignored during execution. See **explicit parallelism** and Chapters 3, 17 and 18.

Impure functional language/imperative language: A (functional) language that allows implicit side-effects, e.g. through providing assignments. See **functional language, pure functional language**.

Instrumentation: Altering a program in order to provide information about the execution of the program. See **profiling, monitoring** and Chapter 10.

Irregular parallelism: Each computation has its own description, and/or the costs of independent computations may vary considerably. See **regular parallelism**.

Lambda calculus, or λ-calculus: A simple and elegant mathematical theory of functions, comprising at its simplest three fundamental concepts: variables, function applications, and function abstractions. A function abstraction (or λ-abstraction) is written $\lambda x.e$. This is the (unnamed) function that takes one argument x, and returns e as its result. For example, $\lambda x.x$ is the identity function (the function that returns its argument). Function abstractions may be applied to some argument expression, in which case that expression is substituted for the variable that has been "bound" by the λ-abstraction. So, for example, $(\lambda x.x)(\lambda y.z)$ yields $(\lambda y.z)$. See **function application, beta reduction, alpha renaming, eta reduction, substitution,** and Chapter 2.

Latency: The time between initiating and receiving an item of communication. See **bandwidth**.

Latency-hiding: Reducing the effect of high latency, for example by switching execution to a different thread whilst awaiting a reply to a message, so that communication can be overlapped with execution. Similar to the use of asynchronous file I/O at an operating systems level. See **latency, message, thread**.

Lazy evaluation: Avoids duplicating work unnecessarily by sharing the results of evaluation. See **eager evaluation, graph reduction, call-by-need** and Chapter 6.

Lifting: A process whereby some implicit property is made explicit. For example, lambda lifting (Chapter 2), where free variables become additional function arguments.

Linear speedup: Speedup that is directly proportional to the number of processors in use. See **speedup**.

Livelock: Livelock occurs when tasks fail to terminate, typically carrying out work which does not contribute to overall program progress. Can be avoided either by careful program design and good discipline, by the use of livelock detection tools, or by delegating resource management to a livelock-free run-time system. See **deadlock** and Chapter 16.

Locality: The degree to which tasks or data are located within close proximity, whether in physical terms or in terms of communication costs.

Locking (node): The process of tagging a node to prevent it being evaluated by more than one thread in a parallel graph reduction system. See **graph reduction**.

Loosely coupled: A loosely coupled parallel architecture is one which is capable of tolerating failures of communication links or processors, such as a network of workstations. Such machines are characterised by high latency, and low bandwidth. See **tightly coupled**.

Map: An operation that applies the same function to all elements of a collection type, returning the results as a new collection type with the same shape as the original. For example on lists:

```
map f [] = []
map f (x:xs) = f x : map f xs
```

This *higher-order function* is very commonly used in functional programs. It can often be used as the basis for introducing data parallelism across the elements of a collection type. It is therefore one of the most commonly encountered algorithmic skeletons. See **farm, fold, scan, higher-order function** and Chapters 7 and 13.

Glossary

Message: A logically indivisible item that is communicated between two (or occasionally more) processors. Includes information about the message's destination and content (usually in the form of tags). See **packet**.

Message passing: A model in which all communication occurs through messages. See **shared-memory**.

MIMD: Multiple Instruction Multiple Data. Anarchy. In this class of architecture, any processor may execute any instruction independently of any other processor. Processors may or may not run instantiations of the same program. See **SPMD** and **SIMD**.

Monomorphism: Having exactly one type. For example, simple types, such as integers, are monomorphic. See **polymorphism**.

MPI: Message Passing Interface. A communication library that aims to be a successor to PVM. See **message passing, PVM** and Chapter 18.

Multi-threaded: A multi-threaded system allows many threads to execute concurrently. See **thread, concurrency, single-threaded**.

Nested parallelism: The language property that some parallel structure may contain further parallelism, perhaps of a different kind. For example, a function that is contained within a pipeline may use data parallelism across its arguments. In this case, data parallelism is nested within a pipeline. See **pipeline, data parallelism, skeleton**.

Network: The logical or physical communication system that connects the processors in a parallel machine. See **communication**.

Non-blocking: Non-blocking communication splits a message into a request and a reply which may be handled asynchronously. See **blocking, asynchronous communication, latency hiding**.

Non-strictness: See **strictness**.

Non-termination: See **termination**.

Normal form: A normal form is one which is the result of using a reduction strategy. In full normal form (often abbreviated "normal form"), no further reduction is possible. Head normal form, and weak head normal form are, in contrast "intermediate" forms that may allow further reductions to take place. Also known as full normal form. See **reduction, head normal form, weak head normal form**.

Notification: A thread/task may be notified when the response to some outstanding communication is received. If it is blocked, and responses have been received to all outstanding communications, it may then be resumed. See **blocking, resumption**.

Packet: A primitive item of communication that contains routing, sequencing etc information. Long messages may be subdivided into many packets for transmission. These packets may take alternative routes through the communication network, perhaps arriving in a different order from that of transmission, and be subsequently reassembled using sequencing information in the packets. See **message**.

Parallelism: Solving a problem by using multiple cooperating agents to collectively produce the required solution. The usual target of parallelism is to improve performance by yielding speedup compared with some sequential system. Some parallel systems, however, target improvements in throughput (quantity of work), or real-time response. See **concurrency, speedup, sequential**.

Partial application: If a function has N formal parameters, partial application involves applying that function to the first $N - A$ actual parameters. The result is a function of A formal parameters that when it is given A actual parameters will yield the same result as a full application to all N actual parameters. For example, a function to increment all the values in a list could be defined as the partial application of the `map` function to the incrementing function, `add1 = map (+ 1)`. Note that it is possible for a multi-parameter function to be partially applied several times, gradually accumulating all the actual parameters that it needs. See **eta reduction, function application**.

Partial evaluation: An expression to expression transformation, that typically involves reducing or evaluating an expression, in the absence of all free variable bindings or with free variables bound to symbolic values. The aim is to evaluate those parts of a program that are not dependent on the program's input at compile-time, so eliminating the need to re-evaluate the same expressions every time the program is executed. See also **execution, evaluation**.

Partitioning: Creating parallel tasks from a sequential program.

Performance model: See **cost model**.

Performance monitoring: Measuring and evaluating a program's dynamic run-time behaviour. See **instrumentation** and **profiling**.

Pipeline: A series of stages which are combined so that the output of one stage is passed as input to the next in the pipeline, and so on to the end of the pipeline. Each of the stages in the pipeline may be executed in parallel. See also **farm, map, skeleton**.

Placement: How tasks or data are allocated are allocated to processors. See **partitioning** and **scheduling**.

Polymorphism: Having many types. So variables that can range over all possible types are polymorphic. For example, the type of the standard map function:

```
map f [] = []
map f (x:xs) = f x : map f xs
```

is:

```
map :: (a -> b) -> [a] -> [b]
```

This function is polymorphic: it takes two arguments, a function of some argument type `a` to some result type `b`, and a list of the same type as the function argument `[a]`, and returns a list of the same type as the function result [b]. The types a and b may be any legal type, either different or the same. It follows that map can be applied in many different contexts. See **monomorphism**.

Process: A logically independent unit of computation with its own set of resources, which are obtained competitively. A concurrent system will normally contain many processes, each of which may perhaps be divided into several parallel tasks. Interprocess communication is normally explicit using message passing. See **task, thread, concurrency, parallelism**.

Processor: A hardware or software agent that is capable of independent execution. See **SIMD, MIMD, SPMD, parallelism**.

Process calculus: A formal system for describing concurrent systems with explicit (often synchronous) communication. Common examples include CSP, CCS and π-calculus. See Chapter 16.

Profiling: The process of assessing the dynamic performance of a program, by periodically monitoring system activity. The result is a "profile" of the program's performance. See **instrumentation, performance monitoring** and Chapter 10.

Pure functional language: A functional language that is free from implicit side-effects, such as assigning a new value to an implicitly shared variable. See **functional language, impure functional language**.

PVM: Parallel Virtual Machine. A collection of communication libraries and utilities based on a portable message passing interface. See **message passing, MPI**.

Recursion: see **recursion**.

Redex: A *reducible expression*, i.e. an expression that can be transformed to some normal form using λ-calculus reduction rules. See **reduction, beta reduction, delta reduction, normal form**.

Reduction: The process of rewriting a λ-calculus term to a canonical (or "normal") form using beta reduction, alpha renaming and perhaps eta-reduction. See **beta reduction, alpha renaming, eta reduction, normal form, head normal form** and **weak head normal form**.

Reduction strategy: A reduction strategy defines how to choose the next of several possible terms to be reduced. Reduction strategies may be either sequential or parallel, and may have properties that affect termination. See **reduction, beta reduction** and Chapter 2.

Referential transparency: The property that the value of an expression will never change during program execution. Used to distinguish pure and impure functional languages.

Refinement: Successively transforming part of a program whilst preserving meaning. Used as part of the program development process, typically to meet some operational criterion. For example, a pure functional prototype might be refined into an parallel, imperative implementation. Compilation could be considered to be automatic program refinement with limited freedom.

Regular parallelism: All parallel computations are described in the same way and the cost of each computation is approximately the same. See **irregular parallelism**.

Relative speedup: Speedup measured relative to one processor on a parallel machine. See **speedup** and **absolute speedup**.

Routing: Choosing the path that is taken by a communication through the communication network. See **communication, message passing**.

Scalability: The property that performance results obtained on a small system are representative of results on a larger system. See **speedup** and **efficiency**.

Scan: One of the essential data parallel operations, related to fold. The scan function successively applies a function to a sequence of values, starting from some initial value.

```
scan f q [] = [q]
scan f q (x:xs) = q : scan f (f q x) xs
```

So scan f z [x1,x2,..] == [z, f z x1, f (f z x1) x2, ...] etc. See **map, fold** and **skeleton**.

Scheduling: Determining the order in which the possible parallel threads or tasks are executed. See **partitioning, placement**.

SECD machine: Peter Landin's Stack Environment Control Dump abstract machine which uses an eager evaluation mechanism. This formed the basis of much early work on functional language implementation. See **abstract machine** and Chapter 5.

Semi-explicit parallelism: A term used in this book to distinguish models of parallelism which unlike implicit parallelism expose the sources of parallelism in the source of the parallel program, but which do not control all details of evaluation as would be the case for explicit parallelism. See **implicit parallelism, explicit parallelism** and Chapter 3.

Sequential: Occurring in sequence. Sequential behaviour ensures that values are produced consecutively, as in normal program execution. Such behaviour is often over-specified – it is frequently not necessary to introduce dependencies between the order in which results are constructed, but only in the final result. This is the observation that allows dataflow execution by exploiting a serial, but non-sequential semantics. See **serial, parallel, concurrent**.

Serial: Having an ordering, but not requiring consecutive evaluation. For example, file I/O usually has a serial semantics – once I/O is completed the file forms a completely ordered entity. It is, however, legitimate to construct later parts of the file before earlier parts have been produced. See **sequential, parallelism, concurrency**.

Shape: The shape of an object is its logical structure together with size information. See **regular parallelism, topology** and Chapter 9.

Glossary

Shared memory: A shared memory architecture allows multiple processors to access the same physical memory locations. Hardware ensures consistency between different copies of the same memory location. See **cache coherence, distributed memory, distributed shared memory, virtual shared memory**.

SIMD: Single Instruction Multiple Data. In this class of architecture, all processors in a machine will execute the same instruction simultaneously, but on different data. See **MIMD**.

Single threaded: A task is single-threaded if it cannot be subdivided into more than one thread. See **sequential, multi-threaded**.

Skeleton: A pattern of parallel computation that can be detected automatically, and mapped efficiently to some target machine. For example, a map may be implemented by a data parallel operation, such as a farm, that applies the function to each element of the collection type on a different processor. Often rely on sophisticated cost models to determine applicability. See **map, farm, pipeline**.

SMP: Symmetric Multiprocessor. A multiprocessor in which any processor can run threads that affect the state of the operating system kernel. Typically, but not necessarily, a shared-memory architecture. See **shared memory, distributed memory**.

Spark: A closure that has been annotated to be potentially parallel. Unlike threads, which are executable entities, sparks are lightweight entities with no attached state. See **closure, spark pool, thread, task**.

Spark pool: A collection of sparks, which can be mined to produce threads. See **spark, thread**.

Speculative evaluation: Involves creating parallel threads or tasks in advance of knowing whether these will be necessary to produce the final result of the program. See **conservative evaluation**.

Speedup: The improvement in performance over a base case. See **absolute speedup, relative speedup**.

SPMD: Single Program Multiple Data. A recent model of parallel execution, in which each processor executes its own copy of the same program, but using different data. More rigid definitions require computation to proceed in a series of supersteps as with BSP, but relax the requirement that all communication must have completed between supersteps. See **BSP, MIMD** and Chapters 12 and 18.

Starvation: See **deadlock** and **livelock**.

Strictness: The language property that a function needs the value of its argument in order to return a result. By extension, strict languages always need all arguments to all functions. See **eager evaluation, non-strictness, bottom**.

Strict evaluation: See **eager evaluation**.

Substitution: The replacement of one or more named variables in a term by the corresponding given terms. A general notion, used in reduction, type inference etc. $t[x/a]$ is used to denote the substitution of x by a in the term t. See **beta reduction**.

Supercombinator: In supercombinator approaches each user-defined function definition is compiled into a single combinator [459]. Since combinators cannot contain free variables, it follows that supercombinators do not implicitly "inherit" arguments from definitions in which they are enclosed, but must be passed these arguments along with those that the user has defined. Supercombinator lifting, which converts normal nested definitions into definitions defined only in terms of supercombinators, is a widely used technique for identifying sites of lazy parallelism in graph reduction based systems. See **combinator, free variable** and Chapter 2.

Suspension: A suspension is a closure that is not a (weak head) normal form. When evaluated, it will be reduced to some normal form. See **closure, normal form, lazy evaluation**.

Synchronous communication: With this form of communication a thread or task will block until a response to the communication is received. See **blocking, asynchronous communication**.

Task: Parallel tasks work collectively to implement some logical process. Each task has its own independent state and communicates with other tasks either explicitly or implicitly. Tasks may sometimes be subdivided into several parallel *threads*, lighter weight agents which all share the state associated with their task. See **process, thread** and **spark**.

Task/thread pool: A collection of tasks/threads which is used to schedule the allocation of tasks/threads to processors. See **spark pool**.

Task/thread resumption: Occurs when a task becomes unblocked, usually as a result of receiving the reply to some communication. See **blocking, notification, message passing**.

Termination: The property that a program will halt and deliver some valid result. Non-termination may be a result of deadlock, livelock, infinite recursion, etc. See **deadlock, livelock**.

Thread: A lightweight parallel processing agent, with minimal state. Typically a single task may be divided into many threads, which can all share the task state. In some uses (derived from dataflow), a thread is a small unit corresponding to a basic block. That is, it comprises a sequence of computations without communication or branching. In this model, a thread terminates when it initiates a communication or branches; a new *continuation* thread is created to continue execution when the response is received. See **task, spark**.

Throughput: A measure of overall system performance in terms of the amount of work that can be accomplished in a given time. Parallel systems generally aim to optimise speedup for an individual program rather than throughput for a number of programs. See **speedup, efficiency**.

Tightly coupled: A tightly coupled parallel architecture is one which cannot tolerate failures of communication links or processors. Typically this means a machine with lower latency than one which is loosely coupled, and usually one which is specifically designed as a multiprocessor. See **loosely coupled**.

Topology: The logical structure of a parallel communication system. Typical modern communication topologies are meshes, hypercubes, or clusters. See Chapter 2.

Virtual shared memory: A system in which memory can be logically shared across the machine. Unlike distributed shared memory, support for virtual shared memory is provided by language-level software, rather than by the hardware or operating system. See **distributed shared memory**.

Weak head normal form: An expression which is not itself reducible at the top level but which may contain reducible subexpressions. All full normal forms and head normal forms are also weak head normal forms. See **normal form**, **head normal form**, **redex** and **lambda calculus**.

Index

\# shape combinator   221
\# =, shape equality   221
⊥, undefined value   6, 67, 109, 466
≡, equivalence   96
*T dataflow system   60
(.), function composition   26
(:), list constructor   34
[], null list   34
'`..`' notation in Haskell   37

ABC Machine   172–174, 338
– parallel   174, 178, 185
abstract interpretation   47, 465
abstract machine   123, 465
– definition of   20–21
accumulating parameter   38, 356
active data structures   201–206
Alfalfa system   179–180
algebraic data types   38, 39, 99
algorithmic skeleton   *see* skeleton
ALICE architecture   19, 150, 176–177
α-conversion   41–42, 465
analysis
– cost   66, 208
– granularity   66, 208
– shape   221
– sharing   163
– static   361–362
– strictness   9, 47, **66–68**
`Annot` in Caliban   308
annotations   11, 70–71, 145
– Concurrent Clean   70–71, 323–325
applications   **399–426**
– accident blackspots   411
– AGNA database   404
– Boyer-Moore theorem prover   404
– BSP   407
– circuit test package   414
– climate modelling   414
– computational fluid dynamics   402
– computer algebra   411
– constructive solid geometry   409
– data mining   414–415
– data-intensive   404, 411–412
– database   411
– explicit parallelism   416–419
– `Gamteb` photon transport program   403
– global ocean circulation   402–403
– implicit parallelism   400–405
– in Hope$^+$ 409
– in Caliban   415
– in Concurrent Clean   408
– in DPFL   405
– in GpH   409–411
– in Id   403
– in MultiLisp   410
– in P3L   414
– in ParLisp   404
– in PCN   414
– in SAC   403
– in SCL   413
– in Skil   406
– in Strand   414
– linear system solving   414
– Lolita natural language system   409
– LR(0) parser generator   410
– Monte Carlo photon transport   403
– multigrid applications   407
– n-body problem   407, 414
– Naira compiler   409
– nucleic acids   410
– numerical applications   400–407, 413–415, 420–422
– `paraffins`   404
– partial differential equations   402, 403
– Pseudoknot   411
– ray tracing   294, 302, 308, 408, 415
– semi-explicit parallelism   405–412
– `Simple`   402
– symbolic applications   404, 407–411, 422

- tidal prediction   407
- transaction processing   411
- using evaluation strategies   409
- using skeletons   407–409
- Veritas theorem-prover   410
- vision   400, 407–408
- weather prediction   400

apply-to-each in NESL   79
Arc in Caliban   83, 306, 308
arrays
- accumulator array in Id   265
- array comprehensions   249
- distributed   395
- distribution in Clean   327–330
- in Haskell   255
- in Id   249
- in SISAL   250
- slices   251, 254, 255

ASM, Abstract Stack Machine   136
associativity in fold   352
asynchronous communication   148, 331, 465
automatic parallelisation   66–68

bags, conversion to lists example   357–358
bandwidth   15–18, 207, 216, 465
barrier synchronisation   129, 213, 465
- in BSP   268, 269
- in Id   250
basic types in Haskell   31
behaviour signatures in SCL   299
behaviours in CML   366–372
benchmarks
- dataflow   251–264
- Impala implicit suite   404
- NAS benchmark FT   251, 254–257
- NAS benchmark MG   403, 404
- NAS benchmarks in BSP   287
- Wisconsin database suite   404

β-reduction   40–42, 52, 53, 466
binomial coefficient example
- d&c skeleton   80
- evaluation strategies   77–78
- in Caliban   83
- in Concurrent Clean   70–71
- in Eden   84
- in Facile   89
- in GpH   71–72, 77–78
- sequential   65

Bird-Meertens Formalism   see BMF notation
bisimulation   112–113, 115

block cyclic distribution   219
block decomposition   226, 229–230
blocking   61, 134, 146, 159, 161, 466
- communication   332
- of threads   241

BMF notation   26, 118, 214, 223, 226, 228, 292, 359, 466
- and skeletons   421–422

Bool type   see boolean type
boolean type (Bool)   33
bound variable   41
boxed representation   51
branch-and-bound   466
Brent's theorem   211
broadcast in SCL   298
Broadcasting Sequential Processes   331

$BS\lambda$ calculus   284
BSML language   284
BSP   **267–287**, 466
- and GOLDFISH   231
- applications   407
- automatic mode   270
- BSPlib   271
- communication   213
- cost modelling   212–214, 217, 271–275
- direct mode   270
- h-relation   272
- NAS parallel benchmarks   287
- parallel scan   275
- sample sort   277–283
- superstep   213, 268

Buckwheat system   179–180
Bulk Synchronous Parallelism   see BSP
Bundle in Caliban   83, 306
byte-code, Java   151, 338

cache coherency   19, 466
cactus stack   141
Caliban language   12, 82–83, 305–321, 415
- applications   415
- Arc annotation   83, 306
- avoiding unwanted compile-time computation   317
- binomial coefficient example   83
- Bundle annotation   83, 306
- compile-time evaluation   310, 317
- garbage collection   313
- introduction to   305
- keywords   306
- **moreover** clause   83, 306

Index

- nested **moreover** clause   312
- network forming operators   83, 310
- process placement rule   307
- ray tracing application   415
- run-time system   313
- thread scheduling   313
- threads   307

call-by-name   50, 108, 466
call-by-need   50, 67, 108, 466
call-by-value   67, 467
CAM, Categorical Abstract Machine   50, 58, 151
Caml language   86, **379–396**, 416
- Caml-Flight   284, 395

Categorical Abstract Machine   *see* CAM
category theory   118, 467
CCOZ system   177–178
CCS process calculus   26, 87, 114
channel in CML   363
channels   145, 157
- Clean   331–334
- CML   146
- Concurrent Haskell   90
- CSP   340
- dynamic communication of   331
- dynamic creation of   85
- Eden   84
- Facile   88, 147, 148

Char type   *see* character type
character type (**Char**)   32
choice
- deterministic   130
- non-deterministic   131

choose in CML   365
Church, Alonzo   39
Church-Rosser property   21, 42, 43, 46, 66, 74, 121, 140
Church-Rosser theorems   42–43
CIP transformation project   342
circuit test generation   302
Clean language   86–87, 303, **322–338**
- ABC Machine   338
- annotations   70–71
- applications   408
- binomial coefficient example   70–71
- channels   331–334
- communication   324, 332
- communication of dynamic channels   331
- communication performance   334
- Concurrent Clean   **322–338**
- conjugate gradient algorithm   330
- **copyTo** function   327
- **CreateCyclicProcs** example   326
- **CurrentP** annotation   70
- data parallelism   323, 327–330
- defining skeletons   326
- distributed arrays   327–330
- **distributeVector** function   330
- *Dynamics*   335
- dynamic types   331, 332, 334–338
- **getRemote** function   327
- {| **I** |} annotation   70, 324
- lazy graph copying   323, 324
- **localMatMulVec** function   330
- **mapDArray** function   329
- matrix multiplication example   329–330
- message ordering   332
- multicast communication   331
- on ZAPP   177–178
- {| **P** |} annotation   70, 324
- {| **P at** processor |} annotation   324
- parallel annotations   323–325
- parallel **Fib** example   325
- **parMap** function   71, 327
- pattern matching on types   335
- pipeline   325
- **Primes** example   325
- producer-consumer example   333
- **putRemote** function   327
- **rap** functions   328
- **receive** primitive   332
- remote application   328
- **send** primitive   332
- sparse matrix multiplication example   71
- *Statics*   335
- strictness annotation   332
- task distribution   328
- type dependent functions   337
- uniqueness type   323, 334
- **zipwithDarray** functions   329

closure   47, 138, 467
cluster   18, 467
CM-LISP language   284
CML language   8, 87, 145–147, 361–378, 389
- **accept**   146
- **recEvt**   365
- **recv**   363
- **acquire**   146
- behaviours   366–372
- causal type and effect system   368–372

- channel   363
- choose   146, 365
- event-based communication   364–366
- events   146, 364–366
- exit   146
- fork   146
- implementation on Mach   146
- introduction to   362
- map   367
- mappar   364, 367
- parmap function   364, 368
- production cell example   372–376
- receive   146
- release   146
- select   365
- send   146, 364
- sendEvt   365
- seqmap   368
- spawn   363
- sync   365
- thread   145
- threads   363
- transmit   146
- wait   146
- wrap   146, 365

coinduction   113–114
- for infinite lists   112–113
combinator   56, 151, 467
- par   71–72
- data parallel   192–201
- parallel   71–72
combinatory logic   56
communication   467
- and cost   207
- and dependencies   5
- and PRAM model   212
- asynchronous   148, 331, 465
- blocking   332
- broadcast   214
- BSP   213
- channels   see channels
- event-based   364–366
- explicit   364–366
- implicit   157
- in Clean   323, 324
- lazy graph copying   323, 324
- message passing   381–382
- multicast   331
- nearest neighbour topology   193
- notification   168, 176, 179, 473
- of dynamic channels   331
- performance of   334
- selective in Scampi   389
- SIMD shifts   193
- synchronous   88, 147, 340, 478
- topology   18–19

comp in P3L   302
compilation
- FISH   223
- P3L   302
compiled graph reduction   58
composition
- of cost models   214–217, 221
- of cost monads   231
- of parallel components   305
compute-ahead   306, 315, 318
Concert system   141
concessions   130–132
- for task creation   126
- π-RED$^+$ 137
concurrency   81, 87–91, 339, 467
- definition of   7
- implementation   145–148
Concurrent Clean   see Clean language
Concurrent Haskell   87, 89–90, 363
Concurrent ML   see CML language
concurrent systems   64, 81
condition variables   146
conditionals   35, 97–98
confluence   42, 218
conjugate gradient algorithm in Clean   330
cons, list constructor   34
conservative evaluation   467
constructive type theory   116–117
constructor function
- list   34
- user-defined   38, 39
continuation   140
control flow   467
control parallelism   see function parallelism
controlled parallelism   11–12, 75–81
controller sponsors   144
coordination language   12, 83, 305–321, 467
- applications   412–415
- GOLDFISH as   228
- numerical applications   413–415
copyTo function in Clean   327
copyToDiagonal function in Clean   329
cost analysis   66
cost calculus   see cost model
cost model   66, 207–218, 468

Index

- BSP   212–214, 217, 220, 271–275
  - composition of   214–217, 221
  - convex   215, 218
  - for GOLDFISH   227, 231–232
  - in NESL   79, 212
  - locality-based   214
  - monadic   221, 231
  - PRAM   211–212
  - RAM   208
  - size of data   207
  - skeleton   213–214, 216–217
  - space   208, 217
  - von Neumann   208
- cost monad   221, 231
- cover   230, 292
- Cray T3D architecture   217
- CreateCyclicProcs example in Clean   326
- critical path   208
- CSG, Constructive Solid Geometry   295, 303, 409
- CSP process calculus   26, 114, 331, **339–360**
  - ACC process   343
  - CAT2 process   340
  - channels   340
  - COPY process   343
  - FILTER process   343
  - firing rules   339
  - FOLDL process   357
  - FOLDR process   354, 355
  - INSERT process   344, 355
  - insertion sort   355–356
  - ISORT process   355
  - list to bag example   357–358
  - MAP process   343, 350
  - notation   339–344
  - pipeline   349–350, 353, 355
  - polynomial evaluation example   350–352
  - POLYS process   351
  - primitive processes   339
  - refinement to sequential process   343–344
  - SPEC process   350
  - synchronous communication   340
- CurrentP annotation in Clean   70
- Curry and Fey's standardisation theorem   43
- Curry/Howard isomorphism   116
- Currying   36

- d&c skeleton   80

- DACTL intermediate language   177, 179
- data parallelism
  - fold   198
- data distribution   219, 221, 228–231
  - GOLDFISH   227
  - shape operators   228–229
- data mining   414–415
- data parallelism   14, 72–75, 148, **191–206**, 271, 327–330, 352, 468
  - cost modelling   212
  - DPFL   391, 395, 405
  - DPHaskell   284
  - fold   195–196, **197–352**
  - heat equation example   194–195
  - high-level   78–79
  - in Clean   323, 327–330
  - index intervals example   202–206
  - maximum segment sum example   199
  - maximum segment sum example   200
  - nested   78–79
  - paraML   148
  - recursive doubling network   200–201
  - scan   **196–198**
  - versus task parallelism   206
- data structures
  - active   201–206
  - and cost   207
  - concrete, CDS   284
  - dataflow   251
  - non-strict   248
- data type
  - recursive   39
  - user-defined   38, 39, 99
- dataflow   **58–61**, 74, 247–265, 468
  - *T system   60
  - benchmarks   251
  - data structures   251
  - dataflow graph   208, 210
  - dataflow token   59
  - dynamic dataflow   59
  - I-structures   59, 74, 249
  - Id   see Id language
  - k-bounded loops   61, 254, 403
  - lambda-S calculus   61
  - languages   249–250
  - latency hiding   61
  - M-structures   59, 74, 250, 261, 265, 403
  - macro-dataflow   61
  - memory performance   247–265

- model   247–248
- non-strictness   250, 251
- P-RISC system   60
- parallelism profile   248
- programming   251
- SISAL   *see* SISAL language
- static dataflow   59
- structure store   248
- synchronisation   248
- tag bits   248
- TAM abstract machine   402
- task throttling   61
- tokens   247
- TTDA system   60
dataflow machine   **60**, 73
- ELS   60
- Manchester   19, 60, 177
- Monsoon   19, 60, 402, 404
- PIM-D   60
- SIGMA-1   60
de Bruijn indices   42, 136
deadlock   6, 8, 161, 468
debugging   5–6
decomposition   468
- of `foldl` in CSP   356–357
- of `foldr` in CSP   352–355
- of `map` in CSP   345–352
defer bit   248
definition, local   36, 98
`delay` function in MultiLisp   141
δ-rule   468
δ-rules   50, 55
denotational semantics   109–111, 339
dependencies   4–5, 83, 210
- and cost   208
- time   85
dependent type   116–117
design patterns   222
destructive update   251
determinacy   6
diamond property   42
DIGRESS system   162, 182–183
distributed arrays in Clean   327–330
distributed shared memory   468
distributed systems   *see* reactive systems
distributed-memory and π-RED$^+$ 136–139
distributed-memory implementation   134–135
distributed-memory system   17, 150, 468

`distributeVector` function in Clean   330
distributivity of `map`   345
divide-and-conquer   66, 80, 142, 143, 145, 252, 289, 292, 293, 325, 468
- paraML   148
- skeleton   294
`dmpa` skeleton   294
Dongarra-Sorensen Eigensolver   251, 259, 403
"dotdot" notation in Haskell   37
`Double` type   *see* double-precision type
double-precision type (`Double`)   32
DPFL, Data Parallel Functional Language   395, 405
DREAM Machine   162, 174–175
dump, in SECD Machine   47
Dutch Parallel Reduction Machine Project   407
dynamic channel creation   85
dynamic dataflow   59
dynamic linking   338
dynamic types   86, 331, 332, 334–338

E-R, Entity-Relationship   240
eager evaluation   47–50, 469
eager task creation   127, 142
Eden language   8, 12, 82, **83–85**, 174–175
- binomial coefficient example   84
- dynamic channels   85
- non-deterministic merge   85
- `parmap` function   84
- process instantiation   84
- `Process` type   84
- sparse matrix multiplication example   84–85
- time dependency   85
- `Transmissible` class   84
efficiency   469
Eigensolvers
- Dongarra-Sorensen   251, 259, 403
- for symmetric matrices   257–259
- Jacobi   257–259
ELS dataflow machine   60
environment, in SECD Machine   47
equational reasoning   95–96, 422
Erlang language   87, 363
Estelle notation   26
η-reduction   469
Euler totient function example   233
evaluate-and-die model   158, 159, 162, 245

Index

evaluation   469
- conservative   467
- eager   47–50, 469
- lazy   *see* lazy evaluation, 472
- parallel   66
- partial   474
- speculative   *see* speculative evaluation, 477
evaluation order independence   43
evaluation strategies   11, 77–78, 206, 415
- applications   409
- binomial coefficient example   77–78
- r0, rwhnf, rnf   78
evaluation transformer   67
evaluation transformers   10
events in CML   146, 364–366
execution   469
explicit parallelism   8, 12, 64, 81–91, 191, **379–396**, 469

Facile language   87, **88–89**, 145, 147–148, 363
- alternative   90
- binomial coefficient example   89
- channel primitive   88
- choice operator   90
- guards   90
- receive primitive   88
- recvguard   90
- send primitive   88
- sendguard   90
- spawn primitive   88
fair scheduling   129, 145
fairness   129–131, 469
FAM, Functional Abstract Machine   50
fan in Caliban   310
farm   469
- and map   26
- in P3L   300
- in paraML   148
- in SCL   297
- skeleton   294
FAST project   181–182
FDR support tool for CSP   341
FFT application   220, 251, 403
- one dimensional   252–254
Fib example in Clean   325
filter in Haskell   37
first-class schedules   11, 12
first-class synchronous operations   146
first-order function   470

FISH notation   221, **223–227**
- β-reduction   224
fixed point   470
Flagship architecture   177, 179
FLARE project   179, 411
flattening   212, 219
- of skeletons   298
Float type   *see* floating-point type
floating-point type (Float)   32
fold   470
- bidirectional   198
- cost   232
- data parallel   **195–198**
- decomposition in CSP   352–357
- fold in CSP   341
- folding functions   37–38, 118
- in GOLDFISH   227
- mapDArray function in Clean   329
foldl   **38**, 221
- data parallel   195
- decomposition of   356–357
- relationship with foldr   357
FOLDL process in CSP   358
foldl1, data parallel   195
foldr   **37**
- data parallel   195
- decomposition of   352–355
- transformation to CSP pipeline   353–355
foldr1, data parallel   195
fork pseudo-function   126
fork-and-join   470
Fortran-S language   298
Four-Stroke Reduction Engine   162–163, 179
FP language   26, 93, 117
frame   150
- stubbing   150
free variable   41, 470
Fujitsu AP1000 architecture   148, 315, 318, 415
full normal form   42, 78
function
- λ-calculus   40
- as a CSP process   341–343
- composition (.)   26
- conditional   35
- constructor   38, 39
- filter in Haskell   37
- folding   37, 38, 118, 195
- higher-order   36–38, 82, 192
- -- skeleton   289
- identity, id   36

– in Haskell 34–38
– map in Haskell 36
– partial application 36, 136, 154
– polymorphic 36
– recursive 34–35
– remote application in Clean 328
– scanning 38
– zipping 113
function application 470
function composition 470
function parallelism 14, 73
fusion law 118
future 146, 410
– MultiLisp 140
FX system 284

G-Machine 58, 150–162, 470
– execution 152–156
– G-code 151
– optimisation 156
– parallel 157–162
– state 151–152
garbage collection 150
– in Caliban 313
Gaussian elimination 298
getRemote function in Clean 327
Gofer language 323
GOLDFISH language **227–228**
Goldrush architecture 177
GpH language 71, 77, 409
– applications 409–411
– binomial coefficient example 71–72, 77–78
– parList strategy 78
– parMap function 78
– Strategy type 77
– using function 77
GranSim simulator 183–185, 234–239
– GranCC 236, 241
– GranSim-light 242
– GranSP 241
granularity 12, 18, **60–61**, 135, 143, 195, 403, 415
– analysis 66, 208
graph reduction 21, 50–59, 125, 470
– blocking 159, 161
– combinator 56
– compiled 58, 151
– copying graph 135
– efficiency of 50
– implementation 149–150
– interpretive 57, 151, 162–163
– lazy parallel copying 323, 324

– locking 159–161
– parallel 58, 291
– parallel model 240–246
– shared-memory implementation 132
– sharing 50–52, 55, 157, 159–160
– Stack-based 58
– supercombinator 57
– template instantiation 151
– unwinding 153–155
– update 156, 160
– with constants 55–56
– without constants 52–55
graph rewriting 323
GRIP architecture 19, 162, 177–179
Group-SPMD model 420–421
guards 35, 97–98
– in Facile 90
GUM system 183–185, 233, 380, 382

Haskell language **31–39**, 82, 83, 89, 174, 191, 195, 233, 255, 262, 323
– DPHaskell 284
HBC-PP 242
HDG Machine 149, 162, 163, 168–169, 182
head normal form 46, 471
heat equation example 194–195
heterogeneous system 17
High Performance Fortran *see* HPF language
high-level data parallelism 78–79
higher-order function 36–38, 82, 192, 471
– and data parallelism 192
– skeleton as 289
HNF *see* head normal form
Hope$^+$ language 295
Householder tridiagonalisation 259
HPF language 191, 219, 270, 285

{| **I** |} annotation in Clean 70, 324
I-structures 59, 74, 249
I/O 14, 82, 89
Id language 61, 72, 74, 249–250, 252, 254, 258, 259, 261–263, 402
– accumulator array 265
– applications 403
– array comprehensions 249
id, identity function 36
identity function, id 36, 343
Illiac IV architecture 14
imperative language 471
implementation

Index

- concurrent 145
- non-strict language 149–187
- Scampi 386–390
- shared-memory 132–134
- strict language 121–148
implicit parallelism 8, 10–11, 63, 65–75, 353, 400–405, 471
impure functional language 9–10, 251, 471
index intervals example 202–206
indirection nodes 52
infinite list 108
inlet 60
instrumentation 233–246, 471
integer type (Int) 32
interactive systems 81, 94, 145
irregular parallelism 471
iteration 34

Jacobi Eigensolver 257–259
Java byte-code 151
join pseudo-function 127
just-in-time compilation 338

k-bounded loops 61, 254, 403
KiR language 91, 136

lambda lifting 57, 151, 472
λ-calculus 39, 136, 471
- and FISH 225
- bound variable 40–41
- free variable 41
- function 40
- function application 40
- normal form
-- head 46
-- weak head 45–46
- syntax 39
- variable 39
lambda-S calculus 61
latency 15–18, 472
- hiding 61, 472
law
- composition of maps 118
- fusion 118
- map decomposition laws 345–346
- relating foldl and foldr 357
laziness 50–58, 66, 263
lazy evaluation 50–58, 66, 82, 93, 149–187, 472
lazy task creation 142, 245, 411
let keyword 36
let, parallel 69–70
letpar construct 69, 70

Linda language 12
Lisp language 139
list constructor, (:) 34
list type 33–34
lists **33–34**
- and data parallelism 193
- coinduction for infinite lists 112–113
- converting to bags in parallel 357–358
- equality on infinite lists 112
- infinite 108, 112–113, 115
- list comprehensions 249, 404
-- in NESL 79
- ranges in Haskell 37
livelock 161, 472
load balancing 135
locality 16, 19, 472
localMatMulVec function in Clean 330
locking 132, 134, 159–161, 472
loop in P3L 301
loops 34
- k-bounded 61, 254, 403
- parallel 61, 73, 254, 403
loosely-coupled system 17–18, 472
LOTOS notation 26

M-structures 59, 74, 250, 261, 265, 403
M-trees 232
M/M/1 queueing system 210
Mach operating system 146
macro-dataflow 61
Manchester dataflow machine 19, 60, 177
mandatory evaluation 123, 133
MANNA simulator 404
map 472
- and farm 26
- CML 367
- composition law 118
- cost 232
- data parallel 193
- decomposition for recursive arguments 346
- decomposition in CSP 345–352
- decomposition laws 345–346
- in GOLDFISH 227
- map in CSP 341
- map in GpH 78
- map in Haskell 11, 36
- map in NESL 79
- map in SCL 297, 298

- map in SML 363
- transformation to CSP pipeline 349–350

map
- strictness of 67

mappar in CML 364, 367
Martin-Löf type theory 116
master/worker systems 81, 85, 389
matrix multiplication 298
- in Clean 71, 329–330
- in Eden 84–85
- in NESL 79
- in Scampi 391–393
maximum segment sum example 199–200
MCode for Concert 141
memory performance 247–265
message 472
message passing 216, 473
MIMD 15, 473
Miranda language 323
MKBAG process in CSP 358
monad 14, 31, 94
- composition of cost monads 231
- cost monad 221, 231
- for concurrency 89
monitor 132
monomorphism 473
Monsoon dataflow machine 19, 60
Monte Carlo photon transport application 259–264, 403
moreover in Caliban 83, 306
- nested 312
MPI library 174, 381–382, 473
MPIRE project 309
MultiLisp language 139–145, 410
multithreading 60–61, 75, 473
mutual exclusion 146
MVar type in Concurrent Haskell 89

NAS benchmark FT 251, 254–257
NAS benchmark MG 403, 404
NAS benchmarks in BSP 287
nCUBE/2 architecture 136
nCX operating system 137
neededness 46–47
NESL language 11, 79, 219, 284
- applications 402
- apply-to-each 79
- cost modelling 79, 212
- map 79
- sequences 79
- sparse matrix multiplication example 79

- write function 79
nested data parallelism 78–79
nested parallelism 473
nested skeletons 291, 298, 299
network 473
network forming operators
- in Caliban 83, 310
newMVar primitive in Concurrent Haskell 89
NFData type class in GpH 78
nil, [] 34
non-deterministic merge 85
non-preemptive scheduling 125
non-strict language 107–108
- implementation 149–187
non-strictness 8–9, 248, 250, 251, 257, 259, 473
non-termination 67, 94, 115–118, 161, 473
normal form 473
- decidability of 42
- full 42, 67, 78, 136
- head 46, 471
- root 70, 324
- spine 67
- weak head 45–46, 50, 67, 70, 71, 78, 149, 151, 159, 479
notification 168, 176, 179, 473
novel architecture 19–20, 187
$<\nu, G>$-Machine 150, 162, 163, 166–167, 180–181
ν-STG Machine 149
null list, [] 34
numerical applications 413–415

offloading in π-RED$^+$ 137
operational semantics 112–113, 339
optical character recognition 302
optimisation, due to inexpressiveness 192

{| P |} annotation in Clean 70, 324
{| P at processor |} annotation in Clean 70, 324
P-RISC system 60
P3L language 80, 299–302, 414
PABC machine *see* ABC machine, parallel
packet 166, 473
PAM Machine 168
par combinator 71–72
para-functional programming 76–77, 233

Index

Parade project 411
Paralation Model 284
parallel annotations 70
parallel combinators 71–72
parallel let 69–70
parallel OR 131
parallel streams 82–85
parallelism
 – automatic 66–68
 – average parallelism 248
 – BSP **267–287**
 – control parallelism *see* function parallelism
 – controlled 11–12, 75–81
 – data parallelism 72–75, 148, **191–206**, 212, 271, 327–330, 352, 468
 – definition of 7, 473
 – dependencies 4–5
 – divide-and-conquer 66, 289, 292–294, 325
 – evaluation strategies 77
 – explicit 8, 12, 64, 81–91, 191, **379–396**, 469
 – function parallelism 14, 72, 73
 – high-level data parallelism 78–79
 – implicit 8, 10–11, 63, 65–75, 353, 400–405, 471
 – indicating 4–5, 68–72
 – irregular 471
 – nested 473
 – nested data parallelism 78–79
 – para-functional programming 76–77
 – partitioning 4
 – pipeline 6–7, 27–28, 214, 294, 301, 325, 342, 349–350, 353–355, 474
 – pipeline parallelism 73
 – producer-consumer 6–7, 73, 333
 – regular 476
 – scaling up 191
 – semi-explicit 11–12, 75–81, 405–412
 – serial combinators 126
 – skeletons 79
 – stream parallelism 73
paraML language 145, 148
`ParArray` in SCL 296
ParLisp language 404
`parList` strategy in GpH 78
`parMap` function
 – in Clean 71
 – in GpH 78
`parMap` function
 – in Clean 327

 – in CML 364, 368
 – in Eden 84
partial application 36, 136, 154, 474
partial evaluation 474
partial evaluation in Caliban 310, 317
partitioning 474
pattern matching 35, 97
 – on types in Clean 335
 – sequential 97
PCN language 414
pD language 411
Pearl intermediate language 174–175
pending stack
 – MultiLisp 141
performance
 – `nfib` results 185–186
 – communication v. computation 135
 – cost model 207–218
 – memory usage in dataflow programs 247–265
 – modelling 218
 – monitoring 233–246, 474
 – – relational views of 246
 – of applications 399–426
 – of Clean communication 334
 – of matrix multiplication in Clean 330
 – of paraML on AP1000 148
 – of process networks 342
 – of task creation 143
 – simple benchmarks 179
 – threads and context switching 146
performance model 474
PERT chart 208
pH – parallel Haskell 10, 74
π-calculus 26, 87, 88, 115
π-RED$^+$ system 136–139
 – closure 138
 – concessions 137
 – distributed-memory 136–139
 – offloading 137
 – speculative evaluation 139
 – thread 137
 – thread scheduler 137
PIM-D dataflow machine 60
`pipe` in P3L 301
pipeline 6–7, 27–28, 73, 214, 294, 301, 325, 342, 349–350, 353–355, 474
 – skeleton 294
platform-independent object code 338
Poisson process 210
polydimensionality 223, 226
polymorphism 36–38, 474

– FISH   225
– Scampi   386–388
polytypic programming   222
ports in paraML   148
PRAM cost model   211–212, 270
presence bit   248
Primes example in Clean   325
process abstraction
– in Eden   83
process algebra   *see* process calculus
process calculus   114–115, 475
– π-calculus   88
– and CML behaviours   366, 377
– CCS   87, 114
– CSP   114
– mobile ambients   377
– π-calculus   87, 377
– TCSP   87
process instantiation
– in Eden   84
process modelling   **339–360**
process networks   82–85, 145, 305–321, 323, 325–326
– cyclic   326
– dynamic   147
– performance of   342
Process type in Eden   84
processes   475
– CSP   339
– Eden   83–85
– paraML   148
processor   475
producer-consumer   6–7, 73, 333
profiling   233–246, 475
– dataflow   248
– per-thread profiles   237
– Scampi   389–390
proof   24–28, 93–119, 339–360
– and recursion   99–100
– proof obligation   117
– structural induction   99–100
pure functional language   9–10, 475
putMVar primitive in Concurrent Haskell   89
putRemote function in Clean   327
PVM library   380, 382, 475

r0 evaluation strategy   78
race conditions   6
RAM cost model   208
ramp skeleton   294
rap functions in Clean   328
ray tracing   302

– Caliban example   308, 415
– in SkelML   408
– using skeletons   294
reactive systems   64, 85, 145
receive
– Clean   332
– Facile primitive   88
recEvt in CML   365
recursion   34–35, 475
– and proof   99–100
– general   105–106
– primitive   118
– structural   100
– tail recursion   353, 356
– – with shared data   346
recursive doubling network   200–201
recv in CML   363
redex   42, 475
– needed   46
reduce   226
reduce in P3L   301
reduceCSG skeleton   295
reduction   475
– applicative order   21, 44–45, 123
– efficiency   44–45
– leftmost innermost   *see* reduction, applicative order
– leftmost outermost   *see* reduction, normal order
– normal order   21, 42, 44–45, 50
– normalising   43, 45
– parallel   46
– strategies   43
– termination   *see* reduction, normalising
reduction rule   112
– big step   112
– one step   112
reduction strategy   475
referential transparency   134, 475
refinement   **339–360**, 475
– notation in CSP   342
– of functions to processes   341–343
– of performance models   246
– of programs   24, 419–423
– to a sequential CSP process   343–344
regular parallelism   476
relative speedup   476
RNF   *see* root normal form
rnf evaluation strategy   78
root normal form   70, 324
routing   476

Index

rwhnf evaluation strategy 78

SAC language 8, 11, 74, 403
scalability 17, 476
Scampi system 8, 85–86, 92, **379–396**
- comm_rank 385
- comm_size 385
- error handling 388
- implementation 386–390
- issend 385
- matrix multiplication example 391–393
- polymorphism 386–388
- profiling 389–390
- recv 385
- selective communication 389
- SPMD programs 386
- ssend 385
- wait 385
scan 219, 476
- bidirectional, mscan 198
- data parallel **196–198**
- parallel scan in BSP 275
- scanning functions 38
scanr function **38**
scheduling 128–129, 209, 476
- fair 129, 145
- greedy 209
- MultiLisp 141
- of threads in Caliban 313
- optimal 210
- preemptive 133
- unfair 134, 141
Scheme language *see also* MultiLisp
scientific computing 72
SCL language 80, 296–299, 413
scripts in Facile 147
SECD Machine 21, 47–50, 476
select in CML 365
selector terms 128
semantics
- denotational 109–111
- operational 112–113
semi-explicit parallelism 11–12, 75–81, 405–412, 476
send
- Clean 332
- Facile primitive 88
send in CML 364
sendEvt in CML 365
SeqArray in SCL 296
seqmap in CML 368
sequences

- finite 192–193
- in NESL 79
Sequent Symmetry architecture 402
sequential 476
sequential construct in P3L 300
serial 476
serial combinators 126
shape 219–232, 476
- analysis 221
- and skeletons 292
- combinator, # 221
- equality, # = 221
- operators for block decomposition 229–230
- operators for data distribution 228–229
- polymorphism 222
- theory 222–223
shared-memory implementation 132–134
shared-memory system 16–17, 150, 157, 476
sharing analysis 163
sharing graph *see* graph reduction, sharing, 50
side- effect 14
side-effect 9, 14–145
- FISH 224
- Lisp 144
SIGMA-1 dataflow machine 60
SIMD 14–15, 193, 477
single assignment *see* dataflow
single-threaded 477
SISAL language 8, 11, 61, 72–74, 250, 262–264, 400
- applications 400–402
- SISAL 90 73
- sparse matrix multiplication example 73
SK-combinators 56, 151
skeleton 7, 11, 26, 79–81, 118, 212, 228, 289–303, 339, 477
- and BMF 421–422
- and BSP 284
- applications 407–409
- binomial coefficient example 80
- classes 293
- composition of 291, 298, 299
- computational skeleton in SCL 297
- cost modelling 213–214, 216–217
- d&c skeleton 80
- d&c skeleton 289, 294
- data skeleton 213

- elementary skeleton in SCL 297
- **farm** 294
- for program derivation 421–422
- homomorphic 214, 216
- in Caliban 310
- in Clean 326
- in P3L 80
- in paraML 148
- in SCL 80
- in SML 408
- iterative combination 303
- nested 291, 298, 299
- **pipe** skeleton 294
- **ramp** 294
- **Sandwich** 407
- shape 292
- SkelML 408
- static iterative transformation 303
- transformation 292, 294

SkelML language 408
Skil language 303, 406
SMP, Symmetric Multiprocessor 477
SNF *see* spine normal form
software re-use 305
sort
- insertion sort in CSP 355–356
- sample sort in BSP 277–283

space, cost modelling 208, 217
spark 71, 149, 157, 159, 477
- GranSim 236
- spark pool 132, 149

spark pool 477
sparse matrix multiplication example
- in SISAL 73
- in Clean 71
- in Eden 84–85
- in NESL 79
- sequential 65
- strictness properties of 67–68

spawn in CML 363
spawn primitive in Facile 88
speculative evaluation 128–131, 133, 415, 477
- aborting 128–131
- MultiLisp 144–145
- order-based 131
- π-RED$^+$ 139

speedup 477
- absolute 465
- linear 472
- regular 476

SPF language 413
spine normal form 67

Spineless G-Machine 156, 163–164
SPMD 15, 267, 270, 382–383, 386, 477
SPMD in SCL 297
stack, in SECD machine 47
Standard ML 303, 363
- concurrent implementations 145–148
- semantics 112

standardisation theorem 43
starvation 477
static analysis 361–362
static dataflow 59
stencilling 230–231
STG Machine 150, 156, 162–164, 169–171
- parallel 171, 172

Strand language 414
Strategy type in GpH 77
stream parallelism 73
strict language 107
- implementation 121–148

strictness 8–9, 46–47, 67, 257, 477
- analysis 9, 47, **66–68**
- annotation in Clean 332
- data structures 67
- hyper-strict 67
- of **map** 67
- of multiplication, (∗) 68
- of sparse matrix multiplication 67
- of **sum** 68

string type (**String**) 33–34
strong functional programming 106, 115–118
structural induction 99–100
- finding proofs by 104

structure store 248
structured operational semantics 112
substitution 477
supercombinator 57, 125, 151, 155, 478
- instantiation 57–58

suspension 50, 478
sync in CML 365
synchronic distance 129
synchronisation 124, 132, 133, 140, 146, 149
- dataflow 248

synchronous communication 88, 147, 340, 478
syntax of heap cells 51

tagged token dataflow architecture, TTDA 60
takeMVar primitive in Concurrent Haskell 89

Index

task 60, 478
- *see also* thread
- defined as triple 124
- garbage collection of 145
- offloading 135, 328
- placement 159, 474
- speculative 129
- stealing 159
- task graph 306
- throttling 61, 126, 134
- throttling of 162
- vital 129
task context blocks 132
task creation 126
- eager 127, 142
- inline 142
- lazy 142, 245, 411
- MultiLisp 141–144
task interaction 123–125
task management 125
task pool 137, 149, 157–158, 478
task priorities 129–131, 144–145
- downgrading 131
- effective 144
- upgrading 131
task resumption 478
task scheduler 132, 134
- π-RED$^+$ 137
task sponsoring 144
task stealing 135
- oldest first 143
task table 132
TCSP process calculus 87
template instantiation 57
termination 67, 94, 115–118, 161, 478
test-and-set 140, 158
theorem
- Brent's 211
- Church-Rosser 42–43
- Curry and Fey's standardisation 43
thread 60, 145, 149, 478
- *see also* task
- and context switches 146
- blocking 61
- in Caliban 307
- in CML 145, 363
- in Facile 147
- in GranSim 236
- in paraML 148
- in π-RED$^+$ 137
- latency hiding 61
- multithreading 61
- scheduling in Caliban 313

thread pool *see* task pool, 478
throttling of tasks 61, 126, 134, 162
- MultiLisp 141, 142
throughput 478
tightly-coupled system 16–17, 478
TIM Machine 150, 164–166
time dependency 85
tokens
- dataflow 59, 247
- for task creation 126
tomography, visualisation 309
topology 18–19, 193, 194, 268, 272, 284, 295, 323, 325–326, 479
toucher sponsors 144
transformation 24, 26–28, 199, 298, **339–360**
- CIP project 342
- cost-directed 218
- improving cost 211
- of foldr to CSP pipeline 353–355
- of map to CSP pipeline 349–350
- of skeleton programs 292, 294
- tractability of 28
transformational systems 64, 81
transformCSG skeleton 295
Transmissible class in Eden 84
TTDA system 60
tuple type 33
TwoL model 206, 420–421
type 12–14
- algebraic 38, 39
- basic types in Haskell 31
- boolean 33
- causal type and effect in CML 368–372
- character 32
- dependent 116–117
- dynamic 331, 332, 334–338
- floating-point 32
- integer 32
- list 33–34
- string 33–34
- tuple 33
- type class in Haskell 31
- type dependent functions 337
- uniqueness type in Clean 323, 334
- user-defined 38, 39

unboxed representation 51
undefined value *see* $\bot$
unfair scheduling 134
- MultiLisp 141
uniqueness type 323, 334
unwinding graph 53, 153–155

update, destructive   251
updating graph   156, 160
using function in GpH   77

verification   96
virtual machine, Facile   147
virtual shared memory   19, 150, 178, 479
vision application   303, 400, 407–408, 415
VisualNets support tool for CSP   341
volume visualisation   302
von Neumann cost model   208

weak head normal form   45–46, 50, 67, 70, 71, 78, 149, 151, 159, 479

where keyword   36
WHNF   *see* weak head normal form
With in Caliban   307
With-loops in SAC   11, 61, 75, 404
work, preservation of   211
wrap in CML   365
write function in NESL   79

ZAPP system   177–178
zipping function   113
– in parallel   328
zipWith function   113
zipwithDarray functions in Clean   329
ZPL system   230